D0555402

Minoli–Cordovana's
Authoritative
Computer & Network Security
Dictionary

Minoli–Cordovana's Authoritative Computer & Network Security Dictionary

by

Daniel Minoli

James Cordovana

A JOHN WILEY & SONS, INC., PUBLICATION

Copyright © 2006 by John Wiley & Sons, Inc. All rights reserved.

Published by John Wiley & Sons, Inc., Hoboken, New Jersey.
Published simultaneously in Canada.

No part of this publication may be reproduced, stored in a retrieval system, or transmitted in any form or by any means, electronic, mechanical, photocopying, recording, scanning, or otherwise, except as permitted under Section 107 or 108 of the 1976 United States Copyright Act, without either the prior written permission of the Publisher, or authorization through payment of the appropriate per-copy fee to the Copyright Clearance Center, Inc., 222 Rosewood Drive, Danvers, MA 01923, (978) 750-8400, fax (978) 750-4470, or on the web at www.copyright.com. Requests to the Publisher for permission should be addressed to the Permissions Department, John Wiley & Sons, Inc., 111 River Street, Hoboken, NJ 07030, (201) 748-6011, fax (201) 748-6008, or online at http://www.wiley.com/go/permission.

Limit of Liability/Disclaimer of Warranty: While the publisher and author have used their best efforts in preparing this book, they make no representations or warranties with respect to the accuracy or completeness of the contents of this book and specifically disclaim any implied warranties of merchantability or fitness for a particular purpose. No warranty may be created or extended by sales representatives or written sales materials. The advice and strategies contained herein may not be suitable for your situation. You should consult with a professional where appropriate. Neither the publisher nor author shall be liable for any loss of profit or any other commercial damages, including but not limited to special, incidental, consequential, or other damages.

For general information on our other products and services or for technical support, please contact our Customer Care Department within the United States at (800) 762-2974, outside the United States at (317) 572-3993 or fax (317) 572-4002.

Wiley also publishes its books in a variety of electronic formats. Some content that appears in print may not be available in electronic format. For information about Wiley products, visit our web site at www.wiley.com.

Library of Congress Cataloging-in-Publication Data is available.

Minoli, Daniel, 1952–
    Minoli-Cordovana's authoritative computer & network security dictionary / Daniel Minoli, James Cordovana.
        p. cm.
    Includes bibliographical references and index.
    ISBN-13: 978-0-471-78263-6
    ISBN-10: 0-471-78263-7
    1. Computer security—Dictionaries. 2. Computer networks—Security measures—Dictionaries. 1. Cordovana, James, 1973– II. Title. III. Title: Minoli-Cordovana's authoritative computer & network security dictionary. IV. Title: Authoritative computer & network security dictionary.
    QA76.9.A25M583 2006
    005.8003—dc22   2006041021

Printed in the United States of America.

10 9 8 7 6 5 4 3 2 1

For Anna
(Dan)

For Sabrina and Sophie
(James)

Acknowledgments

Ted Demopoulos, Demopoulos Associates, is herewith thanked for valuable inputs and guidance.

Any potential imperfections in this dictionary are solely the responsibility of the authors.

Preface

Recent well-documented studies show that cyber attacks continue to remain a substantial threat to organizations of all types. On average, companies experience 30 attacks per week on their Information Technology resources. Around 20 percent of large companies suffer at least two severe events a year. It is estimated that the worldwide financial impact of malicious code is around $100 billion per year. The challenge to corporate planners just continues to get more onerous. It has been conservatively forecasted that in 2010 around 100,000 new vulnerabilities will be discovered in software applications in that year alone. This will force companies to assess and mitigate one new risk every five minutes of every hour each day. Considering that with each infraction threat discovered the vulnerability has the potential to disrupt or bring a company's business to a complete halt, organizations must take risk assessment seriously and determine how each risk will be handled. The increased number of vulnerabilities being discovered also drives up the number of security incidents worldwide, and it will increase to a point where 8000 incidents per week will happen to organizations that have not properly addressed and mitigated their risks.

Corporate information security must become the fiduciary concern of the CEO, the CSO, the CFO, the CIO, and the COO. If a company loses its information technology (computer and/or voice/data networking) resources for more than a day or two, the company may well find itself in financial trouble. Obviously, brokerage firms, banks, airports, medical establishments, and homeland security concerns would be impacted faster than, say, a manufacturing firm or a book publishing firm. However, the general concern is universal. If a company is unable to conduct business for more than a week, the company may well be permanently incapacitated. Therefore, there is a clear need to protect the enterprises from random, negligent, malicious, or planned attacks on its Information Technology (IT) resources. As more and more companies sent their IT business abroad under the rubric of "outsourcing," the potential IT (and, hence, corporate) risks are arguably growing at a geometric pace; these risks can have ultimate negative implications, particularly in view of cumulative exposures to risks which, in the aggregate, take on not trivial probability.

Complexities associated with security threats will continue for the foreseeable future at an accelerated rate, potentially for a long time to come. The purpose of this publication is to gather clear, concise, authoritative, and up-to-date definitions of terms, concepts, methods, solutions, tools, means, and methodologies in the field of computer and networking security. About 5500 security and IT-related terms are authoritatively defined in this dictionary. We make this work authoritative by making reference to definitions developed by a number of authorities and practitioners, including our own, as documented in the reference list. In particular, as a foundation we have made some use of R. Shirey's *Internet Security Glossary,* IETF Request for Comments 2828, May 2000 (RFC 2828 only defines about 1000 terms.)

In this dictionary we have focused less on grammatical aspects of the field (whether a term is a noun, adjective, verb, etc.) and more on the practical insight of a term and its applicability/implication in the field of IT asset protection. Furthermore, our work aims to be more than just a simple dictionary. A simple dictionary would provide terse but often not all-encompassing formal definitions of terms. Our approach is to also provide some context and applicability of the concepts. Therefore, this work can also be seen as a "handbook" and/or "commentary" on security topics.

This book serves the same purpose of *Newton's Telecom Dictionary,* a well-respected, long-available book on telecom terms, now in its 21st edition, but our dictionary has a pragmatic focus on networking- and host-security.

IT security does not exist in a vacuum as a discipline. The field and mechanisms of IT security have evolved to meet the need to protect IT resources.

These resources include, but are not limited to, hosts, systems, OSs, databases, storage, information, communications links, communications network elements, clients, PCs, PDAs, wireless devices, e-mail, and so on. Hence, the reader will find terms related to a description of this "ecosystem" also defined and discussed in this dictionary; other dictionaries have taken on a more sterile view of the discipline and have tended to be more narrowly focused onto distilled security mechanisms.

There is only one other book that comes close to the project that we have undertaken herewith, in terms of terms defined. A few products have appeared over the years, but they tended to be limited in scope, covering 2000–4000 terms but failing to be kept up-to-date. There were a handful of products in the 1980s and then a big void in the 1990s. With the field evolving rapidly, the absolute necessity exists to keep the product up-to-date. While there always will be a number of online glossaries, the value of a book is to refine, streamline, authenticate, normalize, and rationalize terms from a variety of sources, and to have a stable, aggregated point-of-reference. It is the intent of the authors and publisher to keep this dictionary up-to-date and keep it a comprehensive reference document, to assist industry professionals, managers, and planners, as well as those who wish to get their arms around the discipline and its jargon.

Because the security techniques and approaches discussed herewith are intended to support networking and computing, a set of core IT and networking topics and terms are also defined. Little can be accomplished if it does not make financial sense, even in the risk-calculated probabilistic manner (expected gain or expected loss); hence, a set of core financial topics and terms are also defined.

DANIEL MINOLI
JAMES CORDOVANA

The Authors

Daniel Minoli has over 30 years of IT, telecom, and networking experience with end-users, carriers, academia, and venture capitalists, including work at AIG, ARPA think tanks, Bell Telephone Laboratories, ITT, Prudential Securities, Bell Communications Research (Bellcore/Telcordia), AT&T, Capital One Financial, NYU, Rutgers University, Stevens Institute of Technology, and Societé General de Financiament de Quebec. Recently he also played a founding role in the launching of two networking companies through the high-tech incubator Leading Edge Networks Inc., which he ran in the early 2000s: Global Wireless Services, a provider of broadband secure hotspot mobile Internet, hotspot VoIP, and sensor services to high-end marinas; and InfoPort Communications Group, an optical and Gigabit Ethernet metropolitan carrier supporting Data Center/SAN/channel extension and Grid Computing network access services.

Mr. Minoli has worked and published extensively in the field of IT security. His work in security started in the late 1970s with extensive efforts on ARPA-sponsored research on defensible and survivable packet networks under malicious attack. In the 1980s he researched the design and development of security services on behalf of service providers and enterprises. The author was vigorously advocating advanced data networking security measures as far back as 1987. At that time, about 20 years ago, he was (already) advising Local Exchange Carriers (e.g., Verizon, SBC/AT&T, BellSouth, QWEST) to deploy security mechanisms and end-user security services such as (among others): (i) security on dial-up (port security); (ii) authentication; (iii) data encryption; (iv) network transmission service without external observability; (v) closed user groups (i.e., VPNs); (vi) incoming call screening with target-host participation; (vii) nonrepudiation security service; (viii) network-based computer virus filter; (ix) accountability and audit trail service; and (x) e-mail filtering (for spam, and so on) (he advocated these in Bellcore Special Report SR-NPL-000790, December 1987, which had a 45-page section on potential carrier-provided/carrier-supported network security services).

His work on security was encapsulated in a long

chapter in the *Telecommunications Technology Handbook* (Artech House, 1991), a broadly circulated reference book that was on the shelf for well over a decade. In the 1990s he was involved with secure e-commerce applications, as encapsulated in the well-received co-authored handbook *Web Commerce Handbook* (McGraw-Hill, 1998.) Recently he has been involved with the novel design of secure Wi-Fi hotspot networks for interference- and risk-laden public places such as marinas, and has written the first book on the market on hotspot networks and subtending security issues (*Hotspot Networks— WiFi for Public Access Locations,* McGraw-Hill, 2002). Most recently he has been involved in secure services for grid computing applications (*A Networking Approach to Grid Computing,* Wiley, 2004) and for sensor networks.

Mr. Minoli has also written columns for *ComputerWorld, NetworkWorld,* and *Network Computing* (1985–1995). He has taught at New York University (Information Technology Institute), Rutgers University, Stevens Institute of Technology, and Monmouth University (1984–2003). Also, he was a Technology Analyst At-Large, for Gartner/DataPro (1985–2001); based on extensive hand-on work at financial firms and carriers, he tracked technologies and wrote numerous CTO/CIO-level technical/architectural scans in the area of telephony and data communications systems, including topics on security, disaster recovery, IT outsourcing, network management, LANs, WANs (ATM and MPLS), wireless (LAN and public hotspot), VoIP, network design/economics, carrier networks (such as metro Ethernet and CWDM/DWDM), and e-commerce. Over the years he has advised Venture Capitalists for investments of $150 million in a dozen high-tech companies.

James Cordovana has a decade of experience as a security and networking professional, acquired at a premiere financial services company and in academia. In recent years he has focused on the deployment of advanced information security architectures in enterprise environments. Mr. Cordovana enjoys a broad technical understanding of numerous aspects of information security, including, but not limited to, encryption mechanisms, browser-based services, wired and wireless networks, architectural patterns development, application and database development, enterprise Single Sign-On, Directory Service integration solutions, web services security, and e-commerce security. He holds a number of security industry certifications. In his role as Security Architect, he has directed the evolution of the information security posture for a Fortune 200 financial services company.

Mr. Cordovana's experience encompasses operational analysis and process reengineering, physical security audits, and corporate policy compliance checks. Along the way, he has created tiered application architectures with flexible role-based access control. Mr. Cordovana has also worked hands-on with several types of Relational Database Management Systems, applications, and operating systems, while also creating a web-based security framework, including a custom authentication and authorization system. As a Java middleware developer, he worked on reusable enterprise components. He also developed an enterprise Java cryptography component that allowed for software-based symmetrical encryption, hashing, and PKI-based encryption. He has performed audits of third parties and internal systems, creating detailed risk assessments with detailed risk mitigation strategies. He also provided subject matter experience in the revision of corporate security standards, especially those relating to application security. At the current time, Mr. Cordovana's efforts are focused on architecting security solutions for a full range of enterprise applications, systems, and networks.

Acronyms

0x (aka 0X) A prefix often used to indicate that a hexadecimal number representation of a number is to follow.

10-Gigabit Ethernet (10GbE) Ethernet Local Area Network (LAN) systems operating at 10,000-Mbps (10 Gbps) (IEEE Std. 802.3ae-2002). The 10-Gbps IEEE P802.3ae solution extends Ethernet capabilities providing higher bandwidth for multimedia, distributed processing, imaging, and other super-high-speed applications by improving the performance of: (i) LAN-, Backbone-, Server-, and Gateway-Connectivity; (ii) Switch aggregation functions; and (iii) Metropolitan Area Network (MAN), Wide Area Network (WAN), Regional Area Network (RAN), and Storage Area Network (SAN) connectivity environments. Goals of the standardization initiative were [r001–r003]: Preserve the 802.3/Ethernet frame format at the Media Access Control (MAC) Client service interface; preserve minimum and maximum FrameSize of current 802.3 Std.; support full-duplex operation only; support star-wired local area networks using point-to-point links and structured cabling topologies; specify an optional Media-Independent Interface (MII); support a speed of 10.000 Gbps at the MAC/Physical Signaling (MAC/PLS) service interface; define two families of PHYs (a LAN Physical Layer (PHY), operating at a data rate of 10.000 Gbps, and a WAN PHY, operating at a data rate compatible with the payload rate of OC-192c/SDH VC-4-64c); and define a mechanism to adapt the MAC/PLS data rate to the data rate of the WAN PHY.

The following depict PHYs defined in the standard [r004]:

10GBASE-SR/SW: 62.5-micron MultiMode Fiber (MMF); 33 m

10GBASE-SR/SW: 50-micron MMF; 66 m or 300 m (2 GHz)

10GBASE-LR/LW: 9-micron SingleMode Fiber (SMF); 10 km

10GBASE-ER/EW: 9-micron SMF; 40 km

10GBASE-LX4/LW4: 50- or 62.5-micron MMF; 300 m

10GBASE-LX4/LW4: 9-micron SMF; 10 km

10 GBASE-T (10000BASE-TX): Copper [uses installed base of Category 5e Unshielded Twisted Pair (UTP) cable (upgrade transmission functionality from 1000 BASE-T)]; 100 m.

1000BASE-CX 1000BASE-X Local Area Network (LAN) over specialty shielded balanced copper jumper cable assemblies. Described in IEEE 802.3 Clause 39.

1000BASE-LX 1000BASE-X Local Area Network (LAN) using long-wavelength laser devices over multimode and single-mode fiber. Described in IEEE 802.3 Clause 38.

1000BASE-SX 1000BASE-X Local Area Network (LAN) using short-wavelength laser devices over multimode fiber. Described in IEEE 802.3 Clause 38.

1000BASE-T A physical layer communications specification for 1-Gbps IEEE 802 Local Area Networks (LANs), baseband data transmission over a twisted-pair copper wire. IEEE 802.3 Physical Layer specification for a 1000-Mbps Carrier Sense Multiple Access/Collision Detect (CSMA/CD) LAN using four pairs of Category 5 balanced copper cabling. Described in IEEE 802.3 Clause 40.

1000BASE-X IEEE 802.3 Physical Layer specification for a 1000-Mbps Carrier Sense Multiple Access/Collision Detect (CSMA/CD) Local Area Network (LAN) that uses a Physical Layer derived from ANSI X3.230-1994 (FC-PH). Described in IEEE 802.3 Clause 36.

100BASE-FX IEEE 802.3 Physical Layer specification for a 100-Mbps Carrier Sense Multiple Access/Collision Detect (CSMA/CD) Local Area Network (LAN) over two optical fibers. Described in IEEE 802.3 Clauses 24 and 26.

100BASE-T A physical layer communications specification for 100-Mbps IEEE 802 Local Area Networks (LANs), baseband data transmission over a twisted-pair copper wire. IEEE 802.3 Physical Layer specification for a 100-Mbps Car-

rier Sense Multiple Access/Collision Detect (CSMA/CD) LAN. Described in IEEE 802.3 Clauses 22 and 28.

100BASE-T2 IEEE 802.3 specification for a 100-Mbps Carrier Sense Multiple Access/Collision Detect (CSMA/CD) Local Area Network (LAN) over two pairs of Category 3 or better balanced cabling. Described in IEEE 802.3 Clause 32.

100BASE-T4 IEEE 802.3 Physical Layer specification for a 100-Mbps Carrier Sense Multiple Access/Collision Detect (CSMA/CD) Local Area Network (LAN) over four pairs of Category 3, 4, and 5 unshielded twisted-pair (UTP) wire. Described in IEEE 802.3 Clause 23.

100BASE-TX IEEE 802.3 Physical Layer specification for a 100-Mbps Carrier Sense Multiple Access/Collision Detect (CSMA/CD) Local Area Network (LAN) over two pairs of Category 5 unshielded twisted-pair (UTP) or shielded twisted-pair (STP) wire. Described in IEEE 802.3 Clauses 24 and 25.

100BASE-X IEEE 802.3 Physical Layer specification for a 100-Mbps Carrier Sense Multiple Access/Collision Detect (CSMA/CD) Local Area Network (LAN) that uses the Physical Medium-Dependent (PMD) sublayer and Medium-Dependent Interface (MDI) of the ISO/IEC 9314 group of standards developed by ASC X3T12 (FDDI). Described in IEEE 802.3 Clause 24.

10BASE2 (practically outmoded) IEEE 802.3 Physical Layer specification for a 10-Mbps Carrier Sense Multiple Access/Collision Detect (CSMA/CD) Local Area Network (LAN) over RG 58 coaxial cable. Described in IEEE 802.3 Clause 10.

10BASE5 (practically outmoded) IEEE 802.3 Physical Layer specification for a 10-Mbps Carrier Sense Multiple Access/Collision Detect (CSMA/CD) Local Area Network (LAN) over coaxial cable (i.e., thicknet). Described in IEEE 802.3 Clause 8.

10BASE-F A physical layer communications specification for 10-Mbps IEEE 802 Local Area Network (LAN) for baseband data transmission over a fiber-optic cable. IEEE 802.3 Physical Layer specification for a 1-Mbps Carrier Sense Multiple Access/Collision Detect (CSMA/CD) LAN over fiber-optic cable. Described in IEEE 802.3 Clause 15.

10BASE-FB Port A port on a repeater that contains an internal 10BASE-FB Medium Attachment Unit (MAU) that can connect to a similar port on another repeater. Described in IEEE 802.3 Clause 9.

10BASE-FB Segment A fiber-optic link segment providing a point-to-point connection between two 10BASE-FB ports on repeaters.

10BASE-FL Segment A fiber-optic link segment providing point-to-point connection between two 10BASE-FL Medium Attachment Units (MAUs).

10BASE-FP Segment A fiber-optic mixing segment, including one 10BASE-FP Star and all of the attached fiber pairs.

10BASE-FP Star A passive device that is used to couple fiber pairs together to form a 10BASE-FP segment. Optical signals received at any input port of the 10BASE-FP Star are distributed to all of its output ports (including the output port of the optical interface from which it was received). A 10BASE-FP Star is typically comprised of a passive-star coupler, fiber-optic connectors, and a suitable mechanical housing. Described in IEEE 802.3 Clause 16.5.

10BASE-T A physical layer communications specification for 10-Mbps IEEE 802 Local Area Networks (LANs) for baseband data transmission over a twisted-pair copper wire. IEEE 802.3 Physical Layer specification for a 10-Mbps Carrier Sense Multiple Access/Collision Detect (CSMA/CD) LAN over two pairs of twisted-pair telephone wire. Described in IEEE 802.3 Clause 14.

10BROAD36 (practically outmoded) IEEE 802.3 Physical Layer (PHY) specification for a 10-Mbps Carrier Sense Multiple Access/Collision Detect (CSMA/CD) Local Area Network (LAN) over a single broadband cable. Described in IEEE 802.3 Clause 11.

10GBASE-LR/LW PHY for 10 GbE (long range)

Local Area Network (LAN) on long-wavelength fiber cabling systems.

10GBASE-SR/SW PHY for 10 GbE (short range) Local Area Network (LAN) on short-wavelength fiber cabling systems.

10GBASE-T (10000BASE-TX) PHY for 10 GbE. Copper-based transmission, 100 m or less. Uses installed base of Category 5e Unshielded Twisted Pair (UTP) cable (upgrade transmission functionality from 1000 BASE-T).

10GbE See 10-Gigabit Ethernet

1BASE5 (practically outmoded) IEEE 802.3 Physical Layer (PHY) specification for a 1-Mbps Carrier Sense Multiple Access/Collision Detect (CSMA/CD) Local Area Network (LAN) over two pairs of twisted-pair telephone wire. Described in IEEE 802.3 Clause 12.

1G Wireless Networks The first generation of systems for mobile telephony was analog and circuit-switched, and it only carried voice traffic. The analog phones used in 1G were less secure and prone to interference in situations where the signal is weak. Analog systems include Advanced Mobile Phone System (AMPS), Nordic Mobile Telephone Network (NMT), and Extended Total Access Communications System (ETACS). AMPS is an analog mobile phone network that was used mainly in the United States and also Latin America, Australia, New Zealand, parts of Russia, and Asia-Pacific; NMT was an analog network used in Scandinavia, some European countries and small parts of Russia, the Middle East and Asia (there are two NMT systems; the original at 450 MHz and one at 900 MHz); ETACS was the analog mobile phone network developed in the United Kingdom and available in Europe and Asia. 2G and 3G networks are replacing 1G networks. These advanced networks support richer applications, such as Short Message Service (SMS), Multimedia Messaging Service (MMS), and games [r005]. (The 1G term has also been used in other technological contexts.)

2.5G Wireless Networks Technology that extends 2G systems, adding features such as packet-switched connection and enhanced data rates.

2.5G networks include Enhanced Data rates for Global Evolution (EDGE) and General Packet Radio Services (GPRS). These networks support Wireless Application Protocol (WAP), Multimedia Messaging Service (MMS), Short Message Service (SMS), mobile games, and search and directory [r005]. (The 2G term has also been used in other technological contexts.)

2G Wireless Networks   The second generation of mobile telephony systems that make use of digital encoding. 2G networks support high bit rate voice, limited data communications, and different levels of encryption. 2G networks include Global System for Mobile Communications (GSM), Digital Advanced Mobile Phone System (D-AMPS) [a Time Division Multiple Access (TDMA) technology] and Code Division Multiple Access (CDMA). 2G networks can support Multimedia Messaging Service (MMS) applications [r005].

3A's   See Authentication, Authorization, and Auditing or Authentication, Authorization, and Administration.

3DES   See Triple DES

3G Wireless Networks   The third generation of mobile systems; these provided high-speed data transmissions of 144 kbps and higher. 3G will support multimedia applications such as full-motion video, video conferencing, and Internet access [r005]. (The 3G term has also been used in other technological contexts.)

3GPP   See 3rd-Generation Partnership Project

3GPP IP Multimedia Core Network Subsystem (IMS)   In the late 1990s there were discussions for the development of standards for a 3G mobile system with a core network based on evolutions of the Global System for Mobile Communications (GSM) and an access network based on all the radio access technologies (i.e., both frequency- and time-division duplex modes) supported by the plethora of different carriers (in different countries). This project was called the Third-Generation Partnership Project (3GPP).

IP Multimedia Subsystem (IMS) will support both telephony and multimedia services. IMS' role in the Universal Mobile Telecommunication System (UMTS) architecture is to interact both with the Public Switched Telephone Network (PSTN) and the Internet to provide all types of multimedia services to users. The Call State Control Function (CSCF) element in the IMS infrastructure is responsible for signaling messages between all IMS components in order to control multimedia sessions originated by the user. For a particular cellular device, the 3GPP IMS network is further decomposed in a home network and a visited network. An IMS subscriber belongs to his or her home network. Services are triggered and may be executed in the home network. One or more Session Initiation Protocol (SIP) servers are deployed in the SIP home network to support the IMS. Among those SIP servers, there is a SIP serving proxy, which is also acting as a SIP registrar.

Authentication/Authorization servers may be part of the home network as well. Users are authenticated in the home network. A SIP outbound proxy is provided to support the User Agent (UA). The SIP outbound proxy is typically located in the visited network, although it may be located in the home network as well. The SIP outbound proxy maintains security associations between itself and the terminals, and interworks with the resource management in the packet network. The SIP outbound proxy is assigned after the mobile device has connected to the access network. Once this proxy is assigned, it does not change while the mobile remains connected to the access network. Thus the mobile can move freely within the access network without SIP outbound proxy reassignment. The home network may also support one or more SIP edge proxies. These nodes may act as the first entry points for SIP signaling to the home network and may determine (with the help of location servers) which SIP registrar server to assign to a particular user. Typically the address of the home network SIP edge proxy is configured in Domain Name System (DNS) in the form of a DNS Naming Authority Pointer (NAPTR) and Service (SRV) records for SIP. Additionally, home and visited networks may deploy, if required, a SIP-hiding proxy. The main purpose of the SIP-hiding proxy is to hide the network configuration. The 3GPP IP Multimedia Core Network (IM CN) Subsystem is designed to be access independent. Access is granted from 3GPP cellular terminals or from other terminals that use other accesses out of the scope of 3GPP. 3GPP cellular IP Multimedia terminals use the existing General Packet Radio Service (GPRS) as a transport network for IP datagrams. The terminals first connect to the GPRS network to get an IPv6 prefix. In order to do this, the terminals must perform a GPRS Attach procedure followed by a GPRS Packet Data Protocol (PDP) Context Activation procedure. These GPRS procedures are required to be completed before any IP Multimedia session can be established [r006].

3R   See Regeneration with Retiming and Reshaping

3rd-Generation Partnership Project (3GPP) (3G Wireless context) The 3rd-Generation Partnership Project is responsible for setting the Universal Mobile Telecommunication System (UMTS) standards. Here, the network operators, equipment developers, and national standardization committees bundle their activities [r007]. 3GPP has selected Session Initiation Protocol (SIP) as the protocol to establish and tear down multimedia sessions in the IP Multimedia Subsystem (IMS) [r006].

4D-PAM5   The symbol encoding method used in 1000BASE-T. The four-dimensional quinary symbols (4D) received from the 8B1Q4 data encoding are transmitted using five voltage levels (PAM5). Four symbols are transmitted in parallel each symbol period. Described in IEEE 802.3 Clause 40.

4G Wireless Networks   The fourth generation of mobile systems, expected by the end of the decade. Functional definition and capability set is still being defined.

4-Way Handshake   As defined in IEEE 802.11i, the 4-Way Handshake creates an additional key (Pairwise Transient Key) that is used to reduce exposure of the shared secret key (Pairwise Master Key) created by the Extensible Authentication Protocol (EAP) exchange. Another key (Group Temporal Key) is created as well.

6over4   An IPv6 technology designed to favor the coexistence with IPv4 that provides unicast and multicast connectivity through an IPv4 infrastructure with multicast support, using the IPv4 network as a logical multicast link [r008].

6over4 Address   A |64-bit prefix|:0:0:WWXX:YYZZ address, where WWXX:YYZZ is the hexadecimal representation of w.x.y.z (a public or private IPv4 address), used to represent a device in 6over4 technology [r008].

6to4   An IPv6 technology designed to favor the coexistence with IPv4 that provides unicast connectivity between IPv6 networks and devices through an IPv4 infrastructure. 6to4 uses a public IPv4 address to build a global IPv6 prefix [r008].

6to4 Address   A |64-bit prefix|:0:0:WWXX:YYZZ address, where WWXX:YYZZ is the hexadecimal representation of w.x.y.z (a public or private IPv4 address), used to represent a devices on 6over4 technology. A 2002:WWXX:YYZZ:|SLA ID|:|interface ID| address, where WWXX:YYZZ is the hexadecimal representation of w.x.y.z (a public or private IPv4 address), used to represent a device on 6to4 technology [r008].

6to4 Machine   An IPv6 device that is configured, at least, with one 6to4 address (a global address with a 2002::/16 prefix). 6to4 devices do not require manual configuration, and they create 6to4 addresses by means of classical autoconfiguration mechanisms [r008].

6to4 Router   Router designed to favor the coexistence with IPv4 that provides unicast connectivity between IPv6 networks and devices through an IPv4 infrastructure. 6to4 uses a public IPv4 address to build a global IPv6 prefix [r008].

72 Rule   (aka Rule of 72) (financial term) The estimation of doubling time on an investment, for which the compounded annual rate of return times the number of years must equal roughly 72 for the investment to double in value [r009].

78 Rule   (aka Rule of 78) (financial term) The rule of 78 is one way that lenders use to calculate how much interest one should have paid at any stage during the repayment period of a fixed rate installment loan. Also, it represents the revenue that a carrier or Application Service Provider (ASP) will collect at the end of the year (namely, the Run Rate) from adding one customer a month (from January to December), each paying a Monthly Recurring Charge (MRC) of $1 (for any other values in the number of customers or in the MRC, multiply accordingly).

The number 78 arises from the 12 monthly parts of a one-year period. The sum of those parts $(12 + 11 + 10 + 9 + 8 + 7 + 6 + 5 + 4 + 3 + 2 + 1)$ is 78. For example, for a loan with a one-year duration, the lender expects the borrower to pay 12/78ths of the interest in month one, 11/78ths in month two, and so on, down to 1/78th in month twelve. The rule of 78 takes into consideration the fact that one pays more interest in the beginning of a loan when one has the use of more of the money and one pays less interest as the debt is reduced. Because each repayment installment is the same size, the part going to pay off the amount borrowed increases over time and the part representing interest decreases [r010].

8B/10B (8 bits/10 bits)   A dc-balanced octet-oriented data encoding. Transmission code used in high-speed Local Area Networks/Storage Area Networks (LANs/SANs).

8B1Q4   For IEEE 802.3, the data encoding technique used by 1000BASE-T when converting Gigabit Media Independent Interface (GMII) data (8B: 8 bits) to four quinary symbols (Q4) that are transmitted during one clock (1Q4). Described in IEEE 802.3 Clause 40.

A (GSM context) The A interface transmits user and signaling data between the Mobile Services Switching Center (MSC) and the Transcoder [r011].

A3 (GSM context) An algorithm that uses the key Ki and the Random Number (RAND) to generate the Signed Response (SRES) [r011].

A5 (GSM context) An algorithm that uses the 64-bit key Kc and a 22-bit Time Division Multiple Access (TDMA) frame number to generate a 114-bit key, which encodes and decodes speech and signaling data at both ends of the air interface [r011].

A8 (GSM context) An algorithm generates the key Kc using the key Ki and the Random Number (RAND) [r011].

AA See Attribute Authority

AAA See Authentication, Authorization, and Accountability, or Authentication, Authorization, and Administration.

AAL See ATM Adaptation Layer

AAL Connection Association established by the AAL between two or more next-higher layer entities.

AAL-1 See ATM Adaptation Layer Type 1

AAL-2 See ATM Adaptation Layer Type 2

AAL-3/4 See ATM Adaptation Layer Type 3/4

AARL See Attribute Authority Revocation List

AAL-5 See ATM Adaptation Layer Type 5

ABAC See Attribute-Based Access Control

ABC See Authentication & Billing Center

A-bis (GSM context) The A-bis interface connects the Base Transceiver Station (BTS) with the Base Station Controller (BSC). A-bis transmits

Minoli–Cordovana's Authoritative Computer and Network Security Dictionary. By Daniel Minoli and James Cordovana
Copyright © 2006 John Wiley & Sons, Inc.

four types of information: user information, signaling information, synchronization information, and information for the operation and maintenance of the BTS, so-called O&M alarms [r011].

ABL   See Arbitrary Block Length

ABR   See Available Bit Rate

Absorption   (optical transmission term) Impairment affecting optical transmission. This is caused by interactions of the signal with impurities in the glass, causing unwanted radiation of the signal. For silica, loss peaks at a wavelength of about 1390 nm caused by Oxygen–Hydrogen (OH)-radical impurity. Losses for high-quality fiber are typically less than 0.40 dB/km and 0.22 dB/km at 1310 nm and 1550 nm, respectively. New fibers have been developed that eliminate the 1385-nm water peak.

Abstract Syntax   A description of a data structure that is independent of machine-oriented structures and encodings.

Abstract Syntax Notation One (ASN.1)   The abstract syntax (language) used by the Open Systems Interconnection Reference Model (OSIRM) protocols, specifically a standard for describing data objects. (OSIRM standards utilize ASN.1 to specify data formats for protocols.) OSIRM defines functionality in layers. Information objects at higher layers are abstractly defined to be implemented with objects at lower layers. A higher layer may define transfers of abstract objects between computers, and a lower layer may define transfers concretely as strings of bits. Syntax is needed to define abstract objects and encoding rules are needed to transform between abstract objects and bit strings [r013, r020a]. As an example, ASN.1 is used to encode Simple Network Management Protocol (SNMP) packets. ASN.1 is defined in International Organization for Standardization (ISO) International Standard (IS) ISO 8824.2 and ISO 8825.2. [ASN.1 was originally described in CCITT/ITU-T Recommendation X.208: Specification of Abstract Syntax Notation One (ASN.1), 1988.]

ACC   See Access Control Center

Accelerated Depreciation   (financial term) A de-

preciation method that allows faster write-offs than the straight-line method, hence yielding a greater tax advantage than the former method. Firms with large tax exposure often use accelerated depreciation methods, even though it reduces the income shown on financial statement. Accelerated depreciation methods are popular for writing-off equipment that might be replaced before the end of its useful life since the equipment might be obsolete (e.g., computers) [r009].

Acceptable Use Policy (AUP)   A policy that documents permitted system uses and activities, as well as the consequences of noncompliance. Organizations often require users to agree to AUPs prior to granting users access to a network or system.

Access   In the Information Technology (IT) context, the ability to interact with a system in order to use resources that are associated with that system.

Access Control   Preventing the unauthorized use of system resources by regulating access according to a predefined security policy.

Access Control Center (ACC)   A system that defines and stores security policies for an Access Control Service.

Access Control Entry (ACE)   A single entry in an Access Control List (ACL).

Access Control List (ACL)   A file that defines the permissions of an object (such as user, system, or IP address) affiliated with a computer system.

Access Control Service   A security service that protects system resources against unauthorized access.

Access Grant Channel (AGCH)   (GSM context) A Common Control Channel utilized for the downlink. The channel is used to grant the mobile station a Stand-alone Dedicated Control Channel (SDCCH) for resource allocation [r011].

Access Point (AP)   Wireless hubs/bridges that transmit and receive data, serving as point of interconnection between the Wireless Local Area Network (WLAN) and the Local Area Network (LAN).

Access Point Name (APN) (GSM context) A reference point—that is, an address that can be either an IP address or a logical name [r014].

Access Rules (in the context of Presence Services) constraints on how a presence service makes presence information available to watchers. For each presentity's presence information, the applicable access rules are manipulated by the presence user agent of a principal that controls the presentity. Motivation: One needs some way of talking about hiding presence information from people [r016].

Access Slots (AS) (3G Wireless context) Periodically recurring moments at which the User Equipment is allowed to access the network. Two frames contain a total of 15 access slots [r007].

Access Token (aka Token) A type of credential that satisfies the "what you have" element of an authentication transaction. The token is in the form of a hardware device [such as a one-time password fob, smart card, or portable Universal Serial Bus (USB) device] or a software asset (such as an X.509 certificate or a secured cookie). A token is often used along with a password which "unlocks" the token, thereby creating a multifactor authentication mechanism.

Account A set of privileges associated with a particular user.

Account Linking Mapping entity identifiers across various applications (or systems, or businesses) in order to provide cross-application behavior (federation).

Account Termination Inactivating or deleting an entity identifier when system access is no longer authorized.

Accountability The property of a system (including all of its system resources) that ensures that the actions of a system entity may be traced uniquely to that entity, which can be held responsible for its actions [r013].

Accounting (financial term) The systematic recording, reporting, and analysis of financial transactions of a firm [r009].

Accounts Payable (financial term) Money that a company owes to vendors for products and services purchased on credit. This item appears on the company's balance sheet as a current liability, since the expectation is that the liability will be fulfilled in short order. When accounts payable are paid off, it represents a negative cash flow for the company [r009].

Accounts Receivable (financial term) Money that is owed to a company by a customer for products and services provided on credit. This is treated as a current asset on a balance sheet. A specific sale is generally only treated as an account receivable after the customer is sent an invoice [r009].

Accreditation An administrative declaration by a designated authority that an information system is approved to operate in a particular security configuration with a prescribed set of safeguards [r013].

Accreditation Body An independent organization responsible for assessing the performance of other organizations against a recognized standard, as well as for formally confirming the status of those that meet the standard [r016].

Accredited Formally confirmed by an accreditation body as meeting a predetermined standard of impartiality and general technical, methodological, and procedural competence [r016].

Accrual Basis Accounting (financial term) The most commonly used accounting method, which reports income when earned and expenses when incurred, as opposed to cash basis accounting, which reports income when received and expenses when paid. Under the accrual method, companies do have some discretion as to when income and expenses are recognized, but there are rules governing the recognition. In addition, companies are required to make prudent estimates against revenues that are recorded but may not be received, called a bad debt expense [r009].

Accrue (financial term) To accumulate and/or increase.

Accumulated Depreciation (financial term) The depreciation that has taken place on a particular asset up to the present time [r009].

ACE See Access Control Entry

ACL See Access Control List

Acquirer   (financial term) "The financial institution that establishes an account with a merchant and processes payment card authorizations and payments" [r017]. "The institution (or its agent) that acquires from the card acceptor the financial data relating to the transaction and initiates that data into an interchange system" [r018].

Acquisition Indication Channel (AICH) (3G Wireless context) Channel used to confirm a User Equipment's successful random access [r007].

ACRL   See Attribute Certificate Revocation List

Activation Data   Data values, other than keys, that are required to operate cryptographic modules and that need to be protected. Examples include a Personal Identification Number (PIN), a pass phrase, or a manually held key share [r011].

Active Attack   An active attack that causes alterations of some aspect of a system or system interaction. Examples include changing system files and Transmission Control Protocol (TCP) Session Hijacking.

Active Directory (AD)   A centralized and standardized directory service in the Microsoft Windows architecture that automates network management of user data, security, and distributed resources and enables interoperation with other directories in a distributed networking environment [r020]. Active Directory features include:

- Support for the X.500 standard for global directories
- The capability for secure extension of network operations to the Web
- A hierarchical organization that provides a single point of access for system administration (management of user accounts, clients, servers, and applications, for example) to reduce redundancy and errors
- An object-oriented storage organization that allows easier access to information
- Support for the Lightweight Directory Access Protocol (LDAP) to enable inter-directory operability
- Support for the ability to be both backward compatible and forward compatible

Active Fingerprinting   An active attack against a system that is targeted at determining the hardware and software configuration of a system. This is often done by sending carefully crafted packets to the system and noting specific responses.

Active Network Architecture   Network architecture embodying a (relatively) new networking paradigm in which the routers perform customized computation on the data flowing through them (e.g., in the case of sensor networks [r021]). May make use of network-resident proxies (e.g., application-layer proxies). Conceptually speaking, a single IP datagram can carry not only upper-layer protocol headers and user data, but also "code," a set of executable instructions to be interpreted by the intermediate routers, for describing, provisioning, or tailoring network resources and services, and to achieve the delivery and management requirements [r022].

Active Scripting   A generalized term used to describe scripting languages (such as JavaScript or VBScript) that help to create a more dynamic and richer web browsing user experience than would be possible with (static) HyperText Markup Language (HTML). The use of Active Scripting can lead to security exploits, such as Cross-Site Scripting (XSS or CSS).

Active Threat   The threat of a deliberate unauthorized change to the state of the system. (*Note:* Examples of security-relevant active threats may be: modification of messages, replay of messages, insertion of spurious messages, and masquerading as an authorized entity and denial of service) [r068].

ActiveX   A set of technologies from the Microsoft Corporation that extend an application's functionality, such as linking desktop applications with the web browser. ActiveX components often require more access to local system resource than systems traditionally require. This has led to numerous security exploits.

AD   See Active Directory

Add-On Security   (aka remediation) The (often un-architected) overlay of security mechanisms onto a system that is already operational.

Address   Network layer identifier assigned to an interface or set of interfaces that can be used as source or destination field in IP datagrams [r008].

(IPv6 context) The IPv6 128-bit address is divided along 16-bit boundaries. Each 16-bit block is then converted to a 4-digit hexadecimal number, separated by colons. The resulting representation is called colon-hexadecimal. This is in contrast to the 32-bit IPv4 address represented in dotted-decimal format, divided along 8-bit boundaries, and then converted to its decimal equivalent, separated by periods [r023].

The following example shows a 128-bit IPv6 address in binary form:

0010000111011010000000001101001100000000000000000
0101111001110110000001010101010000000001111111111
11111000101000100111000101011010

The following example shows this same address divided along 16-bit boundaries:

0010000111011010 0000000011010011 0000000000000000
0010111100111011 0000000101010101010 0000000011111111
1111111000101000 1001110001011010

The following example shows each 16-bit block in the address converted to hexadecimal and delimited with colons.

21DA:00D3:0000:2F3B:02AA:00FF:FE28:9C5A

IPv6 representation can be further simplified by removing the leading zeros within each 16-bit block. However, each block must have at least a single digit. The following example shows the address without the leading zeros:

21DA:D3:0:2F3B:2AA:FF:FE28:9C5A

Address Autoconfiguration   (IPv6 context) The automatic configuration process for IPv6 addresses in an interface. The process for configuring IP addresses for interfaces in the absence of a stateful address configuration server, such as Dynamic Host Configuration Protocol version 6 (DHCPv6) [r024].

Address Class A   Class A IP addresses use the first bit of the 32-bit space (bit 0) to identify it as a Class A address; this bit is set to 0. Bits 1 to 7 represent the network ID and bits 8 through 31 identify the PC, terminal device, or host/server on the network. This address space supports $2^7 - 2 = 126$ networks and approximately 16 million devices (2^{24}) on each network. By convention, the use of an "all 1s" or "all 0s" address for both the Network ID and the Host ID is prohibited (which is the reason for subtracting the 2 above).

Address Class B   Class B uses the first two bits (bit 0 and bit 1) of the 32-bit space to identify it as a Class B address; these bits are set to 10. Bits 2 to 15 represent the network ID and bits 16 through 31 identify the PC, terminal device, or host/server on the network. This address space supports $2^{14} - 2 = 16,382$ networks and $2^{12} - 2 = 65,134$ devices on each network.

Address Class C   Class C uses the first three bits (bit 0, bit 1, and bit 2) of the 32-bit space to identify it as a Class C address; these bits are set to 110. Bits 3 to 23 represent the network ID and bits 24 through 31 identify the PC, terminal device, or host/server on the network. This address space supports about 2 million networks ($2^{21} - 2$) and $2^8 - 2 = 254$ devices on each network.

Address Class D   This class is used for broadcasting: multiple devices (all devices on the network) receive the same packet. Class D uses the first four bits (bit 0, bit 1, bit 2, and bit 3) of the 32-bit space to identify it as a Class D address; these bits are set to 1110.

Address Maximum Valid Time   Time during a unicast address, obtained by means of stateless autoconfiguration mechanism, keeps in valid state [r008].

Address Resolution   Procedure of link addresses resolution for the next-hop address in a link. In an IPv6 context, the process by which a node resolves a neighboring node's IPv6 address to its link-layer address. The resolved link-layer address becomes an entry in a neighbor cache in the node. The link layer address is equivalent to ARP in IPv4, and the neighbor cache is equivalent to the Address Resolution Protocol (ARP) cache.

The neighbor cache displays the interface identifier for the neighbor cache entry, the neighboring node IPv6 address, the corresponding link-layer address, and the state of the neighbor cache entry [r024].

Address Resolution Protocol (ARP)   A protocol for mapping an IP address to a physical machine address that is recognized in the local network. In an Ethernet Local Area Network (LAN) layer 2 addresses for attached devices are 48 bits long (the physical machine address is also known as a Media Access Control (MAC) address.) A table, usually called the ARP cache, is used to maintain a correlation between each MAC address and its corresponding IP address. ARP provides the protocol rules for making this correlation and providing address conversion in both directions [r19].

Address Types   There are four types of addresses in common use within the Internet described in RFC 1983. They are (in order of increasing protocol model layering): (i) hardware/ Media Access Control (MAC) address; (ii) IP, Internet or Internet address; (iii) e-mail address; and (iv) Uniform Resource Locator (URL).

Address-of-Record (AOR)   (SIP context) A Session Initiation Protocol (SIP) or SIP Secure (SIPS) Uniform Resource Identifier (URI) that points to a domain with a location service that can map the URI to another URI where the user might be available. Typically, the location service is populated through registrations. An AOR is frequently thought of as the "public address" of the user [r025].

Adjacency Down   (OSPF context) The time needed for an Open Shortest-Path First (OSPF) implementation to recognize a link down/adjacency loss based on hello timers alone, to propagate any information as necessary to its remaining adjacencies, and to perform other actions necessary to converge [r026].

Adjacent Channel Crosstalk   (optical transmission term) The relative power level coming from an adjacent channel, referenced to 0 dB power level. It is usually measured at the wavelengths of the pass band boundaries, at the center of a pass band. Note that Adjacent Channel Isolation is interchangeably used, but it is referenced to the peak power of the given channel.

ADLs   See Architecture Description Languages

Administrative Security   Management controls (such as system controls, logging, policies, and procedures) designed to allow for the administration of security systems while providing a high degree to accountability in the execution of these controls.

Administrator   In general the person, entity, or organization that has the responsibility of managing an Information Technologies (IT) systems at various levels such as, but not limited to, proper operation, capacity/performance assessments, security, and user access.

   (instant messaging/presence context) A principal with authority over local computer and network resources, who manages local domains or firewalls. For security and other purposes, an administrator often needs or wants to impose restrictions on network usage based on traffic type, content, volume, or endpoints. A principal's administrator has authority over some or all of that principal's computer and network resources [r027].

Advanced Encryption Standard (AES)   A specific encryption standard (also known as Rijndael) that is a symmetric block cipher adopted by the U.S. Government. The standard was adopted by National Institute of Standards and Technology (NIST) as US FIPS PUB 197 in 2001 after a 5-year standardization process. The cipher was developed by two Belgian cryptographers, Vincent Rijmen and Joan Daemen, and submitted to the AES selection process under the name "Rijndael." As of 2004, no successful attacks against AES had been documented. The block size is 128 bits; the key typically is 128, 192, or 256 bits. AES is intended as a more robust replacement for the Data Encryption Standard (DES) and for the Triple Data Encryption Standard (Triple DES). The algorithm is royalty-free, and it is perceived to offer security of a sufficient level to protect data for the next 20 to 30 years.

Advanced Encryption Standard Galois Message Authentication Code (AES-GMAC) A proposed IPsec Encapsulating Security Payload (ESP) mechanism to provide data origin authentication, but not confidentiality. Galois Message Authentication Code is based on the Galois/Counter Mode (GCM) of operation, and can be efficiently implemented in hardware for speeds of 10 gigabits per second and above, and is also well-suited to software implementations [r028].

Advanced Mobile Phone System (AMPS) Analog cell phone technology deployed in the United States in the 1990s. This technology is now being replaced with digital services such as Time Division Multiple Access (TDMA), Code Division Multiple Access (CDMA), and Global System for Mobile Communications (GSM).

Advanced Research Projects Agency Network (ARPANET) A pioneer packet-switched network that was built in the early 1970s under contract to the U.S. Government, led to the development of today's Internet. ARPANET was decommissioned in 1990 [r013].

Advanced Technology Attachment (ATA) See AT Attachment

Adversary In the security context, an entity that attacks, or is a threat, to a system.

Advice of Charge (AOC) (GSM context) A supplementary service that allows a mobile user to get detailed billing information on the services he/she is subscribed to [r011].

Adware Software applications that present advertising content to screen, usually in the form of a pop-up window or a bar that appears on the screen. These software programs are often downloaded to the workstation without the user's knowledge or consent. When the software tracks on behalf of, and on occasion sends information to, a third party, the software is often called spyware.

AES See Advanced Encryption Standard

AES-GMAC See Advanced Encryption Standard Galois Message Authentication Code

Affiliate (financial term) A company in which another company has a financial interest and/or stake.

AFIWC See Air Force Information Warfare Center

AGCH See Access Grant Channel

Agent Specific meaning: As defined in International Telecommunications Union (ITU) Recommendation X.701, the Systems Management Overview (SMO), a software entity that collects management information which is then sent transmitted to the manager; the agent can also change certain management-related parameters/functionality of the monitored Network Element (NE). With respect to a particular telecommunications service (or resource) instance, it is therefore possible to manage the service with one system playing the manager role while the other plays the agent role [r068a].

Agent-Unique (MIDCOM context) An agent-unique value is unique in the context of the agent. This context includes all MIDCOM sessions the agent participates in. An agent-unique value is assigned by the agent [r030].

Aggregable Unicast Global Address (IPv6 context) Also known as global addresses, these addresses are identified by means of the prefix format 001 (2000::/3). IPv6 global addresses are equivalent to IPv4 public addresses and they are whole routable and reachable in the IPv6 Internet fragment [r008].

Aggregated Risk (aka aggregation) A situation where the sum of the risks of all the elements is higher than the risk of any one element. For example, a collection of Confidential documents may need to be classified as Secret.

Aggregation (aka aggregated risk) A situation where the sum of the risks of all the elements is higher than the risk of any one element. For example, a collection of Confidential documents may need to be classified as Secret.

Aggregation Box (MPLS context) The aggregation box is typically a Layer 2 switch that is service unaware and is used only to aggregate traffic to more function rich points in the network.

AH See Authentication Header

AICH   See Acquisition Indication Channel

AIIM   See Association for Information and Image Management

AIMS   See Automated Intrusion Monitoring System

Air Force Information Warfare Center (AFIWC) (Formerly the Air Force Electronic Warfare Center—AFEWC) USAF organization responsible for planning, implementing, and managing the annual worldwide SERENE BYTE exercise to assess EWIR effectiveness. The term SERENE BYTE refers to exercising Air Force electronic warfare system changes; EWIRDB (Electronic Warfare Integrated Reprogramming Database) is the primary Department of Defense (DoD) approved source for technical parametric and performance data on noncommunications electronic emitters and associated systems. AFIWC was activated in 1993. AFIWC is responsible to develop/acquire/deploy in software tools and systems to help win the war on the information operations battlefield. AFIWC was established by combining the securities functions of the Air Force Cryptologic Support Center with the functions performed by AFEWC. The center is the focal point for development and application of information dominance in future warfare. It provides commanders with products and services to wage command and control warfare. The center is charged with protecting friendly command and control capability including U.S. Air Force computer security. It is the primary source of electronic warfare and command, control, and communications countermeasure analysis and advice for the Air Force; it also maintains a database of electronic combat-related information that is used throughout the DoD. The data assists air component commanders in making electronic combat decisions [r031].

AIS   See Automated Information System and/or Audit Trail Software

ALE   See Annualized Loss Expectancy

Alert   A message describing an event relevant to operations staff, including security staff.

ALG   See Application Level Gateway

Algorithm   An unambiguous formula or set of rules for solving a problem in a finite number of steps. For example, algorithms for encryption are usually called ciphers.

An explicit description of how a particular computation should be performed (or a problem solved). The efficiency of an algorithm can be measured as the number of elementary steps it takes to solve the problem. An algorithm is $O(f(n))$, if its worst-case running time divided by $f(n)$ is bounded by a fixed (positive) constant as the input size n increases [r036].

More formally, an *algorithm* is a Turing machine that halts after a finite number of steps, regardless of input. It has an input tape and an output tape. The algorithm may have access to a *random tape,* in which case the algorithm is called *probabilistic.* The random tape is just a tape containing random zeros and ones, and is sometimes called the *coin tosses* of the algorithm. One usually considers the random tape to be infinitely long. A probabilistic algorithm should terminate after a finite number of steps, regardless of input and random tape [r032].

Alias   A name used in place of an actual name, typically for the purpose of deception or anonymity.

Alliance for Telecommunications Industry Solutions (ATIS)   A technical planning and standards development organization that is committed to rapidly developing and promoting technical and operations standards for the communications and related information technologies industry worldwide using a pragmatic, flexible, and open approach. Participants from more than 350 communications companies are active in ATIS' 22 industry committees and Incubator Solutions Program. An ATIS standard defines frameworks for service and performance requirements, defines interfaces and physical characteristics for technologies, systems, and business processes, and ensures interoperability. The key goal of standards is to support interoperability of networks, network equipment, and customer premise equipment, which in turn reduces costs and coordinates industry efforts to produce solutions that role out new services and products to end users of communications and information services. ATIS standards are not only technical requirements but also those that standardize processes for systems and businesses processes.

Ambient Data A form of computer evidence where the data comes from an area of the computer system where temporary or residual information is stored. Examples of this include Windows operating system temporary files, and in unallocated disk space where the user thought that he or she deleted the data [r066].

American Bar Association (ABA) Guidelines A set of guidelines published by the ABA in the document *American Bar Association (ABA) Digital Signature Guidelines* which are a framework of legal principles for the use of digital signatures and digital certificates in e-commerce.

American National Standards Institute (ANSI) An association of manufacturers, users, and other stakeholders, that administers U.S. voluntary standards. ANSI is the U.S. representative to the International Organization for Standardization (ISO). ANSI has served in the capacity as administrator and coordinator of the United States private sector voluntary standardization system for more than 80 years. ANSI has enhanced the global competitiveness of U.S. business and the American quality of life by (i) facilitating voluntary consensus standards, (ii) improving the conformity assessment system, and (iii) maintaining integrity [r033].

AML See Anti-Money Laundering

Amortization (financial term) (1) The gradual elimination of a liability, such as a mortgage, in regular payments over a specified period of time. Such payments must be sufficient to cover both principal and interest. (2) Writing off an intangible asset investment over the projected life of the assets [r009].

Amortization Method (financial term) (1) A distribution calculation method for making penalty-free early withdrawals from retirement accounts. An assumed earnings rate is applied over the du-

ration of the individual's life expectancy, while the life expectancy is determined using Internal Revenue Service (IRS) tables. Generally, the rate must be within 120% of the applicable federal long-term rate. Once the rate is determined, the withdrawal remains fixed each year [r009]. (2) A distribution calculation method for making penalty-free early withdrawals from retirement accounts. An assumed earnings rate is applied over the duration of the individual's life expectancy. Generally, the rate must be within 120% of the applicable federal long-term rate. Once the rate is determined, the withdrawal remains fixed each year [r009].

AMPS See Advanced Mobile Phone System

Angel (aka angel investor) (financial term) An individual who provides capital to one or more startup companies. The individual is usually affluent or has a personal stake in the success of the venture. Such investments are characterized by high levels of risk and a potentially large return on investment [r009].

Ankle-Biter (aka Script Kiddie) Young individuals (teenage and sometimes even younger), that act as hackers or crackers by utilizing readily available toolkits containing applications and "canned scripts." These users do not always understand how the attack actually works, nor do they always fully understand the consequences of such an attack.

Annual Report (financial term) Audited financial document required by the Securities Exchange Commission (SEC) and sent to a public company's or mutual fund's shareholders at the end of each fiscal year, reporting the financial results for the year (including the balance sheet, income statement, cash flow statement, and description of company operations) and commenting on recent business accomplishments. The term sometimes refers to the colorful brochure and sometimes to Form 10-K, that is sent along with the brochure and contains more detailed financial information. All 10-Ks for public companies and mutual funds incorporated in the United States are available for free on the SEC's website [r009].

Annual Return   (financial term) The increase in value of an investment, expressed as a percentage per year. If the annual return is expressed as annual percentage yield, then the number takes into account the effects of compounding interest. If it is expressed as annual percentage rate, then the annual rate will usually not take into account the effect of compounding interest [r009].

Annualized Loss Expectancy (ALE)   Annual expected loss to an organization based on a security threat.

Anomaly Detection Model Intrusion Detection System   Approach where the intrusion detection system detects intrusions first creating a baseline of "normal" system or network behavior. This is usually done by recording activities over several days. An anomaly is detected when the current activity exceeds the baseline by certain thresholds.

Anonymous   The condition of having a name or identity that is unknown or concealed. An application may require security services that maintain anonymity of users or other system entities, perhaps in order to preserve their privacy or hide them from attack [r013].

Anonymous File Transfer Protocol (Anonymous FTP)   A method of using FTP that does not require the user (system) to login and/or identify himself/herself/itself before downloading files. Often Anonymous FTP is used to deliver signal files informing the system of the status of a job. Because of the lack of accountability inherent with Anonymous FTP, it is preferable to not allow this facility.

Anonymous Login   Enabling an entity to access a system without individual authentication. Anonymous logins are usually where the entity either (a) is not required to authenticate to the system or (b) uses an "anonymous" or "guest" account. Anonymous logins must be avoided when accountability is a requirement.

ANSI   See American National Standards Institute

Ant-Keylogging Software   A program designed to limit the effectiveness of keystroke logging software. Generally, these programs either look for files that match signatures of known keystroke logging software or interact with host-specific mechanisms (listeners or hooks) to identity keystroke logging activity. For example, a hook process in Microsoft Windows uses the function SetWindowsHookEx(). Some hook-based anti-keyloggers block this passing of control from one hook procedure to another.

Anti-Money Laundering (AML)   (financial term) A program in place in a firm (particularly a financial firm) that helps to define: (i) What procedures to follow when obtaining and verifying a new customer's identity; (ii) what activities are suspicious, and how and when to file a Suspicious Activity Report (SAR); (iii) whom to contact about an activity that may warrant filing a SAR; and (iv) how and when to file a Currency Transaction Report (CTR).

Anti-Spyware Software/Products   Application for detection and removal of spyware. Some of the tools for detecting and removing spyware include (but are not limited to): Microsoft Antispyware, Ad-Aware, PestPatrol, and Spy Sweeper.

Antitrust Laws   (financial term) Federal laws precluding a business from monopolizing a market (or restraining free trade).

Anti-Virus Software (AV Software)   A program that is used to detect and remediate a system infected with viruses, worms, Trojans, and other forms of malicious code. In an enterprise, Anti-Virus checks can happen prior to the file being downloaded onto the target system or after the file has been downloaded but before it is first executed.

Anycast Address   A unicast address that identifies several interfaces and is used for the delivery from one to one-between-several. With an appropriate route, datagrams addressed to an anycast address will be deliver to a single interface, the nearest [r008].

AOC   See Advice of Charge

AOR   See Address-of-Record

AP   See Access Point

API   See Application Programming Interface

APN   See Access Point Name

Applet   In general, a program designed to be executed from within another application. Applets cannot be executed directly from the operating system.

In particular, a program written in the Java programming language that can be included in a web page. Java applets are small Java applications that can be downloaded from a web server and run on a computer by a Java-compatible web browser. Browsers (which are almost invariably equipped with a Java Virtual Machine) can interpret applets downloaded from web servers and execute them.

Because applets are small in size and are cross-platform compatible, they are common for Internet applications accessible from a browser. Security may be an issue; however, applets are generally considered to be more secure than ActiveX objects because of Java's robust security features. Often called the Java sandbox, applets "play" in the Java sandbox, but are not allowed to execute, write, or read files outside the sandbox.

Applet class loader   Mechanism used in a Java sandbox. All Java objects belong to classes. The applet class loader determines when and how an applet can add classes to a running Java environment. The loader ensures that elements of the Java run-time environment are not replaced by extraneous code that an applet attempts to install (illegally).

Appliance   A stand-alone element (such as a proxy, firewall, or load balancer) that supports a small set of well-defined functions running on dedicated hardware, Operating System, and often application software. Because appliances are dedicated to a single purpose, they sometimes perform significantly better and are more hardened against attack than nondedicated devices (such as software-based firewalls).

Application Association   A cooperative relationship between two application entities, formed by their exchange of application protocol control information through their use of presentation services [r068a].

Application Content Filtering   Services providing Internet Protocol (IP) filtering, malicious code detection and isolation, and limiting what websites or information may be access or sent by a system or entity.

Application Context   An explicitly identified set of application service elements, related options, and any other necessary information for the interworking of application entities on an application association [r068a].

Application Entity   The aspects of an application process pertinent to Open Systems Interconnection Reference Model (OSIRM) [r068a].

Application Defenses   Mechanisms (sometimes in the form of appliances) that provide resiliency against attacks targeted at all relevant layers of the Open Systems Interconnection Reference Model (OSIRM). These products aim at successfully defended against attack methodologies across OSIRM Layers 2 though 7, while simpler firewalls can only defend against attacks at lower networking levels up to Layer 3.

Application-Layer Proxies/Agents   (aka Application Proxy) Some Internet routers can provide application-layer services. For example, an intermediate router can become a transparent web proxy when it snoops through the Transmission Control Protocol (TCP) and then looks at the HyperText Transfer Protocol (HTTP) header of an Internet Protocol (IP) datagram to determine the web page request and subsequently serves it with the web page from the local cache. Proxies are transparent to end-users but can improve the responsiveness because (in the case of local caching) the delivery paths for web request and data between the intermediate router and the website server are eliminated in a number of instances (e.g., based on the age of the cache and the type of request) [r022].

Application-Layer Proxy Service   A proxy service that is set up and torn down in response to a client request using application protocol information, rather than existing on a static basis. It can be implemented in a firewall, server, or mediation appliance. Circuit proxies always forward packets containing a given port number if that port number is permitted by the rule set, while application proxies forward packets only once a connection has been established using some known protocol and when the connection closes a firewall supporting application layer proxy service rejects individual packets even if they contain port numbers allowed by a rule set [r040].

Application Level Gateway (ALG) A type of firewall that examines the packets more thoroughly than a circuit-level gateway when making forwarding decisions. An application gateway is considered more secure, but uses more memory and processor resources [r035, r036].

The ALG acts as a proxy for applications, performing all data exchanges with the remote system in their behalf. This can render a computer behind the firewall all but invisible to the remote system.

An ALG can allow or disallow traffic according to very specific rules—for instance, permitting some commands to a server but not others, limiting file access to certain types, varying rules according to authenticated users, and so forth. This type of firewall may also perform very detailed logging of traffic and monitoring of events on the host system, and it can often be instructed to sound alarms or notify an operator under defined conditions. ALGs are generally regarded as the most secure type of firewall (they have the most sophisticated capabilities.) A disadvantage is that setup may be very complex, requiring detailed attention to the individual applications that use the gateway. An application gateway is normally implemented on a separate computer on the network whose primary function is to provide proxy service.

(MIDCOM context) Entities that possess the application-specific intelligence and knowledge of an associated middlebox function. An ALG examines application traffic in transit and assists the middlebox in carrying out its function. An ALG may be a co-resident with a middlebox or reside externally, communicating through a middlebox communication protocol. It interacts with a middlebox to set up state, access control filters, use middlebox state information, modify applica-

tion-specific payload, or perform whatever else is necessary to enable the application to run through the middlebox. ALGs are different from proxies. ALGs are not visible to end-hosts, unlike the proxies that are relay agents terminating sessions with both end-hosts. ALGs do not terminate sessions with either end-host. Instead, ALGs examine, and optionally modify, application payload content to facilitate the flow of application traffic through a middlebox. ALGs are middlebox centric, in that they assist the middleboxes in carrying out their function, whereas, the proxies act as a focal point for application servers, relaying traffic between application clients and servers. ALGs are similar to proxies, in that both ALGs and proxies facilitate application-specific communication between clients and servers [r037, r038].

Application Level Gateway Operation A description of typical interactions with an Application Level Gateway. All internal computers (in a network) establish a connection with the proxy server. The proxy server performs all communications with the Internet. External computers only see the IP address of the proxy server and never communicate directly with the internal client [r035].

Application Programming Interface (API) (aka Application Programmer Interface) A published open specification supplied by the owners of a software application that allows developers to program to a preconstructed interface (the API) instead of programming a device or piece of software directly. This can greatly reduce the programming effort because knowledge of the inner workings of the software application are not required. However, functionality exposed via the API is often limited. Many APIs exist; an example of an API is the Java Swings API that allows for easier creation of Java-based Graphical User Interfaces (GUI).

Application Protocol A protocol that normally layers directly on top of the transport layer [e.g., Transmission Control Protocol/Internet Protocol (TCP/IP)]. Examples include HyperText Transfer Protocol (HTTP), TELNET, File Transfer Protocol (FTP), and, Simple Mail Transfer Protocol (SMTP) [r039].

Application Proxy   See Application-Layer Proxies/Agents

Application Servers   Intranet-, Internet-, or extranet-resident computer systems that run business (or other) applications.

Applications Service Provider (ASP)   A company that offers services (typically web-server-based) that can be accessed by consumers of the service over a network. Consumers of these services are often small (sometimes even large-scale) businesses looking to reduce the need for internal support of applications as well as an acknowledgment that the ASP may have specialized tools and expertise in a particular field. However, by externalizing application access, companies are potentially at a greater information security risk. Rigor must be taken in the selection and compliance program for ASPs to ensure that they are meeting the (consumer) company's security requirements.

Application-Specific Data (ASD)   An application-specific field in the IPSec header that along with the destination IP address provides a unique number for each Security Association (SA).

Approved Changes   In a Change Control system, there are a series of approvals that must take place prior to granting personnel the permission to make operation changes. An approved change is a change that has successfully passed the approval workflow.

Arbitrage   (financial term) Attempting to profit by exploiting price differences of identical or similar financial instruments, on different markets or in different forms [r009].

Arbitrary Block Length (ABL)   Pseudo-Integrity Protection algorithm discussed in the context of Institute of Electrical and Electronic Engineers (IEEE) P1619 (Security for Storage Data at Rest). A change in ciphertext produces random plaintext; the upper-layer applications will likely be "confused" by the result and detect the anomaly. Pseudo-integrity is provided by "nonmalleable" encryption modes—for example, EME-32-AES (Encrypt-Mix-Encrypt). ABL (Arbitrary Block Length) (D. Mcgrew and J. Viega) is a recently-proposed as an Intellectual Property free alternative to EME-32-AES.

Architecture   Formal descriptions of a computer system, network, software, and/or application program that define the macro-level organization of the system in question. Typically, an architecture consists of the identification of a set of abstract Functional Blocks, the logical interrelationships of these Functional Blocks (interfaces), the connection/protocols means between the Functional Blocks, and the data exchanged over the interfaces.

Architecture Description   A formal description of an information system, organized in a way that supports reasoning about the structural properties of the system. It defines the components or building blocks that make up the overall information system and provides a plan from which products can be procured, and systems developed, that will work together to implement the overall system. It thus enables one to manage one's own overall Information Technology (IT) investment in a way that meets the needs of the business.

Architecture Description Languages (ADLs)   Mechanisms to describe software architectures via special-purpose languages.

Architecture Description, IEEE 1471-2000   A collection of artifacts that document an architecture.

Architecture Framework   A tool that can be used for developing a broad range of different architectures. Typically, the framework is a collection of guidance for developing and/or documenting Architectures. Namely, the framework provides rules and guidance for developing and presenting architecture descriptions. The products defined by the framework are the work products of architecture development, the descriptive artifacts that communicate the architecture.

The Framework should describe a method for designing an information system in terms of a set of building blocks and for showing how the building blocks fit together. The Framework should contain a set of tools and provide a common vocabulary. It should also include a list of recommended standards and compliant products that can be used to implement the building blocks.

Architecture, American National Standards Institute (ANSI)   Per ANSI/IEEE Std 1471-2000 is: "the fundamental organization of a system, embodied in its components, their relationships to each other and the environment, and the principles governing its design and evolution."

Architecture, IEEE 1471-2000   A system's fundamental organization that embodies its components, their relationships to each other and to the environment, and the principles guiding its design and evolution. This definition/formulation is more focused on the architecture of a single system rather than an entire Enterprise.

Architecture, The Open Group Architecture Framework (TOGAF)   TOGAF embraces but does not strictly adhere to ANSI/IEEE Std 1471-2000 terminology. In TOGAF, "Architecture" has two meanings depending upon its contextual usage: (1) A formal description of a system, or a detailed plan of the system at component level to guide its implementation. (2) The structure of components, their interrelationships, and the principles and guidelines governing their design and evolution over time.

Archival   A means of storing and preserving information that has long-term value. Unlike a backup, archiving typically implies saving application data for the purposes of meeting data retention requirements (for regulatory purposes) or to have data available for future account inquiries. The recovery of archived data may take several minutes, days, or weeks, depending on how long before the data were archived and the importance of the data. Archival is based on a policy and occurs on a predetermined schedule.

Archival Data   The data saved in the archival process.

Archive   The physical location (server, removable media, etc.) of the archival data.

Archive, Backup, and Restore Components   Se-

curity services for security system management. The archival policy specifies at what intervals and for which elements application data are stored. Backup and restore components ensure that a snapshot of the software and application state can be successfully retrieved at any given time.

Archiving   Transferring (electronic) files no longer being used to secondary (and usually less expensive) storage media for safe keeping and future reference.

ARIB   See Association of Radio Industry Business

Arithmetic Mean   Simple average, equal to the sum of all values divided by the number of values.

$$\bar{x} = \text{arithmetic mean} = (x_1 + \cdots + x_n)/n$$

Arithmetic-Geometric Mean   The arithmetic–geometric mean $M(x, y)$ of two positive real numbers x and y is defined as follows: Let $a_1 = (x + y)/2$ and $g_1 = (xy)^{1/2}$; next define a_n and g_n as follows:

$$a_{n+1} = \frac{a_n + g_n}{2} \qquad \text{and} \qquad g_{n+1} = \sqrt{a_n g_n}.$$

Let n go to infinity. Then these two sequences converge to the same number, namely, the arithmetic–geometric mean $M(x, y)$ of x and y (actually this sequence converges fairly rapidly and usually with less than a couple dozen iterations).

ARL   See Authority Revocation List

ARM   See Automated Resource Management

Arm's Length Transaction   (financial term) A transaction between two related or affiliated parties that is conducted as if they were unrelated, so that there is no question of a conflict of interest. Or, sometimes, a transaction between two otherwise unrelated or affiliated [r009].

ARP   See Address Resolution Protocol

ARPANET   See Advanced Research Projects Agency Network

Array Controllers   The intelligent component of a disk subsystem where control software executes [r029].

AS   See Access Slots or Autonomous System

ASD   See Application-Specific Data

ASIM   See Automated Security Incident Measurement

ASN.1   See Abstract Syntax Notation One

ASON   See Automatically Switched Optical Network

ASP   Applications Service Provider

Assessment   In the context of security, an evaluation of the information security risks for system or solution, using as much analytics as possible. The security assessment should be done both in a quantitative manner (e.g., computing the Expected Loss, the Expected Cost, the variance of the outcomes, etc.) as well as in a qualitative manner (what alternative scenarios are possible, what risk mediation techniques are available, etc.)

Assessment & Design   A methodical approach that a company performs in order to identity key areas to focus on and the effort to remediate those key areas.

Asset   (financial term) Any item of economic value owned by an individual or corporation, especially that which could be converted to cash. Examples are cash, securities, accounts receivable, inventory, office equipment, a house, a car, and other property. On a balance sheet, assets are equal to the sum of liabilities, common stock, preferred stock, and retained earnings [r009].

ASSET   See Automated Security Self-Evaluation Tool

Asset Management   Mechanisms that allow companies to learn and record what systems are in the company's purview, what systems are connected to the network, and what applications are on each system.

ASSIST   See Automated Systems Security Incident Support Team

Associated Alarms   Alarms directly related to a given identified trouble [r068a].

Association   A cooperative relationship between system entities—for example, for the purpose of transferring information between them.

Association for Information and Image Management (AIIM)   Industry advocacy group focusing on Enterprise Content Management (ECM) and document imaging.

Association of Radio Industry Business (ARIB)   (GSM context) In the global standardization process, ARIB has the mandate of ascertaining that the Asian guidelines are taken into account [r011].

Assurance   Measure of confidence that the security features, practices, procedures, and architecture of an information system accurately mediates and enforces the security policy [r041].

Assurance Level   A specific level on a hierarchical scale representing successively increased confidence that a target of evaluation adequately fulfills the requirements [r013].

Asymmetric Algorithm for Key Agreement   A key agreement algorithm (e.g., Diffie–Hellman) that operates as follows: Alice and Bob each send their own public key to the other person; then each uses their own private key and the other's public key to compute the new key value [r013].

Asymmetric Algorithm for Signature   A digital signature algorithm (DSA) that operates as follows: when Alice wants to ensure data integrity or provide authentication for data she sends to Bob, she uses her private key to sign the data (i.e., create a digital signature based on the data); to verify the signature, Bob uses the matching public key that Alice has provided [r013].

Asymmetric Algorithms for Encryption   An encryption algorithm [e.g., Rivest–Shamir–Adleman (RSA)] that operates as follows: When Alice wants to ensure confidentiality for data she sends to Bob, she encrypts the data with a public key provided by Bob; only Bob has the matching private key that is needed to decrypt the data [r013].

Asymmetric Cipher   See Public Key Cryptography

Asymmetric Cryptographic Algorithm   An algorithm for performing encipherment or the corresponding decipherment in which the keys used for encipherment and decipherment differ. (*Note:* With some asymmetric cryptographic algorithms, decipherment of ciphertext or the generation of a digital signature requires the use of more than one private key) [r068a]. See Asymmetric Cryptography

Asymmetric Cryptography A branch of cryptography (popularly known as "public-key cryptography") in which the algorithms employ a pair of keys (a public key and a private key) and use a different component of the pair for different steps of the algorithm [r013]. Asymmetric algorithms have key management advantages over equivalently strong symmetric ones, as follows: One key of the pair does not need to be known by anyone but its owner; so it can more easily be kept secret; also, although the other key of the pair is shared by all entities that use the algorithm, that key does not need to be kept secret from other, nonusing entities; so the key distribution part of key management can be done more easily.

Asymmetric Key-based Algorithms (aka public key/private key encryption) Encryption method that uses one key to encrypt information and a different key to decrypt the information later on.

Asynchronous Communication Transmission method where the sender and the receiver do not need to have synchronized clocks. Term also refers more generally to information transfers such as e-mail, voicemail, and videomail where the sender and the receiver do not need to be simultaneously present.

Asynchronous Receipt Receipt returned to the sender on a different communication session than the sender's original message session.

Asynchronous Transaction (MIDCOM context) An asynchronous transaction is not triggered by an agent. It may occur without any agent participating in a session with the middlebox. Potentially, an asynchronous transaction includes the transfer of notification messages from the middlebox to agents that participate in an open session. A notification message is sent to each agent that needs to be notified about the asynchronous event. The message indicates the state transition at the middlebox [r030].

Asynchronous Transfer Mode (ATM) (aka Cell Relay Service) A broadband, cell-based service developed in the late 1980s and deployed in the early to mid-1990s. Cells are 53 bytes long (of which 5 bytes are for overhead). Supports access speeds of T1, DS3, OC-3, and OC-12. Fine-grain Quality of Service (QoS) is supported via traffic policing/shaping mechanisms. Several service categories are supported—for example, Constant Bit Rate (CBR), Variable Bit Rate (VBR), Variable Bit Rate Real Time (rtVBR), Variable Bit Rate Non-Real Time (nrtVBR), and Available Bit Rate (ABR). Connectivity is supported via Virtual Channels (VCs), which are identified by locally significant labels (VPIs/VCIs). ATM can support Switched Virtual Circuits (or Connections) (SVCs), but nearly all implementations relay on permanent Virtual Circuits (or Connections) (PVCs); SVCs require the implementation/support of a signaling channel/protocol. The support of typical enterprise connectivity (e.g., IP PDU transport, voice support, video support, etc.) is accomplished via appropriate ATM Adaptation Layer (AAL) protocols. While the service has been used for the past decade (as a "step-up" from Frame Relay Service), it appears that in the future it will be supplanted by Multi-Protocol Label Switching (MPLS). ATM/cell relay is not "too friendly" to IP connectivity because a typical IP Protocol Data Unit (PDU) needs to be segmented into about 30 cells and then be re-assembled at the remote end; this is both time-consuming and can impact Transmission Control Protocol (TCP) timers/reassembly. For example, see [r042] and [r044–r055].

(GSM context) ATM is used in Universal Mobile Telecommunications System (UMTS) and provides symmetrical or asymmetrical connections for each carrier service used. The connections are not limited to 64 kbps as in GSM, and they offer sufficient capacity even for broadband services [r011].

AT Attachment (ATA) (aka Advanced Technologies Attachment) The proper name for the mass storage device interface that is frequently called (in marketing circles) IDE (Integrated Drive Electronics) or Enhanced IDE (EIDE). The AT part is from the IBM PC/AT (1984). ATAPI is short for ATA Packet Interface. ATAPI allows SCSI devices to be attached to the ATA interface [r043]. The American National Standards Institute (ANSI) InterNational Committee for Information Technology Standards (INCITS) T13 is the standards committee that develops and maintains the ATA and ATA/ATAPI standards. The specification was published in 1994 as ANSI standard X3.221-1994, entitled "AT Attachment Interface for Disk Drives" [r029]. Some additional definitions are:

- ATA or PATA—Parallel ATA—the traditional parallel ATA interface—used by disk drives.
- ATAPI or PATAPI—ATAPI using PATA—used by CD, DVD and tape devices.
- SATA—Serial ATA—serial version of parallel ATA—mostly used by disk drives.
- SATAPI—Serial ATAPI—ATAPI using SATA—used by CD, DVD, and tape devices.

ATA   See AT (Advanced Technology) Attachment

A-ter   (GSM context) The A-ter interface is situated between the Transcoder and the Base Station Controller. A-ter is a multiplexed and transcoded A interface [r011].

Athermal   (optical transmission term) The thermal stability of the devices. If the performance parameters, such as wavelength and insertion loss, are well below some defined critical values over the operating temperature, the device is said to be athermal. To claim a multiplexing/demultiplexing device as athermal, its thermal wavelength stability should be better than 1.0 pm/°C and temperature-dependent insertion loss should be smaller than 0.015 dB/°C.

ATIS   See Alliance for Telecommunications Industry Solutions

ATM   See Asynchronous Transfer Mode

ATM Adaptation Layer (AAL)   The protocol layer that allows multiple applications to have data converted to and from the Asynchronous Transfer Mode (ATM) cell. A protocol used that translates higher layer services into the size and format of an ATM cell [r042, r044–r052].

ATM Adaptation Layer Type 1 (AAL-1)   AAL functions in support of constant bit rate, time-dependent traffic such as voice and video [r042, r044–r052].

ATM Adaptation Layer Type 2 (AAL-2)   AAL for packet-oriented variable bit rate video transmission [r042, r044–r052].

ATM Adaptation Layer Type 3/4 (AAL-3/4)   (effectively defunct) AAL functions in support of variable bit rate, delay-tolerant data traffic requiring some sequencing and/or error detection support. Originally two AAL types (i.e., connection-oriented and connectionless) that have been combined [r042, r044–r052].

ATM Adaptation Layer Type 5 (AAL-5)   AAL functions in support of variable bit rate, delay-tolerant connection-oriented data traffic requiring minimal sequencing or error detection support [r042, r044–r052].

Attachment Circuit (AC)   In a layer 2 VPN the Customer Edge (CE) is attached to the Provider Edge (PE) via an Attachment Circuit (AC). The AC may be a physical or logical link.

Attachment Unit Interface (AUI)   In Ethernet LAN systems (more specifically at the 10-Mbps range), the interface between the Medium Attachment Unit (MAU) and the Data Terminal Equipment (DTE) within a data station. Note that the AUI carries encoded signals and provides for duplex data transmission. Described in IEEE 802.3 Clauses 7 and 8.

Attack   (aka penetration, violation) An attempt to gain unauthorized access (bypassing security controls) to an information system's services, resources, or information; and/or the attempt to compromise an information system's confidentiality, integrity, or availability [r056].

Attacks against PPVPN Routing Protocols   (PPVPN context) This encompasses attacks against routing protocols that are run by the service provider and that directly support the PPVPN service. In layer 3 Virtual Private Networks (VPNs) this typically relates to membership discovery or to the distribution of per-VPN routes.

In layer 2 VPNs this typically relates to membership and endpoint discovery. Attacks against the use of routing protocols for the distribution of backbone (non-VPN) routes are beyond the scope of this document [r058].

Attacks on Address Space Separation (PPVPN context) In layer 3 Virtual Private Networks (VPNs), the IP address spaces of different VPNs have to be kept separate. In layer 2 VPNs, the Media Access Control (MAC) address and Virtual Local Area Network (VLAN) spaces of different VPNs have to be kept separate. A control plane breach in this addressing separation may result in unauthorized data plane cross-connection between VPNs [r058].

Attacks on Hash-and-Sign Signature Schemes Attacks on hash-and-sign signature schemes in which the adversary is allowed to replace the original hash function (description). Given a signature s for the hash value hash(m) of a message, the adversary tries to find a hash function hash* and message m* such that hash*(m*) = hash(m) [r016, r059].

Attacks on Route Separation (PPVPN context) "Route separation" refers to keeping the per-VPN (Virtual Private Network) topology and reachability information for each Provider Provisioned Virtual Private Network (PPVPN) separate from, and unavailable to, any other PPVPN (except as specifically intended by the service provider). This concept is only a distinct security concern for layer-3 VPN types for which the service provider is involved with the routing within the VPN. A breach in the route separation can reveal topology and addressing information about a PPVPN. It can also cause black hole routing or unauthorized data plane cross-connection between PPVPNs [r058].

Attacks on Service Provider Equipment via Management Interfaces (PPVPN context) This includes unauthorized access to service provider infrastructure equipment, in order, for example, to reconfigure the equipment or to extract information (statistics, topology, etc.) about one or more Provider Provisioned Virtual Private

Networks (PPVPNs). This can be accomplished through malicious entrance of the systems, or as an inadvertent consequence of inadequate inter-VPN (Virtual Private Network) isolation in a PPVPN user self-management interface. (The former is not necessarily a PPVPN-specific issue.) [r058].

Attempt Address (IPv6 context) Unicast address where uniqueness is no longer checked.

Attribute Information concerning a managed object used to describe (either in part or in whole) that managed object. This information consists of an attribute type and its corresponding attribute value (single-valued) or values (multivalued) [r068a].

Attribute Authority (AA) A Certification Authority (CA), trusted by the verifier to delegate privileges, which issues attribute certificates [r060].

Attribute Authority Revocation List (AARL) A revocation list containing a list of references to attribute certificates issued to Attribute Authorities (AAs) that are no longer considered valid by the issuing authority [r068a].

Attribute-Based Access Control (ABAC) An access security mechanism that allows access control decisions to depend on multiple attributes of the requester, not just their identity or role.

Attribute Certificate A data structure in a public-key certificate that includes some attribute values and identification information about the owner of the attribute certificate, all digitally signed by an Attribute Authority (AA). This authority's signature serves as the guarantee of the binding between the attributes and their owner [r060].

Attribute Certificate Revocation List (AARL) A revocation list containing a list of references to attribute certificates that are no longer considered valid by the issuing authority [r068a].

Attribute Type The component of an attribute that indicates the class of information given by that attribute [r068a].

Attribute Value A particular instance of the class of information indicated by an attribute type.

AuC   See Authentication Center

Audit   The process of examining the history of a transaction to find out what happened. An operational audit can be an examination of ongoing activities to determine what is happening [r056].

(financial term) (1) An examination and verification of a company's financial and accounting records and supporting documents by a professional, such as a Certified Public Accountant. (2) An Internal Revenue Service (IRS) examination of an individual or corporation's tax return, to verify its accuracy. An audit is an IRS examination of an individual or corporation's tax return, to verify its accuracy. There are three types of IRS audits: correspondence audits (the IRS mails a request for additional information), office audits (an interview is conducted at a local IRS office), and field audits (an interview is conducted at a taxpayer's place of business, for a corporate tax return). Since there is always the chance of an audit, experts recommend keeping good records to support all the information in a return. The reason detailed and accurate bookkeeping is so important is that the burden of proof is on the filer, not the IRS [r009].

Audit Service   A security service that records information needed to establish accountability for system events and for the actions of system entities that cause them [r013].

Audit Trail   A chronological record of system activities or message routing that permits reconstruction and examination of a sequence of events [r064, r065].

AUI   See Attachment Unit Interface

AUP   See Acceptable Use Policy

AUTACK   Authentication and acknowledgment message defined in ISO 9735 for Electronic Data Interchange (EDI) EDIFACT security. AUTACK is a message authenticating *sent,* or providing secure acknowledgment of *received* interchanges, groups, messages, or packages. It can be used for both national and international trade. It is based on universal practice related to administration, commerce, and transport, and is not dependent on the type of business or industry. It is employed to:

(i) give secure authentication, integrity, or non-repudiation of origin to messages, packages, groups, or interchanges; (ii) give secure acknowledgment or nonrepudiation of receipt to secured messages, packages, groups, or interchanges.

Authentic Copy   A reproduction that has been officially certified, especially so that it may be admitted as evidence [r067].

Authentic Signature   A (digital) signature that can be trusted because it can be verified.

Authenticate   The act of performing authentication.

Authentication   The process of verifying an identity claimed by or for a system entity. An authentication process consists of two steps: (1) Identification step: Presenting an identifier to the security system. An example of an identifier is a User ID. (2) Verification step: Presenting or generating authentication information that corroborates the binding between the entity and the identifier. An example would be presenting the password that is associated with the User ID [r013].

(financial term) Verification that a legal document is genuine or valid, such as through a seal from an authorized public official [r009].

Authentication & Billing Center (ABC)   (GSM context) The Authentication & Billing Center transfers customer data to the relevant Network Subsystem (NSS) registers. Connection information from the Mobile Services Switching Center (MSC), so-called Call Detail Records, are used in the Billing Center for billing [r011].

Authentication Center (AuC)   (GSM context) The Authentication Center checks the Subscriber Identity Module (SIM) cards and disables them if necessary [r011].

Authentication Chain   (DNSSEC context) An alternating sequence of Domain Name System (DNS) public key (DNSKEY) RRsets and Delegation Signer (DS) RRsets forms a chain of signed data, with each link in the chain vouching for the next. A DNSKEY Resource Record (RR) is used to verify the signature covering a DS RR and allows the DS RR to be authenticated. The

DS RR contains a hash of another DNSKEY RR and this new DNSKEY RR is authenticated by matching the hash in the DS RR. This new DNSKEY RR, in turn, authenticates another DNSKEY RRset and, in turn, some DNSKEY RR in this set may be used to authenticate another DS RR, and so forth, until the chain finally ends with a DNSKEY RR whose corresponding private key signs the desired DNS data. For illustrative purposes, the root DNSKEY RRset can be used to authenticate the DS RRset for "example."; the "example." DS RRset contains a hash that matches some "example." DNSKEY, and this DNSKEY's corresponding private key signs the "example." DNSKEY RRset. Private key counterparts of the "example." DNSKEY RRset sign data records such as "www.example." and DS RRs for delegations such as "subzone.example" [r069].

Authentication Exchange   A mechanism to verify the identity of an entity by means of information exchange.

Authentication Function   The security functional entity in the home domain that maintains security relationship with the subscribed mobile users and the subscribed mobile terminals.

Authentication Header (AH)   A record containing a Ticket and an Authenticator to be presented to a server as part of the authentication process [r070].

Also, an Internet IP Security (IPsec) protocol designed to provide connectionless data integrity service and data origin authentication service for Internet Protocol (IP) datagrams, and (optionally) to provide protection against replay attacks. In this context, AH provides for integrity but without confidentiality [r013, r071].

AH may be used alone, or in combination with the IPsec Encapsulating Security Payload (ESP) protocol, or in a nested fashion with tunneling. Security services can be provided between a pair of communicating hosts, between a pair of communicating security gateways, or between a host and a gateway. ESP can provide the same security services as AH and ESP can also provide data confidentiality service. The main difference between authentication services provided by ESP and AH is the extent of the coverage; ESP does not protect IP header fields unless they are encapsulated by AH [r013].

Authentication Information   Information used to verify an identity claimed by or for an entity (i.e., authentication, credential.) Authentication information may exist as, or be derived from, one of the following [r013]:

- Something the entity knows (e.g., password)
- Something the entity possesses [e.g., token (bank card, one-time password fob, etc.)]
- Something the entity is [e.g., biometric authentication (fingerprints, retinal scans, etc.)]

Authentication Key   (DNSSEC context) A public key that a security-aware resolver has verified and can therefore use to authenticate data. A security-aware resolver can obtain authentication keys in three ways. First, the resolver is generally configured to know about at least one public key; this configured data is usually either the public key itself or a hash of the public key as found in the Delegation Signer (DS) Resource Record (RR). Second, the resolver may use an authenticated public key to verify a DS RR and the DNSKEY RR to which the DS RR refers. Third, the resolver may be able to determine that a new public key has been signed by the private key corresponding to another public key that the resolver has verified. Note that the resolver must always be guided by local policy when deciding whether to authenticate a new public key, even if the local policy is simply to authenticate any new public key for which the resolver is able verify the signature [r069].

Authentication Methods   Authentication methods typically consist but is not limited to One Time Passwords (OTP), Public Key Infrastructure (PKI), biometrics, or Subscriber Identity Module (SIM) approaches.

Authentication Path   When communicating from one realm to another, a sequence of intermediate realms transited in support of the authentication process.

Authentication Process Steps A two-step process for authentication. These include:

- Identification step: Presenting an identifier to the security system
- Verification step: Presenting or generating authentication information that corroborates the binding between the entity and the identifier [r013]

Authentication Service A security service that verifies an identity claimed by or for an entity, be it a process, computer system, or person. At the internetwork layer, this includes verifying that a datagram came from where it purports to originate. At the application layer, this includes verifying that the entity performing an operation is who it claims to be [r072]. Two general forms of authentication service are data origin authentication service and peer entity authentication service [r013].

Authentication Support The technical mechanism(s) that are used by the service to establish and possibly authenticate connections. These mechanisms include unauthenticated Dynamic Host Configuration Protocol (DHCP), Point-to-Point Protocol (PPP), Remote Authentication Dial-In User Service (RADIUS), and HyperText Transfer Protocol (HTTP) [r034].

Authentication Token (aka token) Information conveyed during a strong authentication exchange, which can be used to authenticate its sender [r068a].

Authentication, Authorization, and Accounting (AAA) Collection of techniques for verifying the identity of, granting access to, and tracking the actions of remote users.

Authentication, Authorization, and Accounting (AAA) Entity A network node processing messages according to the requirements for Authentication, Authorization, and Accounting (AAA protocols). Described in RFC 3127, "Authentication, Authorization, and Accounting: Protocol Evaluation," June 2001.

Authentication, Authorization, and Accounting (AAA) Operation, Mobile Devices A mechanism to allow a mobile node belonging to one administrative domain (called the home domain) to use resources provided by another administrative domain (called the foreign domain). This is often necessitated by an agent in a foreign domain, being called on to provide access to a resource by a mobile user, requests or requires the client to provide credentials which can be authenticated before access to resources is permitted. Described in RFC 2977, "Mobile IP Authentication, Authorization, and Accounting Requirements," October 2000.

Authentication, Authorization, and Accounting (AAA) Security Association A security association between an AAA entity and another node needing the services of that AAA entity.

In mobile environments all AAA Security Associations are between a mobile node and its home AAA server (AAAH). A mobile node's AAA Security Association with its AAAH may be based either on the mobile node's IP address or on its Network Access Identifier (NAI). The key is referred to as "AAA-key" in this specification [r012].

Authentication, Authorization, and Accounting (AAA) Server A server program that handles user requests for access to computer resources and, for an enterprise, provides authentication, authorization, and accounting (AAA) services. The AAA server typically interacts with network access and gateway servers and with databases and directories containing user information. The means by which many current devices or applications communicate with an AAA server is the Remote Authentication Dial-In User Service (RADIUS) [r19].

Authentication, Authorization, and Accounting, (AAA) Servers, Mobile Environment Servers such as Remote Authentication Dial-In User Service (RADIUS) and DIAMETER are utilized for mobile nodes using Mobile IP, when the nodes are attempting to connect to foreign domains with AAA servers. In this context, AAA servers authenticate and authorize network access requests from mobile nodes. The interactions between AAA and Mobile IP are outlined in RFC 2977; the document describes an infrastructure that enables AAA servers to authenticate and authorize network access requests from mobile nodes [r012].

Authentication, Authorization, and Accounting, Home (AAAH) AAA home authority; used in Mobile IP applications.

Authentication, Authorization, and Accounting, Local (AAAL) AAA local authority (namely, AAA of the visited network); used in Mobile IP (MIP) applications.

Authentication, Authorization, and Administration (AAA) The mnemonic "AAA" or "3A's" is often used in conjunction with a collection of techniques for verifying the identity of users, granting access to users, and administrative management and controls of user access. Related to Authentication, Authorization, and Auditing.

Authentication, Authorization, and Auditing (AAA) Techniques for verifying the identity of users, granting access to users, and tracking the actions of users in order to hold them responsible for their actions. Related to Authentication, Authorization, and Administration.

Authenticator A record containing information that can be shown to have been recently generated using the session key known only by the client and server [r070].

(EAP context) The end of the link initiating Extensible Authentication Protocol (EAP) authentication. The term authenticator is used in Institute of Electrical and Electronics Engineers (IEEE) 802.1X with the same meaning [r073].

Authenticity The condition of being genuine and able to be verified and be trusted.

Authoritative Data Source (aka System of Record) The source of information on which all other system entities rely. Oftentimes, it is necessary to identify the system of record because numerous copies of data are sometimes performed in an enterprise.

The use of a common, authoritative data source for call server, endpoint, user, authentication, and white pages in large-scale multimedia conferencing environments [r074].

Authoritative RRset (DNSSEC context) Within the context of a particular zone, an RRset is "authoritative" if and only if the owner name of the RRset lies within the subset of the name space that is at or below the zone apex and at or above the cuts that separate the zone from its children, if any. All RRsets at the zone apex are authoritative, except for certain RRsets at this domain name that, if present, belong to this zone's parent. These RRset could include a Delegation Signer (DS) RRset, the Next Secure (NSEC) RRset referencing this DS RRset (the "parental NSEC"), and Resource Record Signature (RRSIG) RRs associated with these RRsets, all of which are authoritative in the parent zone. Similarly, if this zone contains any delegation points, only the NSEC RRset, DS RRsets, and any RRSIG RRs associated with these RRsets are authoritative for this zone [r069].

Authority Certificate A certificate issued to an authority (e.g., either to a certification authority or to an attribute authority) [r068a].

Authority A server or set of servers containing (registry) information.

Authority Revocation List (ARL) A revocation list containing a list of public-key certificates issued to authorities, which are no longer considered valid by the certificate issuer [r060].

Authorization A right or a permission that is granted to an entity to access a system resource.

Authorization Hook Within the context of an Operating System (OS) an authorization hook is a hook function identifier (i.e., the policy-level operation for which authorization is checked) and a set of arguments to the security module's hook function.

Authorization Process A procedure for granting authorization (rights).

Authorize To grant a right or permission.

Authorize Processing (Certification & Accreditation) Certification is a comprehensive analysis of information technology systems' technical and nontechnical security controls. Accreditation, or "authorize processing," is the official management authorization for the operation of a system or application and is based on the certification process as well as other management considerations [r067].

Authorized Monitoring Software   Software that monitors and records system activity in order to assure accountability and system reliability. Unlike spyware, the security administrators have approved the use of these tools.

Auto Loaders   A robotics-based tape drive with robotics and multiple tape cartridges.

Automated Information System (AIS)   Computing and communications equipment and services, with their supporting facilities and personnel, that collect, record, process, store, transport, retrieve, or display information to accomplish a specified set of functions [r013].

Automated Intrusion Monitoring System (AIMS)   An Intrusion Detection System (IDS) that was developed in the mid-1990s for the U.S. Army and is intended to provide local and "theater-level" monitoring of computer attacks [r075].

Automated Resource Management (ARM)   Storage software solutions which combine elements of Storage Network Management (SNM), Storage Resource Management (SRM), and Policy Management in order to provide user-defined Service Level Agreements (SLA) enforcement and auto-provisioning of capacity [r029].

Automated Security Incident Measurement (ASIM)   An Intrusion Detection System (IDS) designed (in the mid-1990s) for the U.S. Military to measure the level of unauthorized activity against its systems. Under this project, several automated tools are used to examine network activity and detect and identify unusual network events, for example, Internet addresses not normally expected to access Department of Defense (DoD) computers [r075, r076].

Automated Security Monitoring   A set of security features needed to provide an acceptable level of protection for hardware, software, and classi-

fied, sensitive, unclassified or critical data, material, or processes in the system [r063, r077].

Automated Security Self-Evaluation Tool (AS-SET)   A tool used to automate the completion of the questionnaire contained in National Institute of Standards and Technology (NIST) Special Publication 800-26, "Security Self-Assessment Guide for Information Technology Systems." As described in NIST Special Publication 800-26, the results of the questionnaire provide a "method of evaluating the security of a particular system or group of systems." Through interpretation of the questionnaire results, users are able to assess the Information Technology (IT) security posture for any number of systems within their organization and, in particular, assess the status of the organization's security program plan. ASSET consists of two tools: The ASSET-System and the ASSET-Manager. Within ASSET-System, the questionnaire is presented in a progressive format, allowing users to move backward and forward in the questionnaire at their discretion. The ASSET-Manager provides the ability to sort and summarize the questionnaire results for all systems assessed and to display the results through several formatted reports or through an export capability. Both ASSET-System and the ASSET-Manager are developed and designed to meet the GSA Section 508 accessibility standards, as is required by law [r067].

Automated Systems Security Incident Support Team (ASSIST)   The Department of Energy (DoE) Headquarters' ASSIST was formed in 1992 to provide education and protection to the DoE user community in the containment of computer viruses. The team developed and maintains the Headquarters Virus Protection Program, trains and manages the Virus Response Team (ViRT), and provides user, management, and support education, as well as guidance and assistance to various DoE entities concerning virus issues.

Automatic Identification (Auto-ID) Systems   Tools and techniques used in point of sale, inventory, and manufacturing processes to quickly identify products. Examples include optical bar codes such as the Universal Product Code (UPC), and more recently, Radio Frequency Identification (RFID).

Automatic IPv6 Tunnel Automatic creation of tunnels using IPv4 compatible addresses [r008].

Automatic Protection Switching (APS) Mechanism for network survivability in the event of failure on a network element or link. APS schemes involve reserving a protection channel (dedicated or shared) with the same capacity as the channel or facility to be protected. For example, a number of protection-switching mechanisms are available with Synchronous Optical Network/Synchronous Digital Hierarchy (SONET/SDH) networks; other mechanisms are used for different communication services.

Automatic Tunnel (IPv6 context) An IPv6 over IPv4 tunnel in which endpoints are specified by means of the use of tunnels logical interfaces, routes, and IPv6 source and destination addresses [r008].

Automatically Switched Optical Network (ASON) (Optical transmission term) Switched optical architecture for very-high-speed networking. Makes use of an automated control plane for supporting both call and connection management services (ITU G.8080). The ASON architecture describes a reference architecture (i.e., it describes functional components, abstract interfaces, and interactions). The ASON model distinguishes reference points (representing points of information exchange) defined (1) between a user (service requester) and a service provider control domain, aka user–network interface (UNI), (2) between control domains, aka external network–network interface (E-NNI), and (3) within a control domain, aka internal network–network interface (I-NNI). The I-NNI and E-NNI interfaces are between protocol controllers and may or may not use transport plane (physical) links. It must not be assumed that there is a one-to-one relationship between control plane interfaces and transport plane (physical) links, control plane entities and transport plane entities, or control plane identifiers for transport plane resources

[r079]. Functionality supported includes: (a) soft permanent connection capability; (b) call and connection separation; (c) call segments; (d) extended restart capabilities during control plane failures; (e) extended label association; (f) crankback capability; (g) additional error cases.

ASON defines a reference model and functions (information elements) to enable end-to-end call and connection support by a protocol across the respective interfaces, regardless of the particular choice of protocol(s) used in a network. ASON does not restrict the use of other protocols or the protocol-specific messages used to support the ASON functions. Therefore, the support of these ASON functions by a protocol shall not be restricted by (i.e., must be strictly independent of and agnostic to) any particular choice of UNI, I-NNI, or E-NNI used elsewhere in the network. To allow for interworking between different protocol implementations, ITU-G.7713 recognizes that an interworking function may be needed.

Autonomic Management Intelligent self-regulation of grid resources in a Grid Computing environment [r080].

Autonomous System (AS) In IP networks, a carrier-type network domain that belongs to the same administrative authority.

AV See Anti-Virus Software (AV Software)

Availability A measure of the system's readiness for use by a system entity. Availability is diminished when the system entity does not have reliable access to data or a system. An example cause of this is a Denial of Service (DoS) attack. Related to uptime and downtime.

Availability Security Dimension Mechanism that ensures that there is no denial of authorized access to network elements, stored information, information flows, services and applications due to events impacting the network. Disaster recovery solutions are included in this category [r068a].

Availability Service A service that provides controls in order to assure the availability of a system.

Available Bit Rate (ABR) An Asynchronous

Transfer Mode (ATM) service category for which the limiting ATM layer transfer characteristics provided by the network may change subsequent to connection establishment. A flow control mechanism is specified that supports several types of feedback to control the source rate in response to changing ATM layer transfer characteristics. It is expected that an end-system that adapts its traffic in accordance with the feedback will experience a low cell loss ratio and obtain a fair share of the available bandwidth according to a network-specific allocation policy. Cell delay variation is not controlled in this service, al-though admitted cells are not delayed unnecessarily.

Average Accounting Return   (financial term) A measure of the return on an investment over a given period, equal to average projected earnings minus taxes, divided by average book value over the duration of the investment. This measure can also be calculated using average projected earnings without excluding taxes, or average projected earnings less taxes and depreciation. This ratio measures how well investment assets are being used to generate income [r009].

B (GSM context) The B interface is situated between the Mobile Services Switching Center (MSC), and the Visitor Location Register (VLR) [r011].

B2B See Business-to-Business

B2BUA See Back-to-Back User Agent

B2C See Business-to-Consumer

Back Door A hardware or software mechanism that provides access to a system and its resources by other than the usual procedure, that was deliberately left in place by the system's designers or maintainers, and is usually not publicly known. For example, a way to access a computer other than through a normal login. Such access paths do not necessarily always have malicious intent. For example, operating systems sometimes are shipped by the manufacturer with privileged accounts intended for use by field service technicians or the vendor's maintenance programmers [r013].

Back Office (financial term) (1) The administrative functions at a brokerage that support the trading of securities, including trade confirmation and settlement, recordkeeping, and regulatory compliance. (2) More generally, administrative functions that support but are not directly involved in the operations of a business, such as accounting and personnel [r009].

Back Up See Backup

Backdoor Links Links between Customer Edge/Equipment (CE) devices that are provided by the end customer rather than by the Service Provider (SP). They may be used to interconnect CE devices in multiple-homing arrangements [r081, r082].

Back-end Authentication Server An entity that

Minoli–Cordovana's Authoritative Computer and Network Security Dictionary. By Daniel Minoli and James Cordovana
Copyright © 2006 John Wiley & Sons, Inc.

provides an authentication service to an authenticator. When used, this server typically executes Extensible Authentication Protocol (EAP) methods for the authenticator. This terminology is used in IEEE802.1X [r073].

Back-End Demilitarized Zone (DMZ) A DMZ that is protected by an additional layer of firewall rules, separating it from the Front-End DMZ. Usually application and business logic resources are positioned in this network segment. Data typically does not reside within this network segment. If there is a business reason to locate data within this network segment, the data should be encrypted.

Back-to-Back User Agent (B2BUA) (SIP context) A logical entity that receives a request and processes it as a user agent server (UAS). In order to determine how the request should be answered, it acts as a user agent client (UAC) and generates requests. Unlike a proxy server, it maintains dialog state and must participate in all requests sent on the dialogs it has established. Since it is a concatenation of a UAC and UAS, no explicit definitions are needed for its behavior [r025].

Backup (aka back up) A copy of all (or portions of) software- or data-files on a system kept on storage media, such as tape or disk, or on a separate system, so that the files can be restored if the original data is deleted or damaged. Also, the activity involved in creating such copies of data [r069]. Unlike archival, a backup typically does not imply saving application data for the purposes of meeting data retention requirements (for regulatory purposes) or to have data available for future account inquiries.

Backup and Disaster Recovery Services to provide backup and recovery needs, particularly in situations where the primary data center has been destroyed or otherwise incapacitated.

Backup Path (MPLS context) The Label Switched Path (LSP) that is responsible for backing up one protected LSP. A backup path refers to either a detour LSP or a backup tunnel [r083].

Backup Tunnel (MPLS context) The Label Switched Path (LSP) that is used to back up one of the many LSPs in many-to-one backup.

Balance (financial term) (1) The amount of money in an account, equal to the net of credits and debits at that point in time for that account. Also called account balance. (2) The outstanding debt on a loan [r009].

Bank (financial term) An organization, usually a corporation, chartered by a state or federal government, which does most or all of the following: receives demand deposits and time deposits, honors instruments drawn on them, and pays interest on them; discounts notes, makes loans, and invests in securities; collects checks, drafts, and notes; certifies depositor's checks; and issues drafts and cashier's checks [r009].

Bank Identification Number (BIN) The digits of a credit card number that identify the issuing bank.

Bank Rate (financial term) (1) The interest rate charged by a bank for loans. (2) The discount rate set by a central bank.

Bank Secrecy Act (BSA) (financial term) Legislation that requires financial institutions to detect and report suspicious activity through Suspicious Activity Reports (SARs), to keep records of certain financial transactions, and to file Currency Transaction Reports (CTRs) to report large (over $10,000) cash transactions. SARs provide law enforcement with information about possible criminal activity, and CTRs and other transaction records provide a paper trail for law enforcement, which helps them build a better case against money launderers and other criminals.

Banking Act of 1933 (financial term) A U.S. Congressional Act designed to restore financial stability to the country during the Great Depression, through the creation of federal deposit insurance and the separation of commercial banking and investment banking through the Glass–Steagall Act [r009].

Bankruptcy (financial term) A proceeding in a federal court in which an insolvent debtor's assets are liquidated and the debtor is relieved of further liability. Chapter 7 of the Bankruptcy Reform Act deals with liquidation, while Chapter 11 deals with reorganization [r009].

Barriers to Entry   (financial term) Circumstances particular to a given industry that create disadvantages for new competitors attempting to enter the market. These may include government regulations, economic factors, and marketing conditions [r009].

Base Certificate Revocation List (CRL)   A CRL that is used as the foundation in the generation of a Delta-CRL (DCRL) [r068a].

Base Interest Rate   (financial term) The minimum interest rate investors will accept for investing in a non-Treasury security. In general, this is the yield that is being earned on the most recent on-the-run Treasury security of similar maturity plus a premium. Also called benchmark interest rate [r009].

Base Station Color Code (BCC)   (GSM context) A code that is part of the Base Station Identity Code (BSIC); it is used to distinguish cells that use the same frequency as the serving cell [r011].

Base Station Controller (BSC)   (GSM context) In GSM, a device that controls and supervises a number of Base Transceiver Stations (BTSs). Furthermore, the BSC monitors the transmitting power of the BTSs and initiates the handover [r011].

Base Station Identity Code (BSIC)   (GSM context) The identity code that identifies the network operator a base station belongs to. It is broadcast by every Base Transceiver Station (BTS), and it is compared with the relevant entry on the subscriber's Subscriber Identity Module (SIM) card. Furthermore, the BSIC is used to distinguish cells that use the same frequency as the serving cell. It consists of the Network Color Code (NCC) and the Base Station Color Code BCC [r011].

Base Station Subsystem (BSS)   (GSM context) The Base Station Subsystem is the radio network component of the GSM network. Like the Network Subsystem (NSS) and the Operation & Maintenance System (OMS). It forms a subnet and is responsible for radio coverage and radio resource control [r011].

Base Station Subsystem Application Part (BSSAP)   (GSM context) A protocol layer in Signaling System No. 7 (SS7) that is responsible for communication between the Mobile Services Switching Center (MSC) and the Base Station Controller (BSC) in GSM [r011].

Base Station System GPRS Protocol (BSSGP)   (GSM context) A protocol that provides the Serving GPRS Support Node (SGSN) with information concerning routing and quality of service [r014].

Base Transceiver Station (BTS)   (GSM context) In the GSM system, the Base Transceiver Station provides coverage for one or more radio cells [r011].

Basic Encoding Rules (BER)   An International Organization for Standardization (ISO) standard for representing Abstract Syntax Notation One (ASN.1) data types (in protocols) as strings of octets.

Basic Input/Output System (BIOS)   The program (microcode) that a microprocessor (say in a personal computer) uses to get the computer system started after it has turned it on. BIOS also manages data flow between the computer's operating system (OS) and devices such as the hard disk, video adapter, keyboard, mouse, and printer. BIOS is pre-integrated into the system: it is typically stored on an erasable programmable read-only memory (EPROM) chip. When the user turns on the computer, the microprocessor passes control to the BIOS program, which is always located at the same memory location on EPROM.

Bastion Host   An older term that describes a strongly protected computer that is in a network protected by a firewall (or is part of a firewall) and is the only host (or one of only a few hosts) in the network that can be directly accessed from networks on the other side of the firewall [r013]. The term is derived from medieval castle architectural terminology for a fortified area that overlooks, as well as protects, critical areas of the castle.

BCA   See Brand Certification Authority

BCC   See Base Station Color Code

BCCH   See Broadcast Control Channel

BCH   See Broadcast Channel

BCI   See Brand CRL Identifier

BCR   See Benefit–Cost Ratio

BCS   See Block Check Sequence

Beige Book   (financial term) Report on current economic conditions, published by the Federal Reserve Board eight times each year. The Beige Book is part of the Federal Open Market Committee's (FOMC) preparations for its meetings. The report is released two Wednesdays before each FOMC meeting at 2:15 pm EST. The book is a summary of economic conditions in each of the Fed's regions. The report is primarily seen as an indicator of how the Fed might act at its upcoming meeting [r009].

Bell–LaPadula Model   A formal, mathematical, state-transition model of security policy for multilevel-secure computer systems. The model separates computer system elements into a set of subjects and a set of objects. To determine whether or not a subject is authorized for a particular access mode on an object, the clearance of the subject is compared to the classification of the object. The model defines the notion of a "secure state," in which the only permitted access modes of subjects to objects are in accordance with a specified security policy. It is proven that each state transition preserves security by moving from secure state to secure state, thereby proving that the system is secure [r013]. In this model, a multilevel-secure system satisfies several rules, including the following:

- Confinement property (also called "*-property," pronounced "star property"): A subject has write access to an object only if classification of the object dominates the clearance of the subject.
- Simple security property: A subject has read access to an object only if the clearance of the subject dominates the classification of the object.
- "Tranquility" property: The classification of

an object does not change while the object is being processed by the system.

Bending   (optical transmission term) Impairment affecting optical transmission, specifically macrobending and microbending. Fiber bends result from optical fiber coating, cabling, packaging, installation, and aging. Macrobending is the loss that is due to macroscopic deviations of the axis from a straight line. Microbending loss occurs due to the sharp curvatures involving local axis displacements of a few micrometers and spatial wavelengths of a few millimeters.

Benefit–Cost Ratio (BCR)   (financial term) The ratio between discounted total benefits and costs. Thus, if the discounted benefits are $150 million and the discounted costs are $100 million, the BCR is 1.5 (and the NPV is $50 million). The BCR is a useful check to the NPV process, as a way of spotting program options that offer attractive NPVs only because they are large. Reporting of BCRs requires mention of the discount rate used [r085].

BER   See Basic Encoding Rules or Bit Error Rate

Best Practices   Techniques related to a discipline (e.g., Information Technology, Security, and so on) that represent the consensus of many organizations in the field and are subjected to stringent open review. Practices validated by experience and "common sense."

Best-in-Class Security Practices   Secure systems and networks can, in part, be created by developing, managing, and promoting security assessment tools, techniques, and services and by supporting programs for testing, evaluation, and validation. They address such areas as: development and maintenance of security metrics; security evaluation criteria and evaluation methodologies; tests and test methods; security-specific criteria for laboratory accreditation; guidance on the use of evaluated and tested products; research to address assurance methods and system-wide security and assessment methodologies; security protocol validation activities; and appropriate coordination with assessment-related activities of voluntary industry standards bodies and other assessment regimes [r067].

Beta   (financial term) A quantitative measure of the volatility of a given stock, mutual fund, or portfolio, relative to the overall market, usually the S&P 500. Specifically, the performance the stock, fund, or portfolio has experienced in the last 5 years as the S&P moved 1% up or down. A beta above 1 is more volatile than the overall market, while a beta below 1 is less volatile [r009].

Beyond A1   Formally, a level of security assurance that is beyond the highest level of criteria specified by the Trusted Computer System Evaluation Criteria (TCSEC).

Informally, a level of trust so high that it cannot be provided or verified by currently available assurance methods and, in particular, cannot be verified by currently available formal methods [r013].

BG   See Border Gateway

BGP   See Border Gateway Protocol

BHOs   See Browser Helper Objects

Billing Cycle   (financial term) The period between billings for products and services, usually a month [r009].

BIN   See Bank Identification Number

Binary Backup   A true bit backup of a given medium or environment (e.g., disk drive).

Bind   To associate things by utilizing some (appropriate) mechanism—for example, when a Certification Authority (CA) uses a digital signature to bind an entity name and a public key in a public-key certificate.

Biometric Authentication   (aka Biometrics) A method of generating authentication information for a person by measuring (and digitizing) a physical characteristic of the person in question (that is, by using biometrics). Examples include a fingerprint, a hand shape, a retina pattern, a speech pattern (voiceprint), or handwriting.

Biometric Data Interchange Formats   Industry efforts that focus on the standardization of the content, meaning, and representation of biometric data interchange formats. Active projects include:

- Finger Pattern Based Interchange Format
- Finger Minutiae Format for Data Interchange
- Face Recognition Format for Data Interchange
- Iris Interchange Format
- Finger Image-Based Interchange Format
- Signature/Sign Image-Based Interchange Format
- Hand Geometry Interchange Format

Biometric Scanner   A device connected to a computer system that recognizes physical characteristics of an individual (e.g., fingerprint, voice, retina).

Biometrics   See Biometric Authentication

BIOS   See Basic Input/Output System

Birthday Paradox   Observation that states that given a hash function mapping any message to an 128-bit hash digest, one can expect that the same digest will be computed twice when 2^{64} randomly selected messages have been hashed. As cheaper memory chips for computers become available, it may become necessary to require larger than 128-bit message digests (for example, a 160-bit digest has become a standard recently) [r036].

Bit   "Binary digit." Comprised of two symbols: "0" (zero) and "1" (one). Bits are used to represent binary numbers.

Bit Stream Backups   (aka mirror image backups) Involve the backup of all areas of a computer in hard disk drive or another type of storage media (e.g., Zip disks, floppy disks, etc.). Such backups exactly replicate all sectors on a given storage device. Hence, all files and ambient data storage areas are copied. Bit stream backups are sometimes also referred to as "evidence grade" backups; these backups differ substantially from traditional computer file backups and network server backups. When computer evidence is involved, accuracy is extremely important and the making of a bit stream backup is sometimes described as the preservation of the "electronic crime scene" [r066].

Bit Time (BT)   The duration of one bit as transferred to and from the Media Access Control (MAC). The bit time is the reciprocal of the bit rate. For example, for 100BASE-T the bit rate is 10^{-8} s or 10 ns.

BLACK Designation for information system equipment or facilities that handle (and for data that contains) only ciphertext (or, depending on the context, only unclassified information), and for such data itself (U.S. Government COMSEC terminology) [r013].

Black Hat Consulting, Inc. Commercial organization involved in the annual Defcon and Black Hat computer security conferences. The organization focuses on challenging the security environments of a client firm at the request of the client firm, with the goal of identifying vulnerabilities.

Black Hat Hacker (term originates from old Western movies, where heroes often wore white hats and the "bad guys" wore black hats.) An individual who penetrates a computer system or network with malicious intent. A black hat hacker takes advantage of the break-in—for example, destroying files or appropriating information for some future use. The black hat hacker may also make the exploit known to other hackers and/or the public, giving others the opportunity to exploit the vulnerability before the organization is able to secure it.

Black-Box Cryptosystem A cryptosystem that is implemented in such a way that the underlying implementation (source code or circuitry) cannot be scrutinized. A black-box cryptosystem has a public Input/Output (I/O) specification and its general functionality is disclosed (though the true functionality could differ). Cryptovirology relies heavily on the notion of a "black-box" cryptosystem when it comes to developing provably-secure malware attacks against cryptosystems. A black-box cryptosystem is both a theoretical abstraction as well as a common everyday reality [r089].

By definition, a black-box cryptosystem can only be used without verifying the correctness of its implementation. A smartcard is a black-box cryptosystem unless the user disassembles it, verifies the circuitry and the data that resides in memory, and then reassembles it. Similarly, a cryptosystem that is implemented in software is a black-box cryptosystem unless its code is disassembled and verified. Note that this definition states that the implementation in question must be verified, not the design specification for the whole product line. A manufacturer can sell thousands of cryptosystems and put a backdoor in just one of them [r089].

Millions of people use black-box cryptosystems every day. When an item is purchased online, often the secure sockets layer (SSL) is used. When a user does not verify the implementation of SSL, then SSL is a black-box cryptosystem.

Blade Servers High-density compact server arrangement that places and packs these "slim format" computers in high-count cabinets (chassis) with shared assets (e.g., power, cooling, networking, etc.). This arrangement requires less power and physical space than a traditional rack of servers. Blades are typically arranged vertically (like books in a bookshelf). A blade generally includes a limited number of components (processor, memory, and optional hard drive); the chassis support in-rack power distribution, local server access/console (keyboard/mouse); and networking access.

Blaster Worm A worm that spreads by exploiting a buffer overflow in the Windows Distributed Component Object Model (DCOM) Remote Procedure Call (RPC) service on Windows 2000 and Windows XP and also launched a SYN flood attack against port 80 of Microsoft's windowsupdate.com site that is used to distribute security patches (2003). Microsoft temporarily redirected the site, but the media soon "discovered" the story and forced the company to make major changes to its patching schedule to help customers cope with the patch management nightmare [r090].

Blazing Tools' *Perfect Keylogger* Keystroke logging system intended for security monitoring and parental oversight; however, it has also been found in some malicious code.

Blended Threats   Threats that combine the characteristics of viruses, worms, Trojan horses, and other malicious code with server and Internet vulnerabilities to initiate, transmit, and spread an attack.

Blind Signatures   A means of allowing another entity to digitally sign a message without revealing the original message content. This is achieved by incorporating a random value in the original message prior to having a second party sign the message. Blind signatures have numerous uses including timestamping, anonymous access control, and digital cash.

Block Check Sequence (BCS)   (GSM context) A kind of calculation model that later allows the tracing of errors [r014].

Block Cipher   An encryption algorithm that processes plaintext in groups of bits. A common block size is 64 bits, and is used in common encryption algorithms such as Data Encryption Standard (DES). Examples include Blowfish, Data Encryption Algorithm (DEA), International Data Encryption Algorithm (IDEA), Rivest Cipher 2 (RC2), and SKIPJACK.

Blocking of Outbound Applications Services   Mechanisms to disallow access from the host computer. Examples include blocking the use of Simple Mail Transfer Protocol (SMTP) or mail submission to servers, blocking file transfer protocols, and Hypertext Transfer Protocol (HTTP) traffic to external websites.

Blowfish   A symmetric block cipher with variable-length key (32 to 448 bits) designed in 1993 by Bruce Schneier. It is an unpatented, license-free, royalty-free replacement for Data Encryption Standard (DES) or International Data Encryption Algorithm (IDEA) [r013].

Bluejacking   A Bluetooth-targeted hacking technique where the attacker gains access to the victim's phone book, missed, received, or dialed contacts.

Bluesnarf   A sniffer tool used to sniff Bluetooth systems.

Bluetooth Attacks   Attacks against wireless Bluetooth systems. Include: service theft, traffic sniffing, Personal Identification Number (PIN) attacks, profile and implementation vulnerabilities, and audio recording attacks.

Blum Blum Shub Sequence Generator   A random sequence generator that has the strongest public proof of strength. The Blum Blum Shub generator, is named after its inventors [r091]. It is based on quadratic residues but it is computationally intensive compared to the traditional techniques. This is not a major drawback if it is used for moderately infrequent purposes, such as generating session keys. Simply choose two large prime numbers (say, p and q) that each gives a remainder of 3 when divided by 4. Let $n = p * q$. Then choose a random number, x, that is relatively prime to n. The initial seed for the generator and the method for calculating subsequent values are then [r166]:

$$s_0 = (x^2) \pmod{n}$$

$$s_{i+1} = (s_i^2) \pmod{n}$$

(Use only a few bits from the "tail" of each s.) It is always safe to use only the lowest-order bit. If one uses no more than the

$$\log_2 (\log_2 (s_i))$$

low-order bits, then predicting any additional bits from a sequence generated in this manner is provably as hard as factoring n. As long as the initial x is secret, n can be made public if desired.

BML   See Business Management Layer

Board of Directors   (aka directorate) (financial term) Individuals elected by a corporation's shareholders to oversee the management of the corporation. The members of a Board of Directors are paid in cash and/or stock, meet several times each year, and assume legal responsibility for corporate activities [r009].

Board of Governors   (financial term) (1) The governing body of the Federal Reserve System, which is responsible for U.S. monetary policy. (2) The members of a stock exchange that supervise the functioning of the exchange [r009].

Board of Trustees (financial term) A group of people that oversees a nonprofit organization.

Bomb (aka crash) A software or operating system failure. Also see Logic Bomb.

Bona Fide (financial term) In good faith, genuine.

Bond (financial term) A certificate of debt that is issued by a government or corporation in order to raise money with a promise to pay a specified sum of money at a fixed time in the future and carrying interest at a fixed rate. Generally, a bond is a promise to repay the principal along with interest (coupons) on a specified date (maturity). The main types of bonds are corporate bond, municipal bond, treasury bond, treasury note, treasury bill, and zero-coupon bond. It is a tradable debt instrument that might be sold at above or below par (the amount paid out at maturity). Bonds are rated by bond rating services such as Standard & Poor's and Moody's Investors Service, to specify likelihood of default. The Federal Government, states, cities, corporations, and many other types of institutions sell bonds. A bond is relatively more secured than equity and has priority over shareholders if the company becomes insolvent and its assets are distributed [r009].

Bookkeeping (financial term) The systematic recording of a company's financial transactions. The two most common bookkeeping methods are single entry and double entry [r009].

Boot Disk (aka bootable floppy) A removable media such as a compact disk or floppy disk containing a copy of the hard disk master boot record (MBR). In the event that the master boot record is unavailable or corrupted, a boot disk allows one to access system files instead of having to reformat the hard drive.

Bootable Floppy (aka boot disk) A floppy disk that contains enough Operating System (OS) core instructions to bring up a computer with a minimum set of functionality.

Border Gateway (BG) (GSM context) The interface between two InterPLMN networks and behaves like a "firewall" [r014].

Border Gateway Protocol (BGP) A protocol used for exchanging routing information between gateway hosts in an Autonomous System (AS) network. It is an interautonomous system routing protocol. An autonomous system is a network or group of networks under a common administration and with common routing policies. The protocol is used for exchanging routing information between gateway hosts (each with its own router) in a network of autonomous systems. BGP is used to exchange routing information for the Internet and is the protocol used between Internet Service Providers (ISP); that is, BGP is often the protocol used between gateway hosts on the Internet. The routing table contains a list of known routers, the addresses they can reach, and a cost metric associated with the path to each router so that the best available route is chosen [r092]. BGP operates on port 179.

Intranets used by corporations and institutions generally employ an Interior Gateway Protocol (IGP) such as Open Shortest Path First (OSPF) for the exchange of routing information within their networks. Customers connect to ISPs, and ISPs use BGP to exchange customer and ISP routes. When BGP is used between ASs, the protocol is referred to as External BGP (EBGP). If a service provider is using BGP to exchange routes within an AS, then the protocol is referred to as Interior BGP (IBGP).

Border Gateway Protocol (BGP) Device A system that has one or more BGP instances running on it, each of which is responsible for executing the BGP state machine [r086].

Border Gateway Protocol (BGP) Neighbor A device that can be configured as a BGP peer.

Border Gateway Protocol (BGP) Peer A BGP peer is another BGP instance to which the Device Under Test (DUT) is in the established state.

Border Gateway Protocol (BGP) Route A BGP route is an n-tuple <prefix, nexthop, ASpath, [other BGP attributes]>. BGP Attributes, such as Nexthop or AS path, are defined in RFC 1771, where they are known as Path Attributes, and they are the qualifying data that define the route. From RFC 1771: "For purposes of this protocol a route is defined as a unit of information that pairs a destination with the attributes of a path to that destination" [r086].

Border Gateway Protocol (BGP) Session   A session between two BGP instances.

Border Gateway Protocol (BGP) UPDATE Message   An UPDATE message contains an advertisement of a single Network Layer Reachability Information (NLRI) field, possibly containing multiple prefixes and multiple withdrawals of unfeasible routes. From RFC 1771: "A variable length sequence of path attributes is present in every UPDATE. Each path attribute is a triple <attribute type, attribute length, attribute value> of variable length" [r086].

Border Gateway Protocol (BGP)/Multiprotocol Label Switching (MPLS) IP Virtual Private Networks (VPNs)   A Provider Edge (PE)-based VPN approach in which the PE router maintains a separate forwarding environment and a separate forwarding table for each VPN. In order to maintain multiple forwarding table instances while running only a single BGP instance, BGP/MPLS IP VPNs mark route advertisements with attributes that identify their VPN context [r082, r088].

Borrow   (financial term) To receive something of value with the promise of giving something of (usually greater) value at some point in the future [r009].

Botnet   (aka zombie army) A cluster of Internet computers that, unbeknownst to their owners, has been set up to forward transmissions (including spam, viruses, or Distributed Denial of Service attacks) to other computers on the Internet. Any such computer is referred to as a zombie—in effect, a computer robot (bot) that serves the wishes of some master spam or virus originator [r093].

Bottom Line   (financial term) Gross sales minus taxes, interest, depreciation, and other expenses. Also called net earnings or net income or net [r009].

BPM   See Business Process Modeling

BPML   See Business Process Modeling Language

BPMN   See Business Process Modeling Notation

BPO   See Business Process Outsourcing

BPP-Complexity Problem   BPP (bounded probabilistic polynomial-time) is the class of problems that can be solved using a randomized polynomial-time algorithm with at most exponentially small error of probability on every input [r094].

BPR   See Business Process Reengineering

Brand   (financial term) A distinctive mark or name that identifies a product or business entity. For example, financial institutions and other companies have founded payment card brands, protect and advertise the brands, establish and enforce rules for use and acceptance of their payment cards, and provide networks to interconnect the financial institutions. These brands combine the roles of issuer and acquirer in interactions with cardholders and merchants [r013, r018].

Brand Certification Authority (BCA)   A Certification Authority (CA) owned by a payment card brand, such as MasterCard.

Brand CRL Identifier (BCI)   A digitally signed list, issued by a Brand Certification Authority (BCA), of the names of Certificate Authorities (CAs) for which certificate revocation lists (CRLs) need to be processed when verifying signatures in Secure Electronic Transaction™ (SET) messages [r018].

Breach   The successful circumvention of security controls.

Break-Even Analysis   (financial term) A calculation of the approximate sales volume required to just cover costs, below which production would be unprofitable and above which it would be profitable. Break-even analysis focuses on the relationship between fixed cost, variable cost, and profit [r009].

Break-Even Point   (financial term) (1) The price at which an option's cost is equal to the proceeds acquired by exercising the option. For a call option, it is the strike price plus the premium paid. For a put option, it is the strike price minus the premium paid. (2) The price at which a securities transaction produces neither a gain nor a loss. (3) The volume of sales at which a company's net sales just equals its costs [r009].

Bricks and Mortar (financial term) A description of a company or portion of a company with a physical presence, as opposed to one that exists only on the Internet [r009].

Bridge [aka Local Area Network (LAN) bridge] A Layer 2 interconnection device that does not form part of a Carrier Sense Multiple Access/ Collision Detect (CSMA/CD) collision domain but conforms to the ISO/IEC 15802-3:1998 (ANSI/IEEE 802.1D, 1998 Edition) International Standard. A bridge appears as a Media Access Control (MAC) to the collision domain. There exist two basic types of bridges: those that interconnect LANs directly, called Local Bridges, and those that interconnect LANs via an intermediate Wide Area Network (WAN) medium such as a leased line, called Remote Bridges [r095].

Bridge Loan (financial term) Short-term financing which is expected to be paid back relatively quickly, such as by a subsequent longer-term loan. Also called swing loan or bridge financing [r009].

British Standard 7799 A two-part standard. Part 1 is a standard code of practice and provides guidance on how to secure an information system. Part 2 specifies the management framework, objectives, and control requirements for information security management systems. The certification scheme is similar in concept to the International Organization for Standardization (ISO) 9000 standard. The standard is in use in the United Kingdom, the Netherlands, Australia, and New Zealand and might be proposed as an ISO standard or adapted to be part of the Common Criteria (CC) [r013].

British Standards Organization (BSO) British standards organization that published key security standards, including BS 7799—*Code of Practice for Information Security Management and BSO 7799 Community Portal*. ISO/IEC 17799 (*Code of Practice for Information Security Management*) elevates the British Standard BS 7799, which has been adopted in many countries, to an International Standard.

Broadcast Mechanism to transmit certain information to all users on a network. The broadcast address is a special address that every host on the network listens to in addition to its own unique address. This address is the one that datagrams are sent to if every host on the network is meant to receive it. Certain types of data like routing information and warning messages are transmitted to the broadcast address so that every host on the network can receive it simultaneously. There are two commonly used standards for what the broadcast address should be. The most widely accepted one is to use the highest possible address on the network as the broadcast address. An example on an internal network would be 192.168.1.255. Every host on the network must be configured with the same broadcast address [r084].

Broadcast Channel (BCH) (3G Wireless context) A downlink transport channel that is used to broadcast system and cell specific information [r007].

Broadcast Control Channel (BCCH) (GSM context) A control channel that belongs to the group of the Broadcast Channels and exists only in the downlink. The channel is used to inform the mobile station of the parameters of the relevant cell system configuration [r011].

Broker (financial term) An individual or firm that acts as an intermediary between a buyer and seller, usually charging a commission. For securities and most other products, a license is required [r009].

Broker Function A mechanism that identifies appropriate and available resources that can/ should be used within a computing grid, based on the application and application-related parameters provided by the user of the application. The broker functionality provides information about the available resources on the grid and the working status of these resources [r080].

Browser Application (software) for retrieving and displaying websites, HyperText Markup Language (HTML) files, and related content. Examples include Microsoft Internet Explorer, Netscape Navigator, and Firefox.

Browser Helper Objects (BHOs) A dynamic-link library (DLL) module designed to be used as a plug-in for Microsoft's Internet Explorer browser to provide advanced functionality.

Browser-Based Attack Attacks that originate via a web-link. Pharming is an example of a browser-based attack and occurs when a user types in a legitimate web address but is instead redirected to a fraudulent page. Sometimes users are "hooked" into these schemes through fake e-mail messages, a technique known as phishing. Such attacks can be used to unleash unwanted software and malicious code on a user's computer [r096] as well as obtain personal information.

Brute Force A cryptanalysis technique or other kind of attack method involving an exhaustive procedure that tries all possibilities, one-by-one. For example, for ciphertext where the analyst already knows the decryption algorithm, a brute force technique for finding the original plaintext is used to decrypt the message with every possible key [r013]. In theory, any cryptographic method can be broken by trying all possible keys in sequence. If using brute force, one would try all keys; the required computing power increases exponentially with the length of the key. A 32-bit key takes 2^{32} (about 10^9) steps. To give some idea of the complexity for the Rivest–Shamir–Adleman (RSA), cryptosystem, a 256-bit modulus is easily factored by a home Personal Computer (PC), and 512-bit keys can be broken by university research groups within a few months. Keys with 768 bits are probably not secure in the long term. Keys with 1024 bits and more should be safe for now unless major cryptographical advances are made against RSA. RSA Security claims that 1024-bit keys are equivalent in strength to 80-bit symmetric keys and recommends their usage until 2010. 2048-bit RSA keys are claimed to be equivalent to 112-bit symmetric keys and can be used at least up to the year 2030 [r036].

BSA See Bank Secrecy Act

BSC See Base Station Controller

BSIC See Base Station Identity Code

BSO See British Standards Organization

BSS See Base Station Subsystem

BSSAP See Base Station Subsystem Application Part

BSSGP See Base Station System GPRS Protocol

BT See Bit Time

BTS See Base Transceiver Station

Budget (financial term) An itemized forecast of an individual's or company's income and expenses expected for some period in the future [r009].

Buffer Overflow In a programming language, memory buffers are allocated (or reserved) in order to perform some task. If the buffer limit is exceeded, a number of errors can occur. Individuals with malicious intent can create a buffer overflow situation and create an information security risk. Also see Buffer Overflow Attack.

Buffer Overflow Attack The attempted exploitation of a buffer overflow vulnerability. This attack is often most successful against programs written in a C-based programming language. For example, a HyperText Markup Language (HTML) form asks the user to type in their password; the application sets aside a certain amount of memory (a buffer) to hold that password. If the attacker exceeds the buffer allotted, the attacker may be able to cause a "spill over" outside the buffer. If this occurs, it may be possible to execute commands that the attacker was not authorized to use.

Bulk Cipher A symmetric encryption algorithm used to encrypt large quantities of data.

Burn Rate (financial term) For a firm with negative cash flow, the rate of that negative cash flow, usually per month. Often used by venture capitalists to measure how much time a startup has to reach positive cash flow before they run out of money or require additional funding [r009].

Business and Functional Managers Consumers (customers) of the Information Technology (IT) development process.

Business Architecture An architectural formulation of the Business Function.

Business Case (financial term) A financial assessment of initiatives that may include the Net Present Value (NPV) of the initiatives, the internal rate of return, and the total cost of ownership.

Business Continuity Management   A security service that typically includes Business Impact Analysis and Business Continuity Planning.

Business Continuity Planning   Written plan describing the procedures the company takes in case of potentially disruptive events short of a disaster (for which the Disaster Recovery Plan is applicable) in order to assure that the operations of the company can continue unimpeded.

Business Continuity Planning Components   Technical and business process/functional planning for how to deal with operational disruptions. Examples include a Technical Recovery Plan and a Business Recovery Plan.

Business Cycle   (financial term) A predictable long-term pattern of alternating periods of economic growth (recovery) and decline (recession), characterized by changing employment, industrial productivity, and interest rates. Also called economic cycle [r009].

Business Function   A description of all the business elements and structures that are covered by the enterprise.

Business Impact Analysis Components   Analysis that determines the impact that an operational disruption would cause on each business unit and the organization as a whole.

Business Management Layer (MML)   A telecom-related management layer responsible for the total enterprise and not subject to standardization [r068a].

Business Model   (financial term) A description of the operations of a business including the components of the business, the functions of the business, and the revenues and expenses that the business generates [r009].

Business Plan   (financial term) A document prepared by a company's management, detailing the past, present, and future of the company, usually designed to attract capital investment [r009].

Business Process Modeling (BPM)   Business function modeling mechanisms that seeks to standardize the management of business processes that span multiple applications, multiple data repositories, multiple corporate departments, or even multiple companies (or government agencies). BPM provides the foundation for interoperability, whether among departments or among affiliated organizations. BPM typically has the following objectives:

1. Obtain knowledge about the business processes of the enterprise.
2. Utilize business processes knowledge in business process reengineering projects to optimize the operation.
3. Facilitate the decision-making efforts of the enterprise.
4. Support interoperability of the business processes.

Ultimately the idea of "re-use," with the goal of saving Run the Engine costs, relies on (i) being able to apply a certain number of modeled processes from one department or application to another department or application and/or (ii) linking the various departmental models into an enterprise model. BPM is important within the context of an enterprise; however, the shift toward the "extended enterprise" paradigm makes objective #4, interoperability of business process models, even more critical.

Business Process Modeling Language (BPML)   BPML is a meta-language for the modeling of business processes; it provides an abstracted execution model for collaborative and transactional business processes based on the concept of a transactional finite-state machine. BPML is promulgated by the Business Process Management Initiative (BPMI.org).

Business Process Modeling Notation (BPMN)   BPMN is a graphical notation intended to be understandable by business users, business analysts that create the initial drafts of the processes, technical developers responsible for implementing the technology that will perform those processes, and the business people who will manage and monitor those processes. BPMN is promulgated by the Business Process Management Initiative (BPMI.org).

Business Process Outsourcing (BPO)   A strategy

utilized by firms to attempt to save costs. In this arrangement the firm seeks to focus on core competencies and let other providers that specialize in a given function (e.g., Information Technology, Human Resources, Document Production, etc.) operate these "back-office" functions. The service supplier is monitored using a set of Service Level Agreements (SLAs).

Business Process Reengineering (BPR) Business process redesign activities that seek to streamline operations and improve cost, time-to-market, and the reliability of the underlying business process.

Business Risk   (financial term) Risk arising from the uncertainty of the future outcome (revenues, expenses, contingencies, liabilities, losses) (but not usually including debt interest) of a firm.

Business-to-Business (B2B)   (financial term). A transaction that occurs between a company and another company, as opposed to a transaction involving a consumer. The term may also describe a company that provides goods or services for another company [r009].

Business-to-Consumer (B2C)   (financial term) A transaction that occurs between a company and a consumer, as opposed to a transaction between companies (called B2B). The term may also describe a company that provides goods or services for consumers [r009].

Bypass Tunnel   (MPLS context) A Label Switched Path (LSP) that is used to protect a set of LSPs passing over a common facility.

Byte   (aka octet) A fundamental unit of computer storage (eight bits); the smallest addressable unit in a computer's architecture. Usually represents one character of information.

Byte Code Verifier   Mechanism used in a Java sandbox to automatically check untrusted outside code before it is allowed to run. The Java source program is compiled to a platform-independent Java byte code, which is verified before it can run.

C

C   (GSM context) The C interface is situated between the Mobile Services Switching Center (MSC) and the Home Location Register (HLR) [r011].

CA   See Certification Authority

CA Certificate   A (digital, X.509) certificate for one Certification Authority (CA) issued by another CA.

Cable Modem Termination Systems (CMTS) (DOCSIS context) A device (possibly assisted by other IP service devices) that acts as a network edge, separating the physical outside-plant cable television network from the operator's IP network [r097]. See diagram.

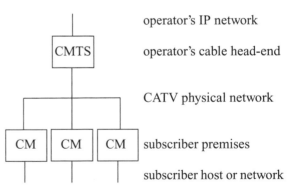

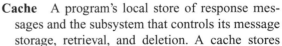

operator's IP network

operator's cable head-end

CATV physical network

subscriber premises

subscriber host or network

Cache   A program's local store of response messages and the subsystem that controls its message storage, retrieval, and deletion. A cache stores

Minoli–Cordovana's Authoritative Computer and Network Security Dictionary. By Daniel Minoli and James Cordovana
Copyright © 2006 John Wiley & Sons, Inc.

cacheable responses in order to reduce the response time and network bandwidth consumption on future, equivalent requests.

Cache Array Routing Protocol (CARP)   Protocol described in a now-expired *Internet Draft*. The draft describes CARP is an algorithm for dividing "Uniform Resource Locator (URL)-space" among an array of loosely coupled proxy caches. CARP is designed to maximize hit ratios, and to minimize the duplication of content among a set of caches.

Cacheable   A response is cacheable if a cache is allowed to store a copy of the response message for use in answering subsequent requests. Even if a resource is cacheable, there may be additional constraints on whether a cache can use the cached copy for a particular request.

Caching   An information-distribution approach that involves storing frequently accessed content closer to the consumers of the content (users) so they have to cross fewer networks to reach it. A typical cache mechanism is an Internet Proxy server, which resides at the edge of an enterprise infrastructure to mediate access to the Internet for users, potentially provide authentication and authorization to sites, and cache frequently downloaded content.

Caching Protocols   Internet Engineering Task Force (IETF) protocols to support caching include the following: Web Cache Control Protocol (WCCP), Network Element Control Protocol (NECP), and Internet Content Adaptation Protocol (ICAP).

CAGR   See Compound Annual Growth Rate

CALEA   See Communications Assistance for Law Enforcement Act of 1994

Calendar Year   (financial term) A year that ends on December 31.

Call   (SIP context) An informal term that refers to some communication between peers, generally set up for the purposes of a multimedia conversation [r025].

Call Back   An authentication technique for terminals that remotely access a computer via telephone lines. The host system disconnects the caller and then calls back on a telephone number that was previously authorized for that terminal.

Call Forwarding Unconditional (CFU)   (GSM context) A supplementary telephony service that ensures that all incoming calls are diverted to the number given by the customer [r011].

Call Holding Service (HOLD)   (GSM context) A supplementary telephony service that allows the customer to interrupt an active call for another call without losing the connection to the first call [r011].

Call Leg   (SIP context) Another name for a dialog.

Call Server   A protocol-specific signaling engine that routes video or voice calls on the network. In International Telecommunication Union (ITU) H.323 this entity is a gatekeeper. In Session Initiation Protocol (SIP), this entity is SIP Proxy Server. Note that not all signaling protocols use a call server [r074].

Call Stateful   (SIP context) A proxy is call stateful if it retains state for a dialog from the initiating INVITE to the terminating BYE request. A call stateful proxy is always transaction stateful, but the converse is not necessarily true [r025].

Call Waiting (CW)   (GSM context) A supplementary telephony service: It notifies the customer of an incoming call when no traffic channel is available, and the customer is currently engaged in an active or held call [r011].

Calling Line Identification Presentation (CLIP)   (GSM context) A supplementary service that allows the called party to receive the line identity of the calling party [r011].

Calling Line Identification Restriction (CLIR)   (GSM context) A supplementary service that allows the calling party to restrict its number so that it cannot be identified by the called party [r011].

CAM   See Content-Addressable Memory

Camellia   An encryption algorithm developed by NTT and Mitsubishi Electric Corporation in 2000 that was designed to withstand all known cryptanalytic attacks. Camellia supports 128-bit block size and 128-, 192-, and 256-bit key sizes—that is, the same interface specifications as the Advanced Encryption Standard (AES) [r098].

Canadian Standards Association (CSA) A Canadian testing and certification agency comparable in function to UL, and it is primarily concerned with the safety of devices, materials, and components in the electrical industry [r033].

Canned Scripts A colloquialism meaning predefined scripts.

Canonical Encoding Rules (CER) Abstract Syntax Notation One (ASN.1) encoding rules specified in ITUX690.2002, International Telecommunications Union, "Information Technology—ASN.1 encoding rules: Specification of Basic Encoding Rules (BER), Canonical Encoding Rules (CER) and Distinguished Encoding Rules (DER)," ITU-T Recommendation X690.2002.

Canonicalization The process of resolving various equivalent forms of a filename into a standard name.

Capability A token (sometimes called a "ticket") that grants the bearer permission to access an object or service. In the Kerberos model, this might be a ticket whose use is restricted by the contents of the authorization data field, but which lists no network addresses, together with the session key necessary to use the ticket [r070].

Capex See Capital Expenditure

CAPI See Cryptographic Application Programming Interface

Capital Asset (financial term) All tangible property that cannot easily be converted into cash and that is usually held for a long period, including real estate, equipment, and so on [r009].

Capital Expenditure (Capex) (financial term) Money spent to acquire or upgrade physical assets such as buildings and machinery. This tends to be a very large expense for companies with significant manufacturing facilities, but usually much less of an expense in the services sector. Also called capital spending or capital expense [r009].

Capital-intensive (financial term) Requiring a large amount of assets to finance a given amount of sales.

Cardholder (SET context) The holder of a valid payment card account and user of software supporting electronic commerce [r018].

Cardholder Certificate A digital certificate that is issued to a cardholder in the Secure Electronic Transaction (SET) system upon approval of the cardholder's issuing financial institution. The digital certificate is transmitted to merchants with purchase requests and encrypted payment instructions, thus carrying assurance that the account number has been validated by the issuing financial institution and cannot be altered by a third party [r017].

Cardholder Certification Authority (CCA) A Certification Authority (CA) responsible for issuing digital certificates to cardholders in the Secure Electronic Transaction system. The CCA is operated on behalf of a payment card brand, an issuer, or another party according to brand rules. A CCA maintains relationships with card issuers to allow for the verification of cardholder accounts. A CCA does not issue a certificate revocation list (CRL) but does distribute CRLs issued by root CAs, brand CAs, geopolitical CAs, and payment gateway CAs [r018, r013].

Cardholder Information Security Program (CISP) Defines a standard of due care and enforcement for protecting sensitive information associated with Visa credit cards. Among other things, CISP specifies the "Digital Dozen," a list of 12 basic security requirements with which all Visa payment system constituents need to comply. For example, CISP requires a firewall to protect data, encryption of data sent across public networks, and use of regularly updated anti-virus software).

CARL See Certification Authority Revocation List

Carnivore (aka DCS1000) An e-mail surveillance tool developed by the Federal Bureau of Investigation (FBI). When installed at an Internet Service Provider (ISP), it monitors the communication that passes through the servers.

CARP See Cache Array Routing Protocol

Carrier File In steganography, a file where information is hidden. For example, an image that contains hidden digitally-coded text.

Carrier Sense Multiple Access/Collision Detect (CSMA/CD)   Original Ethernet protocol for carrier transmission access in Local Area Networks (LANs). It is no longer needed/used for switched LAN systems and/or at the 10-GbE level. One of many Random Access Protocols that emerged in the past quarter century [r100, r047, r002]. CSMA provides the mechanism to detect whether the medium is in use; CD provides the mechanism to detect a collision and retry transmission after some length of time [r101].

Cash Flow   (financial term) A measure of a company's financial health. Equals cash receipts minus cash payments over a given period of time; or equivalently, net profit plus amounts charged off for depreciation, depletion, and amortization [r009].

Cash Flow Statement   (financial term) A summary of a company's cash flow over a given period of time.

CAST   A design procedure for symmetric encryption algorithms, and a resulting family of algorithms, invented by C.A. (Carlisle Adams) and S.T. (Stafford Tavares)—hence, the acronym [r013].

Category   A grouping of sensitive information items to which a non-hierarchical restrictive security label is applied to increase protection of the data.

Category 1 Cabling   Cabling media that supports applications such as voice communications or very low speed data applications (no specific upper limits of use but not suited for Local Area Networks (LANs)) [r102].

Category 2 Cabling   Cabling media that supports Integrated Services Digital Network (ISDN), T1, and Local Area Networks (LANs) operating at 1 Mbps or less [r102].

Category 3 Balanced Cabling   Cabling media that supports Local Area Networks (LANs) at speeds up to 10 Mbps and in some cases (such as 100VG-AnyLAN and 10BASE-T4) 100 Mbps [r102]. Balanced 100- and 120-ohm LAN cables and associated connecting hardware whose trans-

mission characteristics are specified up to 16 MHz (i.e., performance meets the requirements of a Class C link as per ISO/IEC 11801: 1995). Commonly used by IEEE 802.3 10BASE-T environments. In addition to the requirements outlined in ISO/IEC 11801: 1995, IEEE 802.3 Clauses 14, 23, and 32 specify additional requirements for cabling when used with 10BASE-T, 100BASE-TX, and 1000BASE-T.

Category 4 Balanced Cabling   Cabling media that supports Local Area Networks (LANs) at speeds up to 100 Mbps [r103]. Balanced 100- and 120-ohm LAN cables and associated connecting hardware whose transmission characteristics are specified up to 20 MHz as per ISO/IEC 11801: 1995. In addition to the requirements outlined in ISO/IEC 11801: 1995, IEEE 802.3 Clauses 14, 23, and 32 specify additional requirements for this cabling when used with 10BASE-T, 100BASE-T4, and 100BASE-T2, respectively.

Category 5 Balanced Cabling   Cabling media that supports Local Area Network (LAN) speeds of 100 Mbps or greater [r102]. Balanced 100- and 120-ohm LAN cables and associated connecting hardware whose transmission characteristics are specified up to 100 MHz (i.e., cabling components meet the performance specified in ISO/IEC 11801:1995). In addition to the requirements outlined in ISO/IEC 11801:1995, IEEE 802.3 Clauses 14, 23, 25, and 40 specify additional requirements for this cabling when used with 10BASE-T and 100BASE-T.

Category 5e Cabling   Cabling media that supports Local Area Network (LAN) speeds of 1000 Mbps. Also known as Class D, Category 5e. Cable standard: IEC 61156-5, Cat 5e (UTP and screened); Connector standard: IEC 60603-7-2 (UTP) and IEC 60603-7-3 (screened). Used in Gigabit Ethernet (GbE) and 10 Gigabit Ethernet (10GbE).

Category 6 Cabling   Improved Local Area Network (LAN) cabling system. Also known as Class E, Category 6. Cable standard: IEC 61156-5, Cat6 (UTP and screened); Connector standard: IEC 60603-7-4 (UTP) and IEC 60603-7-5 (screened). Performance in the range of 600 MHz with crosstalk isolation > 20 dB than Class D (cat 5e). Used in Gigabit Ethernet (GbE) and 10 Gigabit Ethernet (10GbE).

Category 7 Cabling   Improved Local Area Network (LAN) cabling system. Also known as Class F, Category 7. Cable standard: IEC 61156-5 Cat7 (screened); Connector standard: IEC 60603-7-7. Performance in the range of 600 MHz with crosstalk isolation > 30 dB than Class D (cat 5e). Used in Gigabit Ethernet (GbE) and 10 Gigabit Ethernet (10GbE).

CAW   See Certification Authority Workstation

CBC   See Cipher Block Chaining

CBCH   See Cell Broadcast Control Channel

CBR   See Constant Bit Rate

CC   See Country Code or Common Criteria

CCA   See Cardholder Certification Authority

CCCH   See Common Control Channel

CCEVS   See Common Criteria Evaluation and Validation Scheme

CCG   See Central Clock Generator

CCPCH   See Common Control Physical Channel

CCS7   See Common Channel Signaling System No. 7

CD-I   (video formats and coding) Early digital consumer-electronic format.

CDMA   See Code Division Multiple Access

CE   See Customer Edge (Equipment)

CE-Based Virtual Private Network (VPN)   A VPN approach in which the shared service provider network does not have any knowledge of the customer VPN. This information is limited to Customer Edge (CE) equipment. All the VPN-specific procedures are performed in the CE devices, and the Provider Edge (PE) devices are not aware in any way that some of the traffic they are processing is VPN traffic [r082] (see also [r081]).

Cell Broadcast Control Channel (CBCH)   (GSM context) A control channel responsible for the transmission of short messages [r014].

Cell Global Identity (CGI)   (GSM context) A number code identifying each cell within a Location Area of a particular Global System for Mobile communications (GSM) network [r011].

Cell Identity (CI)   (GSM context) The Cell Identity is part of the Cell Global Identity (CGI), which indicates a particular cell within a Location Area [r011].

Cell Relay Service (CRS)   See Asynchronous Transfer Mode

Cellular Telecommunications and Internet Association (CTIA)   An international organization representing all sectors of wireless communications: cellular, personal communication services, and enhanced specialized mobile radio. As a nonprofit membership organization founded in 1984, the organization represents service providers, manufacturers, wireless data and Internet companies, and other wireless stakeholders. It sees itself as the voice of the wireless industry—representing its members in a constant dialogue with policy makers in the Executive Branch, in the Federal Communications Commission, in Congress, and on the state, regulatory, and legislative levels.

CENELEC   See European Committee for Electrotechnical Standardization

Center for Internet Security (CIS)   A nonprofit enterprise whose mission is to help organizations reduce the risk of business and e-commerce disruptions resulting from inadequate technical security controls. CIS members develop and encourage the widespread use of security configuration benchmarks through a global consensus process involving participants from the public and private sectors.

The practical CIS Benchmarks support available high level standards that deal with the "Why, Who, When, and Where" aspects of Information Technology (IT) security by detailing "How" to secure an ever widening array of workstations, servers, network devices, and software applications in terms of technology-specific controls. CIS Scoring Tools analyze and report system compliance with the technical control settings in the Benchmarks.

Center Wavelength   (optical transmission term) The wavelength (nm) at which a particular signal channel is centered. The International Telecommunications Union (ITU) has defined the standard optical frequency grid (channel center frequency) with 100-GHz spacing based on the reference frequency of 193.10 THz (1552.52 nm), the so-called ITU Grid. A channel's center wavelength is chosen at the wavelength corresponding to the ITU Grid, and should be distinguished from the actual center position of each pass band of the device.

Center Wavelength Offset   (optical transmission term) A relative drift of the actual central wavelength of a particular channel with respect to the standard ITU Grid. Note that the center wavelength offset is a cumulative value resulting from optical misalignment, aging, and temperature change over the operating temperature range.

Central Clock Generator (CCG)   (GSM context) The Central Clock Generator object represents the system time of the Base Transceiver Station (BTS) (Frame Information Signal); there is only one CCG object per BTS [r014].

Central Office (CO)   A telephone carrier's hardened location that houses Public Switched Telephone Network (PSTN) switches and transmission equipment to support telephony services and other transport services. Usually a fiber-rich hub that connects local users to the long-haul network.

Central Processing Unit (CPU) No-Execute Bit A no-execute feature that has been folded in the newest processors by chipmakers Intel and AMD to ward off malicious attacks. Considered not to be a panacea. AMD calls the feature "Enhanced Virus Protection" (EVP) and Intel calls it eXecute Disable (or XD). More generically, it is known as NX (for No eXecute). Essentially, it is a way to specify protected portions of memory so that processor instructions cannot execute there. The idea behind setting some areas of memory as off-bounds is to prevent worms and other malicious code from inserting functions into memory and executing them. AMD has presented EVP within its 64-bit Athlon processors as a security technology that lets "you enjoy peace of mind." AMD calls EVP a "preventative measure" that will not prevent malicious code attacks, but will make them "localized, short-lived, and nonconta-

gious." Intel, takes a similar line, saying that the impact of future mass-mailed worms in the Slammer and MSBlast vein would be "substantially reduced" by XD. NX will not stop all attacks that are aimed at creating a buffer overflow, the most commonly used tactic today for compromising a system. One can still execute code on an NX-enabled machine; it just requires a slightly more complex technique. A "return-to-libc attack," for instance, in which the return address on the stack is replaced by the address of another function, could be the basis for assaults on a non-executable memory stack. Attackers could also create fake stack frames to bypass the memory protection that NX provides. Microsoft calls NX by yet another name, Data Execution Prevention (DEP), in Windows XP SP2 and Windows Server 2003 SP1. Microsoft indicates that the feature will also be enabled by default on critical Windows services in Windows Vista [r161].

Centrex   Traditional Time Division Multiplexing (TDM) voice service offered by the local carriers to provide a function/service comparable to that of a Private Branch Exchange (PBX), but without requiring the customer to deploy and/or maintain equipment. A managed service for campus voice switching.

CEO   See Chief Executive Officer

CEPT   (GSM context) Conférence Européenne des Postes et Télécommunications, the European conference on post (surface mail) and telecommunications [r011].

CER   See Canonical Encoding Rules

CE-R   See Customer Edge Router

CERT® Coordination Center (CERT/CC)   Established in 1988, the CERT® Coordination Center (CERT/CC) is a center of Internet security expertise, located at the Software Engineering Institute, a federally funded research and development center operated by Carnegie Mellon University. The CERT/CC is a major reporting center for Internet security problems. Staff members provide technical advice and coordinate responses to security compromises, identify trends in intruder activity, work with other security experts to identify solutions to security problems, and disseminate information to the broad community. The CERT/CC also analyzes product vulnerabilities, publishes technical documents, and presents training courses. CERT/CC was the first computer security incident response team.

Certificate (General English context) A document that attests to the truth of something or the ownership of something.

(Security context) capability, digital certificate, and in Public Key Infrastructure (PKI), attribute certificate and public-key certificate [r013].

(PKI context) Users of a public key need to be confident that the associated private key is owned by the correct remote subject (person or system) with which an encryption or digital signature mechanism will be used. This confidence is obtained through the use of public key certificates that are data structures that bind public key values to subjects. The binding is asserted by having a trusted Certification Authority (CA) digitally sign each certificate. The CA may base this assertion upon technical means (aka proof of possession through a challenge–response protocol), presentation of the private key, or on an assertion by the subject. A record used for authenticating entities such as a server or a client. A certificate typically contains X.509 [aka International Organization for Standardization (ISO) Authentication Framework] information pieces about its owner (called the subject) and the signing Certification Authority (called the issuer), along with the owner's public key and the signature made by the CA. Network entities verify these signatures using CA certificates. A certificate has a limited valid lifetime that is indicated in its signed contents. Because a certificate's signature and timeliness can be independently checked by a client, certificates can be distributed via untrusted communications and server systems, and the certificates can be cached in unsecured storage in certificate-using systems [r103].

Certificate Authority See Certification Authority, which is the more formal term.

Certificate Creation The act or process by which a Certification Authority (CA) sets the values of a digital certificate's data fields and signs it [r013].

Certificate Expiration The event that occurs when a certificate ceases to be valid because its assigned lifetime has been exceeded [r013].

Certificate Management The functions that a Certification Authority (CA) may perform during the life cycle of a digital certificate, including the following [r013]:

- Acquire and verify data items to bind into the certificate.
- Encode and sign the certificate.
- Store the certificate in a directory or repository.
- Renew, rekey, and update the certificate.
- Revoke the certificate and issue a certificate revocation list (CRL).

Certificate Policy (CP) A named set of rules that indicate the applicability of a certificate to a particular community and/or class of application with common security requirements [r061, r013].

A certificate policy can help a certificate user decide whether a certificate should be trusted in a particular application. For example, a particular certificate policy might indicate applicability of a type of certificate for the authentication of electronic data interchange transactions for the trading goods within a given price range [r104, r105].

(Secure Electronic Transaction [SET] context) Every SET certificate specifies at least one certificate policy: that of the SET root Certification Authority (CA). SET uses certificate policy qualifiers to point to the actual policy statement and to add qualifying policies to the root policy.

Certificate Policy Qualifier Information that pertains to a certificate policy and is included in a "certificatePolicies" extension in a v3 X.509 public-key certificate [r013].

Certificate Reactivation The act or process by which a digital certificate, which a Certification Authority (CA) has designated for revocation but not yet listed on a Certificate Revocation List (CRL), is returned to the valid state [r013].

Certificate Rekey   The act or process by which an existing public-key certificate has its public key value changed by issuing a new certificate with a different (usually new) public key [r013].

Certificate Renewal   The act or process by which the validity of the data binding asserted by an existing public-key certificate is extended in time by issuing a new certificate [r013].

Certificate Revocation   The event that occurs when a Certification Authority (CA) declares that a previously valid digital certificate issued by that CA has become invalid. This is stated with a revocation date [r013].

Certificate Revocation List (CRL)   A time-stamped list identifying revoked certificates. This list signed by a Certification Authority (CA) and made freely available in a public repository [r106].

   The term CRL is also commonly used as a generic term applying to all the different types of revocation lists, including Authority Revocation Lists (ARLs), Attribute Certificate Revocation Lists (ACRLs), and so on [r060, r013].

Certificate Revocation List (CRL) Distribution Point   In X.509 a directory entry or other distribution source for CRLs; a CRL distributed through a CRL distribution point may contain revocation entries for only a subset of the full set of certificates issued by one Certification Authority (CA) or may contain revocation entries for multiple CAs [r068a].

Certificate Revocation Tree   A mechanism for distributing notice of certificate revocations that offers an alternative to issuing a Certificate Revocation List (CRL), but is not supported in X.509 [r013].

Certificate Serial Number   An integer value that is associated with, and may be carried in, a digital certificate, is assigned to the certificate by the certificate's issuer, and is unique among all the certificates produced by that issuer [r013].

Certificate Signing Request (CSR)   An unsigned certificate for submission to a Certification Authority (CA), which signs it with the Private Key of their CA Certificate. After the CSR is signed, it becomes a real certificate.

Certificate Status Responder   (Federal Public-key Infrastructure context) A trusted on-line server that acts for a Certification Authority (CA) to provide authenticated certificate status information to certificate users [r106]. Offers an alternative to issuing a Certificate Revocation List (CRL), but is not supported in X.509 [r013].

Certificate Update   The act or process by which non-key data items bound in an existing public-key certificate, especially authorizations granted to the subject, are changed by issuing a new certificate. For an X.509 public-key certificate, the essence of this process is that fundamental changes are made in the data that is bound to the public key, such that it is necessary to revoke the old certificate. Otherwise, the process is only a "certificate rekey" or "certificate renewal") [r013].

Certificate User   An entity (system or user) that depends on the validity of information (such as another entity's public key value) provided by a digital certificate [r013].

Certificate-Using System   In X.509 an implementation of those functions defined in this Directory Specification that are used by a certificate-user.

Certificate Validation   The process of ensuring that a certificate is valid, including possibly the construction and processing of a certification path, and ensuring that all certificates in that path have not expired or been revoked. To validate a certificate, a certificate user checks the signature, the syntax and semantics, and whether the certificate is expired or has been revoked [r013, r060].

Certification   (Information System context) Technical evaluation (usually made in support of an accreditation action) of an information system's security features and other safeguards to establish the extent to which the system's design and implementation meet specified security requirements [r107, r013].

   (Digital Certificate context) The act or process of vouching for the truth and accuracy of the binding between data items in a certificate [r013].

(Public-Key context) The act or process of vouching for the ownership of a public key by issuing a public-key certificate that binds the key to the name of the entity that possesses the matching private key. In addition to binding a key to a name, a public-key certificate may bind those items to other restrictive or explanatory data items [r013].

[Secure Electronic Transaction (SET) context] The process of ascertaining that a set of requirements or criteria has been fulfilled and attesting to that fact to others, usually with some written instrument. A system that has been inspected and evaluated as fully compliant with the SET protocol by duly authorized parties and process would be said to have been certified compliant [r018, r013].

Certification Authority (CA) (aka Certificate Authority—Certification Authority is the more formal term) An authority trusted by one or more users to create and assign public key certificates. Optionally, the CA may create the user's keys. It is important to note that the CA is responsible for the public-key certificates during their whole lifetime, not just for issuing them [r105]. The main obligations of a CA are [r105]:

(1) Handle certificate requests and issue new certificates:
- Accept and confirm certification requests from entities requesting a certificate according to the agreed procedures contained in this policy and in the Certificate Policy Statement (CPS).
- Authenticate entities requesting a certificate, possibly by the help of separately designated Registration Authorities (RA).
- Issue certificates based on authenticated entities' requests.
- Send notification of issued certificate to requesters.
- Make issued certificates publicly available.

(2) Handle certificate revocation requests and certificate revocation:
- Accept and confirm revocation requests from entities requesting a certificate to be revoked according to the agreed procedures contained in CPS/policy.
- Authenticate entities requesting a certificate to be revoked.
- Make certificate revocation lists (CRLs) publicly available.

Certification Authority (CA) Certificate A certificate for one CA issued by another CA.

Certification Authority Revocation List (CARL) In X.509 a CARL is a revocation list containing a list of public-key certificates issued to certification authorities, which are no longer considered valid by the certificate issuer [r068a].

Certification Authority Workstation (CAW) A computer system that enables a Certification Authority (CA) to issue digital certificates and supports other certificate management functions as required [r013].

Certification Hierarchy A tree-structured (loop-free) topology of relationships among Certificate Authorities (CAs) and the entities to whom the CAs issue public-key certificates. In this structure, one CA is the top CA, the highest level of the hierarchy. The top CA may issue public-key certificates to one or more additional CAs that form the second-highest level. Each of these CAs may issue certificates to more CAs at the third-highest level, and so on. The CAs at the second-lowest level of the hierarchy issue certificates only to non-CA entities, called "end entities" that form the lowest level. Thus, all certification paths begin at the top CA and descend through zero or more levels of other CAs. All certificate users base path validations on the top CA's public key [r013].

[Multilevel Information System Security Initiative (MISSI) context] A MISSI certification hierarchy has three or four levels of CAs [r013]:

- A CA at the highest level, the top CA, is a "policy approving authority."
- A CA at the second-highest level is a "policy creation authority."
- A CA at the third-highest level is a local authority called a "Certification Authority."
- A CA at the fourth-highest (optional) lev-

el is a "subordinate Certification Authority."

[Privacy Enhanced Mail (PEM) context] A PEM certification hierarchy has three levels of CAs [r109]:

- The highest level is the "Internet Policy Registration Authority."
- A CA at the second-highest level is a "policy Certification Authority."
- A CA at the third-highest level is a "Certification Authority."

[Secure Electronic Transaction (SET) context] A SET certification hierarchy has three or four levels of CAs [r013]:

- The highest level is a "SET root CA."
- A CA at the second-highest level is a "brand Certification Authority."
- A CA at the third-highest (optional) level is a "geopolitical Certification Authority."
- A CA at the fourth-highest level is a "cardholder CA," a "merchant CA," or a "payment gateway CA."

Certification Path   An ordered sequence of certificates that, together with the public key of the initial object in the path, can be processed to obtain that of the final object in the path [r011].

Certification Practice Statement (CPS)   A statement of the practices that a Certification Authority (CA) employs in issuing, managing, revoking, and renewing or re-keying certificates [r011, r104].

Certification Practice Statement (CPS) Summary   (aka CPS Abstract) A subset of the provisions of a complete CPS that is made public by a Certification Authority (CA) [r011].

Certification Request   An algorithm-independent transaction format defined by PKCS #10 and used in Public-Key Infrastructure X.509 (PKIX). It contains a Distinguished Name (DN), a public key, and optionally a set of attributes, collectively signed by the entity requesting certification, and sent to a Certification Authority (CA). The CA transforms the request to an X.509 public-key certificate or another type of certificate [r013].

Certified Information System Security Professional (CISSP)   Commercial Certification Programs for Personnel offered by the International Information Systems Security Certification Consortium (ISC)^2—note that the exponent is part of the acronym.

Certify   To issue a digital certificate and thus vouch for the truth, accuracy, and binding between data items in the certificate (e.g., X.509 public-key certificate). The data items include elements such as the identity of the certificate's subject and the ownership of a public key. To "certify a public key" means to issue a public-key certificate that vouches for the binding between the certificate's subject and the key.

Also, the act by which a Certification Authority (CA) employs measures to verify the truth, accuracy, and binding between data items in a digital certificate. A description of the measures used for verification should be included in the CA's Certification Practice Statement (CPS) [r013].

CE-S   See Customer Edge Switch

CFB   See Supplementary Service Call Forwarding on Mobile Subscriber Busy or Cipher Feedback

CFO   See Chief Financial Officer

CFU   See Call Forwarding Unconditional

CGA   See Cryptographically Generated Addresses

CGI   See Cell Global Identity or Common Gateway Interface

Chaining Attacks Modality, Domain Name System (DNS)   Mechanism is as follows [r111]:

- Victim issues a query, perhaps at the instigation of the attacker or some third party; in some cases the query itself may be unrelated to the name under attack (that is, the attacker is just using this query as a means to inject false information about some other name).
- Attacker injects response, whether via packet interception, query guessing, or by being a legitimate name server that's involved at some point in the process of answering the query that the victim issued.

- Attacker's response includes one or more Resource Records (RRs) with DNS names in their RDATA; depending on which particular form this attack takes, the object may be to inject false data associated with those names into the victim's cache via the Additional section of this response, or may be to redirect the next stage of the query to a server of the attacker's choosing (in order to inject more complex lies into the victim's cache than will fit easily into a single response, or in order to place the lies in the Authority or Answer section of a response where they will have a better chance of sneaking past a resolver's defenses).

Any attacker who can insert resource records into a victim's cache can almost certainly do some kind of damage, so there are cache poisoning attacks which are not name chaining attacks in the sense discussed here. However, in the case of name chaining attacks, the cause and effect relationship between the initial attack and the eventual result may be significantly more complex than in the other forms of cache poisoning, so name chaining attacks merit special attention.

The common thread in all of the name chaining attacks is that response messages allow the attacker to introduce arbitrary DNS names of the attacker's choosing and provide further information that the attacker claims is associated with those names; unless the victim has better knowledge of the data associated with those names, the victim is going to have a hard time defending against this class of attacks.

This class of attack is particularly insidious given that it is quite easy for an attacker to provoke a victim into querying for a particular name of the attacker's choosing, for example, by embedding a link to a 1 × 1-pixel "web bug" graphic in a piece of Text/HTML (HyperText Markup Language) mail to the victim. If the victim's mail reading program attempts to follow such a link, the result will be a DNS query for a name chosen by the attacker.

Challenge Handshake Authentication Protocol (CHAP)   A peer authentication method for Point-to-Point Protocol (PPP) defined in RFC 1994 [r112]. The process is as follows:

- The client and the server share a secret key.
- The server generates a randomly generated challenge and an identifier.
- The client performs a one-way hash (using MD5) of the concatenation of the identifier, the randomly generated challenge, and the secured key.
- The client responds with the hashed value and the server compares this value to its calculation of hash with the same input values.
- If the values match, then authentication is allowed.

Challenge–Response   An authentication mechanism that requires a valid response to a challenge.

Challenge–Response Authentication Mechanism (CRAM)   IMAP4 usage: A mechanism, intended for use with Internet Message Access Protocol, version 4 (IMAP4) AUTHENTICATE, by which an IMAP4 client uses a keyed hash to authenticate itself to an IMAP4 server [r013, r113, r114]. The server includes a unique timestamp in its ready response to the client; the client replies with the client's name and the hash result of applying Message Digest 5 (MD5) to a string formed from concatenating the timestamp with a shared secret that is known only to the client and the server.

Change Control   See Change Management (CM)

Change Coordination   The goal of the change coordination process is to ensure that standardized methods and techniques are used for efficient and prompt handling of all changes within a specified Information Technology (IT) domain, so that change-related problems are prevented. Also see Change Management (CM).

Change Management (CM)   Mechanisms to make system changes more quickly and with more confidence, saving an enterprise time and financial resources.

Changes to the Organization's Risk Profile   Information, usually in the form of a report, that describes how the vulnerabilities, threats, and assets have changed over time.

Channel   An information transfer path within a system.

(Optical transmission term) A single signal channel consists of a frequency band that has a finite pass bandwidth and is centered at a given frequency such as one specified by the International Telecommunications Union (ITU) Grid. In Dense Wavelength Division Multiplexing (DWDM), each channel corresponds to one particular wavelength and carries an individual data stream.

Channel (Communications) Bandwidth   Term used to mean the capacity of a communication channel to transfer data through the channel in a given amount of time. Usually expressed in bits per second.

Channel Bandwidth   Actual rate at which information can be transferred over the channel. While the potential channel rate depends on a number of factors, including modulation scheme, the actual rate is the de facto transfer rate in a given environment.

Channel Overhead Due to Encryption   While physical-level encryption does not impact the message length and, consequently the required channel bandwidth, network layer encryption (e.g., IPsec) does impact the message length and required network bandwidth because of the overhead involved in the tunneling process (that is, the encapsulation of an IP datagram/packet inside another packet. This is particularly problematic for short packets (small payload) such as for Voice over IP (VoIP) applications.

Channel Pass Bandwidth   (optical transmission term) A maximum wavelength (or frequency) range (nm) around the corresponding center wavelength (or frequency) at a given relative power level, for example, specified at 0.5 dB down power level referenced to 0 dB.

Channel Spacing   (optical transmission term) The frequency interval (GHz) between the center frequencies of any two neighboring channels in Dense Wavelength Division Multiplexing (DWDM) components or modules.

Channel Uniformity   (optical transmission term) The maximum difference (dB) of insertion loss across all signal channels for all polarization states over the operating temperature rang. Channel uniformity is a measure of how evenly power is distributed between the output ports of the devices.

CHAP   See Challenge Handshake Authentication Protocol

Check_Password   A program used for cracking passwords.

Checksum   A value that is computed by a function that is dependent on the contents of a data object and is stored or transmitted together with the object, for the purpose of detecting changes in the data. Related terms include cyclic redundancy check, message authentication codes, data integrity service, error detection code, hash, keyed hash, and protected checksum. To gain confidence that a data object has not been changed, an entity that later uses the data can compute a checksum and compare it with the checksum that was stored or transmitted with the object [r013].

Checksum Mechanism   A mechanism that provides proof of the integrity of the associated message and that preserves the confidentiality of the message in case it is not sent in the clear. Finding two plaintexts with the same checksum should be infeasible. It is not required that an eavesdropper be unable to determine whether two checksums are for the same message, as the messages themselves would presumably be visible to any such eavesdropper [r115].

Chernobyl Packet   (aka Kamikaze Packet) A Protocol Data Unit (PDU) that creates a broadcast storm and network incapacitation due to ensuing overload. Typically a datagram that passes through a gateway with both source and destination Ethernet address and IP address set as the (respective) broadcast addresses.

Chief Executive Officer (CEO)   (financial term) The executive who is responsible for a company's operations, usually the President or the Chairman of the Board.

Chief Financial Officer (CFO)   (financial term)

Officer who oversees the treasurer and comptroller and sets overall financial strategy (financial planning) for the firm. Also responsible for record-keeping for a company.

Chief Information Officer (CIO)   Senior individual responsible for the organization in a firm or government agency that architects, develops, deploys, manages, and operates the Information Technology (IT) function. Often also owns the security function. Typically is responsible for assisting in the development of the Business Architecture and then for translating that into a System Architecture (along with a Data Architecture), which in turn runs over a set IT assets, as described in a Technology Architecture

Chief Operating Officer (COO)   (financial term) The executive who is responsible for the day-to-day management of a company.

Chief Security Officer (CSO)   [aka Information system security officer (ISSO) or Chief Information Security Offices (CISO)] Executive responsible for the information security of an enterprise.

Chief Technology Officer (CTO)   Senior individual responsible for the organization in a firm or government agency that tracks technology developments and determines how these can be deployed within the firm.

Chip   A set of microminiaturized, electronic circuits that are designed for use as processors and memory in computers and countless consumer and industrial products [r029].

Chosen-ciphertext Attack   A cryptanalysis technique in which the analyst tries to determine the key from knowledge of plaintext that corresponds to ciphertext selected (i.e., dictated) by the analyst [r013].

Chosen-plaintext Attack   A cryptanalysis technique in which the analyst tries to determine the key from knowledge of ciphertext that corresponds to plaintext selected (i.e., dictated) by the analyst [r013].

Chromatic Dispersion   (optical transmission term) The worst-case dispersion (ps/nm) within any clear window for all polarization states of a device.

CI   See Cell Identity

CIA   See Confidentiality, Integrity, and Availability or CIA Triad

CIA Triad   [aka Confidentiality, Integrity, and Availability (CIA)] A grouping that is a simple way to encapsulate three of the most important concepts in information security (confidentiality, integrity, and availability). Refer to the individual terms for their definition.

CIAC   See Computer Incident Advisory Capability

CIDR   See Classless Interdomain Routing

CIK   See Cryptographic Ignition Key

CIO   See Chief Information Officer

CIP   See Customer Identification Program or Critical Infrastructure Protection

Cipher   A cryptographic algorithm for encryption and decryption of data. Examples include Data Encryption Standard (DES), Advanced Encryption Standard (AES), and Rivest Cipher 4 (RC4).

Cipher Block Chaining (CBC)   A block cipher mode that enhances electronic codebook mode by chaining together blocks of ciphertext it produces [r116–r118, r013]. A feedback mechanism is used in the encryption scheme. In CBC, the plaintext is XORed with the previous ciphertext block prior to encryption.

Cipher Feedback (CFB)   A block cipher mode that enhances electronic code book mode by chaining together the blocks of ciphertext it produces and operating on plaintext segments of variable length less than or equal to the block length [r013].

Cipher State   This describes any information that can be carried over from one encryption or decryption operation to the next, for use with a given specific key. For example, a block cipher used in CBC (Cipher Block Chaining) mode may put an initial vector of one block in the cipher state [r115].

Ciphersuite   A set, which must contain both an encryption algorithm and a message authentication algorithm [e.g., a Message Authentication Code (MAC) or a Hashed Message Authentication Code (HMAC)].

Ciphertext   The output that results when plaintext is passed through a cipher—that is, the encrypted data.

Ciphertext-Only Attack   A cryptanalysis technique in which the analyst tries to determine the key solely from knowledge of intercepted ciphertext (although the analyst may also know other clues, such as the cryptographic algorithm, the language in which the plaintext was written, the subject matter of the plaintext, and some probable plaintext words) [r013].

CIPSO   See Common IP Security Option

Circuit-Level Gateway   A kind of firewall where all internal computers establish a "circuit" with the proxy server. The proxy server, in turn, performs all communications with the outside network. External computers only see the IP address of the proxy server and do not communicate directly with the internal clients [r035].

Circuit-Switched (CS)   (GSM context) Circuit-switched refers to a transmission mode: messages like speech or data are transmitted as a continuous data stream between two terminals. The resources are allocated—and charged—for the whole duration of the connection. This very stable transmission is particularly well suited for real-time services such as voice or video; it is used in the Public Switched Telephone Network (PSTN) and 2G mobile radio networks (e.g., in GSM). Its drawback is that resources are not used very efficiently [r011].

CIRT   See Computer Incident Response Team (CIRT)

CIS   See Center for Internet Security

CISA   See Certified Information Systems Auditor

CISP   See Cardholder Information Security Program

CISSP   See Certified Information System Security Professional

CKL   See Compromised Key List

Class 2, 3, 4, or 5   The U.S. Department of Defense has defined several levels of Public Key Infrastructure (PKI) assurance based on risk and value of information to be protected. These levels are [r013]:

- Class 2: For handling low-value information (unclassified, not mission-critical, or low monetary value) or protection of system-high information in low- to medium-risk environment.
- Class 3: For handling medium-value information in low- to medium-risk environment. Typically requires identification of a system entity as a legal person, rather than merely a member of an organization.
- Class 4: For handling medium- to high-value information in any environment. Typically requires identification of an entity as a legal person, rather than merely a member of an organization, and a cryptographic hardware token for protection of keying material.
- Class 5: For handling high-value information in a high-risk environment.

Class A IP Address   See Address Class A

Class B IP Address   See Address Class B

Class C IP Address   See Address Class C

Class D IP Address   See Address Class D

Classification Level   A categorization of the sensitivity of data. The data are labeled, and controls are put in place to protect the labeled data according to a security policy. Corporate labels may include Confidential, Sensitive, Private, or Proprietary. Military labels include Secret and Top Secret.

Classification of Virtual Private Networks (VPNs)   The terminology used in RFC 3809 [Nagarajan, A., "Generic Requirements for Provider Provisioned Virtual Private Networks (PPVPN)", RFC 3809, June 2004] is defined based on the figure below [r082].

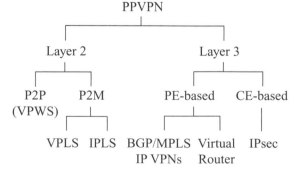

Classified Information Data that has a classification level associated with it. Related to classified status.

Classified Status The term used in government, especially in the military sectors to indicate classification level. In the U.S. Department of Defense (DoD), for example, it refers to information that has been determined pursuant to Executive Order 12958, Classified National Security Information, April 1995 (or any predecessor order), to require protection against unauthorized disclosure and is marked to indicate its classified status when in documentary form [r013].

Classless Interdomain Routing (CIDR) CIDR is a mechanism developed to help alleviate the problem of exhaustion of IP addresses and growth of routing tables. The idea behind CIDR is that blocks of multiple addresses (for example, blocks of Class C address) can be combined, or aggregated, to create a larger classless set of IP addresses, with more hosts allowed. Blocks of Class C network numbers are allocated to each network service provider; organizations using the network service provider for Internet connectivity are allocated subsets of the service provider's address space as required. These multiple Class C addresses can then be summarized in routing tables, resulting in fewer route advertisements. (Note that the CIDR mechanism can be applied to blocks of Class A, B, and C addresses; it is not restricted to Class C.) [r119].

CIDR is described further in RFC 1518, *An Architecture for IP Address Allocation with CIDR,* and RFC 1519, *Classless Inter-Domain Routing (CIDR): An Address Assignment and Aggregation Strategy.* RFC 2050, *Internet Registry IP Allocation Guidelines,* specifies guidelines for the allocation of IP addresses.

Most CIDR debates revolve around summarizing blocks of Class C networks into large blocks of addresses. As a general rule, Internet Service Providers (ISPs) implement a minimum route advertisement standard of /19 address blocks. A /19 address block equals a block of 32 Class C networks. [In some cases, smaller blocks might be advertised, such as with a /21 mask (eight Class C networks).] Addressing is now so limited that networks such as 12.0.0.0/8 are being divided into blocks of /19 that are assigned to major Internet Service Providers (ISPs), which allows further allocation to customers. CIDR combines blocks of addresses regardless of whether they fall within a single classful boundary or encompass many classful boundaries [r119].

Clean System A computer system in which the operating system and application system software and files have just been freshly installed from trusted software distribution media. A clean system is not necessarily in a secure state [r013].

Clear Window (optical transmission term) Defined as a wavelength band (nm) around each International Telecommunications Union (ITU) center wavelength. The worst-case values are specified within the "clear window" of all channels and for all polarizations. This approach eliminates the need to calculate the effects of the filter line shape, center channel accuracy, and polarization. Typically, the clear window is defined as 25% of the channel spacing. For 100 GHz spacing, the clear window is defined as the ITU center wavelength ±12.5 GHz (±0.10 nm).

Clearance Level (aka security clearance) The security level of classified information to which an individual is authorized to have access.

Clearing Trouble Reports An assertion by an agent that actions which are identified in the trouble report or the repair activity object instances have been satisfactorily performed to resolve the trouble, or that such actions are no longer necessary, such that in either case the trouble report is a candidate for closure [r068a].

Cleartext (aka plaintext) Data that is not encrypted. Usually used in the context of the input for an encryption cipher and/or the output of a decryption cipher.

Client A user of something. In the context of information systems, a client can include a user or a program [running on a desktop (PC) system or any type of host] that establishes connections with a server for the purpose of sending requests.

(SIP context) A client is any network element that sends Session Initiation Protocol (SIP) requests and receives SIP responses. Clients may or may not interact directly with a human user. User agent clients and proxies are clients [r025].

Client Connectivity Only, Public Address (Internet Connectivity context) This service provides access to the Internet without support for servers or most peer-to-peer functions. The IP address assigned to the customer is in the public address space. It is usually nominally dynamic or otherwise subject to change, but it may not change for months at a time. Most Virtual Private Networks (VPNs) and similar connections will work with this service. The provider may prohibit the use of server functions by either legal (contractual) restrictions or by filtering incoming connection attempts. Filtering Web proxies are uncommon with this type of service, and the provider should indicate if one is present [r034].

Client Connectivity Only, Without a Public Address (Internet Connectivity context) This service provides access to the Internet without support for servers or most peer-to-peer functions. The IP address assigned to the customer is dynamic and is characteristically assigned from non-public address space. Servers and peer-to-peer functions are generally not supported by the Network Address Translation (NAT) systems that are required by the use of private addresses. Filtering Web proxies are common with this type of service, and the provider should indicate whether or not one is present [r034].

Client Write Key The key used to encrypt data written by the client [r039].

Client Write MAC Secret The secret data used to authenticate data written by a client [r039].

Clinger–Cohen Act of 1996 Also known as the Information Technology Management Reform Act (ITMRA). Act authorized a Chief Information Officer (CIO) for all federal agencies and it makes the CIO responsible for developing, maintaining, and facilitating the implementation of a sound and integrated information technology architecture (ITA) (i.e., Enterprise Architecture).

CLIP See Calling Line Identification Presentation

CLIPPER Chip The Mykotronx, Inc. MYK-82, an integrated microcircuit with a cryptographic processor that implements the SKIPJACK encryption algorithm and supports key escrow. The key escrow scheme for a chip involves a SKIPJACK key common to all chips that protects the unique serial number of the chip, and a second SKIPJACK key unique to the chip that protects all data encrypted by the chip. The second key is escrowed as split key components held by National Institute of Standards and Technology (NIST) and the U.S. Treasury Department [r013].

CLIR See Calling Line Identification Restriction

Closed (Presence Services context) A distinguished value of the status marker. In the context of instant messages, this value means that the associated instant inbox address, if any, corresponds to an instant inbox that is unable to accept an instant message. This value may have an analogous meaning for other communication means, but any such meaning is not defined by this model. Contrast with open [r015].

Closed Out A trouble report is considered "closed out" when the agent determines that the reported trouble either has been cleared or no longer exists, and the agent updates the trouble report status to indicate the trouble report is "closed-out." Only an agent can change the trouble report status to "closedOut" [r068a].

Closed Security Environment (U.S. Department of Defense context) A system environment that meets both of the following conditions [r013, r120]:

(1) Authorizations to provide an acceptable presumption that they have not introduced malicious logic.

(2) Configuration control provides sufficient assurance that system applications and the equipment they run on are protected against the introduction of malicious logic prior to and during the operation of applications.

Closed User Group (CUG) (GSM context)

Closed User Group is a supplementary service that gives a particular group of customers the possibility to communicate with each other in a Public Land Mobile Network (PLMN) or an Integrated Services Digital Network (ISDN) [r011]. More generally, it refers to a 1970s version of Layer 3 Virtual Private Network (VPN) in an X.25 packet network; this VPN did not employ encryptions.

Closing Trouble Reports   An assertion by an Agent that the trouble is resolved such that the cleared trouble report may only be processed further to generate a trouble history record and/or be deleted [r068a].

Cluster   (1) Groupings of memory sectors that are used to allocate the data storage area in all Microsoft operating systems.

(2) Aggregating of processors in parallel-based configurations, typically in local environment (within a Data Center); all nodes work cooperatively as a single unified resource. Resource allocation is performed by a centralized resource manager and scheduling system. A cluster is comprised of multiple interconnected independent nodes that cooperatively work together as a single unified resource; unlike computational grids, cluster resources are typically owned by a single organization [r080].

(3) In storage environment, technology used to ensure the greatest available uptime of any system. This includes redundant hardware and intelligence that allows hardware and applications to "fail over," restart and maintain proper business functions [r029].

CM   See Change Management or Connection Management

CMIP   See Common Management Information Protocol

CMS   See Cryptographic Message Syntax

CMTS   See Cable Modem Termination Systems

CN   See Core Network

CNSS   See Committee on National Security Systems

CO   See Central Office

Coarse Wavelength Division Multiplexing

(CWDM)   (optical transmission term) An optical WDM system where only a few channels are needed or supported. Here wider wavelength spacing is possible compared to a Dense Wavelength Division Multiplexing (DWDM) system. CWDMs do not need to support optical amplification; this typically reduces cost by allowing uncooled lasers and simpler termination equipment.

COAST   See Computer Operations, Audit, and Security Technology

COBIT   See Control Objectives for Information and related Technology

Code   The term has several meanings, including: (i) programming source data (human readable) code or compiled (machine readable and executable) code; (ii) the act of programming; and (iii) symbols, words, or phrases used to represent or conceal the original information.

Code Division Multiple Access (CDMA)   A channel (transmission) technology for cellular service. A (wireless) transmission method in which signals are encoded using a random sequence, or code, to define a channel. CDMA offers improved spectral efficiency over analog transmission in that it allows for greater frequency reuse. Characteristics of CDMA systems include reduce dropped calls, increase battery life, and offer more security. CDMA was originally a military technology first used during World War II. Because Qualcomm Inc. created communications chips for CDMA technology, it was privy to the classified information that later became public. Qualcomm has since claimed patents on the technology and was the first to commercialize it. From Qualcomm . . . "CDMA works by converting speech into digital information, that is then transmitted as a radio signal over a wireless network. Using a unique code to distinguish each different call, CDMA enables many more people to share the airwaves at the same time—without static, cross-talk or interference." Standard: CDMA (IS-95) [r121].

(3G Wireless context) Multiple Access method where each user is assigned an individual code. As the Node B uses one frequency to send data to several users, the User Equipments need the matching codes in order to decipher the data [r007].

Code Red Worm   A worm that spread via a flaw in Microsoft's Internet Information Server (IIS) web server beginning in July 2001. The worm exploited a vulnerability in the indexing software distributed with IIS and caused widespread panic by defacing websites with the stock phrase "Hacked By Chinese!" Code Red spread itself by looking for more vulnerable IIS servers on the Internet and, in August 2001, launched a denial-of-service attack against several U.S. Government websites, including the White House portal. Less than a month later, a new mutant identified as Code Red II appeared and wreaked even more havoc [r090].

Code Reuse   A software approach that utilized pre-built and well-tested components in order to minimize development time. One of the concerns with code reuse is that when developers leverage components developed as Open Source Software or from purchase libraries, these components may behave in ways that were unintended.

Coding Theory   A mathematical field (discipline) deals with the properties of codes and thus with their fitness for a specific application [r122]. It is a well-developed mathematical theory [r123–r133].

The aim of Coding Theory is to find codes that transmit quickly, contain many valid code words, and can correct or at least detect many errors. These aims are mutually exclusive however, so different codes are optimal for different applications. The needed properties of this code mainly depend on the probability of errors happening during transmission [r122].

The term algebraic coding theory denotes the subfield of coding theory where the properties of codes are expressed in algebraic terms and then further researched. It analyzes the following three properties of a code: (i) code word length; (ii) total number of valid code words; and (iii) the minimum Hamming distance between two valid code words.

Another concern of Coding Theory is design-

ing codes that help synchronization. A code may be designed so that a phase shift can be easily detected and corrected and that multiple signals can be sent on the same channel [r122].

Collaborative Engineering   Applications that entail high-bandwidth access to shared virtual spaces, utilizing interactive manipulation of shared datasets and management of complex simulations, in order to support collaborative design of high-end systems [r080].

Collision (LAN Environments)   A condition that results from concurrent transmissions from multiple Data Terminal Equipment (DTE) sources within a single collision domain. Typical of a shared Local Area Network (LAN) (Ethernet).

The result of two devices on the same Ethernet network attempting to transmit data at exactly the same time [r101]. Would have been managed by Carrier Sense Multiple Access/Collision Detect (CSMA/CD). No longer an issue in modern switched LANs.

Collision Domain   A single, half-duplex mode Carrier Sense Multiple Access/Collision Detect (CSMA/CD) network. If two or more Media Access Control (MAC) sublayers are within the same collision domain and both transmit at the same time, a collision will occur. MAC sublayers separated by a repeater are in the same collision domain. MAC sublayers separated by a bridge are within different collision domains. Described in IEEE 802.3 Clauses 8 and 12. No longer an issue in modern switched Local Area Networks (LANs).

Collision Presence   A signal generated within the Physical Layer (PHY) by an end station or hub to indicate that multiple stations are contending for access to the transmission medium. No longer an issue in modern switched Local Area Networks (LANs).

Colon Hexadecimal Notation   (IPv6 context) The notation used to represent IPv6 addresses. The 128-bit address is divided in 8 blocks of 16 bits. Each block is represented as an hexadecimal number and moves apart from next block by means of colon orthographic sign (:). Inside each block, zeros left placed are removed. An example of an IPv6 unicast address represented in hexadecimal notation is 3FFE:FFFF:2A1D:48C:2AA:3CFF:FE21:81F9 [r008].

COLP   See Connected Line Identification Presentation

COLR   See Connected Line Identification Restriction

Comite Consultatif Internationale de Telegraphique et Telephonique (CCITT)   Original name for the International Telecommunications Union—Telecommunications (sector) (ITU-T). An international consultative committee that sets international communications recommendations that are frequently adopted as standards [r033].

Commercial and Federal Chief Information Officers   Senior managers that ensure the implementation of risk management for agency Information Technology (IT) systems and the security provided for these IT systems.

Commercial Certification Programs for Personnel   Among others, the following are well-known: International Information Systems Security Certification Consortium (ISC)^2 offers the designation of Certified Information System Security Professional (CISSP); the Information Systems Audit and Control Association (ISACA) provides the Certified Information Systems Auditor (CISA) certification; the Institute for Certification of Computer Professionals (ICCP) offers the Certified Computing Professional credential for a number of subject areas including system security; the American Society of Industrial Security (ASIS) offers generalist certification in security management [r067].

Commercial off-the-Shelf (COTS)   Commercially available products such as firewalls, routers, and third-party intrusion detection tools. Also refers to software (application) packages.

Commit/Decommit (Commitment Protocols Context)   In a basic commitment protocol, to commit the sender typically creates a key pair and sends a ciphertext of the message together with the public key; to decommit, the sender transmits the message with the random bits used to create the ci-

phertext, or simply sends the secret key (if appropriate). If the encryption scheme is completely nonmalleable, then the resulting commitment scheme in this basic construction is nonmalleable in the ordinary sense. Commitment schemes can be derived from encryption schemes [r134].

Commitment Protocols   These protocols represent fundamental cryptographic primitives, used as subprotocols in such applications as zero-knowledge proofs, secure multiparty computation, contract signing, and many others. Commitment protocols can also be used directly; for example, in remote (electronic) bidding. In this setting, parties bid by committing to a value; once bidding is complete, parties reveal their bids by decommitting. In many of these settings, it is required that participants, upon viewing the commitment of one party, be unable to generate a commitment to a related value. For example, in the bidding scenario it is unacceptable if one party can generate a valid commitment to $x + 1$ upon viewing a commitment to x. Note that the value of the original commitment may remain unknown (and thus secrecy need not be violated); in fact, the second party may only be able to decommit his bid after viewing a decommitment of the first. Unfortunately, most known commitment protocols are easily susceptible to these types of attacks. Two types of commitment schemes have been considered in the literature: perfectly binding and perfectly hiding (one typically refers to the former as standard and the latter as perfect). In a standard commitment scheme, each commitment is information-theoretically bound to only one possible (legal) decommitment value; on the other hand, the secrecy of the commitment is guaranteed only with respect to a computationally bounded receiver. In a perfect commitment scheme, the secrecy of the commitment is information-theoretic, while the binding property guarantees only that a computationally bounded sender cannot find a commitment which can be opened in two possible ways. The type of commitment scheme to be used depends on the application [r134].

Committee on National Security Systems (CNSS)

Under Executive Order (E.O.) 13231 of October, 2001, Critical Infrastructure Protection in the Information Age, the President redesignated the National Security Telecommunications and Information Systems Security Committee (NSTISSC) as the Committee on National Security Systems (CNSS). The Department of Defense (DoD) continues to chair the Committee under the authorities established by NSD-42. This was reaffirmed by Executive Order 13284, dated January, 2003, Executive Order Amendment of Executive Orders and Other Actions, in Connection with the Transfer of Certain Functions to the Secretary of Homeland Security. The CNSS provides a forum for the discussion of policy issues, sets national policy, and promulgates direction, operational procedures, and guidance for the security of national security systems. National security systems are information systems operated by the U.S. Government, its contractors, or agents that contain classified information or that:

1. Involve intelligence activities.
2. Involve cryptographic activities related to national security.
3. Involve command and control of military forces.
4. Involve equipment that is an integral part of a weapon or weapons system(s).
5. Are critical to the direct fulfillment of military or intelligence missions (not including routine administrative and business applications).

Committee on Uniform Securities and Identification Procedures (CUSIP) Number   A nine-character number that uniquely identifies a particular security (namely, a stock). The Committee on Uniform Securities and Identification Procedures is the standards body which created and maintains the classification system. Foreign securities have a similar number, called the CINS number (CUSIP International Numbering System) [r009].

Committee T1 and T1 X1 Subcommittee   Committee T1 sponsored by the Alliance for Telecom-munications Industry Solutions (ATIS) and accredited by the American National Standards Institute (ANSI), develops technical standards and reports on the interconnection and interoperability of telecommunications networks in the U.S. T1X1 is a subcommittee of Committee T1; it has developed the Synchronous Optical Network (SONET) standards over the years.

Common Channel Signaling System No. 7 (CCSS7)   (aka SS7) The out-of-band "Common Channel" signaling apparatus (network) used in the Public Switched Telephone Network (PSTN). It is defined by the International Telecommunication Union (ITU).

Common Control Channel (CCCH)   (3G Wireless context) A bidirectional logical channel used for the exchange of control data between the User Equipment and the network as long as a Radio Resource Control (RRC) connection has not been established [r007].

Common Control Physical Channel (CCPCH) (3G Wireless context) The Common Control Channel (CCCH) used for signaling. This channel is comprised of a Primary Common Control Physical Channel (P-CCPCH) and of a Secondary Common Control Physical Channel (S-CCPCH) [r007].

Common Criteria (CC) Evaluation and Validation Scheme (CCEVS)   The program developed by National Institute of Standards and Technology (NIST) and National Security Agency (NSA) as part of the National Information Assurance Partnership (NIAP) establishing an organizational and technical framework to evaluate the trustworthiness of Information Technology (IT) Products and protection profiles [r016]. The assessment of an IT product against the CC using the Common Evaluation Methodology to determine whether or not the claims made are justified; or, the assessment of a protection profile against the Common Criteria using the Common Evaluation Methodology to determine if the profile is complete, consistent, technically sound, and hence suitable for use as a statement of requirements for one or more Target of Evaluation

(TOE) that may be evaluated (a TOE is an IT product or group of IT products configured as an IT system and associated documentation that is the subject of a security evaluation under the CC; also, a protection profile that is the subject of a security evaluation under the CC) [r0167].

Common Criteria (CC) for Information Technology Security [aka The Common Criteria (CC)] A standard (common language to express common needs) for evaluating information technology products and systems, such as operating systems, computer networks, distributed systems, and applications. It states requirements for security functions and for assurance measures [r135].

In 1993, the sponsoring organizations of the existing United States, Canadian, and European criteria started the CC Project to align their separate criteria into a single set of IT security criteria. Version 1.0 of the CC was completed in January 1996. Based on a number of trial evaluations and an extensive public review, Version 1.0 was extensively revised and CC Version 2.0 was produced in 1998. This became International Organization for Standardization (ISO) International Standard 15408 in 1999. The CC Project subsequently incorporated the minor changes that had resulted in the ISO process, producing CC version 2.1 in 1999. Today the international community has embraced the CC through the Common Criteria Recognition Arrangement (CCRA) whereby the signers have agreed to accept the results of CC evaluations performed by other CCRA members. The Common Criteria Project is represented on the Web at www.CommonCriteriaPortal.org. The United States is represented within the CC Project by the National Information Assurance Partnership (NIAP), a joint National Institute of Standards and Technology (NIST) and National Security Agency (NSA) project. NIAP, in turn, has established the Common Criteria Evaluation and Validation Scheme (CCEVS) to implement the CCRA-compliant evaluation scheme within the United States [r016].

Common Gateway Interface (CGI) (aka CGI scripts) A script-based mechanism for the creation of dynamic web content. Nearly all major web servers support CGI scripts. However, CGI scripts do not inherently have built in security controls. CGI scripts are largely being phased out by more robust means of generating dynamic content, such as Java and .NET.

Common Gateway Interface (CGI) Scripts Early script-based means for the creation of dynamic web content. CGI scripts are supported by nearly all major web servers. However, CGI scripts do not inherently have built in security controls. CGI scripts are largely being phased out more robust means of generating dynamic content, such as Java and .NET.

Common Management Information Protocol (CMIP) Common Management Information Protocol (CMIP), an International Organization for Standardization (ISO) protocol used with the Common Management Information Services (CMIS), supports information exchange between network management applications and management agents. CMIS defines a system of network management information services [r136]. It is occasionally used by carriers to support network management of PSTN Network Elements, although SNMP is becoming more prevalent.

CMIP supplies an interface that provides functions which may be used to support both ISO and user-defined management protocols. The CMIP specification for Transmission Control Protocol/Internet Protocol (TCP/IP) networks is called CMOT (CMIP Over TCP) and the version for IEEE 802 LANs is called CMOL (CMIP Over LLC). CMIP/CMIS are proposed as competing protocols to the Simple Network Management Protocol (SNMP) in the TCP/IP suite. CMIP uses a reliable ISO connection-oriented transport mechanism and has built in security that supports access control, authorization and security logs. The management information, is exchanged between the network management application and management agents through managed objects. Managed objects are a characteristic of a managed device that can be monitored, modified, or controlled and can be used to perform tasks. CMIP does not specify the functionality of the network management application, it only defines the information exchange mechanism of the managed objects and not how the information is to be used or interpreted [r136].

Common Name   A character string that may be a part of the X.500 Distinguished Name (DN) of a Directory object ("commonName" attribute). This is a (possibly ambiguous) name by which the object is commonly known in some limited scope (such as an organization) and conforms to the naming conventions of the country or culture with which it is associated [r137].

Common Object Request Broker Architecture (CORBA)   CORBA-based object request brokers (ORBs) are one example of a service-oriented architecture. More recently, companies have been using Web Services (WS) to connect applications. CORBA is a standardized blueprint worked out by the Object Management Group defining how application objects and ORBs can cooperate to deliver services or perform processes independent of platform, network, or location. In CORBA, ORBs can communicate across a Transmission Control Protocol/Internet Protocol (TCP/IP) network via the Internet Inter-ORB Protocol (IIOP). This protocol that lets both applications (such as web browsers) and object request brokers communicate over a TCP/IP-based network.

Common Open Policy Service (COPS)   A query and response protocol that can be used to exchange policy information between a policy server and its clients. Defined in RFC 2748 [r257].

Common Packet Channel (CPCH)   (3G Wireless context) An uplink transport channel used to transmit data. As with the Random Access Channel, several User Equipments compete with each other for transmission capacity. In contrast to the Random Access Channel (RACH), it uses a fast power control, the closed-loop power control. This power control is realized via a dedicated downlink channel [r007].

Common Pilot Channel (CPICH)   (3G Wireless context) A downlink physical channel that carries the reference phase of the other physical downlink channels. It also measures the signal power of the cells—for example, to decide whether a handover is required, or to determine whether the current cell must be reselected or whether a new one must be selected [r007].

Common Threats: Catastrophic Incidents   These include (among others): fire; flood; earthquake; severe storm; terrorist attack; civil unrest/riots; landslide; avalanche; and industrial accident.

Common Threats: Malicious Persons   These include (among others): hacker, cracker; computer criminal; industrial espionage; government sponsored espionage; social engineering; disgruntled current employee; disgruntled former employee; terrorist; negligent employee; dishonest employee (bribed or victim of blackmail); and malicious mobile code.

Common Threats: Mechanical Failure   These include (among others): power outage; hardware failure; network outage, environmental controls failure; and construction accident.

Common Threats: Nonmalicious Persons   These include (among others) uninformed employees and uninformed users.

Common Traffic Channel (CTCH)   (3G Wireless context) A logical point-to-multipoint channel in the downlink. It is used to broadcast information to a group of User Equipments [r007].

Communication Address   (Presence Services context) It consists of communication means and contact address [r015].

Communication Means   (Presence Services context) These indicate a method whereby communication can take place. Instant message service is one example of a communication means [r015].

Communications Assistance for Law Enforcement Act (CALEA) "Safe Harbor"   Section 107(a)(2) of CALEA contains a "safe harbor" provision, stating that "[a] telecommunications carrier shall be found to be in compliance with the assistance capability requirements under Section 103, and a manufacturer of telecommunications transmission or switching equipment or a provider of telecommunications support services shall be found to be in compliance with Section 106 if the carrier, manufacturer, or support service provider is in compliance with publicly available technical requirements or standards adopted by an industry association or standard-setting organization, or by the Federal Communications Communication (FCC) under subsection (b), to meet the requirements of Section 103" [r139].

Communications Assistance for Law Enforcement Act (CALEA) Goals The purpose of CALEA is to preserve the ability of Law Enforcement to conduct electronic surveillance in the face of rapid advances in telecommunications technology [r139].

Communications Assistance for Law Enforcement Act (CALEA) Responsibilities of Telecommunications Equipment Manufacturers Under CALEA, a manufacturer of telecommunications transmission or switching equipment and a provider of telecommunications support services must, on a reasonably timely basis and at a reasonable charge, make available to the telecommunications carriers using its equipment, facilities, or services such features or modifications as are necessary to permit such carriers to comply with the assistance capability requirements and the capacity requirements [r139].

The Federal Bureau of Investigation (FBI) has implemented a reimbursement strategy that allows telecommunications carriers to receive CALEA software at no charge for certain high priority switching platforms. Under nationwide right-to-use (RTU) license agreements, the Government pays for the development of CALEA software solutions for certain high-priority switching platforms. This allows carriers to receive CALEA software at a nominal charge for equipment, facilities, or services installed or deployed now and in the future [r139].

Communications Assistance for Law Enforcement Act (CALEA), Call Content Defined in 18 U.S.C. 2510(8) it is an intercept "when used with respect to any wire or electronic communications, includes any information concerning the substance, purport, or meaning of that communications" [r139].

Communications Assistance for Law Enforcement Act (CALEA), Call-Identifying Information Section 102(2) of CALEA defines call-identifying information as "dialing or signaling information that identifies the origin, direction, destination, or termination of each communication generated or received by a subscriber by means of any equipment, facility, or service of a telecommunications carrier" [r139].

Communications Assistance for Law Enforcement Act (CALEA), J-STD-025 Subcommittee TR-45.2 of the Telecommunications Industry Association (TIA), along with Committee T1 of the Alliance for Telecommunications Industry Solutions, developed interim standard J-STD-025 to serve as a CALEA standard for wireline, cellular, and broadband PCS carriers and manufacturers. The standard defines services and features required by wireline, cellular, and broadband Personal Communication Services (PCS) carriers to support lawfully authorized electronic surveillance, and it specifies interfaces necessary to deliver intercepted communications and call-identifying information to a Law Enforcement agency [r139].

Communications Assistance for Law Enforcement Act (CALEA), Packet-Mode Communication Technologies CALEA is technology-neutral in its coverage. A telecommunications carrier remains subject to CALEA whether it uses packet-mode or any other technology [r139]; this has implications for services such as Voice over IP (VoIP) and Video over IP.

Communications Assistance for Law Enforcement Act (CALEA), Punch List Technical Requirements In 1999 the Federal Communications Commission (FCC) found that J-STD-025 was deficient in certain technical respects and remanded the standard to TR-45.2 for revision. The additional requirements (commonly referred to as "punch list" items) were required to be implemented June 30, 2002, and they are stated in the FCC Third Report and Order 99-230 and in the

Order on Remand, FCC 02-108 as [r139]: (1) Provide the content of subject-initiated conference calls supported by the subject's service (including the call content of parties on hold). (2) Identify the active parties of a multiparty call. (3) Provide access to all dialing and signaling information available from the subject including a subject's use of features (such as the use of flash-hook and other feature keys). (4) Notify the Law Enforcement agency when a subject's service sends a tone or other network message to the subject or associate (e.g., notification that a line is ringing or busy). (5) Provide timing information to correlate call-identifying information with the call content of a communications interception. And (6) Provide digits dialed by a subject after the initial call "cut-through" is completed to another carrier.

Communications Assistance for Law Enforcement Act (CALEA)-Compliance   All telecommunications carriers as defined by Section 102(8) of CALEA must comply with legislation; this includes all entities engaged in the transmission or switching of wire or electronic communications as a common carrier for hire [r139].

Communications Assistance for Law Enforcement Act of 1994 (CALEA)   In October 1994, Congress took action to protect public safety and ensure national security by enacting the Communications Assistance for Law Enforcement Act of 1994 (CALEA), Pub. L. No. 103-414, 108 Stat. 4279. The law further defines the existing statutory obligation of telecommunications carriers to assist Law Enforcement in executing electronic surveillance pursuant to court order or other lawful authorization [r139].

CALEA is about access, not authority. CALEA does not expand Law Enforcement's fundamental statutory authority to conduct electronic surveillance. It simply seeks to ensure that after Law Enforcement obtains the appropriate legal authority, telecommunications carriers will have the necessary capability, and sufficient capacity, to assist Law Enforcement regardless of their specific systems or services [r139].

The objective of CALEA implementation is to preserve Law Enforcement's ability to conduct lawfully authorized electronic surveillance while preserving public safety, the public's right to privacy, and the telecommunications industry's competitiveness. CALEA implementation responsibilities are delegated to the Federal Bureau of Investigation by the Attorney General [r139].

Communications Security (COMSEC)   Measures that implement and assure security services in a communication system, particularly those that provide data confidentiality and data integrity and that authenticate communicating entities. Usually understood to include cryptographic algorithms and key management methods and processes, devices that implement them, and the life cycle management of keying material and devices [r013].

Communications Security Establishment (CSE)   The Canadian Federal Government lead agency that delivers information technology solutions to the Government of Canada.

Communications Vulnerabilities   Vulnerabilities such as unencrypted communications, "broadcast" transmissions, and lack of robust filtering between networks and/or network segments.

Community String   Simple Network Management Protocol (SNMP) version 1 and version 2c used a string (called the "community string") as a form of authentication between SNMP management consoles and local SNMP management agents. Because the string is passed in cleartext, this should not be set to "public" (readable by all).

Compartment   A grouping of sensitive information items that require special access controls beyond those normally provided for the basic classification level of the information. The term is usually understood to include the special handling procedures to be used for the information [r013].

Compatibility Addresses   IPv6 addresses used when IPv6 traffic is sent through an IPv4 infrastructure. Some examples are: IPv4 compatible addresses, 6to4 addresses, and Automatic Internal Tunnel Addressing Protocol (ISATAP) addresses [r008].

Competition The existence within a market for some good or service of a sufficient number of buyers and sellers such that no single market participant has enough influence to determine the going price of the good or service. Opposite of monopoly [r009].

Competitive Bid (i) An offering procedure in which underwriters submit sealed bids to the issuer and the issuer selects the underwriter with the best terms. (ii) More generally, the sealed bid process, which is sometimes used in construction contracts and other circumstances [r009].

Complete Mediation (aka Principle of Complete Mediation) One of Saltzer and Schroeder's Design Principles. All access to objects must be checked to ensure that they are allowed [r139a]. Security mechanisms that require that all accesses to resources (hardware, middleware, or software) be checked to ensure that they are legitimate/permissible for the user in question. For example, privileges may have changed since the last operation and caching of access checks can cause problems. Also, for an Operating System (OS) access, one must verify that each controlled operation in the kernel is mediated by some authorization hook. A software system that requires access checks to an object each time a user requests access, especially for security-critical objects, decreases the chances of erroneously giving elevated permissions to that user.

Completely Non-Malleable Cryptographic Schemes A cryptographic framework intended to prevent the construction of ciphertexts for related plaintexts (i.e., resistant to chosen ciphertext attacks). These schemes have applications in zero-knowledge proofs of possession of knowledge.

Compound Annual Growth Rate (CAGR) (financial term) The year over year growth rate applied to an investment or other part of a company's activities over a multiple-year period.

Compressing Zeros (IPv6 context) Some types of addresses contain long sequences of zeros. In IPv6 addresses, a contiguous sequence of 16-bit blocks set to 0 in the colon-hexadecimal format can be compressed to :: (known as double-colon). The following list shows examples of compressing zeros [r023]:

- The link-local address of FE80:0:0:0:2AA: FF:FE9A:4CA2 can be compressed to FE80::2AA:FF:FE9A:4CA2.
- The multicast address of FF02:0:0:0:0:0:0:2 can be compressed to FF02::2.

Zero compression can only be used to compress a single contiguous series of 16-bit blocks expressed in colon-hexadecimal notation. One cannot use zero compression to include part of a 16-bit block. For example, one cannot express FF02:30:0:0:0:0:0:5 as FF02:3::5.

Zero compression can be used only once in an address, which enables one to determine the number of 0 bits represented by each instance of a double-colon (::). To determine how many 0 bits are represented by the ::, one can count the number of blocks in the compressed address, subtract this number from 8, and then multiply the result by 16. For example, in the address FF02::2, there are two blocks (the FF02 block and the 2 block). The number of bits expressed by the :: is 96 (96 = (8 − 2) × 16) [r023].

Compression Standards Include but are not limited to the following:

- Lempel, A. and J. Ziv, "A Universal Algorithm for Sequential Data Compression," *IEEE Transactions on Information Theory*, Vol. IT-23, No. 3, September 1977.
- Friend, R. and R. Monsour, "IP Payload Compression Using LZS," RFC 2395, December 1998.
- Friend, R. and W. Simpson, "PPP Stac LZS Compression Protocol," RFC 1974, August 1996.
- Schneider, K. and R. Friend, "PPP LZS-DCP Compression Protocol (LZS-DCP)," RFC 1967, August 1996.
- American National Standards Institute, Inc.,

"Data Compression Method for Information Systems," ANSI X3.241-1994, August 1994.

Compromise   An intrusion into a computer and/or networking system.

Compromised Key List (CKL)   A list issued by a Certification Authority (CA) that identifies the Public Key Infrastructure (PKI) certificates and keys that are believed to have been tampered with or are otherwise untrusted. Related to a Certificate Revocation List (CRL).

COMPUSEC   See Computer Security

Computational Complexity   A problem is *polynomial time* or *in P* if it can be solved by an algorithm which takes less than $O(n^t)$ steps, where t is some finite number and the variable n measures the size of the problem instance [r036].

If a guessed solution to a problem can be verified in polynomial time, then the problem is said to be in NP (nondeterministic polynomial time). The set of problems that lie in NP is very large, and it includes the problem of integer factorization.

A problem is NP-hard if there is no other problem in NP that is easier to solve. There is no known polynomial time algorithm for any NP-hard problem, and it is believed that such algorithms in fact do not exist.

In public-key cryptography, the attacker is interested in solving particular instances of a problem (factoring some given number), rather than providing a general solution (an algorithm to factor any possible number efficiently). This causes some concern for cryptographers, as some instances of a problem that is NP-hard in general may be easily solvable.

Computational Grid   Grid used to allocate resources specifically for computing power; in this situation, most of the processors are high-performance servers. (Processors are *sometimes called nodes, resources, members, donors, clients, hosts, engines, or machines*) [r080].

Computer Abuse   Unauthorized activity that affects the confidentiality, integrity, or availability of computer systems. Examples include denial of service attacks, malicious code, unauthorized access, and data theft.

Computer Bug   An undesirable and unintended condition of a program or piece of hardware that causes a malfunction.

Computer Evidence   Digital evidence of computer activity. This term is often associated with data used in the identification and/or prosecution of computer abuse. Computer evidence can be found on computer hard disk drives, floppy diskettes, zip disks, and other types of removable computer storage media. Computer evidence is quite unique when compared with other forms of "documentary evidence." Unlike paper documentation, computer evidence is fragile. A copy of a document stored in a computer file is identical to the original. The legal 'best evidence' rules change when it comes to the processing of computer evidence. Another unique aspect of computer evidence is the potential for unauthorized copies to be made of important computer files without leaving behind a trace that the copy was made. Ambient computer data is a form of computer evidence where the data comes from an area of the computer system where temporary or residual information is stored. Examples of this include Windows operating system temporary files, and in unallocated disk space where the user thought that they deleted the data [r066].

Computer Fraud and Abuse Act   (aka The United States Code, Title 18, Section 30) Legislation that (among other provisions) specifies civil and criminal remedies for Information Technology (IT) security misconduct. It criminalizes attacks on computer networks and damage to IT assets.

Computer Forensics   The preservation, identification, extraction, and documentation of computer evidence, often in conjunction with investigations of computer abuse. This is performed in such a way as to be admissible in a court of law. The term "Computer Forensics" was coined in 1991 in the first training session held by the International Association of Computer Specialists (IACIS). Like any other forensic science, computer forensics involves the use of sophisticated technology tools and procedures that must be followed to guarantee the accuracy of the preservation of evidence and the accuracy of results concerning computer evidence processing. Typically, computer forensic tools exist in the form of computer software. Computer forensic specialists guarantee accuracy of evidence processing results through the use of time-tested evidence-processing procedures and through the use of multiple software tools, developed by separate and independent developers. The use of different tools that have been developed independently to validate results is important to avoid inaccuracies introduced by potential software design flaws and software bugs [r066].

Computer Incident Advisory Capability (CIAC) A computer emergency response team in the U.S. Department of Energy.

Computer Incident Response Team (CIRT) (aka Computer Security Incident Response Team) A security incident response team established by medium-to-large firms to rapidly recognize, analyze, and respond to a security incident.

Computer Network A set of computer devices (hosts, terminals, PCs, nodes, etc.) together with the subnetwork or internetwork through which they can exchange information.

Computer Operations, Audit, and Security Technology (COAST) A laboratory in computer security research in the Computer Sciences Department at Purdue University focusing on real-world needs and limitations, with a special focus on security for legacy computing systems.

Computer Oracle and Password System (COPS) A computer network monitoring system for Unix-based systems; the software tool for checks security on shell scripts and C programs.

Computer Security (COMPUSEC) Approaches, methods, measures, and controls that ensure confidentiality, integrity, and availability of the information processed and stored by a computer.

Computer Security Incident Response Team (CSIRT) (aka Computer Incident Response Team) An organization that receives, reviews, and responds to computer security incident reports. A CSIRT can be a formalized team or an ad hoc team. A formalized team performs incident response work as its major job function; an ad hoc team is pulled together during an ongoing computer security incident or to respond to an incident when the need arises. A CSIRT operates for a specified constituency (e.g., a corporation, governmental, or educational organization; a region or country; a research network; or a commercial client). Some CSIRTs support an entire country, for example, the Japan Computer Emergency Response Team Coordination Center (JPCERT/CC); others may provide assistance to a particular region, such as AusCERT does for the Asia-Pacific area.

Computer Security Object   The definition or representation of a resource, tool, or mechanism used to maintain a condition of security in computerized environments. Includes many elements referred to in standards that are either selected or defined by separate user communities [r140, r013].

Computer Security Objects Register (CSOR) A service operated by National Institute of Standards and Technology (NIST) that is establishing a catalog for computer security objects to provide stable object definitions identified by unique names. The use of this register enables the unambiguous specification of security parameters and algorithms to be used in secure data exchanges. The CSOR follows registration guidelines established by the international standards community and American National Standards Institute (ANSI). Those guidelines establish minimum responsibilities for registration authorities and assign the top branches of an international registration hierarchy.

Computing: Autonomic Computing Self-managed computing environments with a minimum of required human interference. The use of the term "autonomic" originates from an analogy with the human body's autonomic nervous system, which controls key functions without conscious awareness or involvement [r141, r080].

Computing: Grid Computing (aka Utility Computing) An environment that can be built at the local (data center), regional, or global level, where individual users can access computers, databases, and scientific tools in a transparent manner, without having to directly take into account as where the underlying facilities are located [r080].

Computing: Massively Parallel Computing Mechanisms where large-scale problems can be tackled in an independently parallelized fashion. For example, sequencing and assembling the genome required teraflop clusters; proteomics could require 10 to 100 times as much computing power; optimal target identification with design of intervention may require petascale computing [r142]. Simulation and optimization are dependent on floating point operations, involve less input–output, and require an effective communications fabric among processors. Quantum Computing promises (at least in theory) to be the parallel computing mechanisms of choice in a few years.

Computing: Molecular Computers Computers whose input, output, and state transitions are carried out by biochemical interactions and reactions. At this time, researchers are exploring physical processes that can be put to use as computing substrates: chemical, biomolecular, optical computing via photonics, and quantum systems. Applications for non-silicon-based computing, including cryptography, pharmaceutical development, protein folding, data storage, and data mining [r143, r144].

Computing: Pervasive Computing   An emerging trend in which computing devices are increasingly ubiquitous, numerous, and mobile [r145]. Specific security issues need consideration.

Computing: Quantum Computing A mechanism of computing where the underlying computer takes advantage of Quantum Theory properties (e.g., entanglement) present at the nanoscale [r144]. The idea of a computational device based on Quantum Theory was first explored in the 1970s and early 1980s by physicists and computer scientists such as Charles H.

Bennett of the IBM Thomas J. Watson Research Center, Paul A. Benioff of Argonne National Laboratory in Illinois, David Deutsch of the University of Oxford, and Richard P. Feynman of the California Institute of Technology (Caltech) [r142, r146]. The concept of quantum computing emerged when scientists were pondering the fundamental limits of computation: scientists understood that if technology continued to abide by Moore's Law, then the continually shrinking size of circuitry packed onto silicon chips would eventually reach a point where individual elements would be no larger than a few atoms. Here a problem arose because at the atomic scale the physical laws that govern the behavior and properties of the circuit are inherently quantum mechanical in nature, not classical. This then raised the question of whether a new kind of computer could be devised based on the principles of quantum physics. Feynman was among the first to attempt to provide an answer to this question by producing an abstract model in 1982 that showed how a quantum system could be used to do computations. In 1985, Deutsch realized one could conceive a general-purpose quantum computer; Deutsch published a seminal paper showing that *any* physical process, in principle, could be modeled perfectly by a quantum computer; hence a quantum computer would have capabilities far beyond those of any traditional classical computer. Work has continued in earnest since that time [r146–r149].

Computing: Ubiquitous   Computing   Term coined by Mark Weiser in 1988; concept envisions computers embedded in walls, in tabletops, and in common objects. In this environment, an individual could interact with hundreds of computers at a time, each invisibly embedded in the environment and wirelessly communicating with each other. In this environment, the technology recedes into the background. Some call this "Third Paradigm" Computing (the first paradigm being mainframes and the second paradigm being the personal computer). Related to the ubiquitous computing paradigm is the idea of smart rooms, where a room might contain multiple sensors that keep track of the comings and goings of the people around [r142, r150]. Specific security issues need consideration.

Computing: Utility Computing   (aka Grid Computing) Computing power on-demand (similar to an electric grid providing ready-access to electricity). IBM, Sun Microsystems, and HP, among others, provide utility computing systems/services [r080]. Specific security issues need consideration.

COMSEC   See Communications Security

Conditionally Trusted Entity   An entity that is trusted in the context of a security policy, but that cannot violate the security policy without being detected [r068a].

Conference   (SIP context) A multimedia session that contains multiple participants [r025].

Confidentiality   (aka Data Confidentiality) A security service that protects against unauthorized disclosure of information. Confidentiality is typically assured by encryption, access controls, and legal agreements.

Confidentiality Agreement   An agreement designed to protect trade secrets and expertise from being misused by those who have learned of them.

Confidentiality, Integrity, and Availability (CIA)   (aka CIA Triad) A grouping that is a simple way to encapsulate three of the most important concepts in information security. Refer to the individual terms for their definition.

Configuration Control   (aka Configuration Management) The process of regulating changes to hardware, firmware, software, and documentation throughout the development and operational life of a system. Configuration control helps protect against unauthorized or malicious alteration of a system and thus provides assurance of system integrity [r013].

Configuration Management (CM)   See Configuration Control

Configuration Transaction   (MIDCOM context) A configuration transaction is a request transaction containing a request for state change in the middlebox. If accepted, it causes a state change at the middlebox [r031].

Conformant Management Entity   A real, open system that supports the interoperable interface defined in an Open Systems Interconnection Reference Model (OSIRM) management standard.

CONNECT   A command that can be utilized for "proxying" data channels over HyperText Transfer Protocol (HTTP). For example, it can be used to encapsulate other protocols, such as the Secure Sockets Layer (SSL) protocol.

Connected Line Identification Presentation (COLP)   (GSM context) A supplementary service used by the caller to identify the called party [r011]. (Please note the nonobvious acronym.)

Connected Line Identification Restriction (COLR)   (GSM context) A supplementary service used by the called party to withhold its identity from the caller [r011]. (Please note the nonobvious acronym.)

Connection   A connection is a transport [in the Open Systems Interconnection Reference Model (OSIRM) definition] that provides a suitable type of service. For Transport Layer Security (TLS), such connections are peer-to-peer relationships. The connections are transient. Every connection is associated with one session [r039].

Connection Management (CM)   (3G Wireless context) A management capability takes care of a number of functions between the User Equipment and the Core Network: Bearer Management, Call Control, Supplementary Services, and Short Message Service [r007].

Connectionless Data Integrity Service   A security service that provides data integrity service for an individual IP datagram, by detecting modification of the datagram, without regard to the ordering of the datagram in a stream of datagrams. A connection-oriented data integrity service would be able to detect lost or reordered datagrams within a stream of datagrams [r013].

Consortium   A group of individuals or companies formed to undertake an enterprise or activity that would be beyond the capabilities of the individual members [r009].

Constant Bit Rate (CBR)   An Asynchronous Transfer Mode (ATM) service category that supports a constant or guaranteed rate to transport services such as video or voice as well as circuit emulation that requires rigorous timing control and performance parameters.

Constant Dollars   (financial term) Dollars as if in some base year, used to adjust for the effects of inflation.

Constraint-based Shortest Path First (CSPF)   An extension to the traditional shortest-path (SPF) algorithm with a set of constraints attached. CSPF is designed with traffic engineering in mind; it can adapt to the network condition and select paths to route around overloaded portion of the network at the cost of increased complexity in dealing with multiple constraints. In Generalized MultiProtocol Label Switching (GMPLS) networks, it is important to provide a protection/ restoration mechanism for fast service restoration in the presence of a network failure. CSPF plays a key role in selection of restoration paths to achieve mesh protection, as Synchronous Optical Network (SONET)-based optical networks migrate from ring topology to mesh topology for the benefits of increased resource utilization [r152–r156].

Traditional SPF only has a polynomial-time complexity and thus it is a relatively easy problem to solve. Among a number of available algorithms, the Dijkstra algorithm is the most well known in solving the SPF problem. CSPF, on the other hand, is an intrinsically more complex problem because of the introduction of multiple constraints. Even with only one additive constraint it can be proved to be an NP-complete problem; hence a heuristic approach is typically used to look for a near-optimal solution.

Contact   A person who can provide additional information about something—for example, about a trouble on behalf of the manager or the agent.

Contact Address   (Presence Services context) A specific point of contact via some communication means. When using an instant message service, the contact address is an instant inbox address [r015].

Containment   The step in responding to a security incident focused on limited further damage or unauthorized access.

Content Filtering   (General context) Limiting users' access to content or stripping out objectionable content from data send to or received by the users. Examples include e-mail content filtering and Uniform Resource Locator (URL) filtering.

(Web Access context, that is, URL filtering) Limiting users' access to certain Internet sites (or stripping out the content that is obtained) in order to restrict objectionable content (such as pornography), productivity-reducing content (such as humor or news sites), or performance-reducing content (such as video streams or music files).

Content Monitoring System   A specialized Intrusion Detection System (IDS) that monitors the network for misuse according to an organization's Acceptable Use Policy (AUP). May be used to monitor employee's use of corporate Information Technology (IT) resources such as e-mail, web access, and so on.

Content-Addressable Memory (CAM)   Memory tables that maintain source addresses located on Layer 2 switch ports. Layer 2 switches are able to regulate the flow of data between their ports by logically creating "instant" networks that contain only the two end devices communicating with each other at that moment in time; data frames are sent by end systems and their source and destination addresses are not changed throughout the switched domain. Switches maintain CAM lookup tables to track the source addresses located on the switch ports; these lookup tables are populated by an address-learning process on the switch. If the destination address of a frame is not known or if the frame received by the switch is destined for a broadcast or multicast address, the switch forwards the frame out all ports. With their ability to isolate traffic and create the "instant" networks, switches can be used to divide a physical network into multiple logical, or virtual LANs (VLANs) through the use of Layer 2 traffic segmentation [r156].

Content-Addressable Memory (CAM) Table

Overflow Attack   The CAM table in a switch contains information such as the Media Access Control (MAC) addresses available on a given physical port of a switch, as well as the associated Virtual Local Area Network (VLAN) parameters. When a Layer 2 switch receives a frame, the switch looks in the CAM table for the destination MAC address. If an entry exists for the MAC address in the CAM table, the switch forwards the frame to the port designated in the CAM table for that MAC address. If the MAC address does not exist in the CAM table, the switch forwards the frame out every port on the switch, effectively acting like a hub. If a response is seen, the switch updates the CAM table. CAM tables are limited in size. If enough entries are entered into the CAM table before other entries are expired, the CAM table fills up to the point that no new entries can be accepted. Typically a network intruder will flood the switch with a large number of invalid-source MAC addresses until the CAM table fills up. When that occurs the switch will flood all ports with incoming traffic because it cannot find the port number for a particular MAC address in the CAM table. The switch, in essence, acts like a hub. If the intruder does not maintain the flood of invalid-source MAC addresses, the switch will eventually time out older MAC address entries from the CAM table and begin to act like a switch again. CAM table overflow only floods traffic within the local VLAN so the intruder will see only traffic within the local VLAN to which he or she is connected. In 1999 the tool macof was released. It was written in approximately 100 lines of PERL code and was later ported to C language code and incorporated into the dsniff package. This tool floods a switch with packets containing randomly generated source and destination MAC and IP addresses [r156].

Contingency Plan   A plan for emergency response, backup operations, and post-disaster recovery in a system as part of a security program to ensure availability of critical system resources and facilitate continuity of operations in a crisis [r121, r013]. Short-term arrangements an agency makes to carry out its mission.

Continuity of Operations Plan   A long-term strategy for operations during national crisis.

Contraband Detection   Mechanisms to address Physical Security (PHYSEC) issues related to the detection/prevention of unauthorized contraband items that may enter a facility.

Contractor   A person or business that provides goods or services to another entity under terms specified in a contract. Unlike an employee, a contractor does not work regularly for a company. Also called independent contractor [r009].

Control Components   The major elements of an internal control process. For example, Basel Committee on Banking Supervision identifies the following control components that integrate internal control into the management process: (i) Management oversight and control culture; (ii) Risk recognition and assessment; (iii) Control activities and segregation of duties; (iv) Information and communications; and (v) Monitoring activities and correcting deficiencies.

Control Documentation   Formal documentation of a firm's internal control such as policies, procedures, standards, and so on.

Control Objectives   The primary goals of an internal control system, e.g., safeguarding of assets, compliance with regulations, and data integrity.

Control Objectives for Information and Related Technology (COBIT)   An Information Technology (IT) governance framework, defined by the IT Governance Institute (ITGI). This framework can be used in ensuring proper control and governance over information and the systems that create, store, manipulate, and retrieve it. Effective IT governance helps ensure that IT supports business goals, maximizes business investment in IT, and appropriately manages IT-related risks and opportunities [r157]. COBIT is increasingly gaining momentum as a leading tool for IT governance. ITGI is a research think tank established in 1998 in recognition of the increasing criticality of information technology to enterprise success. In many organizations, success depends on the ability of IT to enable achievement of business goals; in such an environment, governance over IT is as critical a board and management discipline as corporate governance or enterprise governance. Effective IT governance helps ensure that IT supports business goals, maximizes business investment in IT, and appropriately manages IT-related risks and opportunities. By conducting original research on IT governance and related topics, ITGI helps enterprise leaders understand and have the tools to ensure effective governance over IT within their enterprise.

Control Plane   The signaling plane in Integrated Services Digital Network (ISDN), Asynchronous Transfer Mode (ATM), and Automatically Switched Optical Network (ASON).

Controlled Domain (CD)   Network point (zone) where all inbound and outbound communications are mediated (such as the firewall complex). Environment where the physical access, the Information Technology (IT) administration, and the security authority are controlled by the firm is question. This domain separates the Externally Controlled Domain (ECD) and Uncontrolled Domain (UCD) from the Restricted Domain (typically the "inner reaches" of intranet, say where the payroll system is) of the firm.

Controlled Security Mode   The term refers to a mode of operation of an information system, wherein at least some users with access to the system have neither a security clearance nor a need-to-know for all classified material contained in the system. However, separation and control of users and classified material on the basis, respectively, of clearance and classification level are not essentially under operating system control like they are in "multilevel security mode" [r013].

Controller   A hardware device that controls the transfer of information to/from a computer and a peripheral device.

Converged Network   (OSPF context) A network is termed as converged when all the devices within the network have a loop-free path to each possible destination [r026]. Note that the word "convergence" has two distinct meanings: the process of a group of individuals meeting at the same place, and the process of an individual coming to the same place as an existing group.

Cookie   A small text file that a website places on a user's computer. The information stored in this file allows the website to store content, including user names and passwords, a list of items selected at an online store (such as the contents of a shopping cart), and user preferences for a website. Cookies have also been used for the collection of personal information. As a result of privacy and security concerns, browsers have increasing provided more user control and knowledge or cookies and the content within them.

Coordinated Universal Time (CUT)   Time derived from International Atomic Time (TAI) by adding a number of leap seconds. The International Bureau of Weights and Measures computes TAI once each month by averaging data from many laboratories.

COPS   See Common Open Policy Service or Computer Oracle and Password System.

Coptologist   Term totally unrelated to security, but has a resemblance with "cryptologist" and is included for "fun": an expert in ancient manuscripts written in Coptic, an upper-Egyptian language of old that made use of Greek characters.

Copy-and-Paste Attack   (aka Cut-and-Paste Attack) An active attack on the data integrity of ciphertext, effected by replacing sections of ciphertext with other ciphertext, such that the result appears to decrypt correctly but actually decrypts to plaintext that is forged to the satisfaction of the attacker [r013].

Copyright   The exclusive right to make and dispose of copies of a literary, musical, or artistic work [r009]. The Copyright laws applicable in the United States are the laws contained in title 17 of the U.S. Code (http://www.copyright.gov/).

Copyright is a form of protection provided by the laws of the United States (title 17, U.S. Code) to the authors of "original works of authorship," including literary, dramatic, musical, artistic, and certain other intellectual works. This protection is available to both published and unpublished works. Section 106 of the 1976 Copyright Act generally gives the owner of copyright the exclusive right to do and to authorize others to do the following:

- *To reproduce* the work in copies or phono records.
- To prepare *derivative works* based upon the work.
- *To distribute copies or phonorecords* of the work to the public by sale or other transfer of ownership, or by rental, lease, or lending.
- To perform the work publicly, in the case of literary, musical, dramatic, and choreographic works, pantomimes, and motion pictures and other audiovisual works.
- *To display the copyrighted work publicly,* in the case of literary, musical, dramatic, and choreographic works, pantomimes, and pictorial, graphic, or sculptural works, including the individual images of a motion picture or other audiovisual work.
- In the case of *sound recordings, to perform the work publicly* by means of a *digital audio transmission.*
- In addition, certain authors of works of visual art have the rights of attribution and integrity as described in section 106A of the 1976 Copyright Act. For further information, request Circular 40, "Copyright Registration for Works of the Visual Arts."

It is illegal for anyone to violate any of the rights provided by the copyright law to the owner of copyright. These rights, however, are not unlimited in scope. Sections 107 through 121 of the 1976 Copyright Act establish limitations on these rights. In some cases, these limitations are specified exemptions from copyright liability. One major limitation is the doctrine of "fair use," which is given a statutory basis in section 107 of the 1976 Copyright Act. In other instances, the limitation takes the form of a "compulsory license" under which certain limited uses of copyrighted works are permitted upon payment of specified royalties and compliance with statutory conditions.

CORBA See Common Object Request Broker Architecture

Core (SIP context) Term designates the functions specific to a particular type of Session Initiation Protocol (SIP) entity—that is, specific to either a stateful or stateless proxy, a user agent, or a registrar. All cores, except those for the stateless proxy, are transaction users [r025].

Core Network (CN) (3G Wireless context) The Core Network is responsible for call setup and release in the Universal Mobile Telecommunications System (UMTS) network. In the first deployment phase it will consist of Global System for Mobile Communication (GSM) components (circuit-switched) and General Packet Radio Service (GPRS) components (packet-switched) [r007].

Core Router A provider router internal to the provider's network, typically using Border Gateway Protocol (BGP) to that provider's edge routers, other intra-provider core routers, or the provider's inter-provider border routers [r086].

Corporate Governance Review Board A designated approving authority responsible for the ultimate decision on whether to allow operation of an Information Technology (IT) system.

Corporate Portal An internal website (an intranet website) that provide web-based services to corporate personnel. Common features of portal include single sign-on (SSO) functionality links to company-related websites, the ability to customize content, and a search engine.

Corrective Action (Security context) An action intended to reduce or eliminate a known weakness or gap in a security environment.

Corrective Controls Mechanisms to address Physical Security (PHYSEC) risks. May include air conditioning, pumps, backup power supplies, generators, etc.

Correctness Integrity Concerned with the accuracy and consistency of the information that data values represent, rather than the accuracy and consistency of the data itself.

Correctness Proof   A mathematical proof of consistency between a specification for system security and the implementation of that specification [r013].

Correspondent Node   A node that communicates with a mobile node that is out of its own network [r008].

Corruption   An action or event that causes undesirable alteration of data or a system.

Cost of capital   The opportunity cost of an investment—that is, the rate of return that a company would otherwise be able to earn at the same risk level as the investment that has been selected [r009].

Cost–Benefit Analysis   An assessment of the cost of providing protection or security commensurate with the risk and magnitude of asset loss or damage [r056].

COTS   See Commercial off-the-Shelf

Counterfeiting Threats   Counterfeiting has becomes one of the most challenging issues for the Information Technology (IT) industry, with illegal replicas of brand-name high-technology products flooding the marketplace. Manufacturers are encouraged to adopt a comprehensive program targeting the sale and distribution of counterfeit high-tech products to be successful in protecting consumers from poor-quality goods as well as securing the brand integrity inherent in their products. Despite the sophisticated design and complex manufacturing of most IT products, counterfeiting is a pervasive problem. As many as one in 10 IT products sold may actually be counterfeit, according to interviews conducted with electronics industry executives. Some estimate that about US$100 billion of global IT industry revenue is lost to counterfeiters annually. In addition, estimates by the International Chamber of Commerce suggest that counterfeit goods accounted for 6 percent of world trade in 2003, valued at US$456 billion. By reducing revenue and harming brand equity, counterfeiting IT and electronics products are eroding the integrity of the "supply and demand" business model. Counterfeiting not only steals the value of intellectual capital, it stifles innovation and robs customers of the quality they expect from a brand. Early warning signs that can signal when a company has a counterfeiting problem include [r087]: sudden drop in raw-materials orders; increased orders for proprietary components; increased gray-market availability; increase in service returns; and large volume of discounted product available.

Countermeasure   An action, device, procedure, or technique that reduces a threat, a vulnerability, or an attack by eliminating or preventing it, by minimizing the harm it can cause, or by discovering and reporting it so that corrective action can be taken [r013].

Country Code   An identifier that is defined for a nation by International Organization for Standardization (ISO) (Standard I.3166). For each nation, ISO Standard 3166 defines a unique two-character alphabetic code, a unique three-character alphabetic code, and a three-digit code. Among many uses of these codes, the two-character codes are used as top-level domain names.

(GSM context) The Country Code is part of the Mobile Station Roaming Number (MSRN) and the Handover Number (HON) [r011].

Covert Channel   A means by which entities (systems, users, etc.) exchange information that is not in accordance with the security policy and is unknown to system administrators. A concrete example explains what a covert channel is. Suppose that Alice and Bob are connected to a computer that is running a multiuser operating system. In a secure operating system that can be used for sensitive (e.g., military) applications it should not be possible for a process that Alice is running to transmit information covertly to a process that Bob is running. But, suppose that a printer is connected to this machine. Each process can make an operating system call to print data. This call will return a result code indicating success or failure. The result code will also indicate if the printer is busy printing out a document. Alice's process can utilize a special communication protocol to speak with a process that Bob is running. For example, printing out two short documents with a brief pause in between could correspond to a binary "1" and printing out one document could be a binary "0." Bob's process calls the operating system routine in a busy waiting fashion to receive bits from Alice's process. This is not a subliminal channel, but it is a covert channel [r162].

Covert Channel Types   A covert channel is a system feature that the system architects neither designed nor intended for information transfer. Types include [r013]:

- "Timing channel": A system feature that enables one system entity to signal information to another by modulating its own use of a system resource in such a way as to affect system response time observed by the second entity.
- "Storage channel": A system feature that enables one system entity to signal information to another entity by directly or indirectly writing a storage location that is later directly or indirectly read by the second entity.

The cooperating entities can be either two insiders or an insider and an outsider (an outsider has no access authorization at all).

CP   See Certificate Policy

CPCH   See Common Packet Channel

CPE   See Customer Premises Equipment

CPICH   See Common Pilot Channel

CPS   See Certification Practice Statement

CPS Abstract   See CPS Summary

Cracker   (aka hacker or intruder) An individual who attempts to gain unauthorized access to a system.

Crafted Packet   A packet constructed manually (for example, by a hacking tool) rather than being built by a legitimate protocol state machine; typically employed in an attack and/or to detect vulnerabilities.

CRAM   See Challenge–Response Authentication Mechanism

Cramer–Shoup Encryption Scheme   A public key cryptography system that has an arbitrary key length and relies on the discrete log problem (as opposed to factoring prime numbers) is resistant to chosen ciphertext attacks. The encryption algorithm is probabilistic, that is, if the same text is encrypted twice, the ciphertext will usually be different.

Crash   An unexpected, problematic failure of a computer system.

CRC   See Cyclic Redundancy Check

Credentials   Information that is presented as a claim of identity for the purpose of being authenticated. Examples include user name/ID, password, Public Key Infrastructure (PKI) certificate, and biometric information.

Credit Bureau   (financial term) An agency that collects and sells information about the creditworthiness of individuals. A credit reporting agency does not make any decisions about whether a specific person should be extended credit or not. However, it does collect information that it considers relevant to a person's credit habits and history, and uses this information to assign a credit score to indicate how creditworthy a person is. When a prospective creditor approaches a credit reporting agency to inquire about a particular person, they are sold a credit report which contains all the information relevant to the person and the credit score calculated by the agency (some creditors might have an ongoing subscription to credit bureau). The prospective creditor then uses that information to decide whether to extend the applicant the desired credit or not. Also called consumer reporting agency [r009].

Crisis Management   A firm's response to a severe event that could impair its function—for example, a major, publicly disclosed security infraction.

Critical   A determination that the system or resource is crucial. Inability to access the system or degraded performance causes significant detriment to the operation or bottom line of an enterprise.

Critical Extension   Each extension of an X.509 certificate [or Certificate Revocation List (CRL)] is marked as being either critical or noncritical. If an extension is critical and a certificate user (or

CRL user) does not recognize the extension type or does not implement its semantics, then the user is required to treat the certificate (or CRL) as invalid. If an extension is noncritical, a user that does not recognize or implement that extension type is permitted to ignore the extension and process the rest of the certificate (or CRL) [r013].

Critical Infrastructure Protection (CIP)   A U.S. Government program that seeks to synthesize in an integrative manner the disciplines of law, policy, and technology for enhancing the security of cyber-networks, physical systems, and economic processes supporting the nation's critical infrastructures.

Critical infrastructures drive all of the necessary functions upon which society depends, yet for the most part, completely ignores. These systems, which have increased in complexity over the past century, rarely faced serious or eminent danger from hostile forces due to the proximity of friendly neighbors to the north and south, Canada and Mexico. Prior to an attack on American soil, little thought was given to the brittle nature of these complex systems. The only real threats facing infrastructures, prior to the previous decade, came from natural disasters, which tend to be localized to one region and have a fixed, and at times, predictable duration. Additionally, human error, Murphy's Law, and, inevitably, the aging process requiring routine maintenance brought most attention to these systems. Fall-out from post-9/11 events and the 2003 blackout of the Northeast of the United States have all served as reminders of just how fragile and brittle these systems have and can become. Critical infrastructures are the complex and highly interdependent systems that provide the services required in daily life. Electric power, water, transportation, and telecommunications are just a few of the major services that we depend upon every waking moment, and even to run our homes while we sleep. With society's increasing dependence upon these systems comes the inevitable growth in complexity, as these sectors seek to expand upon their already stretched capacity to provide new services,

and products to a growing population [r159].

The systems which support our daily way of life are complex and vulnerable, yet also reliable and resilient. Everything from banking to emergency response to government operations depend on normal operation of electricity, water, telecommunications, and transportation. Society must continue to explore ways to ensure the reliability of infrastructures and to protect systems from various threats. Government agencies, private industries, educational institutions, and citizens all have a vested interest in our complex infrastructure systems and should strive to have a better understanding of the relationships between the sectors [r159].

CRL   See Certificate Revocation List

Cross-Certification   The act or process by which two Certification Authorities (CAs) each certify a public key of the other, issuing a public-key certificate to that other CA. Cross-certification enables users to validate each other's certificate when the users are certified under different certification hierarchies [r013].

Cross-Connection of Traffic Between Provider Provisioned Virtual Private Networks (PPVPNs)   Refers to events where expected isolation between separate PPVPNs is breached. This includes cases such as [r058]: a site being connected into the "wrong" Virtual Private Network (VPN); two or more VPNs being improperly merged; a point-to-point VPN connecting the wrong two points, or any packet or frame being improperly delivered outside the VPN it is sent in. Misconnection or cross-connection of VPNs may be caused by service provider or equipment vendor error, or by the malicious action of an attacker. The breach may be physical (e.g., user-to-carrier links misconnected) or logical (improper device configuration). Anecdotal evidence suggests that the cross-connection threat is one of the largest security concerns of PPVPN users (or would-be users) [r058].

Cross-Forest Trust   A mechanism in the Windows Operating System (OS) environment to set up trust between two forests.

Cross-Site Scripting (XSS) An attack that aims to cause a computer to execute commands it should not. In cross-site scripting, the attacker hides malicious code (a script) in a HyperText Markup Language (HTML) link on an innocuous-looking web page (or in an e-mail). For example, a user may obtain a link that a web page from an Instant Messaging chat room. Unbeknownst to the user, the link includes an embedded HTML script. When the user clicks the link, the user's browser goes to that website's host and requests the page for that URL. If the host computer is vulnerable to cross-site scripting, it dynamically generates a web page in response to the request, but the web page it generates includes the embedded HTML script. Because the user's browser trusts that web host, it executes the malicious script [r062].

CRS See Cell Relay Service

Cryptanalysis The process of recovering the plaintext of a message or the encryption key without access to the key. The analysis of a cryptographic system and/or its inputs and outputs to derive confidential variables and/or sensitive data including cleartext [r068a].

Cryptanalysis Techniques Techniques include: Ciphertext-only attack, Known-plaintext attack, Chosen-plaintext attack, Man-in-the-middle attack, Correlation, Attack against or using the underlying hardware, Faults in cryptosystems, Quantum computing, and DNA cryptography.

Cryptanalysis, Chosen-Plaintext Attack The attacker is able to have any text he/she likes encrypted with the unknown key. The task is to determine the key used for encryption. An example of this attack is the differential cryptanalysis which can be applied against block ciphers (and in some cases also against hash functions). Some cryptosystems, particularly Rivest–Shamir–Adleman (RSA), are vulnerable to chosen-plaintext attacks. When such algorithms are used, care must be taken to design the application (or protocol) so that an attacker can never have chosen plaintext encrypted [r036].

Cryptanalysis, Ciphertext-Only Attack This is the situation where the attacker does not know anything about the contents of the message, and must work from ciphertext only. In practice, it is quite often possible to make guesses about the plaintext, as many types of messages have fixed format headers. Even ordinary letters and documents begin in a very predictable way. For example, many classical attacks use frequency analysis of the ciphertext, however, this does not work well against modern ciphers. Modern cryptosystems are not weak against ciphertext-only attacks, although sometimes they are considered with the added assumption that the message contains some statistical bias [r036].

Cryptanalysis, Correlation Correlation between the secret key and the output of the cryptosystem is the main source of information to the cryptanalyst. In the easiest case, the information about the secret key is directly leaked by the cryptosystem. More complicated cases require studying the correlation (basically, any relation that would not be expected on the basis of chance alone) between the observed (or measured) information about the cryptosystem and the guessed key information. For example, in linear attacks against block ciphers the cryptanalyst studies the known plaintext and the observed ciphertext. Guessing some of the key bits of the cryptosystem the analyst determines by correlation between the plaintext and the ciphertext whether she guessed correctly. This can be repeated, and has many variations. The differential cryptanalysis introduced by Eli Biham and Adi Shamir in late 1980s was the first attack that fully utilized this idea against block ciphers [especially against Data Encryption Standard (DES)]. Later Mitsuru Matsui came up with linear cryptanalysis which was even more effective against DES. More recently, new attacks using similar ideas have been developed. The correlation idea is fundamental to cryptography and several researchers have tried to construct cryptosystems which are provably secure against such attacks. For example, Knudsen and Nyberg have studied provable security against differential cryptanalysis [r036].

Cryptanalysis, Known-Plaintext Attack   The attacker knows or can guess the plaintext for some parts of the ciphertext. The task is to decrypt the rest of the ciphertext blocks using this information. This may be done by determining the key used to encrypt the data, or via some shortcut. One of the best known modern known-plaintext attacks is linear cryptanalysis against block ciphers [r036].

Cryptanalysis, Man-in-the-Middle Attack   The idea is that when two parties, A and B, are exchanging keys for secure communication (for example, using Diffie-Hellman), an adversary positions himself between A and B on the communication line. The adversary then intercepts the signals that A and B send to each other, and performs a key exchange with A and B separately. A and B will end up using a different key, each of which is known to the adversary. The adversary can then decrypt any communication from A with the key he shares with A, and then resends the communication to B by encrypting it again with the key he shares with B. Both A and B will think that they are communicating securely, but in fact the adversary is hearing everything. The usual way to prevent the man-in-the-middle attack is to use a public-key cryptosystem capable of providing digital signatures. For setup, the parties must know each other's public keys in advance. After the shared secret has been generated, the parties send digital signatures of it to each other. The man-in-the-middle fails in his attack, because he is unable to forge these signatures without the knowledge of the private keys used for signing. This solution is sufficient if there also exists a way to securely distribute public keys. One such way is a certification hierarchy such as X.509. It is used, for example, in IPSec [r036].

Crypto   See Cryptography, Cryptoanalysis, and/or Cryptology.

Cryptographic (Crypto) Accelerators   Additional hardware added to a router, server, or proxy that shifts the burden taxing cryptographic calculations away from the main processor. Accelera-tors are particularly useful in environments where a large number of encrypted transactions are being processed [r062].

Cryptographic Algorithm   Mathematical function that computes a result from one or several input values.

Cryptographic Algorithms Depreciation   A measure of the ability of a cryptographic means to ensure the integrity and confidentiality of data when compared to increasing computer processing power.

Cryptographic Application Programming Interface (CAPI)   The source code formats and procedures through which an application program accesses cryptographic services, which are defined abstractly compared to their actual implementation [r163, r013].

Cryptographic Break   To successfully perform cryptanalysis and thus succeed in decrypting data or performing some other cryptographic function, without initially having knowledge of the key that the function requires. (This term applies to encrypted data or, more generally, to a cryptographic algorithm or cryptographic system.) [r013].

Cryptographic Card   A cryptographic token in the form of a smart card or a PC card [r013].

Cryptographic Chaining   A mode of use of a cryptographic algorithm in which the transformation performed by the algorithm depends on the values of previous inputs or outputs [r068a].

Cryptographic Checkvalue   Information that is derived by performing a cryptographic transformation (see Cryptography) on the data unit. (*Note:* The derivation of the checkvalue may be performed in one or more steps and is a result of a mathematical function of the key and a data unit. It is usually used to check the integrity of a data unit.) [r068a].

Cryptographic Component   A generic term for any system component that involves cryptography.

Cryptographic Hash Function   A process that derives a value (hashword) from a data frame, such that manipulation of the data frame along the way is detectable by the receiving end when the receiving end independently re-derives the hashword from the data frame itself and compares it with the received hashword that is embedded with (typically at the end of) the frame.

Cryptographic Ignition Key (CIK)   A physical (usually electronic) token used to store, transport, and protect cryptographic keys. (The term is sometimes abbreviated as "crypto ignition key") [r013].

Cryptographic Key   An input parameter that varies the transformation performed by a cryptographic algorithm. If a key value needs to be kept secret, the sequence of symbols (usually bits) that comprise it should be random, or at least pseudorandom, because that makes the key hard for an adversary to guess. (The term is sometimes also simply called a "key") [r160, r013].

Cryptographic Message Syntax (CMS)   An Internet Engineering Task Force (IETF) syntax used to digitally sign, digest, authenticate, or encrypt arbitrary messages. It describes an encapsulation syntax for data protection. CMS supports digital signatures, message authentication codes, and encryption. The syntax allows multiple encapsulation, hence, one encapsulation envelope can be nested inside another. Likewise, one party can digitally sign some previously encapsulated data. It also allows arbitrary attributes, such as signing time, to be signed along with the message content, and provides for other attributes such as countersignatures to be associated with a signature. The CMS can support a variety of architectures for certificate-based key management [r138, r165].

Cryptographic Min entropy   Defined as

$$\text{Min entropy} = -\log (\text{ maximum } (p_i))$$

where i counts from 1 to the number of possible secret values and p_i is the probability of the value numbered i [r166].

Cryptographic Module   A set of hardware, software, firmware, or some combination thereof that implements cryptographic logic or processes, including cryptographic algorithms, and is contained within the module's cryptographic bound-

ary, which is an explicitly defined contiguous perimeter that establishes the physical bounds of the module [r167, r013].

Cryptographic Random Number Generators   Algorithms to generate random numbers for use in cryptographic applications, such as for keys.

Cryptographic System   A set of cryptographic algorithms together with the key management processes that support use of the algorithms in some application context [r013, r061].

Cryptographic Techniques   Techniques used to provide a variety of services, including confidentiality and authentication. Such services are based on quantities, traditionally called "keys," that are unknown to and unguessable by an adversary [r166].

Cryptographic Techniques in Layer 2 Provisioned Virtual Private Networks (PPVPNs)   Layer 2 PPVPNs will generally not be able to use IPsec to provide encryption throughout the entire network. They may be able to use IPsec for Provider Edge/Equipment (PE)-PE traffic where it is encapsulated in IP packets, but IPsec will generally not be applicable for Customer Edge/Equipment (CE)-PE traffic in Layer 2 PPVPNs. Encryption techniques for Layer 2 links are widely available. Layer 2 encryption could be applied to the links from CE to PE, or it could be applied from CE to CE, as long as the encrypted Layer 2 packets can be handled properly by the intervening PE devices. In addition, the upper-layer traffic transported by the Layer 2 Virtual Private Network (VPN) can be encrypted by the user. In this case, confidentiality will be maintained [r058].

Cryptographic Token   A portable, user-controlled, physical device used to store cryptographic information and possibly perform cryptographic functions [r013].

Cryptographically Generated Addresses (CGA)   A method described in Internet Engineering Task Force (IETF) RFC 3972 for binding a public signature key to an Internet Protocol version 6 (IPv6) address in the Secure Neighbor Discovery (SEND) protocol. CGAs are IPv6 addresses for which the interface identifier is generated by computing a cryptographic one-way hash function from a public key and auxiliary parameters. The binding between the public key and the address can be verified by re-computing the hash value and by comparing the hash with the interface identifier. Messages sent from an IPv6 address can be protected by attaching the public key and auxiliary parameters and by signing the message with the corresponding private key. The protection works without a certification authority or any security infrastructure: no additional security infrastructure, such as a public-key infrastructure (PKI), certification authorities, or other trusted servers, is needed [r168, r169].

Cryptographically Generated Addresses (CGA), Goals The purpose of CGAs is to prevent stealing and spoofing of existing IPv6 addresses. The public key of the address owner is bound cryptographically to the address. The address owner can use the corresponding private key to assert its ownership and to sign Secure Neighbor Discovery (SEND) messages sent from the address [r168].

Cryptographically Strong Sequences A series of random numbers that is computationally infeasible to guess.

Cryptography The mathematical science that deals with transforming data to render its meaning unintelligible (i.e., to hide its semantic content), prevent its undetected alteration, or prevent its unauthorized use. If the transformation is reversible, cryptography also deals with restoring encrypted data to intelligible form [r013].

Cryptography Costs A measure of the financial costs for encryption technology, key distribution, and management. While the technology cost is dropping rapidly, Moore's Law, plus the easy availability of cryptographic components and toolkits, makes it relatively easy to use strong protective techniques. Although there are exceptions, public-key operations are still expensive, perhaps prohibitively so, if the cost of each public-key operation is spread over too few transactions. Careful engineering design can generally lets one spread this cost over many transactions [r170].

Cryptology The science that includes both cryptography and cryptanalysis, and sometimes is said to include steganography [r013].

Cryptonet A group of system entities that share a secret cryptographic key for a symmetric algorithm.

Cryptoperiod The time span during which a particular key is authorized to be used in a cryptographic system. A cryptoperiod is usually stated in terms of calendar or clock time, but sometimes is stated in terms of the maximum amount of data permitted to be processed by a cryptographic algorithm using the key. Specifying a cryptoperiod involves a tradeoff between the cost of rekeying and the risk of successful cryptanalysis [r013].

Cryptosystem, Formal Definition A three-tuple (G, E, D) where [r171]:

G, algorithm for generating keys: this algorithm is probabilistic and always outputs a pair of keys (k_e, k_d), k_e to be used for encryption and k_d to be used for decryption. One can think of the keys simply as strings of bits. One can distinguish two types of cryptosystems: (1) In a conventional or symmetric system, we always have $k_e = k_d$. Furthermore, there are two fixed finite sets given: P, the set of plaintexts, and C, the set of ciphertexts. In most conventional systems, there is also a fixed set of keys K given, and G takes no inputs, but simply outputs a key chosen uniformly from K. Furthermore, it is often the case that $P = C$. For instance in Shift Cipher, or Caesar substitution on the English alphabet, we always have $P = C = Z26$. Moreover, a key is generated by choosing a random element from Z26. (2) In a public-key or asymmetric system, k_e is different from k_d, in fact we want that it is a hard computational problem to find k_d, even if k_e is known. Furthermore, G takes a security parameter k as input, and it outputs the key pair (k_e, k_d) as well as the sets of plaintexts and ciphertexts P, C. The length of the keys produced as well as the sizes of the sets P, C now depend on k, and we require that the key length be polynomial in k. The idea is that we can control the security through the choice of k: The larger we choose k, the harder it will be to break the encryption.

E, algoriithm for encryption: This algorithm takes as input k_e and $x \in P$ ($\in$ = belongs to) and produces as output $E\,k_e(x) \in C$. Note that E may be probabilistic; that is, even though we fix x and k_e, many different ciphertexts may be produced as output from E, as a result of random choices made during the encryption process. In other words, the ciphertext will have a probability distribution that is determined from x and k_e, typically uniform in some subset of the ciphertexts. For instance, consider a cipher, where P is the ordinary alphabet Z26, whereas C is Z100—that is, a much larger set than P. The key then consists of information that splits C into 26 subsets A0, A1, . . . , A25, and to encrypt letter number i, one chooses a random element in Ai.

D, algorithm for decryption: This algorithm takes as input k_d, $y \in C$ and produces as output $Dk_d(y) \in P$. It is allowed to be probabilistic, but is in most cases deterministic. For a cryptosystem, one always require that for any pair of keys (k_e, k_d) output by G, correct decryption is possible—that is, it holds that for any $x \in P$, $x = Dk_d(E\,k_e(x))$.

The most popular public-key cryptosystems are based on the problem of factorization of large integers and discrete logarithm problem in finite groups, in particular in the multiplicative group of finite field and the group of points on elliptic curve over finite field.

Cryptoviral Extortion Cryptoviral extortion is a three-round protocol that is carried out by an attacker against a victim. The attack is carried out via a cryptovirus that uses a hybrid cryptosystem to encrypt host data while deleting or overwriting the original data in the process [r172]. The protocol is as follows [r089]:

(protocol setup phase) An asymmetric key pair is generated by the virus author on a smartcard and the public key is placed within the virus. The private key is designated as "nonexportable" so that even the virus author cannot obtain its bit representation. Thus, the private key is generated,

stored, and used on the smartcard. Ideally, the smartcard will implement two-factor security: something the virus author knows [a Personal Identification Number (PIN)] and something the virus writer has (the smartcard that contains the private key). Also, the card will ideally be immune to differential power analysis, timing attacks, and so on, to prevent the virus author from ever learning the bits of the private key. A standards-based approach can be used—for example, the use of an approved FIPS 140-2 level 2 or higher device (e.g., when it is level 4 the private key will be destroyed if the casing is breached). In the United States the virus author cannot be forced to bear witness against himself or herself (Fifth Amendment), and so the PIN can remain confidential. The purpose of this setup phase is to limit the effectiveness of seizing and analyzing the smartcard under subpoena or warrant (competent evidence).

(1) (virus author → victim) The virus author deploys the cryptovirus. At a later time the virus activates on what could be tens or even hundreds of thousands of machines. The remainder of this description will cover the protocol for just one such machine. When the virus activates, it uses a true random bit generator (TRBG) to generate a symmetric key and initialization vector (IV) uniformly at random. It is essential that the TRBG produce truly random bits to prevent the symmetric key and IV from being guessed or otherwise determined by the victim at a later date. The virus then encrypts host data with this random symmetric key and IV [e.g., using cipher-block chaining (CBC) mode]. The virus concatenates the IV with the symmetric key and then encrypts the resulting string using the public key of the virus author [e.g., using Rivest Shamir Adleman Optimal Asymmetric Encryption Padding (RSA-OAEP)]. The encrypted plaintext is then held ransom. The virus notifies the victim that the attack has occurred (e.g., via a dialog box on the victim's screen) and states that the asymmetric ciphertext will be needed to restore the data. The virus author states his or her demands in return for the

data. The virus author and victim can send asymmetrically encrypted messages to each other via a public bulletin board to try to preserve the attacker's anonymity. Alternatively, digital pseudonyms and mix-networks can be used.

(2) (victim → virus author) If the victim complies by paying the ransom and transmitting the asymmetric ciphertext to the virus author then the virus author decrypts the ciphertext using the private key that only the virus author has access to (the one on his or her smartcard). This reveals the symmetric key and IV that was used in the attack.

(3) (virus author → victim) The virus author sends the symmetric key and IV to the victim. These are then used to decrypt the data that was held ransom.

(security) The attack is ineffective if the data can be recovered from backups. Antiviral experts cannot retrieve the private decryption key by analyzing the virus since only the public key will be found. The importance of using hybrid encryption can be seen from the following argument. Suppose that a smartcard was not used and asymmetric encryption were performed using electronic code-book (ECB) mode. It follows that if the private key were revealed to one victim then that victim could give the private key to others. In this case the virus author cannot hope to victimize very many people (perhaps even just one person). The alternative would be for the virus author to demand the entire ECB ciphertext of the data that was held ransom so that it could be deciphered without revealing the private decryption key. However, this is unacceptable for two reasons. First, the file could be huge and therefore make transmission cumbersome. Second, many victims may refuse to cooperate since it would reveal to the virus author the data that was held ransom (privacy violation). This makes the use of hybrid encryption (not just public-key encryption) essential.

One question that is typically asked in regards to cryptoviral extortion is the following. How could an extortionist ever expect to receive payment? Truly anonymous e-cash (which may be minted off-shore) could provide a safe medium for ransom. Mix networks are also a critical infrastructure for allowing the extortionist to maintain his or her anonymity. Also, the extortionist could seek information that resides on the host machine instead of money. In this case it may be possible for the malware to asymmetrically encrypt the following: cryptographic hash of the desired data concatenated with the randomly generated symmetric key. This would make it so that the symmetric key could not be recovered without revealing the correct hash [r172]. See reference [r173] for attacks of this nature.

This leads to an important consideration for organizations that rely heavily on information technology. It is important to be able to estimate the value of an exploit to an outside thief. A model for doing exactly this has been proposed, and it can be used by an organization to gauge its attractiveness to outside thieves [r174]. One needs to consider the notion of economic threat modeling, and notes that a cryptoviral extortion attack may allow a thief to profit without taking anything.

Cryptovirology Cryptovirology is the study of the applications of cryptography to malicious software [r089, r175, r172]. It is an investigation into how modern cryptographic paradigms and tools can be used to strengthen, improve, and develop new malicious software (malware) attacks. Cryptovirology attacks have been devised to: give malware enhanced privacy and be more robust against reverse-engineering; give the attacker enhanced anonymity when communicating with deployed malware [r176]; improve the ability to steal data; improve the ability to carry out extortion; enable new types of denial-of-service; enable fault-tolerance in distributed cryptoviral attacks, and so on. Also, a worm can install a back door on each infected system that opens only when the worm is presented with a system-specific ticket that is generated by the worm's author; this is called an access-for-sale worm [r177]. Cryptography has traditionally been used for defensive purposes. Ciphers defend against a passive eavesdropper. Public-key infrastructures defend against an active adversary that mounts a man-in-the-middle attack. Digital signature algorithms defend against a forger. E-cash systems defend against a counterfeiter and a double-spender. Pseudo-random bit generators defend against a next-bit predictor, and so on. Cryptovirology extends beyond finding protocol failures and design vulnerabilities; it is a forward-engineering discipline that can be used for attacking rather than defending [r089].

Of particular relevance to cryptovirology is the Federal Information Processing Standard FIPS 140-2 standard entitled, "Security Requirements for Cryptographic Modules" [r178] and its annexes. The annexes employ the FIPS 186-2 standard entitled, "Digital Signature Standard (DSS)" [r179] for such things as key generation.

Cryptovirus   In computer security, a cryptovirus is defined as a computer virus that contains and uses a public key [r089, r173]. Usually the public key belongs to the author of the virus, though there are other possibilities as well. For instance, a virus or worm may generate and use its own key pair at run-time [r172, r180]. Cryptoviruses may utilize secret sharing to hide information and may communicate by reading posts from public bulletin boards [r172]. Cryptotrojans and cryptoworms are the same as cryptoviruses, except they are Trojan horses and worms, respectively. Note that under this definition, a virus that uses a symmetric key and not a public key is not a cryptovirus (this is particularly relevant in the case of polymorphic viruses). (The term cryptovirus was first coined in reference to plant viruses.)

Cryptovirus, Polymorphic Forms   If a polymorphic virus [r183, r182, r089] contains and uses a public key then it is a cryptovirus. A polymorphic virus usually contains and uses a symmetric key for the purposes of obfuscating and de-obfuscating its own code. So, if this is the only cryptographic key it uses then it is not a cryptovirus. Polymorphic viruses often decrypt and then send control to the main portion of their code, called the virus body, at run-time. They may generate new keys periodically and produce new ciphertexts of their bodies to make virus detection more difficult. The body also contains code that alters (morphs) the decryption code at the beginning of the virus. This makes it such that the virus changes its entire appearance. Although it would make sense to call this a "cryptovirus," this is not the way the computer term was originally defined [r172].

Cryptoviruses Cures   There is no cure-all for cryptovirus attacks [r089]. Cryptoviruses attack computer systems using the same tools that are used to protect computer systems. Hence, a weakness in the design of a secure cryptovirus implies a weakness in a block cipher, stream cipher, asymmetric cryptosystem, and so on. A product that claims to protect one specifically from the threat of cryptoviruses is making exaggerated claims; the best defense is to: verify the authenticity of all programs that one runs, protect one's machine from infiltration, use existing antiviral tools, be diligent about archiving data, and so forth.

CS   See Circuit-Switched

CSA   See Canadian Standards Association

CSE   See Communications Security Establishment

CSIRT   See Computer Security Incident Response Team

CSMA/CD   See Carrier Sense Multiple Access/ Collision Detect

CSO   See Chief Security Officer

CSOR   See Computer Security Objects Register

CSPF   See Constraint-based Shortest Path First

CSR   See Certificate Signing Request

CSS   See Cross-Site Scripting

CTCH   See Common Traffic Channel

CTIA   See Cellular Telecommunications and Internet Association

CTO   See Chief Technology Officer

CTR   See Currency Transaction Report

CUG   See Closed User Group

Cumulative   Crosstalk   (optical   transmission term) The relative power level (dB) coming from all other channels including adjacent and nonadjacent channels, referenced to 0-dB power level.

Currency Transaction Report (CTR)   (financial term) The Bank Secrecy Act (BSA) requires financial institutions to detect and report suspicious activity through Suspicious Activity Reports (SARs), to keep records of certain financial transactions, and to file CTRs to report large (over $10,000) cash transactions. SARs provide law enforcement with information about possible criminal activity, while CTRs and other transaction records provide a paper trail for law enforcement. This helps Law Enforcement agencies to build better cases against money launderers and other criminals.

CUSIP   See Committee on Uniform Securities and Identification Procedures

Customer   A user of telecommunications services provided by a service provider.

Customer Edge (CE)   (aka Customer Edge/Equipment) The name of the device with the functionality needed on the customer premises to access Provider-Provisioned Virtual Private Network (PPVPN) services specified [r081, r082]. The concept has been modified—for example, when Layer 2 Virtual Private Networks (L2VPNs) and CE-based Virtual Private Networks (VPNs) were defined. A router or a switch in the customer network interfacing with the service provider's network.

There are two different aspects that have to be considered in naming CE devices. One could start with the type of device that is used to implement the CE. It is also possible to use the service the CE provides whereby the result will be a set of "prefixed CEs." It is common practice to use "CE" to indicate any of these boxes, as it is often unambiguous in the specific context [r082].

Customer Edge Router (CE-R)   A router in the customer network interfacing the provider network. There are many reasons to use a router in the customer network; for example, in a Layer 3 Virtual Private Network (L3VPN) using private IP addressing, this is the router that is able to do forwarding based on the private addresses. Another reason to require the use of a CE-R on the cus-

tomer side is that one wants to limit the number of MAC addresses that need to be learned in the provider network. A CE-R could be used to access both Layer 2 and Layer 3 services [r082].

Customer Edge Switch (CE-S)   A service aware Layer 2 switch in the customer network interfacing the provider network. In a Virtual Private Wire Service (VPWS) or a Virtual Private LAN Service (VPLS), it is not strictly necessary to use a router in the customer network; a layer 2 switch might very well do the job [r082].

Customer Identification Program (CIP)   Section 326 of the USA PATRIOT Act includes specific requirements regarding obtaining and verifying the identity of new customers. The regulation requires all financial institutions to develop and follow a CIP; at account-opening time, financial institutions must collect the following data: (i) Name of individual or business customer; (ii) Date of birth (for individuals only); (iii) Official Identification number (e.g., SSN, TIN, EIN, passport number, etc.); and (iv) Address—Place of residence or business address. This must be a physical address; a Post Office box is not sufficient (with an exception for certain military personnel.)

Customer Premises Equipment (CPE)   The CPE equipment is the device that a provider places with the customer. It serves two purposes: giving the customer ports to plug in to and making it possible for a provider to monitor the connectivity to the customer site. The CPE is typically a low cost device with limited functionality and, in most cases, is not aware of the Virtual Private Network (VPN) services offered by the provider network. The CPE equipment is not necessarily the equipment to which the Customer Edge/Equipment (CE) functions are allocated, but it is part of the provider network and is used for monitoring purposes. The CPE name is used primarily in network operation and deployment contexts and should not be used in protocol specifications [r082].

CUT   See Coordinated Universal Time

Cut-and-Paste Attack   (aka Copy-and-Paste Attack) An active attack on the data integrity of ciphertext, effected by replacing sections of ciphertext with other ciphertext, such that the result appears to decrypt correctly but actually decrypts to plaintext that is forged to the satisfaction of the attacker [r013].

CW   See Call Waiting

CWDM   See Coarse Wavelength Division Multiplexing

Cybercrime   Illegal acts and computer crimes for computers connected to the Internet or perpetrated through the use of the Internet.

Cyberextortion   A form of criminal activity where the network, the computers, the website, or the e-mail server of an organization are subjected to denial of service (DoS) or other attacks by malicious hackers for the purpose of extorting money in return for a promise to halt the attacks. These crackers are called cyberextortionists.

Cyberspace   The collection (or "universe") of computers and the user community that organizes around them.

Cyberterrorism   Group-sanctioned security infractions undertaken as a political agenda or unfriendly military action.

Cyclic Redundancy Check (CRC)   A noncryptographic checksum used to assure the integrity of data. Typically 16 or 32 bits, but can also be longer. Generated via a specified polynomial operation (specified in the Layer 2 standard of interest).

D

D D D D D D D D D D D D D D D D D D D D D D D

D (GSM context) The D interface connects the Visitor Location Register (VLR) and the Home Location Register (HLR) [r011].

D1 See Digital Video Tape Standard D1

D16 See Digital Video Tape Standard D16

D2 See Digital Video Tape Standard D2

D2D See Disk-to-Disk Backup

D3 See Digital Video Tape Standard D3

D5 See Digital Video Tape Standard D5

D6 See Digital Video Tape Standard D6

D7 See Digital Video Tape Standard D7

DAA See Designated Approving Authority or Data Authentication Algorithm

DAC See Discretionary Access Control or Data Authentication Code

Daemon A server-running process.

DACL See Discretionary Access Control List (DACL)

DAP See Directory Access Protocol

DARPA See Defense Advanced Research Projects Agency

DAS See Direct Attached Storage

DASS See Distributed Authentication Security Service

Data Authentication Algorithm (DAA) A keyed hash function equivalent to Data Encryption Standard (DES) Cipher Block Chaining where the Initialization Vector (IV) is equal to zero [r099].

Data Authentication Code (DAC) A U.S. Government standard [r184] for a checksum that is computed by the Data Authentication Algorithm. Also known as the American National Standards Institute (ANSI) Message Authentication Code Standard [r099, r013].

Data Communication Network In general, a network that is specialized to the movement of data, such as the Internet. In particular, a communication network within a Telecommunications Man-

Minoli–Cordovana's Authoritative Computer and Network Security Dictionary. By Daniel Minoli and James Cordovana
Copyright © 2006 John Wiley & Sons, Inc.

agement Network (TMN) or between TMNs which support the data communication function (DCF).

Data Communications Channel (DCC) An in-band channel used in Synchronous Optical Network (SONET) to carry network management information between Network Elements (e.g., Add/Drop Multiplexers).

Data Compromise An intrusion into a computer and/or networking system, where data have been exposed to unauthorized entities or have been altered inappropriately.

Data Confidentiality (aka confidentiality) The property that data have been protected against unauthorized disclosure. Confidentiality is typically assured by encryption, access controls, and legal agreements.

Data Confidentiality Service A security service that protects against, and audits for, unauthorized disclosure of data.

Data Defenses Means to protect data against unauthorized disclosure.

Data Encryption Algorithm (DEA) A 1970s symmetric block cipher, defined as part of the U.S. Government's Data Encryption Standard (DES). DEA uses a 64-bit key, of which 56 bits are independently chosen and 8 are parity bits. DEA maps a 64-bit block into another 64-bit block [r185]. The algorithm has also been adopted in standards outside the U.S. Government [r013].

Data Encryption Key (DEK) A cryptographic key that is used to encipher application data.

Data Encryption Standard (DES) A cryptographic algorithm developed at IBM in 1977 and later adopted by the U.S. Department of Defense. DES was published in Federal Information Processing Standard (FIPS) 46 [r192]. This widely used method of data encryption using a private (secret) key that was originally judged so difficult to break by the U.S. Government that it was restricted for exportation to other countries. DES applies a 56-bit key to each 64-bit block of data. Although this is considered "strong" encryption, many companies now use "triple DES"; "triple

DES" applies three keys in succession. The reason that DES has fallen out of favor is that DES-encrypted messages are vulnerable to being deciphered considering the advancements in computing, particularly grid computing (in 1997 a grid-computing cooperative effort deciphered a DES encrypted message) [r185].

Data Grid A kind of Grid Computing grid used for housing and providing access to data files across multiple organizations; users are not focused on where this data is located as long as they have access to the data [r080].

Data Integrity (aka integrity) The property that data has not been altered, destroyed, or lost in an unauthorized or accidental manner. A state where the data are protected from unauthorized, unanticipated, or unintentional modification.

Data Integrity Service A security service that protects against, and audits for, unauthorized or accidental changes to data.

Data Leakage The successful circumvention of security controls, particularly focused on obtaining authorized access to data.

Data Lifecycle Management (DLM) The infrastructural element of (storage) data management. Information Lifecycle Management (ILM) is the macro-level element that assigns both subjective and objective value; ILM relates not only to an application, but also to where the information itself resides in the company as a whole. DLM—the infrastructural piece of what goes where and when—is very similar to the traditional Hierarchical Storage Management (HSM) that has existed in the mainframe world since inception [r284].

DLM architectures almost exclusively comprise two physical tiers. There is the physical tier of actual storage where data resides, including disk arrays of all sizes and types, and then there is the process tier for moving data between those elements. Today, by and large, the physical tier involves manual processes. There are many different attributes: performance, availability, cost, replication, disaster recovery, retention—to name a few. All of these elements have to be taken into account at various points in time to help one de-termine the right physical asset that data should reside on at a particular moment [r284].

Data Link Connection Identifier (DLCI)   A la-bel used in Frame Relay networks to identify frame relay circuits. It is a Layer 2 relative ad-dressing scheme with local significance. More precisely: the identifier of a Frame Relay Service Virtual Circuit hop (an end-to-end connection is the concatenation of multiple hops).

Data Management   (Grid Computing context) A mechanism for reliable movement of files and data to various nodes within the computational grid [r080].

(Storage context) A category of storage man-agement software designed to migrate data from primary storage to secondary storage in order to protect primary data sets or to create a replica copy of primary data [r029].

Data Mapping   (aka keyless searching) data mapping looks for, finds, or suggests associa-tions between files within a large body of data, that may not be apparent using other techniques. Data mapping well beyond basic search capabil-ities [r057].

Data Origin Authentication   A security service that verifies the identity of the claimed source of data. This service is usually bundled with connec-tionless integrity service [r186].

Data Origin Authentication Service   A service that assures data origin authentication.

Data Over Cable Service Interface Specification (DOCSIS)   A specification for delivery of data (e.g., Internet access channel) within a Cable TV system.

Data Over Cable Service Interface Specification (DOCSIS) Management Information Base (MIB)   A MIB (described in RFC 4036) that provides a set of objects required for the manage-ment of DOCSIS Cable Modem Termination Sys-tems (CMTS). These managed objects facilitate protection of the cable network from misuse by subscribers. This misuse might include, for exam-ple, address spoofing, service spoofing, or opera-tion of unauthorized services. This MIB module controls IP packet forwarding to and from each cable modem, at the CMTS (this is not to be con-fused with the DOCSIS Cable Device MIB of RFC 2669). Although it is expected that the Cable Device MIB will be used to prevent unwanted traffic from entering the cable network, it is also possible that a malicious user might tamper with cable modem software, disabling its filtering policies. The CMTS MIB provides a more secure mechanism, as physical access to the CMTS is controlled by the network operator. In particular, this MIB provides two capabilities: first, to limit the IP addresses behind a modem, and second, to provide address and protocol filtering to and from a modem.

Data Protection Directives   Norms for the protec-tion of client data, particularly in an outsourced environment. The purpose of these directives is to document what a supplier (business partner) may and may not do with client company information. A number of standards have been developed in this arena, including the EU (European Union) Data Protection Directive, ISO 17799, Bank of International Settlements' Outsourcing in Finan-cial Services, and the Federal Financial Institu-tions Examination Council's Outsourcing Tech-nology Services [r187].

Data Security   The protection of data from disclo-sure, alteration, destruction, or loss that either is accidental or is intentional but unauthorized. Both data confidentiality service and data integri-ty service are needed to achieve data security [r013].

Data Terminal Equipment (DTE)   Older term re-ferring to the equipment side of the interface that a computer uses to exchange data with a modem or other serial device, in contrast to the Data Cir-cuit Terminating Equipment, on the communica-tion side of the interface (this used to be on the carrier side in the original definition, at it related to interfaces on modems).

Data-at-Rest, Risks   Data can be stored locally (such as on a hard drive) or in removable media [such as tapes or compact disks (CDs)]. Intruders can gain access to this information by attacking a system (through the application or the operating system), or having physical access to the system. Data on removable media can be obtained by unauthorized persons in onsite storage facilities, off-site storage facilities, or when the physical media is in transit.

Data-Driven Attack   An attack where data sent in a seemingly normal transaction can contain malicious executable code or be in excess so as to cause a denial of service.

Datagram   (aka Protocol Data Unit) A packet or frame. "A self-contained, independent entity of data carrying sufficient information to be routed from the source to the destination" [r194].

DC   See Differential Cryptanalysis

DCC   See Data Communications Channel

DCCH   See Dedicated Control Channel

DCH   See Dedicated Channel

DDoS   See Distributed Denial-of-Service

Debt/asset Ratio   (financial term) Total liabilities divided by total assets. The debt/asset ratio shows the proportion of a company's assets which are financed through debt. If the ratio is less than one, most of the company's assets are financed through equity. If the ratio is greater than one, most of the company's assets are financed through debt. Companies with high debt/asset ratios are said to be "highly leveraged," and could be in danger if creditors start to demand repayment of debt [r009].

Deception   A means by which to trick a system or user into believing that an unauthorized entity is a legitimately authorized entity, where inappropriate data appears to be appropriate, or falsifying the origin of the entity or data.

Decipherment   The reversal of a corresponding reversible encipherment.

Decode   To convert encoded data back to its original form of representation. Related to decrypt.

Decrypt   Process to cryptographically restore ciphertext to the plaintext form it had before encryption.

Decrypt Function   Function with parameters (specific-key, state, octet string) $\rightarrow$ (state, octet string). This function takes the specific key, ci-

pher state, and ciphertext as inputs and verifies the integrity of the supplied ciphertext. If the ciphertext's integrity is intact, this function produces the plaintext and a new cipher state as outputs; otherwise, an error indication must be returned, and the data discarded [r115].

DECT   See Digital Enhanced Cordless Telecommunications

DECT-Level Encryption   Encryption mechanism for cordless handsets. European standard.

Dedicated Channel (DCH)   (3G Wireless context) A bidirectional transport channel. It is dedicated to one particular User Equipment and uses Closed Loop Power Control. The channel's transfer rate can be adjusted every 10 ms [r007].

Dedicated Control Channel (DCCH)   (3G Wireless context) A bidirectional logical channel used to transmit dedicated control information between the User Equipment and the Network. The DCCH is set up together with a Radio Resource Control (RRC) connection [r007].

Dedicated Physical Channel (DPCH)   (3G Wireless context) A downlink channel that takes over the same tasks as the uplink channels Dedicated Physical Control Channel (DPCCH) and Dedicated Physical Data Channel (DPDCH). This means that control information and data is multiplexed in a determined sequence [r007].

Dedicated Physical Control Channel (DPCCH)   (3G Wireless context) In the uplink, there is exactly one Dedicated Physical Control Channel. It is used to control data transfer; the data are transferred in several associated Dedicated Physical Data Channels (DPDCHs) [r007].

Dedicated Physical Data Channel (DPDCH)   (3G Wireless context) A data channel to support data transmission in the uplink. A DPCCH is associated with it to control the data transfer; it is also possible to use several DPDCHs simultaneously [r007].

Dedicated Security Mode   A mode of operation of an information system, wherein all users have the clearance or authorization, and the need-to-know, for all data handled by the system. In this mode, the system may handle either a single classification level or category of information or a range of levels and categories [r195]. This mode is defined formally in U.S. Department of Defense policy regarding system accreditation, but the term is also used outside the Defense Department and outside the Government [r013].

Dedicated Traffic Channel (DTCH) (3G Wireless context) A logical channel that exists in both the uplink and the downlink. It is a point-to-point channel, dedicated to one User Equipment [r007].

Deep Packet Inspection The examination of the payload of a Protocol Data Unit (PDU), or packet [such as a Transmission Control Protocol (TCP) PDU], to determine if there are potential security issues; for example, if the packet was a crafted packet. Typically, this is done by an Intrusion Detection System (IDS); these may also use shallow packet inspection.

Default Account The user or system identification set for a system or application prior to its first use by a consumer of the system. Examples include "system," "root," and "admin." Default accounts are often a source of attack and default password for this account, and preferably the account name itself, should be changed upon first login.

Default Password The password for the default account.

Default Path (IPv6 context) The route with a ::/0 prefix. The default route gathers all destinations and is the route used to obtain next destination address when there are no more matching routes [r008].

Default Route A default route can match any destination address. If a router does not have a more specific route for a particular packet's destination address, it forwards this packet to the next hop in the default route entry, provided that its Forwarding Table [Forwarding Information Base (FIB), contains one]. The notation for a default route for IPv4 is 0.0.0.0/0 and for IPv6 it is 0:0:0:0:0:0:0:0 or ::/0 [r086].

Default Route, Default-Free Table, and Full Table An individual router's routing table may not necessarily contain a default route. Not hav-

ing a default route, however, is not synonymous with having a full default-free table (DFT). Also, a router that has a full set of routes as in a DFT, but that also has a "discard" rule for a default route would not be considered default free [r086].

Default Routers List (IPv6 context) A list supported by each device where all routers, from which a no null router lifetime value advertisement has been received, appear [r008].

Default-Free Routing Table A routing table that has no default routes and is typically seen in routers in the core or top tier of routers in the network [r086].

Default-Free Zone The default-free zone is the part of the Internet backbone that does not have a default route [r086].

De-federation (aka de-referencing) How a user's account linking is "broken up" between Identity and Service Providers, without necessarily destroying a user's account itself [r278].

Defendant A person charged in a legal action.

Defense Advanced Research Projects Agency (DARPA) DARPA is the central research and development organization for the Department of Defense (DoD). It manages and directs selected basic and applied research and development projects for DoD, and it pursues research and technology where risk and payoff are both very high and where success may provide dramatic advances for traditional military roles and missions.

Defense in Depth See Principle of Separation of Privilege

Defense Information Systems Agency (DISA) The Defense Information Systems Agency is a combat support agency of the U.S. the Department of Defense (DoD) responsible for planning, engineering, acquiring, fielding, and supporting global net-centric solutions to serve the needs of the President, Vice President, the Secretary of Defense, and other DoD Components, under all conditions of peace and war.

Defensive Techniques for PPVPN Service Providers For Provider Provisioned Virtual Private Networks (PPVPNs), techniques include encryption, authentication, filtering, firewalls, access control, isolation, and aggregation.

Defer   To postpone work on, or set aside, an activity such as resolution of a trouble report until such time as when appropriate conditions are met and it can be progressed further.

Degauss   Apply a magnetic field to permanently remove, erase, or clear data from a magnetic storage medium, such as a tape or disk [r013].

Degausser   An electrical device that can degauss magnetic storage media.

Degaussing   To degauss a magnetic storage medium.

DEK   See Data Encryption Key

Delegation   Conveyance of privilege from one entity that holds such privilege to another entity.

Delegation Path   In X.509, an ordered sequence of certificates which, together with authentication of a privilege asserter's identity, can be processed to verify the authenticity of a privilege asserter's privilege [r068a].

Delegation Point   (DNSSEC context) Term used to describe the name at the parental side of a zone cut. That is, the delegation point for "foo.example" would be the foo.example node in the "example" zone (as opposed to the zone apex of the "foo.example" zone). See also Zone Apex [r069].

Delivery Rules   (Presence Services context) Constraints on how an instant message service delivers received instant messages to instant inboxes. For each instant inbox, the applicable delivery rules are manipulated by the inbox user agent of a principal that controls the instant inbox. Motivation: one needs a way of talking about filtering instant messages [r016].

Delta Certificate Revocation List (CRL)   A partial CRL that only contains entries for X.509 certificates that have been revoked since the issuance of a prior, base CRL. This method can be used to partition CRLs that become too large and unwieldy [r013].

Demilitarized Zone (DMZ)   A computing environment creating an area of protection that lies between the corporate computing environment and the Internet or network. The DMZ is typically where the firewalls, gateways, application proxies, and other protective computing devices are connected, and where protective software such as filtering and intrusion detection applications are deployed. The term was originally used in a military context.

Demon Dialer   A program that repeatedly calls the same telephone number. This can be a benign and legitimate tool for access or it can be a malicious mechanism when used as a denial of service attack.

Denial of Service (DoS)   The prevention of authorized access to a system resource or the delaying of system operations and functions [r013]. Oftentimes, a DoS attack involves flooding an application or network with messages such that the system does not have sufficient resources to be able to respond to the high volume of messages in a timely manner. This type of flooding attack can be done via a Distributed Denial of Service Attack (DDoS). DoS prevents normal use of computer or network by legitimate users. A DoS attack can cause abnormal termination of the applications, flood the network with traffic, or block traffic [r057].

Denial of Service (DoS) Attacks on a Provider Provisioned Virtual Private Network (PPVPN)   (PPVPN context) DoS attacks are those in which an attacker attempts to disrupt or prevent the use of a service by its legitimate users. For PPVPNs, taking network devices out of service, modifying their configuration, or overwhelming them with requests for service are several of the possible avenues for DoS attack. Overwhelming the network with requests for service, otherwise known as a "resource exhaustion" DoS attack, may target any resource in the network—for example, link bandwidth, packet forwarding capacity, session capacity for various protocols, and processing power. DoS attacks of the resource exhaustion type can be mounted against the data plane of a particular PPVPN by attempting to insert (spoof) an overwhelming quantity of nonauthentic data into the VPN from outside of that VPN. Potential results might be to exhaust the bandwidth available to that

VPN or to overwhelm the cryptographic authentication mechanisms of the VPN. Data plane resource exhaustion attacks can also be mounted by overwhelming the service provider's general (VPN-independent) infrastructure with traffic. These attacks on the general infrastructure are not usually a PPVPN-specific issue, unless the attack is mounted by another PPVPN user from a privileged position. For example, a PPVPN user might be able to monopolize network data plane resources and thus to disrupt other PPVPNs) [r058].

Denial of Service (DoS) Attacks on Network Infrastructure   (PPVPN context) Control plane DoS attacks can be mounted specifically against the mechanisms that the service provider uses to provide Provider Provisioned Virtual Private Networks (PPVPNs) [e.g., IPsec, MultiProtocol Label Switching (MPLS)] or against the general infrastructure of the service provider [e.g., Provider Edge (PE) routers or shared aspects of PE routers.] Attacks against the general infrastructure are within the scope of this document only if the attack happens in relation to the VPN service; otherwise, they are not a PPVPN-specific issue. Of special concern for PPVPNs is DoS to one PPVPN user caused by the activities of another; this can occur, for example, if one PPVPN user's activities are allowed to consume excessive network resources of any sort that are also needed to serve other PPVPN users [r058].

Dense Wavelength Division Multiplexing (DWDM)   (optical transmission term) An optical wavelength division multiplexing system where many channels are needed or supported (e.g., 64, 128, or 256 channels). A typical DWDM may be able to handle 100 2.5-Gbps signals (250 Gbps total) or 50 10-Gbps signals (500 Gbps total). This is in contrast with Coarse Wavelength Division Multiplexers (CWDMs), where only a few channels (e.g., 8 or 16) are present.

Department of Defense (DoD)   U.S. Government department that deals with military defense. The department is a major promoter/consumer of technologies in general, information technology in particular, and information security in practice.

Dependability Theory   Dependability is a combination of reliability (the probability that a system operates through a given operation specification), and availability (the probability that the system will be available at any instant required). Concept typically used in software engineering/quality: "dependability" provides plausible predictions of software quality [r196]. Dependability is an umbrella term for safety, reliability, security, trustworthiness, availability. A dependable system is one known to have all its required properties. One needs dependable processes as well as dependable systems to build systems on time and budget, and to be able to rely on what one delivers [r197].

Depreciated Cost   (financial term) The original cost of an asset minus total its depreciation thus far. Also called net book value or written-down value.

Depreciation   (financial term) The allocation of the cost of an asset over a period of time for accounting and tax purposes. Also, a decline in the value of a property due to general wear and tear or obsolescence; opposite of appreciation [r009].

DER   See Distinguished Encoding Rules

De-referencing   (aka de-federation) How a user's account linking is "broken" between Identity and Service Providers, without necessarily destroying a user's account itself [r288].

Derf   The act of exploiting a PC or system that someone else has absent-mindedly left logged on.

DES   See Data Encryption Standard

Desiderata   A wish list of desired properties, capabilities, mechanisms.

Design Principles for Security (by Saltzer and Schroeder)   These are eight well-known principles [r139a] as follows: (i) Least Privilege; (ii) Fail-Safe Defaults; (iii) Economy of Mechanism; (iv) Complete Mediation; (v) Open Design; (vi) Separation of Privilege; (vii) Least Common Mechanism; and (viii) Psychological Acceptability. Refer to each entry for explanation.

Designated Approving Authority (DAA)   The official with the authority to formally assume responsibility for operating a system at an acceptable level of functionality, risk, and security.

De-skewing Approach used to shape the distribution of quantities gathered for the entropy to produce the random numbers. The original distribution need not be uniform; one can than use a de-skew techniques generate a new bit stream. A technique, originally due to von Neumann is to examine a bit stream as a sequence of nonoverlapping pairs; one could then discard any 00 or 11 pairs found, interpret 01 as a 0 and 10 as a 1 [r166].

Desktop Partitioning Mechanisms to quickly and easily manage workstation hard drives: create, resize, merge, and convert partitions.

Destination Cache (IPv6 context) Table supported by each IPv6 node that maps each destination address (or addresses range) with the next router address to which the datagram has to be sent. Moreover it stores the associated path Maximum Transfer Unit (MTU) [r008].

Detective Control Control introduced to discover events that have occurred or to test the effectiveness of preventive control. Also, PHYSEC (Physical security) mechanisms to physically monitor an environment, such as smoke detectors, heat sensors, humidity sensors, and so on.

Deterministic Algorithm An algorithm whose behavior can be completely predicted from the input. When a deterministic, nonrandomized, algorithm is run multiple times on a given input, it will always execute the same path of instructions and output the same result [r094].

Deterministic Cryptosystems In 1976, Diffie and Hellman introduced a revolutionary new concept called public-key cryptography based on the simple observation that the encryption and decryption could be separated; that is, they recognized that a knowledge of the encryption key (or equivalently, the encryption algorithm) need not imply a knowledge of the decryption key (or algorithm). In such a system, the encryption key can be made public, say in a public directory, while the decryption key can be kept secret. Anyone wishing to send a message to a person in the directory can simply look up the public encryption key for that person and use it to encrypt the message. Then, assuming the decryption key is known only to the intended receiver of the message, only that person can decrypt the message. In such a public-key system it must be computationally infeasible to deduce the decryption key (or the decryption algorithm) from the public key (or the public encryption algorithm), even when general information about the system and how it operates is known. This leads to the idea of one-way functions.

A (deterministic) public-key cryptosystem consists of the following components [r390]:

(1) A set K called the key space whose elements are called keys.
(2) A rule by which each $k \in K$ is associated with a trap-door one-way function E_k with domain M_k (the plaintext space) and range C_k (the ciphertext space).
(3) A procedure for generating a random key $k \in K$ together with a trap-door d for E_k and the inverse map $D_k : C_k \rightarrow M_k$ such that $D_k(E_k(m)) = m$; for all $m \in M_k$.

The key space K is also called the public-key space, and the set of trap-doors d is called the private-key space. Relative to (3), it is also required that random keys $k \in K$ and their corresponding trap-doors d be easy to generate.

In practice, the complete description of all the components (1)–(3) of a cryptosystem is public knowledge. A person (user) who wants to become a part of the communication network can proceed as follows:

• Use (3) to generate a random key $k \in K$ and the corresponding trap-door d.
• Place the encryption function E_k (or equivalently the key k) in a public directory (say in the user's directory or home page), keeping d and the decryption function D_k secret.

Deterrent Controls Physical Security (PHYSEC) mechanisms such as locks, guards, signs, etc.

Detour Label Switched Path (LSP) (MPLS context) The LSP that is used to re-route traffic around a failure in one-to-one backup.

Detour Merge Point (DMP) (MPLS context) In the case of one-to-one backup, this is a Label Switch Router (LSR) where multiple detours converge; only one detour is signaled beyond that LSR.

Developer Tools Grid Tools Tools for developers of grid-enabled applications focused on file transfer, communications, environment control; they range from utilities to Application Programming Interfaces (APIs) [r080].

Device Convergence in the Control Plane A routing device is said to have converged at the point in time when the device under test (DUT) has performed all actions in the control plane needed to react to changes in topology in the context of the test condition. The convergence process, in general, can be subdivided into three distinct phases [r086]: (i) convergence across the entire Internet, (ii) convergence within an Autonomous System (AS), and (iii) convergence with respect to a single device. Convergence with respect to a single device can be (a) convergence with regard to data forwarding process(es) and (b) convergence with regard to the routing process(es).

DHCP See Dynamic Host Configuration Protocol

Dialog (SIP context) A dialog is a peer-to-peer Session Initiation Protocol (SIP) relationship between two User Agents (UAs) that persists for some time. A dialog is established by SIP messages, such as a 2xx response to an INVITE request. A dialog is identified by a call identifier, local tag, and a remote tag. A dialog was formerly known as a call leg in RFC 2543 [r025].

DIAMETER An Authentication, Authorization, and Accounting (AAA) server [similar to Remote Authentication Dial-In User Service (RADIUS)] used to provide authentication and authorization services for dial-up computers.

Dictionary Attack An attack that uses a brute-force technique of successively trying all the words in some large, exhaustive list. Examples include an attack on an authentication service by trying all possible passwords or an attack on encryption by encrypting some known plaintext phrase with all possible keys. This has the effect that the key for any given encrypted message containing that phrase may be obtained by lookup [r013].

Differential Cryptanalysis (DC) A general form of cryptanalysis applicable primarily to block ciphers (the technique can also be applied to stream ciphers and cryptographic hash functions). In the case of a block cipher, it refers to a set of techniques for tracing differences through the network of transformations, discovering where the cipher exhibits nonrandom behavior, and exploiting such properties to recover the secret key. More generally, DC is the study of how differences in an input can affect the resultant difference at the output. DC arose in the late 1980s and is traced to Eli Biham and Adi Shamir.

Differentiated Services (DS) (aka diffserv) A need has emerged in the past decade for relatively simple and coarse methods of providing differentiated classes of service for Internet and intranet traffic, to support various types of applications, and specific business requirements, including but not limited to Voice over IP (VoIP). The differentiated services approach to providing quality of service in networks employs a small, well-defined set of building blocks from which a variety of aggregate behaviors may be built. A small bit-pattern in each packet, in the IPv4 Type of Service (TOS) octet or the IPv6 Traffic Class octet, is used to mark a packet to receive a particular forwarding treatment, or per-hop behavior, at each network node. A common understanding about the use and interpretation of this bit-pattern is required for interdomain use, multivendor interoperability, and consistent reasoning about expected aggregate behaviors in a network. Thus, the Internet Engineering Task Force (IETF) has standardized a common layout for a six-bit field of both octets, called the "DS field." RFC 2474 and RFC 2475 define the architecture, and the general use of bits within the DS field (superseding the IPv4 TOS octet definitions of RFC 1349).

The IETF has standardized a small number of specific per-hop behaviors (PHBs), and recommended a particular bit pattern or "code-point" of the DS field for each one, in RFC 2474, RFC 2597, and RFC 2598. The IETF has also investigated the additional components necessary to support differentiated services, including such traffic conditioners as traffic shapers and packet markers that could be used at the boundaries of networks. Furthermore, the IETF develop a format for precisely describing various Per-Domain Behaviors (PDBs). A PDB is a collection of packets with the same codepoint, thus receiving the same PHB, traversing from edge to edge of a single diffserv network or domain. Associated with each PDB are measurable, quantifiable characteristics which can be used to describe what happens to packets of that PDB as they cross the network, thus providing an external description of the edge-to-edge quality of service that can be expected by packets of that PDB within that network. A PDB is formed at the edge of a network by selecting certain packets through use of classifiers and by imposing rules on those packets via traffic conditioners. The description of a PDB contains the specific edge rules and PHB type(s) and configurations that should be used in order to achieve specified externally visible characteristics.

Diffie–Hellman Algorithm   A key agreement algorithm published in 1976 by Whitfield Diffie and Martin Hellman. Diffie–Hellman does key establishment, not encryption. However, the key that it produces may be used for encryption, for further key management operations, or for any other cryptography. The difficulty of breaking Diffie–Hellman is considered to be equal to the difficulty of computing discrete logarithms modulo a large prime. The algorithm in brief is as follows: Alice and Bob together pick large integers that satisfy certain mathematical conditions, and then use the integers to each separately compute a public–private key pair. They send each other their public key. Each person uses their own private key and the other person's public key to compute a key, k, such that, because of the mathematics of the algorithm, is the same for each of them.

Passive wiretapping cannot learn the shared k, because k is not transmitted, and neither are the private keys needed to compute k. However, without additional mechanisms to authenticate each party to the other, a protocol based on the algorithm may be vulnerable to a man-in-the-middle attack [r013].

Diffie–Hellman Exponential Key Exchange   A technique that yields a shared secret between two parties. It can be computationally infeasible for a third party to determine this secret even if they can observe all the messages between the two communicating parties. This shared secret is a mixture of initial quantities generated by each of the parties. If these initial quantities are random and uncorrelated, then the shared secret combines their entropy but, of course, cannot produce more randomness than the size of the shared secret generated. Although this is true if the Diffie–Hellman computation is performed privately, an adversary who can observe either of the public keys and knows the modulus being used need only search through the space of the other secret key in order to be able to calculate the shared secret. Hence, conservatively, it would be best to consider public Diffie–Hellman to produce a quantity whose guessability corresponds to the worse of the two inputs. Because of this and the fact that Diffie–Hellman is computationally intensive, its use as a mixing function is not recommended [r167].

Diffie–Hellman's Encryption Scheme   Algorithm where there is an encryption function E_K and a decryption function D_K which work on a plaintext P such that $D\_K(E\_K(P)) = P$, that is, running the decryption function over the encrypted form of P results in P, the plaintext, returned. In Diffie–Hellman's scheme, E_K can be computed from a publicly published key X, which is computed from K, a private key held secret by the owner. K is required by D_K for decrypting a message, but anyone who wishes to encrypt a message to send to the private key owner can use the published key X to encrypt a message and then send it to them. The idea is that X is easy to compute from K, but that K is computationally difficult to produce from X. How this is achieved is dependent on the algorithm, but, for example, Rivest–Shamir–Adleman (RSA) uses prime numbers and the fact that factoring large prime numbers is currently extremely difficult without a huge amount of computing power [r203].

diffserv   Popular mechanism to provide Quality of Service (QoS) in enterprise IP networks. It is based on using codepoints in the IP packet that specify the priority of the packet. Routers and switches need to understand the codepoints and appropriately manage queues in order to deliver the intended service. Mechanism is indispensable for Voice over IP (VoIP) and IPTV (video over IP) applications.

Digest Algorithm   A message digest is a compact digital signature for an arbitrarily long stream of binary data. An ideal message digest algorithm would never generate the same signature for two different sets of input, but achieving such theoretical perfection would require a message digest as long as the input file. Practical message digest algorithms compromise in favor of a digital signature of modest size created with an algorithm designed to make preparation of input text with a given signature computationally infeasible. Message digest algorithms have much in common with techniques used in encryption, but to a different end; verification that data have not been altered since the signature was published. Older applications requiring digital signatures employed 16- or 32-bit cyclical redundancy codes (CRC) originally developed to verify correct transmission in data communication protocols, but these short codes, while adequate to detect the kind of transmission errors for which they were intended, are insufficiently secure for applications such as electronic commerce and verification of security related software distributions.

The most commonly used present-day message digest algorithm is the 128-bit Message Digest 5 (MD5) algorithm, developed by Ron Rivest of the MIT Laboratory for Computer Science and RSA Data Security, Inc. The algorithm, with a reference implementation, was published as Internet RFC 1321 in 1992 and was placed into the public domain at that time. Message digest algorithms such as MD5 are not deemed "encryption technology" and are not subject to the export controls some governments impose on other data security products.

Digital   The characteristic of taking on only discrete values. Information that has been created, transmitted, or stored as a string of symbols specifically "1" (on) or "0" (off). Data in digital form (text, numbers, graphics, voice, video, etc.) can be stored and processed by computers and communicated over computer networks. Analog data, such as voice, video, physical parameters (temperature, pressure, oscillations), and so on, can be digitized via an analog-to-digital process which is either lossless or lossy.

Digital Certificate   (aka certificate) A certificate document in the form of a digital data object (a data object used by a computer) to which is appended a computed digital signature value that depends on the data object [r013].

The electronic equivalent of an ID card, which works in conjunction with public-key encryption to sign digital signatures. A digital certificate, which may contain a users name and other information, is issued by a Certification Authority (CA), which also keeps track of digital certificates that have been revoked [r057, r062].

Digital Document   An electronic data object that represents information originally written in a nonelectronic, nonmagnetic medium (usually ink on paper) or is an analogue of a document of that type [r013].

Digital Dozen   A list of 12 basic security requirements with which all Visa payment system constituents need comply under the Visa Cardholder Information Security Program. These 12 requirements are:

- Install and maintain a working firewall to protect data.
- Keep security patches up-to-date.
- Protect stored data.

- Encrypt data sent across public networks.
- Use and regularly update anti-virus software.
- Restrict access by "need to know."
- Assign unique ID to each person with computer access.
- Do not use vendor-supplied defaults for passwords and security parameters.
- Track all access to data by unique ID.
- Regularly test security systems and processes.
- Implement and maintain an information security policy.
- Restrict physical access to data.

Digital Enhanced Cordless Telecommunications (DECT)   Digital Enhanced (former European) Cordless Telecommunications is a short-range transmission protocol to support cordless handsets; it pre-dates Bluetooth technology.

Digital Envelope   A combination of encrypted content data (of any kind) and the content encryption key in an encrypted form that has been prepared for the use of the recipient. This is a hybrid encryption scheme to "seal" a message so that no one other than the intended recipient can "open" the message [r013].

Digital Evidence   (aka electronic evidence) Information stored or transmitted in binary form that may be relied upon in court.

Digital Fingerprint   A characteristic of a data item, such as a cryptographic checkvalue or the result of performing a one-way hash function on the data, that is sufficiently peculiar to the data item that it is computationally infeasible to find another data item that will possess the same characteristics [r068a].

Digital Identity   Digital artifacts created (in cyberspace) by users as they access websites and make use of services such as on-line banking, on-line trading, on-line shopping, access to paid-information, and so on. Target organizations create identities to provide individuals with secure access to on-line resources and services. As a consequence, multiple identities typically exist: End-users often employ different user names, passwords, and other identifying attributes in var-

ious on-line contexts due to practical limitations or out of a desire for anonymity. Also, the same person may have links to many organizations. The proliferation of digital identities creates challenges; for example, users may have difficulty remembering multiple usernames and passwords. There is a desire for maintaining security while enabling ever-increased access to information. "Federated Identity" is one solution to issue [r204].

Digital Linear Tape (DLT)   A family of tape device and media technologies developed by Quantum Corporation [r029].

Digital Media Network   Term can refer to a variety of arrangements ranging from multiple websites, to multiple television stations being centrally owned and operated. With the reduction in cost of custom controllable player devices, a new breed of digital media network is emerging, known under many different terms. The industry appears to be settling on the term digital signage to describe these new digital media networks, where custom images are digitally delivered to sign-like devices located throughout retail environments, or the enterprise [r203].

Digital Money   (financial term) A form of electronic money that can be used to pay for goods and services, most often on the Internet or another electronic medium. Upon receiving the buyer's authorization of the payment, the vendor contacts the issuing bank and receives a transfer of funds [r009].

Digital Notary   An analogous solution to a notary public, providing a trusted date-and-time stamp for a document, so that someone can later prove that the document existed at a point in time. A digital notary may also verify the signature(s) on a signed document before applying the stamp.

Digital Rights Management (DRM)   Set of capabilities to protect digital content. The goal of DRM is to manage all rights, not only the rights applicable to permissions over digital content. DRM includes security and encryption as a means to preclude unauthorized copying. More broadly, DRM covers the description, identification, trading, protection, monitoring, and tracking of all forms of rights usages over both tangible and intangible assets including management of rights holders' relationships.

Digital Signature   A unique cryptographic checksum (or signature) of data created with the use of Public Key Infrastructure (PKI) and one-way hash functions. The digital signature can be authenticated to ensure that the appropriate party signed the data. A digital signature is difficult to forge or repudiate. With the passage of the Electronic Signatures Act, digital signatures are finding increasing acceptance for conducting transactions, such as in contract exchange. Digital signatures, in the context of Message Authentication Codes, are used to verify the integrity of data, such as in financial transactions.

Digital Signature Algorithm (DSA)   An asymmetric cryptographic algorithm that produces a digital signature in the form of a pair of large numbers. The signature is computed using rules and parameters such that the identity of the signer and the integrity of the signed data can be verified.

Digital Signature Algorithm (DSA) Signature   A signature using DSA. DSA is a U.S. Government standard for digital signatures advanced by National Institute of Standards and Technology (NIST) in 1991 as part of the Digital Signature Standard (DSS). The DSA signature algorithm is defined in FIPS-186, the first version of the official DSA specification. DSA is always used with the Secure Hash Algorithm 1 (SHA-1) (RFC 3174) message digest algorithm. FIPS-186 has been updated over time as follows: (i) FIPS-186, change notice No.1, the first change notice to the first version of the specification; (ii) FIPS-186-1, the first revision to the official DSA specification; (iii) FIPS-186-2, the second revision to the official DSA specification.

Digital Signature Applications   Principally used for authentication. The Digital signature can also be used to certify that a public key belongs to a particular entity. This is done by signing the combination of the public key and the information about its owner by a trusted key. The resulting data structure is often called a public-key certificate (or simply, a certificate) [r036].

Digital Signature Archive   An archive of digital signatures for the purpose of verifying digital signatures long after the original signing event. This is necessary because the Certification Authority that originally issued the certificate used the sign the data may no longer be in operation.

Digital Signature Schemes   A Digital Signature is "data appended to, or a cryptographic transformation of, a data unit that allows a recipient of the data unit to prove the source and integrity of the data unit and protect against forgery—for example, by the recipient" [r160]. Typically, the data object is first input to a hash function, and then the hash result is cryptographically transformed using a private key of the signer. The final resulting value is called the digital signature of the data object. The signature value is a protected checksum, because the properties of a cryptographic hash ensure that if the data object is changed, the digital signature will no longer match it. The digital signature is unforgeable because one cannot be certain of correctly creating or changing the signature without knowing the private key of the supposed sign [r013].

Some digital signature schemes use a asymmetric encryption algorithm [e.g., Rivest–Shamir–Adleman (RSA)] to transform the hash result. Thus, when Alice needs to sign a message to send to Bob, she can use her private key to encrypt the hash result. Bob receives both the message and the digital signature. Bob can use Alice's public key to decrypt the signature, and then compare the plaintext result to the hash result that he computes by hashing the message himself. If the values are equal, Bob accepts the message because he is certain that it is from Alice and has arrived unchanged. If the values are not equal, Bob rejects the message because either the message or the signature was altered in transit [r013].

Other digital signature schemes [e.g., Digital Signature Standard (DSS)] transform the hash result with an algorithm [e.g., Digital Signature Algorithm (DSA), El Gamal] that cannot be directly used to encrypt data. Such a scheme creates a signature value from the hash and provides a way to verify the signature value, but does not provide a way to recover the hash result from the signature value. In some countries, such a scheme may improve exportability and avoid other legal constraints on usage [r013].

Digital Signature Schemes, Taxonomy of   Two classes: (i) Signature schemes with message recovery and (ii) Signature schemes with appendix.

Signature schemes with message recovery: a digital signature scheme that does not require prior knowledge of the message for the verification; the message is recovered from the signature itself. Examples include Rivest–Shamir–Adleman (RSA), Rabin, Nyberg–Rueppel, and so on.

Signature schemes with appendix: schemes that require the message as input to the verification algorithm. These schemes are more commonly used scheme as opposed to schemes with message recovery. The schemes rely on cryptographic hash functions rather than customized redundancy functions. Examples include Digital Signature Algorithm (DSA), ElGamal, Schnorr, and so on.

Digital Signature Standard (DSS)   A standard for digital signing, including the Digital Signature Algorithm (DSA), approved by the National Institute of Standards and Technology [r039, r205, r206].

Digital Signatures, Goals   Digital Signatures provide authentication, data integrity, and non-repudiation. A Digital Signature is a data string that associates a message with some originating entity. A Digital Signature Scheme is comprised of a signature generation algorithm and an associated verification algorithm.

Digital Subscriber Line (DSL)   A transmission technology that allows existing copper loops in the Public Switched Telephone Network (PSTN) to be upgraded to support digital transmission and to operate in the 384–768 kbps in the uplink and 1.544–3.128 Mbps in the down link. Typically used for Internet access by individuals or small businesses.

Digital Video   Video signal that has been digitized so that it can be stored on digital media, transmitted over a digital network, and/or controlled from a PC (and displayed directly on a computer monitor). Techniques of lossy digitization now generally involve Moving Pictures Expert Group 2 (MPEG-2) or MPEG-4.

Digital Video Tape Standard D1   A traditional format for digital video tape recording supporting the ITU-R 601, 4:2:2 standard using 8-bit sampling. The tape is 19 mm wide and allows up to 94 minutes to be recorded on a cassette. Being a component recording system, it is ideal for studio or post-production work with its high chrominance bandwidth allowing excellent chroma keying. Also multiple generations are possible with very little degradation and D1 equipment can integrate without transcoding to most digital effects systems, telecines, graphics devices, disk recorders, and so on. Since the stored signal is component-based there are no color framing requirements. Despite the advantages, D1 equipment is not extensively used in general areas of TV production, at least partly due to its high cost [r207].

Digital Video Tape Standard D16   A traditional recording format for digital film images that makes use of standard D1 recorders. The scheme was developed specifically to handle Quantel's Domino pictures and record them over the space that sixteen 625 line digital pictures would occupy. This way three film frames can be recorded or played every two seconds. Playing the recorder allows the film images to be viewed on a standard monitor; running at x16 speed shows full motion direct from the tape [r207].

Digital Video Tape Standard D2   A traditional recording format standard for digital composite (coded) Phase Alternating Line (PAL) or National Television Standards Committee (NTSC) signals. It uses 19 mm tape and records up to 208 minutes on a single cassette. Neither cassettes nor recording formats are compatible with D1. D2 has often been used as a direct replacement for 1-inch analogue Video Tape Recorders (VTRs). Although offering good stunt modes and multiple generations with low losses, being a coded system means coded characteristics are present: the user must be aware of cross-color, transcoding footprints, low chrominance bandwidths and color framing sequences. Employing an 8-bit format to sample the whole coded signal results in reduced amplitude resolution making D2 more susceptible to contouring artifacts [r207].

Digital Video Tape Standard D3   A traditional Video Tape Recorder (VTR) standard using 1/2-inch tape cassettes for recording digitized composite (coded) Phase Alternating Line (PAL) or National Television Standards Committee (NTSC) signals sampled at 8 bits. Cassettes are available for 50 to 245 minutes. Since this uses a composite signal the characteristics are generally as for D2 except that the 1/2-inch cassette size has allowed a full family of VTR equipment to be realized in one format, including a camcorder.

Digital Video Tape Standard D4   There is no D4. Most Digital Video Tape Recorder (DVTR) formats originate from Japan where 4 is regarded as an unlucky number [r208].

Digital Video Tape Standard D5   A traditional Video Tape Recorder (VTR) format that uses the same cassette as D3 but records component signals sampled to ITU-R 601 recommendations at 10-bit resolution. With internal decoding, D5 VTRs can play back D3 tapes and provide component outputs. Being a noncompressed component digital video recorder means that D5 enjoys all the performance benefits of D1, making it suitable for high-end post production as well as more general studio use. Besides servicing the current 625 and 525 line TV standards, the format also has provision for HDTV recording by use of about 4:1 compression (HD D5) [r208].

Digital Video Tape Standard D6   A traditional digital tape format that uses a 19-mm helical-scan cassette tape to record uncompressed High-Definition Television (HDTV) material at 1.88 GB/s. D6 is currently the only High Definition recording format defined by a recognized standard. D6 accepts both the European 1250/50 interlaced format and the Japanese 260M version of the 1125/60 interlaced format that uses 1035 active lines. It does not accept the International Telecommunication Union (ITU) format of 1080 active lines. ANSI/SMPTE 277M and 278M are D6 standards [r207].

Digital Watermark   An identifying embedded mark (embedded bits of data) in a media, file, or document that cannot be removed from a digital document. The watermark contains hidden identification information and is typically used to track the propagation of copyrighted materials or to assure data integrity.

Digital Watermarking   The act of placing a digital watermark on an electronic object.

Direct Attached Storage (DAS)   Storage technology that provides individual (dedicated) storage for each server on a network. Storage hardware that connects to a single server. DAS technology utilizes either dedicated Fibre Channel (FC) or Small Computer System Interface (SCSI) host connectivity. Reliability is an issue in this context. Some vendors address this by eliminating of all single points of failure, providing centralized management and monitoring of all DAS subsystems. Typical Applications for DAS Subsystems: Clustering, Enterprise High-Performance Systems, Disk-to-Disk Backup, Audio/Video Application Storage.

Direct Evidence   Evidence such as oral testimony by an incident handler or system administrator that may be presented in a Court of Law.

Direct Financing   Financing without the use of underwriting.

Direct Sequence Spread Spectrum (DSSS) Radio   Wireless Local Area Network (WLAN) radio transmission technology in the 2.4-GHz band.

Directivity   (optical transmission term) (also called near-end crosstalk) the ratio of the optical power launched into an input port to the optical power returning to any other input port (dB).

Director of Central Intelligence   Individual that has authority (among other responsibilities) for computer systems that contain intelligence information.

Director of the Office of Management and Bud-

get **(OMB)**   Individual authorized to oversee the development of, and ensure compliance with, policies, principles, standards, and guidelines governing the security of all U.S. federal computer systems, except for national security computer systems [r208].

Directors   (Communications context) High-end version of storage switches [Fibre Channel (FC), Fibre Connectivity (FICON), Enterprise System Connection (ESCON)] that are designed specifically with 32+ ports and are highly available. These usually have redundant switch cores and are based upon a bladed architecture [r028].

Directory   A repository of information, oftentimes containing user identity information.

Directory Access Protocol (DAP)   An Open Systems Interconnection Reference Model (OSIRM) protocol for communication between a Directory User Agent (a client) and a Directory System Agent (a server) [r209].

Directory Recursion Attack   Distributed denial-of-service (DDoS) attacks against the Internet's domain name system (DNS).

Directory Services Grid Tools   Applications and systems on a grid must be capable of discovering what services are available to them; this is done via a Directory Service. The tolls are typically based on the Lightweight Directory Access Protocol (LDAP) [r080].

directory vs. Directory   Not capitalized: The term "directory" refers generically to a database server or other system that provides information—such as a digital certificate or certificate revocation list (CRL)—about an entity whose name is known [r013].

Capitalized: "Directory" refers specifically to the X.500 Directory [r013].

DISA   See Defense Information Systems Agency

Disaster Recovery   The steps that are taken to continue support for critical functions.

Disaster Recovery Planning   Documented, detailed plan describing the steps a company would take to restore computer operations in the event of a disaster. The disaster recover plan typically contains four components: the emergency plan, the backup plan, the recovery plan, and the test plan [r202].

Disaster Recovery Testing   Documented, detailed plan describing the steps to test the Disaster Recovery Plan.

Disclosure   (financial term) The act of revealing to shareholders any company information (financial or operational) that has or may have a material impact on a company's public financial statements.

Discontinuous Transmission (DTX)   (GSM context) In Discontinuous Transmission, the Voice Activity Detection algorithm deactivates the sender of a mobile station when there is no data to be transmitted [r011].

Discount Factor   (financial term) Present value of a $1 future payment.

Discount Rate   (financial term) The rate that describes the difference between the face value (e.g., the face value of a bond) and the actual market value (e.g., market value of a bond). Rate used to compute present values of future cash flows (e.g., 15%).

Discrete Logarithms   Addresses the problem of finding n given only some y such that $y = g^n$. One divides the infinite set of integers into a finite set of remainder classes. One can map the set of integers onto a circle (say with circumference of length m). The numbers $0, m, 2m, 3m, \ldots$ all cover the same point on the circle, and therefore are said to be in the same equivalence class [we also write "$0 = m = 2m = \ldots (mod\ m)$"]. Each equivalence class has a least representative in $0 \ldots m - 1$. So one can write any integer n as $t + km$ for any integer t, where $0 \le t < m$. It is a convention to write $n = t\ (mod\ m)$ in this case. Here m is said to be the *modulus*. It can be shown that one can add, subtract, and multiply with these classes of integers (modulo some m). This structure, when $m = p$ with p a prime number, is often called a prime field or a Galois field, GF(p). When m is prime, the division of nonzero integer classes is well defined. It is a *finite field* of characteristic p, where p is the modulus. If m is not a prime number then the structure is called a (finite) *ring*. The discrete logarithm problem in the finite field GF(p) is then stated as follows: given two positive nonzero integers a, g (both less than p), compute n such that $a = g^n \ (mod \ p)$. We can choose g so that a solution for n exists for any nonzero a. To make this problem cryptographically hard p should be a large prime number (about 10^{300}) and n, in general, of same magnitude. This problem is currently considered as hard as factoring. The best method known at this time is the Number Field Sieve (NFS) for discrete logarithms (which uses similar ideas as the NFS for factoring) [r036].

Discretionary Access Control (DAC)   An access control service that enforces a security policy based on the identity of system entities and their authorizations to access system resources. This service is termed "discretionary" because an entity might have access rights that permit the entity, by its own volition, to enable another entity to access some resource [r013, r215].

Discretionary Access Control List (DACL)   A security mechanism used in the New Technology File System (NTFS), which is used in modern Windows Operating Systems (OSs). DACLs represent a set of NTFS permissions. Individual permissions in the DACL are called Access Control Entities. Permissions include, for example, file read, write, etc.

Disk Operating System (DOS)   Original Operating system for PCs developed by Microsoft in the early to mid-1980s.

Disk-to-Disk Backup (D2D)   (aka Virtual Tape) A relatively new storage technology where data are transferred in real time to a local or remote backup device for the purpose of recovery protection. Provides the ability to randomly store and retrieve data. Considered to support a lower cost per megabyte for small to enterprise-class environments: D2D solutions provide disk-based backup alternatives of similar capacity that are two to ten times less expensive than tape based on initial purchase costs [the total cost of ownership (TCO) also demonstrates increased savings]. D2D backup solutions provide a high degree of reliability and availability utilizing Redundant Array of In-

expensive Disks (RAID) sets, full hot-pluggable redundancy, predictive and preemptive on-line monitoring, higher data rates, on-site on-line random file accessibility, off-site on-line random file accessibility for disaster recovery and the simplicity of disk storage compared to conventional tape backup operations.

Performance: When evaluating a medium for backup and recovery functions, the speed with which the medium accesses files and reads and writes data is probably the most significant factor in determining the medium's value. D2D systems can access files much more quickly than tape because of D2D's ability to randomly store and retrieve data. Its read/write heads fly directly to a new location as soon as it receives an address from the CPU. File access on tape media occurs much more slowly than on hard disk. A system must find the location on the tape at which the desired file is stored. Accessing an address on linear media that must be wound or unwound to make the location available for read/write takes substantially more time than accessing an address on a circular disk [r213].

On-Line Immediate Recovery: D2D provides unrestricted restore options, including double-click restores for ease of use. D2D provides the availability of immediate file access. Backup files appear to the operating systems as the original files. In the event of a server crash or a virus attack, D2D users can immediately redirect the data path to the last known best version. This provides the ability to be up and running immediately allowing for an off-line server restore or rebuild [r213].

Hot Disaster Recovery: D2D not only supports a primary on-line, on-site system but also makes it possible to co-locate a secondary D2D on-line disaster recovery system off-site. This solution provides immediate access to data in the event of the catastrophic loss of a data center via LAN, WAN, Fibre Channel, Copper, and Internet connections [r213].

Capacity and Scalability: D2D offers capacity starting at 400 GB to multi-TB. The data is secured on a disk-based RAID system in a compressed format, delivering fault-tolerant unrestricted configuration options at an overall, industry-wide, lowest cost per megabyte. D2D offers significant advantages in terms of scalability compared to tape; with D2D, a manager can increase storage capacity with no additional application-based tape library slots or drive license charges [r213].

Dispersion-Shifted Fiber (DSF) (optical transmission term) Transmission fibers optimized for operation at 1550 nm. Regular single-mode fibers exhibit lowest attenuation performance at 1550 nm and optimum bandwidth at 1310 nm. DSFs are made so that both attenuation and bandwidth are optimal at 1550 nm. Fiber suitable for Synchronous Optical Network/Synchronous Digital Hierarchy/Time Division Multiplexing (SONET/SDH/TDM) use in the 1550-nm region, but not suitable for Dense Wavelength Division Multiplexing (DWDM) in this region.

Disruption A circumstance or event that interrupts or prevents the correct operation of system services and functions [r013].

Distance Vector A routing protocols technology that propagates routing information as network identifier and its distance as hops numbers [r008].

Distinguished Encoding Rules (DERs) Abstract Syntax Notation One (ASN.1) encoding rules specified in ITU.X690.2002, International Telecommunications Union, "Information Technology—ASN.1 encoding rules: Specification of Basic Encoding Rules (BERs), Canonical Encoding Rules (CERs) and Distinguished Encoding Rules (DER)," ITU-T Recommendation X.690, July 2002.

A subset of the BERs which gives exactly one way to represent any ASN.1 value as an octet string [r210]. Since there is more than one way to encode ASN.1 in BERs, DERs are used in applications in which a unique encoding is needed, such as when a digital signature is computed on an ASN.1 value [r013].

Distinguished Name (DN) An identifier that uniquely represents an object in the X.500 Directory Information Tree (DIT) [r211]. A DN is a set of attribute values that identify the path leading from the base of the Directory Information Tree (DIT) to the object that is named. An X.509 public-key certificate or Certificate Revocation List (CRL) contains a DN that identifies its issuer, and an X.509 attribute certificate contains a DN or other form of name that identifies its subject [r013].

Distinguishing Identifier Data that uniquely identifies an entity.

Distributed Authentication Security Service (DASS) An experimental Internet protocol [r212] that uses cryptographic mechanisms to provide strong, mutual authentication services in a distributed environment [r013].

Distributed Denial of Service Attack (DDoS) A Denial of Service (DoS) attack in which malicious code is installed on a very large number of machines. These machines are then coerced to act in concert with the other compromised machines, sending out messages to flood the systems of the target.

Distribution Point An X.500 Directory entry or other information source that is named in a version 3 X.509 public-key certificate extension as a location from which to obtain a Certificate Revocation List (CRL) that might list the certificate [r013].

Diversifying Risk A risk management technique that spreads the risk from a single activity or asset to multiple activities or assets to minimize losses.

DLCI See Data Link Connection Identifier

DLM See Data Lifecycle Management

DLT See Digital Linear Tape

DMP See Detour Merge Point

DMZ See Demilitarized Zone

DN See Distinguished Name

DNS See Domain Name System

DNSBL See Domain Name System (DNS) Blacklist

DNSSEC See DNS Security Extensions

DOCSIS See Data Over Cable Service Interface Specification

Document Management [aka document imaging

system, enterprise content management (ECM)] Mechanisms to manage the document life-cycle, versions, metadata, and so on, namely, record retention and archiving. Typically entails a storage capability; it may also include a workflow capability. Features include the ability to manage both electronic and paper records, and supporting at long-term availability and legal admissibility of electronic documents.

Document Timestamping   Method to authoritatively add a date to a document. Digital signatures can be used to timestamp documents: A trusted party signs the document and its timestamp with his/her private key, thus testifying that the document existed at the stated time [r036].

Documentation   In the current context, the codification and storage of information, algorithms, data, design approaches, architecture, and so on, associated with an Information Technology (IT) system. Documentation is important to the security of the system in that it explains how software/hardware is to be used and formalizes security and operational procedures specific to the system. Examples of documentation for a system includes descriptions of the hardware and software, policies, standards, procedures, and approvals and agreements related to automated information system security, backup and contingency activities as well as descriptions of user and operator procedures [r067].

DoD   See Department of Defense

DOI   See Domain of Interpretation

Domain   (Security context) An environment or context that is defined by a security policy, security model, or security architecture to include a set of system resources and the set of system entities that have the right to access the resources [r013].

(Instant Messaging/Presence context) A portion of a Namespace [r027].

(Internet context) That part of the Internet domain name space tree that is at or below the name that specifies the domain [r218]. A domain is a subdomain of another domain if it is contained within that domain. For example, D.C.B.A is a subdomain of C.B.A. [r013].

(Multilevel Information System Security Initiative context) The set of MISSI users whose certificates are signed by the CA [r013].

Domain Controller   A server in a Windows environment that helps to manage the Active Directory (AD) database on behalf of the computers and users in the organization.

Domain Name   The style of identifier—a sequence of case-insensitive American Standard Code for Information Interchange (ASCII) labels separated by dots ("bbn.com.")—defined for subtrees in the Internet Domain Name System [r218] and used in other Internet identifiers, such as host names (e.g., "rosslyn.bbn.com."), mailbox names (e.g., "minoli@att.net."), and Uniform Resource Locators (URLs) (e.g., "http://www.cnn.com") [r013].

The domain name space of the DNS is a tree structure in which each node and leaf holds records describing a resource. Each node has a label. The domain name of a node is the list of labels on the path from the node to the root of the tree. The labels in a domain name are printed or read left to right, from the most specific (lowest, farthest from the root) to the least specific (highest, closest to the root). The root's label is the null string, so a complete domain name properly ends in a dot. The top-level domains, those immediately below the root, include COM, EDU, GOV, INT, MIL, NET, ORG, and two-letter country codes (such as U.S.) from International Organization for Standardization (ISO) International Standard (IS) 3166 [r219]. New extensions are added over time [r013].

Domain Name System (DNS)   The main Internet operations database, which is distributed over a collection of servers and used by client software for purposes such as translating a domain name-style host name into an IP address (e.g., "rosslyn.bbn.com" is "192.1.7.10") and locating a host that accepts mail for some mailbox address [r218, r013].

The DNS has three major components [r013]:

- Domain name space and resource records: Specifications for the tree-structured domain name space, and data associated with the names.
- Name servers: Programs that hold information about a subset of the tree's structure and data holdings, and also hold pointers to other name servers that can provide information from any part of the tree.
- Resolvers: Programs that extract information from name servers in response to client requests; typically, system routines directly accessible to user programs.

Extensions to the DNS [r220, r222] support (a) key distribution for public keys needed for the DNS and for other protocols, (b) data origin authentication service and data integrity service for resource records, (c) data origin authentication service for transactions between resolvers and servers, and (d) access control of records.

Domain Name System (DNS) Blacklist (DNSBL) (aka an RBL or Real-time Blackhole List) A type of filter based on the Internet address of an incoming e-mail connection. Basically, mail arrives with a hello from another e-mail server. The DNSBL filter is built to lookup and compare the incoming IP address to an online listing of undesirable IP addresses. This listing resides as a zone or a special domain on a DNS server. If the incoming address is blacklisted, (i.e., if a match on the IP address is found) the connection is rejected. This process happens early in a Simple Mail Transport Protocol (SMTP) transaction [r216].

The DNSBL is maintained in the form of IP zone data on a particular DNS server, or hierarchy of servers. This data can be supplied through complaints, through automated testing, through statistics, through information derived from WHOIS information, and so on [r216].

Domain Name System (DNS) Protocol Changes to Support DNS Security Extensions (DNSSEC) The DNSSEC mechanisms require changes to the DNS protocol. DNSSEC adds four new resource record types: Resource Record Sig-

nature (RRSIG), DNS Public Key (DNSKEY), Delegation Signer (DS), and Next Secure (NSEC). It also adds two new message header bits: Checking Disabled (CD) and Authenticated Data (AD). In order to support the larger DNS message sizes that result from adding the DNSSEC Resource Records (RRs), DNSSEC also requires EDNS0 support (RFC 2671). Finally, DNSSEC requires support for the DNSSEC OK (DO) EDNS header bit (RFC 3225) so that a security-aware resolver can indicate in its queries that it wishes to receive DNSSEC Resource Records (RRs) in response messages. DNSSEC provides authentication by associating cryptographically generated digital signatures with DNS RRsets. These digital signatures are stored in a new resource record, the RRSIG record. Typically, there will be a single private key that signs a zone's data, but multiple keys are possible. For example, there may be keys for each of several different digital signature algorithms. If a security-aware resolver reliably learns a zone's public key, it can authenticate that zone's signed data. An important DNSSEC concept is that the key that signs a zone's data is associated with the zone itself and not with the zone's authoritative name servers. (Public keys for DNS transaction authentication mechanisms may also appear in zones [r069].)

Domain Name System (DNS) Security Extensions (DNSSEC) Refers to the core hierarchical public key and signature mechanism specified in the DNSSEC documents. A collection of new Resource Records (RR) and protocol modifications that add data origin authentication and data integrity to the DNS [r216]. The DNS security extensions provide origin authentication and integrity protection for DNS data, as well as a means of public-key distribution. These extensions do not provide confidentiality.

Effort was under development for most of the last decade [the earliest organized work on DNSSEC within the Internet Engineering Task Force (IETF) was performed by the DNS working group in November 1993]. This group was interested in protecting against disclosure of DNS data to unauthorized parties. The design team has made an explicit decision that "DNS data is public." Backwards compatibility and coexistence with "insecure DNS" has been an explicit requirement. The resulting list of desired security services was (1) data integrity and (2) data origin authentication. The design team noted that a digital signature mechanism would support the desired services. While a number of detail decisions were yet to be made (and in some cases remade after implementation experience) over the subsequent decade, the basic model and design goals have remained fixed [r111].

DNSSEC (when used properly) does provide an end-to-end data integrity check. Note, however, that DNSSEC does not provide any protection against modification of the DNS message header, so any (paranoid) resolver must [r111]:

- Perform all of the DNSSEC signature checking on its own.
- Use TSIG (or some equivalent mechanism) to ensure the integrity of its communication with whatever name servers it chooses to trust. Or
- Resign itself to the possibility of being attacked via packet interception.

RFC 4033 (*DNS Security Introduction and Requirements the Domain Name System Security Extensions*) and its two companion documents RFC 4034 and RFC 4035, update, clarify, and refine the security extensions defined in RFC 2535 and its predecessors. These security extensions consist of a set of new resource record types and modifications to the existing DNS protocol (RFC 1035).

Domain Name System (DNS) Security Extensions (DNSSEC), Weaknesses   DNSSEC weaknesses include [r112]:

- DNSSEC is complex to implement and includes some nasty edge cases at the zone cuts that require very careful coding. Testbed experience to date suggests that trivial zone configuration errors or expired keys can cause serious problems for a DNSSEC-aware resolver, and that the current protocol's error reporting capabilities may leave something to be desired.
- DNSSEC significantly increases the size of DNS response packets; among other issues, this makes DNSSEC-aware DNS servers even more effective as denial of service amplifiers.
- DNSSEC answer validation increases the resolver's workload, since a DNSSEC-aware resolver will need to perform signature validation and in some cases will also need to issue further queries. This increased workload will also increase the time it takes to get an answer back to the original DNS client, which is likely to trigger both timeouts and re-queries in some cases. Arguably, many current DNS clients are already too impatient even before taking the further delays that DNSSEC will impose into account, but that topic is beyond the scope of this note.
- Like DNS itself, DNSSEC's trust model is almost totally hierarchical. While DNSSEC does allow resolvers to have special additional knowledge of public keys beyond those for the root, in the general case the root key is the one that matters. Thus any compromise in any of the zones between the root and a particular target name can damage DNSSEC's ability to protect the integrity of data owned by that target name. This is not a change, since insecure DNS has the same model.
- Key rollover at the root is hard. Work to date has not even come close to adequately specifying how the root key rolls over, or even how it is configured in the first place.
- DNSSEC creates a requirement of loose time synchronization between the validating resolver and the entity creating the DNSSEC signatures. Prior to DNSSEC, all time-related actions in DNS could be performed by a machine that only knew about "elapsed" or "relative" time. Because the validity period of a DNSSEC signature is based on "absolute" time, a validating resolver must have the same

concept of absolute time as the zone signer in order to determine whether the signature is within its validity period or has expired. An attacker that can change a resolver's opinion of the current absolute time can fool the resolver using expired signatures. An attacker that can change the zone signer's opinion of the current absolute time can fool the zone signer into generating signatures whose validity period does not match what the signer intended.

- The possible existence of wildcard Resource Records (RRs) in a zone complicates the authenticated denial mechanism considerably. For most of the decade that DNSSEC has been under development these issues were poorly understood. At various times there have been questions as to whether the authenticated denial mechanism is completely airtight and whether it would be worthwhile to optimize the authenticated denial mechanism for the common case in which wildcards are not present in a zone. However, the main problem is just the inherent complexity of the wildcard mechanism itself. This complexity probably makes the code for generating and checking authenticated denial attestations somewhat fragile, but since the alternative of giving up wildcards entirely is not practical due to widespread use, we are going to have to live with wildcards. The question just becomes one of whether or not the proposed optimizations would make DNSSEC's mechanisms more or less fragile.

- Even with DNSSEC, the class of attacks discussed earlier is not easy to defeat. In order for DNSSEC to be effective in this case, it must be possible to configure the resolver to expect certain categories of DNS records to be signed. This may require manual configuration of the resolver, especially during the initial DNSSEC rollout period when the resolver cannot reasonably expect the root and Top-Level Domain (TLD) zones to be signed.

Domain Name System (DNS) Service   A service (mechanism) that allows users to employ names

(e.g., www.cnn.com) to identify web servers, rather than using native IP addresses (e.g., 216.17.43.102). It provides a mechanism to translate domain names (such as cnn.com) to their actual network IP addresses (for example 165.137.228.156). It is more convenient for users to remember the domain name than to remember the actual IP address. The DNS server maintains a mapping of domain names and IP addresses. The server(s) takes an incoming request and point the session to the corresponding IP address. Key Request For Comments (RFCs) include RFC 1034, RFC 1035, RFC 1123, RFC 2181, RFC 2308, RFC 2671, RFC 2845, RFC 2930, RFC3007, and RFC 2535.

Managing a single database of all domain names and IP addresses in the world would be taxing, hence the burden has been distributed around the world. Firms can also choose to do so maintain their own DNS servers; this may be done at a proxy. At press time there were 13 root servers that contain the authoritative name server information for every top-level domain (e.g., .com, .net, .us, .uk).

The clients can be pointed to the internal DNS server as the primary server and to the external server as the secondary server; otherwise, all clients can be pointed directly to the primary external server.

Domain Name System (DNS) Spoofing   Situation where a DNS server accepts and uses incorrect information from a host that has no authority giving that information. Can be described as malicious cache poisoning where forged data is placed in the cache of the DNS servers. Spoofing attacks can cause serious security problems—for example, causing users to be directed to wrong Internet sites or e-mail being routed to non-authorized mail servers. In order to prevent attacks, it is necessary to have the security built into DNS systems.

Domain Name System (DNS) Threats   There are several classes of threats to the DNS, most of which are DNS-related instances of more general problems, but a few of which are specific to peculiarities of the DNS protocol [r111]: (1) Packet Interception, (2) ID Guessing and Query Prediction, (3) Name Chaining, (4) Betrayal By Trusted Server, (5) Denial of Service, (6) Spoofing, and (7) Wildcards.

Domain Name System (DNS) Threats, Betrayal By Trusted Server   A variation on the packet interception attack where the trusted server that turns out not to be so trustworthy, whether by accident or by intent [r111]. Many client machines are only configured with stub resolvers, and use trusted servers to perform all of their DNS queries on their behalf. In many cases the trusted server is furnished by the user's Internet Service Provider (ISP) and advertised to the client via Dynamic Host Configuration Protocol (DHCP) or Point-to-Point Protocol (PPP) options. Besides accidental betrayal of this trust relationship (via server bugs, successful server break-ins, etc.), the server itself may be configured to give back answers that are not what the user would expect, whether in an honest attempt to help the user or to promote some other goal such as furthering a business partnership between the ISP and some third party. This problem is particularly acute for frequent travelers who carry their own equipment and expect it to work in much the same way wherever they go. Such travelers need trustworthy DNS service without regard to who operates the network into which their equipment is currently plugged or what brand of middle devices the local infrastructure might use.

Domain Name System (DNS) Threats, Denial of Service   As with any network service (or, indeed, almost any service of any kind in any domain of discourse), DNS is vulnerable to denial of service attacks. DNS Security Extensions (DNSSEC) may in fact make the problem worse for resolvers that check signatures, since checking signatures both increases the processing cost per DNS message and in some cases can also increase the number of messages needed to answer a query [r111]. Transaction Authentication for DNS (TSIG) (and similar mechanisms) has

equivalent problems. DNS servers are also at risk of being used as denial of service amplifiers, since DNS response packets tend to be significantly longer than DNS query packets.

Domain Name System (DNS) Threats, ID Guessing, and Query Prediction   Since DNS is for the most part used over User Datagram Protocol/Internet Protocol (UDP/IP), it is relatively easy for an attacker to generate packets which will match the transport protocol parameters [r111]. The ID field in the DNS header is only a 16-bit field and the server UDP port associated with DNS is a well-known value, so there are only 2^{32} possible combinations of ID and client UDP port for a given client and server. This is not a particularly large range and is not sufficient to protect against a brute force search; furthermore, in practice both the client UDP port and the ID can often be predicted from previous traffic, and it is not uncommon for the client port to be a known fixed value as well (due to firewalls or other restrictions), thus frequently reducing the search space to a range smaller than 2^{16} [r111].

By itself, ID guessing is not enough to allow an attacker to inject bogus data, but combined with knowledge (or guesses) about QNAMEs and QTYPEs for which a resolver might be querying, this leaves the resolver only weakly defended against injection of bogus responses. Since this attack relies on predicting a resolver's behavior, it is most likely to be successful when the victim is in a known state, whether because the victim rebooted recently, or because the victim's behavior has been influenced by some other action by the attacker, or because the victim is responding (in a predictable way) to some third-party action known to the attacker. A resolver that checks DNSSEC signatures will be able to detect the forged response; resolvers that do not perform DNS Security Extensions (DNSSEC) signature checking themselves should use TSIG or some equivalent mechanism to ensure the integrity of their communication with a recursive name server that does perform DNSSEC signature checking [r111].

Domain Name System (DNS) Threats, Name Chaining   Name chaining attacks are a subset of a larger class of name-based attacks, sometimes called "cache poisoning" attacks [r112]. Most name-based attacks can be partially mitigated by the long-standing defense of checking Resource Records (RRs) in response messages for relevance to the original query, but such defenses do not catch name chaining attacks. There are several variations on the basic attack, but what they all have in common is that they all involve DNS RRs whose RDATA portion (right-hand side) includes a DNS name (or, in a few cases, something that is not a DNS name but which directly maps to a DNS name). Any such RR is, at least in principle, a hook that lets an attacker feed bad data into a victim's cache, thus potentially subverting subsequent decisions based on DNS names.

The worst examples in this class of RRs are CNAME, NS, and DNAME RRs because they can redirect a victim's query to a location of the attacker's choosing. RRs like MX and SRV are somewhat less dangerous, but in principle they can also be used to trigger further lookups at a location of the attacker's choosing. Address RR types such as A or AAAA do not have DNS names in their RDATA, but since the IN-ADDR.ARPA and IP6.ARPA trees are indexed using a DNS encoding of IPv4 and IPv6 addresses, these record types can also be used in a name chaining attack [r111].

Domain Name System (DNS) Threats, Packet Interception   Some of the simplest threats against DNS are various forms of packet interception: monkey-in-the-middle attacks, eavesdropping on requests combined with spoofed responses that beat the real response back to the resolver, and so forth [r111]. In any of these scenarios, the attacker can simply tell either party (usually the resolver) whatever it wants that party to believe. While packet interception attacks are far from unique to DNS, DNS's usual behavior of sending an entire query or response in a single unsigned, unencrypted User Datagram Protocol (UDP) packet makes these attacks particularly easy for any "bad guy" with the ability to intercept packets on a shared or transit network. To further complicate things, the DNS query the attacker intercepts may just be a means to an end for the attacker: the attacker might even choose to return the correct result in the answer section of a reply message while using other parts of the message to set the stage for something more complicated, for example, a name chaining attack.

While it is possible to sign DNS messages using a channel security mechanism such as Transaction Authentication for DNS or IPsec, or even to encrypt them using IPsec, this would not be a very good solution for interception attacks. First, this approach would impose a fairly high processing cost per DNS message, as well as a very high cost associated with establishing and maintaining bilateral trust relationships between all the parties that might be involved in resolving any particular query. For heavily used name servers (such as the servers for the root zone), this cost would almost certainly be prohibitively high. Even more important, however, is that the underlying trust model in such a design would be wrong, since at best it would only provide a hop-by-hop integrity check on DNS messages and would not provide any sort of end-to-end integrity check between the producer of DNS data (the zone administrator) and the consumer of DNS data (the application that triggered the query [r111].

Domain Name System (DNS) Threats, Spoofing   The act of assuming the DNS name of another system by either corrupting the name service cache of a victim system, or by compromising a domain name server for a valid domain [r057].

Domain Name System (DNS) Threats, Wildcards   The issue relates to "wildcard" DNS names [r111]. Conceptually, Resource Records (RRs) with wildcard names are patterns for synthesizing RRs on the fly according to the matching rules described in RFC 1034. While the rules that control the behavior of wildcard names have a few quirks that can make them a trap for the unwary zone administrator, it is clear that a number of sites make heavy use of wildcard RRs, particularly wildcard MX RRs.

Domain Name System (DNS), Basic References
Basic DNS references include the following:

- Mockapetris, P., "Domain names—concepts and facilities," STD 13, RFC 1034, November 1987.
- Mockapetris, P., "Domain names—implementation and specification," STD 13, RFC 1035, November 1987.
- Braden, R., "Requirements for Internet Hosts—Application and Support," STD 3, RFC 1123, October 1989.
- Elz, R. and R. Bush, "Clarifications to the DNS Specification," RFC 2181, July 1997.
- Andrews, M., "Negative Caching of DNS Queries (DNS NCACHE)," RFC 2308, March 1998.
- Vixie, P., "Extension Mechanisms for DNS (EDNS0)," RFC 2671, August 1999.
- Vixie, P., Gudmundsson, O., Eastlake, D., 3rd, and B. Wellington, "Secret Key Transaction Authentication for DNS (TSIG)," RFC 2845, May 2000.
- Eastlake, D., 3rd, "Secret Key Establishment for DNS (TKEY RR)," RFC 2930, September 2000.
- Wellington, B., "Secure Domain Name System (DNS) Dynamic Update," RFC 3007, November 2000.
- Eastlake, D., 3rd, "Domain Name System Security Extensions," RFC 2535, March 1999.

Domain Names System (DNS)   A storage hierarchical system and its associated protocol to store and recover information about names and IP addresses [r008].

Domain of Interpretation (DOI)   IPsec usage: An Internet Security Association and Key Management Protocol (ISAKMP)/IKE (IPsec Key Exchange) DOI defines payload formats, exchange types, and conventions for naming security-relevant information such as security policies or cryptographic algorithms and modes [r223].

Dominate   Security level A is said to "dominate" security level B if the hierarchical classification level of A is greater (higher) than or equal to that of B and the nonhierarchical categories of A include all of those of B [r013].

Dongle   A portable, physical, electronic device that is required to be attached to a computer to enable a particular software program to run. A dongle is essentially a physical key used for copy protection of software, because the program will not run unless the matching dongle is attached. When the software runs, it periodically queries the dongle and quits if the dongle does not reply with the proper authentication information [r013].

DoS   See Denial of Service

DOS   See Disk Operating System

Double Colon   (IPv6 context) Compressing continuous series of 0 blocks, into IPv6 addresses like "::". For example, FF02:0:0:0:0:0:0:2 multicast address is expressed as FF02::2 [r008].

Downgrade   Reduce the classification level of information in an authorized manner

Downlink Shared Channel (DSCH)   (3G Wireless context) Channel used by several User Equipments simultaneously. The DSCH is always associated with a Dedicated Channel (DCH) [r007].

Downstream   (SIP context) A direction of message forwarding within a transaction that refers to the direction that requests flow from the user agent client to user agent server [r025].

Downtime   A measure of the system's inability to be used by a system entity. Downtime is increased when the system entity does not have reliable access to data or a system. An example cause of downtime is a Denial of Service (DoS) attack. Related to availability (uptime).

DPA   See Negotiated Data Protection Agreement

DPCCH   See Dedicated Physical Control Channel

DPCH   See Dedicated Physical Channel

DPDCH   See Dedicated Physical Data Channel

Draft Standard Protocol, Internet Engineering Task Force (IETF)   A specification from which at least two independent and interoperable implementations from different code bases have been developed, and for which sufficient successful operational experience has been obtained, may be elevated to the "Draft Standard" level. For the purposes of this definition, "interoperable" means to be functionally equivalent or inter-changeable components of the system or process in which they are used. If patented or otherwise controlled technology is required for implementation, the separate implementations must also have resulted from separate exercise of the licensing process. Elevation to Draft Standard is a major advance in status, indicating a strong belief that the specification is mature and will be useful [r290, r281].

DRM   See Digital Rights Management

Drift Radio Network Subsystem (DRNS)   (3G Wireless context) The main connection of a User Equipment to the network is realized via the Serving Radio Network Subsystem (RNS); further connections to the Node Bs of another RNS are possible. They are then called Drift RNS [r007].

Drive-by Downloads   Malicious spyware that requires no permission, interaction, or knowledge by the user in order to be downloaded and installed. The spyware application is delivered when the user visits a particular website, opens zipped files, or clicks on a malicious pop-up ad that contains some active content such as ActiveX, Java Applets, and so on. Spyware can also be hidden in image files or in some cases has been shipped along with the drivers that come with a new hardware device [r224].

DRNS   See Drift Radio Network Subsystem

DSA   See Digital Signature Algorithm

DSCH   See Downlink Shared Channel

DSF   See Dispersion-Shifted Fiber

DSL   See Digital Subscriber Line

DSS   See Digital Signature Standard

DSS Pseudo-random Number Generation   160-bit Pseudo-random numbers generated in the manner prescribed in the National Institute of Standards and Technology (NIST) Digital Signature Standard (DSS) Appendix 3.

DSSS   See Direct Sequence Spread Spectrum

DSV   See Dynamic Signature Verification

DTCH   See Dedicated Traffic Channel

DTE   See Data Terminal Equipment

DTX   See Discontinuous Transmission

Dual Control   A procedure that uses two or more entities (usually persons) operating in concert to protect a system resource, such that no single entity acting alone can access that resource [r013].

Dual Signature   A single digital signature defined by the Secure Electronic Transaction (SET) Specification that protects two separate messages by including the hash results for both sets in a single encrypted value [r013, r018]. This is generated by hashing each message separately, concatenating the two hash results, and then hashing that value and encrypting the result with the signer's private key. A dual signature is done to reduce the number of encryption operations and to enable verification of data integrity without complete disclosure of the data.

Dual Stack Communications   (IPv6 context) An IPv6/IPv4 nodes architecture in which two complete protocols stack implementations exist, one for IPv4 and another one for IPv6, each with its own implementations of the transport layer (Transmission Control Protocol (TCP) and User Datagram Protocol (UDP)) [r008].

Due Diligence   The process of investigation, performed by investors, into the details of a potential investment, such as an examination of operations and management and the verification of material facts [r009].

Duplicate Address Detection   The process by which a node determines that an address considered for use is not already in use by a neighboring node; this is equivalent to the use of gratuitous Address Resolution Protocol (ARP) frames in IPv4 [r024].

DVD-Video   (video formats and coding) Digital consumer-electronic format.

Dynamic Addresses   A number of systems, including several "blacklist" systems, are based on the assumption that most undesired e-mail originates from systems with dynamic addresses, especially dial-up and home broadband systems.

Consequently, they attempt to prevent the addresses from being used to send mail, or perform some other services, except through provider systems designated for that purpose. Different techniques are used to identify systems with dynamic addresses, including provider advertising of such addresses to blacklist operators, heuristics that utilize certain address ranges, and inspection of reverse-mapping domain names to see if they contain telltale strings such as "dsl" or "dial." In some cases, the absence of a reverse-mapping Domain Name System (DNS) address is taken as an indication that the address is "dynamic." [Prohibition on connections based on the absence of a reverse-mapping DNS record was a technique developed for File Transfer protocol (FTP) servers many years ago; it was found to have fairly high rates of failure, both prohibiting legitimate connection attempts and failing to prevent illegitimate ones.] Service providers should describe what they are doing in this area for both incoming and outgoing message traffic, and users should be aware that, if an address is advertised as "dynamic," it may be impossible to use it to send mail to an arbitrary system even if Full Internet Connectivity is otherwise provided [r034].

Dynamic Host Configuration Protocol (DHCP) Protocol is used to assign IP addresses to hosts or workstations on the network. A mechanism for passing configuration information to hosts on a Transmission Control Protocol/Internet Protocol (TCP/IP) network, using an options field; a development from the BOOTP Bootstrap Protocol. That is, a configuration protocol with "stateful" state that provides IP addresses and other configuration parameters to connect to an IP network [r008].

Internet Engineering Task Force (IETF) protocol (described in RFC 1533 and RFC 1534 and updated in RFC 2132) used to automate the assignment of private IP addresses to devices (Hosts) on a network. Rather than having (i) to manually inventory (tracking which ones are in use and remembering to place addresses back in the pool when devices go away), (ii) to assign, and then (iii) to load the IP address into the device, which would be the case without the services of DHCP, DHCP handles these tasks automatically. Each device that is configured to use DHCP communicates with the DHCP server on the network when it boots up, to request a network-unique IP address. The DHCP server assign an IP address from the address range it has been configured to use (e.g., from 192.3.4.1 to 192.3.4.255). The address has time horizon (lease duration). When the device leaves the network (e.g., it roams, it connects to another Ethernet segment on another subnet, or the machine is turned off), or when the lease expires, the IP address is placed back in the pool to be used by another device.

Dynamic Host Configuration Protocol (DHCP) Message Exchange   The DHCP protocol uses a 4-message exchange procedure. The 4-message exchange procedure allows for redundancy (multiple DHCP servers) without wasting addresses, as addresses are only provisionally assigned to a client until the client chooses and requests one of the provisionally assigned addresses. In some environments, such as those in which high mobility occurs and the network attachment point changes frequently, it is beneficial to rapidly configure clients. And, in these environments it is possible to more quickly configure clients because the protections offered by the 4-message exchange procedure. A 2-message exchange may therefore be used when only one server is present or when addresses are plentiful and having multiple servers commit addresses for a client is not a problem [r198].

Dynamic Host Configuration Protocol (DHCP) Spoofing   DHCP is used to automatically configure machines with an IP address so that the hosts do not have to be statically assigned IP addresses (DHCP helps reduce administration as a central server issues IP addresses to network cards upon request; DHCP also helps address the problem of a shortage of IP version 4 address as DHCP allows more machines than there are available IP addresses). Most Internet Service Providers (ISPs) that have dial up access use DHCP to set a modems IP address, as they assume that not every modem will be online at the same time) [r199].

An attacker by spoofing the clients' packet exchange will cause the DHCP server to give all the available leases to spoofed [Media Access Control (MAC)] address thus causing a denial of service (DoS). Any device wishing to join the network after the attack would not be allocated an IP address as the whole of the DHCP range will have been either allocated to valid interfaces (i.e., interfaces already joined to the network before the attack took place) or spoofed MAC addresses (from the attack). Any interface already joined to the network would not notice the effect of the attack as they have already been assigned an IP address, but interfaces without an IP address would not be able to join the network as the DHCP server will have no available IP addresses. Some DHCP servers issue Address Resolution Protocol (ARP) requests or Internet Control Message Protocol (ICMP) pings to detect for IP addresses that may be reclaimed by the server. This is done as Operating Systems (OS) and/or interfaces do not release there assigned IP address when shutdown. Basic testing of the denial of service code often successfully defeat the ARP method of reclaiming IP addresses as the number and speed of requests for IP addresses is significantly higher than the number of ARP requests issued by the DHCP server (when running multiple copies of the source code in a script) [r200].

Dynamic Host Configuration Protocol (DHCP) Starvation   A DHCP starvation attack works by broadcasting DHCP requests with spoofed Media Access Control (MAC) addresses. This is easily achieved with attack tools such as gobbler. If enough requests are sent, the network attacker can exhaust the address space available to the DHCP servers for a period of time. This is a simple resource starvation attack just like a SYN flood is a starvation attack. The network attacker can then set up a rogue DHCP server on his or her system and respond to new DHCP requests from clients on the network. Exhausting all of the DHCP addresses is not required to introduce a rogue DHCP server, though. As stated in RFC 2131: "The client collects DHCPOFFER messages over a period of time, selects one DHCPOFFER message from the (possibly many) incoming DHCPOFFER messages (for example, the first DHCPOFFER message or the DHCPOFFER message from the previously used server) and extracts the server address from the 'server identifier' option in the DHCPOFFER message. The time over which the client collects messages and the mechanism used to select one DHCPOFFER are implementation dependent." By placing a rogue DHCP server on the network, a network attacker can provide clients with addresses and other network information. Since DHCP responses typically include default gateway and DNS server information, the network attacker can supply his or her own system as the default gateway and DNS server resulting in a "man-in-the-middle" attack [r156].

Dynamic Signature Verification (DSV)   Signature verification technology uses conventional signature-captures devices but employs biometric verification using signature dynamics (e.g., pen flow, movement, etc.). DSV uses the behavioral biometrics of a hand-written signature to confirm the identity of a computer user.

E (GSM context) The E interface transmits signaling data as well as user data (i.e., speech) between two Mobile Services Switching Centers (MSCs) [r011].

E0 The cipher used in Bluetooth systems.

E.164 Addressing mechanism defined by the International Telecommunication Union (ITU) in recommendation ITU E.164 for the global numbering plan of the Public Switched Telephone Network (PSTN).

E.164 Domain Names A representation of an International Telecommunication Union (ITU) E.164 number that has been translated to conform to domain name syntax, as described in the ENUM specification [r225].

EAI See Enterprise Application Integration

EAM See Enterprise Access Management

EAP-TTL See Extensible Authentication Protocol Tunneled Transport Layer Security Authentication Protocol

EARL See End-Entity Attribute Certificate Revocation List

Earnings Before Interest and Taxes (EBIT) (financial term) Earnings before key expenses such as debit interest and income taxes are deducted. A measure of a company's earning power from ongoing operations, equal to earnings before deduction of interest payments and income taxes. EBIT excludes income and expenditure from unusual, non-recurring or discontinued activities. In the case of a company with minimal depreciation and amortization activities, EBIT is watched closely by creditors, since it represents the amount of cash that such a company will be able to use to pay off creditors. Also called operating profit [r009].

Earnings Before Interest, Taxes, Depreciation,

 Minoli–Cordovana's Authoritative Computer and Network Security Dictionary. By Daniel Minoli and James Cordovana
Copyright © 2006 John Wiley & Sons, Inc.

and Amortization (EBIDTA) (financial term) An approximate measure of a company's operating cash flow based on data from the company's income statement. Calculated by looking at earnings before the deduction of interest expenses, taxes, depreciation, and amortization. This earnings measure is of particular interest in cases where companies have large amounts of fixed assets which are subject to heavy depreciation charges (such as manufacturing companies) or in the case where a company has a large amount of acquired intangible assets on its books and is thus subject to large amortization charges (such as a company that has purchased a brand or a company that has recently made a large acquisition). EBIDTA is a good way of comparing companies within and across industries. This measure is also of interest to a company's creditors, since EBIDTA is essentially the income that a company has free for interest payments. In general, EBIDTA is a useful measure only for large companies with significant assets and/or for companies with a significant amount of debt financing. It is rarely a useful measure for evaluating a small company with no significant loans. Sometimes also called operational cash flow [r009].

Easter Egg   A type of Trojan Horse where an undocumented, unauthorized program functions in a production program.

Eavesdropping   Passive wiretapping done secretly, that is, without the knowledge of the originator or the intended recipients of the communication.

eBGP   See External Border Gateway Protocol

EBIDTA   See Earnings Before Interest, Taxes, Depreciation and Amortization

EBIT   See Earnings Before Interest and Taxes

EC   See Electronic Commerce

ECB   See Electronic Codebook

ECC   See Elliptic Curve Cryptography

ECDSA   See Elliptic Curve Digital Signature Algorithm

ECM   See Enterprise Content Management

E-commerce   Commercial transactions where the goods-ordering, goods-tracking, goods-paying are handled over the Internet or other network.

Environment where money is exchanged for valuable goods and services with either the money and/or the goods and services being transported over computer networks, specifically the Internet [r226, r057].

Economic Growth   (financial term) A positive change in the level of production of goods and services by a country over a certain period of time. Nominal growth is defined as economic growth including inflation, while real growth is nominal growth minus inflation. Economic growth is usually brought about by technological innovation and positive external forces [r009].

Economic Sanctions Administered by the Office of Foreign Assets Control (OFAC)   (financial term) OFAC administers economic sanctions against governments, individuals, and entities that are prohibited from engaging in transactions in the United States or with U.S. persons. These sanctions govern all U.S. persons and corporations, wherever they are located. OFAC maintains a list of named persons subject to sanctions known as the SDN List (Specially Designated Nationals and Blocked Persons). This list contains thousands of names and is updated several times a year. These sanctions target narcotics traffickers, members of rogue governments, terrorists, and supporters of terrorism. A financial firm must report to OFAC within ten days of a confirmed hit against OFAC's SDN List. Capital One also reports to OFAC on an annual basis on any property owned by an SDN that has been blocked or frozen by the bank.

Economic Value Added (EVA)   (financial term) The monetary value of an entity at the end of a time period minus the monetary value of that same entity at the beginning of that time period [r009].

Economy of Mechanism   (aka Principle of Economy of Mechanism) One of Saltzer and Schroeder's Design Principles. The principle that each security mechanism should be designed to be as simple as possible, so that the mechanism can be correctly implemented and so that it can be verified that the operation of the mechanism enforces the containing system's security policy [r013].

EDFA   See Erbium-Doped-Fiber Amplifier

EDGE   See Enhanced Data Rates for Global Evolution

Edge Presence Server   (Instant Messaging/Presence context) An edge presence server is a presence agent that is co-located with a Presence User Agent (PUA). It is aware of the presence information of the presentity because it is co-located with the entity that manipulates this presence information [r227].

EDI   See Electronic Data Interchange

EES   See Escrowed Encryption Standard

EFS   See Encrypted File System

EFT   See Electronic Funds Transfer

EGP   See Exterior Gateway Protocol

EIA   See Electronic Industry Association

EIGRP   See Enhanced Interior Gateway Routing Protocol

EIR   See Equipment Identity Register

El Gamal Algorithm   An algorithm for asymmetric cryptography, invented in 1985 by Taher El Gamal, that is based on the difficulty of calculating discrete logarithms and can be used for both encryption and digital signatures [r013].

Electrical Testing Laboratories (ETL)   An organization that provides product safety testing and certification, Electromagnetic Compatibility (EMC) testing, performance testing, and quality management systems registration for global clients [r033].

Electrical–Optical–Electrical (EOE) Conversions   (optical transmission term) Intermediary Electrical–Optical–Electrical conversions—for example, in a transmission system. These are ultimately undesirable because they add cost and could impact (in some cases) signal quality. At the very least this is currently required to deal with voice switch interfaces. Ultimately carriers would like to deploy all-optical networks (also including optical switching.)

Electromagnetic Compatibility (EMC)   EMC is defined as the ability of a product to operate within its intended electromagnetic environment and to accept or emit Radio Frequency (RF) disturbances within defined limits with the electromagnetic spectrum.

Electromagnetic Compatibility (EMC) Testing   Tests related to EMC. EMC testing can be partitioned into two areas: (i) electromagnetic immunity (EMI) testing, the ability of a product to accept disturbance; and (ii) emissions testing [Electromagnetic Interference (EMI)], the level of disturbance produced by the product.

Electromagnetic Field   The field associated with a particle or object in motion that has an electric charge. An interaction takes place between the electric and magnetic fields and gives rise to an electromagnetic phenomenon [r228, r229].

Electronic Codebook (ECB)   A block cipher mode in which a plaintext block is used directly as input to the encryption algorithm and the resultant output block is used directly as ciphertext [r013]. Two identical plaintext blocks always generate the same ciphertext block.

Electronic Commerce (EC)   (aka E-commerce) General usage: Business conducted through paperless exchanges of information, using electronic data interchange, electronic funds transfer (EFT), electronic mail, computer bulletin boards, facsimile, and other paperless technologies [r013].

SET usage: "The exchange of goods and services for payment between the cardholder and merchant when some or all of the transaction is performed via electronic communication" [r018].

Electronic Commerce Modeling Language (ECML)   Electronic commerce frequently requires a substantial exchange of information in order to complete a purchase or other transaction, especially the first time the parties communicate. A standard set of hierarchically organized payment-related information field names in an Extensible Markup Language (XML) syntax is defined so that this task can be more easily automated. This is the second version of an Electronic Commerce Modeling Language (ECML) and is intended to meet the requirements of RFC 3505 [r233]. Numerous parties are conducting business on the Internet using ad hoc fields and forms. The data formats and structure can vary considerably from one party to another. Where forms are filled out manually, some users find the diversity confusing, and the process of manually filling in these forms can be tedious and error prone. Software tools, including electronic wallets, can help this situation. Such tools can assist in conducting online transactions by storing billing, shipping, payment, preference, and similar information and using this information to complete the data sets required by interactions automatically. For example, software that fills out forms has been successfully built into browsers, as proxy servers, as helper applications to browsers, as stand-alone applications, as browser plug-ins, and as server-based applications. But the proliferation of more automated transaction software has been hampered by the lack of standards. ECML provides a set of hierarchical payment-oriented data structures that will enable automated software, including electronic wallets from multiple vendors, to supply and query for needed data in a more uniform manner. Version 2.0 extends ECML Versions 1.0, RFC 2706, and 1.1, RFC 3106.

Electronic Data Interchange (EDI)   A set of specifications to support high volume business to business (B2B) electronic commerce. Computer-to-computer exchange, between trading partners, of business data in standardized document formats. Concept originally developed in the 1960s to expedite procurement. EDI formats have been standardized primarily by American National Standards Institute (ANSI) X12 and by EDIFACT (EDI for Administration, Commerce, and Transportation), which is an international, UN-sponsored standard primarily used in Europe and Asia. X12 and EDIFACT have sought to align to create a single, global EDI standard [r013].

Electronic Data Interchange (EDI) Security   The most common EDI standards bodies, ANSI X12 and EDIFACT, have defined internal provisions for security. X12.58 is the security mechanism for ANSI X12, and AUTACK provides security for EDIFACT [r164].

Electronic Evidence   (aka digital evidence) Information stored or transmitted in binary form that may be relied upon in court.

Electronic Funds Transfer (EFT)   Any transfer of funds that is initiated by electronic means, such as an electronic terminal, telephone, computer, Automated Teller Machine (ATM), or magnetic tape.

Electronic Industry Association (EIA)   A U.S. trade organization that specializes in the development of standards for the electrical and functional characteristics of interface equipment [r033].

Electronic Signatures Act   (Officially named the Electronic Signatures in Global and National Commerce Act) Legislation stating that electronic signatures may be legally binding for contracts and transactions. The law does not specify what type of technology can be used. Digital signatures are popular types of electronic signatures, but simple click-through agreements at websites also may be legally binding. Electronic signatures also may involve biometrics or digitized versions of handwritten signatures [r057].

Electronic Surveillance   Either the interception of call content (commonly referred to as wiretaps) and/or the interception of call-identifying information (commonly referred to as dialed-number extraction) through the use of pen registers and/or trap and trace devices. Lawfully authorized electronic surveillance is considered to be an invaluable tool for Law Enforcement in its fight against crime and terrorism [r139].

Electronic Surveillance Laws (Current)   Applicable legislation. The National Conference of State Legislatures provides a website listing of all of the electronic surveillance laws in the United States (*http://www.ncsl.org/programs/lis/CIP/surveillance.htm*) [r139].

Electronic Surveillance Legislation (Historical)   In 1968, the U.S. Congress carefully considered and passed the Omnibus Crime Control and Safe Streets Act, Pub. L. No. 90-351, 82 Stat. 212, which laid out the meticulous procedures Law Enforcement must follow to obtain the necessary judicial authorization to conduct electronic surveillance. The law was enacted after Congress exhaustively debated issues concerning Law Enforcement's need to effectively address serious criminal activity and an individual's right to privacy [r139].

In 1970, the U.S. Congress amended the federal wiretap statute to make clear the duty of service providers and others to provide Law Enforcement with the technical and other assistance necessary to accomplish the intercept [r139].

In 1978, the U.S. Congress passed the Foreign Intelligence Surveillance Act (FISA), 50 U.S.C. §§ 1801–1843, to safeguard national security by authorizing select government agencies to conduct electronic surveillance of a foreign power or an agent of a foreign power for the purpose of obtaining foreign intelligence information [r139].

In 1986, as a result of developments in telecommunications and computer technologies, the U.S. Congress found it necessary to enact the Electronic Communications Privacy Act, Pub. L. No. 99-508, 100 Stat. 1848, which amended the Omnibus Crime Control and Safe Streets Act by broadening its coverage to include electronic communications (including e-mail, data transmissions, faxes, and pagers) [r139].

The provisions of Title III of the Omnibus Crime Control and Safe Streets Act, as amended, continue to govern the U.S. procedures for obtaining legal authority for initiating and conducting lawful interceptions of wire, oral, and electronic communications [r139].

Element Management Layer   A management layer which is responsible for management of network elements on an individual or collective basis.

Elliptic Curve Cryptography (ECC)   An approach to public-key cryptography based on the mathematic discipline of elliptic curves. The application of elliptic curves in cryptography originated in the mid-1980s (proposed by N. Koblitz and V. Miller). Under a number of situations, ECC uses smaller keys than other cryptographic methods, while providing a comparable or better level of security; a drawback, however, is that the algorithms for encryption and decryption operations may take longer to execute on hardware

than in other schemes. An elliptic curve is a plane curve defined by an equation of the type

$$y^2 = x^3 + ax + b$$

which is nonsingular (i.e., its graph has no cusps or self-intersections).

This type of asymmetric cryptography based on mathematics of groups that are defined by the points on a curve. The most efficient implementation of ECC is claimed to be stronger per bit of key (against cryptanalysis that uses a brute force attack) than any other known form of asymmetric cryptography [r013]. Thus, ECC may increasingly be used in devices with limited processing power or memory, such as portable devices.

Elliptic Curve Digital Signature Algorithm (ECDSA)   A standard that is the elliptic curve cryptography analog of the Digital Signature Algorithm [r235]. Algorithm proposed to be used with Extensible Markup Language (XML) Signatures to provide integrity, message authentication, and/or signer authentication services for data of any type, whether located within the XML that includes the signature or included by reference [r231].

ECDSA is defined in the ANSI X9.62 standard. ECDSA incorporates the use of a hash function. Currently, the only hash function defined for use with ECDSA is the Secure Hash Algorithm One (SHA-1) message digest algorithm (described in FIPS-180-1). ECDSA signatures are smaller than Rivest–Shamir–Adleman (RSA) signatures of similar cryptographic strength. ECDSA public keys (and certificates) are smaller than similar strength Digital Signature Algorithm (DSA) keys and result in improved communication efficiency [r234].

E-Mail Archiving   Archiving solutions enable organizations to automatically migrate e-mail messages, with or without attachments, to nearline storage. The automated migration is managed to administrator-defined policies, and archived e-mail can be searched and retrieved easily from a user mailbox. Utilizing a policy- or schedule-driven disk-to-disk archiving solution enables an organization to move less frequently accessed business-critical data to nearline storage [r236].

E-Mail Content Filtering   (aka content filtering) Limiting users' access to content or stripping out objectionable content from e-mail data (or attachments) send to or received by the users. Attachments with document extensions that can carry malicious logic (.zip, .exe, etc.) are often blocked (stripped) either based on policy for not allowing these types of files to be transmitted or if they have been found to carry malicious logic.

E-Mail Labeling Requirements   The U.S. Congress and President have enacted the Controlling the Assault of Non-Solicited Pornography and Marketing Act of 2003 (CAN-SPAM Act of 2003) which requires that the Federal Trade Commission sets forth a plan for requiring commercial electronic mail to be identifiable from its subject line [r237].

E-Mail Security   Security mechanism that entails the following three areas: delivery assurance (including non-misrouting), confidentiality (encryption), and spam-prevention.

E-Mail Spoofing   The act of forging the Simple Mail Transfer Protocol (SMTP) header information in an e-mail in order to falsify the identity of the origin of the e-mail. Technique is used by individuals distributing malicious e-mail content and spam.

Emanation   A signal (electromagnetic, acoustic, or other medium) that is emitted by a system (through radiation or conductance) as a consequence (i.e., byproduct) of its operation, and that may contain information [r013].

Emanations Security   See Emission Security

Emanations Security (EMSEC)   Physical constraints to prevent information compromise through signals emanated by a system, particular the application of TEMPEST technology to block electromagnetic radiation [r013].

Embezzle   (financial term) To fraudulently appropriate an asset for one's own use.

EMC   See Electromagnetic Compatibility

EMC/VMWare's VMware   (Vendor-specific) virtualization technology that aims at lowering the cost of "Intel server farms." Converts the workloads of all of a specified set of servers to run as a single hardware pool without inhibiting any application [r080].

Emergency Alert Systems   Systems allowing for the rapid dissemination of late-breaking news and information.

Emergency Disk   Floppy disk/compact disks (CDs) that contains an unaffected copy of operating system.

Emission Security (EMSEC)   Measures taken to prevent the interception of electromagnetic and (in the case of fiber optics) light emissions from systems transmitting confidential data.

EMSEC   See Emanation Security or Emission Security

EMSK   See Extended Master Session Key

Encapsulating Security Payload (ESP)   (IPv6 context) An IPv6 extension header and trailer that provides data source authentication, data integrity and confidentiality, and a not-reply service for the loading of the datagram encapsulated by the header and trailer.

(IP Security context) An IPsec protocol designed to provide a mix of security services, especially data confidentiality service, in the Internet Protocol [r238]. ESP may be used alone, or in combination with the IPsec Authentication Header (AH) protocol or in a nested fashion with tunneling. Security services can be provided between a pair of communicating hosts, between a pair of communicating security gateways, or between a host and a gateway. The ESP header is encapsulated by the IP header, and the ESP header encapsulates either the upper layer protocol header (transport mode) or an IP header (tunnel mode). ESP can provide data confidentiality service, data origin authentication service, connectionless data integrity service, an anti-replay service, and limited traffic flow confidentiality [r013].

Encipherment   (aka encryption) The process of making data unreadable to unauthorized entities by applying a cryptographic algorithm (an encryption algorithm). Decipherment (decryption) is the reverse operation by which ciphertext is transformed to plaintext. The cryptographic transformation of data (see cryptography) to produce ciphertext. (*Note:* Encipherment may be irreversible, in which case the corresponding decipherment process cannot feasibly be performed.) [r068a].

Encode To use a system of symbols to represent information, which might originally have some other representation. Examples include Morse code, American Standard Code for Information Interchange (ASCII), and Basic Encoding Rules (BERs) [r013].

Encrypt Cryptographically transform data to produce ciphertext [r013].

Encrypt Function Function with parameters (specific-key, state, octet string) → (state, octet string). This function takes the specific key, cipher state, and a nonempty plaintext string as input and generates ciphertext and a new cipher state as outputs. If the basic encryption algorithm itself does not provide for integrity protection, then some form of verifiable Message Authentication Code (MAC) or checksum must be included [r116]. If the integrity is intact, this function produces the ciphertext; otherwise, an error indication must be returned.

Encrypted File System (EFS) A file system used in (recent) Windows Operating System (OS) environments that provides encryption of data files. EFS is transparent to the user.

Encrypting Storage A technique to safeguard stored information. This ensures that even if the encrypted data is obtained by an attacker (and the attacker does not have the corresponding key), there is reasonable assurance that the data will not be compromised.

Encryption (aka encipherment) A security mechanism used to transform data from an intelligible form (plaintext) into an unintelligible form (ciphertext), to provide confidentiality. The inverse transformation process is called decryption. Often this term is used to generically refer to both processes [r186].

Encryption Certificate A public-key certificate that contains a public key that is intended to be used for encrypting data, rather than for verifying digital signatures or performing other cryptographic functions [r013].

Encryption Desiderata An encryption mechanism must provide for confidentiality and integrity of the original plaintext. (Incorporating a checksum may permit integrity checking, if the encryption mode does not provide an integrity check itself.) It must also provide nonmalleability. Use of a random confounder prepended to the plaintext is recommended. It should not be possible to determine if two ciphertexts correspond to the same plaintext without the key [r115].

Encryption for Device Configuration and Management in Provider Provisioned Virtual Private Networks (PPVPN) (PPVPN context) For configuration and management of PPVPN devices, encryption and authentication of the management connection at a level comparable to that provided by IPsec is desirable. Several methods of transporting PPVPN device management traffic offer security and confidentiality [r058]:

- Secure Shell (SSH) offers protection for TELNET or terminal-like connections to allow device configuration.
- Simple Network Management Protocol Version 3 (SNMP v3) provides encrypted and authenticated protection for SNMP-managed devices.
- Transport Layer Security (TLS) (RFC 2246) and the closely related Secure Sockets Layer (SSL) are widely used for securing Hypertext Transfer Protocol (HTTP)-based communication, and thus can provide support for most Extensible Markup Language (XML)- and Simple Object Application Protocol (SOAP)-based device management approaches.
- As of 2004, extensive work is proceeding in several organizations (OASIS, W3C, WS-I, and others) on securing device management traffic within a "Web Services (WS)" frame-

work. This work uses a wide variety of security models and supports multiple security token formats, multiple trust domains, multiple signature formats, and multiple encryption technologies.

- IPsec provides the services with security and confidentiality at the network layer. With regard to device management, its current use is primarily focused on in-band management of user-managed IPsec gateway devices.

Encryption Overhead   When deciding about whether or not to encrypt data, especially for transmission channel encryption, it is important to consider the ramifications of any performance or processor utilization overhead that the encryption may require. While physical-level encryption does not usually impact the message length and, consequently the required channel bandwidth, network layer encryption (e.g., IPsec) does impact the message length and required network bandwidth. This is because of the overhead involved in the tunneling process (that is, the encapsulation of an IP datagram/packet inside another packet. This is particularly problematic for short packets (small payload) such as for Voice over IP (VoIP) applications.

End-Entity   A certificate subject that uses its private key for purposes other than signing certificates or an entity that is a relying party [r068a].

End-Entity Attribute Certificate Revocation List (EARL)   A revocation list containing a list of attribute certificates issued to holders; these certificates are not also Attribute Authorities (AAs) and are no longer considered valid by the certificate issuer [r068a].

End-Entity Public-Key Certificate Revocation List (EPRL)   A revocation list containing a list of public-key certificates issued to subjects; these certificates are not also Certification Authorities (CAs) and are no longer considered valid by the certificate issuer [r068a].

End-to-End Encipherment   (aka End-to-End Encryption) Encipherment of data within or at the source end system, with the corresponding deci-

pherment occurring only within or at the destination end system [r068a].

End-User   (General usage) A system entity, usually an individual, that makes use of system resources, primarily for application purposes as opposed to system management purposes [r013].

End-User License Agreement (EULA)   A legal contract between the manufacturer and the end-user of an application. EULA is type of licensing used for most software. The EULA describes how the software can be used and any restrictions that the manufacturer imposes (e.g., most EULAs prohibit the user from sharing the software with others).

End-hosts   Entities that are party to a networked application instance. End-hosts referred to in this document, are specifically those terminating Real-time streaming Voice-over-IP applications, such as Internet Engineering Task Force (IETF) Session Initiation Protocol (SIP) and ITU H.323, and peer-to-peer applications such as Napster and NetMeeting [r037].

Endogenous   That which originates from within.

Endpoint   (Multimedia context) a logical device that provides video and/or voice media encoding/decoding, and signaling functions. Examples include [r074]: (i) a group teleconferencing appliance that is located in a conference room; (ii) an IP telephone; and (iii) a software program that takes video and voice from a camera and microphone and encodes it and applies signaling using a host computer.

Endpoint Discovery   Endpoint discovery is the process by which the devices that are aware of a specific Virtual Private Network (VPN) service will find all customer facing ports that belong to the same service [r236].

Endpoint Security   Security measure implemented at the termination (and/or origination) point in a system relationship. This is often used to discuss security measures for desktop systems connecting to server resources and includes such controls as personal firewalls, anti-virus, and operation system path compliance checks.

Endsystem   (aka End System) An Open Systems

Interconnection (OSI) Reference Model (OSIRM) term for a computer that implements all seven layers of the OSIRM and may attach to a subnetwork. (In the context of the Internet Protocol Suite, usually called a "host.")

End-to-end Encryption   Encryption of data that is not decrypted at any intermediate nodes in a network or system. This assures that intermediate nodes cannot affect or circumvent the confidentiality and integrity of the data.

Enhanced Data Rates for Global Evolution (EDGE)   (GSM context) A transmission technology that achieves higher bit rates than Global System for Mobile Communications (GSM) and General Packet Radio Service (GPRS) on the basis of a new modulation procedure [r011].

Enhanced Interior Gateway Routing Protocol (EIGRP)   A vendor-specific network protocol [an Interior Gateway Protocol (IGP)] that lets routers exchange information more efficiently than with earlier network protocols. EIGRP evolved from Interior Gateway Routing Protocol (IGRP).

Enterprise   A(ny) collection of corporate or institutional task-supporting functional entities that has a common set of goals and/or a single mandate. In this context, an enterprise is, but is not limited to, an entire corporation, a division or department of a corporation, a group of geographically dispersed organizations linked together by common administrative ownership, a government agency (or set of agencies) at any level of jurisdiction, and so on. This also encompasses the concept on an "extended enterprise," which is a logical aggregation that includes internal business units of a firm along with partners and suppliers.

Enterprise Access Management (EAM)   A security mechanism, typically in the form of an application, that supports a single sign-on (SSO) solution in order to authenticate users of the enterprise's Web portal and authorize access to critical back-end resources.

Enterprise Application Integration (EAI)   Information Technology (IT) efforts aimed at integrating the back-office applications (systems) so that they interconnect in an efficient and reliable man-

ner. This way, the System of Record of a given function can indeed provide appropriate functional support and data extracts to all other systems that need such function and data without having to replicate the function and data within multiple systems.

Enterprise Architecture   A plan-of-record, a blueprint of the permitted structure, arrangement, configuration, functional groupings/partitioning, interfaces, data, protocols, logical functionality, integration, technology, of an Information Technology (IT) resource needed to support a corporate business function. Typically resources that need architectural formulations include applications, security subsystems, data structures, networks, hardware platforms, storage, desktop systems, to name just a few. The following are considered part of the Enterprise Architecture:

- The Enterprise Architecture Description (of the current or target state)
- The Enterprise standards set
- The Enterprise Approved Equipment List
- The Roadmap along with (migration) strategies

Enterprise Architecture Program Management Office   Program Management Office established in 2002, in accordance with direction issued by the Associate Director for Information Technology and E-Government, Office of Management and Budget (OMB).

Enterprise Architecture, Minoli   Define a Function Block m at version n, FB(m, n), as being comprised of the following

$$FB(m, n) = \{F(m, n), I(m, n, j), D(m, n, j), \\ PI(m, n, j)\} \text{ for some } 1 \leq m \leq w$$

where

$F(m, n)$ is a set of (enterprise IT) functions that Function Block m can undertake at version n;

$I(m, n, j)$ is equal to "1" if Function Block FB(m, n) has an interface with Function Block FB(j, n) for $j = 1, 2, \ldots, x$ where x is the number of Function Blocks under consideration in this architecture, and "0" otherwise;

$D(m, n, j)$ is the set of data that is exchanged over interface $I(m, n, j)$ for all j where $I(m, n, j) = 1$; and

$PI(m, n, j)\}$ is the protocol used to exchange data over interface $I(m, n, j)$ for all j where $I(m, n, j) = 1$.

Finally assume that a (non-overlapping) partition exists such that $\{FB(m, n)\} = P(1, n) \cup P(2, n) \cup P(3, n) \ldots \cup P(y, n)$ for $m = 1, 2, \ldots, x$.

Then Enterprise Architecture $A(n)$ is defined as

$$A(n) = \{P(k, n)\}, k = 1, 2, \ldots, y$$

Note: we also call the set $\{P(k, n)\}$, $k = 1, 2, \ldots, y$, the "architecture description."

Enterprise Content Management (ECM) The set of technologies used to capture, manage, store, preserve, and deliver content and documents related to organizational processes. ECM tools and strategies allow the management of an organization's unstructured information, wherever that information exists.

Enterprise Directory A canonical collection of information about users in an organization. Typically, this information is collected from a variety of organizational units to create a whole. For example, Human Resources may provide name and address, Telecommunications may provide the telephone number, Information Technology may provide the e-mail address, etc. Generally an enterprise directory is accessible via Lightweight Directory Access Protocol (LDAP).

Enterprise Risk Management A structured and disciplined risk management approach that takes into account strategy, process, people, technology and knowledge with the purpose of continually evaluating and managing risks to business strategies and objectives on an enterprise-wide basis.

Enterprise System Connection (ESCON) A 200-Mbps serial Input/Output (I/O) bus used on IBM Corporation's Enterprise System 9000 data center computers. Similar to Fibre Channel (FC) in many respects, ESCON is based on redundant switches to which computers and storage subsystems connect using serial optical fiber cable [r029]; it predates FC by a number of years.

Entity (Instant Messaging/Presence context) Any of Presentity, Subscriber, Fetcher, Poller, or Watcher [r027].

Entity Class A group of entities with a common type or common set of characteristics [r237].

Entity Name The identifier used to refer to a single entity within an entity class [r237].

Entity Reference A pointer to an entity composed of an authority, an optional resolution method, a registry type, an entity class, and an entity name. One type of entity reference is the Internet Registry Information Service (IRIS) Uniform Resource Identifier (URI) [r237].

Entrapment "The deliberate planting of apparent flaws in a system for the purpose of detecting attempted penetrations or confusing an intruder about which flaws to exploit" [r238].

Entropy Sources In the security context, entropy is a mechanism employed to generate random numbers. Entropy sources are implementation-dependent. Once one has gathered sufficient entropy, it can be used as the seed to produce the required amount of cryptographically strong pseudo-randomness [r166]. Thermal noise (sometimes called Johnson noise in integrated circuits) or a radioactive decay source and a fast, free-running oscillator would do the trick directly. This is a trivial amount of hardware, and it could easily be included as a standard part of a computer system's architecture. Most audio (or video) input devices are usable. Furthermore, any system with a spinning disk or ring oscillator and a stable (crystal) time source or the like has an adequate source of randomness. All that is needed is the common perception among computer vendors that this small additional hardware and the software to access it is necessary and useful [r166].

Entropy, Renyi See Renyi Entropy

ENUM Proposed numbering scheme (defined in RFC 3761) for Voice over IP (VoIP)/IP telephony applications involving public-switched networks. (ENUM is not an acronym.) Specification that describes how the Domain Name System (DNS) can be used to identify services associated with an E.164 number [r225].

Environmental Variables   Those aspects of policy required for an authorization decision, that are not contained within static structures, but are available through some local means to a privilege verifier (e.g., time of day or current account balance) [r068a].

EOE   See Electrical-Optical-Electrical Conversion

EOI   See Event of Interest

Ephemeral Key   A public key or a private key that is relatively short-lived.

Ephemeral Port   A client-selected port at the transport layer where communication is taking place or can take place. Typically, this is a high-numbered port (e.g., 32345). This is in contrast with well-known ports which are low-numbered ports.

Ephemeral-Static Diffie–Hellman   A variant of the Diffie–Hellman key agreement.

EPRL   See End-Entity Public-Key Certificate Revocation List

Equipment Identity Register (EIR)   (GSM context) With the help of the International Mobile Equipment Identity (IMEI) number, the Equipment Identity Register can recognize mobile stations that are trying to get unauthorized access to the network and deny them access. EIR is an optional Global System for Mobile Communications (GSM) network element [r011].

Eradication   The phase in Incident Handling that makes sure the problem is eliminated and the avenue of entry is closed off [r057].

Erasing   Purging, clearing, or removing file allocation.

Erbium-Doped-Fiber Amplifier (EDFA)   (optical transmission term) Amplifier based on optical fibers doped with erbium; commercially successful technology being used in the context of WDM. An amplifier is a device that boosts the strength of an electronic signal; an EDFA acts as an all-optical amplifier. A device that uses doped fiber and a secondary pump laser to optically amplify a signal. EDFAs operate as basic transmission network elements that eliminate the need for intermediate regeneration and re-transmission functions. The doped fiber can amplify light in the 1550-nm region when pumped by an external light source. In a cable system (including fiberoptic-based systems), amplifiers are spaced at regular intervals throughout the system to maintain signal strength. EDFAs are optical fibers that are doped with the rare earth element, erbium; as a result, they can amplify light in the 1550-nm region when pumped by an external light source.

Error Detection Code   A checksum designed to detect, but not correct, accidental (i.e., unintentional) changes in data.

Escalating a Trouble Report   Identifying a trouble report that is to receive urgent and immediate supervisory attention to resolve the trouble [r068a].

ESCON   See Enterprise System Connection

Escrowed Encryption Standard (EES)   A U.S. Government standard that specifies use of a symmetric encryption algorithm (SKIPJACK) and a Law Enforcement Access Field (LEAF) creation method to implement part of a key escrow system that provides for decryption of encrypted telecommunications when interception is lawfully authorized [r239]. Both SKIPJACK and the LEAF are to be implemented in equipment used to encrypt and decrypt unclassified, sensitive telecommunications data.

Esoterica   Secrets known only to an initiated minority.

ESP   See Encapsulating Security Payload

Estelle   A language for formal specification of computer network protocols. Specified in ISO 9074-1989.

Ethereal   A graphical-based sniffer that can be used to decode Voice Over IP (VoIP) packets.

Ethernet   Local Area Network (LAN) technology. More precisely, LAN protocol synonymous with IEEE 802.3 family of standards. Originally based on wireless transmission (hence the term from Ether), later coaxial, and later yet, Unshielded Twisted Pair (UTP) cable.

Ethernet Over Synchronous Optical Network

(SONET) Communication service that provides direct Ethernet-to-Ethernet communication in the Metropolitan Area Network (MAN) or in the Wide Area Network (WAN). This service uses ITU.G7041 Generalized Framing Procedure (GFP) and ITU G.7042 Link Capacity Adjustment Scheme (LCAS) standards to provide Ethernet leased line service over SONET Virtual Concatenation (VCAT) transport infrastructure.

Ethernet Sniffing The monitoring of Ethernet Local Area Network (LAN) interface for traffic content using appropriate monitoring software. When the software detects a packet that fits certain criteria, it typically logs the packet to a file (the most common criteria for an interesting packet is one that contains words like login or password) [r057].

Ethernet-Based WANs See WANs, Ethernet-based and/or Virtual Private Local Area Network (LAN) Service.

Ethical Hacking Performing scans and attacks on a system in order to discover (and not exploit) vulnerabilities. This is usually done with the prior knowledge and consent of the system administrators. However, individuals who do not have prior consent of system administrators sometimes perform ethical hacking, but the results of the hacking effort are provided to the system owners.

ETL See Electrical Testing Laboratories

ETSI See European Telecommunications Standards Institute

EUI See Extended Unique Identifier

EULA See End-User License Agreement

European Committee for Electrotechnical Standardization (CENELEC) Organization that promotes European harmonization and publishes standards for the European market [r033].

European Telecommunications Standards Institute (ETSI) A not-for-profit organization that develops the specifications and determines the European standards of telecommunication [r011]. The mission is to produce the telecommunications standards that will be used for decades to come throughout Europe and beyond. ETSI unites about 1000 members from over 50 countries inside and outside Europe, and represents administrations, network operators, manufacturers, service providers, research bodies, and users.

EVA See Economic Value Added

Evaluated Products List A list of information system equipment items that have been evaluated against, and found to be compliant with, a particular set of criteria.

(U.S. Department of Defense context) A listing of items that have been evaluated against the Trusted Computer System Evaluation Criteria (TCSEC) by the National Computer Security Center (NCSC), or against the Common Criteria by the NCSC or one of its partner agencies in another county. The List forms Chapter 4 of National Security Agency (NSA) "Information Systems Security Products and Services Catalogue" [r013].

Evaluated System Refers to a system that has been evaluated against security criteria such as the Trusted Computer System Evaluation Criteria (TCSEC) or the Common Criteria [r013].

Event An instantaneous occurrence that changes the global status of the environment of an object. This status change may be persistent or temporary, thus allowing for surveillance, monitoring, and performance measurement functionality, and so on. Events may or may not generate reports; they may be spontaneous or planned; they may trigger other events or may be triggered by one or more other events [r068a].

Event Message Message capturing a single portion of a connection.

Event of Interest (EOI) An Activity on a network or host that may have security implications. Typically, an Intrusion Detection System (IDS) will identify EOIs.

Exogenous That which originates from the outside.

Experimental Protocol, Internet Engineering Task Force (IETF) The "Experimental" designation typically denotes a specification that is part of some research or development effort. Such a specification is published for the general information of the Internet technical community and as an archival record of the work, subject only to editorial considerations and to verification that there has been adequate coordination with the standards process. An Experimental specification may be the output of an organized Internet research effort (e.g., a Research Group of the IRTF), an IETF Working Group, or it may be an individual contribution [r290, r281].

Expert System   A system based on Artificial Intelligence (AI) principles that can be used in a variety of applications, such as fraud detection, trend analysis, network management, intrusion detection analysis, and so on [e.g., r240].

Exploit   A technique or code that leverages a vulnerability in order to gain unauthorized access to the system or data.

Exponential Encryption System (TESS)   A system of separate but cooperating cryptographic mechanisms and functions for the secure authenticated exchange of cryptographic keys, the generation of digital signatures, and the distribution of public keys. TESS employs asymmetric cryptography, based on discrete exponentiation, and a structure of self-certified public keys [r241, r013].

Export-Crippled   A system with "watered-down" cryptographic strength (and security) in order to comply with the United States' Export Administration Regulations (EAR). Export-crippled cryptographic software is limited to a small key size, resulting in Ciphertext that usually can be decrypted by brute force techniques.

Exposure   A situation where sensitive data is directly released to an unauthorized entity. This includes deliberate exposure, scavenging systems or data for residual sensitive information, human error, and system error [r013].

Extended Authentication (Xault) Message   Message used in Internet Engineering Task Force (IETF) Remote Access Dial-In User Service (RADIUS). Xauth lets an administrator deploy IP Security (IPsec) on Virtual Private Networks (VPNs) using Terminal Access Controller Access Control System (TACACS+) or RADIUS as the user authentication method within the Internet Key Exchange (IKE) protocol [r242].

Extended Master Session Key (EMSK)   Additional keying material derived in an Extensible Authentication Protocol (EAP) exchange between the EAP client and server that is exported by the EAP method. The EMSK is at least 64 octets in length and is reserved for future uses that are not yet defined [r073].

Extended Unique Identifier (EUI)   Link layer address defined by the Institute of Electrical and Electronic Engineers (IEEE) [r008].

Extended Unique Identifier (EUI)-64 Address in IPv6   (IPv6 context) 64-bit link layer address that is used as basis to generate interface identifiers in IPv6 [r008].

Extended Unique Identifier (EUI)-Based Interface Identifiers   The 64-bit EUI-64 address is defined by the Institute of Electrical and Electronic Engineers (IEEE). EUI-64 addresses are either assigned to a network adapter or derived from IEEE 802 addresses. It is an extension of the traditional Media Access Control (MAC) address and is employed in IPv6.

Traditional interface identifiers for network adapters use a 48-bit IEEE 802 MAC address (also called the physical or hardware address). This address consists of a 24-bit company ID (also called the manufacturer ID) and a 24-bit extension ID (also called the board ID). The concatenation of the company ID, which is uniquely assigned to each manufacturer of network adapters, and the board ID, which is uniquely assigned to each network adapter at the time of assembly, generates a globally unique 48-bit address. The IEEE EUI-64 address is a newer standard for network interface addressing. The company ID is still 24 bits in length, but the extension ID is 40 bits; this creates a larger address space for a network adapter manufacturer. To create an EUI-64 address from an IEEE 802 address, the 16 bits of 11111111 11111110 (0xFFFE) are inserted into the IEEE 802 address between the company ID and the extension ID.

eXtensible Access Control Markup Language (XACML)   An eXtensible Markup Language

(XML)-based security policy language standardized by Organization for the Advancement of Structured Information Standards (OASIS).

Extensible Authentication Protocol (EAP) A framework that supports multiple, optional authentication mechanisms for Point-to-Point Protocol (PPP), including cleartext passwords, challenge-response, and arbitrary dialog sequences [r243]. This protocol is intended for use primarily by a host or router that connects to a PPP network server via switched circuits or dial-up lines [r013].

IEEE 802.1x standard that allows the passing of security authentication data between Remote Access Dial-In Service (RADIUS) and the access point (AP) and wireless client. EAP has a number of variants, including: EAP MD5, EAP-Tunneled TLS (EAP-TTLS), Lightweight EAP (LEAP), and Protected EAP (PEAP).

Extensible Authentication Protocol (EAP) Authentication Requirements A set of criteria for EAP authentication methods to ensure secure wireless LAN authentication [r073].

Extensible Authentication Protocol (EAP) Server The entity that terminates the EAP authentication method with the peer. In the case where no backend authentication server is used, the EAP server is part of the authenticator. In the case where the authenticator operates in pass-through mode, the EAP server is located on the backend authentication server [r073].

Extensible Authentication Protocol Tunneled Transport Layer Security Authentication Protocol (EAP-TTLS) EAP-TTLS is an Internet Draft protocol. It is an Authentication Protocol (EAP) type that utilizes Transport Layer Security (TLS) to establish a secure connection between a client and server, through which additional information may be exchanged. The initial TLS handshake may mutually authenticate client and server; or it may perform a one-way authentication, in which only the server is authenticated to the client. The secure connection established by the initial handshake may then be used to allow the server to authenticate the client using existing, widely deployed authentication infrastructures such as Remote Authentication Dial-In User Service (RADIUS). The authentication of the client may itself be EAP, or it may be another authentication protocol. Thus, EAP-TTLS allows legacy password-based authentication protocols to be used against existing authentication databases, while protecting the security of these legacy protocols against eavesdropping, man-in-the-middle, and other cryptographic attacks.

Extensible Markup Language (XML) Firewall A (relatively) new type of firewall intended to secure Extensible Markup Language (XML) messages and Web Services (WSs). Traditional firewalls are not designed to understand/interpret the XML message-level security and they cannot defend against new XML message-based attacks. The majority of packet-inspection firewalls are designed to secure and apply policy to the transport level, therefore they generally do not scan for content in Simple Object Access Protocol (SOAP), Universal Description, Discovery and Integration (UDDI), Security Assertion Markup Language (SAML), or other Web Services protocols. The difference between an XML firewall and other firewalls is that many of the features in an XML firewall exist at the application layer and within the data payload or content, as opposed to the transport and session layer. Many modern XML firewalls act like high-performance proxies: they can approach wire speed performance by offloading crypto and XML validation functions to dedicated hardware (features such as message routing, encryption, and forwarding are somewhat of a commodity). In this role, the XML firewall performs security services such as authentication, authorization, auditing (AAA), and XML validation at a message level. The features are a separation of message-level security from transport-level security (these XML features do not act as transport-level connection security such as done in Secure Sockets Layer (SSL) [r276].

Extensible Markup Language (XML) Firewall Operation XML firewalls protect Web Services where it provides security policy enforcement for Web Services and XML messages. To enforce security policy, the XML firewall validates message source, reads and modifies message headers, inspects the message content, and validates message elements/attributes to enforce fine-grained security policies. Just as traditional firewalls protect the private IP addresses and ports from hackers, the XML firewall protects the Web service listener, the XML parser and the Web Service application from a variety of attacks [r276].

Extensible Markup Language (XML) Firewall Operation with Simple Object Access Protocol (SOAP)   An XML firewall can scan SOAP message attachments for potentially hostile payloads and executables before they reach the private network and Web Service applications. By stripping binary data and other indicators of executable code, the XML firewall is able to stop a variety of payload attacks [r276].

Extensible Markup Language (XML) Security   A set of mechanisms such that Web Services and XML streams can be used without compromising security over variety of non-secure transport methods [File Transfer protocol (FTP), Hyper-Text Transfer Protocol (HTTP), Simple Mail Transfer Protocol (SMTP), etc.] because the message itself is secure [r276].

Extensible Provisioning Protocol (EPP) Extension Mapping for the Provisioning and Management of E.164   A mechanism defined in RFC 4059 for the provisioning and management of E.164 numbers stored in a shared central repository. Information exchanged via this mapping can be extracted from the repository and used to publish Domain Name System (DNS) resource records [r225].

eXtensible Rights Markup Language™ (XrML™)   A general-purpose, eXtensible Markup Language (XML)-based specification grammar for expressing rights and conditions associated with digital content, services, or any digital resource.

Extension   A data item defined for optional inclusion in a v3 X.509 public-key certificate, a v2 X.509 Certificate Revocation List (CRL), or private extensions [r013].

Extension Headers (IPv6 context)   Headers placed between IPv6 header and higher level protocol headers, and are used to provide additional functionalities to IPv6 [r008].

Exterior Gateway Protocol (EGP)   A protocol for distribution of routing information to the routers that connect autonomous systems (here "gateway" means "router").

External Border Gateway Protocol (eBGP)   An exterior gateway protocol (EGP), used to perform interdomain routing in Transmission Control Protocol/Internet Protocol (TCP/IP) networks. A Border Gateway Protocol (BGP) router needs to establish a connection (on TCP port 179) to each of its BGP peers before BGP updates can be exchanged. The BGP session between two BGP peers is said to be an external BGP (eBGP) session if the BGP peers are in different autonomous systems (AS).

External Security Threats   Threats that arise from outside the corporate intranet, typically from the Internet. This is the venue used by hackers who can exploit flaws and characteristics of computer operating systems and software applications.

Extra Tracks   Most hard disks have several more than the rated number of tracks. These extra tracks are used to make up for flaws that might occur during manufacture that would otherwise require that the entire disk be rejected for failing its quality control requirements. Often these tracks are not required or used; they are accessible with special tools and provide a place for hiding or storing sensitive data [r057].

Extranet   A network of controlled-access resources that are available only to specific users, such as customers or trading partners [r158, r244]. A network that an organization uses to carry application data traffic between the organization and its business partners. An extranet can be implemented securely by constructing the extranet as a Virtual Private Network (VPN) [r013].

Extranet Data/Tangible Assets   These assets require protection considerations: partner contract data; partner financial data; partner contact data;

partner collaboration application; partner crypto-graphic keys; partner credit reports; partner pur-chase order data; supplier contract data; supplier financial data; supplier contact data; supplier col-laboration application; supplier cryptographic keys; supplier credit reports; supplier purchase or-der data [r190].

Extrinsic Data   Information about the file such as file signature, author, size, name, path, creation, and modification dates. These data are the accu-mulation of what is in the file, on the media label, discovered by the operator, and contributed by the client. Collectively, it represents the real value of examining an electronic file as opposed to its printed version [r057].

F

F F F F F F F F F F F F F F F F F F F F F F F

F (GSM context) The F interface is situated between the Mobile Services Switching Center (MSC) and the Equipment Identity Register (EIR) [r011].

FA See Foreign Agent

FACCH See Fast Associated Control Channel

FACH See Forward Access Channel

Facility Backup (MPLS context) A local repair method in which a bypass tunnel is used to protect one or more protected Label Switched Paths (LSPs) that traverse the Point of Local Repair (PLR), the resource being protected, and the Merge Point in that order [r083].

Factoring Every nonprime integer can be represented uniquely as a product of prime numbers. One possible algorithm for factoring an integer is to divide the input by all small prime numbers iteratively until the remaining number is prime. This is efficient only for integers that are, say, of size less than 10^{16} because this already requires trying all primes up to 10^8. In public-key cryptosystems based on the problem of factoring, numbers are of size 10^{300} and this would require trying all primes up to 10^{150} and there are about 10^{147} such prime numbers according to the prime number theorem. In cryptography we want to use only those integers that have only large prime factors. Preferably one should select an integer with two large prime factors, as is done in the Rivest–Shamir–Adleman (RSA) cryptosystem [r036].

Fail Safe A mode of system termination that automatically leaves system processes and components in a secure state when a failure occurs or is detected in the system [r013].

 Minoli–Cordovana's Authoritative Computer and Network Security Dictionary. By Daniel Minoli and James Cordovana
Copyright © 2006 John Wiley & Sons, Inc.

Fail-Safe Defaults (aka Principle of Fail-Safe Defaults) One of Saltzer and Schroeder's Design Principles. Unless a subject is given explicit access to an object, it should be denied access to that object, namely [r139a]: (i) default access to an object is NONE; (ii) the default settings of a system should offer a secure configuration; (iii) do not set default values for passwords; (iv) administrator sets (only) one password during installation; and (v) administrator disables features by default that might open holes if not configured carefully (this is only a partial list).

Fail Soft Selective termination of affected nonessential system functions and processes when a failure occurs or is detected in the system [r013].

Failure Control A methodology used to provide fail-safe or fail-soft termination and recovery of functions and processes when failures are detected or occur in a system [r238].

Fair Credit Reporting Act (financial term) Federal law giving individuals the right to examine their own credit history. The provisions of this law enable consumers to approach credit reporting agencies to see what the agencies may be saying about them, find out if their credit information has been used by any third parties, and approach an agency to dispute wrongful use or interpretation of their information [r009].

Fair Market Value (financial term) The price that an interested but not desperate buyer would be willing to pay and an interested but not desperate seller would be willing to accept on the open market assuming a reasonable period of time for an agreement to arise [r009].

Fake Word It has been an old tradition in encyclopedias, dictionaries, and maps to include a fake entry to protect ones' own copyright: If someone copied the fake term, then the publisher would know that someone had taken that material from that specific source or publication.

False Denial of Origin Action whereby the originator of data denies responsibility for its generation.

False Denial of Receipt Action whereby the recipient of data denies receiving and possessing the data.

False Negative Occurs when an actual intrusive action has occurred but the system allows it to pass as nonintrusive behavior [r057, r062].

False Positive Occurs when the system classifies an action as anomalous (a possible intrusion) when it is a legitimate action [r057, r062].

False Sense of Security To have a misplaced, ill-based, yet risk-laden belief that an Information Technology (IT) environment is secure, when in fact it is not, and where an infraction can be perpetrated with rather limited effort by an inimical agent (firm is at risk of nefarious exogenous and endogenous IT infractions) [r406].

Falsification A threat action where false data deceives an authorized entity by substituting or inserting data.

Fast Associated Control Channel (FACCH) (GSM context) A control channel that transmits information for handover and call setup. Similarly to the Slow Associated Control Channel (SACCH) and the Stand-alone Dedicated Control Channel (SDCCH), FACCH belongs to the group of the Dedicated Control Channels [r011].

Fast Data Encipherment Algorithm (FEAL) A family of algorithms that maps 64 plaintext to 64-bit ciphertext blocks under a 64-bit secret key. It is similar to Data Encryption Standard (DES) but with a far simpler function. It was designed for speed and simplicity, making it suitable for less complex microprocessors (e.g., smartcards) [r068a].

Fast Ethernet (FE) Another name for Ethernet systems operating at 100 Mbps. Originally defined in IEEE 802.3u.

FAT See File Allocation Table

Fault, Configuration, Accounting, Performance, and Security Management (FCAPS) Set of techniques and principles to handle the five management areas (Fault, Configuration, Accounting, Performance, and Security) defined in International Organization for Standardization (ISO) standard ISO/IEC 7498-4:1989: Information Processing Systems, Open Systems Interconnection,

Basic Reference Model, Part 4: Management Framework.

FCAPS   See Fault, Capacity, Accounting, Performance, and Security Management

FCAPS, Accounting Management   The ability to track network usage to detect inefficient network use, abuse of network privileges, or usage patterns is included in accounting management, a key component for planning network growth [r245].

FCAPS, Configuration Management   Configuration management activities include the configuration, maintenance, and updating of network components. Configuration management also includes notification to network users of pending and performed configuration changes [r245].

FCAPS, Fault Management   Fault management encompasses the activities of detection, isolation, and correction of abnormal network operation. Fault management provides the means to receive and present fault indication, determine the cause of a network fault, isolate the fault, and perform a corrective action [r245].

FCAPS, Performance Management   Performance management tools are used to recognize current or impending performance issues that can cause problems for network users. Activities include the monitoring and maintenance of acceptable network performance, and collection and analysis of statistics critical to network performance [r245].

FCAPS, Security Management   Security management encompasses the activities of controlling and monitoring the access to the network and associated network management information. This includes controlling passwords and user authorization, as well as collecting and analyzing security or access logs. The goal of a network management system is to provide the above functionality in a concise manner that views the entire network as one homogeneous entity [r245].

FCC   See Federal Communications Commission

FCCH   See Frequency Correction Channel

FCIP   See Fibre Channel over IP

FDD   See Frequency Division Duplex

FDMA   See Frequency Division Multiple Access

FE   See Fast Ethernet

FEAL   See Fast Data Encipherment Algorithm

FEC   See Forwarding Equivalence Class or Forward Error Correction

Federal Agency Security Practices (FASP)   The FASP effort was initiated as a result of the success of the Federal CIO Council's Federal Best Security Practices (BSP) pilot effort to identify, evaluate, and disseminate best practices for Critical Infrastructure Protection (CIP) and security.

Federal Communications Commission (FCC)   A U.S. government agency charged with the task of regulating all forms of interstate and international communication. A board of seven commissioners appointed by the President under the Communications Act of 1934 (and newer legislation), having the power to regulate all electrical communications systems originating in the United States including radio, television, facsimile, telegraph, telephone, and cable systems [r033].

Federal Computer Security Program Managers' Forum   This Forum is an informal group sponsored by the National Institute of Standards and Technology (NIST) to promote the sharing of computer security information among federal agencies.

Federal Financial Institutions Examination Council's (FFIEC)   The Council is a formal interagency body empowered to prescribe uniform principles, standards, and report forms for the federal examination of financial institutions by the Board of Governors of the Federal Reserve System (FRB), the Federal Deposit Insurance Corporation (FDIC), the National Credit Union Administration (NCUA), the Office of the Comptroller of the Currency (OCC), and the Office of Thrift Supervision (OTS) and to make recommendations to promote uniformity in the supervision of financial institutions [r246].

Federal Information Processing Standards (FIPS)   The Federal Information Processing Standards Publication (FIPS PUB) series issued by the U.S. National Institute of Standards and Technology are technical guidelines for U.S. Government procurements of information processing system equipment and services. They were issued under the provisions of section 111(d) of the Federal Property and Administrative Services Act of 1949 as amended by the Computer Security Act of 1987, Public Law 100-235 [r013].

Federal Information Processing Standards (FIPS) 140   Important standards documents of the Federal Information Processing Standards (FIPS). The two key documents are:

- *FIPS 140-1, "Security Requirements for Cryptographic Modules."* This standard specifies the security requirements to be satisfied by a cryptographic module used within a security system protecting unclassified information within computer and telecommunications systems (including voice systems) [r250].
- *FIPS 140-2, "Security Requirements for Cryptographic Modules, Version 2."* This is the second version of the standard that describes the Security Requirements for Cryptographic Modules.

FIPS 140-1 has been made mandatory and binding by the Secretary of Commerce and is applicable to all U.S. Government departments and agencies that use cryptographic-based security systems to protect unclassified information within computer and telecommunication systems (including voice systems) that are not national security systems. The National Security Telecommunications and Information Systems Security Policy No. 11 requires that effective July 1, 2002, such systems use only approved information assurance products. According to the rule, systems that enter, process, store, display, or transmit national security information must include information assurance products validated against the International Common Criteria for Information Security Technology or Federal Information Processing Standard FIPS 140-2 [r078].

Within the FIPS 140-2 (or 140-1) validations,

there are four possible Security Levels for which a product may receive validation.

- *Security Level 1* provides the lowest level of security. It specifies basic security requirements for a cryptographic module.
- *Security Level 2* improves the physical security of a Security Level 1 cryptographic module by adding the requirement for tamper evident coatings or seals, or for pick-resistant locks.
- *Security Level 3* requires enhanced physical security, attempting to prevent the intruder from gaining access to critical security parameters held within the module.
- *Security Level 4* provides the highest level of security. Level 4 physical security provides an envelope of protection around the cryptographic module to detect a penetration of the device from any direction.

Federal Information Processing Standards (FIPS) 140 Validation Certificate   A vendor developing a cryptographic module must select a laboratory that the National Institute of Standards and Technology (NIST) has accredited for FIPS validation testing and pay a testing fee. The lab tests the cryptographic algorithms and then the cryptographic module for conformance to the FIPS standard. The lab then writes a test report and sends this report to National Institute of Standards and Technology/Communications Security Establishment (NIST/CSE) for validation. A NIST/CSE representative reviews the report and, if everything is correct, issues a validation certificate and publishes the module on the list of FIPS 140 validated modules [r078].

Federal Information Processing Standards PUB 140-1   See Federal Information Processing Standards (FIPS) 140

Federal Information Security Act (FISMA) of 2002   Provides the basic statutory requirements for securing federal computer systems. FISMA requires each agency to inventory its major computer systems, to identify and provide appropriate security protections, and to develop, document, and implement an agency-wide information security program. FISMA authorizes the National Institute of Standards and Technology (NIST) to develop security standards and guidelines for systems used by the federal government. It authorizes the Secretary of Commerce to choose which of these standards and guidelines to promulgate. FISMA authorizes the Director of the Office of Management and Budget (OMB) to oversee the development and implementation of (including ensuring compliance with) these security policies, principles, standards, and guidelines [r208].

Federal Information Security Management Act (FISMA) Implementation Project The E-Government Act (Public Law 107-347) passed by the 107th Congress and signed into law by the President in December 2002 recognized the importance of information security to the economic and national security interests of the United States. Title III of the E-Government Act, entitled the Federal Information Security Management Act, requires each federal agency to develop, document, and implement an agency-wide program to provide information security for the information and information systems that support the operations and assets of the agency, including those provided or managed by another agency, contractor, or other source. FISMA Implementation Project seeks to promote the development of standards and guidelines to support the Federal Information Security Management Act including: Security categorization of information and information systems; selection of appropriate security controls for information systems; verification of security control effectiveness and determination of information system vulnerabilities; and, operational authorization for processing (security accreditation) of information systems [r067].

Federal Information Systems Security Educators' Association (FISSEA) Vision of the Association: be a national forum in information technology systems security awareness, training, and education. Mission of the Association: Encourage the professional development of mem-

bers to result in an elevated level of information systems security awareness, training, and education; and facilitate a meaningful exchange of related information.

Federal Public-Key Infrastructure (FPKI) A Public-Key Infrastructure (PKI) being planned to establish facilities, specifications, and policies needed by the U.S. Federal Government to use public-key certificates for Information Security (INFOSEC), Communications Security (COMSEC), and electronic commerce involving unclassified but sensitive applications and interactions between Federal agencies. FPKI also includes interactions with entities of other branches of the Federal Government, state, and local governments, business, and the public [r013].

Federal Reserve Bank (financial term) One of 12 regional banks established to maintain reserves, issue bank notes, and lend money to member banks. The Federal Reserve Banks are also responsible for supervising member banks in their areas, and are involved in the setting of national monetary policy [r009].

Federal Standard 1027 A U.S. Government document defining emanation, anti-tamper, security fault analysis, and manual key management criteria for Data Encryption Standard (DES) encryption devices, primary for Open Systems Interconnection reference Model (OSIRM) layer 2. It was renamed "FIPS PUB 140" when responsibility for protecting unclassified, sensitive information was transferred from the National Security Agency (NSA) to National Institute of Standards and Technology (NIST), and then it was superseded by FIPS PUB 140-1 [r013].

Federal Trade Commission (FTC) Federal agency whose purpose is to encourage free enterprise and prevent restraint of trade and monopolies. Among other functions, the agency manages an Identity Theft Hotline (1-877-IDTHEFT).

Federal Wiretap Act The Federal Wiretap Act (18 U.S.C. 25112c), sometimes referred to as Title III, was adopted in 1968 and expanded in 1986. It sets procedures for court authorization of real-time surveillance of all kinds of electronic communications, including voice, e-mail, fax, and Internet, in criminal investigations. It normally requires, before a wiretap can commence, a court order issued by a judge who must conclude, based on an affidavit submitted by the government, that there is probable cause to believe that a crime has been, is being, or is about to be committed. Terrorist bombings, hijackings, and other violent activities are crimes for which wiretaps can be ordered.

Federated Logically/physically (inter)connected and treated as a single entity. For example, related to databases, it refers to a collection of databases all of which can be viewed through a single user interface.

Federated Authentication In this context, the term "federated" refers to multiple authentication types as well as multiple authentication sources. Often, information systems that seek to enforce access control rules must be prepared to accept authentication information from any number of sources. Federated authentication holds the promise of permitting organizations to utilize their existing relationships with customers, business affiliates, and users, through linked accounts, single sign-on, and greatly improved ease of use.

Authentication takes place both within an organization and among multiple organizations. Even when within an organization, there may be multiple sources; however, traditional authentication systems assume the existence of single authentication source and type. Federated authentication is an environment that permits an organization to use authentication sources that belong to themselves or to their customers, partners, suppliers and any other third party. There are three types of players with respect to federated authentication: (i) *Identity Managers*—The organizational units that manage electronic identity information and provide identity information and authentication services for their campuses/sites. (ii) *Service Providers*—The organizational units that manage services. These services are generally network-based, but may not necessarily be so.

(iii) *Community Members*—The people who have an established affiliation with a campus; they are the people who use the Service Providers' services and whose electronic identity is managed by Identity Managers.

Federated Directories An environment where multiple directories (dispersed throughout the entire enterprise) (multiple forests in an Active Directory environment) can be combined and treated as a single hierarchical directory; the directories can then also share rights and privileges.

Federated Identity The Burton Group defines a federated identity as a portable identity, and its associated entitlements, that can be used across autonomous domains or business boundaries. Identity federation is based upon linking a user's otherwise distinct identities at two or more locations [r078].

While existing identity management solutions can help increase security and reduce inefficiencies associated with managing internal users and access to internal information, increasingly the users that require access are outside of any one company's control. Federated Identity and the standards for federation established by Organization for the Advancement of Structured Information Standards (OASIS) and the Liberty Alliance Project define mechanisms for companies to share identity information between domains. Federated identity provides companies with an open-standards approach of enabling increased access to cross-boundary information. As a result of federation, companies are able to create identity-based applications (such as federated single sign-on) that enable increased access to cross-boundary information [r204].

Federation The concept of unifying security information (especially across an extended enterprise, group of companies, etc.) by making use of agreed and standardized lines. An example would be federated identity where it has been agreed to utilize a standard for sharing identity with multiple parties with multiple privileges. As a result of federation, companies are able to create identity-based applications (such as federated single sign-on) that enable increased access to cross-boundary information [r205].

Federation means that local identities and their associated data stay in place, but they are linked together through higher-level mechanisms. The driving concept behind federated identity is that the existing, heterogeneous nature of enterprise Information Technology (IT) architecture should not have to be changed. Federation is the notion that by securely and efficiently enabling access to cross-domain resources, enterprises are able to improve productivity, operational efficiency, and competitive differentiation. But there is more to federation than extending single sign-on. Federation respects the distributed, heterogeneous architecture of the current IT environment. Efforts to implement unique, all-encompassing identifiers tend to be ineffectual. By contrast, federated identity organizes controlled linkages among the distributed identities of a user. It allows for efficient management, control, and movement in a radically distributed world. As organizations integrate more tightly with trading partners and outsourcers, federated identity provides a flexible mechanism to authenticate users from partner organizations and provide them with seamless access to protected online resources [r204].

Feistel Cipher (aka Feistel structure or Feistel network) A block cipher named after IBM cryptographer Horst Feistel. The Feistel structure is a structure where the encryption and decryption operations are very similar (often requiring only a reversal of the key schedule). Because of this property the size of the software, microcode, or hardware required to implement such a cipher is approximately 50% of what it otherwise need to be. Many block ciphers use this scheme, including the Data Encryption Standard (DES). Feistel ciphers have been publicly cryptanalyzed for more than two decades, and no systematic weaknesses have been uncovered. Feistel ciphers are reasonably fast and simple to implement in both hardware and software.

Fetcher (Presence Services context) A form of watcher that has asked the presence service for the presence information of one or more presentities, but has not asked for a subscription to be created [r015].

FHSS See Frequency Hopping Spread Spectrum

Fiat–Shamir Signatures [aka Feige–Fiat–Shamir (FFS) signature scheme] The Fiat–Shamir signature scheme is a scheme that uses a one-way hash function $h: \{0; 1\}^* \rightarrow \{0; 1\}^k$ for some fixed positive integer k. $\{0; 1\}^k$ denotes the set of bitstrings of bitlength k, and $\{0; 1\}^*$ denotes the set of all bitstrings (of arbitrary bitlengths). The method provides a digital signature with appendix, and is a randomized mechanism. Fiat–Shamir is predicated on (a) the difficulty of factoring large numbers and (b) a hash function whose range size is (exponential in) the security parameter. The Fiat–Shamir approach for transforming identification schemes into signature schemes has been popular in recent years because it yields efficient signature schemes; it has received renewed interest of late as a tool in deriving forward-secure signature schemes.

Note that any identification scheme involving a witness-challenge response sequence can be converted to a signature scheme by replacing the random challenge of the verifier with a one-way hash function.

Fibre Channel (FC) A high-speed transport technology used to build storage area networks (SANs). Although Fibre Channel can be used as a general-purpose network carrying Asynchronous Transfer Mode (ATM), IP and other protocols, it has been primarily used for transporting Small Computer System Interface (SCSI) traffic from servers to disk arrays. The Fibre Channel Protocol (FCP) serializes SCSI commands into FC frames; however, IP is used for in-band Simple Network Management protocol (SNMP) network management. FC not only supports single-mode and multimode fiber connections, but coaxial cable and twisted pair as well [r029].

FC can be configured point-to-point, via a switched topology or in an arbitrated loop (FC-AL) with or without a hub, which can connect up to 127 nodes. It supports transmission rates up to

2.12 Gbps in each direction, and 4.25 Gbps is expected. FC uses the Gigabit Ethernet physical layer and IBM's 8B/10B encoding method, where each byte is transmitted as 10 bits. FC provides both connection-oriented and connectionless services. Following are the class and functional levels of the architecture [r029].

Fibre Channel over IP (FCIP)   A protocol for transmitting Fibre Channel (FC) data over an IP network. Internet Protocol (IP)-based storage networking technology developed by the Internet Engineering Task Force (IETF). It allows the encapsulation/tunneling of FC packets and transport via Transmission Control Protocol/Internet Protocol (TCP/IP) networks (gateways are used to interconnect FC Storage Area Networks (SANs) to the IP network and to set up connections between SANs. Protocol enables applications developed to run over FC SANs to be supported under IP, enabling organizations to leverage their current IP infrastructure and management resources to interconnect and extend FC SANs [r029].

Fibre Connectivity (FICON)   IBM Corporation's Implementation of ESCON over Fibre Channel [r029].

FICON   See Fibre Connectivity

Field Sieve Algorithm   One of the best factoring algorithms. It consists of a sieving phase and a matrix step. The sieving phase can be distributed (and has been several times) among a large number of participants, but the matrix step needs to be performed on large supercomputers. The effectiveness of the Number Field Sieve (NFS) algorithm becomes apparent for very large integers, it can factor any integer of size 10^{150} in a few months time. The NFS algorithm takes subexponential time (which is still not very efficient). There is no known proof that integer factorization is an NP-hard problem nor that it is not polynomial time solvable. If any NP-hard problem were polynomial time solvable, then also factoring would, but there is very little hope that this is the case. It is plausible under current knowledge that factoring is not polynomial time solvable [r036].

File Allocation Table (FAT)   A term used by DOS (Disk Operating System) to describe the table that outlines the location of all of the files on disk. There are two FATs, and in a properly operating computer they are identical [r057].

File Encryption   The encryption of files for the purpose of either storing them securely on any kind of storage media or for the purpose of transmitting the files over a communications network.

File Integrity Monitoring   The use of (tools that perform) cryptographic hashes on files to determine if alterations have been made at a point after an initial file hash was created.

File Server   Network-resident (intranet or Internet) server that controls distributed file usage; it provides a central location for shared information [r247].

File Slack Space   The space between the logical end and the physical end of file and is called the file slack. The logical end of a file comes before the physical end of the cluster in which it is stored. The remaining bytes in the cluster are remnants of previous files or directories stored in that cluster [r057].

File System   A system that organizes files and metadata in a hierarchical structure and is responsible for managing the physical placement of blocks that make up the files [r029].

File Transfer Protocol (FTP)   An Internet Engineering Task Force (IETF) standard for file transfer. FTP is Transmission Control Protocol (TCP)-based and runs at the application layer. The objectives of FTP are to:

- Promote sharing of files (computer programs and/or data).
- Encourage indirect or implicit (via programs) use of remote computers.
- Shield a user from variations in file storage systems among hosts.
- Transfer data reliably and efficiently.

FTP, though usable directly by a user at a terminal, is designed mainly for use by programs [r248]. FTP requires user identification/password combinations and these credentials (along with all other data) are transmitted in clear text.

File Virus   Malicious code that becomes part of a program file. When the infected program is executed, the malicious code is leaded into memory and executed.

Filter   Packet-matching information that identifies a set of packets to be treated a certain way by a middlebox. A set of terms and/or criteria used for the purpose of separating or categorizing. This is accomplished via single- or multi-field matching of traffic header and/or payload data. 5-Tuple specification of packets in the case of a firewall and 5-tuple specification of a session in the case of a Network Address Translation (NAT) middlebox function are examples of a filter [r037] (the connection state information typically consists of a 5-tuple entry, which includes the protocol, the source and destination port numbers, and the source and destination IP addresses).

Filtering or Security Issues   The effort to control or limit objectionable network traffic has led to additional restrictions on the behavior and capabilities of Internet services. Such objectionable traffic may include unsolicited mail of various types (including spam), worms, viruses, and their impact, and in some cases, specific content [r034]. In general, significant restrictions are most likely to be encountered with Web connectivity and non-public-address services. Because users may have legitimate reasons to access remote file services, e-mail services, and so on, it is important that providers disclose the services they are making available and the filters and conditions they are imposing.

Filtering Router   An internetwork router that selectively prevents the passage of data packets according to a security policy. A filtering router may be used as a firewall or part of a firewall. A router usually receives a packet from a network and decides where to forward it on a second network. A filtering router does the same, but first decides whether the packet should be forwarded at all, according to some security policy. The policy is implemented by rules (packet filters) loaded into the router. The rules mostly involve values of data packet control fields [especially In-

ternet Protocol (IP) source and destination addresses and Transmission Control Protocol (TCP) port numbers] [r013, r249].

Final Response   (SIP context) A response that terminates a Session Initiation Protocol (SIP) transaction, as opposed to a provisional response that does not. All 2xx, 3xx, 4xx, 5xx, and 6xx responses are final [r025].

Financial Institution   (financial term) "An establishment responsible for facilitating customer-initiated transactions or transmission of funds for the extension of credit or the custody, loan, exchange, or issuance of money" [r018].

Finger   An Operating System (OS) service that returns information about users on a particular system. The command can be used in reference to a particular user (user name); more generally, it can be used to establish who is logged on a system. Many installations disable this command.

Fingerprint   Literally: A pattern of curves formed by the ridges on a fingertip.

FIPS   See Federal Information Processing Standards

Firewall   An internetwork gateway that restricts data communication traffic to and from one of the connected networks (the one said to be "inside" the firewall) and thus protects that network's system resources against threats from the other network (the one that is said to be "outside" the firewall).

A firewall typically protects a smaller, secure network [such as a corporate Local Area Network (LAN), or even just one host] from a larger network (such as the Internet). The firewall is installed at the point where the networks connect, and the firewall applies security policy rules to control traffic that flows in and out of the protected network.

A firewall is not always a single device. For example, a firewall may consist of a pair of filtering routers and one or more proxy servers running on one or more bastion hosts, all connected to a small, dedicated LAN between the two routers. The external router blocks attacks that use IP to break security (IP address spoofing, source routing, packet fragments), while proxy servers block attacks that would exploit a vulnerability in a higher layer protocol or service. The internal router blocks traffic from leaving the protected network except through the proxy servers. The difficult part is defining criteria by which packets are denied passage through the firewall, because a firewall not only needs to keep intruders out, but usually also needs to let authorized users in and out [r013].

(Instant Messaging/Presence context): A point of administrative control over connectivity. Depending on the policies being enforced, parties may need to take unusual measures to establish communications through the firewall [r027].

Firewalled Internet Connectivity A service that provides access to the Internet and supports most servers and most peer-to-peer functions, with one or (usually) more static public addresses. It is similar to full Internet connectivity, however, this service places a provider-managed firewall between the customer and the public Internet, typically at customer request and at extra cost compared to non-firewalled services. Typically by contractual arrangements with the customer, this may result in blocking of some services. Other services may be intercepted by proxies, content-filtering arrangements, or application gateways. The provider should specify which services are blocked and which are intercepted or altered in other ways. In most areas, this service arrangement is offered as an add-on, extra-cost option with what would otherwise be full Internet connectivity. It is distinguished from the models above by the fact that any filtering or blocking services are ultimately performed at customer request, rather than being imposed as service restrictions [r034].

FireWire Marketing name for the 1394 IEEE standard. It specifies a serial connection mechanism that support transfer rates 200–800 Mbps. Apple Computer Inc. and manufacturers of digital video cameras have adopted this connection standard; for PCs the adoption has been relatively limited up to now.

Firmware Computer programs and data stored in hardware—typically in read-only memory (ROM) or programmable read-only memory (PROM)—such that the programs and data cannot be dynamically written or modified during execution of the programs [r013].

FIRST See Forum of Incident Response and Security Teams

First-Generation Grids Computing grids that involved local "Metacomputers" with basic services such as distributed file systems and site-wide single sign on, upon which early-adopters developers created distributed applications with proprietary communications protocols [r080].

Fishbowl (aka honey pot) A system is designed to lure (or decoy) individuals with malicious intent away from the true target systems. It is also a means to observe malicious behavior in an attempt to better understand cracker methodologies and system weaknesses, and is utilized to find out more details on the cracker in order to determine more information about the individual and from where the attack is initiated. Fishbowls may not be legal in some instances.

FISA See Foreign Intelligence Surveillance Act

FISMA See Federal Information Security Management Act

FISSEA See Federal Information Systems Security Educators' Association

Flat-Top Pass Band (optical transmission term) Specifies a class of Dense Wavelength Division Multiplexing (DWDM) Mux/Demux devices whose transmission spectrum profiles within the pass band are relatively flat by comparison with the Gaussian profile (nm).

Flaw Hypothesis Methodology An evaluation or attack technique in which specifications and documentation for a system are analyzed to hypothesize flaws in the system. The list of hypothetical flaws is prioritized on the basis of the estimated probability that a flaw exists and, assuming it does, on the ease of exploiting it and the extent of control or compromise it would provide. The prioritized list is used to direct a penetration test or attack against the system [r120, r013]

Flooding Flooding is a function related to Layer 2

services; when a Provider Edge (PE) device receives a frame with an unknown destination Media Access Control (MAC) address, that frame is sent out over (flooded) every other interface [r082].

An attack that attempts to cause a failure in (especially, in the security of) a computer system or other data processing entity by providing more input than the entity can process properly [r013].

Flow (IPv6 context) Datagram series exchanged between a source and a destination that require a special treatment at middle routers, and defined by a specific source and destination IP address, just as by a flow label with a non 0 value [r008].

Flow Analysis An analysis performed on a non-procedural formal system specification that locates potential flows of information between system variables. By assigning security levels to the variables, the analysis can find some types of covert channels [r013].

Flow Control A procedure or technique to ensure that information transfers within a system are not made from one security level to another security level, and especially not from a higher level to a lower level [r013].

Flow Control Standard, Layer 2 Defined in IEEE 802.3x Flow Control.

Follow-Up The phase in Incident Handling that identifies lessons learned, improves incident handling capability, and tabulates the findings in a report format. Also, information given to the person when the person logs into or otherwise access a system [r057].

Foreign Agent (FA) (Mobile IP context) As defined in RFC 3220, a router on a mobile node's visited network which provides routing services to the mobile node while registered. The foreign agent detunnels and delivers datagrams to the mobile node that were tunneled by the mobile node's home agent. For datagrams sent by a mobile node, the foreign agent may serve as a default router for registered mobile nodes. A Foreign Network is any network other than the mobile node's Home Network.

In contrast, as defined in RFC 3220, a Home Agent is a router on a mobile node's home network which (a) tunnels datagrams for delivery to the mobile node when it is away from home and (b) maintains current location information for the mobile node. A Home network is a network, possibly virtual, having a network prefix matching that of a mobile node's home address (a traditional IP routing mechanism will deliver datagrams destined to a mobile node's Home Address to the mobile node's Home Network).

Foreign Intelligence Surveillance Act (FISA) Legislation passed by the U.S. Congress in 1978 intended to safeguard national security by authorizing select government agencies to conduct electronic surveillance of a foreign power or an agent of a foreign power for the purpose of obtaining foreign intelligence information [r139].

Forest Mechanism to define hierarchical domains in the Windows Operating System (OS) environment. A set of Active Directory (AD) domains that replicate their AD databases with each other.

Forgery An illegal modification or reproduction of an instrument, document, signature, or legal tender, or any other means of recording information. An item is also considered forged if it is claimed that it was made by someone who did not make it [r009].

Fork Bomb (aka Logic Bomb) Malicious code that recursively spawn copies of itself. This can cause a memory "explosion" that can consume system resources to the point where it can create a denial of service.

Formal Specification A specification of hardware or software functionality in a computer-readable language; usually a precise mathematical description of the behavior of the system with the aim of providing a correctness proof [r013].

Format Prefix (IPv6 context) High-order bits with a fixed value that define an IPv6 type address [r008].

Formulary A technique for enabling a decision to grant or deny access to be made dynamically at the time the access is attempted, rather than earlier when an access control list or ticket is created [r013].

FORTEZZA A cryptographic module that implements the Digital Signature Algorithm Standard, Secure Hash Algorithm Standard, Key Exchange Algorithm Standard, and the Skipjack Encryption Algorithm Standard. The card complies with Personal Computer Memory Card International Association (PCMCIA) specification Standard Release 2.1. The card provides 41 individual commands that can be used to support cryptographic based authentication and encryption applications. U.S. Government documents describe the Security Policy for the FORTEZZA Crypto Card. The Security Policy specifies the security rules under which the FORTEZZA card operates [r108].

Forum of Incident Response and Security Teams (FIRST) An international consortium of Computer Security Incident Response Teams (CSIRTs) that work together to handle computer security incidents and promote preventive activities. FIRST was founded in 1990. Its mission includes [r013]:

- Provide members with technical information, tools, methods, assistance, and guidance.
- Coordinate proactive liaison activities and analytical support.
- Encourage development of quality products and services.
- Improve national and international information security for government, private industry, academia, and the individual.
- Enhance the image and status of the CSIRT community.

Forward Access Channel (FACH) (3G Wireless context) A downlink transport channel used to transmit small bursty data. The FACH uses a slow power control. The bitrate can be changed every 10 ms [r007].

Forward Error Correction (FEC) Algorithm (based on Coding Theory principles) used in one-way data communications where additional data is added onto the data packet to allow the receiving end to ensure that no errors are received [r251].

Forward Secrecy One concept of "forward secrecy" is that, given observations of the operation of a key establishment protocol up to time t and also given some of the session keys derived from those protocol runs, one cannot derive unknown past session keys or future session keys. A related property is that, given observations of the protocol and knowledge of the derived session keys, one cannot derive one or more of the long-term private keys. For some this is a synonym for public-key forward secrecy. This refers to the effect of the compromise of long-term keys [r013].

All three concepts involve the idea that a compromise of "this" encryption key is not supposed to compromise the "next" one. There also is the idea that compromise of a single key will compromise only the data protected by the single key. In Internet literature, the focus has been on protection against decryption of back traffic in the event of a compromise of secret key material held by one or both parties to a communication [r013].

Forwarding Equivalence Class (FEC) (for MPLS networks) A group of IP packets that are forwarded in the same manner (e.g., over the same path, with the same forwarding treatment) [r053–r055].

Forwarding Information Base (FIB) The table containing the information necessary to forward IP datagrams is called the Forwarding Information Base. At minimum, this contains the interface identifier and next hop information for each reachable destination network prefix.

Four-Wave Mixing (optical transmission term) Optical transmission impairment that limits multi-channel transmission on dispersion-shifted fiber that has its zero dispersion in the Erbium-Doped-Fiber Amplifier (EDFA) bandwidth range. Monitoring of input power levels into the EDFA can address this problem when conventional fiber is used for transmission. New fiber designs (including Non-Zero-Dispersion Shifted Fiber (NZ-DSF) designs) have been introduced to address the issue.

FPKI See Federal Public-Key Infrastructure

FQDN See Fully Qualified Domain Name

Fragment (IPv6 context) A portion from a message sent by a host into an IPv6 datagram. Fragments contain a fragmentation header [r008].

Fragmentation (IPv6 context) Process in which the source device divides the message of an IPv6 datagram in some number of fragments, so all fragments have a properly Maximum Transfer Unit (MTU) to its destination [r008].

Fragmentation Header (IPv6 context) An IPv6 extension header that contains information needed for reassembly to be used in the receiving node [r008].

Frame Merge (for frame relay networks) Label merging, when it is applied to operation over frame-based media, so that the potential problem of cell interleave is not an issue.

Frame Relay Services (FRS) A broadly deployed wide area network (WAN) data communication service offered by carriers that supports frame relaying (movement of Layer 2 frames containing/ encapsulating IP packets) at speeds generally up to 1.544 Mbps.

Fraud Intentional misrepresentation or concealment of information in order to deceive or mislead.

Fraud Discovery Mechanisms and processes to identify fraud as well as actions to discover and/or prevent fraud.

Fraud Interdiction Actions to recover from and/or prevent future fraud.

French Security Incident Response Team (FrSIRT) A security research group based in France.

Frequency Correction Channel (FCCH) (GSM context) A broadcast channel utilized for the downlink. Information is broadcast at short regular intervals; with this the mobile station can correct and adjust its frequency [r011].

Frequency Division Duplex (FDD) Mode (3G Wireless context) A multiplexing method where multiple access is made possible by a combination of different spreading codes and different frequencies [r007].

Frequency Division Multiple Access (FDMA) (GSM context) A multiplexing method that assigns several frequency channels to one Base Transceiver Station (BTS) [r011].

Frequency Hopping Spread Spectrum (FHSS) Radio Less common Wireless Local Area Net-

work (WLAN) radio transmission technology in the 2.4-GHz band. More generally, this technique is used in (some) military systems.

Front-End Demilitarized Zone (DMZ) A DMZ that is closest to the public Internet where the least critical assets are located within a layered network architecture. Usually, the Web presentation layer and related services are located within this segment. Data typically does not reside within this network segment.

FRS See Frame Relay Services

FTC See Federal Trade Commission

FTP See File Transfer Protocol

Full Certificate Revocation List (CRL) A complete revocation list that contains entries for all certificates that have been revoked for the given scope [r068a].

Full Cone Network Address Translation (NAT) A full cone NAT is one where all requests from the same internal IP address and port are mapped to the same external IP address and port. Furthermore, any external host can send a packet to the internal host, by sending a packet to the mapped external address [r252].

Full Default-Free Table A full default-free table is the union of all sets of Border Gateway Protocol (BGP) routes taken from all the default-free BGP routing tables collectively announced by the complete set of autonomous systems making up the public Internet. Due to the dynamic nature of the Internet, the exact size and composition of this table may vary slightly depending on where and when it is observed [r086].

Full Internet Connectivity A connectivity service that provides the user full Internet connectivity, with one or more static public addresses. Dynamic addresses that are long-lived enough to make operating servers practical without highly dynamic Domain Name System (DNS) entries are possible, provided that they are not characterized as "dynamic" to third parties. Filtering Web proxies, interception proxies, Network Address Translation (NAT), and other provider-imposed restrictions on inbound or outbound ports and traffic are incompatible with this type of service. Servers on a connected customer Local Area Networks (LANs) are typically considered normal. The only compatible restrictions are bandwidth limitations and prohibitions against network abuse or illegal activities [r034].

Full Provider-Internal Table   A superset of the full routing table that contains infrastructure and nonaggregated routes [r086].

Full-Duplex   A communications channel that carries data in both directions simultaneously [r200].

Fully Qualified Domain Name (FQDN)   The unique name of a network entity, consisting of a hostname and a domain name that can resolve to an IP address. For example, www is a hostname, att.com is a domain name, and www.att.com is a fully qualified domain name.

Function Block   The smallest (deployable) unit of Telecommunications Management Network (TMN) management functionality that is subject to standardization. More generally, a grouping of related functions, for example, in the context of architectural descriptions.

Fuzzy Logic   Fuzzy Logic is an extension of Boolean logic, introduced in the mid-1960s by Lotfi Zadeh and dealing with the concept of partial truth. In classical Boolean logic everything can be expressed in binary terms (0 or 1, black or white, yes or no); Fuzzy Logic replaces Boolean truth values with degrees of truth. (Degrees of truth are often confused with probabilities, although they are conceptually distinct, because fuzzy truth represents membership in vaguely defined sets, not likelihood of some event or condition.) Fuzzy sets are based on vague definitions of sets, not randomness. Fuzzy Logic allows for set membership values between and including 0 and 1, shades of gray as well as black and white, and in its linguistic form, imprecise concepts like "slightly," "quite," and "very." Specifically, Fuzzy Logic allows partial membership in a set. Some applications can be found in the following areas, among others: cameras, digital image processing, such as edge detection, and video game artificial intelligence [r253].

G

G G G G G G G G G G G G G G G G G G G G G G G G

G Reference Points A reference point located outside the Telecommunications Management Network (TMN) between the human users and the workstation function block (WSF). It is not considered to be part of the TMN even though it conveys TMN information.

GAAP See Generally Accepted Accounting Principles

Galois Message Authentication Code (GMAC) A block cipher mode of operation providing data origin authentication. It is defined in terms of the Galois/Counter Mode (GCM) authenticated encryption operation as follows. The GCM authenticated encryption operation has four inputs: a secret key, an Initialization Vector (IV), a plaintext, and an input for Additional Authenticated Data (AAD). It has two outputs, a ciphertext whose length is identical to the plaintext, and an Authentication Tag. GMAC is the special case of GCM in which the plaintext has a length of zero. The (zero-length) ciphertext output is ignored so that the only output of the function is the Authentication Tag. Implementations make use of an automated key management system, such as the Internet Key Exchange (IKE) (as defined in RFC 2409) [r028].

Gateway (1) In the networking context, the term "gateway" is the historical nomenclature for "router." More generally, it enables two technologically different networks to communicate (here the gateway is a network point that acts as an entrance to another network [r029]). Hence, it is a relay mechanism that attaches to two (or more) computer networks that have similar functions but dissim-

Minoli–Cordovana's Authoritative Computer and Network Security Dictionary. By Daniel Minoli and James Cordovana
Copyright © 2006 John Wiley & Sons, Inc.

ilar implementations and that enables host computers on one network to communicate with hosts on the other; an intermediate system that is the interface between two computer networks. In theory, gateways are conceivable at any Open Systems Interconnection Reference Model (OSIRM) layer. In practice, they operate at OSIRM layer 3 (bridge, router) or layer 7 (proxy server). When the two networks differ in the protocol by which they offer service to hosts, the gateway may translate one protocol into another or otherwise facilitate interoperation of hosts [r013].

(2) A server that acts as an intermediary for some other server.

Gateway GPRS Support Node (GGSN) (3G Wireless context) The Gateway GPRS (General Packet Radio Service) Support Node represents the gateway to the GPRS network. It takes over a number of important functions in the GPRS network [r007].

Gateway Mobile Services Switching (GMSC) (GSM context) Mobile Services Switching Centers (MSCs) that provide connections to another mobile radio network [i.e., a Public Land Mobile Network (PLMN)], or to a Public Switched Telephone Network (PSTN), and which are connected to the Home Location Register (HLR), are also referred to as Gateway-MSCs [r011].

Gateway Mobile Services Switching Center (GMSC) (GSM context) A network element (node) used to interconnect two networks. The gateway is often located at or is integral to a mobile services switching center (MSC). The MSC performs the switching functions of the system. The MSC serves as a network node in a wireless telecommunications network and as a point of access to the Public Switched Telephone Network (PSTN). The MSC supervises and controls voice/data path connections to the PSTN and other mobility switches. It controls calls to and from other telephone and data systems, including network interfacing and signaling. The MSC is then referred to as the GMSC.

Gaussian Minimum Shift Keying (GMSK) (GSM context) A phase modulation technique used to transmit data over the air interface [r011].

Gaussian Pass Band   (optical transmission term) Specifies a class of DWDM Mux/Demux devices whose transmission spectrum profiles within the pass band are essentially Gaussian (nm).

Gb (GSM context) Interface between a Serving General Packet Radio Service (GPRS) Support Node and a Base Station [r014].

GbE   See Gigabit Ethernet

Gc (GSM context) Interface between a Gateway General Packet Radio Service (GPRS) Support Node and a Home Location Register (HLR) [r014].

Gd (GSM context) Interface between a Short-Message Service Center (SMSC) and a Serving General Packet Radio Service (GPRS) Support Node [r014].

GDOI   See Group Domain of Interpretation Group Keying

General Number Field Sieve (GNFS) Algorithm   Currently the fastest known method for factoring large integers (e.g., for integers with over 110 digits). GNFS techniques have facilitated factorizations of integers that were once speculated to require thousands of years of supercomputer time to accomplish. This makes GNFS the best algorithm for attempting to unscramble keys in ciphers that use public-key cryptography. A specialized version of GNFS, the Special Number Field Sieve (SNFS) is asymptotically faster than FNFS when used for factoring integers in the form $r^e + s$ or $r^e - s$ with r, e, s integers and $e > 0$.

General Packet Radio Service (GPRS)   A packet-based technology that enables high-speed wireless Internet and other communications over a Global System for Mobile Communications (GSM) network. GPRS is well-suited for sending and receiving small bursts of data. GPRS enables information to be sent or received immediately and users are considered to be "always connected" as no dial-up modem connection is required. Benefits include: Faster data speeds and "always on" mobility; almost instantaneous connection setup; connection to an abundance of data sources around the world, through support for multiple protocols, including IP; and a step toward full 3G services. GPRS provides users with fast file download, and effective Internet searching, while GPRS subscribers are charged only for data sent and received and not for time online [r011].

Generalized Mersenne Numbers/Generalized Mersenne Primes   The sequence $\{m_{n,t}\} = \{n^t - (n-1)\}$ for $t = 2$ to infinity is called a "Mersenne sequence routed on n." For example, if $n = 2$, then the well-known Mersenne sequence $2^t - 1$ is generated; if $n = 3$ then the sequence $3^t - 2$ is generated. And so on. If n is a prime the sequence is called a "Legitimate Mersenne sequence." Any $j \in \{m_{n,t}\}$ is called a "Generalized Mersenne Number"; if j is prime then it is called a "Generalized Mersenne Prime." For example for $n = 3$, the sequence is $\{3^1 - 2 = 1, 3^2 - 2 = 7, 3^3 - 2 = 25, 3^4 - 2 = 79, 3^5 - 2 = 241, 3^6 - 2 = 727, 3^7 - 2 = 2185, 3^8 - 2 = 6559, 3^9 - 2 = 19681, ...\}$; note that 7, 79, 241, 727, 19681 are primes. These numbers have applicability to cryptography. See [r053] pages 114–124 for an extensive discussion of this (novel) topic.

Generalized Multiprotocol Label Switching (GMPLS)   (aka Generalized MPLS) Protocol aims to extend Multiprotocol Label Switching (MPLS) to encompass a number of transport architectures, including optical networks that incorporate a number of all-optical and optoelectronic elements, such as optical cross-connects with both optical and electrical fabrics, transponders, and optical add–drop multiplexers [r349]. It provides Control plane mechanisms: routing of lightpaths through an all-optical network. Optical networking poses a number of challenges for GMPLS. Fundamentally, optical technology is an analog rather than digital technology whereby the optical layer is lowest in the transport hierarchy and hence has an intimate relationship with the physical geography of the network [r349].

As described in RFC 3945, GMPLS extends MPLS from supporting packet (Packet-Switching Capable—PSC) interfaces and switching to include support of four new classes of interfaces and switching: Layer 2 Switch Capable (L2SC), Time-Division Multiplex (TDM), Lambda-Switch Capable (LSC) and Fiber-Switch Capable (FSC). A functional description of the extensions to MPLS signaling needed to support the new classes of interfaces and switching is provided in RFC 3471. RFC 3473 describes ReSerVation Protocol with Traffic Engineering (RSVP-TE) specific formats and mechanisms needed to support all five classes of interfaces, and Constraint-based Label Distribution Protocol (CR-LDP) extensions can be found in RFC 3472 [r254].

Suite of protocols defined to control different switching technologies and different applications. These include support for requesting TDM connections, including Synchronous Optical Network (SONET)/Synchronous Digital Hierarchy (SDH) and Optical Transport Networks (OTNs) [r079]. GMPLS signaling protocol also support capabilities of an Automatically Switched Optical Network (ASON) (architecture is defined in ITU-T G.8080). These include generic capabilities such as call and connection separation, along with more specific capabilities such as support of soft permanent connections.

GeneralizedTime   The ASN.1 data type "GeneralizedTime" (specified in ISO 8601) contains a calendar date (YYYYMMDD) and a time of day, which is either (a) the local time, (b) the Coordinated Universal Time, or (c) both the local time and an offset allowing Coordinated Universal Time to be calculated. (See Coordinated Universal Time, UTCTime.) [r013].

Generally Accepted Accounting Principles (GAAP)   (financial term) A widely accepted set of rules, conventions, standards, and procedures for reporting financial information, as established by the Financial Accounting Standards Board [r009].

Generic Framing Procedure (GFP)   A recently introduced protocol for Synchronous Optical Network (SONET) environments that allows efficient encapsulation of Ethernet, Fibre Channel, and other data traffic onto the SONET payload.

Similar to, but more efficient than, Packet Over SONET (POS) schemes.

Generic Security Service Application Program Interface (GSS-API) An Internet Standard protocol that specifies calling conventions by which an application (typically another communication protocol) can obtain authentication, integrity, and confidentiality security services independently of the underlying security mechanisms and technologies, thus allowing the application source code to be ported to different environments [r255, r013].

A GSS-API caller accepts tokens provided to it by its local GSS-API implementation and transfers the tokens to a peer on a remote system; that peer passes the received tokens to its local GSS-API implementation for processing. The security services available through GSS-API in this fashion are implementable (and have been implemented) over a range of underlying mechanisms based on symmetric and asymmetric cryptography [r255].

Generic Upper Layer Security (GULS) Service A five-part standard (ISO 11586) for the exchange of security information and security-transformation functions that protect confidentiality and integrity of application data [r013].

Geometric Mean The geometric mean is defined as the product of all the numbers (assuming they are positive), raised to a power equal to the reciprocal of the number of members.

In a formula: The geometric mean of $a_1, a_2, \ldots, a_n$ is

$$(a_1 \cdot a_2 \cdots a_n)^{1/n} = \sqrt[n]{a_1 \cdot a_2 \cdots a_n}$$

The geometric mean of a data set is always smaller than or equal to the set's arithmetic mean (the two means are equal if and only if all members of the data set are equal).

Geopolitical Certificate Authority (GCA) (Secure Electronic Transaction (SET) context) A SET certification hierarchy, with an optional level that is certified by a BCA and that may certify cardholder Certification Authorities (CAs), merchant CAs, and payment gateway CAs. Using GCAs enables a brand to distribute responsibility for managing certificates to geographic or political regions, so that brand policies can vary between regions as needed [r013].

GFP See Generic Framing Procedure

GFP Encapsulation Encapsulation adapts Ethernet, Fibre Channel, and other data traffic for suitability to a constant bitrate carrier.

GFR See Guaranteed Frame Rate

GGF See Global Grid Forum

GGSN See Gateway GPRS Support Node

Ghost A user account that is not associated with an actual person. Often this was an account of an employee who left a company. It can be utilized as an anonymous account for malicious activities. In some cases, the ghost account can also be associated with a payroll account for embezzlement purposes [r062].

Gi (GSM context) Reference point between General Packet Radio Service (GPRS) and an external packet data network [r014].

Gigabit Ethernet (GbE) Another name for Ethernet systems operating at 1000 Mbps. Originally defined in IEEE 802.3z.

GLBA See Gramm–Leach–Bliley Act

Global Address See Global Unicast Aggregatable Address

Global Certificate Infrastructure A universally accepted trust agency. Such an agency currently does not exist. Questions about a suitable business model, as well as privacy considerations, may prevent one from ever emerging [r170].

Global Grid Forum (GGF) An industry advocacy group: a forum for exchanging information and defining standards relating to distributed computing and grid technologies. GGF supports community-driven processes for developing and documenting new standards for Grid Computing.

Global System for Mobile Communication (GSM) A type of cellular service. GSM is an international standard for 2nd generation (2G) digital mobile radio. It was named after the Groupe Spécial Mobile [r011]. GSM service was introduced in 1991. As of the late 1990s, it was already available in more than 100 countries and has become the de facto standard in Europe and Asia. GSM is used on the 900-MHz and 1800-MHz frequencies in Europe, Asia, and Australia, as well as on the MHz-1900 frequency in North America and Latin America. GSM allows eight simultaneous calls on the same radio frequency and uses narrowband Time Division Multiple Access (TDMA) [r121].

Global Unicast Aggregatable Address   (aka global address) An address format (defined in RFC 2374) that is designed to support both the provider-based aggregation and a new type of exchange-based aggregation. The combination allows efficient routing aggregation for sites that connect directly to providers and for sites that connect to exchanges. Aggregatable addresses are organized into a three level hierarchy: (i) Public Topology; (ii) Site Topology; and (iii) Interface Identifier. Public topology is the collection of providers and exchanges who provide public Internet transit services. Site topology is local to a specific site or organization which does not provide public transit service to nodes outside of the site. Interface identifiers identify interfaces on links. Aggregatable Global Unicast Address Format is an improvement over RFC 2073 in a number of areas. The major changes include removal of the registry bits because they are not needed for route aggregation, support of EUI-64 based interface identifiers, support of provider and exchange based aggregation, separation of public and site topology, and new aggregation based terminology.

Globus Toolkit   The de facto standard for several important Connectivity, Resource, and Collective protocols. The toolkit, a "middleware plus" capability, addresses issues of security, information discovery, resource management, data management, communication, fault detection, and portability [r080].

GMAC   See Galois Message Authentication Code

GMPLS   See Generalized Multiprotocol Label Switching

GMSC   See Gateway Mobile Services Switching Center

GMSK   See Gaussian Minimum Shift Keying

Gn   (GSM context) Interface between two General Packet Radio Service (GPRS) Support Nodes within the same Public Land Mobile Network [r014].

GNFS   See General Number Field Sieve Algorithm

Gopher   Pre-World Wide Web (WWW) protocol for menu-based information retrieval over the Internet.

GOTS   See Government Off-the-Shelf

Government Off-the-Shelf (GOTS)   Commercially available off-the-shelf (COTS) products that are directly available (and approved) for government purchase, such as firewalls, routers, and third-party intrusion detection tools.

Gp   (GSM context) Interface between two General Packet Radio Service (GPRS) Support Nodes in different Public Land Mobile Networks [r014].

GPO   See Group Policy Objects

GPRS   See General Packet Radio Service

GPRS Support Node (GSN)   (GSM context) The General Packet Radio Service (GPRS) Support Node is the network element that takes care of communication between the public Packet Data Networks and the Serving GPRS Service Node (SGSN) through an IP-based UMTS/W-CDMA backbone network. It provides IP connectivity between mobile users and public services such as Internet, Content Services Gateway, Wireless Application Protocol (WAP), and multimedia messaging (MMS) and to corporate virtual private networks (VPNs) [r014].

GPRS Tunneling Protocol (GTP)   (GSM context) The General Packet Radio Service (GPRS) Tunneling Protocol is a protocol that exists only between the Gateway GPRS Support Node (GGSN) and the Serving GPRS Support Node (SGSN) and prepares the data for the transmission via the GPRS backbone network [r014].

Gr   (GSM context) Interface between the Serving General Packet Radio Service (GPRS) Support Node and the Home Location Register [r014].

Graded Authentication   Mechanisms to control use access to a network (or asset) based on the log-in method used to authenticate the user. For example, an environment could be setup as follows, and the privileges be based on the login method:

- Biometric + Password + Token: Authentication and access requires a physical attribute, a password, and a token.
- Biometric + Password: Authentication and access requires a physical attribute and a password.
- Biometric + Token: Authentication and access requires a physical attribute and a token.
- Password + Token: Authentication and access requires a password and a token.
- Biometric: Authentication and access requires a physical attribute.
- Password: Authentication and access requires a password.
- Token: Authentication and access requires a token.

(the stronger the authentication, the greater the set of privileges granted after login)

Gramm–Leach–Bliley Act (GLBA)   Legislation that requires financial institutions to protect the security and confidentiality of their customers' nonpublic personal information. The Act authorizes various federal regulatory agencies to coordinate the development of regulations for meeting this requirement. Each of these federal agencies is authorized to enforce the regulations for those institutions in their jurisdiction. The regulations require financial institutions to develop, implement, and maintain a comprehensive information security program that contains appropriate administrative, technical, and physical safeguards. Such a program should include the designation of an employee to coordinate the program, risk assessments, regular tests and monitoring of safeguards, and a process for making adjustments in light of test results and/or changes in operations or other circumstances that may impact the effectiveness of the program [r208].

Grid Computing   (Virtualized) distributed computing environment that enables the dynamic "runtime" selection, sharing, and aggregation of

(geographically) distributed autonomous (autonomic) resources based on the availability, capability, performance, and cost of these computing resources, and, simultaneously, also based on an organization's specific baseline and/or burst processing requirements. Grid Computing enables organizations to transparently integrate, streamline, and share dispersed, heterogeneous pools of hosts, servers, storage systems, data, and networks into one synergistic system, in order to deliver agreed-upon service at specified levels of application efficiency and processing performance. Grid Computing is an approach to distributed computing that spans multiple locations and/or multiple organizations, machine architectures, and software boundaries to provide power, collaboration, and information access. Grid Computing is infrastructure that enables the integrated, collaborative use of computers, supercomputers, networks, databases, and scientific instruments owned and managed by multiple organizations. Grid Computing is a network of computation: namely, tools and protocols for coordinated resource sharing and problem solving among pooled assets; it allows coordinated resource sharing and problem solving in dynamic, multi-institutional virtual organizations [r080].

Grid Computing Synonyms   (some with slightly different connotations): "computational grid"; "computing-on-demand"; "On Demand computing"; "just-in-time computing"; "platform computing"; "network computing", "computing utility"; "utility computing"; "cluster computing"; and "high-performance distributed computing" [r080].

Grid Computing Topologies   Local, metropolitan, regional, national, or international footprint. Systems may be in the same room, or may be distributed across the globe; they may be running on homogenous or heterogeneous hardware platforms; they may be running on similar or dissimilar operating systems; and, they may be owned by one or more organizations [r080].

Grid Computing Types   (i) *Computational grids:* machines with set-aside resources stand by to "number-crunch" data or provide coverage for other intensive workloads; (ii) *Scavenging grids:* commonly used to locate and exploit CPU cycles on idle servers and desktop machines for use in resource-intensive tasks; and, (iii) *Data grids:* a unified interface for all data repositories in an organization, and through which data can be queried, managed, and secured. Computational grids can be local, Enterprise grids (also called Intragrids), and Internet-based grids (also called Intergrids.) Enterprise grids are middleware-based environments to harvest unused "machine cycles," thereby displacing otherwise-needed growth costs [r080].

Grid Service   A Web Service that conforms to a set of conventions (interfaces and behaviors) that define how a client interacts with a grid capability [r080].

Group and Multicast Security   Group and multicast applications in IP networks have diverse security requirements. These include support for internetwork-, transport-, and application-layer security protocols. Some applications achieve simpler operation by running key management messaging over a pre-established secure channel [e.g., Transport Layer Security (TLS) or IPsec]. Other security protocols benefit from a key management protocol that can run over an already-deployed session initiation or management protocol [e.g., Session Initiation Protocol (SIP) or Real Time Streaming Protocol (RTSP)]. Finally, some benefit from a lightweight key management protocol that requires few round trips. For all these reasons, application-, transport-, and IP-layer data security protocols [e.g., Secure Real-time Transport Protocol (SRTP) (RFC 3711) and IPsec (RFC 2401)] benefit from different group key management systems [r256].

Group Domain of Interpretation (GDOI) Group Keying   Process that provides a means for a group of users or devices to share cryptographic keys, get efficient key updates, and efficient remove group members. Defined in RFC 3547 [r257].

Group Identifier   (IPv6 context) Latest 112 bits or latest 32 bits (according to RFC 2373 recom-

mendation) of an IPv6 multicast address, that identifies a multicast group [r008].

Group Key Management (GKM)   A protocol that supports protected communication between members of a secure group. A secure group is a collection of principals, called members, who may be senders, receivers, or both receivers and senders to other members of the group. Group membership may vary over time. A group key management protocol helps to ensure that only members of a secure group can gain access to group data (by gaining access to group keys) and can authenticate group data. The goal of a group key management protocol is to provide legitimate group members with the up-to-date cryptographic state they need for secrecy and authentication [r256].

Group Policy   Mechanisms in the Windows Operating System (OS) environment to manage security for the entities in the domain.

Group Policy Objects (GPOs)   Data objects in the Windows Operating Sytstem (OS) environment that are replicated through the Active Directory (AD). They are used to configure security options in this environment including but not limited to: password policies, account lockout policies, audit policies, custom user rights assignments, and event log sizes.

Groupware   Applications that provide collaboration services, such as e-mail, meeting scheduling, instant messaging, and file sharing.

Gs   (GSM context) Interface between the Serving General Packet Radio Service (GPRS) Support Node and a Mobile Switching Center/Visitor Location Register [r014].

GSM   See Global System for Mobile Communication

GSM Radio Frequency (GSM-RF)   (GSM context) The GSM protocol layer that provides a clear description of the physical layer and the air interface [r014].

GSM-RF   See GSM Radio-Frequency Protocol

GSN   See GPRS Support Node

GSS-API   See Generic Security Service Application Program Interface

Gt   (GSM context) Interface between a Serving

General Packet Radio Service (GPRS) Support Node and an Equipment Identity Register (EIR) [r014].

GTP   See GPRS Tunneling Protocol

Guaranteed Frame Rate (GFR)   GFR optimizes the handling of packet-based Local Area Network (LAN) traffic that otherwise relies on unspecified bit rate (UBR) service across Asynchronous Transfer Mode (ATM) backbones. Networks based on the ATM Forum TM 5.0 GFR deliver entire frames through the network, and not partial frames.

Guard   A gateway that is interposed between two networks (or computers, or other information systems) operating at different security levels (one level is usually higher than the other) and is trusted to mediate all information transfers between the two levels. This is either to ensure that no sensitive information from the first (higher) level is disclosed to the second (lower) level, or to protect the integrity of data on the first (higher) level [r013].

Guest Login/Login   A login (and associated password) for temporary use by users or to provide limited privileges for users. These users are not uniquely identifiable.

Guidelines and Recommendations for Security Incident Processing (GRIP)   The name of the Internet Engineering Task Force (IETF) working group that seeks to facilitate consistent handling of security incidents in the Internet community. Guidelines to be produced by the working group will address technology vendors, network service providers, and response teams in their roles assisting organizations in resolving security incidents. These relationships are functional and can exist within and across organizational boundaries [r013].

GULS   See Generic Upper Layer Security Service

H.261 (video formats and coding) International Telecommunications Union Standardization Sector (ITU-T) digital videoconferencing format for Integrated Services Digital Network (ISDN) environments.

H.263 (video formats and coding) International Telecommunications Union Standardization Sector (ITU-T) digital videoconferencing format for Local Area Network (LAN)/IP networks.

H.264 [aka MPEG-4 Part 10 or Advanced Video Coding (AVC)] A digital video codec standard that achieves very high data compression, developed in 2003 by the International Telecommunications Union (ITU) Video Coding Experts Group (VCEG) in collaboration with the International Organization for Standardization/International Electrotechnical Commission (ISO/IEC) Moving Picture Experts Group (MPEG). The ITU-T H.264 standard and the ISO/IEC MPEG-4 Part 10 standard (formally, ISO/IEC 14496-10) are identical. It is normal to call the standard as H.264/AVC (or AVC/H.264 or H.264/MPEG-4 AVC or MPEG-4/H.264 AVC) to emphasize the common heritage. The intent of the H.264/AVC standard is to provide acceptable (good) video quality at bit rates that are substantially lower (e.g., half or less) than what previous standards would need (e.g., relative to MPEG-2, H.263, or MPEG-4 Part 2), and to do so without an increase in complexity.

H.350 Series of Recommendations Series of Recommendations that specify directory services architectures in support of multimedia conferencing protocols. The goal of the architecture is to "directory enable" multimedia conferencing so

Minoli–Cordovana's Authoritative Computer and Network Security Dictionary. By Daniel Minoli and James Cordovana
Copyright © 2006 John Wiley & Sons, Inc.

that these services can leverage existing identity management and enterprise directories. A particular goal is to enable an enterprise or service provider to maintain a canonical source of users and their multimedia conferencing systems, so that multiple call servers from multiple vendors, supporting multiple protocols, can all access the same data store [r074].

HA   See Home Agent

Hacker   Someone with a strong interest in computers, who enjoys learning about them and experimenting with them. The original meaning of the term (circa 1960) had a neutral or positive connotation of "someone who figures things out and makes something cool happen." At this time the term is frequently misused, especially by journalists, to have the pejorative meaning of cracker [r013].

Hacking Run   A hacking session extended long outside normal working times, especially one longer than 12 hours [r057].

Hacktivism (sometimes spelled Hactivism)   Politically or ideologically motivated vandalism. Defacing a website for no particular reason is vandalism; the same defacement to post political propaganda or to cause harm to an ideological opponent is hacktivism [r057].

Hacktivist   A hacker with an (often political) agenda

Handle   An on-line pseudonym, particularly one used by a cracker. The term is derived from citizens band radio culture [r013].

Handover Number (HON)   (GSM context) Number used for routing between two Mobile Services Switching Centers (MSCs) in an Inter-MSC-Handover [r011].

Handshake   An initial negotiation between client and server that establishes the parameters of their transactions [r039].

Hard Reset   An event that triggers a complete reinitialization of the routing tables on one or more Border Gateway Protocol (BGP) sessions, resulting in exchange of a full routing table on one or more links to the router [r086].

Hardened   A state of a system where the capability of a device has been decreased to the minimum required for its intended purpose [r200]. A system has been hardened after hardening has taken place.

Hardening   Decreasing the capability of a device to the minimum required for its intended purpose [r200].

Hardware   The physical components of a computer system.

Hardware and Systems Software Maintenance Security Issues   To ensure that hardware and software function as intended, there should be controls used to monitor the installation of, and updates to, hardware, operating system software, and other software. The controls may also be used to ensure that only authorized software is installed on the system. Such controls may include a hardware and software configuration policy that grants managerial approval to modifications and requires that changes be documented. Other controls include products and procedures used in auditing for or preventing illegal use of shareware or copyrighted software [r067].

Hardware Keyloggers   Small inline devices placed between the keyboard and the computer. Because of their size they can often go undetected for long periods of time. However, they of course require physical access to the machine. These hardware devices have the power to capture hundreds of keystrokes including banking and e-mail username and passwords [r224].

Hardware or Software Error   An error that causes failure of a system component and leads to disruption of system operation. Also, an error that results in the alteration of system functions or data [r013].

Hardware Vulnerability   Vulnerabilities specific to computing hardware, including outdated firmware, hardware failure, and systems not physically secured.

Hardware-Based Token   (aka access token or token) A type of credential that satisfies the "what you have" element of an authentication transaction. The token is in the form of a hardware device [such as a one-time password fob, smart card, or portable Universal Serial Bus (USB) device]. A token is often used along with a password which "unlocks" the token, thereby creating a multifactor authentication mechanism.

Harmonic Mean   The harmonic mean of the positive real numbers $a_1, a_2, \ldots, a_n$ is defined to be

$$H = \frac{n}{\dfrac{1}{a_1} + \dfrac{1}{a_2} + \cdots + \dfrac{1}{a_n}}.$$

Note that the harmonic mean is never larger than the geometric mean or the arithmetic mean.

Hash   A fixed-length cryptographic output of variables. Often used as term describing the output of a hash function.

Hash Function   An algorithm [e.g., Message Digest 2 (MD2), MD4, MD5, Secure Hash Algorithm One (SHA-1)] that computes a value based on a data object (such as a message or file, which is usually variable length and possibly very large), thereby mapping the data object to a smaller data object (the "hash result") which is usually a fixed-size value [r013].

This (mathematical) function maps values from a large (possibly very large) domain into a smaller range. A "good" hash function is such that the results of applying the function to a (large) set of values in the domain will be evenly distributed (and apparently at random) over the range [r061]. The kind of hash function needed for security applications is called a cryptographic hash function, an algorithm for which it is computationally infeasible to find either a data object that maps to a prespecified hash result (the "one-way" property) or two data objects that map to the same hash result (the "collision-free" property) [r013].

Typical uses of hash functions are to use a one-way hash function to protect passwords in storage or to produce cryptographic message digests of documents (in order to ensure data integrity).

Hash Function Reliability   Message Digest 4 (MD4), Message Digest 5 (MD5), and Secure Hash Algorithm One (SHA-1) have been broken. MD4 and MD5 should be considered insecure. SHA-1 is still widely used, although its stronger counterparts—SHA-256, SHA-384, and SHA-512—are likely to replace it in the future [r036].

Hash Result   The output (result) of a hash function.

Hashing   The act of putting data through a hash function.

Hashing for Message Authentication (HMAC)   A keyed hash that can be based on any iterated cryptographic hash [e.g., Message Digest 5 (MD5) or Secure Hash Algorithm One (SHA-1)] [r114, r013]. The cryptographic strength of HMAC depends on the properties of the selected cryptographic hash [r258–r260].

Hashing for Message Authentication (HMAC)-Based One-Time Password (HOTP) Algorithm   A proposed algorithm to generate one-time password values, based on keyed-hash message authentication code (HMAC). The proposed algorithm can be used across a wide range of network applications ranging from remote Virtual Private Network (VPN) access, to Wi-Fi network logon, to transaction-oriented Web applications. Intended as a common and shared algorithm that will facilitate adoption of two-factor authentication on the Internet by enabling interoperability across commercial and open-source implementations [r263].

HBA   See Host Bus Adapter

HCA/TCA   See Host Channel Adapter/Target Channel Adapter

HCP   See Hypertext Caching Protocol

HDTV   See High Definition Television

Header   Potion of a packet (refer to packet definition) that contains the source and destination addresses, error checking information, message originator, date and time, and subject lines [r057].

(SIP context) A header is a component of a Session Initiation Protocol (SIP) message that conveys information about the message. It is structured as a sequence of header fields [r025].

Header Field   Fields (blocks of bits) in a Protocol Data Unit (PDU) that are appended to the Service Data Unit (SDU) to instantiate (support) a given networking protocol (e.g., the Media Access Control fields in the Ethernet frame).

(SIP context) A header field is a component of

the Session Initiation Protocol (SIP) message header. A header field can appear as one or more header field rows. Header field rows consist of a header field name and zero or more header field values. Multiple header field values on a given header field row are separated by commas. Some header fields can only have a single header field value, and as a result, always appear as a single header field row [r025].

Header Field Value   (SIP context) A header field value is a single value; a header field consists of zero or more header field values [r025].

Health Insurance Portability and Accountability (HIPAA) Act of 1996   Legislation that authorizes the Secretary of Health and Human Services to adopt standards that require health plans, health care providers, and health care clearinghouses to take reasonable and appropriate administrative, technical and physical safeguards to:

- Ensure the integrity and confidentiality of individually identifiable health information held or transferred by them.
- Protect against any reasonably anticipated threats, unauthorized use, or disclosure.
- Ensure compliance with these safeguards by officers and employees [r208].

The compliance date was April 21, 2005 for most organizations and April 21, 2006 for small health plans.

Health Insurance Portability and Accountability (HIPAA) General Rules   Section 164.306 HIPAA provides the General rules that organizations must follow to protect Electronic Personal Health Information (EPHI). They are [r262]:

- Ensure the confidentiality, integrity, and availability of all electronic protected health information the covered entity creates, receives, maintains, or transmits.
- Protect against any reasonably anticipated threats or hazards to the security or integrity of such information.
- Protect against any reasonably anticipated

uses or disclosures of such information that are not permitted.
- Ensure compliance by its workforce.

Hedge   (financial term) An investment made in order to reduce the risk of adverse price movements in a security, by taking an offsetting position in a related security, such as an option or a short sale [r009].

Hewlett-Packard's Utility Data Center (UDC)   Hewlett-Packard's virtualization product family focusing on resource management across its servers [r080].

Hexadecimal (Hex) Notation   (aka hex) Base 16 arithmetic. Hexadecimal notation uses a base of 16: 1 (0001), 2 (0010), 3 (0011), 4, 5, 6, 7, 8, 9, 10, A, B, C, D, E (1110), F (1111). With hex notation, every byte can be shown as two hexadecimal characters. For example, a single byte of information can be represented as eight bits 10011101, or simplified to hex 9D.

HIDS   See Host-Based Intrusion Detection Systems

Hierarchical Public-Key Infrastructure (PKI)   A PKI architecture based on a certification hierarchy.

Hierarchical Storage Management (HSM)   A storage management methodology. The primary difference between Data Lifecycle Management (DLM) and HSM is that HSM was a single-server, single storage stack methodology for moving things down (usually) that physical stack in order to lower the cost of primary storage while DLM is more encompassing. HSM is still used today in the mainframe world and had limited success in some of the open and traditional world. DLM is HSM in the network world where there are lots of ways into and out of a storage environment from a multitude of potential servers, and each server has a multitude of different ways in and out. HSM was more of a single stovepipe. The HSM data migration technologies of the past were predicated on purely objective measures. For example, one might have a policy that if one has not accessed a file or type of data in a certain period of time, the data should be moved from expensive primary storage to less expensive tape storage. That works well if all the value is predicated on those objective measures. Unfortunately, currently that is not true in most applications. Value is not only objective but it is subjective. Just because access might be limited to a certain data set does not necessarily mean that data set lacks great value to the organization. Conversely, data that one accesses all the time (such as PowerPoint, for example) may not be the most important application, in spite of the frequency of access. ILM aims to use the combination of both subjective and objective measures—the data itself combined with overall business policies (which typically do not exist today) to ascertain where things are located at a particular point in time [r284].

Hierarchical Storage Management/Automated Data Management (HSM/ADM) Solutions that migrate data within the storage environment according to user-defined policies [r029].

Hierarchy Management The process of generating configuration data and issuing public-key certificates to build and operate a certification hierarchy [r013].

High-Definition Television (HDTV) High-definition digital scheme for video formats and coding.

High-Speed Circuit Switched Data (HSCSD) (GSM context) An enhancement of the GSM standard. HSCSD supports an increase in bit rates. It is circuit-switched and optimizes the existing transfer rates using a new type of channel encoding and channel bundling [r011].

Higher-Level Checksum (IPv6 context) Calculation of the checksum, realized in Internet Control Message Protocol for the Internet Protocol Version 6 (ICMPv6), Transmission Control Protocol (TCP) and User Datagram Protocol (UDP), that uses the IPv6 pseudo-header [r008].

Higher-Level Protocol (IPv6 context) Protocol that uses IPv6 as transport and it is placed in the upper layer than IPv6, such as Internet Control Message Protocol for the Internet Protocol Version 6 (ICMPv6), Transmission Control Protocol (TCP), and User Datagram Protocol (UDP) [r008].

Higher-Layer Security Mechanisms Mecha-

nisms that operate above Transport Control Protocol (TCP) layer (Layer 4) in the Open Systems Interconnection Reference Model (OSIRM). These mechanisms typically encrypt the TCP data while leaving the TCP header in unencrypted and unauthenticated form. Examples include Secure Hypertext Transfer Protocol (HTTPS) for web content, and Secure Internet Message Access Protocol (SIMAP) for e-mail content.

High-Level Format The process of formatting using the FORMAT command in Windows or Disk Operating System (DOS). This does not destroy the data on the disk; it simply resets the index in the file allocation table so that the operating system sees the disk as empty [r057].

Hijack Attack A form of active wiretapping in which the attacker seizes control of a previously established communication association. Examples include man-in-the-middle attacks, pagejackings, and piggyback attacks [r013].

Hijacking The use of an authenticated user's communication session to communicate with system components [r200].

HIPAA See Health Insurance Portability and Accountability

HIPS See Host-Based Intrusion Prevention Systems

Historical Protocol, Internet Engineering Task Force (IETF) A specification that has been superseded by a more recent specification or is for any other reason considered to be obsolete is assigned to the "Historic" level. (Purists have suggested that the word should be "Historical"; however, at this point the use of "Historic" is historical.) [r280, r281].

HLR See Home Location Register

HMAC See Hashed Message Authentication Code

Hoax E-mail messages highlighting "perceived" security concerns that are usually untrue. Instead of spreading from one computer to another by itself, hoaxes rely on people to pass them along [r057].

HOLD See Call Holding Service

Holder In X.509 an entity to whom some privilege has been delegated either directly from the Source of Authority or indirectly through another Attribute Authority.

Home Agent (HA) Mobile IP was developed for transparently dealing with mobile users; specifically it enables hosts to stay connected to a network (such as the Internet) regardless of the host's location. The HA is a router with additional functionality to handle mobility binding of the Mobile Node's (MN) IP address with its Care-of-address (COA) [the COA is the address that identifies MN's current location; it is sent by the Foreign Agent (FA) to HA when MN attaches; usually it is the IP address of the FA]. The HA is located on home network of MN and it forwards packets to appropriate network when MN is away (through encapsulation.)

Home Domain   (SIP context) The domain providing service to a Session Initiation Protocol (SIP) user. Typically, this is the domain present in the Uniform Resource Identifier (URI) in the address-of-record of a registration [r025].

Home Location Register (HLR)   (GSM context) A database in the Network Subsystem (NSS) that contains the subscriber information [r011].

Homeland Security Presidential Directive No. 7 Among other items, it describes the role of the Department of Homeland Security.

Homologation   (from the verb homologate, meaning to approve or confirm officially) The certification of a product or specification to indicate that it meets regulatory standards. There are companies that specialize in helping manufacturers achieve regulatory compliance. Their services might include the explanation and interpretation of standards and specifications, assistance in plant facility audit and approval, testing and certification of materials, product design consulting, and translation of manuals, legal mandates, and other written material [r019].

HON   See Handover Number

Honey Pot   (aka fishbowl) A system is designed to lure (or decoy) individuals with malicious intent away from the true target systems, much like honey attracts bears. It is also a means to observe malicious behavior in an attempt to better understand cracker methodologies and system weaknesses, and is utilized to find out more details on the cracker in order to determine more information about the individual and from where the attack is initiated. Honeypots may not be legal in some instances.

Honeynet   A network of honeypots; this set of honeypots may emulate an entire corporate intranet. A honeypot is an information system resource whose value lies in unauthorized or illicit use of that resource; the honeypot can be a system (host computer) or something else. Specifically in reference to the last statement, the honeypot does not necessarily have to be a computer, but simply a resource that nefarious agent are "enticed" to interact with.

Honeypot   (aka Honey Pot)

Honeytoken   A honeypot that is not a computer. It can be some type of digital entity; for example, it can be a credit card number, a database entry, a Word document, an Excel spreadsheet, or a bogus login. It is a digital or information system resource whose value lies in the unauthorized use of that resource. Just as a honeypot computer has no authorized value, no honeytoken has any authorized use (no one should be using or accessing it).

Hop-by-Hop Option Header   (IPv6 context) An IPv6 extension header that contains options that must be processed by all intermediate routers as well as final router [r008].

Host   General computer network usage: A computer that is attached to a communication subnetwork or internetwork and can use services provided by the network to exchange data with other attached systems [r013]. A computer system, particularly one that is accessed by a user from a remote location, being that it is connected to a network. A computer that can be accessed over a network. A single computer or workstation [r057].

Specific Internet Protocol Suite usage: A networked computer that does not forward Internet Protocol packets that are not addressed to the computer itself [r013].

Host-Based Intrusion Detection Systems (HIDS) Intrusion Detection Systems (IDSs) that reside on a computer in order to detect, audit, and send alerts about malicious activity on that host.

Host-Based Intrusion Prevention Systems (HIPS) Host-Based Intrusion Detection Systems (HIDS) that not only detect, but also take actions (such as disabling a service) to prevent intrusion if malicious activity is suspected.

Host Bus Adapter (HBA) Any hardware bridge between a storage interconnect and a system's Input/Output (I/O) bus [r029].

Host Channel Adapter/Target Channel Adapter (HCA/TCA) HCAs and TCAs enable servers and Input/Output (I/O) devices to connect to the InfiniBand fabric, respectively. These adapters are comprised of specialized chips that process the InfiniBand link protocol at wire speed and without incurring any host overhead [r029].

Host Defenses The result of actions taken to protect a computing system. These defenses include disabling unnecessary services, keeping system patches up-to-date, and installing anti-virus software.

Hosted Private Branch Exchange (PBX) A situation where the PBX is deployed in the carrier's network rather that in the customer's environment. Managed service for campus voice switching.

Generally similar to Centrex service, except that in with Centrex the carrier would likely use a telephone-carrier-class switch rather than a PBX; this switch is likely Time Division Multiplexing (TDM)-based. The concept of Hosted PBX is more likely to be seen in the context of Voice over IP (VoIP), where a firm may have outsourced the function to an Application Service Provider (ASP) (possibly via an asset transfer arrangement). The PBX here may actually be a softswitch.

Hosts File A text file used to contain name-IP address correspondences. In Windows XP or .NET server is located at \SystemRoot\System32\Drivers\Etc directory. In Unix devices is located at /etc directory [r008].

Host-to-Host Tunnel (IPv6 context) An IPv6 over IPv4 tunnel in which endpoints are devices [r008].

Host-to-Router Tunnel (IPv6 context) An IPv6 over IPv4 tunnel in which the tunnel begins in a host and ends in an IPv6/IPv4 router [r008].

Hotfixes Operating System (OS) patches that typically require immediate attention and implementation.

HOTP See HMAC-Based One-Time Password

Hotspot A geographic location (typically within a radius of 100 meters or so, but sometimes more) where a user can get access to Internet services or Voice over Wi-Fi (Wireless Fidelity) services by using the Wireless Local Area Network (WLAN) capabilities of the laptop (usually employing IEEE 802.11b technology) [r348]. Such locations exist in airports, hotel lobbies, coffeshops, business-serving locations, and sometimes in open metropolitan spaces; often a subscription to a Wireless Internet Service Provider (WISP) is needed.

Hot Zones Hotspots that cover a broad area, such as a downtown city district. Off-the-shelf radio technology such as Wi-Fi (Wireless Fidelity), WiMAX (Worldwide Interoperability for Microwave Access), and cellular 3G are used [r021].

HOVC See Higher-Order Virtual Container

HSCSD See High-Speed Circuit Switched Data

HSM See Hierarchical Storage Management

HSM/ADM See Hierarchical Storage Management/Automated Data Management

HTML See HyperText Markup Language

HTTP See HyperText Transfer Protocol

https When used in the first part of a URL (the part that precedes the colon and specifies an access scheme or protocol), this term specifies the use of HTTP enhanced by a security mechanism, which is usually Secure Sockets Layer (SSL) [r013].

HTTPS See HyperText Transport Protocol—Secure

Human Capital The set of skills which an employee acquires on the job, through training and experience, and which increase that employee's value in the marketplace.

Human Error An action performed (or not performed) by an individual that unintentionally results in the alteration of system functions or data [r013].

Human Vulnerability   Weaknesses in a system due to human error or lack or foresight. Examples include poorly defined procedures, inappropriate credentials stores (such as placing a note with the passwords on the desk), and manual input errors.

Hybrid Encryption   An application of cryptography that combines two or more encryption algorithms, particularly a combination of symmetric and asymmetric encryption. Asymmetric algorithms require more computation than equivalently strong symmetric ones. Thus, asymmetric encryption is not normally used for data confidentiality, rather it is often used in distributing symmetric keys (i.e., key exchange or "handshake") [r013]. The combined use of symmetric (or secret-key) and asymmetric (or public-key) algorithms: A public-key algorithm is used to encrypt a randomly generated encryption key, and the random key is used to encrypt the actual message using a symmetric algorithm [r036].

Hyperlink   In hypertext or hypermedia, an information object (such as a word, a phrase, or an image; usually highlighted by color or underscoring) that points (indicates how to connect) to related information that is located elsewhere and can be retrieved by activating the link (e.g., by selecting the object with a mouse pointer and then clicking) [r013].

Hypermedia   A generalization of hypertext; any media that contain hyperlinks that point to material in the same or another data object.

Hyperperfect Number   A "nice" generalization of the concept of a perfect number now part of Number Theory co-introduced by the senior author of this dictionary in the early 1970s (Minoli-Bear). Hyperperfect numbers are expected to have applications in cryptology and signal processing transforms [r080, r265–r272].

In mathematics, a k-hyperperfect number (sometimes just called hyperperfect number) is a natural number n for which the equality $n = 1 + k(\sigma(n) - n - 1)$ holds, where $\sigma(n)$ is the divisor

function (i.e., the sum of all positive divisors of n). A number is perfect iff it is 1-hyperperfect. The first few numbers in the sequence of k-hyperperfect numbers are 6, 21, 28, 301, 325, 496, ... with the corresponding values of k being 1, 2, 1, 6, 3, 1, 12, ... The first few k-hyperperfect numbers that are not perfect are 21, 301, 325, 697, 1333, ... The following table lists the first few k-hyperperfect numbers for some values of k:

k	Some Known k-Hyperperfect Numbers
1	6, 28, 496, 8128, 33550336, ...
2	21, 2133, 19521, 176661, 129127041, ...
3	325, ...
4	1950625, 1220640625, ...
6	301, 16513, 60110701, 1977225901, ...
10	159841, ...
11	10693, ...
12	697, 2041, 1570153, 62722153, 10604156641, 13544168521, ...
18	1333, 1909, 2469601, 893748277, ...

It can be shown that if $k > 1$ is an odd integer and $p = (3k + 1)/2$ and $q = 3k + 4$ are prime numbers, then p^2q is k-hyperperfect; Judson S. McCraine has conjectured that all k-hyperperfect numbers for odd $k > 1$ are of this form, but the hypothesis has not been proven so far. Furthermore, it can be proven that if $p \neq q$ are odd primes and k is an integer such that $k(p + q) = pq - 1$, then pq is k-hyperperfect.

It is also possible to show that if $k > 0$ and $p = k + 1$ is prime, then for all $i > 1$ such that $q = p^i - p + 1$ is prime, $n = p^{i-1}q$ is k-hyperperfect.

HyperText   A computer document, or part of a document, that contains hyperlinks to other documents—that is, text that contains active pointers to other text. Usually written in Hypertext Markup Language and accessed using a Web browser.

HyperText Caching Protocol (HCP)   A protocol described in RFC 2756 that is an alternative and improvement to Internet Cache Protocol (ICP). HCP permits full request and response headers to be used in cache management, and expands the domain of cache management to include monitoring a remote cache's additions and deletions, requesting immediate deletions, and sending hints about Web objects such as the third-party locations of cacheable objects or the measured uncacheability or unavailability of web objects.

HyperText Markup Language (HTML)   A language to create documents that can be seen and properly displayed by a browser. A platform-independent system of syntax and semantics for adding characters to data files (particularly text files) to represent the data's structure and to point to related data, thus creating hypertext for use in the World Wide Web (WWW) and other applications [r283, r229, r284, r013].

HyperText Transfer Protocol (HTTP)   A TCP-based, application-layer, client–server, Internet protocol [r285] used to carry data requests and responses in the World Wide Web (WWW). The protocol used by the World Wide Web to transfer HyperText Markup Language (HTML) files. The standard transmission protocol used on the World Wide Web. HTTP is a "stateless protocol" [r283, r229].

HyperText Transport Protocol-Secure (HTTPS)   The standard for encrypted communication mechanism on the World Wide Web. This mechanism uses HTTP over Secure Sockets Layer (SSL). The HTTPS (HTTP/SSL) apparatus has been employed for a number of years to secure the "first generation of the Web." SSL basically provides a secure tunnel (channel) between two points [r286].

I

I I I I I I I I I I I I I I I I I I I I I I I I I I I

I/O See Input/Output

IA See Information Assurance

IAB See Internet Architecture Board

IANA See Internet Assigned Numbers Authority

IBGP See Internal Border Gateway Protocol

IBM's on Demand IBM and its partners offer a number of grid computing solutions in several vertical industries (e.g., automotive, financial markets, government, and others). IBM's strategy is to grid-enable all of its products: the company states that they will continue to incorporate virtualization technologies into its server software products and plan to incorporate autonomic capabilities into DB2 and associated content management products [r080].

ICANN See Internet Corporation for Assigned Numbers and Names

ICAP See Internet Content Adaptation Protocol

ICCP See Institute for Certification of Computer Professionals

ICMP See Internet Control Message Protocol

ICMPV6 See Internet Control Message Protocol for IPv6

ICP See Internet Cache Protocol

ICRL See Indirect Certificate Revocation List

IDE See Integrated Drive Electronics or Integrated Development Environment

IDEA See International Data Encryption Algorithm

Identification An act or process that presents an identifier to a system so that the system can recognize a system entity and distinguish it from other entities [r013].

[Public-Key Infrastructure (PKI) context] Establishing that a given name of an individual or organization corresponds to a real-world identity of an individual or organization, and establishing that an individual or organization applying for or seeking access to something under that name is, in fact, the named individual or organization. A person seeking identification may be a certificate applicant, an applicant for employment in a trusted position within a PKI participant, or a person seeking access to a network or software application, such as a Certification Authority (CA) administrator seeking access to CA systems [r011].

Identification Protocol   A client–server Internet protocol for learning the identity of a user of a particular Transmission Control Protocol (TCP) connection [r277]. Given a TCP port number pair, the server returns a character string that identifies the owner of that connection on the server's system. The protocol is not intended for authorization or access control. At best, it provides additional auditing information with respect to TCP [r013].

Identifier   (Instant Messaging/Presence context) A means of indicating a point of contact, intended for public use such as on a business card. Telephone numbers, email addresses, and typical home page Uniform Resource Locators (URLs) are all examples of Identifiers in other systems. Numeric IP addresses such as 10.0.0.26 are not, and neither are URLs containing numerous Common Gateway Interface (CGI) parameters or long arbitrary identifiers [r027].

Identity Provider   An entity establishes, maintains, and distributes identity information. Identity providers include Certification Authorities and Human Resources systems. Often, identity providers manage their services through a directory services.

Identity Theft   The impersonation of the identity of another individual/entity for malicious purposes.

Identity-Based Encryption   A form of public-key encryption for which the public key can be an arbitrary string, and in particular, a string that identifies the user who holds the associated private key, like his e-mail address. The original motivation for identity-based cryptography was to simplify certificate management, but it has many other applications [r078].

Identity-Based Security Policy   A security policy based on the identities and/or attributes of users, a group of users, or entities that act on behalf of the users and the resources/objects being accessed [r160].

IDIOT   See Intrusion Detection in Our Time

IDS   See Intrusion Detection System

IEAK   See Internet Explorer Administration Kit

IEEE   See Institute of Electrical and Electronics Engineers

IETF   See Internet Engineering Task Force

IFCP   See Internet FCP

IGMP   See Internet Group Management Protocol

IGP   See Interior Gateway Protocol

IGRP   See Interior Gateway Routing Protocol

IIOP   See Internet Inter-ORB Protocol

IIPtran   An alternative to tunnel mode Internet Protocol (IP) Security (IPsec) that uses non-IPsec IP within IP (IPIP) encapsulation together with IPsec transport mode, as defined in RFC 3884. IPIP encapsulation occurs as a separate initial step, as the result of a forwarding lookup of the virtual network (VN) packet. IPsec transport mode processes the resulting (tunneled) IP packet with a security association (SA) determined through a security association database (SAD) match on the tunnel header. IIPtran supports dynamic routing inside the VN without changes to the current IPsec architecture [r282]. IIPtran separates the step of IP tunnel encapsulation from IPsec processing. The solution combines a subset of the current IPsec architecture with other Internet standards to arrive at an interoperable equivalent that is both simpler and has a modular specification.

IIS   See Internet Information Service

IISP   See Interim Interswitch Signaling Protocol

IKE   See Internet Key Exchange

iLBC   See Internet Low-Bitrate Codec

ILM   See Information Lifecycle Management

ILMI   See Interim Local Management Interface

ILOVEYOU Worm   Still widely considered one of the most costly viruses to enterprises, the ILOVEYOU worm, also known as VBS/Loveletter or Love Bug, used social engineering and catchy subject lines to trick Windows users into launching the executable (May 2000). The worm spread rapidly by sending out copies of itself to all entries in the Microsoft Outlook address book. Anti-virus researchers also discovered an additional—and dangerous—component called "WIN-BUGSFIX.EXE" that was a password-stealing program that e-mailed cached passwords back to the attacker [r090]. The worm also gained the attention of the mainstream press when it launched a denial-of-service attack against the White House website.

IMA   See Inverse Multiplexed ATM

Image Map   Picture in a web page that acts as a hyperlink to different pages.

IMAP4   See Internet Message Access Protocol, version 4

IMEI   See International Mobile Equipment Identity

Impersonation   Pretending to be an individual with legitimate business purposes, for the purpose of gaining unauthorized access to a facility. To enter a secure location for the purpose. Examples include entering into a site dressed as an employee, or pretending to be maintenance personnel. Impersonation is an element of social engineering.

Implementation & Deployment   Planning, installing, configuring, and maintaining computer system.

Imposter   A person or entity that deceives others under an assumed identity.

IMSI   See International Mobile Subscriber Identity

IMT-2000   See International Mobile Telecommunication System-2000

Imux   See Inverse Multiplexing

IN   See Intelligent Network

In the clear   Having the property of not being encrypted.

Inbox User Agent   (Presence Services context) Means for a principal to manipulate zero or more instant inboxes controlled by that principal. Motivation: this is intended to isolate the core functionality of an instant inbox from how it might appear to be manipulated by a product. This manipulation includes fetching messages, deleting messages, and setting delivery rules. The inbox user agent, instant inbox, and instant message service can be colocated or distributed across machines [r015].

Incapacitation   A threat action that prevents or interrupts system operation by disabling a system component. This includes malicious code, physical destruction, human error, systems errors, and natural disasters [r013].

Incident Management   (aka incident response) A systematic investigation and response to potential violations of security policies. Examples include Computer Incident Response Team (CIRT) and computer forensics tools.

Incident Response   See Incident Management

Incident Response Capability   An incident response capability provides help when an adverse event in a computer system or network causes a failure of a security mechanism or an attempted breach of those mechanisms. The capability should be able to respond quickly and to share information concerning common vulnerabilities and threats [r067].

Independent Evaluations   Reviews of a firm's system of internal control or risk management by internal or external entities.

Indirect Certificate Revocation List (ICRL)   In X.509, a Certificate Revocation List (CRL) that may contain certificate revocation notifications for certificates issued by Certification Authorities (CAs) other than the issuer of the ICRL [r013].

Indistinguishability   An attribute of an encryption algorithm that is a formalization of the notion that the encryption of some string is indistinguishable from the encryption of an equal-length string of nonsense [r013].

Industrial Espionage   Spying on one's competitors to gain a competitive advantage.

Industrial, Scientific, and Medical (ISM) Band

2.4-GHz radio band available on a nonregulated basis in the United States. Employed for Wireless Local Area Networks (WLANs.) This spectrum band is subject to interference, drop-out, and eavesdropping. Transmission power is typically limited by regulation to relatively low levels.

Inference   A threat action whereby an unauthorized entity indirectly accesses sensitive data (but not necessarily the data contained in the communication) by reasoning from characteristics or byproducts of communications. This includes [r013]:

- Traffic analysis: Gaining knowledge of data by observing the characteristics of communications that carry the data.
- Signals analysis: Gaining indirect knowledge of communicated data by monitoring and analyzing a signal that is emitted by a system and that contains the data but is not intended to communicate the data.

InfiniBand   A switched I/O architecture that delivers a high-performance, low-latency interconnect for the data center [r029].

Inflation   (financial term) The overall general upward price movement of goods and services in an economy, usually as measured by the Consumer Price Index and the Producer Price Index. Over time, as the cost of goods and services increase, the value of a dollar is going to fall because a person will not be able to purchase as much with that dollar as he/she previously could. While the annual rate of inflation has fluctuated greatly over the last half century, ranging from nearly zero inflation to 23% inflation, the Fed (Federal Reserve Bank) actively tries to maintain a specific rate of inflation, which is usually 2–3% but can vary depending on circumstances. Opposite of deflation [r009].

Informatics   The sciences dealing with gathering, manipulating, storing, retrieving, and classifying recorded information.

Information   Facts and ideas, which can be represented (encoded) as various forms of data.

Information Architecture   An architectural for-

mulation of the Information Function via a data model.

Information Asset   Information an organization must have to conduct its mission or business.

Information Assurance (IA)   Information operations that protect and defend information and information systems by ensuring their availability, integrity, authentication, confidentiality, and non-repudiation. This includes providing for restoration of information systems by incorporating protection, detection, and reaction capabilities [r057].

Information Assurance Technical Framework Forum   Forum that defines protection profiles. A Protection Profile is an implementation-independent specification of information assurance security requirements. Protection profiles are a complete combination of security objectives, security related functional requirements, information assurance requirements, assumptions, and rationale. Protection profiles are written in accordance with the Common Criteria (CC) standard. The use of protection profiles to define information assurance requirements is part of the National Information Assurance Partnership (NIAP) program [r285].

Information Function   A comprehensive identification of the data, the data flows, and the data interrelations required to support the Business function. The identification, systematization, categorization, and inventory/storage of information are always necessary to run a Business, but these are essential if the data-handling functions are to be automated.

Information Lifecycle Management (ILM)   A process whereby Information Technology (IT) staff makes conscious or unconscious decisions about what data should reside where in the physical infrastructure and how to optimize for use by the appropriate application at the right time. ILM is a process in which people, processes, and technologies deal with data from cradle to grave. Data has different value at inception than it does at death, so it should not be treated the same way during each phase of its lifetime. ILM is a concept more than a product: several products, tools, and services encompass a company's total ILM strategy [r284]. Today most solutions being sold as ILM focus on data migration or data movement, as well as the retention and protection aspects of where data resides.

Information Managers Owners of data stored, processed, and transmitted by the IT systems.

Information Operations (IO) Actions taken to affect adversary information and information systems while defending one's own information and information systems (DODD S-3600.1 of 9 Dec 96) [r057].

Information Retention Policy (IRP) Guidelines and mechanisms that specify how to store, track, and properly destroy "official records" (such as electronic files and e-mails) in order to facilitate compliance with existing laws, regulations, and litigation-related document retention orders.

Information Risk Management A security service that typically includes Risk Assessment and Risk Management.

Information Security (INFOSEC) The protection of information systems against unauthorized access to or modification of information, whether in storage, processing, or transit, and against the denial of service to authorized users or the provision of service to unauthorized users, including those measures necessary to detect, document, and counter such threats [r200].

Information Security and Privacy Advisory Board (ISPAB) ISPAB was originally created by the Computer Security Act of 1987 (P.L. 100-35) as the Computer System Security and Privacy Advisory Board. As a result of Public Law 107-347, The E-Government Act of 2002, Title III, The Federal Information Security Management Act of 2002, the Board's name was changed and its mandate was amended. The scope and objectives of the Board are: (i) to identify emerging managerial, technical, administrative, and physical safeguard issues relative to information security and privacy; (ii) to advise the National Institute of Standards and Technology (NIST), the Secretary of Commerce, and the Director of the Office of Management and Budget on information security and privacy issues pertaining to Federal Government information systems, including thorough review of proposed standards and guidelines developed by NIST; (iii) to annually report its findings to the Secretary of Commerce, the Director of the Office of Management and Budget, the Director of the National Security Agency, and the appropriate committees of the Congress.

Information Security Roles System and user access profiles as part of a Role Based Access Control (RBAC) program. Roles should be assigned based on security principles such as least privilege, separation of duties, and deny before permit.

Information Superiority The capability to collect, process, and disseminate an uninterrupted flow of information while exploiting or denying an adversary's ability to do the same (DODD S-3600.1 of 9 Dec 96) [r057].

Information System Auditors Auditors of Information Technology (IT) systems for financial, regulatory, and functional integrity.

Information System Security Officer (ISSO) Another name for a Chief Security Officer (CSO).

Information Systems (IS) See Information Technology (IT)

Information Systems Audit and Control Association (ISACA) Global organization for information governance, control, security, and audit professionals. Its Information Systems (IS) auditing and IS control standards are followed by practitioners worldwide. Its Certified Information Systems Auditor (CISA) certification is recognized globally and has been earned by more than 40,000 professionals since inception. The Certified Information Security Manager (CISM) is another (newer) certification program for the individual who must maintain a view of the "big picture" by managing, designing, overseeing, and assessing an enterprise's information security. ISACA has more than 170 chapters established in over 60 countries worldwide, and those chapters provide members education, resource sharing, advocacy, professional networking, and other benefits on a local level.

Information Systems Audit and Control Association (ISACA) Certified Information Systems Auditor (CISA) Certification Certification program. Since 1978, the CISA exam has measured excellence in Information Systems (IS) auditing, control, and security. CISA has grown to be globally recognized and adopted worldwide as a symbol of achievement.

Information Technology (IT) [aka Information Technologies, or Information Systems (IS)] The body (universe) of Computer Science and the industry around it that deals with business computers, business computer software, data center management, data center networking, enterprise networking, software development, security, databases, and so on.

IT is essential to manage transactions, information, and knowledge necessary to initiate and sustain economic and social activities. These activities increasingly rely on globally cooperating entities to be successful. In many organizations, IT is fundamental to support, sustain, and grow the business [r157].

Information Technology (IT) Consultants Professionals and contractors supporting clients in risk management.

Information Technology (IT) Quality Assurance Personnel Associates that test and ensure the integrity of the Information Technology (IT) systems and data.

Information Technology (IT) Security Program Managers Managers that implement the security program.

Information Technology (IT) Services as an Asset These assets require protection considerations (among others): messaging (e-mail/scheduling [e.g., Microsoft Exchange]; instant messaging; core infrastructure [e.g., Microsoft Active Directory; core networks; business servers]; Domain Name System (DNS); Dynamic Host Configuration Protocol (DHCP); enterprise management tools; file sharing; storage; dial-up remote access; telephony; Virtual Private Networking (VPN) access; Microsoft Windows Internet Naming Service (WINS); and collaboration services [r190].

Information Technology (IT) System Term refers to a general support system (e.g., mainframe computer, mid-range computer, local area network, agency-wide backbone) or a major application that can run on a general support system and whose use of information resources satisfies a specific set of user requirements [r315].

Information Technology (IT) System and Application Developers (Programmers) Associates that develop and maintain software (e.g., applications, middleware, Web Services-based systems).

Information Technology (IT) System Managers Owners of system software and/or hardware used to support IT functions.

Information Technology (IT) Vendors Suppliers that develop (security) systems or packages that are used by organizations.

Information Technology Laboratory (ITL) A laboratory operated by the National Institute of Standards and Technology (NIST). ITL has the broad mission of supporting U.S. industry, government, and academia with measurements and standards that enable new computational methods for scientific inquiry, assure Information Technology (IT) innovations for maintaining global leadership, and re-engineer complex societal systems and processes through insertion of advanced information technology. Through its efforts, ITL seeks to enhance productivity and public safety, facilitate trade, and improve the quality of life.

Information Theory A branch of the mathematical theory of probability and mathematical statistics that quantifies the concept of information. It is concerned with information entropy, communication systems, data transmission and rate distortion theory, cryptography, data compression, error correction, and related topics [r286].

Claude Shannon has been called "the father of Information Theory" (key articles were "The Mathematical Theory of Communication" in the Bell System Technical Journal in July and October of 1948). His theory for the first time considered communication as a rigorously stated mathematical problem in statistics and gave communications engineers a way to determine the capacity of a communication channel in terms of the common currency of bits. The transmission part of the theory is not concerned with the meaning (semantics) of the message conveyed, though the complementary wing of information theory concerns itself with content through lossy compression of messages subject to a fidelity criterion. These two wings of information theory are joined together and mutually justified by the information transmission theorems, or source-channel separation theorems that justify the use of bits as the universal currency for information in many contexts. In the process of working out a theory of communications that could be applied by electrical engineers to design better telecommunications systems, Shannon defined a measure of entropy [r286, r287]:

$$H = -\sum_i p_i \log p_i$$

(where p_i is the probability of i) that, when applied to an information source, could determine the capacity of the channel required to transmit the source as encoded binary digits. If the logarithm in the formula is taken to base 2, then it gives a measure of entropy in bits. Shannon's measure of entropy came to be taken as a measure of the information contained in a message as opposed to the portion of the message that is strictly determined (hence, predictable) by inherent structures, such as redundancy in the structure of languages or the statistical properties of a language relating to the frequencies of occurrence of different letter or word pairs, triplets, and so on.

Information Warfare   Actions taken to achieve information superiority by affecting adversary information, information-based processes, and information systems, while defending our own information, information-based processes, and information systems. Any action to deny, exploit, corrupt, or destroy the enemy's information and its functions, protect themselves against those ac-

tions; and exploiting their own military information functions [r057].

Informational Response   (SIP context) Same as a provisional response [r025].

INFOSEC   See information security

Infrastructure Grid Tools   Grid computing subsystems that include filesystems, schedulers and resource managers, messaging systems, security applications, certificate authorities, and file transfer mechanisms [r080].

Inherent Risk   The risk before considering the beneficial effect of any risk mitigation, or control.

Inimical Agent   An adversary; an enemy; a person or entity that attacks, or is a threat to, a system.

Initial Cipher State   The generation of the initial value for the cipher state if it is not being carried over from a previous encryption or decryption operation [r115].

Initialization   (OSPF context) The time needed for an Open Shortest Path First (OSPF) implementation to be initialized, to recognize any links across which OSPF must run, to build any needed adjacencies, to synchronize its database, and to perform other actions necessary to converge [r026].

Initialization Vector (IV)   (aka initialization value or message indicator) An input parameter that sets the starting state of a cryptographic algorithm or mode [r013]. An IV can be used to introduce cryptographic variance in addition to that provided by a key (also see the term "salt"), and to synchronize one cryptographic process with another. For an example of the latter, cipher block chaining mode requires an IV [r288].

Initiator, Calling Party, Caller   (SIP context) The party initiating a session (and dialog) with an INVITE request. A caller retains this role from the time it sends the initial INVITE that established a dialog until the termination of that dialog [r025].

Inmarsat   Acronym derived from International Maritime Satellite System. A commercial satellite service that uses a number of satellites in geosynchronous orbit. Available as Inmarsat A, B, C, and M [r121].

Inner Label   "Inner label" is another name for Virtual Channel (VC) label [in Multiprotocol Label Switching (MPLS)].

Innovation   The creation of new products and/or services.

Input/Output (I/O)   The interfaces that different subsystems of an information processing system use to communicate with each other. While the term also has a logical meaning, more often it refers to the physical apparatus used to connect the various peripherals. Furthermore, it generally represents a bus-level connection rather than a communications port (e.g., an Ethernet port) connection.

Insecurity Mechanisms, Address-Based Authentication   A common security mechanism is address-based authentication. At best this approach can work in highly constrained environments. If the environment consists of a small number of machines, all tightly administered, secure systems run by trusted users, and if the network is guarded by a router that blocks source-routing and prevents spoofing of the source addresses, and one knows there are no wireless bridges, and if one restricts address-based authentication to machines on that network, then one is at least in theory probably safe. These conditions, however, are rarely met. Among the threats are Address Resolution Protocol (ARP)-spoofing, abuse of local proxies, renumbering, routing table corruption or attacks, Dynamic Host Configuration Protocol (DHCP), IP address spoofing [a particular risk for User Datagram Protocol (UDP)-based protocols], sequence number guessing, and source-routed packets [r170].

Insecurity Mechanisms, Name-Based Authentication   Name-based authentication has all of the problems of address-based authentication and adds new ones: attacks on the Domain Name System (DNS) and lack of a one-to-one mapping between addresses and names. At a minimum, a process that retrieves a host name from the DNS should retrieve the corresponding address records and cross-check. Techniques such as DNS cache contamination can often negate such checks.

DNSSEC provides protection against this sort of attack. However, it does not enhance the reliability of the underlying address. Furthermore, the technique generates a lot of false alarms. These lookups do not provide reliable information to a machine, though they might be a useful debugging tool for humans and could be useful in logs when trying to reconstruct how and attack took place [r170].

Insecurity Mechanisms, Plaintext Passwords   Plaintext passwords are a common security mechanism in use today. If that system has been compromised or if the encryption layer does not include effective authentication of the server to the client, an enemy can collect the passwords and possibly use them against other targets [r170].

Insertion   Introducing false data that serves to deceive an authorized entity.

Insertion Loss of a Device   (optical transmission term) The relative power level (dB) transmitted to the output end referenced to the 0-dB reference level when a device is inserted for all polarization states and over the operating temperature range. It usually measures the power difference between the lowest peak power among all channels and the 0-dB reference.

Insertion Loss of a Single Channel   (optical transmission term) The relative power level (dB) transmitted to the output end referenced to the 0-dB reference level when a device is inserted for all polarization states and over the operating temperature range. It may be defined as (1) peak transmission within the pass band or (2) the minimum transmission within any clear window.

Insertion of Nonauthentic Data Traffic on a Provider Provisioned Virtual Private Network (PPVPN): Spoofing and Replay   Refers to the insertion (or "spoofing") into the Virtual Private Network (VPN) of packets that do not belong there, with the objective of having them accepted as legitimate by the recipient. Also included in this category is the insertion of copies of once-legitimate packets that have been recorded and replayed [r058].

Inside Attack An attack initiated by an entity inside the security perimeter (an "insider")—that is, an entity that is authorized to access system resources but uses them in a way not approved by those who granted the authorization [r013].

Instant Inbox (Presence Services context) Receptacle for instant messages intended to be read by the instant inbox's principal [r015].

Instant Inbox Address (Presence Services context) Indicates whether and how the presentity's principal can receive an instant message in an instant inbox. The status and instant inbox address information are sufficient to determine whether the principal appears ready to accept the instant message [r015].

Instant Message (Presence Services context) An identifiable unit of data, of small size, to be sent to an instant inbox (this definition seeks to avoid the possibility of transporting an arbitrary-length stream labeled as an "instant message").

Instant Message Protocol (Presence Services context) The messages that can be exchanged between a sender user agent and an instant message service, or between an instant message service and an instant inbox [r015].

Instant Message Service (Presence Services context) A service that accepts and delivers instant messages. Related observations:

- May require authentication of sender user agents and/or instant inboxes.
- May have different authentication requirements for different instant inboxes, and may also have different authentication requirements for different instant inboxes controlled by a single principal.
- May have an internal structure involving multiple servers and/or proxies. There may be complex patterns of redirection and/or proxying while retaining logical connectivity to a single instant message service. Note that an instant message service does not require having a distinct server.
- The service may be implemented as direct

communication between sender and instant inbox.
- May have an internal structure involving other instant message services, which may be independently accessible in their own right as well as being reachable through the initial instant message service [r015].

Instant Messaging Security Issues Organizations have taken varying steps to manage the use of instant messaging (IM) and Internet Relay Chat (IRC). Some agencies have blocked IM and IRC use at the firewall due to the inability to centrally control new vulnerabilities presented by the software manufacture. Other organizations allow the use of IM internally. There are products that can be configured for internal use only (e.g., Lotus Notes' product called Same-Time and the Jabber Inc. product, called Jabber) [r067].

Institute for Certification of Computer Professionals (ICCP) Organization founded in 1973 dedicated to the establishment of high professional standards for the computer industry. ICCP offers internationally recognized certification program. It offers certification in two professional designations: Certified Computing Professional (CCP) and Associate Computing Professional (ACP).

Institute of Electrical and Electronics Engineers (IEEE) A U.S. organization for electrical engineering, the leading authority in technical areas ranging from telecommunications to aerospace and consumer electronics. A Standards Developing Organization (SDO). The IEEE promotes standards related to electrical and information technologies. The 802 Committee is the developer of all Local Area Network (LAN) standards to date, including the Ethernet family of specifications. Active working groups and technical advisory groups include:

- 802.1 High-Level Interface (HILI) Working Group
- 802.3 CSMA/CD Working Group

- 802.11 Wireless LAN (WLAN) Working Group
- 802.15 Wireless Personal Area Network (WPAN) Working Group
- 802.16 Broadband Wireless Access (BBWA) Working Group
- 802.17 Resilient Packet Ring (RPR) Working Group
- 802.18 Radio Regulatory Technical Advisory Group
- 802.19 Coexistence Technical Advisory Group
- Executive Committee Study Group, Mobile Broadband Wireless Access

Hibernating working groups (standards published, but inactive) include:

- 802.2 Logical Link Control (LLC) Working Group
- 802.4 Token Bus Working Group
- 802.5 Token Ring Working Group
- 802.6 Metropolitan Area Network (MAN) Working Group
- 802.7 BroadBand Technical Adv. Group (BBTAG)
- 802.9 Integrated Services LAN (ISLAN) Working Group
- 802.10 Standard for Interoperable LAN Security (SILS) Working Group
- 802.12 Demand Priority Working Group

Institute of Electrical and Electronics Engineers (IEEE) 802.11 Family of Standards The IEEE standard for Wireless Local Area Networks (WLANs). The following standards and task groups exist with the working group:

- IEEE 802.11—The original 2-Mbps, 2.4-GHz standard
- IEEE 802.11a—54-Mbps, 5-GHz standard (1999, shipping products in 2001)
- IEEE 802.11b—Enhancements to 802.11 to support 5.5 and 11 Mbps (1999)
- IEEE 802.11d—New countries
- IEEE 802.11e—Enhancements: QoS, including packet bursting

- IEEE 802.11f—Inter-Access Point Protocol (IAPP)
- IEEE 802.11g—54 Mbps, 2.4-GHz standard (backwards compatible with b) (2003)
- IEEE 802.11h—5-GHz spectrum, Dynamic Channel/Frequency Selection (DCS/DFS) and Transmit Power Control (TPC) for European compatibility
- IEEE 802.11i (ratified 24 June 2004)—Enhanced security
- IEEE 802.11j—Extensions for Japan
- IEEE 802.11n—Higher throughput improvements
- IEEE 802.11p—Adding wireless capabilities to mobile vehicles such as ambulances and passenger cars

A brief description follows [r005]:

802.11a: Operating in the 5-GHz band, 802.11a supports a maximum theoretical data rate of 54 Mbps, but more realistically it achieves throughput somewhere between 20 Mbps and 25 Mbps in normal traffic conditions. In a typical office environment, its maximum range is 50 meters (150 feet) at the lowest speed, but at higher speed, the range is less than 25 meters (75 feet). 802.11a can make use of four, eight, or more channels, depending on the country. WLAN products based on 802.11a have been less popular than the 802.11b and 802.11g standards.

802.11b: Most WLANs deployed at press time used 802.11b technology (however they may soon be upgraded to 802.11g). 802.11b operates in the 2.4-GHz band and supports a maximum theoretical data rate of 11 Mbps, with average throughput falling in the 4- to 6-Mbps range. In a typical office environment, its maximum range is 75 meters (250 feet) at the lowest speed, but at higher speed its range is about 30 meters (100 feet). Bluetooth devices, 2.4-GHz cordless phones and even microwave ovens are sources of interference (and thus create poor performance) for 802.11b networks. Minimizing interference can be difficult because 802.11b uses only three nonoverlapping channels. 802.11b products have been available almost a decade; products are plentiful and affordable.

802.11g: This standard offers the throughput of 802.11a with the backward compatibility of 802.11b. 802.11g operates in the 2.4-GHz band, but it supports data rates from 6 Mbps to 54 Mbps. Like 802.11b, it has up to three nonoverlapping channels. 802.11g uses orthogonal frequency-division multiplexing (OFDM) modulation as does 802.11a, but, for backward compatibility with 11b, it also supports complementary code keying (CCK) modulation and, as an option for faster link rates, allows packet binary convolutional coding (PBCC) modulation. Its "backward compatibility" with 802.11b means that when a mobile 802.11b device joins an 802.11g access point, all connections on that access point slow down to 802.11b speeds.

802.11n: latest WLAN technologies that uses Multiple In Multiple Out (MIMO) antenna approaches to support double the nominal datarate of 802.11g. Products were becoming available at press time.

Institute of Electrical and Electronics Engineers (IEEE) 802.11i Media Access Control (MAC) Security Enhancements Amendment Requires that Extensible Authentication Protocol (EAP) authentication methods be available for Wireless Local Area Network (WLAN) deployments. WLAN deployments are expected to use different credential types, including digital certificates, user-names and passwords, existing secure tokens, and mobile network credentials [Global System for Mobile Communications and Universal Mobile Telecommunications System (UMTS) secrets]. Other credential types that may be used include public/private key (without necessarily requiring certificates) and asymmetric credential support (such as password on one side, public/private key on the other) [r073].

Institute of Electrical and Electronics Engineers (IEEE) 802.11i Wireless Security The Institute of Electrical and Electronics Engineers (IEEE) set up a dedicated task group to create a replacement security solution for the original wired equivalent privacy (WEP). Afterwards, the Wi-Fi Alliance announced an interim specification called Wireless Protected Access (WPA) based on a subset of the current IEEE draft. 802.11i (aka WPA-2) was ratified in June 2004, and uses the Advanced Encryption Standard (AES), instead of Rivest Cipher 4 (RC4), which was used in WEP and WPA.

Institute of Electrical and Electronics Engineers (IEEE) 802.11n In 2004 IEEE announced that it would develop a new standard for wide-area wireless networks. The speed would be at least 108 Mbps, and so up to 2 times faster than 802.11g (about 10 times faster than 802.11b). As projected, 802.11n will also offer a better operating distance than current networks. The standardization progress is expected to be completed by the end of 2006. 802.11n builds upon previous 802.11 standards by adding MIMO (multiple-input multiple-output). The additional transmitter and receiver antennas allow for increased data throughput through spatial multiplexing and increased range by exploiting the spatial diversity.

Institute of Electrical and Electronics Engineers (IEEE) 802.15 Standard for Wireless Personal Area Networks (WPANs.) It has four active task groups [r005].

- 802.15.1 Task Group had the job of delivering the standard for low-speed, low-cost WPANs and is based on the Bluetooth spec.
- The 802.15.2 Task Group developed the recommended practices on how 802.11 WLANs and 802.15 WPANs can coexist in the 2.4-GHz band. It is mainly working on the interference problem between Bluetooth and 802.11.
- The 802.15.3 Task Group developed a standard for higher speed WPANs from 10 Mbps to 55 Mbps at distances less than 10 meters.
- The 802.15.4 Task Group developed a standard for simple, low-cost, low-speed WPANs. Data ranges from 2 kbps to 200 kbps and uses DSSS modulation in the 2.4-GHz and 915-MHz ranges.

Institute of Electrical and Electronics Engineers (IEEE) 802.1Q IEEE standard that supports Quality of Service (QoS) and also Virtual LANs (VLANs). The 802.1Q format is designed to allow VLAN tagged frames to transit between switches from vendors. The Media Access Control (MAC) frame is as follows (in sequential order left to right):

- DA (48 bits): Destination address of the frame. This address is the same in the tagged frame as it is in the untagged frame.
- SA (48 bits): Source address of the frame. This address is the same in the tagged frame as it is in the untagged frame.
- Frame Indicator (16 bits set to hex 8100): Constant field indicates that this frame contains an 802.1Q VLAN tag.
- Priority (3 bits): Three-bit user defined priority field.
- CFI (1 bit): Canonical Format Indicator— One-bit field indicates whether options follow the VLAN tag. Primarily used in Token Ring networks.
- VLAN ID (12 bits): This field is used to indicate the VLAN membership of the tagged frame.
- Ethertype (16 bits): Indicates the Layer 3 protocol contained in the tagged frame.
- Data (368–12,000 bits): The data portion of the tagged frame.
- FCS (32 bits): Frame Check Sequence used to validate the integrity of the frame.

Institute of Electrical and Electronics Engineers (IEEE) 802.1X The IEEE standard for access control for wireless and Wired Local Area Networks (LANs). Specification provides a means of authenticating and authorizing devices to attach to a LAN port. This standard defines the Extensible Authentication Protocol (EAP), which uses a central authentication server to authenticate users on the network.

Institute of Electrical and Electronics Engineers (IEEE) P1363 An IEEE working group, Standard for Public-Key Cryptography, developing a comprehensive reference standard for asymmetric cryptography. It covers discrete logarithm [e.g., Digital Signature Algorithm (DSA)], elliptic curve, and integer factorization [e.g., Rivest–Shamir–Adleman (RSA)]; as well as covering key agreement, digital signature, and encryption [r013].

Institute of Electrical and Electronics Engineers (IEEE) P1619 Goals A standard for the interoperable encryption of storage devices at the physical level. It also can be used for transferring keys between vendors. The Institute of Electrical and Electronics Engineers (IEEE) P1619 provides confidentiality and pseudo-integrity, with the following features [r279]:

- Applied to 512-byte blocks (up to 2^{128} wide blocks)
- Without data expansion (no additional integrity tag)
- Resistant to copy-and-paste attacks
- Parallelizable for high speed hardware

Institute of Electrical and Electronics Engineers (IEEE) P1619 Key Transfer In addition to standardizing algorithms, Institute of Electrical and Electronics Engineers (IEEE) P1619 is exploring ways to back up and transfer key material between vendors. While it may not seem like something an encryption vendor would want to enable, standardization of key transfers will appeal to customers hesitant to deploy products in which the keys to their data are hidden. To support orderly key transfer, exported keys are encoded in a standard Extensible Markup Language (XML) format. Key export supports archiving keys and the potential transfer of these keys to another vendor's equipment.

Institute of Electrical and Electronics Engineers (IEEE) P1619 Standard IEEE P1619, "Standard Architecture for Encrypted Shared Media," addresses the need for secure storage methods to help protect information in comprehensive storage environments. IEEE P1619 enables interoperable encryption of data at rest on storage. P1619 focuses on three types of storage: sector-oriented, object-oriented, and variable-block (tape).

Sector-oriented storage—integrated drive electronics (IDE), Advanced Technology Attachment (ATA), Serial ATA, Small Computer System Interface (SCSI), and Fibre Channel (FC)—most commonly operate on 512-byte sectors. Operations on these sectors always start on a boundary for an integral number of sectors. Sector disks' fixed size makes adding extra data difficult, which in turn prevents traditional integrity checking using standard message authentication codes (MACs). Users must therefore rely on the encryption modes such as cipher block chaining (CBC). However, sectors encrypted in this way are malleable: an attacker can indirectly control unencrypted data (plaintext) by altering the encrypted data (cipher text); for example, an attacker could increase his salary in the company's Human Resources (HR) database without actually having to break the cryptographic algorithm.

Object-oriented storage: Network-attached and object-based storage devices store objects (files) as units that are unlimited in length and can be manipulated on any byte boundary for any number of bytes. Because of this access technique, the inclusion of additional integrity information is nontrivial.

Variable-block storage: Tape storage is a variable-length block device that usually has a well-defined start-of-block/end-of-block protocol. The IEEE was planning to standardize a solution for tape that will allow the addition of integrity fields.

Two P1619 documents aim to standardize solutions to the problem of malleable encryption. "Draft Proposal for Tweakable Wide-Block Encryption," edited by Shai Halevi, and "Draft Proposal for Tweakable Narrow-Block Encryption," edited by Clement Kent, describe a position-dependent encryption algorithm that can encrypt either a wide block (512 bytes) or a narrow block (16 bytes), respectively, as a unit. These modes represent a pseudorandom permutation of the entire unit, which is tweakable by the location on the disk and can only be decrypted at the point of encryption. An attacker who moves or attempts to manipulate the data will obtain unpredictable results. Both of these modes have cryptographic proofs.

Insurance (financial term) A promise of compensation for specific potential future losses in exchange for a periodic payment. Insurance is designed to protect the financial well-being of an individual, company, or other entity in the case of unexpected loss. Some forms of insurance are required by law, while others are optional. Agreeing to the terms of an insurance policy creates a contract between the insured and the insurer. In exchange for payments from the insured (called premiums), the insurer agrees to pay the policy holder a sum of money upon the occurrence of a specific event. In most cases, the policy holder pays part of the loss (called the deductible), and the insurer pays the rest. Examples include car insurance, health insurance, disability insurance, life insurance, and business insurance [r009].

Intangible Assets (financial term) These assets require protection considerations: reputation; goodwill; employee moral; employee productivity [r190].

Integrated Development Environment (IDE) Development environments (tools) for the creation of software. An effective software development environment includes both the Software Development Environment (SDE) and an IDE.

An SDE typically includes: version control system, defect tracking system, loadbuild, update submission process (inspection and testing), load-build process, and sanity testing process.

An IDE typically includes: source-code editor, source-code debugger, low-level debugger, code browsers, compile and build tools, and simulation/emulation capabilities.

Integrated Drive Electronics (IDE) [aka ATA (AT Attachment)] A disk drive implementation designed to integrate the controller onto the drive itself, thereby reducing interface costs and making firmware implementations easier. Since the late 1980s it has become the drive of choice for PC manufacturers.

Integrated Security Client and gateway security

solutions combine firewall, intrusion detection, anti-virus, and other technologies.

Integrated Services Digital Network (ISDN)   All digital narrowband switched communications service ($n \times 64$ kbps with $n = 2$ to 32) developed in the 1980s that allows for transmission of voice, data, video, and graphics, over standard copper loops (communication lines) that have been appropriately upgraded. Has a separate, "out-of-band" signaling channel (the D-channel). Predecessor of Digital Subscriber Line (DSL) services (uses similar transmission technology). ISDN service has seen limited deployment in the United States, but more deployment in Europe and Asia [r289]. Defines a digital telephone network that has been designed for speech telephony, dial-up networking, fax, and other services such as video conferencing [r011].

Integrated Services Digital Network (ISDN) User Part (ISUP)   (GSM context) If the Telephone User Part (TUP) protocol is enhanced with ISDN User Part [r011] functions, it is called Integrated Services Digital Network (ISDN) .

Integrated Services/intserv   One way to provide Quality of Service (QoS) in an enterprise IP network, based on the ReSerVation Protocol (RSVP) mechanism. This approach has not seen much deployment [being modeled after Asynchronous Transfer Mode (ATM)-like approaches]; nearly all enterprise networks now with QoS use the *diffserv* method.

Integrated Storage Network Interface Card (IS-NIC)   A NIC card that incorporates Transmission Control Protocol/Internet Protocol (TCP/IP) offload features and fully implements the TCP/IP stack [r029].

Integrity   (aka data integrity) The property that data has not been altered, destroyed, or lost in an unauthorized or accidental manner. A state where the data is protected from unauthorized, unanticipated, or unintentional modification.

Integrity Components   Mechanisms that ensure data integrity. Examples include session encryption, Message Authentication Codes (MACs), and checksums.

Integrity, IPSec Environment   IPSec supports two forms of integrity: connectionless and a form of partial sequence integrity. Connectionless integrity is a service that detects modification of an individual IP datagram, without regard to the ordering of the datagram in a stream of traffic. The form of partial sequence integrity offered in IPsec is referred to as anti-replay integrity, and it detects arrival of duplicate IP datagrams (within a constrained window). This is in contrast to connection-oriented integrity, which imposes more stringent sequencing requirements on traffic—for example, to be able to detect lost or re-ordered messages. Although authentication and integrity services often are cited separately, in practice they are intimately connected and almost always offered in tandem [r186].

Intelligent Network (IN)   (3G Wireless context) A mechanism that makes supplementary services possible. Service development platforms are used to enable cost-efficient and speedy development [r007].

Intelligent Switching Platforms   Switches that provide a platform for intelligent storage services to reside on, which makes the storage intelligence, such as replication, volume management, virtualization, and file serving, part of the switching infrastructure. These switches are often multiprotocol (Fibre Channel, IP, InfiniBand) [r029].

Intelligent Threat   A circumstance in which an adversary has the technical and operational capability to detect and exploit a vulnerability and also has the demonstrated, presumed, or inferred intent to do so [r013].

Intended Recipient   (Instant Messaging/Presence context) The Principal to whom the sender of an Instant Message is sending it [r027].

Interactive Voice Response (IVR)   Network devices that provide voice replies over the telephonic connection to customers accessing the device to obtain certain type of service information (e.g., account statues). Typically found in Contact Centers and Help Desks.

Interception   A threat action whereby an unauthorized entity directly accesses sensitive data traveling between authorized sources and destinations. This includes theft of physical media, wiretapping, and emanations analysis [r013].

Interception Proxy (aka "transparent proxy," "transparent cache") Proxies used with zero configurations within the user agent.

Interest rate   Interest per year divided by principal amount, expressed as a percentage.

Interface   An architectural concept that provides interconnection between physical blocks at reference points.

Interface Identifier (IPv6 context) The last (rightmost) 64 bits of a unicast or anycast IPv6 address [r008].

Interference   Disruption of system operations by blocking communications or user data or control information [r013].

InterGrid   A global Internet-based computing grid that spans multiple organizations and geographic locations. Generally, an InterGrid may be used to collaborate on "large" projects of common scientific interest. The stringiest levels of security are usually required in this environment [r080].

Interim Interswitch Signaling Protocol (IISP) An Asynchronous Transfer Mode (ATM) Signaling Protocol. Not widely deployed.

Interim Local Management Interface (ILMI) Bidirectional exchange of management information between User-to-Network (UNI) Management Entities (UMEs).

Interior Gateway Protocol (IGP)   A protocol for exchanging routing information between gateways (hosts with routers) within an autonomous network. Two commonly used IGPs: the Routing Information Protocol (RIP) and the Open Shortest Path First (OSPF) protocol.

Interior Gateway Routing Protocol (IGRP)   The Interior Gateway Routing Protocol (IGRP) is a routing protocol [an Interior Gateway Protocol (IGP)] developed in the mid-1980s by Cisco Systems.

Intermediate System to Intermediate System (ISIS)   A protocol for the exchange of configuration and routing information to facilitate the operation of the routing and relaying functions of the network layer (ISO 10589).

Internal Audit   (financial term) Mechanisms to validate control solution effectiveness. An ongoing appraisal of the financial health of a company's operations by its own employees. Employees who carry out this function are called internal auditors. During an internal audit, internal auditors will evaluate and monitor a company's risk management, reporting, and control practices and make suggestions for improvement. Internal auditing covers not only an organization's finance function, but all the operations and systems in a firm. While internal auditors are typically accountants, this activity can also be carried out by other professionals who are well-versed with a company's functions and the relevant regulatory requirements [r009].

Internal Border Gateway Protocol (iBGP)   An exterior gateway protocol (EGP) is used to perform interdomain routing in Transmission Control Protocol/Internet Protocol (TCP/IP) networks. A Border Gateway Protocol (BGP) router needs to establish a connection (on TCP port 179) to each of its BGP peers before BGP updates can be exchanged. A BGP session between two BGP peers is said to be an internal BGP session if the BGP peers are in the same autonomous systems.

Internal Control   A process put in place by (senior) management intended to provide reasonable assurance regarding things such as safeguarding of assets, compliance with regulations, and integrity/reliability of data.

Internal Fraud   Fraud committed by an employee or a supplier to the organization.

Internal Rate of Return (IRR)   (financial term) The discount rate that discounts an investment's (a project's) expected net cash flows to a net present value of zero. That is, the discount rate at which the future streams of costs and benefits are equal. The higher the IRR, the better the project, hence the IRR method is a convenient way to compare different alternative options in labor programs [r085].

Internal Security Threats Threats that arise from within an organinzation. These threats range from outright attempts to steal corporate data, to laptop-borne viruses from employees that may use these laptops in unprotected networks (home, hotels, etc.), to user installation of unapproved software or hardware.

International Data Encryption Algorithm (IDEA) A patented, symmetric block cipher that uses a 128-bit key and operates on 64-bit blocks [r290, r291]. The algorithm was developed as a replacement for the Data Encryption Standard (DES) by X. Lai and J. L. Massey of ETH-Zürich in the early 1990s. IDEA has been used, for example, in Pretty Good Privacy (PGP) V2.0.

International Mobile Equipment Identity (IMEI) (GSM context) An electronic hardware identification that enables network operators to identify, e.g., stolen mobiles [r011].

International Mobile Subscriber Identity (IMSI) (GSM context) Mechanism to identify a particular Subscriber Identity Module (SIM) card, and thus also each mobile subscriber worldwide [r011].

International Mobile Telecommunication System-2000 (IMT-2000) (3G Wireless context) The international term for the European Universal Mobile Telecommunications System (UMTS) [r007].

International Organization for Standardization (ISO) International organization for the development of dejure standards. A nonprofit standards organization whose membership includes standards organizations from participating nations [The American National Standards Institute (ANSI) is the U.S. representative] [r033]. ISO is a voluntary, non-treaty, non-government organization, established in 1947, with voting members that are designated standards bodies of participating nations and non-voting observer organizations. Legally, ISO is a Swiss, non-profit, private organization. ISO and the IEC (the International Electrotechnical Commission) form the specialized system for worldwide standardization. National bodies that are members of ISO or IEC participate in developing international standards through ISO and IEC technical committees that deal with particular fields of activity. Other international governmental and nongovernmental organizations, in liaison with ISO and IEC, also take part. The ISO standards development process has four levels of increasing maturity: Working Draft (WD), Committee Draft (CD), Draft International Standard (DIS), and International Standard (IS). In information technology, ISO and IEC have a joint technical committee, ISO/IEC JTC 1. DISs adopted by JTC 1 are circulated to national bodies for voting, and publication as an IS requires approval by at least three quarters of the national bodies casting a vote [r013].

International Packet Communications Consortium (IPCC) An international industry association dedicated to accelerating the deployment of Voice over IP (VoIP), video over IP, and packet technologies and services over converged wireless, wireline, and cable broadband networks. The association is comprised of service providers, solutions providers, system integrators, and government agencies translating industry standards into revenue generating services. Members aim to develop simple, cost-effective technical frameworks for converged services in wireline, cable, 3G, Wi-Fi (Wireless Fidelity), and WiMAX (Worldwide Interoperability for Microwave Access) networks. The organization continues the groundbreaking work of the International Softswitch Consortium (ISC) founded in 1998.

The mission of the IPCC is to develop the market for all products, services, applications, and solutions that utilize packet-based voice, data, and video communications technologies, regardless of transport medium—wireless, copper, broadband, fiber optics, or other. It positions itself as the industry Forum for Broadband Cable, Wireline, and Wireless Communications Convergence to VoIP and Packet Applications.

International Softswitch Consortium (ISC) The purpose of the organization was to promote open standards and protocols, as well as new application development for a distributed set of hardware and software platforms which can seamlessly interconnect the traditional telephone network with information and applications currently available only over the Internet. This set of technologies operates by distributing functions currently performed by digital circuit switches and is generally referred to as a "Softswitch."

The International Packet Communications Consortium (IPCC) evolved from the ISC, the industry's most longstanding advocate, advancing the maturation of packet-based network technologies and markets. Founded in 1999, the ISC was the premiere forum for the worldwide advancement of softswitch interoperability, promoting the growth of Internet-based multimedia communications and applications. The IPCC continues to build on the groundbreaking work of the ISC. The mission of IPCC is to develop the market for all products, services, applications and solutions that utilize packet-based voice, data, and video communications technologies, regardless of transport medium—wireless, copper, broadband, fiber optics, or other.

International Telecommunications Union (ITU) Grid (Optical transmission term) A standard published by the ITU specifying the wavelengths at which optical signals should be positioned in Dense Wavelength Division Multiplexing (DWDM) in order to ensure interoperability among equipment manufactured by various vendors. The optical frequency grid has 100-GHz spacing.

International Telecommunications Union Telecommunications Standardization Sector (ITU-T) International standards-setting organization for carriers. ITU-T is a subunit of the International Telecommunications Union (ITU), the United Nations body chartered with establishing telecom and radio standards around the globe. It is a treaty organization that is composed mainly of postal, telephone, and telegraph authorities of the member countries and that publishes standards called "Recommendations" (e.g., X.400, X.500). ITU-T was created on 1 March 1993, re-

placing the former International Telegraph and Telephone Consultative Committee (CCITT) whose origins go back to 1865. The public and the private sectors cooperate within ITU-T for the development of standards that benefit telecommunication users worldwide. The Department of State represents the United States. ITU-T works on many kinds of communication systems. ITU-T cooperates with the International Organization for Standardization (ISO) on communication protocol standards, and many Recommendations in that area are also published as an ISO standard with an ISO name and number [r013].

The ITU-T has been instrumental in laying the standardized foundation for wireless [including 3G standards such as International Mobile Telecommunication System-2000 (IMT-2000)] and optical networking [including the basic "ITU-grid" of Dense Wavelength Division Multiplexing (DWDM channels)]. A key relevant standard is Synchronous Digital Hierarchy (SDH) used in networks outside of the United States and Japan.

International Traffic in Arms Regulations (ITAR) Rules issued by the U.S. State Department, by authority of the Arms Export Control Act (22 U.S.C. 2778), to control export and import of defense articles and defense services, including information security systems, such as cryptographic systems, and TEMPEST suppression technology [r013].

Internet The Internet is a global network of independently managed networks and hosts. There is no central authority responsible for the operation of the network [r072].

Internet Architecture Board (IAB) A technical advisory group of the Internet Society (ISOC), chartered by the ISOC Trustees to provide oversight of Internet architecture and protocols and, in the context of Internet Standards, a body to which decisions of the Internet Engineering Steering Group (IESG) may be appealed. Responsible for approving appointments to the IESG from among nominees submitted by the Internet Engineering Task Force (IETF) nominating committee [r013, r293]. ISOC is an international nonprofit organization incorporated in the United States with thousands of individual and corporate members throughout the world. The Internet Society provides a number of services to the IETF including financial and logistical support. Internet standardization is an organized activity of the ISOC, with the ISOC Board of Trustees being responsible for ratifying the procedures and rules of the Internet standards process.

Internet Assigned Numbers Authority (IANA) From the early days of the Internet, the IANA was chartered by the Internet Society (ISOC) and the U.S. Government's Federal Network Council to be the central coordination, allocation, and registration body for parameters for Internet protocols. Superseded by Internet Corporation for Assigned Names and Numbers (ICANN) [r013].

Internet Cache Protocol (ICP) Caching protocol defined in RFC 2186 (ICPv2—Internet Cache Protocol version two). ICP is a User Datagram Protocol (UDP)-based protocol used for locating instances of cached responses in neighbor caches. RFC 2186 addresses only the structure, field definitions, and allowed field values of the protocol; RFC 2187 is an application of ICPv2; it describes how ICP is used in a Web caching hierarchy.

Internet Content Adaptation Protocol (ICAP) The ICAP protocol id defined in RFC 3507. It aims at providing simple object-based content vectoring for HyperText Transfer Protocol (HTTP) services. ICAP is, in essence, a lightweight protocol for executing a "remote procedure call" on HTTP messages. It allows ICAP clients to pass HTTP messages to ICAP servers for some sort of transformation or other processing ("adaptation"). The server executes its transformation service on messages and sends back responses to the client, usually with modified messages. Typically, the adapted messages are either HTTP requests or HTTP responses. ICAP is a request/response protocol similar in semantics and usage to HTTP/1.1. ICAP is *not* an application protocol that runs over HTTP.

Internet Control Message Protocol (ICMP) An Internet Standard protocol that is used to report error conditions during IP datagram processing and to exchange other information concerning the state of the IP network [r013, r292].

Internet Control Message Protocol (ICMP) Flood A denial of service attack that sends a host more ICMP echo request ("ping") packets than the protocol implementation can handle [r013].

Internet Control Message Protocol for IPv6 (ICMPv6) (IPv6 context) A protocol that provides error messages for the routing and delivers IPv6 datagrams and information messages for diagnostics, neighbor discovery, multicast receiver discovery, and IPv6 mobility [r008].

Internet Corporation for Assigned Names and Numbers (ICANN) The nonprofit, private corporation that has assumed responsibility for the Internet Protocol (IP) address space allocation, protocol parameter assignment, Domain Name System (DNS) management, and root server system management [these functions were formerly performed under U.S. Government contract by Internet Assigned Numbers Authority (IANA) and other entities] [r013]. ICANN was formed in October 1998, by a coalition of the Internet's business, technical, and academic communities. The U.S. Government designated ICANN to serve as the global consensus entity.

The Internet Protocol Suite, as defined by the Internet Engineering Task Force (IETF) and the Internet Engineering Steering Group (IESG), contains numerous parameters, such as Internet addresses, domain names, autonomous system numbers, protocol numbers, port numbers, management information base object identifiers, including private enterprise numbers, and many others. The Internet community requires that the values used in these parameter fields be assigned uniquely. ICANN makes those assignments as requested and maintains a registry of the current values [r013].

ICANN is responsible for generic Top-Level Domain (gTLD) and country code Top-Level Domain (ccTLD) name system management, and root server system management functions. As a private–public partnership, ICANN is dedicated to preserving the operational stability of the Internet; to promoting competition; to achieving broad representation of global Internet communities; and to developing policy appropriate to its mission through bottom-up, consensus-based processes.

Internet Data/Tangible Assets   Assets associated with an Internet presence that require protection. Examples include website content and customer credit card data.

Internet Electronic Data Interchange (EDI) Mechanisms specifying Multipurpose Internet Mail Extensions (MIME) content types for EDI data (RFC 1767). RFC 3335 expands on RFC 1767 to specify use of a comprehensive set of data security features, specifically data privacy, data integrity/authenticity, nonrepudiation of origin and non-repudiation of receipt.

Internet Engineering Steering Group (IESG) The IESG is responsible for technical management of Internet Engineering Task Force (IETF) activities and the Internet standards process. As part of the Internet Society (ISOC), it administers the process according to the rules and procedures which have been ratified by the ISOC Trustees. The IESG is directly responsible for the actions associated with entry into and movement along the Internet "standards track," including final approval of specifications as Internet Standards.

Internet Engineering Task Force (IETF)   IETF is an informal body that is responsible for the evolution of the Internet architecture. It is an open global community of network designers, operators, vendors, and researchers producing technical specifications for the evolution of the Internet architecture and the smooth operation of the Internet. IETF is not a corporation: It is an unincorporated, freestanding organization. A self-organized group of people who make contributions to the development of Internet technology. The IETF is partially supported by the Internet Society (ISOC), although not itself a part of the ISOC. ISOC is an international nonprofit or-

ganization incorporated in the United States with thousands of individual and corporate members throughout the world. ISOC provides many services to the IETF, including insurance and some financial and logistical support. Internet standardization is an organized activity of the ISOC, with the ISOC Board of Trustees being responsible for ratifying the procedures and rules of the Internet standards process. However, the IETF is not a formal subset of ISOC; for example, one does not have to join ISOC to be a member of the IETF. There is no board of directors for the IETF, no formally signed bylaws, no treasurer, and so on [r295]. IETF is the principal body engaged in developing Internet Standards. Composed of Working Groups, which are arranged into Areas (such as the Security Area), each coordinated by one or more Area Directors. Nominations to the IAB and the Internet Engineering Steering Group (IESG) are made by a committee selected at random from regular IETF meeting attendees who have volunteered [r293, r294, r013].

Internet Engineering Task Force (IETF) Security Technology   The IETF has several security protocols and standards. IP Security (IPSec, RFC 2411), Transport Layer Security (TLS, RFC 2246) are two well-known protocols. Simple Authentication and Security Layer (SASL), RFC 2222, and the Generic Security Service Application Programming Interface (GSSAPI, RFC 2743) provide services within the context of a "host" protocol. They can be viewed as "toolkits" to use within another protocol [r072].

Internet FCP (iFCP)   A protocol that converts Fibre Channel (FC) frames into Transmission Control Protocol (TCP) enabling native Fibre Channel devices to be connected via an IP network. Encapsulation protocols for IP storage solutions where the lower-layer FC transport is replaced with Transmission Control Protocol/Internet Protocol (TCP/IP) and Gigabit Ethernet. The protocol enables existing FC storage devices or Storage Area Network (SAN) to attach to an IP network. The operation is as follows: FC devices, such as disk arrays, connect to an iFCP gateway or switch. Each FC session is terminated at the local gateway and converted to a TCP/IP session via iFCP. A second gateway or switch receives the iFCP session and initiates a FC session. In iFCP, TCP/IP switching and routing elements complement and enhance, or replace, FC SAN fabric components.

Internet Gateway Routing Protocol (IGRP) A proprietary IGP used by Cisco System's routers.

Internet Governance Bodies Internet-related activities are managed by a number of bodies, notably:

- IAB: Internet Architecture Board; described in RFC 2026, RFC 2850
- IESG: Internet Engineering Steering Group; described in RFC 2026 and RFC 3710
- IETF: Internet Engineering Task Force; described in RFC 3233
- ISOC: Internet Society; described in RFC 2031
- IANA: Internet Assigned Number Authority, described in BCP 98 and BCP 99

Internet Group Management Protocol (IGMP) Protocol used by IP hosts to register their dynamic multicast group membership. It is defined in RFC 988. IGMP is also used by connected routers to discover these group members. Multicasting mechanisms allow a host to create, join, and leave host groups, as well as send IP datagrams to host groups. Multicasting requires implementation of IGMP. IP multicasting is the transmission of an IP datagram to a "host group," a set of zero or more hosts identified by a single IP destination address. A multicast datagram is delivered to all members of its destination host group with the same "best-efforts" reliability as regular unicast IP datagrams; that is, the datagram is not guaranteed to arrive at all members of the destination group or in the same order relative to other datagrams. The membership of a host group is dynamic; that is, hosts may join and leave groups at any time. There is no restriction on the location or number of members in a host group, but membership in a group may be restricted to only those hosts possessing a private access key. A host may be a member of more than one group at a time. A host need not be a member of a group to send datagrams to it.

Internet Infrastructure Services Services that include (among many other): Domain Name System (DNS), Secure Sockets Layer (SSL) digital certificates, managed security, payments, and fraud protection services.

Internet Inter-ORB Protocol (IIOP) Protocol that lets both applications (such as Web browsers) and object request brokers (ORB) communicate over a TCP/IP network. Used in the context of CORBA (Common Object Request Broker Architecture).

Internet Key Exchange (IKE) (aka IPsec Key Exchange) An IPsec standard protocol used to ensure security for Virtual Private Network (VPN) negotiation and remote host or network access. A key-establishment protocol that is intended for putting in place authenticated keying material for use with Internet Security Association and Key Management Protocol (ISAKMP) and for other security associations, such as in Authentication Header (AH) and Encapsulating Security Payload (ESP) [r320, r013]. Specified in Internet Engineering Task force (IETF) Request for Comments (RFC) 2409.

IKE defines an automatic means of negotiation and authentication for IPsec security associations (SA). Security associations are security policies defined for communication between two or more entities; the relationship between the entities is represented by a key. The IKE protocol ensures security for SA communication without the preconfiguration that would otherwise be required. IKE implements two earlier security protocols, Oakley and Secure Key Exchange Mechanism for Internet (SKEME), within an ISAKMP (Internet Security Association and Key Management Protocol) Transmission Control Protocol/Internet Protocol (TCP/IP)-based framework.

Internet Key Exchange (IKE) Version 1 (IKEv1) Basic Requirements IKEv1 specification

(RFC 2409) has the following requirements [r296]:

- Data Encryption Standard (DES) for encryption must be supported.
- Message Digest 5 (MD5) and Secure Hash Algorithm One (SHA-1) for hashing and Hashing for Message Authentication (HMAC) functions must be supported.
- Pre-shared secrets for authentication must be supported.
- Diffie–Hellman More Modular Exponential (MODP) group 1 (discrete log 768 bits) must be supported.
- TripleDES for encryption should be supported.
- Tiger for hashing should be supported.
- Digital Signature Algorithm (DSA) and Rivest–Shamir–Adleman (RSA) for authentication with signatures should be supported.
- RSA for authentication with encryption should be supported.
- Diffie–Hellman MODP group 2 (discrete log 1024 bits) should be supported.

RFC 2409 gives two conflicting requirement levels for Diffie–Hellman MODP groups with elliptic curves. It says that "IKE implementations . . . may support Elliptic Curve Group over GF[P] (ECP) and Elliptic Curve Group over GF[2^N] (EC2N) groups," but other sections say that MODP groups 3 and 4 for EC2N groups should be supported.

Internet Key Exchange (IKE) Version 1 (IKEv1) Enhanced Requirements   The original IKEv1 specification does not reflect the current reality of the Internet Protocol (IP) Security (IPsec) market requirements. The original specification allows weak security and suggests algorithms that are thinly implemented. RFC 4109 updates RFC 2409, the original specification, and is intended for all IKEv1 implementations deployed today. Requirements for IKEv1 as described in RFC 4109 are [r276]:

- TripleDES for encryption must be supported.
- Advanced Encryption Standard (AES-128) in Cipher Block Chaining (CBC) mode (RFC 3602) for encryption should be supported.
- Secure Hash Algorithm One (SHA-1) for hashing and Hashing for Message Authentication (HMAC) functions must be supported.
- Pre-shared secrets for authentication must be supported.
- AES-128 in authenticated-encryption mode (XCBC) mode for pseudo-random functions (PRF) (RFC 3566 and RFC 3664) should be supported.
- Diffie–Hellman More Modular Exponential (MODP) group 2 (discrete log 1024 bits) must be supported.
- Diffie–Hellman MODP group 14 (discrete log 2048 bits) (RFC 3526) should be supported.
- RSA for authentication with signatures should be supported.

Note that some of the requirements are the same as those in RFC 2409, whereas others are changed.

Internet Low-Bitrate Codec (iLBC)   Speech codec (defined in RFC 3951) suitable for robust Voice over IP (VoIP). Some of the applications for which this coder is suitable are real time communications such as telephony and video-conferencing, streaming audio, archival, and messaging. The codec is designed for narrowband speech and results in a payload bit rate of 13.33 kbps for 30-ms frames and 15.20 kbps for 20-ms frames. The codec enables graceful speech quality degradation in the case of lost frames, which occurs in connection with lost or delayed IP packets [r297].

This algorithm is used for the coding of speech signals sampled at 8 kHz. iLBC uses a block-independent linear-predictive coding (LPC) algorithm and has support for two basic frame lengths: 20 ms at 15.2 kbps and 30 ms at 13.33 kbps. When the codec operates at block lengths of 20 ms, it produces 304 bits per block; similarly, for block lengths of 30 ms it produces 400 bits per block. The two modes for the different frame sizes operate in a very similar way. When they differ it is explicitly stated in the text, usually with the notation x/y, where x refers to the 20-ms mode and y refers to the 30-ms mode. The algorithm results in a speech coding system with a controlled response to packet losses similar to what is known from pulse code modulation (PCM) with packet loss concealment (PLC), such as the ITU-T G.711 standard, which operates at a fixed bit rate of 64 kbps. At the same time, the iLBC algorithm enables fixed bit rate coding with a quality-versus-bit rate tradeoff close to state-of-the-art. A suitable Real-time Transport Protocol (RTP) payload format for the iLBC codec is available [r297].

Internet Message Access Protocol (IMAP)   Protocol that provides a means of managing e-mail messages on a remote server, similar to the Post Office Protocol (POP) protocol. IMAP e-mail server allows clients [Message Transfer Agents (MTAs)] to retrieve e-mail from systems remotely. A protocol for retrieving e-mail from a server. Similar to POP3 but instead of downloading messages to the local machine IMAP's default is to work on the server [r084]. Uses Transmission Control Protocol (TCP) port 143.

Internet Message Access Protocol, Version 4 (IMAP4)   An Internet protocol by which a client workstation can dynamically access a mailbox on a server host to manipulate and retrieve mail messages that the server has received and is holding for the client [r309]. IMAP4 has mechanisms for optionally authenticating a client to a server and providing other security services [r298].

Internet Message Access Protocol, Version 4 (IMAP4) AUTHENTICATE   An Internet Message Access Protocol, version 4 (IMAP4) "command" (better described as a transaction type, or a protocol-within-a-protocol) by which an IMAP4 client optionally proposes a mechanism to an IMAP4 server to authenticate the client to the server and provide other security services [r013]. If the server accepts the proposal, the command is followed by performing a challenge-response authentication protocol and, optionally, negotiating a protection mechanism for subsequent Post Office Protocol Version 3 (POP3) interactions. The security mechanisms that are used by IMAP4 AUTHENTICATE—including Kerberos, Generic Security Service Application Program Interface (GSSAPI), and S/Key—are described in [r293, r013].

Internet Policy Registration Authority (IPRA)   An X.509-compliant Certification Authority (CA) that is the top CA of the Internet certification hierarchy operated under the auspices of the Internet Society (ISOC) [r109].

Internet Protocol (IP)   Networking/routing layer datagram service of the Transmission Control Protocol/Internet Protocol (TCP/IP) suite. Layer 3 protocol used by nearly all computer networks now deployed. IPv4 is widely deployed; a transition to IPv6 is expected in the years to come.

An Internet Standard protocol (version 4 [r299] and version 6 [r300]) that moves datagrams (discrete sets of bits) from one computer to another across an internetwork but does not provide reliable delivery, flow control, sequencing, or other end-to-end services that TCP provides [r013].

The original reference for the IP protocol is Postel, J., "Internet Protocol," RFC 760, USC/Information Sciences Institute, January 1980.

Internet Protocol Multicast (IP-M)   The Internet Protocol Multicast exchanges data between the IP-M participants by means of the Internet Protocol [r014].

Internet Protocol Security Option (IPSO)   Refers to one of three types of Internet Protocol (IP) security options, which are fields that may be added to an IP datagram for the purpose of carrying security information about the datagram [r013].

Internet Registries IP addresses on the Internet are assigned in a hierarchical manner. At the top of the hierarchy is ICANN (Internet Corporation for Assigned Names and Numbers). It allocates blocks of IP addresses to regional Internet registries. The regional registries in turn further allocate blocks of IP addresses to local Internet registries within their geographic region. Finally, the local Internet registries assign addresses to end users. There are three regional Internet registries that cover the Americas, Europe, and Asia. These organizations provide the following functions: (i) *Registration services*—Approve organizations to receive allocations of IP address space. (ii) *Routing registry*—A registration service where network operators submit and retrieve router configuration information. The registry serves as a repository for routing policy system information and provides information about IP numbers database.

Internet Registries, Registry Type Each kind of Internet registry is identified by a Registry Type. The identifier for a registry type is a Uniform Resource Name (URN) used within the Extensible Markup Language (XML) instances to identify the XML schema that formally describes the set of queries, results, and entity classes allowed within that type of registry. A registry information server may handle queries and serve results for multiple registry types. Each registry type that a particular registry operator serves is a registry service instance [r237].

Internet Registry Information Service (IRIS) An application layer client-server protocol defined in RFC 3981 for a framework to represent the query and result operations of the information services of Internet registries. Specified in the Extensible Markup Language (XML), the protocol defines generic query and result operations and a mechanism for extending these operations for specific registry service needs. IRIS defines two types of referrals: an entity reference and a search continuation. An entity reference indicates specific knowledge about an individual entity, and a search continuation allows distributed searches. Both referrals may span differing registry types and instances. No assumptions or specifications are made about the roots, bases, or meshes of entities [r237].

The IRIS framework can be thought of as having three layers.

Registry-Specific	|domain |address	etc. . .	
Common Registry	| IRIS |
Application Transport	| beep | iris-lwz | etc. . . |

In this diagram, "beep" refers to the Blocks Extensible Exchange Protocol (BEEP), and "iris-lwz" refers to a theoretical User Datagram Protocol (UDP) binding that uses compression.

The differing layers have the following responsibilities:

Registry-Specific :: defines queries, results, and entity classes of a specific type of registry. Each specific type of registry is identified by a Resource Name (URN).

Common Registry :: defines base operations and semantics common to all registry types such as search sets, result sets, and referrals. It also defines the syntaxes for talking about specific registry types.

Application Transport :: defines the mechanisms for authentication, message passing, connection and session management, and so on. It also defines the Uniform Resource Identifier (URI) syntax specific to the application-transport mechanism.

Internet Relay Channel (IRC) A form of Internet-based instant communication. It is designed for group (many-to-many) communication in discussion forums called channels, but also allows one-to-one communication. IRC is an Internet Engineering Task Force (IETF) protocol that uses Transmission Control Protocol (TCP) and optionally Secure Sockets Layer (SSL). All client-to-server IRC protocols in use today are based on RFC 1459; RFC 2810, RFC 2811, RFC 2812, and RFC 2813 add new features; however, these protocol have not been widely adopted.

Internet Security   The Internet provides no inherent security. The role of the Internet Engineering Task Force (IETF) is to ensure that IETF standard protocols have the necessary features to provide appropriate security for the application as it may be used across the Internet. Making it mandatory to implement mechanisms should provide adequate security to protect sensitive business applications [r072].

Internet Security Association and Key Management Protocol (ISAKMP)   An Internet Protocol (IP) security (IPsec) protocol to negotiate, establish, modify, and delete security associations [r301]. Another aspect of ISAKMP is to exchange key generation and authentication data, independent of the details of any specific key generation technique, key establishment protocol, encryption algorithm, or authentication mechanism. ISAKMP supports negotiation of security associations for protocols at all Transmission Control Protocol/Internet Protocol (TCP/IP) layers. By centralizing management of security associations, ISAKMP reduces duplicated functionality within each protocol [r013].

Internet Service Provider (ISP)   Any commercial entity provides the required access to the Internet [r014].

Internet Small Computer System Interface (iSCSI)   A protocol that serializes Small Computer System Interface (SCSI) commands and converts them to Transmission Control Protocol/Internet Protocol (TCP/IP). Encapsulation protocols for IP storage solutions for the support of Direct Attached Storage (DAS) (specifically SCSI-3 commands) over IP network infrastructures (at the physical layer, iSCSI supports a Gigabit Ethernet interface so that systems supporting iSCSI interfaces can be directly connected to standard Gigabit Ethernet switches and/or IP routers; the iSCSI protocol sits above the physical and data-link layers).

Internet Society (ISOC)   A professional society concerned with Internet development (including technical Internet Standards); with how the Internet is and can be used; and with social, political, and technical issues that result. The ISOC Board of Trustees approves appointments to the Internet Architecture Board (IAB) from among nominees submitted by the Internet Engineering Task Force (IETF) nominating committee [r293].

Internet Standard   A specification, approved by the Internet Engineering Steering Group (IESG) and published as an RFC, that is stable and well-understood, is technically competent, has multiple, independent, and interoperable implementations with substantial operational experience, enjoys significant public support, and is recognizably useful in some or all parts of the Internet [r013, r293]. The Internet Standards Process is an activity of the Internet Society (ISOC) and is organized and managed by the Internet Architecture Board (IAB) and the IESG. The process is concerned with all protocols, procedures, and conventions used in or by the Internet, whether or not they are part of the Internet Protocol Suite. The "Internet Standards Track" has three levels of increasing maturity: Proposed Standard, Draft Standard, and Standard.

internet vs. Internet   (i) Not capitalized: A popular abbreviation for "internetwork." (ii) Capitalized: "The Internet" is the single, interconnected, worldwide system of commercial, government, educational, and other computer networks that share the set of protocols specified by the Internet Architecture Board (IAB) and the name and address spaces managed by the Internet Corporation for Assigned Names and Numbers (ICANN) [r293].

The protocol set is named the "Internet Protocol Suite." It also is popularly known as "Transmission Control Protocol/Internet Protocol (TCP/IP)," because TCP and IP are two of its fundamental components. These protocols enable a user of any one of the networks in the Internet to communicate with, or use services located on, any of the other networks. Although the Internet does have architectural principles, no Internet Standard formally defines a layered reference model for the Internet Protocol Suite that is similar to the Open Systems Interconnection Reference Model (OSIRM) [r302]. However, Internet community documents do refer (inconsistently) to layers: application, socket, transport, internetwork, network, data link, and physical [r013].

internetwork   A system of interconnected networks; a network of networks. Usually shortened to "internet." An internet is usually built using Open Systems Interconnection Reference Model (OSIRM) layer 3 gateways to connect a set of subnetworks. When the subnetworks differ in the OSIRM layer 3 protocol service they provide, the gateways sometimes implement a uniform internetwork protocol (e.g., IP) that operates at the top of layer 3 and hides the underlying heterogeneity from hosts that use communication services provided by the internet [r013].

Inter-provider Border Router   An inter-provider border router is a Border Gateway Protocol (BGP) speaking router that maintains BGP sessions with other BGP speaking routers in other providers' Autonomous Systems (ASes) [r086].

Interrupt   A call to software or hardware to have it do something else than it is already doing. In some cases interrupts can be exploited as part of an attack.

Interworking Function (IWF)   (GSM context) An external data server that is connected to different data networks. The IWF translates the incoming packet-switched data into circuit-switched signals that can be understood by GSM [r011].

Intragrid   Also known as Enterprise Grid. A grid computing environment completely enclosed within one organization [r080].

Intranet   An internal network (possibly using web portal access) offering content and services to employees. A computer network that an organization uses for its own internal, and usually private, purposes and that is closed to outsiders. Although it may link to the Internet, an intranet cannot be accessed by other companies or by the general public; a set of firewalls typically separates the internal and external environments.

Intranet Data/Tangible Assets   Assets associated with an internal network that require protection. Examples include employee data, marketing data, and strategic corporate plans.

Intra-Site Automatic Tunnel Addressing Protocol (ISATAP)   (IPv6 context) A technology of coexistence that provides IPv6 unicast connectivity between devices placed in an IPv4 intranetwork. ISATAP obtains an interface identifier from the IPv4 address (public or private) assigned to the device. This identifier is used for the establishment of automatic tunnels through IPv4 infrastructure [r008]. (Sometimes also called Automatic Internal Tunnels Addressing Protocol.)

Intra-Site Automatic Tunneling Addressing Protocol (ISATAP) Address   (IPv6 context) A |64-bit prefix|:0:5EFE:w.x.y.z address, where w.x.y.z is a public or private IPv4 address, that is allocated to an ISATAP device [r008].

Intra-Site Automatic Tunneling Addressing Protocol (ISATAP) Machine   A device to which an ISATAP address is assigned to [r008].

Intra-Site Automatic Tunneling Addressing Protocol (ISATAP) Name   The name solved by computers with Windows XP Service Pack 1 or Windows .NET Server 2003 operative systems to automatically discover the ISATAP router address. Windows XP equipment tries to resolve the name "_ISATAP" [r008].

Intra-Site Automatic Tunneling Addressing Protocol (ISATAP) Router   (IPv6 context) An IPv6/IPv4 router that answers to ISATAP equipments requests through tunnels and routes traffic between ISATAP equipments and nodes from another ISATAP network or subnetwork [r008].

Intruder   An entity that gains or attempts to gain access to a system or system resource without having authorization to do so [r013].

Intrusion   A threat action whereby an unauthorized entity gains access to sensitive data by circumventing a system's security protections. This includes physical trespass, penetration, reverse engineering, and cryptoanalysis [r013].

Intrusion Detection   A security service that monitors and analyzes system events for the purpose of finding, and providing real-time or near real-time warning of, attempts to access system resources in an unauthorized manner [r013].

Intrusion Detection in Our Time (IDIOT)   A system that detects intrusions using pattern matching.

Intrusion Detection System (IDS)   (aka Attack Detection System) Software systems (or appliances) that detect intrusions. The goal of intrusion detection is to monitor network assets to detect anomalous behavior and misuse. IDS systems can be broadly classified as host-based IDS or server-based IDS. This concept has been around for nearly a quarter century, but only recently has it seen a rise in popularity and incorporation into the overall information security infrastructure. Beginning in 1980, with James Anderson's paper, *Computer Security Threat Monitoring and Surveillance,* the notion of intrusion detection was born. Since then research and development has advanced intrusion detection to its current state [r305, r303, r304]. The most common approaches to IDS are statistical anomaly detection and pattern-matching (signature) detection [r306].

Intrusion Prevention   See Intrusion Prevention System

Intrusion Prevention System (IPS)   A security service that not only acts like an Intrusion detection system (to discover potentially malicious activity), but also which takes actions (such as disabling a service) to prevent further malicious activity. IPS systems can be broadly classified as host-based IPS or server-based IPS. IPSs have been criticized because the activation of IPS services, and the subsequent disabling of services, could be the intent of a denial of service attack.

Intrusion Protection   See Intrusion Prevention System

intserv   See Integrated Services

Invalidity Date   An X.509 certificate revocation list (CRL) entry extension that indicates the date at which it is known or suspected that the revoked certificate's private key was compromised or that the certificate should otherwise be considered invalid [r061].

Inverse Multiplexed Asynchronous Transfer Mode (IMA)   An imux-ed carrier service that enables the delivery on nxT1 Asynchronous Transfer Mode (ATM) services to customers.

Inverse Multiplexing (imux)   Carriers' service multiplexing mechanism that allows several low speed channels to be combined transparently into one higher-speed channel. Typically one combines a few DS1s channels into a 3.2- or 6.4-Mbps stream. One way to solve the DS1-DS3 gap is to bundle together multiple DS1 lines (channels) into one larger channel. Inverse multiplexing can be supported by a number of technologies, including point-to-point Time Division Multiplexing (TDM) equipment; it is more advantageous, however, when it is used with a switched service such as Frame Relay (FR) or Asynchronous Transfer Mode (ATM). Inverse Multiplexed ATM (IMA) has seen some deployment in the late 1990s; MultiLink Frame Service is a more recent service example.

Invitation   (SIP context) An INVITE request [r025].

Invitee, Invited User, Called Party, Callee   (SIP context) The party that receives an INVITE request for the purpose of establishing a new session. A callee retains this role from the time it receives the INVITE until the termination of the dialog established by that INVITE [r025].

IP   See Internet Protocol

IP Address   Address of computer nodes at layer 3. Each device on a network (whether the Internet or an intranet) must have a unique address. An IP version 4 [r299] address is written as a series of four 8-bit numbers separated by periods (32-bit total or 4-bytes). For example, the address of the host named "rosslyn.bbn.com" is 192.1.7.10. An IP version 6 [r307] address is comprised of 128 bytes and is written as x:x:x:x:x:x:x:x, where each "x" is the hexadecimal value of one of the eight 16-bit parts of the address [r013]. For example,   1080:0:0:0:8:800:200C:417A   and   FEDC: BA98:7654:3210:FEDC:BA98:7654:3210.

In IPv4 it is a 32-bit (4-byte) binary address used to identify a hosts' network ID. It is represented by the nomenclature a.b.c.d (each of these being from 1 to 255 - 0 has a special meaning); for example, 67.68.69.70 or 132.133.29.209 or 200.100.200.100, and so on. The network portion can contain either a network ID or a network ID and a subnet [r057]. Legal addresses are assigned by the Internet Assigned Numbers Authority.

The IP address can be from an officially assigned range or from an internal block. Internal intranet addresses may be in other ranges—for example, in the 10.0.0.0 or 192.0.0.0 range. In the latter case a Network Address Translation (NAT) function is employed to map the internal addresses to an external legally assigned number when the private-to-public network boundary is crossed.

IP Control Protocol (IPCP)   Protocol responsible for configuring the IP parameters on both ends of the Point-to-Point Protocol (PPP) link.

IP DF   See IP Don't Fragment

IP Don't Fragment (DF)   This is the "Don't Fragment" field in the IP header.

IP Encapsulation Issues   When an IP packet is encapsulated as payload inside another IP packet, some of the outer header fields can be newly written. Among these fields is the IP Don't Fragment (IP DF) flag. When the inner packet DF flag is clear, the outer packet may copy it or set it; however, when the inner DF flag is set, the outer header must copy it. IPsec defines conflicting rules, where that flag and other similar fields [Type of Service (TOS), etc.] may be copied, cleared, or set as specified by a "Security Association" (SA). The IPsec specification indicates that such fields must be controlled, to achieve security. Otherwise, such fields could provide a covert channel between the inner packet header and outer packet header. However, RFC 2003 requires that the outer fields not be cleared when the inner ones are set, to prevent maximum transmission unit (MTU) discovery "black holes" [r282].

IP Header Compression (IPHC)   Internet Engineering Task Force (IETF) RFC 2507 provides a standard for IP Header Compression. The RFC supports compression of IPv4 and IPv6 headers, multiple IP header compression (in case of tunneling of IP packets), and also User Datagram Protocol (UDP), Transmission Control Protocol (TCP) and Real-time Transport Protocol (RTP) headers on a per-hop basis. This header compression scheme compresses the UDP and TCP headers typically down to 2 to 5 bytes (without UDP or TCP checksum). It is designed to work well over low and medium bandwidth links with nontrivial packet loss (e.g., links such as dial-up and wireless). In general, header compression schemes that use delta encoding of compressed packets require that the lower layer does not reorder packets between compressor and decompressor.

IP Splicing/Hijacking   An action whereby an active, established, session is intercepted and co-opted by the unauthorized user. Internet Protocol (IP) splicing attacks may occur after an authentication has been made, permitting the attacker to assume the role of an already authorized user. Primary protections against IP splicing rely on encryption at the session or network layer [r057].

IP Spoofing   A situation where an attacker impersonates the Internet Protocol (IP) of a legitimate (i.e., authorized) IP address on the network.

IP Storage (Internet Protocol-Based Storage)   Using IP and Gigabit Ethernet to build Storage Area Networks (SANs). Traditional SANs were developed using the Fibre Channel (FC) transport, because it provided gigabit speeds compared to 10- and 100-Mbps Ethernet used to build messaging networks at that time. FC equipment has been costly, and interoperability between different vendors' switches was not completely standardized. Since Gigabit Ethernet and IP have become commonplace, IP storage enables familiar network protocols to be used, and IP allows SANs to be extended throughout the world. Network management software and experienced professionals in IP networks are also widely available [r029].

Internet FCP (iFCP) in a gateway-to-gateway protocol allows the replacement of FC fabric components, allowing attachment of existing FC enabled storage products to an IP network.

Metro Fibre Channel Protocol (mFCP) is another proposal for handling "IP storage." It is identical to iFCP, except that Transmission Control Protocol (TCP) is replaced by User Datagram Protocol (UDP).

Internet Small Computer System Interface (iSCSI) is a transport protocol for SCSI that operates on top of TCP. It provides a new mechanism for encapsulating SCSI commands on an IP network. iSCSI is a protocol for a new generation of storage end-nodes that natively use Transmission Control Protocol/Internet Protocol (TCP/IP) and replaces FCP with a pure TCP/IP implementation. iSCSI has broad industry support.

Fibre Channel Over Internet Protocol (FCIP) is FC over TCP/IP. Here FC uses IP-based network services to provide the connectivity between the SAN islands over Local Area Networks (LANs), Metropolitan Area Networks (MANs), or Wide Area Networks (WANs). FCIP relies on TCP for congestion control and management and upon both TCP and FC for data error and data loss recovery. FCIP treats all classes of FC frames the same as datagrams.

IP Television (IPTV)   Delivery of (entertainment-quality) video programming over an IP-based network. Traditional telecom carriers are looking to compete with Cable TV companies by deploying IP video services over their networks. IPTV technology is gaining industry momentum and aggressive deployment among U.S. service providers. However, open industry standards supporting end-to-end implementation and deployment of IPTV are seriously needed to deliver the functionality and carrier-grade quality that industry requires, as well as the service reliability that users demand [r311].

IP Time-to-Live (TTL) Field   This field in the IP header represents the number of hops that datagram has traversed so far.

IP Type-of-Service (TOS) Field   This is the Type-of-Service field in the IP header (now used to support Quality of Service (QoS) with *diffserv* approaches).

IP Version 6 (IPv6)   Latest version of the Internet Protocol (IP). Advantages are usually perceived as follows: (i) expanded addressing capabilities; (ii) server-less autoconfiguration ("plug-and-play") and reconfiguration; (iii) more efficient and robust mobility mechanisms; (iv) end-to-end security, with built-in, strong IP-layer encryption and authentication; (v) streamlined header format and flow identification; (vi) enhanced support for multicast and Quality of Service (QoS); and (vii) extensibility: Improved support for options/extensions.

IP Virtual Private Network (VPN) Architectures   Include the following three major approaches: MultiProtocol Label Switching (MPLS)-based, IPSec-based, and Secure Sockets Layer (SSL)-based.

IP Virtual Private Network (VPN) Architectures, Selection Criteria   The primary function of an IP VPN is to provide cost-effective, secure connectivity over a shared infrastructure with the same or better policies and service attributes that the enterprise enjoys within its dedicated private network. To achieve this goal, the IP VPN solution must deliver the following essential attributes: high availability, network security, Quality of Service (QoS), scalability, and ease of management. Different IP VPN architectures deliver these attributes to varying degrees, so the best choice for a given enterprise depends on the relative importance of the following business needs [r312].

IP Virtual Private Network (VPN) Class of Service (CoS)   Service providers now (generally) offer granular class of service (CoS) for VPNs, including the following [r312]:

- Level 4: Real time (voice, interactive video)
- Level 3: Business interactive [call signaling, Systems Network Architecture (SNA), Oracle, PeopleSoft, SAP, Telnet, and others]

- Level 2: Real time (streaming video, network management)
- Level 1: Business LAN-to-LAN (Internet Web, IBM Lotus Workplace, Novell Groupwise, and others)
- Level 0: Best-effort data [Simple Mail Transfer Protocol (SMTP), File Transfer Protocol (FTP), Internet web, and others]

IP Virtual Private Network (VPN), IPSec-Based
IPSec protocol, a suite of Engineering Task Force (IETF) open standards, provides the framework for Customer Premises Equipment (CPE)-based Layer 3 VPNs. To protect data as it travels across a public or a closed IP network, IPSec supports a combination of the following network security functions: (i) *Data confidentiality:* encrypts packets before transmission; (ii) *Data integrity:* authenticates packets to help ensure that the data has not been altered during transmission; (iii) *Data origin authentication:* authenticates the source of received packets, in conjunction with data integrity service; and (iv) *Antireplay:* detects aged or duplicate packets, rejecting them to avoid replay attacks.

The IPSec standard also defines several new packet formats, such as Encapsulating Security Payload (ESP), for confidentiality. ESP supports any type of symmetric encryption, including standard 56-bit Data Encryption Standard (DES), the more secure Triple DES (3DES), and the newer Advanced Encryption Standard (AES). IPSec parameters are communicated and negotiated between network devices in accordance with the Internet Key Exchange (IKE) protocol. The IPSec protocol provides protection for IP packets by allowing network designers to specify the traffic that needs protection, define how that traffic is to be protected, and control who can receive the traffic. IPSec VPNs replace or augment existing private networks based on traditional Wide Area Network (WAN) infrastructures such as leased-line, Frame Relay, or Asynchronous Transfer Mode (ATM). They fulfill the same requirements as these WAN alternatives including the support

for multiple protocols. The advantage of IPSec is that it meets network requirements more cost effectively and with greater flexibility by using today's most pervasive transport technologies: the public Internet and service providers' IP-based networks. When an enterprise out-tasks IPSec VPN service management, the service provider typically configures IPSec in a hub-and-spoke topology, where all branches (spokes) maintain a point-to-point connection to the hub, or headend. IPSec inherently supports IP unicast. Enterprises that need other Layer 3 protocols, such as AppleTalk or IPX, can use protected Generic Routing Encapsulation (GRE) tunnels over IPSec [r312].

IP Virtual Private Network (VPN), MultiProtocol Label Switching (MPLS)-Based MPLS blends the intelligence of routing with the performance of switching, providing benefits to service providers with existing native IP architectures, existing native IP plus Asynchronous Transfer Mode (ATM) architectures, or a mixture of other Layer 2 technologies. MPLS-based Layer 3 VPNs conform to a peer-to-peer model that uses Border Gateway Protocol (BGP) to distribute VPN-related information. They are based on the Internet Engineering Task Force (IETF) RFC 2547bis specification for BGP, which defines a VPN solution that uses MPLS to forward customer traffic using per-customer labels. BGP distributes route information across the provider's backbone network so that the provider participates in and manages customer routing information. A primary advantage of MPLS is that it provides the scalability to support both small and very large-scale VPN deployments: up to tens of thousands of VPNs on the same network core. In addition to scalability, its benefits include end-to-end Quality of Service (QoS), rapid fault correction of link and node failure, bandwidth protection, and a foundation for deploying additional value-added services. MPLS technology also simplifies configuration, management, and provisioning, helping service providers to deliver highly scalable, differentiated, end-to-end IP-based services. For example, the service provider can offer Service Level Agreements (SLAs) by enabling MPLS traffic engineering and fast reroute capabilities in the core network. In conjunction with the MPLS VPN service offering, service providers can also offer a multicast service, which is the replication of packets from a single source to multiple destinations, enabling voice or video broadcasts [r312].

IP Virtual Private Network (VPN), Secure Sockets Layer (SSL)-Based   SSL is an alternative to IPSec for remote-access VPNs. It is not designed for site-to-site VPNs. SSL provides access to Web-based applications from any location with a Web browser, an Internet connection, and without special client software. It provides secure connectivity by authenticating the communicating parties and encrypting the traffic that flows between them. Because SSL operates at the session layer, it works only with those applications coded for SSL, such as Web browsers and Web-based e-mail. SSL-based VPNs do not support applications not coded for SSL, including standard e-mail clients, TELNET, File Transfer Protocol (FTP), IP telephony, multicast applications, and applications requiring Quality of Service (QoS). An advantage of SSL as a remote-access VPN solution is that it does not require any special VPN client software other than a Web browser. In addition, the enterprise Information Technology (IT) group or service provider can provide granular access control, limiting individual users' access to specific Web pages or other internal resources. IT infrastructure requirements for SSL-based VPNs include application proxies because SSL must be aware of each individual connection or application session. In addition, the headend needs adequate memory to maintain all individual application connections. SSL is computing-intensive because of encryption processes, so the server needs adequate processing and memory resources to avoid becoming a bottleneck. Most enterprises regard SSL VPN as an enhancement to IPSec VPN for remote access, not as a replacement. Its simplified remote client implementation

and management make it a good choice for partner VPN connectivity when the enterprise does not control the remote client. When enterprises deploy both SSL and IPSec for their VPNs, they generally use SSL to provide limited-duration access to Web-based applications from unmanaged or home computers, airport or library kiosks, and Internet cafés; and they use IPSec for remote access from corporate-managed computers to provide full network access, providing users with the same experience they would have in the office [r312].

IP6.Int   (IPv6 context) The Domain Name System (DNS) domain created for the IPv6 reverse resolution. The reverse resolution has the purpose of fixing the name of a device by means of its address [r008].

IP-Based Private Branch Exchange (IP-PBX)   Newer Ethernet/IP/intranet/on-premises (customer-owned) equipment (often servers or appliances) to handle packet voice/Voice over IP (VoIP) in a building or campus. Technology replacing traditional PBXs. Often based on softswitch technology.

IPCC   See International Packet Communications Consortium

IPCP   See IP Control Protocol

IPHC   See IP Header Compression

IPLS   See IP-Only LAN-Like Service

IP-M   See Internet Protocol Multicast

IP-Only Local Area Network (LAN)-Like Service (IPLS)   An IPLS is very like a Virtual Private LAN Service (VPLS), except that [r082]:

> ✓ It is assumed that the Customer Edge (CE) devices are hosts or routers, not switches.
> ✓ It is assumed that the service will only have to carry IP packets, and supporting packets such as Internet Control Message Protocol (ICMP) and Address Resolution Protocol (ARP) (otherwise layer 2 packets that do not contain IP are not supported).
> ✓ The assumption that only IP packets are carried by the service applies equally to IPv4 and IPv6 packets.

While this service is a functional subset of the VPLS service, it is considered separately because it may be possible to provide it by using different mechanisms, which may allow it to run on certain hardware platforms that cannot support the full VPLS functionality [r308].

IP-PBX   See IP-Based PBX

IPRA   See Internet Policy Registration Authority

IPsec   A collective name for an architecture and set of protocols to provide security services for Internet Protocol (IP) traffic [r013]. IPsec is a framework, a set of protocols (RFC 2401) for security of IP-based networks by encrypting portions of the Protocols Data Unit (PDU) at the network layer. The term can be expanded to be Internet Protocol Security, but most people do not consider IPsec as an acronym.

Also, the name of the IETF working group that is specifying a security architecture [r442] for this set of protocols [r013].

Implementation of IPsec protocols is optional for IP version 4, but mandatory for IP version 6 [r013]. IPsec includes encryption and authentication technologies. It is commonly used to create encrypted Virtual Private Networks (VPNs), both over the internet and in Wide Area Networks (WAN).

IPsec Architecture   The IPsec architecture specifies the following [r013]:

- Security protocols [Authentication Header (AH) and Encapsulating Security Payload (ESP)].
- Security associations (what they are, how they work, how they are managed, and associated processing).
- Key management [IPsec Key Exchange (IKE)].
- Algorithms for authentication and encryption. The set of security services include access control service, connectionless data integrity service, data origin authentication service, protection against replays (detection of the arrival of duplicate datagrams, within a constrained window), data confidentiality service, and limited traffic flow confidentiality.
- There are two IPsec modes: tunnel mode and transport mode

IPsec Conflicts   IPsec can secure the links of a multihop network to protect communication between trusted components—for example, for a secure virtual network (VN), overlay, or virtual private network (VPN). Virtual links established by IPsec tunnel mode can conflict with routing and forwarding inside VNs because IP routing depends on references to interfaces and next-hop IP addresses. The IPsec tunnel mode specification is ambiguous on this issue, so even compliant implementations cannot be trusted to avoid conflicts. An alternative to tunnel mode uses non-IPsec IP-in-IP (IPIP) encapsulation together with IPsec transport mode (called IIPtran in RFC 3884). IPIP encapsulation occurs as a separate initial step, as the result of a forwarding lookup of the VN packet. IPsec transport mode processes the resulting (tunneled) IP packet with a security association (SA) determined through a security association database (SAD) match on the tunnel header. IIPtran supports dynamic routing inside the VN without changes to the current IPsec architecture [r282].

IPsec in Provider-Provisioned Virtual Private Network (PPVPN)   IPsec (RFC 2401, RFC 2402, RFC 2406, RFC 2407, RFC 2411) is the security protocol of choice for encryption at the IP layer (Layer 3), as discussed in RFC 3631. IPsec provides robust security for IP traffic between pairs of devices. Non-IP traffic must be converted to IP packets, or it cannot be transported over IPsec. Encapsulation is a common conversion method. In the PPVPN [r058] model, IPsec can be employed to protect IP traffic between Provider Edges (PEs), between a PE and a Customer Edge (CE), or from CE to CE. CE-to-CE IPsec may be employed in either a provider-provisioned or a user-provisioned model. The user-provisioned CE-CE IPsec model is outside the scope of this document and outside the scope of the PPVPN Working Group. Likewise, data encryption that is performed within the user's site is outside the scope of the RFCs, as it is simply handled as user data by the PPVPN. IPsec can also be used to protect IP traffic between a remote user and the PPVPN. IPsec does not itself specify an encryption algorithm. It can use a variety of encryption algorithms with various key lengths, such as Advanced Encryption Standard (AES) encryption. There are tradeoffs between key length, computational burden, and the level of security of the encryption. A full discussion of these trade-offs is beyond the scope of this document. In order to assess the level of security offered by a particular IPsec-based PPVPN service, some PPVPN users may wish to know the specific encryption algorithm and effective key length used by the PPVPN provider. However, in practice, any currently recommended IPsec encryption offers enough security to substantially reduce the likelihood of being directly targeted by an attacker. Other, weaker, links in the chain of security are likely to be attacked first. PPVPN users may wish to use a Service Level Agreement (SLA) specifying the service provider's responsibility for ensuring data confidentiality rather than to analyze the specific encryption techniques used in the PPVPN service. For many of the PPVPN provider's network control messages and some PPVPN user requirements, cryptographic authentication of messages without encryption of the contents of the message may provide acceptable security. With IPsec, authentication of messages is provided by the Authentication Header (AH) or by the Encapsulating Security Protocol (ESP) with authentication only. Where control messages require authentication but do not use IPsec, other cryptographic authentication methods are available. Message authentication methods currently considered to be secure are based on Keyed-Hashing for Message Authentication (HMAC) (RFC 2104) implemented with a secure hash algorithm such as Secure Hash Algorithm 1 (SHA-1) (RFC 3174) [r058].

IPsec Limitations   IPsec's end-to-end protection model and its strict layering principle are unsuitable for an emerging class of new networking services and applications. Unlike in the traditional minimalistic Internet, intermediate routers begin to play more and more active roles. They often rely on some information about the IP datagram payload, such as certain upper layer protocol header fields, to make intelligent routing decisions. In other words, routers can participate in a layer above IP [r022]. Some examples include "transport-aware link layer mechanisms," traffic engineering, and Network-resident application-layer proxies/agents.

IPsec Modes   IPsec can be used in transport mode or in tunnel mode [r013]:

- *Transport mode:* The protection applies to (i.e., the IPsec protocol encapsulates) the packets of upper-layer protocols, the ones that are carried above IP. A transport mode security association is always between two hosts.
- *Tunnel mode:* The protection applies to (i.e., the IPsec protocol encapsulates) IP packets. In a tunnel mode security association, each end may be either a host or a gateway. Whenever either end of an IPsec security association is a security gateway, the association is required to be in tunnel mode.

IPsec Operation   Before an IP datagram is transmitted over the Internet (or any other untrusted network), it is encrypted and/or signed using an IPsec protocol. When it reaches the destination side, the datagram is decrypted and/or verified. When a Transmission Control Protocol (TCP) session is transported by an IPsec Encapsulating Security Payload (ESP) protocol, the TCP header is encrypted inside the ESP header.

IPsec Request for Comments (RFCs)   The following is a list of RFCs relevant to IPsec:

- RFC 2401: Security Architecture for the Internet Protocol

- RFC 2402: IP Authentication Header (AH)
- RFC 2403: The Use of Keyed-Hashing for Message Authentication (HMAC)-Message Digest 5 (MD5)-96 within Encapsulating Security Payload (ESP) and Authentication Header (AH)
- RFC 2404: The Use of HMAC- Secure Hash Algorithm One (SHA-1)-96 within ESP and AH
- RFC 2405: The ESP Data Encryption Standard- Cipher Block Chaining (CBC) (DES-CBC) Cipher Algorithm with Explicit Initialization Vector (IV)
- RFC 2406: IP Encapsulating Security Payload (ESP)
- RFC 2407: The Internet IP Security Domain of Interpretation for ISAKMP
- RFC 2408: Internet Security Association and Key Management Protocol (ISAKMP)
- RFC 2409: The Internet Key Exchange (IKE)
- RFC 2410: The NULL Encryption Algorithm and Its Use with IPsec
- RFC 2411: IP Security Document Roadmap
- RFC 2412: The OAKLEY Key Determination Protocol
- RFC 3602: The AES-CBC Cipher Algorithm and Its Use with IPsec
- RFC 3775: Mobility Support in IPv6
- RFC 3776: Using IPsec to Protect Mobile IPv6 Signaling Between Mobile Nodes and Home Agents

IPsec Virtual Private Network (VPN)   A common method for providing encrypted, authenticated Virtual Private Networks (VPNs) over an IP network.

IPsec, Conflict with Network Address Translation (NAT)   See NAT Conflict with IPsec

IPsec, Granularity of Security Protection   The granularity of security protection in IPsec is at the datagram level. IPsec treats everything in an IP datagram after the IP header as one integrity unit. Usually, an IP datagram has three consecutive parts: the IP header (for routing purpose only), and the upper layer protocol headers [e.g., the Transmission Control Protocol (TCP) header], and the user data (e.g., TCP data). In transport mode, an IPsec header [Authentication Header (AH) or Encapsulating Security Payload (ESP)] is inserted after the IP header and before the upper layer protocol header to protect the upper layer protocols and user data. In tunnel mode, the entire IP datagram is encapsulated in a new IPsec packet (a new IP header followed by an AH or ESP header). In either mode, the upper layer protocol headers and data in an IP datagram are protected as one indivisible unit. The keys used in IPsec encryption and authentication are shared only by the sender-side and receiver-side security gateways. All other nodes in the public Internet, whether they are legitimate routers or malicious eavesdroppers, see only the IP header and will not be able to decrypt the content, nor can they tamper it without being detected. Traditionally, the intermediate routers do only one thing-forwarding packets based on the IP header (mainly the destination address field); IPsec's "end-to-end" protection model suits well in this layering paradigm [r022].

IPsec, Usage of Triple DES   The algorithm variation proposed for Encapsulating Security Payload (ESP) uses a 168-bit key, consisting of three independent 56-bit quantities used by the Data Encryption Algorithm (DEA), and a 64-bit initialization value. Each datagram contains an initialization value to ensure that each received datagram can be decrypted even when other datagrams are dropped or a sequence of datagrams is reordered in transit [r310, r013].

IPSO   See Internet Protocol Security Option

IPv4   Internet Protocol Version 4. Address space is 32 bits long and the header has a well-defined format [r014].

IPv4 Address Format   The 32-bit address can be represented as AdrType|netID|hosted. Every network and every host or device has a unique address, by definition. The layout that follows depicts the traditional address classes.

IP address

```
|1|2|3|4|5|6|7|8|1|2|3|4|5|6|7|8|1|2|3|4|5|6|7|8|1|2|3|4|5|6|7|8|
| Address Class  |  Network ID    | Host ID                       |
```

Class A

```
|1|2|3|4|5|6|7|8|1|2|3|4|5|6|7|8|1|2|3|4|5|6|7|8|1|2|3|4|5|6|7|8|
|0| Network ID   | Host ID                                       |
```

Class B

```
|1|2|3|4|5|6|7|8|1|2|3|4|5|6|7|8|1|2|3|4|5|6|7|8|1|2|3|4|5|6|7|8|
|1| 0  Network ID|                | Host ID                       |
```

Class C

```
|1|2|3|4|5|6|7|8|1|2|3|4|5|6|7|8|1|2|3|4|5|6|7|8|1|2|3|4|5|6|7|8|
|1|1|0|                                        | Host ID          |
```

Class D

```
|1|2|3|4|5|6|7|8|1|2|3|4|5|6|7|8|1|2|3|4|5|6|7|8|1|2|3|4|5|6|7|8|
|1|1|1|0| Multicast Address                                       |
```

Address Class A. Class A uses the first bit of the 32-bit space (bit 0) to identify it as a Class A address; this bit is set to 0. Bits 1 to 7 represent the network ID and bits 8 through 31 identify the PC, terminal device, or host/server on the network. This address space supports $2^7 - 2 = 126$ networks and approximately 16 million devices (2^{24}) on each network. By convention, the use of an "all 1s" or "all 0s" address for both the Network ID and the Host ID is prohibited (which is the reason for subtracting the 2 above).

Address Class B. Class B uses the first two bits (bit 0 and bit 1) of the 32-bit space to identify it as a Class B address; these bits are set to 10. Bits 2 to 15 represent the network ID and bits 16 through 31 identify the PC, terminal device, or host/server on the network. This address space supports $2^{14} - 2 = 16,382$ networks and $2^{12} - 2 = 65,134$ devices on each network.

Address Class C. Class C uses the first three bits (bit 0, bit 1, and bit 2) of the 32-bit space to identify it as a Class C address; these bits are set to 110. Bits 3 to 23 represent the network ID and bits 24 through 31 identify the PC, terminal

device, or host/server on the network. This address space supports about 2 million networks ($2^{21} - 2$) and $2^8 - 2 = 254$ devices on each network.

Address Class D. This class is used for broadcasting: multiple devices (all devices on the network) receive the same packet. Class D uses the first four bits (bit 0, bit 1, bit 2, and bit 3) of the 32-bit space to identify it as a Class D address; these bits are set to 1110.

IPv4-Compatible Address (IPv6 context) A 0:0:0:0:0:0:w.x.y.z or ::w.x.y.z address, where w.w.y.z is the decimal representation of a public IPv4 address. For example, ::131:107:89:42 is an IPv4-compatible address. These addresses are used in Automatic IPv6 tunnels [r008].

IPv4 Node (IPv6 context) A node that implements IPv4; it can send and receive IPv4 packets. It can be an only IPv4 node or a dual IPv4/IPv6 node [r008].

IPv6 The Internet Protocol Version 6, which is being introduced as the successor of the IPv4.

IPv6 Addresses IP address in which the leftmost 64 bits of a 128-bit address form the subnet prefix and the rightmost 64 bits of the address form the interface identifier as described in RFC 3513. One numbers the bits of the interface identifier starting from bit zero on the left.

IPv6 In IPv4 (IPv6 context) See IPv6 over IPv4 tunnels.

IPv6 Maximum Transfer Unit (MTU) (IPv6 context) The maximum IP packet size that can be sent over a link [r008].

IPv6 Migrations At some point in the future, applications will have to be modified to support IPv6. There are four cases [r314]:

Case 1: IPv4-only applications in a dual-stack node. IPv6 protocol is introduced in a node, but applications are not yet ported to support IPv6.

Case 2: IPv4-only applications and IPv6-only applications in a dual-stack node. Applications are ported for IPv6-only. Therefore there are two similar applications, one for each protocol version (e.g., ping and ping6).

Case 3: Applications supporting both IPv4 and IPv6 in a dual stack node. Applications are ported for both IPv4 and IPv6 support. Therefore, the existing IPv4 applications can be removed.

Case 4: Applications supporting both IPv4 and IPv6 in an IPv4-only node. Applications are ported for both IPv4 and IPv6 support, but the same applications may also have to work when IPv6 is not being used [e.g., disabled from the Operating System (OS)].

The first two cases are not interesting in the longer term; only few applications are inherently IPv4- or IPv6-specific, and should work with both protocols without having to care about which one is being used.

```
+———————+
|     appv4     | (appv4 - IPv4-only applications)
+———————+
| TCP/UDP/others | (transport protocols - TCP, UDP,
+———————+ SCTP, DCCP, etc.)
|   IPv4 | IPv6   | (IP protocols supported/enabled in the OS)
+———————+
```

Case 1. IPv4 applications in a dual-stack node.

```
+———————+ (appv4 - IPv4-only applications)
| appv4 | appv6   | (appv6 - IPv6-only applications)
+———————+
|TCP / UDP / others | (transport protocols - TCP, UDP,
+———————+         SCTP, DCCP, etc.)
|   IPv4 | IPv6   | (IP protocols supported/enabled in the OS)
+———————+
```

Case 2. IPv4-only applications and IPv6-only applications in a dual-stack node.

```
+———————+
|   appv4/v6    | (appv4/v6 - applications supporting
+———————+          both IPv4 and IPv6)
| TCP/UDP/others | (transport protocols - TCP, UDP,
+———————+          SCTP, DCCP, etc.)
|   IPv4 | IPv6   | (IP protocols supported/enabled in the OS)
+———————+
```

Case 3. Applications supporting both IPv4 and IPv6 in a dual-stack node.

```
+———————+
|   appv4/v6    | (appv4/v6 - applications supporting
+———————+          both IPv4 and IPv6)
| TCP/UDP/others | (transport protocols - TCP, UDP,
+———————+          SCTP, DCCP, etc.)
|     IPv4      | (IP protocols supported/enabled in the OS)
+———————+
```

Case 4. Applications supporting both IPv4 and IPv6 in an IPv4-only node.

IPv6 Node   (IPv6 context) Node that implements IPv6; it can send and receive IPv6 packets. An IPv6 node can be an only IPv6 node or a dual IPv6/IPv4 node [r008].

IPv6 Over IPv4 Tunnel   (IPv6 context) Sending IPv6 packets with an IPv4 header, so IPv6 traffic can be sent over an IPv4 infrastructure. In the IPv4 header, the protocol field value is 41 [r008].

IPv6 Point-to-Point Protocol (PPP) Control Protocol (IPv6CP)   Protocol responsible for configuring, enabling, and disabling the IPv6 protocol modules on both ends of a PPP link.

IPv6 Prefixes   (IPv6 context)The prefix is the part of the address that indicates the bits that have fixed values or are the bits of the network identifier. Prefixes for IPv6 routes and subnet identifiers are expressed in the same way as Classless Inter-Domain Routing (CIDR) notation for IPv4. An IPv6 prefix is written in address/prefix-length notation. For example, 21DA:D3::/48 is a route prefix and 21DA:D3:0:2F3B::/64 is a subnet prefix. IPv4 implementations commonly use a dotted decimal representation of the network prefix known as the subnet mask. A subnet mask is not used in IPv6. Only prefix-length notation is used [r023].

IPv6 Routing Table   (IPv6 context) Set of routes used to determine next node address and interface in IPv6 traffic sent by some equipment or redirected by a router [r008].

IPv6/IPv4 Node   (IPv6 context) A node that has IPv4 and IPv6 implementations [r008].

IRC   See Internet Relay Channel

IRIS   See Internet Registry Information Service

Iris Recognition A type of biometric authentication that focuses on the unique characteristics found in the iris of the human eye.

IRP See Information Retention Policy

IRR See Internal Rate of Return

IS See Information Systems

ISACA See Information Systems Audit and Control Association

ISAKMP See Internet Security Association and Key Management Protocol

ISATAP See Intra-Site Automatic Tunneling Addressing Protocol

ISC See International Softswitch Consortium

iSCSI See Internet Small Computer System Interface

ISDN See Integrated Services Digital Network

ISIS See Intermediate System to Intermediate System

Island of Security (DNSSEC context) Term used to describe a signed, delegated zone that does not have an authentication chain from its delegating parent. That is, there is no Delegation Signer (DS) Resource Record (RR) containing a hash of a Domain Name System (DNS) public key (DNSKEY) RR for the island in its delegating parent zone (RFC 4034). An island of security is served by security-aware name servers and may provide authentication chains to any delegated child zones. Responses from an island of security or its descendents can only be authenticated if its authentication keys can be authenticated by some trusted means out of band from the Domain Name System (DNS) protocol.

ISM See Industrial, Scientific, and Medical

IS-NIC See Integrated Storage Network Interface Card

ISO See International Organization for Standardization

ISP See Internet Service Provider

ISPAB See Information Security and Privacy Advisory Board

ISSO See Information System Security Officer

Issue [A Digital Certificate or Certificate Revocation List (CRL)] To generate and sign a digital certificate (or CRL) and, usually, distribute it and make it available to potential certificate users (or CRL users). The American Bar Association (ABA) Digital Signature Guidelines [r110] explicitly limit this term to certificate creation, and exclude the act of publishing. In general usage, however, "issuing" a digital certificate (or CRL) includes not only certificate creation but also making it available to potential users, such as by storing it in a repository or other directory or otherwise publishing it [r013].

Issuer of a Certificate or Certificate Revocation List (CRL) The Certification Authority (CA) that signs the digital certificate or CRL. An X.509 certificate always includes the issuer's name. The name may include a common name value [r013].

Issuer of a Payment Card (SET context) The institution that establishes the account for a cardholder and issues the payment card also guarantees payment for authorized transactions that use the card in accordance with card brand regulations and local legislation [r017, r013].

Issuing Certification Authority (Issuing CA) In the context of a particular certificate, the issuing Certification Authority (CA) is the CA that issued the certificate (see also Subject certification authority) [r011, r105].

ISUP See ISDN User Part

IT See Information Technologies

ITAR See International Traffic in Arms Regulations

ITL See Information Technology Laboratory

ITU or ITU-T See International Telecommunications Union—Telecommunication Standardization Sector

Iu (3G Wireless context) The Iu interface connects the Core Network to the Radio Network Subsystem (RNS) [r007].

Iub (3G Wireless context) The Iub interface connects the Radio Network Controller (RNC) to the Node Bs [r007].

IV See Initialization Vector

IVR See Interactive Voice Response

IWF See Interworking Function

Jabber   A device that is handling electrical signals improperly. In an Ethernet network, a jabber can look like a device that is always sending, effectively bringing the network to a halt. A jabber is usually the result of a bad network interface card (NIC) [r101].

Java   A high-level programming language developed by Sun Microsystems, originally designed for handheld devices and set-top boxes. In 1995 Sun modified the language to make it applicable to World Wide Web. Java is an object-oriented language similar to C++, but simpler. Java source code files are compiled into a format called *bytecode* which can then be executed by a Java interpreter (Java source code files have a *.java* extension and *bytecode* files have a *.class* extension). Java interpreters and runtime environments exist for most operating systems. Small Java applications are called Java applets and can be downloaded from a web server and run on a computer by a Java-compatible web browser.

Java Sandbox   In general, sandboxes are security mechanisms employed when executable code comes from unknown or untrusted sources and allow the user to run untrusted code safely.

A Java Sandbox is a sandbox for use in the Java development environment. It is a set of rules that are used when creating an applet. These rules are intended to prevent certain functions when the applet is sent as part of a web page. When a browser requests a web page with applets, the applets are executed as soon as the page arrives. If the applet is allowed unlimited access to memory and operating system resources, it could be used for mali-

Minoli–Cordovana's Authoritative Computer and Network Security Dictionary. By Daniel Minoli and James Cordovana
Copyright © 2006 John Wiley & Sons, Inc.

cious intent. The sandbox creates an environment where there are limitations on what system resources the applet can use. The Java sandbox relies on a three-tiered defense: (i) byte code verifier; (ii) applet class loader; and (iii) security manager.

Jericho Forum An international group of organizations seeking to facilitate secure interoperability and to develop security standards for open networks.

Job Management and Resource Management Function In a grid-computing environment, this function provides the services to actually launch a job on a particular resource, to check the job's status, and to retrieve the results when the job is complete. Typically, the management component keeps track of the resources available to the grid and which users are members of the grid [r080].

Joint Photographic Experts Group (JPEG) A graphics file compression format for still images that features adjustable levels of compression.

JPEG sacrifices some image quality to achieve high compression [r203, r316].

Joke A harmless program that causes various benign activities to display on a computer (for example, an unexpected screen saver) [r272].

Journal An accounting book of original entry where transactions are initially recorded.

JPEG See Joint Photographic Experts Group

Jumbo Payload Option (IPv6 context) An option in the hop-to-hop options header that shows the size of the jumbogram [r008].

Jumbogram (IPv6 context) An IPv6 packet that has a payload greater than 65,535 bytes. Jumbograms are identified with a 0 value in the payload length IPv6 header field, and including a Jumbo payload option in the hop-to-hop options header [r008].

Jurisdiction In telecom this refers to the functional separation of telecommunications networks.

K-64 Encryption algorithm. The Secure And Fast Encryption Routine with 64-bit key algorithm was introduced by J. L. Massey in 1993 and is an iterated blockcipher with 64-bit plaintext and ciphertext blocks [r068a].

Kamikaze Packet (aka Chernobyl Packet) A Protocol Data Unit (PDU) that creates a broadcast storm and network incapacitation due to ensuing overload. Typically a datagram that passes through a gateway with both source and destination Ethernet address and IP address set as the (respective) broadcast addresses.

Kazaa Popular peer-to-peer (P2P) file sharing protocol. Other P2P protocols/systems include Gnutella and eDonkey.

Kc (GSM context) Together with the Signed Response (SRES) and the random number (RAND), the key Kc belongs to the Authentication Triplet, which is generated in the Authentication Center (AuC) for the authentication of a mobile subscriber. Kc is also used for channel coding [r011].

KDC See Key Distribution Center and/or Kerberos

KEA See Key Exchange Algorithm

KEK See Key-Encrypting Key

Keystream Cipher (aka stream cipher) Encryption where a stream of keys ("keystream") is used to encrypt the information: successive plaintext elements are encrypted with successive keys in a stream. Stream ciphers operate on a single bit, byte, or word at a time and use a feedback mechanism so that the key is constantly changing.

Kerberos A network security package developed

at the Massachusetts Institute of Technology that depends on passwords and symmetric cryptography [e.g. Data Encryption Standards (DES)] to implement ticket-based, peer entity authentication service and access control service distributed in a client-server network environment [r070, r013].

Kerberos Operation   Under Kerberos, a client (generally either a user or a service) sends a request for a ticket to the Key Distribution Center (KDC). The KDC creates a ticket-granting ticket (TGT) for the client, encrypts it using the client's password as the key, and sends the encrypted TGT back to the client. The client then attempts to decrypt the TGT, using its password. If the client successfully decrypts the TGT (i.e., if the client gave the correct password), it keeps the decrypted TGT, that indicates proof of the client's identity. The TGT, that expires at a specified time, permits the client to obtain additional tickets, that give permission for specific services. The requesting and granting of these additional tickets is user-transparent. Since Kerberos negotiates authenticated, and optionally encrypted, communications between two points anywhere on the Internet, it provides a layer of security that is not dependent on which side of a firewall either client is on [r327].

Kerberos Protocols   Protocols are designed to encrypt messages of arbitrary sizes, using block encryption ciphers or, less commonly, stream encryption ciphers. Encryption is used to prove the identities of the network entities participating in message exchanges. However, nothing in the Kerberos protocol requires that any specific encryption algorithm be used, as long as the algorithm includes certain operations [r115].

Kernel   Core elements of the Operating System (OS). Unix systems have a kernel that provides a system call interface to allow programs to interface directly with hardware and files. The Linux kernel provides file systems, networking support for Transmission Control Protocol/Internet Protocol (TCP/IP) and other protocols, and device drivers. These can be built into a kernel *"statically"* or as loadable modules [r084].

Kernel/driver Keyloggers   A type of keylogger that is at the kernel level and receives data directly from the input device (typically, a keyboard). It replaces the core software for interpreting keystrokes. It can be programmed to be virtually undetectable by taking advantage of the fact that it is executed on boot, before any user-level applications start. Since the program runs at the kernel level, one disadvantage to this approach it that it fails to capture autocomplete passwords, as this information is passed in the application layer [r224].

Key   (aka cryptographic key) An input parameter that varies the transformation performed by a cryptographic algorithm.

Key Agreement (Algorithm or Protocol)   The procedure whereby two different parties generate shared symmetric keys such that any of the shared symmetric keys is a function of the information contributed by all legitimate participants, so that no party (alone) can predetermine the value of the key [r339]. For example, a message originator and the intended recipient can each use their own private key and the other's public key with the Diffie–Hellman algorithm to first compute a shared secret value and, from that value, derive a session key to encrypt the message.

Key Authentication   The assurance of the legitimate participants in a key agreement that no non-legitimate party possesses the shared symmetric key [r339].

Key Center   A centralized key distribution process (used in symmetric cryptography), usually a separate computer system, that uses key-encrypting keys (master keys) to encrypt and distribute session keys needed in a community of users [r013]. An American National Standards Institute (ANSI) standard defines two types of key center: key distribution center and key translation center [r340].

Key Confirmation   The assurance of the legitimate participants in a key establishment protocol that the intended parties sharing the symmetric key actually possess the shared symmetric key [r348].

Key Distribution   A process that delivers a cryptographic key from the location where it is generated to the locations where it is used in a cryptographic algorithm [r013].

Key Distribution Center (KDC)   A machine (or system) that issues keys (or Kerberos tickets in a Kerberos-based system). The KDC services both initial ticket and ticket-granting ticket requests. The initial ticket portion is sometimes referred to as the Authentication Server (or service). The ticket-granting ticket portion is sometimes referred to as the ticket-granting server (or service) [r070].

Key Escrow   The system of giving a piece of a key to each of a certain number of trustees such that the key can be recovered with the collaboration of all the trustees [r057].

Key Establishment (Algorithm or Protocol)   The procedure to share a symmetric key among different parties by either key agreement or key transport [r339].

Key Exchange   The swapping of public keys between entities to be used to encrypt communication between the entities.

Key Exchange Algorithm (KEA)   A key agreement algorithm [r063] that is similar to the Diffie–Hellman algorithm, uses 1024-bit asymmetric keys, and was developed and formerly classified at the "Secret" level by the National Security Agency (NSA). (KEA was declassified in 1998.)

Key Generation   A process that creates the sequence of symbols that comprise a cryptographic key.

Key Generation Functions (Kerberos)   Encryption keys must be generated in a number of cases, from different types of inputs. All function specifications must indicate how to generate keys in the proper wire format and must avoid generating keys that significantly compromise the confidentiality of encrypted data, if the cryptosystem has such. Entropy from each source should be preserved as much as possible. Many of the inputs, although unknown, may be at least partly predictable (e.g., a password string is likely to be entirely in the American Standard Code for Information Interchange (ASCII) subset and of fairly short length in many environments or a semi-random string may include time stamps). The benefit of such predictability to an attacker must be minimize [r115].

Key Generation Nonce   Nonce data used for the purpose of creating a key.

Key Generator   An algorithm that uses mathematical rules to deterministically produce a pseudo-random sequence of cryptographic key values [r013].

Also, an encryption device that incorporates a key generation mechanism and applies the key to plaintext (e.g., by exclusive OR-ing the key bit string with the plaintext bit string) to produce ciphertext [r013].

Key Length   The number of symbols (usually bits) needed to be able to represent any of the possible values of a cryptographic key [r013].

Key Lifetime   An attribute of a Multilevel Information Systems Security Initiative (MISSI) key pair that specifies a time span that bounds the validity period of any MISSI X.509 public-key certificate that contains the public component of the pair [r013].

Key Loggers   Same as Keyloggers

Key Management   The activities involving the handling of cryptographic keys and other related security parameters (e.g., initialization vectors and counters) during the entire life cycle of the keys, including their generation, storage, distribution, entry and use, deletion or destruction, and archiving [r167].

Key Management Protocol (KMP)   A protocol to establish a shared symmetric key between a pair (or a group) of users.

Key Material Identifier (KMID)   A 64-bit identifier that is assigned to a key pair when the public key is bound in a Multilevel Information Systems Security Initiative (MISSI) X.509 public-key certificate [r013].

Key Pair   A set of mathematically related keys (a public key and a private key) that are used for asymmetric cryptography and are generated in a way that makes it computationally infeasible to derive the private key from knowledge of the public key [r013]. A key pair's owner discloses the public key to other system entities so they can use the key to encrypt data, verify a digital signature, compute a protected checksum, or generate a key in a key agreement algorithm. The matching private key is kept secret by the owner, who uses it to decrypt data, generate a digital signature, verify a protected checksum, or generate a key in a key agreement algorithm [r013].

Key Recovery   Techniques that provide an intentional, alternate (i.e., secondary) means to access the key used for data confidentiality service in an encrypted association [r013].

There are two classes of key recovery techniques [r013]:

- *Key escrow:* A key recovery technique for storing knowledge of a cryptographic key or parts thereof in the custody of one or more third parties called "escrow agents," that allows for the key to be recovered and used in specified circumstances. Key escrow is typically implemented with split knowledge techniques. For example, the Escrowed Encryption Standard [r239] entrusts two components of a device-unique split key to separate escrow agents. The agents provide the components only to someone legally authorized to conduct electronic surveillance of telecommunications encrypted by that specific device. The components are used to reconstruct the device-unique key; the device-unique key is used to obtain the session key needed to decrypt communications.

- *Key encapsulation:* A key recovery technique for storing knowledge of a cryptographic key by encrypting it with another key and ensuring that only certain third parties called "recovery agents" can perform the decryption operation to retrieve the stored key. Key encapsulation typically allows direct retrieval of the secret key used to provide data confidentiality.

Also, a process for learning the value (through cryptoanalysis) of a cryptographic key that was previously used to perform some cryptographic operation [r013].

Key Signing Key (KSK)   [DNS Security Extensions (DNSSEC) context] An authentication key that corresponds to a private key used to sign one or more other authentication keys for a given zone. Typically, the private key corresponding to a key signing key will sign a zone signing key, which in turn has a corresponding private key that will sign other zone data. Local policy may require that the zone signing key be changed frequently, while the key signing key may have a longer validity period in order to provide a more stable secure entry point into the zone. Designating an authentication key as a key signing key is purely an operational issue. DNSSEC validation does not distinguish between key signing keys and other DNSSEC authentication keys, and it is possible to use a single key as both a key signing key and a zone signing key. Key signing keys are discussed in more detail in RFC 3757 [r069].

Key Space   The range of possible values of a cryptographic key; or the number of distinct transformations supported by a particular cryptographic algorithm [r013].

Key Strength   A measure of how "randomly unguessable" a key is. An adversary can try to determine the "secret" key by trial and error. This is possible as long as the key is enough smaller than the message that the correct key can be uniquely identified. The probability of an adversary succeeding at this must be made acceptably low, depending on the particular application. The size of the space the adversary must search is related to the amount of key "information" present, in an information-theoretic sense. This depends on the number of different secret values possible and the probability of each value, as follows [r166]:

$$\text{bits of information} = \Sigma \ (-p_i) * \log_2(p_i)$$

where i counts from 1 to the number of possible secret values and p_i is the probability of the value numbered i. (Because p_i is less than 1, the log will be negative, so each term in the sum will be non-negative.) If there are 2^n different values of equal probability, then n bits of information are present and an adversary would have to try, on the average, half of the values, or $2^{(n-1)}$, before guessing the secret quantity. If the probability of different values is unequal, then there is less information present, and fewer guesses will, on average, be required by an adversary. In particular, any values that an adversary can know to be impossible or of low probability can be initially ignored by the adversary, who will search through the more probable values first [r166].

For example, consider a cryptographic system that uses 128-bit keys. If these keys are derived using a fixed pseudo-random number generator that is seeded with an 8-bit seed, then an adversary needs to search through only 256 keys (by running the pseudo-random number generator with every possible seed), not 2^{128} keys as may at first appear to be the case. Only 8 bits of "information" are in these 128-bit keys.

Key Translation Center A type of key center (used in a symmetric cryptography) that implements a key distribution protocol to convey keys between two (or more) parties who wish to communicate securely [r013].

Key Transport (Algorithm or Protocol) A key establishment method by which a secret key is generated by one entity in a communication association and securely sent to another entity in the association [r013]. For example, a message originator can generate a random session key and then use the Rivest–Shamir–Adleman (RSA) algorithm to encrypt that key with the public key of the intended recipient.

Key Update A process that derives a new key from an existing key.

Key Validation The procedure for the receiver of a public key to check that the key conforms to the arithmetic requirements for such a key in order to thwart certain types of attacks [r339].

Key-Based Encryption Nearly all modern (commercial) encryption algorithms base their security on the usage of a key. A message can be decrypted only if the key used for decryption matches the key used for encryption. This is in contrast with earlier methods that relied on the secrecy of the encrypting algorithm itself [r036].

There are two types of key-based encryption algorithms: symmetric (or secret-key) and asymmetric (or public-key) algorithms. A symmetric algorithm uses the same key for encryption and decryption (or the decryption key is easily derived from the encryption key). An asymmetric algorithm uses a different key for encryption and decryption, and the decryption key cannot be derived from the encryption key. In general, symmetric algorithms are much faster to execute on a computer than asymmetric ones. Data Encryption Standard (DES) and Advanced Encryption Standard (AES) are well-known examples of symmetric encryption algorithms.

Key-Derivation Function (Kerberos context) In this function, the integer input is the key usage value; (protocol-key, integer) $\rightarrow$ (specific-key). An attacker is assumed to know the usage values [r115].

Keyed Hash A cryptographic hash [e.g., r341] in which the mapping to a hash result is varied by a second input parameter that is a cryptographic key. If the input data object is changed, a new hash result cannot be correctly computed without knowledge of the secret key. Thus, the secret key protects the hash result so it can be used as a checksum even when there is a threat of an active attack on the data. There are at least two forms of keyed hash [r013]:

- A function based on a keyed encryption algorithm (e.g., Data Authentication Code)
- A function based on a keyless hash that is enhanced by combining (e.g., by concatenating) the input data object parameter with a key parameter before mapping to the hash result [e.g., Hashing for Message Authentication (HMAC)]

Key-Encrypting Key (KEK) A cryptographic key that is used to encrypt other keys, either Data Encryption Keys (DEKs) or other KEKs, but is not usually used to encrypt application data [r013].

Key-Generation Seed Length   The length of the random bit string needed to generate a key with the encryption scheme's random-to-key function. This must be a fixed value so that various techniques for producing a random bit string of a given length may be used with key generation functions [r115].

Keying Material   Data (such as keys, key pairs, and initialization values) needed to establish and maintain a cryptographic security association.

Keyloggers   (aka key logger, keystroke logger) Applications that monitor users' keystrokes and stores this information for later retrieval. Keyloggers can be used for legitimate purpose, such as would be found in security administrators' toolkit (in order to monitor a suspicious user's activity). Other uses, such as in spyware programs and/or hacker toolkits, may have malicious intent.

Keylogging Programs, Benign Roles   While keyloggers can be used nefariously, initially software products of this type were designed solely for recording key stroke information (including the system keys), to the special log file (audit trail). Afterwards this would be analyzed by the person who had installed this program. Log files can be sent within the network to the shared server, to the ftp server in the Internet, by e-mail, and so on. New software products perform many additional functions: They intercept information from the windows, capture mouse clicks, snapshots of the screen and active windows, record all received and sent e-mails, monitor file activity, monitor system register, monitor the printer queue, intercept sound from the microphone and video pictures from the Web camera connected to the computer, and so on. Keyloggers can be included in commercial, free and shareware programs, Trojan programs, viruses, and Internet worms [r342].

Keystroke Logger   Same as Keyloggers.

Keystroke Monitoring   An audit trail system that records every keystroke by a user; such a system also captures every character of the response that the system returns to the user.

keytab   A key table file in the Kerberos system containing one or more keys. A host or service uses a keytab file in much the same way as a user uses his/her password [r317].

Ki   (GSM context) The key Ki is a parameter needed for the generation of the Authentication Triplet. This consists of the random number (RAND), the Signed Response (SRES) and Kc [r011].

KISA   See Korea Information Security Agency

Kleptographic Attacks   Attacks that have been devised for factoring-based key generation algorithms [r089, r318]. These attacks leak the private key securely and subliminally through the public key itself. This can potentially affect any implementation of RSA, Rabin, Goldwasser–Micali, Paillier, and so on. Kleptographic attacks have been devised for key exchanges [r319], and for digital signature algorithms as well. These include ElGamal, Schnorr, DSA, Pointcheval–Stern, and others. There is a general way to attack any cryptosystem that displays a modular exponentiation in its output when the exponent is chosen randomly [r320, r321]. Kleptographic attacks also work against elliptic curve cryptosystems [r173].

A kleptographic attack is carried out by building a malicious implementation of a black-box cryptosystem. The malicious implementation is designed to have the same Input/Output (I/O) specifications as the correctly implemented cryptosystem, yet securely and subliminally leaks private information to the attacker. Kleptography grew out of the notion of a cryptovirus and the realization that subliminal channels could be used by cryptotrojans to covertly transmit host data to the attacker. This is for data that has been asymmetrically encrypted using the public key of the attacker. The code that carries out a kleptographic attack is therefore malicious software that contains and uses the public key of the attacker. In other words, the code that carries out a kleptographic attack is a cryptotrojan. So, from the perspective of cryptovirology, kleptography can be thought of as the study of cryptotrojans that only infect hosts that are cryptosystems [r089].

Kleptographic Attacks Against Deterministic Cryptosystems Kleptographic attacks have been devised for symmetric encryption algorithms that are deterministic [r089, r322–r325]. This issue encompasses relatively recent results and is therefore likely to be of interest to cryptographers [r326–r328]. It might seem counterintuitive that information can be leaked within a keyed bijection. However, a block cipher is considered to be secure only if it can withstand a chosen-plaintext attack (or an adaptive chosen plaintext attack). So, it may be assumed that the adversary has plaintext/ciphertext pairs at his or her disposal. In the case of pseudo-random one-time pad encryption (akin to the Vernam cipher), this implies that the pad is known under the bitwise XOR operation. Hence, there can be information transmission outside the black-box cryptosystem. This intuitive explanation closely resembles the principles behind that attacks presented in [r324, r325].

Kleptographic Remedies There is a long line of research geared toward eliminating subliminal channels. By eliminating subliminal channels, the ability to carry out kleptographic attacks is greatly hampered. Gus Simmons introduced the idea of using a protocol involving randomization to destroy subliminal channels [r089, r329]. To destroy a particular subliminal channel that was identified, Simmons has the warden (in the prisoners' problem) generate a random number x and modify the message that is sent from one prisoner to the other prisoner using x. This shows the dual nature of randomization; it can pave the way for subliminal communications, but at the same time it can be used in carefully crafted protocols to virtually eliminate the existence of subliminal channels.

For other early results that use randomization to eliminate subliminal channels, see references [r330] and [r331]. See also references [r331–r333]. There are also concrete methods to protect against kleptographic attacks in particular. The

nature of these solutions varies greatly. For example, some are protocols that involve a third-party verifier that verifies that no kleptographic attacks are taking place [r334]. Some are stand-alone heuristic algorithms [r335, r336], while other solutions involve distributing trust by using multiple, independently designed smartcards. Many of these approaches are covered in reference [r173].

While there are efforts on behalf of the research community to mitigate the threats of subliminal channels and kleptography, not much attention has been paid to this issue.

Kleptography Kleptography is the study of stealing information securely and subliminally [r089, r319, r337, r338]. In a kleptographic attack, there is an explicit distinction between confidentiality of the messages (e.g., the private keys of the users) and awareness that the attack is taking place. A secure kleptographic attack is undetectable as long as the cryptosystem is a black box. Also, if the black-box is opened, it may be evident that a kleptographic attack is underway, but confidentiality is preserved. Kleptography is a natural extension of the theory of subliminal channels.

Kleptographic attacks often utilize subliminal channels to transmit things such as: private signing keys, private decryption keys, symmetric keys, and so on, outside of a cryptosystem (e.g., smartcard). The requirement that kleptographic attacks have (that exceeds the requirements of a subliminal channel) is robustness against reverse engineering. A kleptographic attack is only secure if the confidentiality of the subliminal messages holds even after the black-box is opened and inspected. This must hold for all previously transmitted messages as well as future subliminal messages that may be sent. Asymmetric cryptography is used to achieve this type of confidentiality. It is this added robustness in confidentiality that makes kleptographic attacks more attractive to carry out in practice.

An example will go a long way to explain what a kleptographic attack is. A kleptographic attack against a software based Rivest–Shamir–Adleman (RSA) cryptosystem like Pretty Good Privacy (PGP) has been demonstrated [r318, r173]. In this attack, RSA keys are not generated normally. However, the RSA public modulus n is still the product of two primes p and q. The modulus n is generated such that its upper order bits effectively constitute the asymmetric encryption of a value that allows n to be efficiently factored. Computing such composites n is possible using a well known subliminal channel in the products of two primes. The asymmetric encryption is computed using the public key of the attacker that is embedded in the RSA key generation algorithm. As a result, a database of public keys [i.e., the Certification Authority (CA)] is a database of public keys and ciphertexts of the corresponding private keys from the perspective of the attacker.

The novelty in this kleptographic attack is the following. It can be deployed in software in a single binary program (that may be code-signed) such that everyone obtains the same copy. The key pairs that the program outputs do not reveal that a kleptographic attack is occurring (they appear to be normal). If a reverse-engineer examines the key generation code then he or she will learn that a kleptographic attack is underway. However the reverse-engineer will still be out of luck in actually learning the private key of anyone who uses the binary.

Kleptography Cures   Algorithms and protocols already exist that could greatly reduce the threats of certain subliminal channels and kleptographic attacks [r089]. It is not safe to say that these have achieved "cure-all" status, but they are certainly solid measures that could be taken. They have yet to be adopted in industry standards, let alone de facto industry standards. By their very nature kleptographic attacks are designed not to be found. Combine this with the habit that organizations have of covering up attacks to avoid embar-

rassment, and one has a problem that could be lurking behind the scenes for a very long time.

Klez Worm   An e-mail-borne virus that exploited a flaw in Microsoft's Internet Explorer browser and targeted both Outlook and Outlook Express users. Because Klez required users to click on an embedded e-mail attachment, the damage was limited. When later variants appeared with spoofed sender addresses, it provided the first sign that virus writers would change tactics to avoid detection. The spoofing of e-mail addresses would later become a standard trick to attack nontechnical e-mail (and Windows) users [r090].

KMID   See Key Material Identifier

KMP   See Key Management Protocol

Knapsacks   Given a small set of integers, the knapsack problem consists of determining a subset of these integers such that their sum is equal to a given integer. For example, given $(2, 3, 5, 7)$ and 10, we can find the solution $2 + 3 + 5 = 10$, and thus solved the knapsack problem, by brute-force search. The general knapsack problem is provably Nondeterministic Polynomial (NP)-hard, and thus appears superior to factorization and discrete logarithm used in public-key cryptosystems. Unfortunately, all cryptosystems that have used this underlying idea have been broken, because the used instances of the problem have not been really NP-hard [r036].

Known Viruses   Viruses that have been identified along with their associated exploits methods.

Known-Plaintext Attack   A cryptanalysis technique in which the analyst tries to determine the key from knowledge of some plaintext–ciphertext pairs. The analyst may also have other clues, such as knowing the cryptographic algorithm.

Korea Information Security Agency   Korean agency that deals with computer/networking security issues.

L

LLLLLLLLLLLLLLLLLLLLLLLL

L1 See Layer 1

L2 See Layer 2

L3 See Layer 3

L2F See Layer 2 Forwarding Protocol

L2PE See Layer 2 Provider Edge

L2TP See Layer 2 Tunneling Protocol

L2VPN See Layer 2 Virtual Private Network

Layer 3 Virtual Private Network (L3VPN) VPN based on a tunneling mechanism at Layer 3. VPNs generally include encryption such as IPsec, hence they are more secure than L2 VPNs.

Layer 3 Virtual Private Network (L3VPN) Customer Edge (CE) A device or set of devices on the customer premises that attaches to a provider provisioned L3VPN; for example, a RFC 2547bis implementation.

Layer 3 Virtual Private Network (L3VPN)

Provider Edge (PE) A device or set of devices at the edge of the provider network interfacing the customer network, with the functionality needed for an L3VPN [r082].

L3VPN See Layer 3 Virtual Private Network

Label (MPLS context) A short fixed length physically contiguous identifier that is used to identify a Forwarding Equivalence Class (FEC), usually of local significance [r053–r055].

Label Merging (MPLS context) The replacement of multiple incoming labels for a particular Forwarding Equivalence Class (FEC) with a single outgoing label [r053–r055].

Label Stack (MPLS context) An ordered set of labels [r053–r055].

Label Swap (MPLS context) The basic forwarding operation consisting of looking up an incom-

Minoli–Cordovana's Authoritative Computer and Network Security Dictionary. By Daniel Minoli and James Cordovana
Copyright © 2006 John Wiley & Sons, Inc.

ing label to determine the outgoing label, encapsulation, port, and other data handling information [r053–r055].

Label Swapping   (MPLS context) A forwarding paradigm allowing streamlined forwarding of data by using labels to identify classes of data packets that are treated indistinguishably when forwarding [r053–r055].

Label Switch Router (LSR)   Multiprotocol Label Switching (MPLS) integrates the label swapping forwarding paradigm with network layer routing. In an MPLS environment, when a stream of data traverses a common path, a Label Switched Path (LSP) can be established using MPLS signaling protocols. At the ingress LSR, each packet is assigned a label and is transmitted downstream. At each LSR along the LSP, the label is used to forward the packet to the next hop. To deliver reliable service, MPLS requires a set of procedures to provide protection of the traffic carried on different paths. This requires that the LSRs support fault detection, fault notification, and fault recovery mechanisms, and that MPLS signaling support the configuration of recovery [r053–r055].

Label Switched Hop   (MPLS context) The hop between two Multiprotocol Label Switching (MPLS) nodes, on which forwarding is done using labels [r053–r055].

Label Switched Path   (MPLS context) The path through one or more Label Switch Routers (LSRs) at one level of the hierarchy followed by packets in a particular Forwarding Equivalence Class (FEC) [r053–r055].

Label Switching Router   (MPLS context) A Multiprotocol Label Switching (MPLS) node that is capable of forwarding native Layer 3 (L3) packets [r053–r055].

Label-Switched Path (LSP)   An end-to-end path in a Multiprotocol Label Switching (MPLS) network defined via the label mechanism.

Laboratory Attack   Using sophisticated signal recovery equipment in a laboratory environment to recover stored information from data storage media [r057].

LAC   See Location Area Code

Lacuna (Lacunae)   Gaps, shortcomings, holes, incompletes.

LAI   See Location Area Identity

LAN   See Local Area Network

Language of Temporal Ordering Specification (LOTOS)   A language (ISO 8807-1990) for formal specification of computer network protocols; describes the order in which events occur [r013].

LAP-D   See Link Access Protocol for the ISDN "D" channel

Laser Diode (LD)   (optical transmission term) Semiconductor diode lasers are the standard light sources in fiber-optic systems.

Latency   (security context) The period during which a time bomb, logic bomb, virus, or worm refrains from overt activity or damage (delivery of the payload). Long latency coupled with vigorous reproduction can result in severe consequences for infected or otherwise compromised systems [r057].

Lattice Model   A security model for flow control in a system, based on the lattice that is formed by the finite security levels in a system and their partial ordering [r343], such as those used in military organizations. A lattice is a finite set together with a partial ordering on its elements such that for every pair of elements there is a least upper bound and a greatest lower bound. For example, a lattice is formed by a finite set S of security levels—that is, a set S of all ordered pairs (x, c), where x is one of a finite set X of hierarchically ordered classification levels $(X_1, ..., X_m)$, and c is a (possibly empty) subset of a finite set C of non-hierarchical categories $(C_1, ..., C_n)$ together with the "dominate" relation [r013].

Lattice, Shortest Vector   Defines a vector basis $w_i = <w_1, ..., w_n>$ for $i = 1, ..., m$, and the lattice that is generated by the basis. That is, elements of the lattice are of the form $t_1 w_1 + t_2 w_2 + ... + t_m w_m$, where t_i are integers. The problem of finding the shortest vector in a lattice (using the usual Euclidean distance) is a Nondeterministic Polynomial (NP)-hard problem (for lattices of sufficiently large dimension). However, the LLL algorithm by Lenstra, Lenstra, and Lovasz computes an approximate solution in polynomial time. The effectiveness of the LLL algorithm comes from the fact that in many cases approximate solutions are good enough, and that surprisingly often the LLL algorithm actually gives the shortest vector. This algorithm has been often used to break cryptosystems based on lattice problems or knapsacks [r036].

Launder   To run illegally acquired money through a legitimate business in order to make it more difficult to track.

Law Enforcement Access Field (LEAF)   A data item that is automatically embedded in data encrypted by devices that implement the Escrowed Encryption Standard.

LAWN   See Local Area Wireless Network

Layer 1 (L1)   (aka physical layer) The protocol layer for defining the physical, electrical, and functional properties of a signaling data link as well as of the equipment for accessing the network [r014].

Layer 2 (L2)   (aka datalink layer) The protocol layer for handling message transfer (forwarding) functions for a single communications link. Forwarding, when done by the swapping of short fixed length labels, occurs at layer 2 regardless of whether the label being examined is an Asynchronous Transfer Mode (ATM) Virtual Path Identifier (VPI)/Virtual Channel Identifier (VCI), a frame relay Data Link Connection Identifier (DLCI), or a Multiprotocol Label Switching (MPLS) label.

Layer 2 (L2) Virtual Private Network (L2VPN) (aka Layer 2 VPN) VPN based on a Layer 2 label—for example, a Virtual Local Area Network (VLAN) label, an Asynchronous Transfer Mode (ATM) label [i.e., Virtual Path Identifier (VPI)/ Virtual Channel Identifier (VCI)], a frame relay label [i.e., Data Link Connection Identifier (DLCI)], or a Multiprotocol Label Switching (MPLS) label. Usually does not entail (the automatic inclusion of) encryption, hence by itself it is not a secure service. (L3 VPNs generally include encryption such as IPSec, hence they are more secure that L2 VPNs.)

Layer 2 Forwarding Protocol (L2F)   An Internet protocol (originally developed by Cisco Corporation) that uses tunneling of Point-to-Point Protocol (PPP) over IP to create a virtual extension of a dial-up link across a network, initiated by the dial-up server and transparent to the dial-up user [r013].

Layer 2 Provider Edge (L2PE)   The joint name of the devices in the provider network that implement L2 functions needed for a Virtual Private LAN Service (VPLS) or a Virtual Private Wire Service (VPWS).

Layer 2 Tunneling Protocol (L2TP)   An Internet client-server protocol that combines aspects of Point-to-Point Tunneling Protocol (PPTP) and Layer 2 Forwarding Protocol (L2F) and supports tunneling of Point-to-Point Protocol (PPP) over an IP network or over frame relay or other switched network. PPP can in turn encapsulate any Open Systems Interconnection Reference Model (OSIRM) Layer 3 protocol. Thus, L2TP does not specify security services; rather, it depends on protocols layered above and below it to provide any needed security [r013].

Layer 2 Virtual Private Network (L2VPN) (aka L2 VPN) Three types of L2VPNs are currently defined [r082]: Virtual Private Wire Service (VPWS); Virtual Private LAN Service (VPLS); and IP-only LAN-like Service (IPLS).

Layer 3 (L3)   (aka network layer) The protocol layer handling the routing functions within a network. The protocol layer at which IP and its associated routing protocols operate.

Layer 3 Address   Addresses in Layer 3 packets used to identify destinations. These addresses can be unique within a private enterprise, or can be globally unique when assigned by official agencies. The allocation of Internet Protocol version 4 (IPv4) address space to various registries is listed here. Originally, all the IPv4 address spaces was managed directly by the IANA (Internet Assigned Numbers Authority). Later parts of the address space were allocated to various other registries to manage for particular purposes or regional areas of the world.

Layer 3 Security Mechanisms Encryption mechanisms such as IPsec or Multilayer IP-security (ML-IPsec).

Layer 3 Virtual Private Network (L3VPN) (aka L3 VPN) A VPN that interconnects sets of hosts and routers based on Layer 3 addresses (see reference [r081]).

Layer Two Tunneling Protocol (L2TP) A protocol that provides a method for tunneling Point-to-Point Protocol (PPP) packets.

LC See Linear Cryptanalysis

LCAS See Link Capacity Adjustment Scheme

LD See Laser Diode

LDAP See Lightweight Directory Access Protocol

LDAPS See LDAP over SSL

LEAF See Law Enforcement Access Field

LEAP See Lightweight EAP

Leapfrog Attack Use of userid and password information obtained illicitly from one host to compromise another host. An example of this is the act of TELNETing through one or more hosts in order to preclude a trace (a standard cracker procedure) [r057].

Least Common Mechanism (aka Principle of Least Common Mechanism) One of Saltzer and Schroeder's Design Principles. Mechanisms used to access resources should not be shared (shared resources can serve as "unintended" information channels; may subvert security policy, e.g., confidentiality) [r139a].

Least Privilege (aka Principle of Least Privilege) One of Saltzer and Schroeder's Design Principles [r139a]. The principle that a security architecture should be designed so that each system entity is granted the minimum system resources and authorizations that the entity needs to do its work. This principle tends to limit damage that can be caused by an accident, error, or unauthorized act. Not only should the minimum access necessary to perform an operation be granted but access should be granted only for the minimum amount of time necessary.

LEDs See Light-Emitting Diodes

Legacy System Older software and hardware systems still in use and generally proprietary [r057].

Legal Meeting the requirements under law.

Legal Intercept Intercepts of electronic communications as permitted by Communications Assistance for Law Enforcement Act of 1994 (CALEA), Pub. L. No. 103-414, 108 Stat. 4279 and other applicable legislation.

Lempel–Ziv–Stac (LZS) Compression Method A general-purpose lossless compression algorithm described in RFC 2246 for use with a wide variety of data types. Its encoding method is very efficient, providing compression for strings as short as two octets in length. The LZS algorithm uses a sliding window of 2048 bytes. During compression, redundant sequences of data are replaced with tokens that represent those sequences. During decompression, the original sequences are substituted for the tokens in such a way that the original data is exactly recovered. LZS differs from lossy compression algorithms, such as those often used for video compression, that do not exactly reproduce the original data [r344]. The LZS compression method, encoding format, and application examples are described in RFC 1967, RFC 1974, and RFC 2395.

Letter Bomb E-mail with malicious logic sent in an attempt to do harm to the target computing system.

Liability (financial term) A financial obligation, debt, claim, or potential loss.

Liberty Alliance A consortium of companies that develops specifications for federated identity management. It originally envisioned creating a single comprehensive federated identity specification. In 2003, however, it released a new blueprint that described three separate specifications that can be used together or independently [r204]:

- Identity Federation Framework (ID-FF) allows single sign-on (SSO) and account linking between partners with established trust relationships.
- Identity Web Services Framework (ID-WSF) allows groups of trusted partners to link to other groups and gives users control over how their information is shared.

- Identity Services Interface Specifications (ID-SIS) will build a set of interoperable services on top of the ID-WSF.

Libraries   (Storage context) A large-scale tape device with robotics that can house multiple tape drives and a significant amount of tape cartridges [r029].

Lifetime In Preferred State   Time during a unicast address, obtained by means of stateless autoconfiguration mechanism, stays in the preferred state. This time is specified by the preferred lifetime field in routers advertisement messages prefix information option [r008].

Light-Emitting Diodes (LEDs)   (optical transmission term) A semiconductor diode that emits chromatically pure but incoherent light (spontaneous emission). Light is emitted at the junction between *p*- and *n*-doped materials. Device (manufactured with two semiconductors) such that by running current in one direction across the semiconductor the LED emits light of a particular frequency (hence a particular color). These semiconductors are durable and do not require much power. By packing red, blue, and green LEDs next to each other on a sheet ("substrate"), one can create a full color display.

Lightweight Directory Access Protocol (LDAP)   A client-server protocol that supports basic use of the X.500 Directory (or other directory servers) without incurring the resource requirements of the full Directory Access Protocol (DAP) [r013, r345].

Lightweight Directory Access Protocol (LDAP) over Secure Sockets Layer (SSL) (LDAPS)   LDAP traffic between a client system and a directory that is secured via Secure Sockets Layer (SSL)/Transport Layer Security (TLS) encryption. (By default, LDAP traffic is transmitted unsecured.)

Lightweight EAP (LEAP)   Authentication protocol of the Extensible Authentication Protocol (EAP) family that is used in Wireless Local Area Networks (WLAN) [it is typically utilized with Remote Authentication Dial-In User Service (RADIUS)]. Protected Extensible Authentication Protocol (PEAP) and/or WPA-2 (Wi-Fi Protected Access 2 described in IEEE 802.11i) are phasing out LEAP.

Linear Cryptanalysis (LC)   A cryptanalysis approach invented by Mitsuru Matsui that uses a plaintext-based attack methodology. Input–output correlation is exploited. LC has successfully applied on the Data Encryption Standard (DES). LC is a known-plaintext attack in which a large amount of plaintext–ciphertext pairs are used to determine the value of key bits. LC can also be applied in a ciphertext-only context. A condition for applying linear cryptanalysis to a block cipher is to find "effective" linear expressions.

Linear Tape Open (LTO)   A family of open magnetic tape standards developed by HP, IBM, and Seagate that are licensed to third-party vendors [r029].

Link   (World Wide Web context) a hyperlink.

(Subnetwork context) A point-to-point communication channel connecting two subnetwork relays (especially a channel between two switches or routers) that is implemented at Open Systems Interconnection Reference Model (OSIRM) layer 2. The relay devices assume that links are logically passive. If a device at one end of a link sends a sequence of bits, the sequence simply arrives at the other end after a finite time, although some bits may have been changed either accidentally (errors) or by active intervention (intrusion) [r013].

(IPv6 context) A communication facility or medium over which nodes can communicate at the link layer—that is, the layer immediately below IPv6. Examples are Ethernets (simple or bridged); Point-to-Point Protocol (PPP) links; X.25, Frame Relay, or Asynchronous Transfer Mode (ATM) networks; and Internet (or higher) layer "tunnels," such as tunnels over IPv4 or IPv6 itself.

Link Access Protocol for the Integrated Services Digital Network (ISDN) "D" (LAP-D)   (GSM context) The Base Station Controller (BSC) and the Base Transceiver Station (BTS) communicate via the Link Access Protocol (LAP) for the ISDN "D" channel, or LAP-D. This protocol is also used in ISDN networks between the end user and the network. A slightly modified version of the same protocol exists between the BTS and the mobile station; because of the modifications required due to the characteristics of the air interface, the protocol version is called LAP-Dm [r011].

Link Aggregation Standard, Layer 2   Protocol used in Virtual Local Area Network (VLAN) systems. It is defined in IEEE 802.3ad Link Aggregation.

Link-by-Link Encipherment   The individual application of encipherment to data on each link of a communications system. See also end-to-end encipherment. (*Note:* The implication of link-by-link encipherment is that data will be in cleartext form in relay entities) [r068a].

Link Capacity Adjustment Scheme (LCAS)   A recently introduced International Telecommunication Union (ITU) protocol that enhances the flexibility of Synchronous Optical Network/Synchronous Digital Hierarchy (SONET/SDH) virtual concatenation transport. It enables the addition and removal of virtual link containers in response to an identified change in service bandwidth requirement, or in response to a fault condition in an existing container.

Link Down   (OSPF context) The time needed for an Open Shortest-Path First (OSPF) implementation to recognize a link down based on Layer 2-provided information, to propagate any information as needed to its remaining adjacencies, and to perform other actions necessary to converge [r026].

Link Encryption   Stepwise protection of data that flows between two points in a network, provided by encrypting data separately on each network link—that is, by encrypting data when it leaves a host or subnetwork relay and decrypting when it arrives at the next host or relay. Each link may use a different key or even a different algorithm [r013, r346].

Link Maximum Transmission Unit (MTU)   The number of bytes in the greatest IPv6 packet that can be sent through the link (IPv6 context) or network. Since the frame maximum size includes link layer headers, the link MTU does not equate with the link frame maximum size; rather, the link MTU matches the link layer technology payload maximum size [r008].

Link or Neighbor Device Up   (OSPF context) The time needed for an Open Shortest-Path First (OSPF) implementation to recognize a new link coming up on the device, to build any necessary adjacencies, to synchronize its database, and to perform all other actions necessary to converge [r026].

Link State   Routing protocol technology that exchanges route information. Routing information consists of prefixes of networks connected to a router and its associated cost. Link state information is advertised in boot process, just as when changes are detected in the network topology [r008].

Linux Security Modules (LSM)   A framework for implementing flexible access control in the Linux kernel.

Liskov, Rivest, Wagner (LRW) Cipher   An instantiation of the class of tweakable block ciphers being proposed for use for encryption of storage in IEEE P1619 (it is one of several ciphers being considered) [r279]. The LRW transform (cipher) acts on "narrow" blocks of 16 bytes, under the control of two secret keys (the "keyset"); the logical position of the data is encrypted within the scope of the keys (the range of data locations being encrypted). It is implemented as a mode of operation for the Advanced Encryption Standard (AES) block cipher (with blocks comprised of 16 bytes). When used to encrypt storage data, the tweak value is computed from the logical position of the current narrow block within the scope of the current key. This cipher addresses threats such as copy-and-paste attacks and dictionary attacks, while allowing parallelization of cipher implementations.

LISTSERV   Commercial mailing list. Although LISTSERV refers to a specific mailing list server, the term is occasionally used to refer to any mailing list server.

LLC See Logical Link Control

Load Balancer An appliance or server that is used (e.g., in an enterprise setting) to direct incoming service requests to a number of different servers all running the same application and all having access to the same data (e.g., Web servers) to load-share the tasks among various processors.

Local Address (IPv6 context) An IPv6 unicast address that is not reachable in IPv6 Internet. Local addresses include "link-local" and "site-local" addresses [r008].

Local Area Network (LAN) A networking system spanning a few hundred feet and offering high-speed connections (10 Mbps to 10 Gbps). A communications system that connects devices in a building or group of buildings or data center [r057].

Local Area Network (LAN) Repeater A device as specified in Clauses 9 and 27 of IEEE 802.3 that is used to extend the length, topology, or interconnectivity of the physical medium beyond that imposed by a single segment, up to the maximum allowable end-to-end transmission line length. Repeaters perform the basic actions of restoring signal amplitude, waveform, and timing applied to the normal data and collision signals. For wired star topologies, repeaters provide a data distribution function. In 100BASE-T, a device that allows the inter-connection of 100BASE-T Physical Layer (PHY) network segments using similar or dissimilar PHY implementations (e.g., 100BASE-X to 100BASE-X, 100BASE-X to 100BASE-T4, etc.). Repeaters are only for use in half duplex mode networks.

Local Area Network Segment Link portion that consists of only a single medium limited by bridges or Layer 2 switches [r008].

Local Area Wireless Network (LAWN) Uncommonly used term [better known as Wireless LAN (WLAN)]: a Local Area Network (LAN) that uses radio links rather than cables to support communication between nodes.

Local Interface Internal interface that allows a node to send packets to itself [r008].

Local Loop Address (IPv6 context) IPv6::1 address, assigned to local interface [r008].

Local Repair Techniques used to repair Label Switched Path (LSP) tunnels quickly when a node or link along the LSP's path fails [r083].

Local Site Address (IPv6 context) Local address identified by the 1111 1110 11 (FEC0::/10) prefix. The scope of these addresses is local sites (of an organization), without the necessity of a global prefix. Local site addresses are not accessible from other sites and routers should not direct local site traffic out of such site [r008].

Location Area Code (LAC) (GSM context) Part of the Cell Global Identity (CGI); it identifies a certain Location Area [r011].

Location Area Identity (LAI) (GSM context) A number which is globally unique and which identifies a Location Area [r011].

Location Service (SIP context) A location service is used by a Session Initiation Protocol (SIP) redirect or proxy server to obtain information about a callee's possible location(s). It contains a list of bindings of address-of-record keys to zero or more contact addresses. The bindings can be created and removed in many ways; this specification defines a REGISTER method that updates the bindings [r025].

Log Files Records of system use and activity, with the intent of auditing for security-relevant activities.

Logging Components Security services for security logging. Examples include syslogs and application logs.

Logic Bomb (aka Fork Bomb) Malicious logic that activates when specified conditions are met. Usually intended to cause denial of service or otherwise damage system resources [r013].

Logical Access Controls The system-based mechanisms used to specify who or what is to have access to a specific system resource and the type of access that is permitted. Examples are the access control lists and access control software that a system contains [r067].

Logical Layered Architecture   An architectural concept that organizes the management functions into a grouping of management layers and describes the relationship between the layers [r068a].

Logical Link Control (LLC)   Local Area Network (LAN) protocol that provides a reliable connection between two adjacent endpoints on the LAN. This protocol sits above the Media Access Control (MAC) protocol.

Logical Provider Edge (PE) (LPE)   Dated term used to describe a set of devices used in a provider network to implement a Virtual Private LAN Service (VPLS). In a LPE, VPLS functions are distributed across small devices (PE-Edges/U-PE) and devices attached to a network core (PE-Core/N-PE). In an LPE solution, the PE-edge and PE-core can be interconnected by a switched Ethernet transport network or uplinks. The LPE will appear to the core network as a single PE. In this document, the devices that constitutes, the LPE are called N-PE and U-PE [r082].

Login   (aka logon) The act of a system entity gaining access to a session in which the entity can use system resources. This is usually accomplished by providing a user name and password to an access control system that authenticates the user.

Login/Logon Weaknesses   In private and public computer networks (including the Internet), authentication is commonly done through the use of login passwords. Knowledge of the password is assumed to guarantee that the user is authentic. Each user registers initially (or is registered by someone else), using an assigned or self-declared password. On each subsequent use, the user must know and use the previously declared password. The weakness in this system for transactions that are significant (such as the exchange of money) is that passwords can often be stolen, accidentally revealed, or forgotten. More stringent (often multifactor) authentication processes (e.g., digital certificates) are desired [r347].

Logon   See Login

Long Reach (LR) Wavelength   (optical transmission term) Wavelength group that will pass transparently over a reconfigurable Optical Add-Drop Multiplexers (OADM) to a distant adaptation function [r349].

Loop   (SIP context) A request that arrives at a proxy, is forwarded, and later arrives back at the same proxy. When it arrives the second time, its Request Uniform Resource Identifier (URI) is identical to the first time, and other header fields that affect proxy operation are unchanged, so that the proxy would make the same processing decision on the request it made the first time. Looped requests are errors, and the procedures for detecting them and handling them are described by the protocol [r025].

Loop Detection   (IP/MPLS context) A method of dealing with loops in which loops are allowed to be set up, and data may be transmitted over the loop, but the loop is later detected [r053–r055].

Loop Prevention   (IP/MPLS context) A method of dealing with loops; the goal is to ascertain that the data is never transmitted over a loop [r053–r055].

Loose Routing   (SIP context) A proxy is said to be loose routing if it follows the procedures defined in this specification for processing of the Route header field. These procedures separate the destination of the request [present in the Request-Uniform Resource Identifier (URI)] from the set of proxies that need to be visited along the way (present in the Route header field). A proxy compliant to these mechanisms is also known as a loose router [r025].

Lossless Compression   A compression method where the original data can be recovered exactly. Generally the compression ratio is 10:1. A compression method such as Lempel–Ziv–Stac (LZS).

Lossy Compression   A compression method where the original data cannot be recovered exactly. Generally the compression ratio is 200:1 to 100:1. These methods are used, for example, in video compression [e.g., Moving Pictures Expert Group (MPEG)-2, MPEG-4, H.263].

LOTOS   See Language of Temporal Ordering Specification

LOVC   See Lower Order Virtual Container

Low-Level Format   A process that destroys all data on a disk. The FORMAT command in Disk Operating System (DOS) or Windows does not perform a low-level format [r057].

LPE   See Logical PE

LSP   See Label Switched Path

LSR   See Label Switch Router

LSM   See Linux Security Modules

LTO   See Linear Tape Open

M Reference Points A reference point located outside the Telecommunications Management Network (TMN) between a Q adapter function (QAF) block and managed entities that do not conform to TMN Recommendations [r068a].

MAC See Media Access Control, or Message Authentication Code, or Mandatory Access Control

Machine (Host) (IPv6 context) A node that cannot send datagrams not created by itself. A machine that is both the source and destination of IPv6 traffic, and will discard traffic that is not specifically addressed to it [r008].

Mail Bomb E-mail sent to urge others to send massive amounts of e-mail to a single system or person, specifically for Denial of Service (DoS) purposes. Mailbombing is regarded as an offense.

Mail Servers A firm's or Internet Service Provider (ISP) server that either receives or forwards mail for a defined subscriber user community.

Mail Transport Agent (MTA) The program handling actual delivery of mail. For example, on Unix systems this is usually Sendmail, S-mail, or Z-mailer.

Mail User Agent (MUA) The program the user interacts with to read and write e-mail. For example, in Unix systems MUA's include Elm, Pine, mail, mailx, mush, and so on.

Malicious Code See Malicious Logic

Malicious Logic Hardware, software, or firmware that is intentionally included or inserted in a system for a harmful/security-affecting purpose.

In context of masquerade, any hardware, firmware, or software (e.g., Trojan horse) that ap-

Minoli–Cordovana's Authoritative Computer and Network Security Dictionary. By Daniel Minoli and James Cordovana
Copyright © 2006 John Wiley & Sons, Inc.

pears to perform a useful or desirable function, but actually gains unauthorized access to system resources or tricks a user into executing other malicious logic [r013].

In context of corruption, any hardware, firmware, or software (e.g., a computer virus) intentionally introduced into a system to modify system functions or data.

In context of incapacitation, any hardware, firmware, or software (e.g., logic bomb) intentionally introduced into a system to destroy system functions or resources [r013].

In context of misuse, any hardware, software, or firmware intentionally introduced into a system to perform or control execution of an unauthorized function or service [r013].

Malignant   Negative, virulent, subject to malfeasance, harmful, malicious.

Malleable Encryption   An encryption algorithm that allows transformations on the ciphertext to produce changes in the plaintext: given a plaintext P and the corresponding ciphertext $C = E(P)$, it is possible to generate $C^{\sim} = f(C)$ so that the decryption of $C^{\sim}$ is a function $P^{\sim} = f'(P)$ of the original plaintext P, with arbitrary but known functions f and f'. Stream ciphers are examples of malleable encryption algorithms. Malleability is an undesirable property because it allows an attacker to modify the contents of a message.

Malpractice   Injurious conduct by an individual acting in an official or professional capacity, such as a doctor.

Malware   (aka scumware) Short for malicious software, this term describes a variety of malicious programs that may be installed on a computer (client or server) with or without the users' knowledge. This may include Trojan Horses, viruses, worms, logic bombs, spyware, exploits, and time bombs [r057, r062].

Malware Attacks   Host/network attacks based on malware mechanisms of entry and/or execution.

Managed Objects   Network management-level objects accessed via a virtual information store, termed the Management Information Base (MIB). MIB objects are generally accessed through the Simple Network Management Protocol (SNMP). Objects in the MIB are defined using the mechanisms defined in the Structure of Management Information (SMI). SMIv2 is described in STD 58, RFC 2578, STD 58, RFC 2579, STD 58, RFC 2580 [r097].

Managed Resource   The abstraction of those aspects of a telecommunication resource (logical or physical) required for telecommunications management [r068a].

Managed Security Services (MSS)   Outsourced services that offload a firm's burden of managing and monitoring security devices and events, ensuring rapid response to real threats. MSSs can provide round-the-clock monitoring and management of firewalls, intrusion detection systems, and other network security devices on a global basis by an external provider.

Managed Security Services Provider (MSSP)   A service provider (an outsourcing provider) that handles network security services (such as, but not limited to, intrusion detection and prevention, spam blocking, and firewall management) on behalf of its clients.

Management Application Function   A function that represents (part of) the functionality of one or more management services.

Management Domain   A set of managed resources subject to a common management policy [r068a].

Management Function   The smallest part of a management service as perceived by the user of the service.

Management Function Set   In International Telecommunications Union (ITU) recommendation M.3010 the Telecommunications Management Network (TMN) management function set is a grouping of TMN management functions that contextually belong together; that is, they are related to a specific management capability (e.g., alarm reporting functions, traffic management control). The TMN management function set is the smallest reusable item of functional specification. The TMN management function set must be considered as a whole. It is similar to the requirements part of the Open Systems Interconnect (OSI) system management function (SMF) [r068a].

Management Information Base (MIB) Module Modules (hardware or software) that have the purpose of remotely controlling synthetic sources (or "active" probes) and sinks in order to enhance remote performance monitoring capabilities within IP networks and services. Managed objects are accessed via a virtual information store, termed the Management Information Base (MIB). MIB objects are generally accessed through the Simple Network Management Protocol (SNMP). Objects in the MIB are defined using the mechanisms defined in the Structure of Management Information (SMI) [r357].

Management Information Bases (MIBs) A (set) of specifications for the data collection (database) of network-relevant information used to support many of the Fault, Configuration Accounting, Performance, and Security (FCAPS) management functions. Examples of basic MIBs include: RFC 1213 MIB-2, RFC 2863 Interface MIB, RFC 2665 Ether-Like MIB, RFC 1493 Bridge MIB, RFC 2674 Extended Bridge MIB, RFC 2819 Remote Monitoring (RMON) MIB, RFC2737 Entity MIB, and so on.

Management Layer An architectural concept that reflects particular aspects of management and implies a clustering of management information supporting that aspect [r068a].

Management Service A management service is an offering fulfilling specific telecommunications management needs [r068a].

Mandatory Access Control (MAC) An access control service that enforces a security policy based on comparing security labels (which indicate how sensitive or critical system resources are) with security clearances (which indicate system entities are eligible to access certain resources). This kind of access control is called "mandatory" because an entity that has clearance to access a resource may not, just by its own volition, enable another entity to access that resource [r013].

Mandatory Security Requirements Based on

Public Law OMB Circular A-130 requires a management official to authorize in writing the use of each general support system or major application based on the implementation of its security plan before beginning or significantly changing processing in the system. Use of the system needs to be re-authorized at least every three years. National Institute of Standards and Technology (NIST) Federal Information Processing Standard (FIPS) 102, "Certification and Accreditation" contains standards on certifying and accrediting sensitive unclassified systems. FIPS 102 is being revised as a NIST Special Publication. Certification activities consist primarily of evaluations that result in the development of a recommendation to the authorizing official to accredit the system. Depending on the level of certification, one or several evaluations should be performed [r067].

Man-in-the-Middle (aka Man-in-the-Middle Attack) A form of active wiretapping attack in which the attacker intercepts and selectively modifies communicated data in order to masquerade as one or more of the entities involved in a communication association. For example, suppose Alice and Bob try to establish a session key by using the Diffie–Hellman algorithm without data origin authentication service. A "man in the middle" could block direct communication between Alice and Bob and then masquerade as Alice sending data to Bob, masquerade as Bob sending data to Alice, establish separate session keys with each of them, and function as a clandestine proxy server between them in order to capture or modify sensitive information that Alice and Bob think they are sending only to each other [r013].

Manipulation Detection A mechanism which is used to detect whether a data unit has been modified (either accidentally or intentionally) [r068a].

Mantraps Secure portals that require identification in order for the gateway to open toward the restricted area.

MAP See Mobile Application Part

Mapping IPv4 Address (IPv6 context) A 0:0:0:0:0:FFFF:w.x.y.z or ::FFFF:w.x.y.z address, where w.x.y.z is an IPv4 address. Mapped IPv4 addresses are used to represent an IPv4-only node in the presence of an IPv6 node [r008].

Masquerade   An action of an unauthorized entity that entails posing as an authorized user. Such action by the unauthorized entity seeks to gain access to a system ("spoof") or to perform a malicious act ("malicious logic"). In context of masquerade, "malicious logic" is any hardware, firmware, or software (e.g., Trojan horse) that appears to perform a useful or desirable function, but actually gains unauthorized access to system resources or tricks a user into executing other malicious logic.

Masquerade Attack   (aka spoofing) A type of attack in which one system entity illegitimately poses as (assumes the identity of) another entity [r013].

Master Origin Server   An origin server on which the definitive version of a resource resides.

Master Program   In distributed denial-of-service attacks, a program that communicates with zombie programs on compromised systems. The master program usually transmits encrypted instructions to zombies with details of which targeted system to swamp with transmissions at exactly what time [r057].

Master Secret   Secure secret data used for generating encryption keys, Message Authentication Code (MAC) secrets, and Initialization Vectors (IVs) [r039].

Master Session Key (MSK)   Key material that is derived between the Extensible Authentication Protocol (EAP) peer and server and exported by the EAP method. The MSK is at least 64 octets in length. In existing implementations, an Authentication, Authorization, and Accounting (AAA) server acting as an EAP server transports the MSK to the authenticator [r073].

MAU   See Medium Attachment Unit

Maximum Transfer Unit (MTU)   The longest protocol data unit (PDU) that can be sent (unfragmented) in a computer network. MTUs are defined at the link layer (frame maximum size) and at the network or Internet layer (maximum IPv4/IPv6 packet size) [r008].

Maximum-Level Aggregation Identifier   [aka Top-Level Aggregation Identifier (TLA ID)]. Thirteen bits field inside the global unicast address reserved for large organizations or Internet Service Providers (ISPs) by the Internet Assigned Numbers Authority (IANA)/Internet Corporation for Assigned Names and Numbers (ICANN); hence it identifies the addresses range that they have delegated [r008].

MCA   See Merchant Certification Authority

MCC   See Mobile Country Code

MDA   See Model Driven Architecture

MDN   See Message Disposition Notification

Mean Time to Failure (MTTF)   The expected time before a failure:

$$\mathrm{MTTF} = \int_0^\infty R(t)\, dt,$$

$R(t)$ = the reliability, the chance that the system will fail between $[t_0, t]$.

Mean Time to Repair (MTTR)   The average time to repair a system.

Media   Physical objects that store data, such as paper, hard disk drives, tapes, and compact disks (CDs) [r200].

Media Access Control (MAC)   A sublayer of Open Systems Interconnection (OSI) Reference Model (OSIRM) link layer defined by the Institute of Electrical and Electronic Engineers (IEEE). Layer 2 of the protocol model for local Area Networks (LANs) mostly focused on random access/channel sharing. MAC's functionality is the creation of frames and the management of the medium access [r008]. Random access/channel sharing is not applicable to switched LANs [such as Fast Ethernet (FE), Gigabit Ethernet (GbE), or 10 Gigabit Ethernet (10GbE)], but remains important for Wireless LANs (WLANs). In WLANs, the MAC takes over the assignment of radio resources to the subscribers [r014].

Media Access Control (MAC) Address   (aka as physical address, hardware address, or network adapter address) A link layer address of local network typical technologies such as Ethernet and Token Ring Local Area Networks (LANs). Node address given a layer 2 of the protocol model (MAC layer, with a MAC address). Layer 2 addresses are unique and are assigned by the Institute of Electrical and Electronics Engineers (IEEE) and the manufacturer of the equipment. A 6-byte address space defined/maintained by the IEEE for IEEE 802.3 LANs. A MAC address can be one of two types: (a) *Individual Address:* the address associated with a particular station on the network. Or (b) *Group Address:* a multidestination address, associated with one or more stations on a given network. There are two kinds of multicast address: (1) *Multicast-Group Address;* an address associated by higher-level convention with a group of logically related stations. And, (2) *Broadcast Address;* a distinguished, predefined multicast address that always denotes the set of all stations on a given LAN.

Media Access Control (MAC) Address Learning A function related to Layer 2 services. In a telecom environment, when Provider Edge (PE) equipment receives a frame with an unknown source MAC address, the relationship between that MAC address and interface is learned for future forwarding purposes. In a Layer 2 Virtual Private Network (VPN) this function is allocated to the Virtual Private LAN Service PE (VPLS-PE) [r082].

Media Access Control (MAC) Layer The lower end of the protocol stack for a Local Area Network (LAN) that includes the PHY and a portion of the Data Link Layer (Layer 2). Classically it included collision management [e.g., Carrier Sense Multiple Access/Collision Detect (CSMA/CD)], but with the present-day prevalence of switched LANs, the major remaining function of the lower portion of the Data Link Layer that comprises the MAC is basically the frame structure of the Layer 2 Protocol Data Unit (PDU).

Media Access Control (MAC) Security Enhancements Amendment Security mechanisms for Wireless Local Area Network (WLANs). The Institute of Electrical and Electronics Engineers (IEEE) 802.11i MAC Security Enhancements Amendment makes use of IEEE 802.1X, which

in turn relies on the Extensible Authentication Protocol (EAP) defined in RFC 3748. Today, deployments of IEEE 802.11 wireless LANs are based on EAP and use several EAP methods, including EAP-Transport Level Security (EAP-TLS) (defined in RFC 2716), EAP Tunneled Transport Layer Security Authentication Protocol (EAP-TTLS), Extensible Authentication Protocol (PEAP), and Extensible Authentication Protocol Method for Global System for Mobile Communications (GSM) Subscriber Identity (EAP-SIM). These methods support authentication credentials that include digital certificates, user names and passwords, secure tokens, and Subscriber Identity Module (SIM) secrets [r073].

The Security Enhancements Amendment requires that EAP authentication methods be available. WLAN deployments are expected to use different credential types, including digital certificates, user names and passwords, existing secure tokens, and mobile network credentials [GSM and Universal Mobile Telecommunication System (UMTS) secrets]. Other credential types that may be used include public/private key (without necessarily requiring certificates) and asymmetric credential support (such as password on one side, public/private key on the other).

Media Access Control (MAC) Spoofing Attack MAC spoofing attacks involve the use of a known MAC address of another host to attempt to make the target switch forward frames destined for the remote host to the network attacker. By sending a single frame with the other host's source Ethernet address, the network attacker overwrites the Content-Addressable Memory (CAM) table entry so that the switch forwards packets destined for the host to the network attacker. Until the host sends traffic, it will not receive any traffic. When the host sends out traffic, the CAM table entry is rewritten once more so that it moves back to the original port [r156].

Media Access Control (MAC)-Based Virtual Local Area Networks (VLANs) One problem with port based VLANs is that if the original device is removed from the port and another device is connected, the new device will be in the same VLAN as the original. MAC based VLANs are intended to resolve this problem. In a MAC based VLAN, the VLAN membership is based on the MAC address of the device, not the physical switch port. If a device is moved from one switch port to another, the VLAN membership will follow the device. Unfortunately, the correlation of MAC address to VLAN is a time-consuming process and this type of VLAN is rarely used [r366].

Media Gateway Control Protocol (MGCP)   A protocol used for controlling Voice over IP (VoIP) gateways from external call control elements. Described in RFC 2705 and tracked by the International Softswitch Consortium (ISC).

Media Stream   A stream that can be of type audio, video or data or a combination of any of them. Media stream data conveys user or application data (payload) but no control data [r068a].

Media Vulnerability   Vulnerability to either transmission media (via physical tapping, interference, or even vandalism) or storage media (via penetration, alteration, or theft/vandalism).

Medium Attachment Unit (MAU)   In (older) 10-Mbps Ethernet Local Area Network (LAN) systems, the external device that connects the station to the actual cable. At this juncture, systems generally come with an internal MAU such that the device has a direct Ethernet connector that can be used to connect directly to the LAN cabling system.

MEF   See Metro Ethernet Forum

Melissa Worm   Worm named after a dancer in Florida, the Melissa worm is considered the first destructive mass-mailer targeting Microsoft customers (March 1999). The worm was programmed to spread via Microsoft Word- and Outlook-based systems, and the infection rate was startling. Melissa, created by a hacker who would go to jail for the attack, was released on a Usenet discussion group inside a Microsoft Word file. It spread quickly via e-mail, sending anti-virus vendors scrambling to add detections and prompting immediate warnings from the CERT Coordination Center [r090].

Memory Cards   Removable electronic storage devices, that do not lose the information when power is removed from the card. Used in a variety of devices, including computers, digital cameras, and PDAs. Examples are memory sticks, smart cards, flash memory, and flash cards [r057].

Memory Clusters   All Microsoft operating systems rely upon the storage of data in fixed length blocks of bytes called clusters. Clusters are essentially groupings of sectors that are used to allocate the data storage area in all Microsoft operating systems—that is, DOS, Windows, Windows 95, Windows 98, Windows NT, Windows 2000, and Windows XP. Clusters can be one sector in size to 128 sectors in size and cluster sizes vary depending on the size of the logical storage volume and the operating system involved [r066].

Memory Scavenging   Working through data storage to acquire data. Data may be stored on records, blocks, pages, segments, files, directories, words, bytes, fields, or peripheral devices, such as printers or video displays [r057].

MEMS   See MicroelectroMechanical Systems

Merchant   (SET context) A seller of goods, services, and/or other information who accepts payment for these items electronically [r018].

Merchant Certificate   (SET context) A public-key certificate issued to a merchant. Sometimes used to refer to a pair of such certificates where one is for digital signature use and the other is for encryption.

Merchant Certification Authority (MCA)   (SET context) A Certification Authority (CA) that issues digital certificates to merchants and is operated on behalf of a payment card brand, an acquirer, or another party according to brand rules. Acquirers verify and approve requests for merchant certificates prior to issuance by the MCA. An MCA does not issue a Certificate Revocation List (CRL), but does distribute CRLs issued by root CAs, brand CAs, geopolitical CAs, and payment gateway CAs [r018]. One of the functions of SET is to authenticate all parties in the transaction. Specifically, "Is the merchant who it says he/she is?"

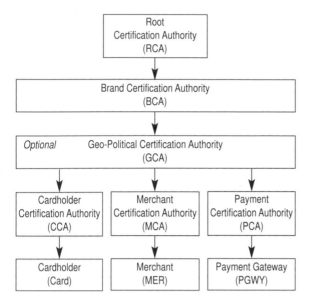

Merge (IP/MPLS context) point a node at which label merging is done.

Merge Point (MP) (MPLS context) The Label Switch Router (LSR) where one or more backup tunnels rejoin the path of the protected Label Switched Path (LSP) downstream of the potential failure. The same LSR may be both an MP and a Point of Local Repair (PLR) simultaneously [r083].

Mersenne Primes Primes of the form $2^q - 1$. For $2^q - 1$ to be prime, q must be prime, but not all numbers of this form are prime [these are named for Marin Mersenne (1588–1648)]. The largest prime yet found (as of 2004) is $2^{20,996,011} - 1$ (which is 6,320,430 digits long in decimal notation), is the 40th known Mersenne prime.

Mesh Public-Key Infrastructure (PKI) A non-hierarchical PKI architecture in which there are several trusted Certification Authorities (CAs) rather than a single root. Each certificate user bases path validations on the public key of one of the trusted CAs, usually the one that issued that user's own public-key certificate. Rather than having superior-to-subordinate relationships between CAs, the relationships are peer-to-peer, and CAs issue cross-certificates to each other.

Message (SIP context) Data sent between Session Initiation Protocol (SIP) elements as part of the protocol. SIP messages are either requests or responses [r025].

Message Authentication Code (MAC) A bit string that is a function of both data (either plaintext or ciphertext) and a secret key, and that is attached to the data in order to allow data authentication. A one-way hash computed from a message and the secret key. Its purpose is to detect if the message has been altered [r039, r354]. Also, data associated with an authenticated message allowing a receiver to verify the integrity of the message [r354].

Message Authentication Code vs. Message Authentication Code (MAC) Capitalized: "(The) Message Authentication Code" refers to an American National Standards Institute (ANSI) standard for a checksum that is computed with a keyed hash that is based on the Data Encryption Standard (DES) [r099]. (Also known as the U.S. Government standard Data Authentication Code) [r013]. The ANSI standard MAC algorithm is equivalent to cipher block chaining with Initialization Vector (IV) = 0.

When people use the uncapitalized "message authentication code" form the term is somewhat ambiguous because it mixes concepts (hence such use should be avoided); it could mean "checksum," "error detection code," "hash," "keyed hash," "Message Authentication Code," or "protected checksum," depending on context. In the uncapitalized form, the word "message" is misleading because it implies that the mechanism is particularly suitable for or limited to electronic mail. The word "authentication" is misleading because the mechanism primarily serves a data integrity function rather than an authentication function. The word "code" is misleading because it implies that either encoding or encryption is involved or that the term refers to computer software [r013].

Message Digest A hash of a message that can be used to verify that the contents of the message have not been altered in transit.

Message Digest 2 (MD2) A cryptographic hash

[r351] that produces a 128-bit hash result, was designed by Ron Rivest, and is similar to MD4 and MD5 but slower.

Message Digest 4 (MD4) A cryptographic hash [r352] that produces a 128-bit hash result and was designed by Ron Rivest.

Message Digest 5 (MD5) A cryptographic hash [r353] that produces a 128-bit hash result and was designed by Ron Rivest to be an improved version of MD4. The MD5 digest algorithm is defined in RFC 1321. Recently MD5 has been shown to have weaknesses.

Message Digest Function (aka one-way hash function) A one-way function that takes a variable-length message and produces a fixed-length hash. Given the hash, it is computationally hard to find a message with that hash. For some one-way hash functions, it is also computationally infeasible to determine two messages which produce the same hash. A one-way hash function can be private or public. Examples include Message Digest 5 (MD5) and Secure Hash Algorithm (SHA). SHA was developed by National Institute of Standards and Technology (NIST) and defined in standard FIPS 180. SHA-1 is a revision published in 1994. It is also described in American National Standards Institute (ANSI) standard X9.30 (Part 2).

Message Disposition Notification (MDN) The Internet messaging format used to convey a receipt. This term is used interchangeably with receipt. A signed MDN is a signed receipt.

Message Handling System (MHS) An International Telecommunications Union/International Organization for Standardization (ITU/ISO) system concept, which encompasses the notion of electronic mail but defines more comprehensive Open Systems Interconnection Reference Model (OSIRM) systems and services that enable users to exchange messages on a store-and-forward basis [r013].

Message Integrity Check (MIC) (aka Message Digest) The MIC is the digest output of the hash algorithm used by the digital signature.

Message Security Protocol (MSP) A secure message handling protocol [r355] for use with X.400 and Internet mail protocols. Developed by National Security Agency (NSA) and used in the United States' Defense Message System.

Message Transfer Part (MTP) (GSM context) The basic protocol in the Signaling System 7 (SS7) environment. It is responsible for message transfer between two network elements [r011].

Metadata Data about data or a definition or description of data. In Information Technology (IT), metadata is definitional data that provides information about, or documentation of, other data managed within an application or environment. For example, metadata would document data about data elements or attributes (name, size, data type, etc.) and data about records or data structures (length, fields, columns, etc.) and data about data (where it is located, how it is associated, ownership, etc.) [r080].

Method (SIP context) The primary function that a request is meant to invoke on a server. The method is carried in the request message itself. Example methods are INVITE and BYE [r025].

Metro Ethernet Forum (MEF) Industry forum for the advancement of Ethernet-based carrier-provided services in Metropolitan Area Network (MAN) and Wide Area Network (WAN) environments. Membership includes service providers, chip companies, and several large equipment vendors. One of the goals is to formalize the idea of carrier-class Ethernet. Carrier-class Ethernet has been loosely defined as an Ethernet environment that matches the reliability and quality of service (QoS) that carriers have enjoyed with Synchronous Optical NETwork (SONET) and Synchronous Digital Hierarchy (SDH) and Asynchronous Transfer Mode (ATM). the other goal is to allow product equipment vendors to prove that their systems make the cut [r356].

MFR See MultiLink Frame Relay

MGCP See Media Gateway Control Protocol

MHS See Message Handling System

MIB See Management Information Base

MIC See Message Integrity Check

MicroelectroMechanical Systems (MEMS)

Generic term to describe micron-scale (one millionth of a meter) electrical/mechanical devices.

Microsoft's Virtual Server   A virtual machine solution for application migration and server consolidation. With Virtual Server, a Windows Server 2003-based server can run multiple operating systems concurrently. The goal is to make it easier to migrate legacy applications. Virtual Server aims at reducing capital expenditures through the use of fewer servers. Virtual Server does not require custom drivers and it does not use any proprietary protocols [r080].

Microsoft's ".NET"   Microsoft's Internet and Web strategy. ".NET" is an Internet and Web based infrastructure that delivers software as Web Services and is a framework for universal services. It is a server-centric computing model [r080].

Microsoft's Defense-in-Depth Model   Microsoft's defense-in-depth model (illustrated below). Similar to publicly available models that other organizations use, Microsoft's multilayer model organizes controls into several broad categories [r190].

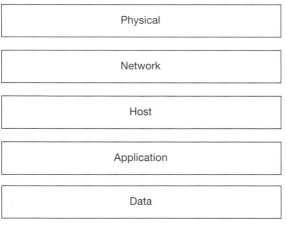

Microsoft's Defense-in-Depth Model

Middlebox   Intermediate devices in the Internet that require application intelligence for their operation. These are described in RFC 3303. Datagrams pertaining to real-time streaming applications, such as Session Initiation Protocol (SIP) and International Telecommunication Union

(ITU) H.323, and peer-to-peer applications, such as Napster and NetMeeting, cannot be identified by merely examining packet headers. Middleboxes implementing Firewall and Network Address Translator services typically embed application intelligence within the device for their operation [r037].

Intermediate devices requiring application intelligence. Many of these devices enforce application specific policy based functions such as packet filtering, Virtual Private Network (VPN) tunneling, Intrusion detection, security, and so forth. Network Address Translator (NAT) service, on the other hand, provides routing transparency across address realms (within IPv4 routing network or across v4 and v6 routing realms), independent of applications. Application Level Gateways (ALGs) are used in conjunction with NAT to examine and optionally modify application payload so the end-to-end application behavior remains unchanged for many of the applications traversing NAT middleboxes. There may be other types of services requiring embedding application intelligence in middleboxes for their operation [r037].

A Middlebox is a network intermediate device that implements one or more of the middlebox services. A NAT middlebox is a middlebox implementing NAT service. A firewall middlebox is a middlebox implementing firewall service. Traditional middleboxes embed application intelligence within the device to support specific application traversal. Middleboxes supporting the Middlebox Communication (MIDCOM) protocol will be able to externalize application intelligence into MIDCOM agents. In reality, some of the middleboxes may continue to embed application intelligence for certain applications and depend on MIDCOM protocol and MIDCOM agents for the support of remaining applications [r037].

Middlebox Communication (MIDCOM) Agent Registration   The process (as defined in RFC 3303) of provisioning agent profile information with the middlebox or a MIDCOM Policy Decision Point (PDP). MIDCOM agent registration is often a manual operation performed by an operator rather than the agent itself. A MIDCOM agent profile may include agent authorization policy [i.e., session tuples for which the agent is authorized to act as Application Level Gateway (ALG)], agent-hosting entity (e.g., Proxy, Gateway, or end-host which hosts the agent), agent accessibility profile (including any host level authentication information), and security profile (for the messages exchanged between the middlebox and the agent) [r037].

Middlebox Communication (MIDCOM) Agents Entities performing Application Level Gateway (ALG) functions, logically external to a middlebox (defined in RFC 3303). MIDCOM agents possess a combination of application awareness and knowledge of the middlebox function. This combination enables the agents to facilitate traversal of the middlebox by the application's packets. A MIDCOM agent may interact with one or more middleboxes [r037].

Middlebox Communication (MIDCOM) Policy Decision Point (PDP) A PDP acts as a policy repository, holding MIDCOM related policy profiles in order to make authorization decisions (as defined in RFC 3303). A logical entity that makes policy decisions for itself or for other network elements that request such decisions; and a policy repository as a specific data store that holds policy rules, their conditions and actions, and related policy data [r037].

Middlebox Communication (MIDCOM) Protocol A protocol to be used by MIDCOM agents for interacting with middleboxes such as firewalls and Network Address Translators (NATs); framework is defined in RFC 3303. Examples are the packet filters and NATs. MIDCOM supports applications that require dynamic configuration of these middleboxes [r030].

The semantics are defined in terms of transactions. Two basic types of transactions are used: request–reply transactions and asynchronous transactions. For each transaction, the semantics are specified by describing (1) the parameters of the transaction, (2) the processing of request messages at the middlebox, (3) the state transitions at the middlebox caused by the request transactions or indicated by the asynchronous transactions, respectively, and (4) the reply and notification messages sent from the middlebox to the agent in order to inform the agent about the state change [r030].

The protocol between a MIDCOM agent and a middlebox allows the MIDCOM agent to invoke services of the middlebox and allow the middlebox to delegate application specific processing to the MIDCOM agent. The MIDCOM protocol allows the middlebox to perform its operation with the aid of MIDCOM agents, without resorting to embedding application intelligence. The principal motivation behind architecting this protocol is to enable complex applications through middleboxes, seamlessly using a trusted third party (i.e., a MIDCOM agent) [r037].

Middlebox Communication (MIDCOM) Session A lasting association between a MIDCOM agent and a middlebox. The MIDCOM session is not assumed to imply any specific transport layer protocol. Specifically, this should not be construed as referring to a connection-oriented Transmission Control Protocol (TCP) protocol [r037].

Middlebox Function/Service A middlebox function or a middlebox service is an operation or method performed by a network intermediary that may require application specific intelligence for its operation (defined in RFC 3303). Policy-based packet filtering (aka firewall), Network Address Translation (NAT), Intrusion detection, load balancing, Policy-based tunneling, and IPsec security are all examples of a middlebox function (or service) [r037].

Middlebox-Unique A value that is unique in the context of the middlebox. This context includes all Middlebox Communication (MIDCOM) sessions the middlebox participates in. A middlebox-unique value is assigned by the middlebox [r030].

Middleware Grid Tools Software plug-ins that facilitate the use of grid technology. For example, the open source Globus Toolkit 3.0, a mature set of tools useful for building a grid, is the first full-scale implementation of the Open Grid Services Infrastructure (OGSI) standard. The toolkit was developed by the Globus Project, a research and development project focused on enabling the application of Grid concepts to scientific and engineering computing [r080].

MIME   See Multipurpose Internet Mail Extensions

Mimicking   (aka impersonation, masquerading, or spoofing) An action of an unauthorized entity that entails posing as an authorized user. Such action is by the unauthorized entity to gain access to a system ("spoof") or to perform a malicious act ("malicious logic"). In context of masquerade "malicious logic" is any hardware, firmware, or software (e.g., Trojan horse) that appears to perform a useful or desirable function, but actually gains unauthorized access to system resources or tricks a user into executing other malicious logic.

MIMO   See Multiple-Input Multiple-Output

Minimum Interoperability Specification for Public Key Infrastructure (PKI) Components (MISPC)   A technical description to provide a basis for interoperation between PKI components from different vendors; this consists primarily of a profile of certificate and Certificate Revocation List (CRL) extensions and a set of transactions for PKI operation [r013].

MIP   See Mobile IP

Mirror Image Backups   Involves the backup of all areas of a computer hard disk drive or another type of storage media, e.g., Zip disks, floppy disks, Universal Serial Bus (USB) memory dongles, and exactly replicate all sectors on a given storage device. (All files and ambient data storage areas are copied.) Such backups are sometimes referred to as bit stream backups or "evidence grade" backups and they differ substantially from standard file backups and network server backups [r057].

Misappropriation   A threat action whereby an entity assumes unauthorized logical or physical control of a system resource via theft of service, theft of functionality, or theft of data [r013].

Misnamed Files   A file, typically of executable code, that is disguised at a superficial level by changing the file's name, in an attempt to make it look like it is innocuous.

MISPC   See Minimum Interoperability Specification for PKI Components

MISSI   See Multilevel Information System Security Initiative

MISTY1   A secret-key cryptosystem described in RFC 2994 which is a block cipher with a 128-bit key, a 64-bit block, and a variable number of rounds. It is designed to achieve high-speed encryption on hardware platforms as well as on software environments. The cryptosystem is designed on the basis of the theory of provable security against differential cryptanalysis (DC) and linear cryptanalysis (LC) [r359].

Misuse   A threat action that causes a system component to perform a function or service that is detrimental to system security. Misuses may come in the form of tampering, malicious logic, or violation of permissions [r013].   The term misuse is sometimes used to describe an attack that originates from the internal network, while intrusion is used to describe attacks from the outside [r306].

Misuse Detection Model Intrusion Detection System   [aka signature-based Intrusion Detection System (IDS)] Approach where the intrusion detection system detects intrusions by looking for activity (i.e., signatures) that corresponds to known intrusion techniques or system vulnerabilities [r076].

Mitigation Plan   The set of actions intended to improve control to mitigate identified risk(s).

Mitnick Attack   A well-known attack that made use of a trust relationship plus reconnaissance plus predictability [of Transport Control Protocol (TCP) sequence numbers] to gain access to a host. These same mechanisms can be used in many types of other attacks.

Mixing   A technique for obtaining unguessable random numbers in the absence of a strong, reliable hardware entropy source. The system obtains input from a number of uncorrelated sources and to mix them with a strong mixing function. Such a function will preserve the entropy present in any of the sources, even if other quantities being combined happen to be fixed or easily guessable (low entropy). This approach may be advisable even with a good hardware source, as hardware can also fail. However, this should be weighed against a possible increase in the chance of overall failure due to added software complexity.

MLF   See MultiLink Frame Service

ML-IPsec   See Multilayer IPsec

MLS   See Multilevel Secure

MM   See Mobility Management

MN   See Mobile Node

MNC   See Mobile Network Code

MNT   See Molecular Nanotechnology

Mobile Application Part (MAP)   (GSM context) A Global System for Mobile Communications (GSM)-specific protocol for non-call-related applications between Network SubSystem (NSS) elements. MAP is based directly on Transaction Capabilities Application Part (TCAP), which coordinates and guarantees smooth MAP communication [r011].

Mobile Country Code (MCC)   (GSM context) Code that constitutes the second part of the Mobile Subscriber Integrated Services Digital Network (ISDN) Number (MSISDN), and indicates the code of the relevant country. It is also part of the Cell Global Identity (CGI) [r011].

Mobile IP (MIP)   A protocol developed for transparently dealing with mobile users. Specifically it enables hosts to stay connected to a network (such as the Internet) regardless of the host's location. Described in RFC 3344, *IP Mobility Support for IPv4*. RFC 3344 describes protocol enhancements that allow transparent routing of IP datagrams to mobile nodes in the Internet. Each mobile node is always identified by its home address, regardless of its current point of attachment to the Internet. While situated away from its home, a mobile node is also associated with a care-of address, which provides information about its current point of attachment to the Internet. The protocol provides for registering the care-of address with a home agent. The home agent sends datagrams destined for the mobile node through a tunnel to the care-of address. After arriving at the end of the tunnel, each datagram is then delivered to the mobile node.

Mobile IP Registration Request   A request for network access. There are considerations to augment the functionality of the Mobile IP mobility agents so that they can translate between Mobile IP registration messages and the messages used within the Authentication, Authorization, and Accounting (AAA) infrastructure, as described in RFC 2977. AAA Security Association can be used to create derivative Mobility Security Associations [r012]. Extensions to Mobile IP registration messages are provided in RFC 3957 that can be used to create Mobility Security Associations between the Mobile Node (MN) and Foreign Agent (FA) and/or MN and Home Agent (HA) based on the AAA Security Association between the MN and AAA server. These new Mobility Security Associations may then be used to calculate the Authentication Data needed by authentication extensions used in Mobile IP control messages.

Mobile Network Code (MNC)   (GSM context) The second part of the International Mobile Subscriber Identity (IMSI). It has a fixed length of 2 digits, and is also part of the CGI [r011].

Mobile Node (MN)   Nomadic node in IP Mobile. The entity in the Mobile IP context that may change its point of attachment from network to network in the Internet. Such a node is expected to be able to detect that it has moved and it registers with a "best" Foreign Agent (FA). A MN is assigned a permanent IP address called its home address to which other hosts send packets regardless of MN's real-time location (because this IP does not change it can be utilized by other entities to communicate with node).

Mobile Originated Call (MOC)   (GSM context) The connection between the network and a mobile station initiated by the mobile station [r011].

Mobile Services Switching Center (MSC)   (GSM context) The Mobile Services Switching Center within the Network SubSystem (NSS) that serves as a digital exchange for the routing of messages and calls, and for connecting mobile subscribers with each other or with subscribers in other networks, such as the Public Switched Telephone Network, the Integrated Services Digital Network (ISDN), or data networks [r011].

Mobile Station (MS)   (GSM context) The cellular telephone itself.

Mobile Station Roaming Number (MSRN) (GSM context) A number generated temporarily for the duration of a mobile station's stay in a particular Location Area. It is required when a Gateway Mobile Services Switching (GMSC) wants to forward an incoming call to a mobile station that is not located in the area controlled by the Visitor Location Register (VLR) of this GMSC [r011].

Mobile Subscriber Identification Number (MSIN)   (GSM context) The fourth part of the Mobile Subscriber Integrated Services Digital Network (ISDN) number (MSISDN). It determines the logical Home Location Register (HLR) where a subscriber is stored, and identifies the subscriber and his services [r011].

Mobile Subscriber ISDN number (MSISDN) (GSM context) The international phone number of a mobile Global System for Mobile Communication (GSM) customer is its Mobile Subscriber Integrated Services Digital Network (ISDN) number (MSISDN). This number is stored on the subscriber's Subscriber Identity Module (SIM) card and in the Home Location Register (HLR) of the Home Network [r011].

Mobile Terminated Call (MTC)   (GSM context) A connection between the network and the mobile station that was initiated by the network [r011].

Mobility Management (MM) (GSM context) Establishes the location of a mobile in order to make a connection [r011]. Mobility Management makes it possible to determine the location of a User Equipment for setting up a connection [r007].

Mobility Routing Proxy (MRP) An optional functional entity that acts as an intermediate functional entity, terminating the security association of a hop-by-hop link [r068a].

Mobility Security Association   A simplex connection that applies security services to RFC 3344 Mobile IP Version 4 (MIPv4) control traffic between a Mobile Node (MN) and the Home Agent (HA) [or MN and Foreign Agent (FA)] using RFC 3344 Authentication Extensions. A Mobility Security Association is uniquely identified by the peer source and destination IP addresses and a Security Parameter Index (SPI). Two nodes may have one or more Mobility Security Associations; however, typically there is no reason to have more than one Mobility Security Association between two nodes, except as a transient condition during re-keying events [r012]. The SPI is the 4-byte opaque index within the mobility security association that selects the specific security parameters to be used to authenticate the peer.

A Mobility Security Association is identified by the two end points, such as a MN IP address and a HA IP address, and a SPI. Authentication, Authorization, and Accounting (AAA) servers typically use the Network Access Identifier (NAI) to uniquely identify the mobile node; the mobile node's home address is not always necessary to provide that function. Thus, it is possible for a mobile node to authenticate itself, and be authorized for connection to the foreign domain, without having any home address. However, for Mobile IP to work, the mobile node is required to have a home address and a Mobility Security Association with its home agent. When a mobile node depends on an AAA infrastructure to obtain authorization for network connectivity and Mobile IP registration, it may lack any preexisting Mobility Security Associations with either its home agent, or the foreign agent controlling the access to the foreign network. The extensions defined in RFC 3957 allows an AAA entity to supply key material to mobile nodes to be used as the basis of its Mobility Security Association with mobile agents.

Mobile IP for IPv4 requires strong authentication between the mobile node and its home agent. When the mobile node shares an AAA Security Association with its home AAA server, however, it is possible to use that AAA Security Association to create derived Mobility Security Associations between the mobile node and its home agent, and again between the mobile node and the foreign agent currently offering connectivity to the mobile node [r012].

Mobility Security Associations to Support Mobile IP Entities Associations between Mobile IP entities (mobile nodes, home agents, foreign agents) that contain both the necessary cryptographic key information and a way to identify the cryptographic transform that uses the key to produce the authentication information that is present in the Mobile-Home Authentication extension or the Mobile-Foreign Authentication extension. In order for the mobile node to make use of key material created by the Authentication, Authorization, and Accounting (AAA) server, the mobile node also has to be able to identify and select the appropriate cryptographic transform that uses the key to produce the authentication [r012]. The Mobility Security Association to be established between the mobile node and the foreign agent has to be communicated to the foreign agent as well as to the mobile node.

The following requirements are placed on the mechanism used by the AAA infrastructure to effect key distribution [r012]:

- The Home AAA (AAAH) must establish strong, fresh session keys.
- The mechanism must maintain algorithm independence, allowing for the distribution of authentication algorithm identification along with the keys.
- The mechanism must include replay detection.
- The mechanism must authenticate all parties, including the AAA servers and the Foreign Agent (FA) and Home Agent (HA).
- The mechanism must provide for authorization of the client, FA, and HA.

- The mechanism must not rely on plaintext passwords.
- The mechanism must maintain confidentiality of session keys.
- The mechanism must uniquely name session keys.
- The mechanism must be such that the compromise of a single FA and HA cannot compromise any other part of the system, including session keys and long-term keys.
- The mechanism must bind key(s) to an appropriate context.
- The mechanism must not expose the keys to entities other than the AAAH and FA (or HA in the case of key distribution to the HA).

The way that the key is distributed to the foreign agent (or home agent) is expected to be handled as part of the AAA protocol processing between the AAAH and AAA server in the visited network (AAAL, and the further AAA protocol processing between the AAAL and the foreign agent.

MOC See Mobile Originated Call

Mockingbird Software that intercepts communications (especially login transactions) between users and hosts, and provides system-like responses to the users while capturing their responses (e.g., account IDs and passwords) for future transmission to, or collection by, some unauthorized/external third party.

Mode of Operation (Encryption context) A technique for enhancing the effect of a cryptographic algorithm or adapting the algorithm for an application, such as applying a block cipher to a sequence of data blocks or a data stream [r013].

(System operation context) A type of security policy that states the range of classification levels of information that a system is permitted to handle and the range of clearances and authorizations of users who are permitted to access the system [r013].

Model Driven Architecture™ (MDA) MDA has the objective of unifying the Modeling and Middleware spaces. MDA supports applications over their entire lifecycle from Analysis and Design, through implementation and deployment, to maintenance and evolution. Based on Unified Modeling Language™ (UML) models which remain stable as the technological landscape changes around them, MDA-based development maximizes software return on investment as it integrates applications across the enterprise, and one enterprise with another. MDA and UML are promulgated by the Object Management Group (OMG).

Modeling   The act of designing of software applications before coding. Modeling is an essential part of any medium-to-large software development projects. A model plays the analogous role in software development that blueprints and other plans (site maps, elevations, physical models) play in the building of a skyscraper. Using a model, those responsible for a software development project's success can assure themselves that business functionality is complete and correct, end-user needs are met, and program design supports requirements for scalability, robustness, security, extendibility, and other characteristics, before implementation in code renders changes difficult and expensive to make [r379].

Modem   A device that enables a computer or other intelligent device (e.g., a Point-of-Sale terminal) to transmit data over analog telephone lines. A cable modem operates over a cable system and may or may not involve analog conversion. (Most cable modems simply provide an Ethernet-to-ATM conversion for transmission over a digital cable system.)

Modes of Operation of IPv6/IPv4 Nodes   Modes include: (i) IPv6-only operation: An IPv6/IPv4 node with its IPv6 stack enabled and its IPv4 stack disabled; (ii) IPv4-only operation: An IPv6/IPv4 node with its IPv4 stack enabled and its IPv6 stack disabled; and (iii) IPv6/IPv4 operation: An IPv6/IPv4 node with both stacks enabled.

Modification of Data Traffic on a PPVPN   Refers to modifying the contents of packets as they traverse the Virtual Private Network (VPN) [r058].

Modular Storage System   Building block system where controller/host connection function is physically separate from storage, and storage and/or controller function may be added independently of each other [r029].

Modulus   The defining constant in modular arithmetic. Usually, this is part of the public key in asymmetric cryptography that is based on modular arithmetic.

Molecular Nanotechnology (MNT)   Techniques for the control of the structure of matter based on molecule-by-molecule engineering; the products and processes of molecular manufacturing. Thorough but inexpensive control of the structure of matter based on molecule-by-molecule control of products and byproducts; the products and processes of molecular manufacturing, including molecular machinery [r360].

Money Laundering Process: Integration   (financial term) The third, and final, step in the money laundering process is integration. This is the step where the laundered funds are legitimized. In the example of layering involving credit cards, the money launderer's subsequent use of the credit, either to make purchases or to obtain cash advances, would be an example of integration. In addition, the money launderer could request a credit balance refund, and the check issued in response to the request would appear to be "clean" funds that could be cashed or deposited at other financial institutions without arousing suspicion.

Money Laundering Process: Layering   (financial term) The second step in the money laundering process is layering. Layering involves moving funds into multiple accounts and/or ventures to hide activity and funds ownership. This is often a series of complex transactions designed to shift the money, while leaving a difficult-to-follow trail.

Money Laundering Process: Layering Methods   (financial term) Unusual payments and credit balances: For example, in the placement stage, a money launderer might recruit friends or associates to take dirty cash in amounts below reporting thresholds to deposit at retail banks, to purchase money orders, or to make wire transfers. After the funds are placed within the financial system, these funds could then be wired, mailed, or sent by check to make a payment against a credit card account owned by the money launderer, perhaps even creating a credit balance in the money launderer's name. Alternatively, these funds may be deposited into an on-line bank deposit account. The money launderer may make ordinary payments or deposits from legitimate checking accounts to his account as well, effectively intermingling the clean and dirty funds. These activities create layers of financial transactions that can obscure the criminal origin of the funds.

Money Laundering Process: Placement (financial term) The first step in the money laundering process is placement. This is the step where the funds are first introduced into the financial system. Placing funds into the system is the most difficult step of the process, due to the many filing requirements and the intense scrutiny of cash transactions by law enforcement and financial institutions. Cash transactions, including large cash transactions, are common and regular occurrences at banks with traditional retail branches, and these entities must ensure that appropriate monitoring and control of cash transactions occurs to minimize the risk of money laundering.

Money Laundering Process: Placement Methods (financial term) Structuring: Laundered funds are typically placed into a financial institution via a series of structured transactions. This is a practice frequently used to hide proceeds from drug sales. Structuring is the process of regularly depositing cash in amounts just below the reporting thresholds amount. These deposits may occur several times a week or several times during a 30-day period. The deposits may even be at several different locations or offices of a financial institution on the same day, in an effort to better disperse the funds. Each of these deposits would be far below the reporting requirement so as not to arouse suspicion.

Smurfing: In the world of money laundering, a "smurf" is a person who deposits cash or monetary instruments into someone else's account. The smurf may be making deposits as a favor for a friend or for a total stranger. Often, the smurf has no idea that the money being deposited was obtained from illegal activities. Smurfing manifests as numerous deposits of small amounts of cash (or monetary instruments such as travelers checks or money orders) into a single account. The deposits may be made by one person or by several people, but none of them owns the account.

Monitoring Programs Scope, Illegal Use (i.e., Spy Programs) Usage of monitoring programs may allow the violator (among other things) to [r342]:

- Illegally intercept another's information.
- Perform economic espionage.
- Perform political espionage.
- Obtain unauthorized access to the "bank–client" systems.
- Obtain unauthorized access to security-specific systems of the personal computer user, such as public and private keys or password phrases.
- Obtain unauthorized access to authorization data of credit cards.

Monitoring Programs Scope, Legal Use Permit firms to (among other) [r342]:

- Define (locate) all attempted cases of unauthorized access to confidential information with exact time report and the networked workstation where from this attempt has been performed.
- Control contacts of children when they are surfing the Internet.
- Conduct information audit.
- Explore and investigate computer incidents.
- Restore critical information after failures of computer systems.

Monitoring Software, Authorized Products used by the security administrator of a computing system (information security service of the company or organization) for ensuring its accountability. This property, depending on quality of its realization, allows inspecting how employees comply with the established rules of safe operation on computers and security policy. There is a vague line between monitoring products for ensuring accountability and spy products [r342].

Products for monitoring and accountability typically have the following special program functions [r342]:

- Possibility of a preliminary configuration of the monitoring module (client, agent, etc.) and obtaining of compiled executable file, that at installation does not display any messages and does not create windows on the screen
- Built-in means of delivery and remote installation of the configured module on the user's computer

Monitoring Transaction   (MIDCOM context) A request transaction containing a request for state information from the middlebox. Monitoring does not cause a state transition at the middlebox [r030].

Monkey-in-the-Middle Attack   A man-in-the-middle attack launched against Secure Shell (SSH) and Secure HyperText Transfer Protocol (HTTPS).

Monolithic   (Storage context) Single box system containing all control and storage in a single system, where the storage is integrated with the other components and cannot be segregated [r029].

Monte Carlo   An analytical technique in which a large number of simulations are run using random quantities for uncertain variables and looking at the distribution of results to infer which values are most likely. The name comes from the city of Monte Carlo, which is known for its casinos [r009].

Moore's Law   In 1965 G. Moore made his now well-known observation that an exponential growth in the number of transistors per integrated circuit could be observed and predicted that this trend would continue. Through technology advances, Moore's Law, the doubling of transistors every 18 months has been maintained, and still

holds true today. Observers (such as Intel) expect that it will continue at least through the end of the current decade [r361].

Morris   The first Internet worm, originating in 1988. Written by Robert T. Morris, Jr., the Morris worm flooded the ARPANET in November 1988, causing problems for thousands of hosts.

MOSS   See Multipurpose Internet Mail Extensions Object Security Services

Motion Joint Photographic Experts Group (Motion JPEG)   (video formats and coding) Digital compression format (principally for still-video, but also for some video) [r316].

Moving Picture Expert Group (MPEG)   An International Organization for Standardization (ISO)-based standards-making group for digital video systems.

Moving Picture Expert Group-1 (MPEG-1)   (video formats and coding) Digital compression full-motion video (low-end entertainment video and multimedia). Compressed rates are usually 1.1–1.5 Mbps.

Moving Picture Expert Group-2 (MPEG-2)   (video formats and coding) Digital compression full-motion video (high resolution). Compressed rates are usually 2–6 Mbps.

Moving Picture Expert Group-4 (MPEG-4)   (video formats and coding) Robust low data-rate compression full-motion video—for example, for use in cellular phones. Compressed rates can be less than 64 kbps.

MP   See Merge Point

MPEG-1   See Moving Picture Expert Group-1

MPEG-2   See Moving Picture Expert Group-2

MPEG-4   See Moving Picture Expert Group-4

MPLS   See Multi-Protocol Label Switching

MRP   See Mobility Routing Proxy

MS   See Multiplex Section or Mobile Station

MSC   See Mobile Services Switching Center

MSEC   See Multicast Security

MSIN   See Mobile Subscriber Identification Number

MSISDN   See Mobile Subscriber ISDN Number

MSK   See Master Session Key

MSO   See Multiple Systems Operator

MSOH   Multiplex Section Overhead

MSP   See Message Security Protocol

MSRN   See Mobile Station Roaming Number

MSS   See Managed Security Services

MSSP   See Managed Security Services Provider

MTA   See Mail Transport Agent

MTBF   See Mean Time Between Failures

MTC   See Mobile Terminated Call

MTP   See Message Transfer Part

MTTF   See Mean Time to Failure

MTTR   See Mean Time to Repair

MTU   See Maximum Transmission Unit or Multi-Tenant Unit

MUA   See Mail User Agent

Multicast Address   An address that identifies several interfaces and is used to deliver data from one-to-several. By means of the multicast routing topology, packets to a multicast address will be delivered to all interfaces identified by it [r008].

Multicast Group   Set of equipments listening to a specific multicast address [r008].

Multicast IPv4 Tunnel   See 6over4

Multicast Requirements   Multicast applications, such as video broadcast and multicast file transfer, typically have the following key management requirements (among others) [r256]:

- Group members receive security associations that include encryption keys, authentication/integrity keys, cryptographic policy that describes the keys, and attributes such as an index for referencing the security association (SA) or particular objects contained in the SA.
- In addition to the policy associated with group keys, the group owner or the Group Controller and Key Server (GCKS) may define and enforce group membership, key management, data security, and other policies that may or may not be communicated to the entire membership.
- Keys will have a predetermined lifetime and may be periodically refreshed.
- Key material should be delivered securely to members of the group so that they are se-

cret, integrity-protected, and verifiably obtained from an authorized source.

- The key management protocol should be secure against replay attacks and Denial of Service (DoS) attacks.
- The protocol should facilitate addition and removal of group members. Members who are added may optionally be denied access to the key material used before they joined the group, and removed members should lose access to the key material following their departure.
- The protocol should support a scalable group rekey operation without unicast exchanges between members and a GCKS, to avoid overwhelming a GCKS managing a large group.
- The protocol should be compatible with the infrastructure and performance needs of the data security application, such as the IPsec security protocols Authentication Header (AH) and Encapsulating Security Payload (ESP), and/or application layer security protocols such as Secure Real-time Transport Protocol (SRTP) (RFC 3711).
- The key management protocol should offer a framework for replacing or renewing transforms, authorization infrastructure, and authentication systems.
- The key management protocol should be secure against collusion among excluded members and nonmembers. Specifically, collusion must not result in attackers gaining any additional group secrets than each of them individually are privy to. In other words, combining the knowledge of the colluding entities must not result in revealing additional group secrets.
- The key management protocol should provide a mechanism to securely recover from a compromise of some or all of the key material.
- The key management protocol may need to address real-world deployment issues such as Network Address Translation (NAT)-tra-

versal and interfacing with legacy authentication mechanisms.

Multicast Security (MSEC)   Key management protocols that support a variety of application, transport, and network layer security protocols. MSEC key management protocols may be used to facilitate secure one-to-many, many-to-many, or one-to-one communication. Described in RFC 4046 [r256]. It is based on the group control or key server model developed for the Group Key Management Protocol (GKMP) (RFC 2093, July 1997).

Multifactor Authentication   A scheme requiring authentication that satisfies two or three of the following conditions:

- Authentication based on what you know—for example, a user identifier/password combination
- Authentication based on what you have—for example, hardware-based token (such as a smart card) or a software-based token [Public-Key Infrastructure (PKI) certificate]
- Authentication based on what you are—for example, fingerprint or retinal scan

Generally, two-factor authentication is stronger than single-factor authentication, while three-factor authentication is stronger than two-factor authentication. Typical deployments of two-factor authentication include the use of a hardware or software-based used along with a password which "unlocks" the token.

Multihost-Based Auditing   Audit data from multiple hosts that is used to detect intrusions.

Multihost-Based Intrusion Detection Systems (IDS)   IDS where audit data from multiple hosts is used to detect intrusions [r076].

Multilayer IPsec (ML-IPsec)   ML-IPsec is a proposed standard that uses a multilayer protection model to replace the single end-to-end model. Unlike IPsec where the scope of encryption and authentication apply to the entire IP datagram payload (sometimes IP header as well), ML-IPsec divides the IP datagram into zones. It applies dif-

ferent protection schemes to different zones. Each zone has its own sets of security associations, its own set of private keys (secrets) that are not shared with other zones, and its own sets of access control rules (defining which nodes in the network have access to the zone) [r022].

Multilayer IPsec applies separate encryption/authentication with different keys on different parts of an IP datagram. It allows intermediate routers to have limited and controllable access to part of IP datagram (usually headers) but not the user data, for applications such as flow classification, diffserv, transparent proxy, and so on (and those "intelligent routing" that need access to higher-layer protocol headers). The idea is to divide the IP datagram into several parts and apply different forms of protection to different parts. For example, the Transmission Control Protocol (TCP) payload part can be protected between two end points while the TCP/Internet Protocol (TCP/IP) header part can be protected but accessible to two end points plus certain routers in the network. It allows TCP with Performance Enhancing Proxies (PEP) to coexist with IPsec, and provides both performance improvement and security protection to wireless networks [r022].

Multilayer IPsec (ML-IPsec) Operation   When ML-IPsec protects a traffic stream from its source to its destination, it will first rearrange the IP datagram into zones and apply cryptographic protections. When the ML-IPsec protected datagram flows through an authorized intermediate gateway, a certain part of the datagram may be decrypted and/or modified and re-encrypted, but the other parts will not be compromised. When the packet reaches its destination, ML-IPsec will be able to reconstruct the entire datagram. ML-IPsec defines a complex security relationship that involves both the sender and the receiver of a security service, but also selected intermediate nodes along the delivery path [r022].

Multilevel Information System Security Initiative (MISSI)   A National Security Agency (NSA) program to foster development of interoperable, modular products for constructing secure network information systems in support of a variety of U.S. Government goals.

Multilevel Information System Security Initiative (MISSI) User   A system entity that is the subject of one or more MISSI X.509 public-key certificates issued under a MISSI certification hierarchy. MISSI users include both end users and the authorities that issue certificates. A MISSI user is usually a person but may be a machine or other automated process. Some machines are required to operate non-stop. To avoid downtime needed to exchange the FORTEZZA cards of machine operators at shift changes, the machines may be issued their own cards, as if they were persons [r013].

Multilevel Secure (MLS)   A class of system that has system resources (particularly stored information) at more than one security level (i.e., has different types of sensitive resources) and that permits concurrent access by users who differ in security clearance and need-to-know, but is able to prevent each user from accessing resources for which the user lacks authorization [r013].

Multilevel Security Mode   A mode of operation of an information system, that allows two or more classification levels of information to be processed concurrently within the same system when not all users have a clearance or formal access authorization for all data handled by the system [r013]. This mode is defined formally in U.S. Department of Defense policy regarding system accreditation [r195], but the term is also used outside the Defense Department and outside the Government.

MultiLink Frame (MLF) Service   [aka Multilink Frame Relay (MFR)] An inverse-multiplexed carrier service that enables the delivery on nxT1 Frame Relay services to customers. The MPLS/Frame Relay Forum FRF.16.1, *Multilink Frame Relay (MFR) UNI/NNI,* that was ratified in 2002, provides economical multilink solutions for increasing bandwidth without using a higher bandwidth transmission facility. Customer Premise Equipment (CPE) devices and Central Office [CO, also called Point of Presence (POP)]

concentrators can be interoperable based on the FRF.16 MFR specification. Users of MFR can increase their bandwidth without making costly changes to their network and can move forward with confidence that FRF.16-compliant equipment is interoperable. CO concentrators enable the carrier to add Frame Relay services without changing the switch.

MultiLink Frame Relay (MFR)   See MultiLink Frame (MLF) Service

Multimode Fiber   Fiber used in localized telecommunication applications (e.g., data centers, central offices, etc.). Multiple optical modes of light propagate. Transmission typically occurs at 850–1300 nm.

Multiple Spanning Trees Standard   Defined in IEEE 802.1s. Supports basic traffic engineering in Virtual Local Area Networks (VLANs).

Multiple Systems Operator (MSO)   Synonymous with cable provider. A cable TV company that operates more than one TV cable system. A cable industry term that describes a company that operates more than one cable TV system.

Multiple-Input Multiple-Output (MIMO)   Antenna systems (and related transmitter and receiver technology) that allows for increased data throughput through spatial multiplexing and increased range by exploiting the spatial diversity.

Multipoint-to-Multipoint Connection   A collection of associated Asynchronous Transfer Mode (ATM) Virtual Channel (VC) or Virtual Path (VP) links, and their associated nodes, with the following properties: (a) All Nodes in the connection, called endpoints, serve as a Root Node in a Point-to-Multipoint connection to all of the $(N - 1)$ remaining endpoints. (b) Each of the endpoints on the connection can send information directly to any other endpoint, but the receiving endpoint cannot distinguish which of the endpoints is sending information without additional (e.g., higher layer) information.

Multipoint-to-Point Connection   A connection that has zero bandwidth from the Root Node to the Leaf Nodes, and nonzero return bandwidth from the Leaf Nodes to the Root Node. Such a connection is also known as a Multipoint-to-Point Connection.

Multiprotocol Label Switching (MPLS)   A newly introduced telecommunications (carrier-provided) service that is IP-based. MPLS is a hybrid Layer 2/Layer 3 service that attempts to bring together the best of both worlds: Layer 2 and Layer 3, Asynchronous Transfer Mode (ATM) and IP. During the past 25 years, corporations have sought improved packet technologies to support intranets, extranets, and public switched data networks such as the Internet. The progression went from X.25 packet switched technology to Frame Relay technology, and also, on a parallel track, cell relay/Asynchronous Transfer Mode (ATM) technology. In the mean time, throughout the 1980s and 1990s, IP-based connectionless packet services (a Layer 3 service) continued to make major inroads. IP, however, has limited Quality of Service (QoS) capabilities by itself. Therefore, the late 1990s and early 2000s saw the development of MPLS, as a way to provide a better QoS framework, based on improved packet handling [r053–r055].

MPLS is a late-1990s set of specifications that provides a link-layer-independent transport mechanism for IP. The specification-development work is carried out by the Internet Engineering Task Force (IETF). MPLS protocols allow high-performance label switching of IP packets: network traffic is forwarded using a simple label apparatus as described in RFC 3031. By combining the attributes of Layer 2 switching and Layer 3 routing into a single entity, MPLS provides (i) enhanced scalability by way of switching technology; (ii) support of Class of Service (CoS) and QoS-based services (Differentiated Services/*diffserv*, as well as Integrated Services/*intserv*); (iii) elimination of the need for an IP-over-ATM overlay model and its associated management overhead; and (iv) enhanced traffic shaping and engineering capabilities. In addition, MPLS provides a gamut of features in support of Virtual Private Networks (VPNs).

The basic idea of MPLS involves assigning short fixed-length labels to packets at the ingress to an MPLS cloud (based on the concept of forwarding equivalence classes). Throughout the interior of the MPLS domain, the labels attached to packets are used to make forwarding decisions (usually without recourse to the original packet headers). A set of powerful constructs to address many critical issues in the (eventually) emerging *diffserv* Internet can be devised from this relatively simple paradigm. One of the most significant initial applications of MPLS is in Traffic Engineering (TE). (It should be noted that even though the focus is on Internet backbones, the capabilities described in MPLS TE are equally applicable to Traffic Engineering in enterprise networks.)

Multiprotocol Label Switching (MPLS) Edge Node   An MPLS node that connects an MPLS domain with a node that is outside of the domain, either because it does not run MPLS, and/or because it is in a different domain. Note that if a Label Switch Router (LSR) has a neighboring host that is not running MPLS, that that LSR is an MPLS edge node [r053–r055].

Multiprotocol Label Switching (MPLS) Egress Node   An MPLS edge node in its role in handling traffic as it leaves an MPLS domain [r053–r055].

Multiprotocol Label Switching (MPLS) Ingress Node   An MPLS edge node in its role in handling traffic as it enters an MPLS domain [r053–r055].

Multiprotocol Label Switching (MPLS) Motivations   MPLS was developed at a time when IP Wide Area Network (WAN) routers could not perform longest prefix match lookups at wire-speed. By tagging an IP packet at the ingress point of an MPLS enabled network, further hops along the path only need to perform a label lookup instead of a longest prefix lookup, which is a simpler operation. This operation is similar to the virtual circuit identifier (VCI) switching found within Asynchronous Transfer Mode (ATM) environments. These tags, known as MPLS labels, are actually used to create a circuit, and hence augment IP with a connection oriented approach [r378].

Multiprotocol Label Switching (MPLS) Node
A node that is running MPLS. An MPLS node will be aware of MPLS control protocols, will operate one or more Layer 3 (L3) routing protocols, and will be capable of forwarding packets based on labels. An MPLS node may optionally be also capable of forwarding native L3 packets [r053–r055].

Multiprotocol Label Switching (MPLS) RFCs
Key MPLS Internet Engineering Task Force (IETF)-defined specifications and RFCs include the following (list not exhaustive).

- Label Distribution Protocol (LDP) specification (RFC3036), LDP State Machine (RFC 3215)
- MPLS Architecture (RFC 3031)
- MPLS Label Stack Encoding (RFC 3032)
- Resource Reservation Protocol Traffic Engineering (RSVP-TE) extensions for LSP tunnels (RFC 3209)
- Virtual Private LAN Service (VPLS) Applications: draft-ietf-l2vpn-vpls-ldp-applic (Internet Draft)
- VPLS LDP usage: draft-ietf-l2vpn-vpls-ldp (Internet Draft)
- VPLS-Multicast: draft-serbest-l2vpn-vpls-mcast (Internet Draft)

IETF RFC 2702, *Requirements for Traffic Engineering over MPLS,* identifies the functional capabilities required to implement policies that facilitate efficient and reliable network operations in an MPLS domain. These capabilities can be used to optimize the utilization of network resources and to enhance traffic-oriented performance characteristics. IETF RFC 3031, *Multiprotocol Label Switching Architecture,* specifies the architecture of MPLS. IETF RFC 3032, *MPLS Label Stack Encoding,* specifies the encoding to be used by a Label Switch Router (LSR) in order to transmit labeled packets on Point-to-Point Protocol (PPP) data links, on LAN data links, and possibly on other data links. Also, this RFC specifies rules and procedures for processing the various fields of the label stack encoding. An array of

supplementary Internet Drafts support the various aspects of MPLS.

Multiprotocol Label Switching (MPLS) Signaling Protocols Dynamic signaling protocols used in MPLS include Label Distribution Protocol (LDP) and Resource Reservation Protocol (RSVP). These protocols allow tunnels to be set up over such a routed network. Such tunnels can be protected with the use of back up paths or RSVP Traffic Engineering (RSVP-TE) fast reroute to deliver sub-1 second restoration time [r362].

Multiprotocol Label Switching (MPLS), Virtual Channel (VC) A VC is transported within a tunnel and identified by its tunnel multiplexer. A virtual channel is identified by a VCI (Virtual Channel Identifier). In the PPVPN context, a VCI is a VC label or tunnel multiplexer, and in the Martini case, it is equal to the VCID [r082].

Multiprotocol Label Switching (MPLS), Virtual Channel (VC) Label In an MPLS-enabled IP network, a VC label is an MPLS label used to identify traffic within a tunnel that belongs to a particular Virtual Private Network (VPN); i.e., the VC label is the tunnel multiplexer in networks that use MPLS labels [r082].

Multiprotocol Label Switching (MPLS) Domain A contiguous set of nodes that operate MPLS routing and forwarding and that are also in one Routing or Administrative Domain.

Multiprotocol Label Switching (MPLS) Label A label that is carried in a packet header, and that represents the packet's Forwarding Equivalence Class (FEC) [r053–r055].

Multipurpose Internet Mail Extensions (MIME) A set of Internet standards used to express, in e-mail format, data beyond plain text. These protocols [r379] enhance the basic format of Internet electronic mail messages [r380] to be able to use character sets other than American Standard Code for Information Interchange (ASCII) for textual headers and text content, and to carry nontextual and multipart content [r013].

Multipurpose Internet Mail Extensions (MIME) Object Security Services (MOSS) An Internet protocol [r381] that applies end-to-end encryption and digital signature to MIME message content, using symmetric cryptography for encryption and asymmetric cryptography for key distribution and signature [r013].

Multipurpose Internet Mail Extensions (MIME)-Based Secure Peer-to-Peer Business Data Interchange over the Internet   Mechanisms (defined in RFC 3335) to exchange structured business data securely using Simple Mail Transfer Protocol (SMTP) transport for Electronic Data Interchange (EDI—either the American Standards Committee X12 or UN/EDIFACT, Electronic Data Interchange for Administration, Commerce and Transport), Extensible Markup Language (XML), or other data used for business-to-business (B2B) data interchange. The data are packaged using standard MIME content types. Authentication and privacy are obtained by using Cryptographic Message Syntax (Secure Multipurpose Internet Mail Extensions (S/MIME)) or OpenPGP security body parts. Authenticated acknowledgments make use of multipart/signed replies to the original SMTP message [r358]. With an enhancement in the area of "receipts," secure Internet MIME based EDI can be accomplished by using and complying with the following RFCs:

- RFC 821 SMTP
- RFC 822 Text Message Formats
- RFC 1767 EDI Content Type
- RFC 1847 Security Multiparts for MIME
- RFC 1892 Multipart/Report
- RFC 2015, 3156, 2440 MIME/PGP
- RFC 2045 to 2049 MIME RFCs
- RFC 2298 Message Disposition Notification
- RFC 2630, 2633 S/MIME v3 Specification

Multi-Tenant Unit (MTU)   (not to be confused with the more general meaning of the term, that is, a multi-dwelling unit) An MTU is typically a Layer 2 (L2) switch placed by a service provider in a building where several customers of that service provider are located. The term was introduced in an Internet Draft specifying a Virtual Private Local Area Network (LAN) Service (VPLS) solution with function distributed between the MTU and the Provider Edge (PE) equipment in the context of a [r366]. The MTU device name is used primarily in network operation and deployment contexts and should not be used in protocol specifications, as it is also an abbreviation used for Maximum Transmit Units [r082].

Mutual Authentication   When two parties have certificates, and if both parties trust the Certification Authorities (CAs) sign each other's certificates, and then the two parties can prove to each other that they are who they say they are. To mutually authenticate, the first person (A) establishes a connection to the second person (B). To start the authentication process, A gives B his certificate. The certificate tells B who A is claiming to be (the identity), what A's public key is, and what CA is being used to certify the certificate. B will first make sure that the certificate is valid by checking the CA's digital signature to make sure that the CA actually signed the certificate and that the certificate has not been tampered with. (This is where B must trust the CA that signed A's certificate.) [r367].

Mutual Suspicion   The state that exists between two interacting system entities in which neither entity can trust the other to function correctly with regard to some security requirement [r013].

MyDoom Worm   The most impactful Internet virus (by propagation) seen by 2004, along with new strains (e.g., MyDoom.B) that followed. A mass-mailer with a payload targeting the Windows operating system, MyDoom quickly surpassed Sobig as the fastest-spreading e-mail worm ever (2004). MyDoom generated more than 100 million infected e-mails in its first 36 hours. At some point in time, between 20 and 30 percent of all e-mail traffic worldwide is generated by this worm. MyDoom.B is designed to attack www.microsoft.com, the main website run by Microsoft Corporation, as well as the website of the U.S.-based software vendor SCO, which had been the target of the original worm. The so-called "back-door Trojan" program could allow a hacker to control an infected PC without the owner's knowledge, creating an army of "zombies" that are used to attack websites. The remote control of other computers could be used for politically oriented attacks or for spam, in an effort to generate money. In addition to seeding Windows machines to create botnets, MyDoom was programmed to launch DDoS (distributed denial-of-service) attacks on Microsoft's website [r090].

NAI See Network Access Identifier

Nak Attack (negative acknowledgment) An infraction technique that capitalizes on a potential weakness in an operating system (OS) where it does not handle asynchronous interrupts properly. This leaves the system in an unprotected mode during such interrupts.

Name Resolution Procedure to obtain an address from a name. In IPv6, the resolution of names allows obtaining addresses from device names or domain names totally qualified (FQDN) [r008].

Namespace (Instant Messaging/Presence context) The system that maps from a name of an entity to the concrete implementation of that entity. A namespace may be composed of a number of distinct domains [r027].

Naming Authority Pointer (NAPTR) Resource Records In ENUM, NAPTAR resource records are used to identify available ways for contacting a specific node identified by a domain name created from the translation of an International Telecommunications Union (ITU) E.164 number [r225].

Nanobiotechnology An emerging area of scientific and technological opportunity. Nanobiotechnology applies the tools and processes of nano- and/or micro-fabrication to build devices for studying biosystems. Researchers also seek to learn from biology how to create better devices operating at the micro- and/or nanoscale.

Nanotechnology The creation and utilization of materials, devices, and systems through the control of matter on the nanometer-length scale, that is, at the level of atoms, molecules, and supramolecular structures [r368].

NAS See Network-Attached Storage

Minoli–Cordovana's Authoritative Computer and Network Security Dictionary. By Daniel Minoli and James Cordovana
Copyright © 2006 John Wiley & Sons, Inc.

NASA   See National Aeronautics and Space Administration

NAT   See Network Address Translation

National Aeronautics and Space Administration   U.S. government agency involved in space exploration. The agency undertakes a lot of research and development, including computer science and security.

National Association of Securities Dealers (NASD) Regulation (NASDR)   An independent subsidiary of the NASD that regulates the activities of broker/dealers in the over-the-counter markets and the Nasdaq Stock Market.

National Computer Security Center (NCSC)   A U.S. Department of Defense organization, housed in the National Security Agency (NSA) that has responsibility for encouraging widespread availability of trusted computer systems throughout the Federal Government. It has established criteria for, and performs evaluations of, computer and network systems that have a trusted computing base [r013].

National Electrical Code (NEC)   A document that describes the recommended safe practice for the installation of all types of electrical equipment in the U.S. The NEC is not a "legal document" unless it is so designated by a municipality as its own statute for safe electrical installations. It is revised every three years [r033].

National Electrical Manufacturers Association (NEMA)   A U.S. industry association that standardizes specifications for electrical components and power wires and cable. NEMA standards are referenced by many consumers in writing specifications for the materials they purchase. NEMA standards generally form the basis for American National Standards Institute (ANSI) standards.

National Information Assurance Partnership (NIAP)   A U.S. Government initiative originated to meet the security testing needs of both Information Technology (IT) consumers and producers. NIAP is a collaboration between the National Institute of Standards and Technology (NIST) and the National Security Agency (NSA) in fulfilling their respective responsibilities under PL 100-235 (Computer Security Act of 1987). The partnership combines the extensive IT security experience of both agencies to promote the development of technically sound security requirements for IT products and systems and appropriate measures for evaluating those products and systems. The long-term goal of NIAP is to help increase the level of trust consumers have in their information systems and networks through the use of cost-effective security testing, evaluation, and validation programs. In meeting this goal, NIAP seeks to: (i) promote the development and use of evaluated IT products and systems; (ii) champion the development and use of national and international standards for IT security; (iii) foster research and development in IT security requirements definition, test methods, tools, techniques, and assurance metrics; (iv) support a framework for international recognition and acceptance of IT security testing and evaluation results; and (v) facilitate the development and growth of a commercial security testing industry within the United States [r066].

National Infrastructure Security Co-ordination Centre   A security research group based in the United Kingdom.

National Institute of Standards and Technology (NIST)   A U.S. agency (under Department of Commerce) that promotes U.S. economic growth by working with industry to develop and apply technology, measurements, and standards. Among many other roles, NIST has the responsibility for developing information security (INFOSEC) standards and guidelines for all federal computer systems, except national security systems. The Computer Security Division at NIST maintains a number of cryptographic standards and coordinates validation programs for many of those standards. The Cryptographic Module Validation (CMV) Program encompasses validation testing for cryptographic modules and algorithms.

National Security Agency (NSA)   A U.S. Department of Defense intelligence agency that has primary Government responsibility for Information Security (INFOSEC) for classified information and for unclassified but sensitive information handled by national security systems [r013].

National Television Standards Committee (NTSC) (video formats and coding) Analog U.S. and Japanese format. Long-standing group that developed such standards in the 1950s and 1960s.

National Voluntary Laboratory Accreditation Program (NVLAP) NVLAP provides third-party accreditation to testing and calibration laboratories. NVLAP's accreditation programs are established in response to Congressional mandates or administrative actions by the Federal Government or from requests by private-sector organizations [r078].

National Vulnerability Database (NVD) A comprehensive cyber security vulnerability database that integrates all publicly available U.S. Government vulnerability resources and provides references to industry resources. It is based on and synchronized with the Common Vulnerabilities and Exposures (CVE®) vulnerability naming standard. The CVE initiative is described at http://cve.mitre.org. CVE aims to standardize the names for all publicly known vulnerabilities and security exposures. It is a dictionary, not a database, and it is a Community-Wide effort and is Freely Available for Review or Download. (CVE is sponsored by the U.S Department of Homeland Security.)

National Vulnerability Database (NVD) Severity Metrics A vulnerability is "high severity" if (i) it allows a remote attacker to violate the security protection of a system (i.e., gain some sort of user, root, or application account), (ii) it allows a local attack that gains complete control of a system, and (iii) it is important enough to have an associated CERT/CC advisory or US-CERT alert.

A vulnerability is "medium severity" if it does not meet the definition of either "high" or "low" severity.

A vulnerability is "low severity" if (i) the vulnerability does not typically yield valuable information or control over a system but instead gives the attacker knowledge that may help the attacker find and exploit other vulnerabilities and (ii) the

vulnerability is inconsequential for most organizations.

Natural Disaster Any "act of God" (e.g., fire, flood, earthquake, lightning, or wind) that disables a system component. Also any "act of God" (e.g., power surge caused by lightning) that alters system functions or data [r013].

Natural Vulnerability Vulnerabilities due to potential nature-related incidents. Examples include data centers in a flood plain, avalanche, or tornado-prone areas.

NCC See Network Color Code or Network Control Center

NCH See Notification Channel

NCSC See National Computer Security Center

ND See Neighbors Discovery

NDA See Non-Disclosure Agreement

NDC See Network Destination Code

NDS See Novell Directory Services

Nearline Storage Technology (along with policy) for disk-based archiving of less frequently accessed business-critical data. Files that are archived are deleted from the primary storage system.

A technique to provide automated access to data from media that must be mounted before being read. Also, the device or media where such data is kept. A contraction of near online storage. Examples of nearline storage include tape and disk libraries. Nearline storage is slower than online storage, that uses media that is permanently mounted on the system. Nearline storage is distinguished from off-line storage because off-line storage requires the media to be mounted manually [r068].

NEC See National Electrical Code

NECP See Network Element Control Protocol

Need-to-Know The necessity for access to, knowledge of, or possession of specific information required to carry out official duties. This criterion is used in security procedures that require a custodian of sensitive information, prior to disclosing the information to someone else, to establish that the intended recipient has proper authorization to access the information [r013].

NEF See Network Element Function

Negotiated Data Protection Agreement (DPA) An agreed-upon and legally binding data protection agreement.

Neighbor Node connected to the same link.

Neighbor Discovery Options Neighbors discovery messages options that show link layer addresses, information about prefixes, Maximum Transfer Unit (MTU), routes, and configuration information for IPv6 mobility [r008].

Neighbor Unreachability Detection The process by which a node determines that neighboring hosts or routers are no longer available on the local network segment. After the link-layer address for a neighbor has been determined, the state of the entry in the neighbor cache is tracked. If the neighbor is no longer receiving and sending back Protocol Data Units (PDUs), the neighbor cache entry is eventually removed [r024].

Neighbors Cache (IPv6 context) A cache supported by each IPv6 node that stores the IP address of its neighbors in the link, its corresponding link layer address, and an indication of its accessibility state. Neighbors cache is equivalent to Address Resolution Protocol (ARP) cache in IPv4 [r008].

Neighbors Discovery (ND) (IPv6 context) A set of messages and Internet Control Message Protocol Version 6 (ICMPv6) processes that fixes the relations between neighbor nodes. Neighbors discovery replaces Address Resolution Protocol (ARP), ICMP routes discovery, and ICMP redirection messages used in IPv4. It also provides inaccessible neighbor detection [r008].

NEMA See National Electrical Manufacturers Association

Net Cash Flow (financial term) A measure of a company's financial health. Equals cash receipts minus cash payments over a given period of time; or equivalently, net profit plus amounts charged off for depreciation, depletion, and amortization. Also called cash flow.

Net Operating Income (NOI) (financial term) Income after deducting for operating expenses but before deducting for income taxes and interest [r009].

Net Present Value (NPV) (financial term) The difference between the discounted streams of future costs and future benefits. The present value of the future cash flows of an investment (e.g., a security infrastructure) less the investment's current costs. Future cash flows are discounted given a certain (compoundable) discount rate (say, 15%) and then summed arithmetically. The present value of an investment's future net cash flows minus the initial investment. If positive, the investment should be made (unless an even better investment exists), otherwise it should not [r009].

If costs exceed benefits, the NPV is negative. If benefits exceed costs, the NPV is positive. The NPV is the value, discounted to the present, of undertaking a work force restructuring project rather than not doing so. NPV assessments require that a predetermined discount rate is selected. One criticism of NPV assessments is that, when comparing alternative restructuring proposals, the decision rule would select the largest project (giving the highest NPV) over a smaller project with a higher IRR but a lower NPV [r085].

Given cash flows C1 in year 1, C2 in year 2, C3 in year 3, and so on, and a discount rate of d, the NPV is calculated as

$$NPV = C1/(1 + d)^1 + C2/(1 + d)^2 + C3/(1 + d)^3 + \ldots .$$

NetBIOS (Network Basic Input Output System) A fundamental instruction set providing network access.

Network Two or more systems interconnected by communications links.

Network Access Identifier (NAI) Term defined in RFC 2486, January 1999, for the user identifier submitted by the client during Point-to-Point Protocol (PPP) authentication. In roaming, the purpose of the NAI is to identify the user as well as to assist in the routing of the authentication request. The NAI may not necessarily be the same as the user's e-mail address or the user identifier submitted in an application layer authentication.

Network Address Translation (NAT)   A method by which IP addresses are mapped from one address realm to another, providing transparent routing to end-hosts. Transparent routing here refers to modifying end-node addresses en-route and maintaining state for these updates so that when a datagram leaves one realm and enters another, datagrams pertaining to a session are forwarded to the right end-host in either realm. Two types of NAT are most common. Basic-NAT, where only an IP address [and the related IP, Transmission Control Protocol (TCP)/User Datagram Protocol (UDP) checksums] of packets is altered and NAPT (Network Address Port Translation), where both an IP address and a transport layer identifier, such as a TCP/UDP port (and the related IP, TCP/UDP checksums), are altered [r037].

Network Address Translation (NAT) Binding   (MIDCOM context) An abstraction that enables communication between two end points through the NAT-type middlebox. An enable action may result in a NAT bind or a NAT session, depending on the request and its parameters [r030].

Network Address Translation (NAT), Conflict with IPsec   The key management for IPsec can use either certificates or shared secrets. For all the obvious reasons, certificates are preferred; however, they may present more of a challenge for the system manager. There is strong potential for conflict between IPsec and NAT (RFC 2993). NAT does not easily coexist with any protocol containing embedded IP address; with IPsec, every packet, for every protocol, contains such addresses, if only in the headers. The conflict can sometimes be avoided by using tunnel mode, but that is not always an appropriate choice for other reasons. There is ongoing work to make IPsec pass through NAT more easily. Most current IPsec usage is for Virtual Private Networks (VPNs). Assuming that the other constraints are met, IPsec is the security protocol of choice for Virtual Private Network (VPN)-like situations, including the remote access scenario where a single machine tunnels back into its home network over the Internet using IPsec [r170].

Network Addresses Translator   An IPv4 router that translate addresses and ports when sending packets between a network with private addresses and Internet [r008]. A router implementing Network Address Translation (NAT).

Network Attached Storage (NAS)   A file-storage device that is accessed through a network [r029]. A specialized file server that connects to the network. A NAS device contains a slimmed-down (microkernel) operating system and file system and processes only I/O requests by supporting popular file sharing protocols such as NFS (Unix) and SMB/CIFS (DOS/Windows). Using traditional LAN protocols such as Ethernet and Transmission Control Protocol/Internet Protocol (TCP/IP), the NAS enables additional storage to be quickly added by plugging it into a network hub or switch. As network transmission rates have increased from Ethernet to Fast Ethernet to Gigabit Ethernet, NAS devices have come up to speed parity with direct attached storage devices [r029].

General-purpose computers with a full-blown operating system such as Windows or Unix are sometimes labeled as NAS products, but the true NAS is built from scratch as a dedicated file I/O device [r029].

A NAS device is a server that is dedicated to file sharing. NAS does not provide any of the activities that a server in a server-centric system typically provides, such as e-mail, authentication, or file management. NAS technology is dedicated storage that is relocated to its own independent platform with the goal of increasing the speed and functionality of one's network. Since applications and storage are now on independent, the file server bandwidth is increased and file sharing in quick and easy.

Network Backbone   High-speed network infrastructure that comprises a major pathway within a network. Tier 1 connections among key nodes—usually these nodes are relatively small in number (typically less than one dozen for enterprise networks and typically less than two or three dozen for carrier networks).

Network Color Code (NCC)   (GSM context) The Network Color Code is part of the Base Station Identity Code (BSIC) and represents a particular Global System for Mobile Communication (GSM) network operator [r011].

Network Control Center (NCC)   [aka Network Operations Center (NOC) and/or Network Management Center (NMC)] A carrier/service provider (hardened) location that has visibility over the entire network for the purpose of managing the operations of such network. Typically, Fault Management functions are supported.

Network Defenses   A well-designed and properly implemented network architecture provides highly available, secure, scalable, manageable, and reliable services. One may have multiple networks in the organization and should evaluate each individually to ensure that they are appropriately secured or that the high value networks are protected from unsecured networks. Implementing internal network defenses includes paying attention to proper network design, wireless network security, and, potentially, using Internet Protocol security (IPsec) to ensure that only trusted computers have access to critical network resources [r190]. (Part of Microsoft's Defense-in-Depth Model.)

Network Destination Code (NDC)   (GSM context) Code that constitutes the third part of an Mobile Subscriber ISDN number (MSISDN). It identifies the relevant national network operator. It is also part of the Mobile Station Roaming Number (MSRN) and of the Handover Number (HON) [r011].

Network Element   Typically, a specialized piece of hardware deployed in a private or public network to support a specific function—for example, an appliance in an intranet; an Add/Drop Multiplexer; an Edge Concentrator; or a switch in a carrier's network.

Network Element Function (NEF)   A function block that represents the telecommunication functions and communicates with the Telecommunications Management Network (TMN) oper-

ations systems function (OSF) block for the purpose of being monitored and/or controlled [r068a].

Network Facing PE (N-PE)   The N-PE is the device to which the signaling and control functions are allocated when a VPLS-PE is distributed across more than one box.

Network Interface Card (NIC)   (aka network adapter) A circuit board that connects a computer or other node to a network, typically a Local Area Network (LAN).

Network Layer   Synonymous with Layer 3.

Network Layer Security Protocol (NLSP)   An International Organization for Standardization (ISO) protocol (ISO 11577) for end-to-end encryption services running above Open System Interconnection reference Model (OSIRM) Layer 3. NLSP is derived from a Secure Data Network System (SDNS) protocol, specifically Security Protocol 3 (SP3), but is much more complex.

Network Level Firewall   A firewall where traffic is examined at the IP level.

Network Level Reachability Information (NLRI)   The NLRI consists of one or more network prefixes with the same set of path attributes. Each prefix in the NLRI is combined with the (common) path attributes to form a Border Gateway Protocol (BGP) route. The NLRI encapsulates a set of destinations to which packets can be routed (from this point in the network) along a common route described by the path attributes [r086].

Network Management   The complexity and reliance of corporate operations on enterprise networks requires the utilization of comprehensive management tools to manage, monitor, and troubleshoot the network. The major goals of a network management system are [r245]: (i) Improve network availability (up time) and service. (ii) Centralize control of network components. (iii) Reduce complexity. (iv) Reduce operational and maintenance costs. The network management system can effectively reduce the cost and complexity of today's ever-growing networks by providing a set of integrated tools that allow a network manager or support staff to quickly isolate and diagnose network issues. The ability to analyze and correct network problems from a central location is critical to the management of both network and personnel resources. The requirements of a network management system have been categorized as part of the International Organization for Standardization (OSI) specification for systems management, which is used as a baseline for the key functional areas of network management on any system [r245].

Network Management Center (NMC) A carrier/service provider (hardened) location that has visibility over the entire network for the purpose of managing the operations of such network. Typically Fault Management functions are supported. (GSM context) The Network Management Center assumes special functions of the Performance Management in the context of Operation & Maintenance System (OMS), that are not defined in the Global System for Mobile Communication (GSM) standard, like the evaluation of alarms, the detection of capacity bottlenecks and the monitoring of the quality of service [r011].

Network Management Layer A management layer responsible for the management, including coordination of activity, of a network view.

Network Management System (NMS) A software system (or collection of systems) that (a) collects information related to Fault, Configuration, Accounting, Performance, and Security Management (FCAPS) events and (b) correlates the information and displays it in a graphical and/or tabular fashion. Protocols are used to communicate with agents that reside in each of the managed devices on the network; e.g., Simple Network Management Protocol (SNMP). Many different software packages are available on the market today. Some are very generic and can communicate with any SNMP-compliant device. Others are for specific manufacturers' equipment but may offer more specialized features than SNMP or Common Management Information Protocol (CMIP) [r369].

Management systems provide a user interface for the network administrator to perform tasks such as manipulating network device settings, capturing and analyzing network activity, and creating and monitoring network events. Another benefit of network management software is that the interface allows a network administrator to quickly make changes to many different systems with a single command. In addition, most software packages are much easier to understand than the archaic interfaces of the network devices—it is much easier to click a button or two than it is to type in long strings of text commands [r369].

Network Mapping A probe that uses Simple Network Management Protocol (SNMP) or broadcast Internet Control Message Protocol (ICMP) "ping" packets to determine the topology/connectivity of the network.

Network Operations Center (NOC) (aka Network Control Center (NCC); and/or Network Management Center, (NMC) A carrier/service provider (hardened) location that has visibility over the entire network for the purpose of managing the operations of such network. Typically Fault Management functions are supported.

Network Prefix The fixed part of the address that is used to determine the subnetwork identifier, the route or the addresses range [r008].

Network Prefix Length The network prefix length is the number of bits, out of the total constituting the address field, that define the network prefix portion of the address. A common alternative to using a bit-wise mask to communicate this component is the use of slash (/) notation. This binds the notion of network prefix length in bits to an IP address. For example, 141.184.128.0/17 indicates that the network component of this IPv4 address is 17 bits wide. Similar notation is used for IPv6 network prefixes; e.g., 2001:db8:719f::/48. When referring to groups of addresses, the network prefix length is often used as a means of describing groups of addresses as an equivalence class. For example, "one hundred/16 addresses" refers to 100 addresses whose network prefix length is 16 bits [r086].

Network Security Protection of networks and

their services from unauthorized access, penetration, use, and exploitation. Ensuring the confidentiality, integrity, and availability of inter-networked systems and related devices, as well as the data that is transmitted across the network. Aims at eliminating modification, destruction, or disclosure of information while in transit. Protects network elements and communication channels from infraction, corruption, and/or compromise.

From the view of a purist, the previous definition encompasses the concept of network security. Others tend to include the protection of hosts as part of network security. One may also view the network simply as a conduit (by analogy: a physical road); the responsibility of host protection is beyond network security (just as the responsibility of home protection is beyond the responsibility of a road maintenance/protection function; that is why a homeowner would have door locks, window locks, electronic alarms, home safes, etc.). One may also view host security as its own discipline. Also, one can view protection of data-at-rest (e.g., data in a database) as yet another discipline. Network security should properly focus on protecting the network and its components, not the hosts on the network, which is an add-on responsibility [r406].

Network Segment   See Subnetwork

Network Services (NS)   (GSM context) The term describes the entirety of all services offered in Global System for Mobile Communication/General Packet Radio Services (GSM/GPRS) [r014].

Network Sniffer (or Packet Sniffer)   A network-monitoring program used to capture user account and password information.

Network Subsystem (NSS)   (GSM context) A subnet within the Global System for Mobile Communication (GSM) network, just like the Base Station Subsystem (BSS) and the Operation & Maintenance System (OMS). It is responsible for all procedures concerning the forwarding of calls and subscriber localization [r011].

Network-Based Intrusion Detection System (NIDS)   Intrusion Detection System where net-work traffic data, along with audit data from one or more hosts, is used to detect intrusions [r076]. These IDSs operate on a host to detect malicious activity on network data flows or network elements (e.g., router, switches).

Network-Based Intrusion Prevention Systems (NIPS)   Enhanced Intrusion Detection Systems (IDSs) that operate on a host to detect and prevent malicious activity on network data flows or network elements (e.g., router, switches).

New Technology File System (NTFS)   File system used by modern Windows Operating Systems (OSs). Note: some make use only of the acronym form at this juncture and drop the original expansion of the acronym.

Next-Hop Obtaining   Process to obtain either address interface or next-hop interface to facilitate sending a packet based on the routing table content [r008].

Next-gen Synchronous Optical Network (SONET)   (aka next-gen SONET) Term applied to recent enhancements and additions of Synchronous Optical Network/Synchronous Digital Hierarchy (SONET/SDH) standards and equipment that enable data services (e.g., Metro Ethernet) to be carried more efficiently and flexibly. Three new technologies are key to next-generation SONET/SDH: (i) Generic Framing Procedure (GFP); (ii) Virtual concatenation; and (iii) Link Capacity Adjustment Scheme (LCAS).

Next-Hop (NHOP) Bypass Tunnel   (MPLS context) A backup tunnel that bypasses a single link of the protected Label Switched Path (LSP) [r083].

Next-Hop Determination   The process by which a node determines the IPv6 address of the neighbor to which a Protocol Data Unit (PDU) is being forwarded. The determination is made based on the destination address. The forwarding or next-hop address is either the destination address of the PDU being sent or the address of a neighboring router. The resolved next-hop address for a destination becomes an entry in a node's destination cache, also known as a route cache. The route cache displays the destination address, the interface identifier and next-hop address, the interface identifier and address used as a source address when sending to the destination, and the path Maximum Transfer Unit (MTU) for the destination [r024].

Next-Level Aggregation Identifier (NLAID) A 24-bit field inside the global unicast aggregatable address that allows the creation of several hierarchical levels of addressing in its networks to organize addresses and routing to other Internet Service Providers (ISPs), as well as to identify organization sites [r008].

NIAP See National Information Assurance Partnership

NIC See Network Interface Card

NIDS See Network-Based Intrusion Detection Systems

NIPC See National Infrastructure Protection Center

NIPS See Network-Based Intrusion Prevention Systems

NIST See National Institute of Standards and Technology

NLAID See Next-Level Aggregation Identifier

NLRI See Network Level Reachability Information

NLSP See Network Layer Security Protocol

NMC See Network Management Center

NMS See Network Management System

No eXecute (NX) See Central Processing Unit (CPU) No-Execute Bit

No-Broadcast Multiple Access Link A link layer technology that supports links with more than two nodes, but without allowing the sending of a packet to several destinations (broadcast). For example, X.25, Frame Relay and Asynchronous Transfer Mode (ATM) [r008].

NOC See Network Operations Center

Node A computer or other device in a network. Every node has a unique network address.

Node Address Typically the address is given a Layer 2 of the protocol model [Medium Access Control (MAC) layer, with a MAC address], as well at Layer 3 (the network layer). Layer 2 addresses (6 bytes) are unique and are assigned by

the Institute of Electrical and Electronic Engineers (IEEE) and the manufacturer of the equipment. Layer 3 addresses (4 bytes in IPv4) can be unique within a private enterprise, or can be globally unique when assigned by official agencies.

Originally, all the IPv4 address spaces were managed directly by the Internet Assigned Numbers Authority (IANA). Later parts of the address space were allocated to various other registries to manage for particular purposes or regional areas of the world. RFC 1466 documents most of these allocations.

Node B (3G Wireless context) The Node B can be compared to a Global System for Mobile Communications (GSM) base station. It provides the air interface to the User Equipment [r007].

Node Security Function A mechanism that supports secure communication between internal elements of a computational grid. A grid is comprised of a collection of hardware and software resources whose origins may not be obvious to a grid user; hence, strong security mechanisms are required [r080].

NOI See Net Operating Income

Noise Any unwanted electrical signal.

No-Lone Zone A room or other space to which no person may have unaccompanied access and that, when occupied, is required to be occupied by two or more appropriately authorized persons [r013].

Non-Adjacent Channel Crosstalk (dB) (optical transmission term) The relative power level coming from all other channels except the two adjacent channels, referenced to 0-dB power level. Commonly, only the first two nonadjacent channels (left- and right-hand sides) are accounted for.

Nonce Term that means "for the present time" or "for a single occasion or purpose." In the context of security a nonce is a "number used once"—for example, a random or pseudo-random number issued in an authentication protocol to ensure that previous communications cannot be reused to unleash "replay attacks." Hence, it is a random or nonrepeating value that is included in data exchanged by a protocol, usually for the purpose of guaranteeing liveness and thus detecting and protecting against replay attacks [r013].

Non-Compete Agreement (financial term) A contract that restricts participation in a certain market by a company or individual under specific circumstances. Employers often require employees to sign a noncompete agreement to deter them from quitting to join a competitor [r009].

Noncompetitive bid (financial term) A method of purchasing treasury bills in which an investor agrees to buy a specified number of securities at the average price of the accepted competitive bids [r009].

Non-Disclosure Agreement (NDA) A legally binding contract where the parties involved agree to not disclose details of subsequent knowledge sharing with any parties not associated with the NDA.

Non-Cryptographic Credentials Credentials in a form not relating to cryptographic means, such as Public-Key Infrastructure (PKI). Examples include user identification (ID) and password, Secure ID token, smartcards, biometrics, and Personal Identification Numbers (PINs).

Non-Dispersion-Shifted Fiber (Standard SM Fiber) (optical transmission term) Workhorse fiber of telecom: accounts for more than 95 percent of deployed plant. Fiber is suitable for Synchronous Optical Network (SONET) use in the 1310-nm region or Dense Wavelength Division Multiplexing (DWDM) use in the 1550-nm region (with dispersion compensators). Fiber can also support 10 Gigabit Ethernet standard at distances over 300 meters.

Non-Persistent Cookies Cookies exist on a per-session basis; they are not written to the browser file system.

Nonmalleability Attacks, Vulnerabilities to Most of the well-known encryption and signature schemes fall prey to complete nonmalleability attacks [r016].

Nonmalleability Encryption Nonmalleability is equivalent to indistinguishability under a "parallel chosen ciphertext attack." This is a kind of chosen ciphertext attack in which the adversary's decryption queries are not allowed to depend on answers to previous queries, but must be made all at once. This characterization simplifies both the notion of nonmalleable encryption and its usage, and enables one to see more easily how it compares with other notions of encryption [r370]. There are two definitions of nonmalleable encryption appearing in the literature: the original one of Dolev, Dwork, and Naor and the later one of Bellare, Desai, Pointcheval and Rogaway.

Bellare, M., Desai, A., Pointcheval, D., and P. Rogaway, "Relations Among Notions of Security for Public-Key Encryption Schemes," Extended abstract published in *Advances in Cryptology-Crypto 98 Proceedings, Lecture Notes in Computer Science,* Vol. 1462, H. Krawcyzk ed., Springer-Verlag, 1998.

Dolev, D., Dwork, C., and M. Naor, "Non-malleable cryptography," *Proceedings of the 23rd Annual Symposium on Theory of Computing,* ACM, 1991.

Nonmalleable Encryption Schemes An encryption scheme where the adversary cannot transform a ciphertext into one of a related message under the given public key. Although providing a very strong security property, some application scenarios like the recently proposed key-substitution attacks show the limitations of this notion. In such settings the adversary may have the power to transform the ciphertext and the given public key, possibly without knowing the corresponding secret key of her own public key [r016]. According to the seminal paper by Dolev et al. [r371, r016], an encryption scheme is called nonmalleable if giving a ciphertext to an adversary does not significantly help this adversary to produce a ciphertext of a related message under the same public key. Analogous requirements can be formulated for other cryptographic primitives like signatures or commitments.

Nonmalleable Encryption, Goals Since the discovery of public-key encryption in the 1970s, several different schemes have been proposed that are secure as far as anyone can tell. We still lack conclusive scientific proof that any of the systems in widespread use are secure, and this motivates further work in the search for provably secure and practical cryptosystems [r372]. In 1991, three IBM Almaden researchers proposed a general framework for constructing "non-malleable" encryption systems that prevent the construction of ciphertexts for related plaintexts [r373]. This led to the proposal of "plaintext aware" cryptosystems by Bellare and Rogaway in 1994 [r374], and more recently Victor Shoup of IBM Zurich and Ronald Cramer of ETH Zurich have proposed a practical plaintext-aware cryptosystem that is resistant to chosen ciphertext attacks [r375]. This is exactly the kind of problem that surfaced that the use of RSA's PKCS#1 encryption in Secure Sockets Layer (SSL) is vulnerable to chosen ciphertext attacks.

Nonpublic Addresses and Network Address Translation (NAT)   The NAT systems that are used to map between private and public address spaces may support connections to distant e-mail systems for outbound and inbound e-mail, but terms of service often prohibit the use of systems not supplied by the connectivity provider and prohibit the operation of "servers" (typically not precisely defined) on the client connection [r034].

Non-Real-Time Variable Bit Rate (nrtVBR)   An Asynchronous Transfer Mode (ATM) service category that supports packet-oriented data traffic. Non-Real-Time VBR (nrtVBR) suited to data (IP)/bulk transfer applications. The Service Level Agreement (SLA) is expressed (by the provider) in terms of end-to-end latency, jittter, and packet loss. The end-user will require the use of ATM Adaptation Layer 5 (AAL-5) in their clients/hosts/routers to utilize VBR-based services.

Nonrepudiation   Ensuring that a transferred message has been sent and received by the parties claiming to have sent and received the message. Nonrepudiation is a way to guarantee that the sender of a message cannot later deny having sent the message and that the recipient cannot deny having received the message [r200]. Techniques

used to ensure nonrepudiation include digital or physical signatures and finger printing.

Nonrepudiation of Receipt (NRR)   A "legal event" that occurs when the original sender of a signed Electronic Data Interchange (EDI)/E-commerce (EC) interchange has verified the signed receipt coming back from the receiver. The receipt contains data identifying the original message for which it is a receipt, including the message-ID and a cryptographic hash [message integrity code (MIC)]. The original sender must retain suitable records providing evidence concerning the message content, its message-ID, and its hash value. The original sender verifies that the retained hash value is the same as the digest of the original message, as reported in the signed receipt. NRR is not considered a technical message, but instead is thought of as an outcome of possessing relevant evidence [r164].

In order to support NRR, a signed receipt, based on digitally signing a message disposition notification, is to be implemented by a receiving trading partner's UA (User Agent). The message disposition notification, specified by RFC 2298 is digitally signed by a receiving trading partner as part of a multipart/signed Multipurpose Internet Mail Extensions (MIME) message [r358].

Nonrepudiation Service   A security service that provides protection against false denial of involvement in a communication. Nonrepudiation service does not and cannot prevent an entity from repudiating a communication. Instead, the service provides evidence that can be stored and later presented to a third party to resolve disputes that arise if and when a communication is repudiated by one of the entities involved. There are two basic kinds of nonrepudiation service [r013]:

- Nonrepudiation with proof of origin: provides the recipient of data with evidence that proves the origin of the data, and thus protects the recipient against an attempt by the originator to falsely deny sending the data. This service can be viewed as a stronger version of a data origin authentication service, in that it proves authenticity to a third party.

- Nonrepudiation with proof of receipt: provides the originator of data with evidence that proves the data was received as addressed, and thus protects the originator against an attempt by the recipient to falsely deny receiving the data.

Non-Return to Zero (NRZ)   (optical transmission term) The optical line coding where a "1" or "0" is designated by a constant levels of opposite polarity. Used by Synchronous Optical Network (SONET) transmission systems.

Nonvalidating Security-Aware Stub Resolver (DNSSEC context) A security-aware stub resolver that trusts one or more security-aware recursive name servers to perform most of the tasks discussed in this document set on its behalf. In particular, a nonvalidating security-aware stub resolver is an entity that sends DNS queries, receives DNS responses, and is capable of establishing an appropriately secured channel to a security-aware recursive name server that will provide these services on behalf of the security-aware stub resolver. See also security-aware stub resolver, validating security-aware stub resolver [r069].

Nonvalidating Stub Resolver   (DNSSEC context) A less tedious term for a nonvalidating security-aware stub resolver [r069].

Non-Zero-Dispersion-Shifted Fiber (NZDSF) (optical transmission term) A fiber that introduces a small amount of dispersion without the zero-point crossing being in the C-band (1528–1565 nm). Fiber usable for both Synchronous Optical Network (SONET) and Dense Wavelength Division Multiplexing (DWDM) use in the 1550-nm region.

no-Personal Identification Number (PIN) Organizational Registration Authority (ORA) (NORA)   [Multilevel Information System Security Initiative (MISSI) context] An ORA that operates in a mode in which it performs no card management functions and, therefore, does not require knowledge of either the Site Security Officer (SSO) PIN or user PIN for an end-user's FORTEZZA PC card.

NORA   See no-Personal Identification Number Organizational Registration Authority

NOS   See Network Operating System

Not Specified Address   (IPv6 context) 0:0:0:0:0: 0:0:0 (::) address is used to show the absence of any address, equivalent to IPv4 0.0.0.0 address.

Notarization   Registration of data under the authority or in the care of a trusted third party, thus making it possible to provide subsequent assurance of the accuracy of characteristics claimed for the data, such as content, origin, time, and delivery [r160, r013].

Notification   (Presence Services context) a message sent from the presence service to a subscriber when there is a change in the presence information of some presentity of interest, as recorded in one or more subscriptions [r015].

Notification Channel (NCH)   (GSM context) Channel that contains the information necessary for notifying the mobile stations about a Point-to-Multipoint Multicast connection [r014].

Novell Directory Services (NDS)   Novell's centralized directory mechanism.

NP-Complexity Problem   NP stands for "nondeterministic polynomial." NP is the class of problems that can be solved in polynomial time by a nondeterministic algorithm. A nondeterministic algorithm is one that can magically get some extra input (usually called a "witness") that helps it to find and verify the answer to the problem at hand. Specifically, a decisional problem is in NP if for every possible input for which the correct answer is "yes," there exists some witness which makes the algorithm output "yes." On the other hand, if the correct answer is "no," then there exists no witness which will cause the algorithm to mistakenly say "yes." An equivalent, and now standard, way of viewing problems that are in NP is to say that a problem is in NP if a solution to the problem can be verified in polynomial time [r094].

Note that NP does not stand for "nonpolynomial time"—a common misunderstanding of the term.

N-PE   See Network Facing PE

NPV   See Net Present Value

NRR   See Nonrepudiation of Receipt

nrtVBR   See Non-Real-Time VBR

NRZ   See Non-Return to Zero

NS   See Network Services

NSA   See National Security Agency

NSS   See Network Subsystem

NTFS   See New Technology File System

NTSC   See National Television Standards Committee

NULL Encryption Algorithm   An algorithm [r376] that does nothing to transform plaintext data—that is, a no-op. It originated because of IPsec Encapsulating Security Payload (ESP) (described in RFC 2406), which always specifies the use of an encryption algorithm to provide confidentiality. The NULL encryption algorithm is a convenient way to represent the option of not applying encryption in ESP (or in any other context where this is needed) [r013].

Number Theory   Traditionally, that branch of pure mathematics concerned with the properties of integers and contains many open problems that are easily understood even by nonmathematicians. More generally, the field has come to be concerned with a wider class of problems that arose naturally from the study of integers. Number theory may be subdivided into several fields according to the methods used and the questions investigated. There are several general subcategories within Number Theory including [r377]

- Algebraic number theory
- Analytic number theory
- Computational number theory Diophantine approximation
- Diophantine equations
- Integer sequences
- Modular arithmetic
- Modular forms
- Number theoretic algorithms

NVD   See National Vulnerability Database

NVLAP   See National Voluntary Laboratory Accreditation Program

NX   See Central Processing Unit (CPU) No Execute Bit

NZDSF   See Non-Zero-Dispersion-Shifted Fiber

O

○ ○

O&M Alarm (GSM context) Warning information—that is, alarms directed to the Operation & Maintenance System (OMS), concerning the operation and maintenance of Base Station Subsystem (BSS) network elements [r011].

OAKLEY (aka Oakley Protocol) A key establishment protocol [proposed for IPsec but superseded by IPsec Key Exchange (IKE)] based on the Diffie–Hellman algorithm and designed to be a compatible component of Internet Security Association and Key Management Protocol (ISAKMP) [r378, r013]. OAKLEY establishes a shared key with an assigned identifier and associated authenticated identities for parties. That is, OAKLEY provides authentication service to ensure the entities of each other's identity, even if the Diffie–Hellman exchange is threatened by active wiretapping. Also, it provides public-key forward secrecy for the shared key and supports key updates, incorporation of keys distributed by out-of-band mechanisms, and user-defined abstract group structures for use with Diffie–Hellman [r013]. Oakley provides the important security property of Perfect Forward Secrecy (PFS).

OATH Algorithm OATH algorithm (http://openauthentication.org), (Initiative for Open Authentication) is the industry-standard One-Time Password (OTP) algorithm ensuring compatible interoperability with any current or future OATH-compatible device.

Object An entity in an object-oriented model, such as Service-Oriented Architecture (SOA) or Common Object Request Broker Architecture (CORBA).

Minoli–Cordovana's Authoritative Computer and Network Security Dictionary. By Daniel Minoli and James Cordovana
Copyright © 2006 John Wiley & Sons, Inc.

Object Identifier (OID)   An official, globally unique name for a thing, written as a sequence of integers [which are formed and assigned as defined in the Abstract Syntax Notation One (ASN.1) standard] and used to reference the thing in abstract specifications and during negotiation of security services in a protocol [r013]. Objects named by OIDs are leaves of the object identifier tree (which is similar to but different from the X.500 Directory Information Tree). Each arc (i.e., each branch of the tree) is labeled with a non-negative integer. An OID is the sequence of integers on the path leading from the root of the tree to a named object. The OID tree has three arcs immediately below the root: {0} for use by the International Telecommunications Union (ITU), {1} for use by the International Organization for Standardization (ISO), and {2} for use by both jointly.

Object Management Group (OMG)   A not-for-profit computer industry specifications consortium; members define and maintain the Unified Modeling Language™ (UML) specification that the OMG publishes in the series of documents. Software providers build tools that conform to these specifications [r379].

Object Method   An action that can be invoked on a resource (e.g., a file system may have read, write, and execute object methods) [r068a].

Object Request Brokers (ORBs)   An ORB establishes a client/server connection between two objects across a network with the goal of allowing applications, which may be running on completely different operating systems, to exchange and act on information. ORBs (i) abstractly define an application's interfaces so that other applications can use them; (ii) discover applications and the associated interfaces elsewhere in a network; and, (iii) allow applications to message and respond to one another.

Neither the programmers who create the objects, nor the object themselves, nor the end-users who use them need to know anything about the other objects in the network because the ORB is designed to handle the interactions. Interfaces are defined with an interface definition language. Common Object Request Broker Architecture (CORBA) is one example of an attempt at ORB specifications.

ORBs were developed before the XML-based protocol Simple Object Application Protocol (SOAP), which attempts to achieve similar goals (some vendors now offer tools to connect ORB and Web-services-based systems).

Object Reuse   The reassignment and reuse of a storage medium (e.g., page frame, disk sector, magnetic tape) that once contained one or more (information) objects. To be securely reused and assigned to a new subject, storage media must contain no residual data (magnetic remanence) from the object(s) previously contained in the media [r120].

Obligation   (financial term) Any debt, written promise, or duty.

Obsolescence   A loss in the utility of an asset due to the development of improved or superior equipment, but not due to physical deterioration [r009].

Obstruction   A threat action that interrupts delivery of system services by hindering system operations through interference of overloading systems [r013].

Occupational Safety and Health Act (OSHA)   A federal law that requires compliance by all to whom it is applicable. OSHA is designed to protect employees at their workplace and covers many types of possible job hazards, including electrical safety. OSHA is not an approval or testing agency [r033].

OCP   See Open Pluggable Edge Services (OPES) Callout Protocol

OCSP   See On-Line Certificate Status Protocol

Octet   A data unit of eight bits (a byte). This term is used in networking [especially in Open System Interconnect Reference Model (OSIRM) standards] in preference to "byte," because some systems use "byte" for data storage units of a size other than eight [r013].

ODBC   See Open Database Connectivity

ODRL   See Open Digital Rights Language

OFAC See Office of Foreign Assets Control

OFDM See Orthogonal Frequency Division Multiplexing

Office of Foreign Assets Control (OFAC) OFAC administers economic sanctions against governments, individuals and entities that are prohibited from engaging in transactions in the United States or with U.S. persons. These sanctions govern all U.S. persons and corporations, wherever they are located. OFAC maintains a list of named persons subject to sanctions known as the SDN List (Specially Designated Nationals and Blocked Persons).

Office of Management and Budget (OMB) Circular A-130 Management of Federal Information Resources. November 2000. U.S. Government Publications of Interest to Risk Management.

Official Records Individual documents (electronic, paper, or other media) that have a legally defined retention period stated in a law, regulation, or statute.

Off-Line Storage Storage not currently accessible to the computer, such as files on a diskette that is not in the diskette drive [r380].

Off-Site Storage Facilities for housing materials away from where they are used; remote storage. Off-site storage may be used to house inactive records, reducing the costs of storing records in expensive office areas to less expensive warehouse facilities. Off-site storage may also be used to keep copies of vital (essential) records to increase the chances that at least one copy will survive a disaster [r068].

Off-the-Record Messaging A system for on-line communication that behaves like a casual, "off-the-record" conversation. In particular [r381]:

- If no one was actively listening in at the time the conversation was taking place, then the conversation's contents are secure forever (unless of course the sender or the receiver divulges the information).
- Even if the receiver (or the sender) goes to a third party with the contents of the conversation, the third party will have to take his word for it. There's nothing that can be used to prove the authenticity of the messages to him.
- On the other hand, the sender and the receiver are assured of the authenticity of each other's messages.

Off-the-Record Secure Messaging In order to achieve "Off-the-record" secure messaging one needs to use cryptographic techniques more esoteric than plain old public-key encryption and signatures, including the following [r381]:

- Perfect forward secrecy: Ensuring that key compromise cannot be used to recover past messages.
- Message authentication codes: Enabling the sender and the receiver to be assured of the authenticity of each others' messages, without third parties being able to.
- Malleable encryption: Allowing anyone to easily modify transcripts of encrypted conversations, to further aid the sender's repudiability as being the originator.

OGSA See Open Grid Services Architecture

OGSI See Open Grid Services Infrastructure

Ohnosecond A colloquialism referring to that minuscule fraction of time in which you realize that your information has been compromised [r013].

OID See Object Identifier

OIF See Optical Internetworking Forum

OMB See Office of Management and Budget

OMC See Operation & Maintenance Center

OMG See Object Management Group

OMS See Operation & Maintenance System

On-Line Certificate Status Protocol (OCSP) An Internet protocol used by a client to obtain from a server the validity status and other information concerning a digital certificate. In some applications, such as those involving high-value commercial transactions, it may be necessary to obtain certificate revocation status that is more timely than is possible with Certificate Revocation Lists (CRLs) or to obtain other kinds of status information. OCSP may be used to determine the current revocation status of a digital certificate, in lieu of or as a supplement to checking against a periodic CRL. An OCSP client issues a status request to an OCSP server and suspends acceptance of the certificate in question until the server provides a response [r013].

On-line Storage Techniques for storing and retrieving data on media that is mounted and directly accessible to the system. On-line storage connotes facilities used principally for storage of data, rather than system memory used as cache or for loading the operating system and applications. Hard drives are examples of on-line storage [r067].

One-Time Pad An encryption algorithm in which the key is a random sequence of symbols and each symbol is used for encryption only one time. Thus, the one-time pad encrypts only one plaintext symbol to produce only one ciphertext symbol. A copy of the key is used similarly for decryption. To ensure one-time use, the copy of the key used for encryption is destroyed after use, as is the copy used for decryption. This is the only encryption algorithm that is truly unbreakable, even given unlimited resources for cryptanalysis, but key management costs and synchronization problems make it impractical except in special situations [r013].

one-time password (OTP) A unique password or key string that can only be used once. One-time passwords are often implemented by one-time password tokens. Another implementation could be a card (or list) of password strings, where the user strikes through each element on the list upon using the password string to access the system.

One-Time Password (OTP) Authentication for system access (login) and other applications requiring authentication that is secure against passive attacks based on replaying captured reusable passwords ("replay attack"). The idea behind OTP authentication was first proposed by Leslie Lamport [r382]. The authentication system for OTP uses a secret pass-phrase to generate a sequence of one-time (single-use) passwords. With this system, the user's secret pass-phrase never needs to cross the network at any time such as during authentication or during pass-phrase changes. Thus, it is not vulnerable to replay attacks. Added security is provided by the property that no secret information need be stored on any system, including the server being protected. The OTP system protects against external passive attacks against the authentication subsystem. It does not prevent a network eavesdropper from gaining access to private information and does not provide protection against either "social engineering" or active attacks [r383, r384].

The use of the OTP system only provides protections against passive eavesdropping/replay attacks. It does not provide for the privacy of transmitted data, and it does not provide protection against active attacks such as session hijacking that are known to be present in the current Internet [r383]. The use of IP Security (IPsec) is recommended to protect against Transmission Control Protocol (TCP) session hijacking [r384].

One-Time Password (OTP)—Supporting Devices Potential devices to support OTP algorithms include Java smart cards, Universal Serial Bus (USB) dongles, and Global System for Mobile Communication (GSM) Subscriber Identity Module (SIM) cards (or cell phones in general). This is technology now under development.

one time password vs. One-Time Password Not capitalized: A "one-time password" is a simple authentication technique in which each password is used only once as authentication information that verifies an identity. This technique counters the threat of a replay attack that uses passwords captured by wiretapping [r013].

Capitalized: "One-Time Password" is an Internet protocol (described in RFC 1938) that is based on S/KEY (described in RFC 1760) and uses a cryptographic hash function to generate one-time passwords for use as authentication information in system login and in other processes that need protection against replay attacks [r385, r013].

One-Time Password Fob See One-Time Password Token

One-Time Password Token   A type of access token that creates and displays a unique password or key string for every access attempt. Often, the one-time password changes based on a set schedule. RSA Security's SecureID is an example.

One-to-One Backup   (MPLS context) A local repair method in which a backup Label Switched Path (LSP) is separately created for each protected LSP at a Point of Local Repair (PLR) [r083].

One-Way Encryption   Irreversible transformation of plaintext to ciphertext, such that the plaintext cannot be recovered from the ciphertext by other than exhaustive procedures even if the cryptographic key is known [r013].

One-Way Function   A (mathematical) function, f, which is easy to compute, but which for a general value y in the range, it is computationally difficult to find a value x in the domain such that $f(x) = y$. There may be a few values of y for which finding x is not computationally difficult [r061, r013].

One-Way Hash   See One-Way Hash Function

One-Way Hash Function   (aka one-way hash) A one-way transformation that converts an arbitrary amount of data into a fixed-length hash. It is computationally hard to reverse the transformation or to find collisions. Message Digest 5 (MD5) and Secure Hash Algorithm (SHA) are examples of one-way hash functions [r039].

Opaque Optical Networks   (optical transmission term) Networks deployed until recently where each link is optically isolated by transponders doing optical-to-electrical-to-optical conversions. They provide regeneration with retiming and reshaping, also called 3R, which eliminates transparency to bit rates and frame format. These transponders are quite expensive and their lack of transparency also constrains the rapid introduction of new services [r365]. It follows that there are strong motivators to introduce "domains of transparency" via all-optical subnetworks. Generalized Multiprotocol Label Switching (GMPLS) may be used for Control Plane mechanisms.

Open   (Presence Services context) A distinguished value of the status marker. In the context of instant messages, this value means that the associated instant inbox address, if any, corresponds to an instant inbox that is ready to accept an instant message. This value may have an analogous meaning for other communication means, but any such meaning is not defined by this model. Contrast with closed [r016].

Open Database Connectivity (ODBC)   A Microsoft designed protocol for relational database interfacing. Many consider ODBC to be a de facto standard programming interface for accessing database data. Because it is applied across many DataBase Management Systems (DBMSs) and applications, in principle (but not always in practice), communications between different platforms and DBMSs are possible using this interface.

Open Design   (aka Principle of Open Design) One of Saltzer and Schroeder's Design Principles. The security of a mechanism should not depend on the secrecy of its design or implementation. E.g., the security of a good encryption algorithm does not depend on the secrecy of its specification [r139a] (information in the software is usually public, and it is relatively easy to reverse engineer the software—e.g., one should not hide sensitive keys in software—do not rely on an algorithm staying secret: there is always someone who reveals or finds out the secret).

Open Digital Rights Language (ODRL)   A specification of an extensible language and vocabulary (data dictionary) for the expression of terms and conditions over any content including permissions, constraints, requirements, conditions, offers, and agreements with rights holders. Developed by the Open Mobile Alliance (www.openmobilealliance.org).

Open Grid Services Architecture (OGSA)   Defines the standard architecture for Grid Computing. Describes the overall structure and the services to be provided in grid environments. A distributed interaction and computing architecture that is based on the Grid Service concept, assuring interoperability on heterogeneous systems allowing different types of systems to communicate and share information. Building on Web Services standards, OGSA takes the view that a Grid Service is simply a Web Service that conforms to a particular set of conventions. OGSA manages resources across distributed heterogeneous platforms; it supports Quality of Service (QoS)-oriented Service Level Agreements; it provides a common base for autonomic management; defines open, published interfaces and protocols for interoperability of diverse resources; exploits industry standard integration technologies and leverages existing solutions where appropriate: the foundation of OGSA is rooted in Web Services [e.g., Simple Object Access Protocol (SOAP) and Web Services Description Language (WSDL)] document published by the Global Grid Forum (GGF) [r080].

Open Grid Services Architecture (OGSA) Architected Grid Services Layer   Services in this layer include: Discovery, Lifecycle, State Management, Service Groups, Factory, Notification, and Handle Map. These services are based on the Web Services layer [r080].

Open Grid Services Architecture (OGSA) Grid Applications Layer   The user-visible layer; it supports user applications [r080].

Open Grid Services Architecture (OGSA) Physical and Logical Resources Layer   Resources comprise the capabilities of the grid. Physical resources include servers, storage, and network; logical resources provide additional function by virtualizing and aggregating the resources in the physical layer. General-purpose middleware such as file systems, database managers, directories, and workflow managers provide these abstract services on top of the physical grid [r080].

Open Grid Services Architecture (OGSA) Web Services Layer   The specification defines Grid Services and builds on standard Web Services technology. It exploits the mechanisms of Web Services such as Extensible Markup Language (XML) and Web Service Definition Language (WSDL) to specify standard interfaces, behaviors, and interaction for all grid resources [r080].

Open Grid Services Infrastructure (OGSI)   A grid computing service specification published by the Global Grid Forum (GGF) that the keystone in the Open Grid Services Architecture (OGSA) architecture. Defines the standard interfaces and behaviors of a Grid Service, building on a Web Services baseline. Defines mechanisms for creating, managing, and exchanging information among Grid Services. This approach provides a common and open standards-based mechanism to access various Grid Services using existing industry standards such as Simple Object Access Protocol (SOAP), Extensible Markup Language (XML), and WS-Security [r080].

Open Grid Services Infrastructure (OGSI) Factory   A mechanism (interface) that provides a way to create new Grid Services. Factories may create temporary instances of limited function, such as a scheduler creating a service to represent the execution of a particular job, or they may create longer-lived services such as a local replica of a frequently used data set [r080].

Open Grid Services Infrastructure (OGSI) HandleMap   Deals with service identity. When factories are used to create a new instance of a Grid Service, the factory returns the identity of the newly instantiated service. This identity is composed of two parts, a Grid Service Handle (GSH) and a Grid Service Reference (GSR). A GSH provides a permanent reference to the Grid Service indefinitely; GSR can change within the Grid Services lifetime [r080].

Open Grid Services Infrastructure (OGSI) Life Cycle   A mechanism architected to prevent Grid Services from consuming resources indefinitely without requiring a large scale distributed "garbage collection" scavenger. Every Grid Service has a termination time set by the service creator or factory. Because Grid Services may be transient, Grid Service instances are created with a specified lifetime [r080].

Open Grid Services Infrastructure (OGSI) Notification   Services interact with one another by exchanging messages based on service invocation. The state information that is modeled for Grid Services changes as the system runs. Many interactions between Grid Services require dynamic monitoring of changing state. Notification applies a traditional publish/subscribe paradigm to this monitoring [r080].

Open Grid Services Infrastructure (OGSI) Service Groups   Service groups are collections of Grid Services that are indexed (using Service Data described above) for some specific purpose [r080].

Open Grid Services Infrastructure (OGSI) State Management   A framework for representing Grid Services' "state" along with a mechanism for inspecting or modifying that state, named Find/SetServiceData [r080].

Open Pluggable Edge Services (OPES)   The OPES architecture described in RFC 3835 enables cooperative application services (OPES services) between a data provider, a data consumer, and zero or more OPES processors. The application services under consideration analyze and possibly transform application-level messages exchanged between the data provider and the data consumer. The OPES processor can delegate the responsibility of service execution by communicating with callout servers. As described in RFC 3836, an OPES processor invokes and communicates with services on a callout server by using an OPES callout protocol (OCP) [r386].

As an application proxy, the OPES processor proxies a single application protocol or converts from one application protocol to another. At the same time, OPES processor may be an OCP client, using OCP to facilitate adaptation of proxied messages at callout servers.

The OPES processor works with messages from application protocols and may relay information about those application messages to a callout server. OCP is also an application protocol. Thus, protocol elements such as "message," "connection," or "transaction" exist in OCP and other application protocols [r386].

Open Pluggable Edge Services (OPES) Callout Protocol (OCP)   A protocol that marshals application messages from other communication protocols. An OPES intermediary sends original application messages to a callout server; the callout server sends adapted application messages back to the processor. OCP is designed with typical adaptation tasks in mind (e.g., virus and spam management, language and format translation, message anonymization, or advertisement manipulation). The OCP Core (RFC 4037) consists of application-agnostic mechanisms essential for efficient support of typical adaptations [r386].

Open Relay   Server that allows anyone from anywhere to send e-mail through an e-mail server, which accounts for a large majority of spam. This is a frequent tactic of commercial spammers who are trying to use a third-party mail server to conceal the source of their messages or bypass an existing block against them [r216].

Open Security   Environment that does not provide sufficient assurance that applications and equipment are protected against the introduction of malicious logic prior to or during the operation of a system [r057].

Open Security Environment   (U.S. Department of Defense context) A system environment that meets at least one of the following conditions:

- Application developers (including maintainers) do not have sufficient clearance or authorization to provide an acceptable presumption that they have not introduced malicious logic.
- Configuration control does not provide sufficient assurance that applications and the equipment are protected against the introduction of malicious logic prior to and during the operation of system applications [r013, r120].

Open Shortest-Path First (OSPF)   A link-state, routing protocol; an Internal Gateway protocol (IGP) defined in RFC 1583 and RFC 1793. The multicast version, Multicast OSPF (MOSPF), is defined in RFC 1584 (some routing protocols are distance-vector type of protocols).

Open Source Software (OSS)   Any software in which the source code is available for users to look at, modify, and/or compile. There are open source operating systems, compilers, cryptographic libraries, and so on. An advantage to open source is that the source can be analyzed for the presence of backdoors and other malicious code. The code can then be compiled and the resulting program used.

Open Systems Interconnection (OSI) Reference Model (OSIRM)   A set of internationally accepted standards that define a protocol model that is comprised of seven hierarchically dependent layers. It is the foundation of protocol development work by the various standards agencies. A joint International Organization for Standardization (ISO)/International Telecommunications Union (ITU) standard [r160] for a seven-layer, architectural communication framework for interconnection of computers in networks. OSIRM-based standards include communication protocols that are mostly incompatible with the Internet Protocol Suite, but also include security models, such as X.509, that are used in the Internet. The OSIRM layers, from highest to lowest, are (7) Application, (6) Presentation, (5) Session, (4) Transport, (3) Network, (2) Data Link, and (1) Physical. In this Glossary, these layers are referred to by number to avoid confusing them with Internet Protocol Suite layers, which are referred to by name. The model, originally developed in the 1980s, is defined in the following four documents:

ISO/IEC 7498-1:1994: Information technology—Open Systems Interconnection—Basic Reference Model: The Basic Model

ISO 7498-2:1989: Information processing systems—Open Systems Interconnection—Basic Reference Model, Part 2: Security Architecture

ISO/IEC 7498-3:1997: Information technology—Open Systems Interconnection—Basic Reference Model: Naming and addressing

ISO/IEC 7498-4:1989: Information processing systems—Open Systems Interconnection—Basic Reference Model, Part 4: Management framework

Open Systems Interconnection (OSI) Standards   (aka OSIRM standards) Networking standards defined by the International organization for Standardization (ISO) to support the Open Systems Interconnection Reference Model (OSIRM) architecture.

Open Systems Security   Provision of tools for the secure internetworking of open systems.

Operating Sytstem (OS)   Middleware code that manages resources on a computer and runs over the processor's hardware. The OS allows application to execute without having to be concerned about the low-level details of the hardware platform (chip).

Operating System (OS) Fingerprinting   Techniques (used by hackers) to infer the kind of OS that a processor is utilizing.

Operating System (OS) Migration   Mechanisms to migrate PCs and servers from an OS to a new one (e.g., from Unix to Linux).

Operating Temperature   (optical transmission term) The temperature range (°C) over which the device can be operated and maintain its specifications.

Operation & Maintenance Center (OMC)   (GSM context) The Global System for Mobile Communication (GSM) network is monitored and controlled from a central point, specifically from the OMC. The OMC is part of the Operation & Maintenance System (OMS) [r011]. The OMC is responsible for error management, configuration management, performance management, and administration management and offers remote access to different network components [r014].

Operation & Maintenance System (OMS)   (GSM context) After the Network Subsystem (NSS) and the Station Subsystem (BSS), the Operation & Maintenance System is the third subnet within Global System for Mobile Communication (GSM). It guarantees network supervision and administration [r011].

Operation Subsystem (OSS)   Part of the Operation & Maintenance System (OMS) within Global System for Mobile Communication (GSM).

Operational Data Security   The protection of data

from either accidental or unauthorized, intentional modification, destruction, or disclosure during input, processing, or output operations [r057].

Operational Integrity   A synonym for "system integrity"; emphasizes the actual performance of system functions rather than just the ability to perform them [r013].

Operations Security (OPSEC)   A process to identify, control, and protect evidence of the planning and execution of sensitive activities and operations, and thereby prevent potential adversaries from gaining knowledge of capabilities and intentions [r013].

Operations System   A physical block which performs operations systems functions (OSFs).

Operations Systems Function (OSF)   A function block that processes information related to the telecommunications management for the purpose of monitoring/coordinating and/or controlling telecommunication functions including management functions [i.e. the Telecommunications Management Network (TMN) itself] [r068a].

Operations Systems Support (OSS)   (aka Operations Support System) The back-office software used for configuration, performance, fault, accounting, and security management [r068a].

OPES   See Open Pluggable Edge Services

OPSEC   See Operations Security

Optical Amplifier   (optical transmission term) A device that amplifies the input optical signal without converting it to electrical form.

Optical Fiber, Newer Generation   (optical transmission term) Examples include Extended Wavelength Band (EWB)/dispersion-flattened fibers that allow the utilization of wavelengths farther from the optimum wavelength without pulse spreading; and fiber that allow the energy to travel further into the cladding, creating a small amount of dispersion to counter four-wave mixing.

Optical Impairments   (optical transmission term) Impairments can be classified into two categories, linear and nonlinear. Linear effects are independent of signal power and affect wavelengths individually. Amplifier spontaneous emission (ASE), polarization mode dispersion (PMD), and chromatic dispersion are examples. Nonlinearities are significantly more complex: they generate not only impairments on each channel, but also crosstalk between channels [r349].

Optical Internetworking Forum (OIF)   (optical transmission term) An industry-bred organization consisting of several hundred equipment manufacturers, telecom service providers, and users whose goal is to foster interoperability among optical equipment. It developed the optical UNI 1.0.

Optical Layer Cross-Connect (OLXC)   (optical transmission term) A crossconnect system (a transmission-level network element) that operates at the optical level. In effect, a "slow" (crossconnect-speed) optical switch.

Optical Mode   (optical transmission term) A "ray" of light. Light entering a waveguide can be regarded as confined and is referred to as an optical mode. The properties of the optical mode are determined from the characteristics of the propagating light and the refractive indices of the absorbing cladding and/or substrate regions. Propagation of the confined mode can be defined unambiguously by a property of the mode called its effective index. Propagation is a function of the wavelength.

Observations show that the optical mode is not totally confined in an ideal fashion within the waveguide region but also extends into the neighboring regions. The shape of the optical modes in these regions is referred to as evanescent.

Single-mode fibers transmit a single (one) mode of light. Multimode fibers transmit multiple modes. Telecom systems are based on single-mode fibers (multimode fibers find some applications in short-run applications in data centers, central offices, and inter-rack and/or collocated inter-rack cabling.)

Propagation is a function of the wavelength. The cut-off wavelength is the wavelength at which an optical fiber operates as singlemode: at wavelengths shorter than cut-off several optical modes may propagate and the fiber operates as multimode. As the cut-off wavelength is approached (usually around 100 nanometers), progressively fewer modes may propagate until, at "Cut-off," only the fundamental mode may propagate. At wavelengths longer than cut-off, the guidance of the fundamental mode becomes progressively weaker until eventually (usually at a wavelength several hundred nanometers above cut-off) the fiber ceases to guide—the fiber loses all optical functionality.

Optical Multiplexer   (optical transmission term) A device that combines two or more optical wavelengths into a single output or fiber.

Optical Routing-Related Functions (optical transmission term) Functions include [r365]: (i) *Adaptation*. These are the functions done at the edges of the subnetwork that transform the incoming optical channel into the physical wavelength to be transported through the subnetwork. (ii) *Connectivity*. This defines which pairs of edge Adaptation functions can be interconnected through the subnetwork.

Optimal Asymmetric Encryption Padding (OAEP)   A method for encoding messages developed by M. Bellare and P. Rogaway. A message is encoded with OAEP and then encrypted with Rivest Shamir Adleman (RSA). This is provably secure in the random oracle model. Informally, this means that if hash functions are truly random, then an adversary who can recover such a message must be able to break RSA.

An OAEP encoded message consists of a "masked data" string concatenated with a "masked random number". In the simplest form of OAEP, the masked data is formed by taking the XOR of the plaintext message M and the hash G of a random string r. The masked random number is the XOR of r with the hash H of the masked data.

Often, OAEP is used to encode small items such as keys. There are other variations on OAEP (differing only slightly from the above) that include a feature called "plaintext awareness." This means that to construct a valid OAEP-encoded message, an adversary must know the original plaintext. To accomplish this, the plaintext message M is first padded (for example, with a string

of zeroes) before the masked data is formed. OAEP is supported in the ANSI X9.44, IEEE P1363, and Secure Electronic Transaction (SET) standards [r430].

ORA   See Organizational Registration Authority

Oracle' 10g Family   10g family of "grid-aware" products; focuses on databases. Oracle's own brand of grid computing: a database system that comprises multiple nodes and lets IT planners shift database resources between them [r080].

ORBs   See Object Request Brokers

Organization for the Advancement of Structured Information Standards (OASIS)   Industry advocacy group that advances a number of Web Services constructs, including Security Assertion Markup Language (SAML).

Organizational Certificate   A type of Multilevel Information System Security Initiative (MISSI) X.509 public-key certificate that is issued to support organizational message handling for the U.S. Government's Defense Message System [r013].

Organizational Registration Authority (ORA) (General context) A registration authority (RA) for an organization.

[Multilevel Information System Security Initiative (MISSI) context] The MISSI implementation of RA. A MISSI end entity that (a) assists a policy creation authority (PCA), Certification Authority (CA), or subordinate certification authority (SCA) to register other end entities, by gathering, verifying, and entering data and forwarding it to the signing authority and (b) may also assist with card management functions. An ORA is a local administrative authority, and the term refers both to the office or role, and to the person who fills that office. An ORA does not sign certificates, Certificate Revocation Lists (CRLs), or Compromised Key Lists (CKLs) [r013].

Origin Server   The server on which a given resource resides or is to be created.

Orthogonal Frequency Division Multiplexing (OFDM)   Transmission technology employed in IEEE 802.11a Wireless Local Area Networks (WLANs).

Orthogonal Variable Spreading Factor Codes (OVSF) (3G Wireless context) Codes used to spread data from its original bandwidth to the bandwidth available. These codes show no cross correlation behavior, i.e., they are fully independent of each other [r007].

OS See Operating System

OSF See Operations Systems Function

OSHA See Occupational Safety and Health Act

OSIRM See Open Systems Interconnection Reference Model

OSPF See Open Shortest-Path First

OSS See Operation Subsystem or Open Source Software or Operations Systems Support

Other Presence Markup (Presence Services context) any additional information included in the presence information of a presentity [r015].

OTP See One-Time Password

Out-of-Band Transfer of information using a channel that is outside (i.e., separate from) the channel that is normally used (e.g., covert channel). Out-of-band mechanisms are often used to distribute shared secrets (e.g., a symmetric key) or other sensitive information items (e.g., a root key) that are needed to initialize or otherwise enable the operation of cryptography or other security mechanisms [r013].

Out of Contact (instant messaging/presence context) A situation in which some entity and the presence service cannot communicate [r027].

Outage Unavailability of a service or resource, e.g., a telecom service.

Outbound Port Filtering from the Provider Security technique that involves blocking connections to servers outside the provider's control by blocking Transmission Control Protocol (TCP) ports that are commonly used for messaging functions. Different providers have different theories about this. Some prohibit their customers from accessing external Simple Mail Transport Protocol (SMTP) servers for message submission, but they permit the use of the mail submission protocol with sender authentication. Others try to block all outgoing messaging-related protocols, including remote mail retrieval protocols; however, this is less common with public-address services than those that are dependent on private addresses and Network Address Translation (NAT). If this type of filtering is present, especially with "Client only, public address" and "Full Internet Connectivity" services, the provider must indicate that fact. Still others may divert (reroute) outbound e-mail traffic to their own servers, on the theory that this eliminates the need for reconfiguring portable machines as they connect from a different network location. Again, such diversion must be disclosed, especially since it can have significant security and privacy implications. More generally, filters that block some or all mail being sent to (or submitted to) remote systems (other than via provider-supported servers), or that attempt to divert that traffic to their own servers, are, as discussed above, becoming common and should be disclosed [r034].

Outbound Proxy (SIP context) A proxy that receives requests from a client, even though it may not be the server resolved by the Request-Uniform Resource Identifier (URI). Typically, a User Agent (UA) is manually configured with an outbound proxy, or can learn about one through auto-configuration protocols [r025].

Output Feedback (OFB) A block cipher mode [r116] that modifies electronic codebook mode to operate on plaintext segments of variable length less than or equal to the block length. This mode operates by directly using the algorithm's previously generated output block as the algorithm's next input block (i.e., by "feeding back" the output block) and combining (exclusive OR-ing) the output block with the next plaintext segment (of block length or less) to form the next ciphertext segment [r013].

Outside Attack An attack initiated from outside the perimeter, by an unauthorized or illegitimate user of the system (an "outsider").

Overhead Due to Encryption While physical-level encryption does not impact the message length and, consequently the required channel bandwidth, network layer encryption (e.g., IPsec) does impact the message length and required network bandwidth because of the overhead involved in the tunneling process (that is, the encapsulation of an IP datagram/packet inside another packet. This is particularly problematic for short packets (small payload) such as for Voice over IP (VoIP) applications.

Overload   Degradation of a system's operation by placing excess burden on its performance capabilities.

Overwriting   Process of writing patterns of data over data stored on a magnetic medium.

OVSF   See Orthogonal Variable Spreading Factor Codes

Own Link   Home link. In Mobile IP, the link in which the mobile node resides in its network. The mobile node uses the own link prefix to create its own address [r008].

P3P See Platform for Privacy Preferences

PA See Presence Agent

PAA See Policy Approving Authority

PACCH See Packet Associated Control Channel

Packet (aka Protocol Data Unit or datagram) Limited-length unit of data formed by the network, transport, presentation, or application layer [layers 3–7 of the Open System Interconnection Reference Model (OSIRM)] in a networked computer system. Data are transported over the network, and larger amounts of data are broken into shorter units and placed into packets [r057]. A packet consists of a header and payload [r008].

Packet Assembler/Dissembler (PAD) (GSM context) A device that establishes a connection to a packet-switched network [r011].

Packet Associated Control Channel (PACCH) (GSM context) A channel that serves as the signaling channel during a packet data transmission [r014].

Packet Control Unit (PCU) (GSM context) A unit that takes over different Channel Access Control functions, such as channel request and channel assignment [r014].

Packet Data Channel (PDCH) (GSM context) A channel that is made available to the Mobile Station simultaneously with the Network Reply for the data transport to the Base Station [r014].

Packet Data Network (PDN) (GSM context) A data network based on the X.25 or the Internet Protocol (IP) and behaves like the Internet [r014].

Packet Data Protocol (PDP) (3G Wireless context) Protocol used to perform signaling tasks in

General Packet Radio Service (GPRS). GPRS is the enhancement to Global System for Mobile Communication (GSM) to provide packet data services to GSM subscribers. GPRS aims at making efficient use of GSM radio resource for bursty packet data transfer; this is in contrast to conventional circuit switched data services available in GSM. GPRS operator can allocate certain number of time slots, called packet data channels (PDCHs), in each Time Division Multiple Access (TDMA) frame (of 8 time slots) of a particular carrier frequency for packet data services. The actual number of PDCHs depends on the volume of packet data traffic in the cell. The data rate for each PDCH varies between 9.05 kbps and 21.4 kbps, depending on the coding scheme used. A special multiframe structure has been defined for GPRS. It specifies a multiframe of 52 TDMA frames which is divided into 12 blocks of 4 TDMA frames each. Each of these blocks can transfer one RLC block over the air interface. Resource assignment to any terminal is based on these blocks of 4 TDMA frames. If the mobile terminal has multislot capability, it can simultaneously receive data on more than one PDCHs. GPRS introduces two new network elements, namely Serving GPRS Support Node (SGSN) and Gateway GPRS Support Node (GGSN), in the GSM architecture in order to support packet data services. SGSN maintains the mobility context for the mobile station (MS) and also performs authentication procedures. SGSN is connected to the Base Station Subsystem (BSS) over a frame relay network on one side and to the GGSN over IP backbone [called core network (CN)] on the other side. GGSN acts as a gateway to public data networks such as the Internet. Note that the GSM BSS is shared by GPRS and GSM circuit switched services. Data packets are transported between SGSN and GGSN using IP tunnels. For example, an IP packet destined to the MS is encapsulated into another IP packet by GGSN. The outer IP header has serving SGSN's IP address as the destination address. The encapsulated packet is then forwarded through the CN using hop-by-hop forwarding. At SGSN, the outer IP header is stripped. The original packet is then forwarded by SGSN to MS via appropriate BSS using link layer procedures, i.e., over a radio access bearer. GPRS Tunneling Protocol (GTP) implemented at SGSN and GGSN is responsible for performing these tasks of encapsulation at GGSN and mapping onto appropriate radio access bearer at SGSN. PDP is used to perform signaling tasks of GTP [r188].

Although GPRS gives to the user the impression of "always-on" Internet connectivity, in reality mobile terminals need to explicitly create data sessions, on demand, to the GPRS part of the GSM network, in order to enable data (as opposed to voice) traffic to flow from and to the mobile phones. For each such session to a data network, such as the Internet, some sort of session description information needs to exist to enable agreement on the characteristics of any data flow between the GSM/GPRS network and the mobile terminal. That session description is called the PDP context [r189].

Packet Data Protocol Address (PDP-Address) (3G Wireless context) The address all data of a particular active service is sent to [r007]. The address where all Protocol Data of a specific active service are sent to [r014].

Packet Data Protocol Context (PDP-Context) (GSM context) A Packet Data Protocol Context is a service profile and it is located in the Serving GPRS Support Node (SGSN). This service profile is necessary for exchanging Protocol Data Units (PDUs) between the mobile station and the Gateway General Packet Radio Services (GPRS) Support Node (GGSN) [r014].

Packet Data Traffic Channel (PDTCH) (GSM context) Channel used for the transmission of General Packet Radio Services (GPRS) data. One PDTCH corresponds to the resource available to a mobile station for the transmission of payload data on a physical channel [r014].

Packet Filtering A feature incorporated into routers and Layer 2 switches to limit the flow of information based on predetermined policy such as source, destination, or type of service being provided by the network. Packet filters allows the administrator limit protocol-specific traffic to one network segment and perform many other traffic/security functions.

Packet-Filtering Firewalls Firewalls that use rules based on a packets source, destination, port, or other basic information to determine whether or not to allow it into the network. More advanced stateful packet filtering firewalls have access to additional information to make their forwarding/deny decisions [r057, r062].

Packet Sniffer A device or program that monitors the information traveling between computers on a network [r057]. This tool (hardware or software) can be used to (mis)appropriate valid Transmission Control Protocol/Internet Protocol (TCP/IP) network addresses by reading packets (units of data). Malicious code can then be labeled with the trusted network address and sent through the network unquestioned [r062].

Packet-Switched (PS) Mode (GSM context) The packet-switched transmission mode segments data into small packets before transmission. The packets can be transmitted across the network flexibly—that is, over different routes, according to the current network capacity. Therefore, PS is mainly suited for non-real-time applications like file transfer and e-mail. This mode is used in public data networks (X.25 networks) and IP networks (e.g., the Internet). However, progress in transmission and router technology now also allows the packet-switched transmission of real-time data, such as Internet telephony (Voice over IP) or video streaming. This is, among other things, the prerequisite for wireless multimedia services in 3G mobile radio networks (e.g., Universal Mobile Telecommunications System (UMTS)) [r011].

Packet-Switched Network (PSN) Typically a generic public network that supports information movement. It can be X.25-based, IP-based, or MultiProtocol Label Switching (MPLS)-based.

Packet Switching A communication technique (invented in the mid-1960s) that segments the transmitted data into individual units or "packets," each of which contains the destination address of the data. The goal is to achieve efficient transmission channel sharing, among multiple users and/or applications. Most typically this is perceived to be segmentation at Layer 3 (network layer) of the Open System Interconnection Reference Model (OSIRM); however, segmentation can take place at other layers. The packets are independently routed through the network and reassembled by the computer at the destination address.

Packet Timing Advance Control Channel (PTCCH) (GSM context) A Control Channel that finds and sends out the signaling delays [r014].

PAD See Packet Assembler/Dissembler

Page File After the boot sector of a partition, it is customary to skip the rest of the track and start the volume on the next track. Since this area is inaccessible to all but low-level disk viewers, it is a hiding spot for information and/or malware code.

Pagejacking A contraction of "Web page hijacking." A masquerade attack in which the attacker copies (steals) a home page or other material from the target server, rehosts the page on a server the attacker controls, and causes the rehosted page to be indexed by the major Web search services, thereby diverting browsers from the target server to the attacker's server [r013].

Paging Channel (PCH) (GSM context) A Common Control Channel in the downlink, broadcast by all base stations within a Location Area to notify a mobile subscriber of an incoming call [r011, r007].

Paging Control Channel (PCCH) (3G Wireless context) A downlink logical channel that is used for pagings.

Paging Indication Channel (PICH) (3G Wireless context) A downlink physical channel. It is used to transmit the Page Indicator for paging support [r007].

PAL See Phase Alternating Line

PAN See Primary Account Number

PAP See Password Authentication Protocol

Paper Asset   (financial term) An asset that is not readily usable or convertible to cash.

Parallel Search   (SIP context) In a parallel search, a proxy issues several requests to possible user locations upon receiving an incoming request. Rather than issuing one request and then waiting for the final response before issuing the next request as in a sequential search, a parallel search issues requests without waiting for the result of previous requests [r025].

Parameter Discovery   The process by which a host discovers additional operating parameters, including the link Maximum Transmission Unit (MTU) and the default hop limit for outbound Protocol Data Units (PDUs) [r024].

Parameters Discovery   Neighbors Discovery process that allows equipment to know configuration parameters, including link Maximum Transfer Unit (MTU) and the default hops limit for outgoing packets [r008].

Participant   An individual or organization that plays a role within a given public-key infrastructure (PKI) as a subscriber, relying party, Certification Authority (CA), Registration Authority (RA), certificate manufacturing authority, repository service provider, or similar entity [r011].

Partition   Before a storage device such as a hard drive can be used by the system, it must be partitioned. A partition is a portion of the whole drive. It defines the boundaries in which the file system can manage. A file system cannot be placed on a storage device without a designated partition [r084].

Partitioned Security Mode   A mode of operation of an information system, wherein all users have the clearance, but not necessarily formal access authorization and need-to-know, for all information handled by the system. This mode is defined in U.S. Department of Defense policy regarding system accreditation [r013, r196].

Partnership   (financial term) A type of unincorporated business organization in which multiple individuals, called general partners, manage the business and are equally liable for its debts. Other individuals called limited partners may invest but not be directly involved in management and are liable only to the extent of their investments. Unlike a limited liability company or a corporation, in a partnership the partners share equal responsibility for the company's profits and losses and for its debts and liabilities. The partnership itself does not pay income taxes, but each partner has to report their share of business profits or losses on their individual tax return [r009]. More generally, the term refers to a relationship of two or more entities conducting business for mutual benefit [r009].

Pass Phrase   (aka password) A secret data value, usually a character string, that is used as authentication information. A pass phrase is usually matched with a user identifier that is explicitly presented in the authentication process, but in some cases the identity may be implicit [r013].

Passback   A method for bypassing access control systems. For example: One person uses a key or keycard to enter a building, then passes the device back to another person who also uses it to gain entry. "Anti-passback" refers to features in access control systems designed to prevent this tactic [r062].

Passive Attack   Attack that does not result in an unauthorized state change. A passive attack seeks to learn or make use of information from the system but does not affect system resources. An example of this is wiretapping.

Passive Fingerprinting   A common technique attackers use when conducting reconnaissance. Passive fingerprinting is the act of trying to determine the type of system information from a captured data stream. Because each system has its own "quirks," it has been found that one can determine signatures/fingerprints by the default settings used in Transmission Control Protocol/Internet Protocol (TCP/IP) headers and in some ICMP message types. Tests can be performed using specially crafted TCP/IP packets, and depending on the response one can determine the remote system. Using this concept, a number of tools have been created to allow a person to remotely "fingerprint" a system to try to determine the operating system [r387].

Passive Threat   The threat of unauthorized disclosure of information without changing the state of the system. A type of threat that involves the interception, not the alteration, of information [r057].

Passive Wiretapping   (aka sniffing) The passive interception of data transmissions.

Password   (aka pass phrase) A secret data value, usually a character string, that is used as authentication information. A password is usually matched with a user identifier that is explicitly presented in the authentication process, but in some cases the identity may be implicit. Using a password as authentication information assumes that the password is known only by the system entity whose identity is being authenticated. Therefore, in a network environment where wiretapping is possible, simple authentication that relies on transmission of static (i.e., repetitively used) passwords as cleartext is often inadequate [r013].

Password Alternatives   Alternatives to traditional password based security include tokens, smart cards, and Single Sign-On (SSO).

Password Authentication Protocol (PAP)   A simple authentication mechanism in the Point-to-Point Protocol (PPP). In PAP, a user identifier and password are transmitted in cleartext [r395].

Password Reset   Mechanisms to reset user passwords. These mechanisms may be driven by a time-event, an infraction, or a user-request.

Password Rules   Security policies that specify parameters for passwords and rules for using them. A well-thought-out and stringently applied password policy can reduce the unauthorized use of system credentials. For example, the following could be the password rules for an enterprise:

- Passwords have to be at least 6 characters.
- Passwords must be alphanumeric.
- Passwords must contain at least one special character.
- Passwords need to be changed every 30 days.
- Password must not be written down.

Password Sniffing   Passive wiretapping, usually on a local area network, to gain knowledge of passwords.

Patch   Software code that replaces or updates other code. Frequently patches are used to correct security flaws. A small update released by a software manufacturer to fix known vulnerabilities (bugs) in existing programs [r200, r062].

Patch Management   Mechanisms to protect network systems from identified vulnerabilities and quickly deploy specific patches. Patches often require pre-distribution testing for possible conflicts.

Patent   The exclusive right, granted by the government, to make use of an invention or process for a specific period of time, usually 14 years.

Path Determination System   (IPv6 context) Procedure to select the route from the routing table the datagram will be forwarded through. That is, how the next router the datagram will be sent to is selected [r008].

Path Discovery   For a digital certificate, the process of finding a set of public-key certificates that comprise a certification path from a trusted key to that specific certificate [r013].

Path Maximum Transfer Unit (MTU)   (IPv6 context) Maximum IPv6 packet size that can be sent without using fragmentation between a source and a destination over an IPv6 network route. The route MTU equates with the smallest link MTU for all links in such route [r008]. Concept is also applicable to IPv4.

Path Overhead   Header bits used at Layer 1 of the Open Systems Interconnection Reference Model (OSIRM) in a Synchronous Optical Network (SONET) environment.

Path Validation   The process of validating (a) all of the digital certificates in a certification path and (b) the required relationships between those certificates, thus validating the contents of the last certificate on the path [r013].

Path Vector   A routing protocol's approach that involves the exchange of hops information sequences showing the path to follow in a route. For example, BGP-4 exchanges sequences of numbers of Autonomous Systems (ASs) [r008].

Path's Maximum Transfer Unit (MTU) Discovery   Process relating to the use of Too Big message by means of Internet Control Message Protocol v6 (ICMPv6) to discover the maximum IPv6 MTU value in all links between two devices [r008].

Payload Units (PU)   (3G Wireless context) In Radio Link Control (RLC), the Packet Data Units (PDUs) are segmented into smaller RLC Payload Units by higher layers, and reassembled in the opposite direction [r007].

Payment Card   (SET context) Collectively refers to credit cards, debit cards, charge cards, and bank cards issued by a financial institution, which reflects a relationship between the cardholder and the financial institution [r018].

Payment Gateway   (SET context) A system operated by an acquirer, or a third party designated by an acquirer, for the purpose of providing electronic commerce services to the merchants in support of the acquirer, and which interfaces to the acquirer to support the authorization, capture, and processing of merchant payment messages, including payment instructions from cardholders [r017, r013].

Payment Gateway Certification Authority   (SET context) A Certification Authority (CA) that issues digital certificates to payment gateways and is operated on behalf of a payment card brand, an acquirer, or another party according to brand rules. This Policy Certification Authority (PCA) issues a Certificate Revocation List (CRL) for compromised payment gateway certificates [r018, r013].

Payout Period   (financial term) Definition 1: Dividends per share divided by earnings per share. Definition 2: The early stage, before a project's startup costs and cumulative operating expenses have been recovered, during which cash flow is negative. Definition 3: The period during which annuity or retirement withdrawals are made [r009].

PBXs   See Private Branch Exchanges

PC   See Personal Computer

PC Card   [aka Personal Computer Memory Card International Association (PCMCIA) card] A type of credit card-sized, plug-in peripheral device that was originally developed to provide memory expansion for portable computers, but is also used for other kinds of functional expansion. The international PC Card Standard defines a nonproprietary form factor in three standard sizes—Types I, II, and III—each of which have a 68-pin interface between the card and the socket into which it plugs. All three types have the same length and width, roughly the size of a credit card, but differ in their thickness from 3.3 to 10.5 mm. Examples include storage modules, modems, device interface adapters, and cryptographic modules [r013].

PCCH   See Paging Control Channel

P-CCPCH   See Primary-Common Control Physical Channel

PCH   See Paging Channel

PCM   See Pulse Code Modulation

PCMCIA   See Personal Computer Memory Card International Association

P-complexity Problem   P stands for a class of decisional problems (problems for which one can answer "yes" or "no") for which any instance of the problem can be solved by a deterministic algorithm in time that can be bounded by a polynomial on the size of the input of the problem [r094].

PCPCH   See Physical Common Packet Channel

PCR   See Peak Cell Rate

PCS   See Physical Coding Sublayer or Personalization Center for SIM card

PCU   Packet Control Unit

PDCH   See Packet Data Channel

PDL   See Polarization Dependent Loss

PDN   See Packet Data Network

PDP   See Packet Data Protocol or MIDCOM Policy Decision Point

PDP-Address   See Packet Data Protocol Address

PDP-Context   See Packet Data Protocol Context

PDS   See PKI Disclosure Statement

PDSCH   See Physical Downlink Shared Channel

PDTCH   See Packet Data Traffic Channel

PDU See Protocol Data Unit

PE See Provider Edge

PE Device See Provider Edge device

Peak Cell Rate Traffic parameter used in Asynchronous Transfer Mode (ATM) services [e.g., Constant Bit Rate (CBR), Variable Bit Rate (VBR)] that corresponds to the maximum arrival rate, measured in cells.

PEAP See Protected EAP

PE-Based Virtual Private Networks (VPNs) A Layer 3 VPN approach in which a service provider network is used to interconnect customer sites using shared resources. Specifically, the Provider Edge (PE) device maintains VPN state, isolating users of one VPN from users of another. Because the PE device maintains all required VPN states, the Customer Edge (CE) device may behave as if it were connected to a private network. Specifically, the CE in a PE-based VPN must not require any changes or additional functionality to be connected to a Provider-Provisioned Virtual Private Network (PPVPN) instead of a private network [r082].

The PE devices know that certain traffic is VPN traffic. They forward the traffic (through tunnels) based on the destination IP address of the packet, and optionally based on other information in the IP header of the packet. The PE devices are themselves the tunnel endpoints. The tunnels may make use of various encapsulations to send traffic over the Service Provider (SP) network [such as, but not restricted to, Generic Routing Encapsulation (GRE), IP-in-IP, IPsec, or Multiprotocol Label Switching (MPLS) tunnels] [r081, r082].

Peer In the Extensible Authentication Protocol (EAP) context, this is the end of the link that responds to the authenticator. In IEEE 802.1X, this end is known as the supplicant.

Peer Entity Authentication The corroboration that a peer entity in an association is the one claimed [r160].

Peer Entity Authentication Service A security service that verifies an identity claimed by or for a system entity in an association. This service is used at the establishment of, or at times during, an association to confirm the identity of one entity to another, thus protecting against a masquerade by the first entity. However, unlike data origin authentication service, this service requires an association to exist between the two entities, and the corroboration provided by the service is valid only at the current time that the service is provided [r013].

Peer-to-Peer (P2P) Communication P2P communication is the communications that travel from one user's computer to another user's computer without being stored for later access on a server. E-mail is not a P2P communication since it travels from the sender to a server, and is retrieved by the recipient from the server. On-line chat, however, is a P2P communication since messages travel directly from one user to another [r200].

Peer-to-Peer (P2P) Computing P2P is concerned with the same general problem as Grid Computing, namely, the organization of resource sharing within virtual communities. Grid community focuses on aggregating distributed high-end machines such as clusters, whereas the P2P community concentrates on sharing low-end systems such as PCs connected to the Internet [r080].

PEM See Privacy Enhanced Mail

Penetration The successful unauthorized access to a host or other system; successful, repeatable, unauthorized access to a protected system resource.

Penetration Signature The description of a situation or set of conditions in which a penetration could occur or of system events that in conjunction can indicate the occurrence of a penetration in progress [r057].

Penetration Test A system test, often part of system certification, in which evaluators attempt to circumvent the security features of the system [r120]. Penetration testing may be performed under various constraints and conditions. However, for a Trusted Computer System Evaluation Criteria (TCSEC) evaluation, testers are assumed to have all system design and implementation documentation, including source code, manuals, and circuit diagrams, and to work under no greater constraints than those applied to ordinary users [r013].

PE-R   See Provider Edge Router

Perceived Severity   The seriousness of the problem as seen by the person reporting the trouble [r068a].

Perfect Forward Secrecy   The assurance that once the receiver has received the sender's message and destroyed his copy, it will be impossible for anyone else to decrypt it later on, even if all of the sender's and receiver's secrets (keys) become compromised [r381]. If a third party has compromised either the sender's or the receiver's computer at the time a message is being composed and sent (or received and read), then he can clearly read the message. However, once the compromise is detected and corrected, future messages should not be exposed. This means that encryption key material has to be generated "freshly," and not derived from some stored state. In addition, a compromise must never expose past messages [r381].

Performance Monitoring   The act of monitoring traffic for the purpose of evaluating a statistic of a metric related to the performance of the system. A performance monitoring system is comprised of traffic generators, measurement, data reduction, and reporting. The traffic generators may be natural sources, synthetic sources, or intrusive sources [r3573].

Perimeter   A security perimeter.

Perimeter-Based Security   The technique of securing a network by controlling access to all entry and exit points of the network. The collection of mechanisms being utilized to create the perimeter layer security may include firewalls, Intrusion Detection Systems (IDS), and other security tools [r057].

Perimeter Network   A network added between a protected network and an external network, in order to provide an additional layer of security. A perimeter network is sometimes called a Demilitarized Zone (DMZ) [r084].

Periods Processing   A mode of system operation in which information of different sensitivities is processed at distinctly different times by the same system, with the system being properly purged or sanitized between periods. [r013].

Permanent Virtual Channel Connection (PVCC)   A Virtual Channel Connection that is provisioned through some network management function and left up indefinitely.

Permanent Virtual Circuit (PVC)   In Asynchronous Transfer Mode (ATM) services, this is a link with static route defined in advance, usually by manual setup.

Permanent Virtual Path Connection (PVPC)   A Virtual Path Connection (VPC) is an Asynchronous Transfer Mode (ATM) connection where switching is performed on the Virtual Path Identifier (VPI) field only of each cell. A Permanent VPC is one that is provisioned through some network management function and left up indefinitely.

Permission   (aka authorization) A right that is granted to a system entity to access a system resource. Sometime the term permission is used interchangeably with the term authorization, but authorization is preferred in the Public-Key Infrastructure (PKI) context [r013] Also, user privileges in the Windows Operating System (OS) environment, such as shared folder permissions, printer permissions, Active Directory (AD) permissions, and so on.

Permutation   (aka transposition) The shuffling of the order in which characters (or bytes) appear.

Perpetrator   The entity that has performed the attack.

Persistent Cookie   A small file (known as a cookie) that is used to track user activity and maintain session state when accessing Web content. Unlike a session cookie, a persistent cookie is stored on the hard drive (instead of in memory) and has an expiration date.

Personal Computer Memory Card International Association (PCMCIA)   A group of manufacturers, developers, and vendors, founded in 1989 to standardize plug-in peripheral memory cards for personal computers and now extended to deal with any technology that works in the PC card form factor.

Personal Identification Number (PIN) A character string (authentication information) used as a password to gain access to a system resource. Despite the words "identification" and "number," a PIN seldom serves as a user identifier, and a PIN's characters are not necessarily all numeric [r013].

(GSM context) The Personal Identification Number is stored on a Global System for Mobile Communication (GSM) customer's Subscriber Identity Module (SIM) card. By keying in this code, the subscriber can enable his mobile station for use in a Public Land Mobile Network (PLMN) [r011].

Personality Label A set of Multilevel Information System Security Initiative (MISSI) X.509 public-key certificates that have the same subject Distinguished Name (DN), together with their associated private keys and usage specifications, that is stored on a FORTEZZA PC card to support a role played by the card's user. When a card's user selects a personality to use in a FORTEZZA-aware application, the data determines behavior traits (the personality) of the application. A card's user may have multiple personalities on the card. Each has a "personality label," a user-friendly character string that applications can display to the user for selecting or changing the personality to be used. For example, a military user's card might contain three personalities: GENERAL HALFTRACK, COMMANDER FORT SWAMPY, and NEW YEAR'S EVE PARTY CHAIRMAN. Each personality includes one or more certificates of different types [such as Signature Algorithm (DSA) versus Rivest–Shamir–Adleman (RSA)], for different purposes (such as digital signature versus encryption) or with different authorizations [r013].

Personalization Center for Subscriber Identity Module (SIM) (GSM context) A SIM card is connected with the Administration Center via an interface, thus it is possible, if necessary, to disable the SIM card and protect it from abuse [r011].

Personnel Security Policies and procedures aimed at ensuring that persons who access a system have proper authorization.

Pervasive Computing Environment/state where computers (and sensors and actuators) become practically invisible and where they are used in almost every aspect of human commerce, interaction, and life.

PE-S See Provider Edge Switch

PFS See Public-Key Forward Secrecy

Phage A program that modifies other programs in an unauthorized manner, especially one that propagates a virus or Trojan horse [r057].

Pharming Security infraction mechanism that redirects users to a fraudulent page after they have typed a legitimate web address. This site could be used to capture personal information, or unwanted or malicious software could be unintentionally downloaded to the user's workstation.

Phase Alternating Line (PAL) The color video and broadcasting standard used mainly in Western Europe and South America. PAL screen resolution is 625 lines and its refresh rate is 50 Hz [r203].

PHF See Phonebook File

PHF Hack A well-known and vulnerable Common Gateway Interface (CGI) script that does not filter out special characters submitted by a user.

Phishing A specific tactic for committing on-line fraud and identity theft. A phisher sends an e-mail that poses as a legitimate business request, an example being a bank asking its customers to verify financial data. The e-mail includes a link that purports to go to a legitimate banking website. However, the site is bogus and when the victim types in passwords or other sensitive information, the data are captured and subsequently used by the phisher to commit fraud [r062].

Phonebook File (PHF) Phonebook file demonstration program that hackers use to gain access to a computer system and potentially read and capture password files [r057].

Photuris A User Datagram Protocol (UDP)-

based, key establishment protocol for session keys, designed for use with the IPsec protocols Authentication Header (AH) and Encapsulating Security Payload (ESP). Superseded by Internet Key Exchange (IKE) [r013].

Phracker   An individual who combines phone phreaking with computer hacking.

Phreaker   An individual fascinated by the telephone system. More specifically, an individual who uses his knowledge of the telephone system to make calls at the expense of other users or institutions.

Phreaking   A contraction of "phone breaking." An attack on or penetration of a telephone system or, by extension, any other communication or information system [r013]. Phreaking is using the telephone network illegally. The classic early example of phreaking was the use of cereal-box toy whistles that, when blown into a telephone handset, hit a pitch normally used by phone technicians to signal the system to allow free calls [r062].

PHY   See Physical Layer Entity

PHYSEC   Physical security mechanisms intended to physically protect Information Technology (IT) resources.

Physical Access   Direct access to systems or networks, allowing passive or active intrusion [r264].

Physical Block   An architectural concept representing a realization of one or more function blocks.

Physical Coding Sublayer (PCS)   Within IEEE 802.3, a sublayer used in 100BASE-T, 1000BASE-X, and 1000BASE-T to couple the Media-Independent Interface (MII) or Gigabit Media-Independent Interface (GMII) and the Physical Medium Attachment (PMA). The PCS contains the functions to encode data its into code-groups that can be transmitted over the physical medium. Three PCS structures are defined for 100BASE-T—one for 100BASE-X, one for 100BASE-T4, and one for 100BASE-T2. (Described in IEEE 802.3, Clauses 23, 24, and 32.) One PCS structure is defined for 1000BASE-X

and one PCS structure is defined for 1000BASE-T. Described in IEEE 802.3 Clauses 36 and 40.

Physical Common Packet Channel (PCPCH)   (3G Wireless context) Packet Channel that serves to transmit data in the uplink [r007].

Physical Destruction   Deliberate destruction of a system component to interrupt or prevent system operation.

Physical Downlink Shared Channel (PDSCH)   (3G Wireless context) Channel is used to receive data by several User Equipments simultaneously. A PDSCH is always associated with a DPCH [r007].

Physical Infrastructure/Tangible Assets   These assets require protection considerations (among others): Data Centers; servers; desktop computers; mobile computers; Personal Data Assistants (PDAs); cell phones; server application software; end-user application software; development tools; routers; network switches; fax machines; Private Branch Exchanges/Voice over IP (PBXs/VoIP) servers; removable media (e.g., tapes, floppy disks, CD-ROMs, DVDs, portable hard drives, PC card storage devices, Universal Serial Bus (USB) storage devices, etc.); power supplies; uninterruptible power supplies; fire suppression systems; air-conditioning systems; air filtration systems; and other environmental control systems [r190].

Physical Layer Entity (PHY)   Within IEEE 802.3, the portion of the Physical Layer between the Medium-Dependent Interface (MDI) and the Media-Independent Interface (MII), or between the MDI and Gigabit Media-Independent Interface (GMII), consisting of the Physical Coding Sublayer (PCS), the Physical Medium Attachment (PMA), and, if present, the Physical Medium-Dependent (PMD) sublayers. The PHY contains the functions that transmit, receive, and manage the encoded signals that are impressed on and recovered from the physical medium. Described in IEEE 802.3 Clauses 23-26, 32, 36, and 40.

Physical Layer Signaling (PLS)   A protocol layer for Local Area Network (LAN) that is a sublayer

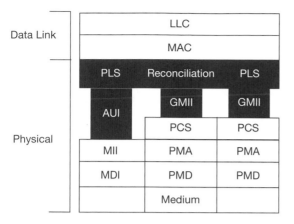

of the Physical Layer (PHY). Early LANs separated the PLS part of the physical layer from the Medium Independent Interface (MII), but the connection between the two was internal to the computer. Transceivers are available; however, to connect AUI interfaces to 10BASE-T cable. Now its function is called the reconciliation layer; it sits at the top of the PHY. PLS translates Layer 2 octets into Layer 1 bits (in doing so, it may introduce overhead bits).

Physical Media   Devices such as disk drives, solid-state disks, and tape drives, that physically hold the data.

Physical Medium Attachment (PMA) Sublayer Within 802.3, that portion of the Physical Layer that contains the functions for transmission, reception, and (depending on the PHY) collision detection, clock recovery and skew alignment. Described in IEEE 802.3, Clauses 7, 12, 14, 16, 17, 18, 23, 24, 32, 36, and 40.

Physical Medium-Dependent (PMD) Sublayer In 100BASE-X, that portion of the Physical Layer responsible for interfacing to the transmission medium. The PMD is located just above the Medium Dependent Interface (MDI). Described in IEEE 802.3 Clause 24.

Physical Random Access Channel (PRACH) (3G Wireless context) Channel used by user equipment to communicate to the network that it wants to be connected. It can also be used to transmit small bursty data in the uplink [r007].

Physical Security   The measures used to provide physical protection of the facilities housing system resources, the system resources themselves, the personnel, and the facilities used to support their operation. Physical security, as it pertains to computer security, covers the following areas: access controls, fire safety, failure of supporting utilities, structural collapse, interception of data, and mobile and portable systems [r067].

Physical Vulnerability   These vulnerabilities include but are not limited to: unlocked doors, unguarded access to computing facilities, insufficient fire suppression systems, poorly designed buildings, poorly constructed buildings, flammable materials used in construction, flammable materials used in finishing, unlocked windows, walls susceptible to physical assault, and interior walls that do not completely seal the room at both the ceiling and floor [r190].

PICH   See Paging Indication Channel

Piggy Back(ing)   Entering secure premises by following an authorized person through the security process. Also, unauthorized access to information by using a device that is already logged on with an authorized ID (identification).

Piggyback Attack   A form of active wiretapping in which the attacker gains access to a system via intervals of inactivity in another user's legitimate communication connection. Sometimes called a "between-the-lines" attack [r013].

PIN   See Personal Identification Number

Ping   A program that randomly identifies potential targets on the Internet. Uses Internet Control Message Protocol (ICMP) echo request packet (a "ping").

Ping of Death   An attack that sends an improperly large Internet Control Message Protocol (ICMP) [r292] echo request packet (a "ping") with the intent of overflowing the input buffers of the destination machine and causing it to crash [r013].

Ping Sweep   An attack that sends Internet Control Message Protocol (ICMP) [r292] echo requests ("pings") to a range of IP addresses, with the goal of finding hosts that can be probed for vulnerabilities [r013].

PKC   See Public-Key Certificate

PKCS   See Public-Key Cryptography Standards

PKCS #10   See Public-Key Cryptography Standards #10

PKCS #11   See Public-Key Cryptography Standards #11

PKCS #7   See Public-Key Cryptography Standards #7

PKI   See Public-Key Infrastructure

PKI Disclosure Statement (PDS)   An instrument that supplements a Certificate Policy (CP) or Certification Practice Statement (CPS) by disclosing critical information about the policies and practices of a Certification Authority/Public-Key Infrastructure (CA/PKI). A PDS is a vehicle for disclosing and emphasizing information normally covered in detail by associated CP and/or CPS documents. Consequently, a PDS is not intended to replace a CP or CPS [r011].

PKIX   See Public-Key Intrastructure X.509

PKIX Private Extension   Defines a private extension to identify an on-line verification service supporting the issuing Certification Authority (CA).

Plaintext   Unencrypted data (text, information). Data that are input to and transformed by an encryption process, or that are output by a decryption process. Usually, the plaintext input to an encryption operation is cleartext; in some cases, the input is ciphertext that was output from another encryption operation [r013].

Platform   Underlying hardware or software for a system. The term is often used as a synonym for operating system, but also to refer to the processor itself.

Platform for Privacy Preferences (P3P)   A project of the World Wide Web Consortium (W3C) that gives consumers an easy way to learn about and react to the way web sites may be using personal information. Essentially, a P3P-enabled web site would generate a snapshot of how it handles personal information. That snapshot would be compared automatically to preferences set by a consumer using a P3P-enabled browser [r057, r062].

PLMN   See Public Land Mobile Network

PLR   See Point of Local Repair

PLS   See Physical Layer Signaling

PMA   See Physical Medium Attachment

PMD   See Polarization Mode Dispersion and/or Physical Medium Dependent.

PMI   See Privilege Management Infrastructure

Podcast   (aka "TiVo for radio") Internet-based streaming audio, specifically tailored for Apple iPod portable media devices.

POH   See Path Overhead.

Point of Local Repair (PLR)   (MPLS context) The head-end Label Switch Router (LSR) of a backup tunnel or a detour Label Switched Path (LSP).

Point-to-Multipoint (PTM)   (GSM context) During a Point-to-Multipoint connection, a sender sends out information to several receivers in a defined area [r014].

Point-to-Multipoint Connection   A collection of associated Asynchronous Transfer Mode (ATM) Virtual Circuit (VC) or Virtual Path (VP) links, with associated endpoint nodes, with the following properties: (a) One ATM link, called the Root Link, serves as the root in a simple tree topology. When the Root Node sends information, all of the remaining nodes on the connection, called Leaf Nodes, receive copies of the information. (b) Each of the Leaf Nodes on the connection can send information directly to the Root Node. The Root Node cannot distinguish which Leaf is sending information without additional (higher layer) information. (The Leaf Nodes cannot communicate directly to each other with this connection type.)

Point-to-Multipoint Group Call (PTM-G)   (GSM context) The Point-to-Multipoint Group Call enables a sender to send messages to many receivers simultaneously. In this case, the connection is two-way respectively n-ways; that is, the receiving mobile stations can react to the received messages and communicate between each other [r014].

Point-to-Point (PTP)   Describes the exchange of data between two users [r014].

Point-to-Point Connection   (telecom context) A connection with only two endpoints.

Point-to-Point Connection-Oriented Network Service (PTP-CONS)   In the case of the Point-to-Point Connection-Oriented Network Service, several packets that belong together are sent [r014].

Point-to-Point Connectionless Network Service (PTP-CNLS)   Describes the sending of small individual packets that are independent of the preceding and following packets [r014]. Protocol is used in Europe and in the General Packet Radio Services (GPRS)/Global System for Mobile Communication (GSM) context.

Point-to-Point Protocol–Bridge Protocol Data Unit (PPP–BPDU)   A protocol defined in Request for Comments (RFC) 1638 that is used to establish the topology/connectivity to Remote Bridges [r095].

Point-to-Point Protocol (PPP)   Protocol defined originally in Request for Comments (RFC) 1661 (also RFC 1548 and RFC 1662) [r396]. PPP provides a standard method for transporting multi-protocol datagrams over point-to-point links. PPP is designed for simple links that support transport packets between two peers. A protocol for encapsulation and full-duplex transportation of network layer protocol data packets over a link between two peers, and for multiplexing different network layer protocols over the same link. Includes optional negotiation to select and use a peer entity authentication protocol to authenticate the peers to each other before they exchange network layer data [r013]. PPP is comprised of three main components:

- A method for encapsulating multi-protocol datagrams.
- A Link Control Protocol (LCP) for establishing, configuring, and testing the data-link connection.
- A family of Network Control Protocols (NCPs) for establishing and configuring different network-layer protocols.

Point-to-Point Tunneling Protocol (PPTP)   An Internet client–server protocol (originally developed by Ascend and Microsoft) that enables a remote user to create a virtual extension of the remote link across a network by tunneling Point-to-Point Protocol (PPP) over IP. PPP can encapsulate any Internet Protocol Suite network layer protocol. Therefore, PPTP does not specify security services, rather, it depends on protocols above and below it to provide any needed security. PPTP makes it possible to divorce the location of the initial remote access server (i.e., the PPTP Access Concentrator, the client, which runs on a special-purpose host) from the location at which the dial-up protocol (PPP) connection is terminated and access to the network is provided (i.e., the PPTP Network Server, which runs on a general-purpose host) [r013].

Polarization-Dependent Loss (PDL)   (optical transmission term) Maximum insertion loss (dB) variation among all polarization states over the operating temperature range. Two definitions of PDL are commonly adopted: (1) PDL at the International telecommunications Union (ITU) center wavelength and (2) worst-case PDL across the entire pass band.

Polarization Mode Dispersion (PMD)   (optical transmission term) Impairment affecting optical transmission. The pulse spreading (ps) caused by a change of polarization properties. Optical transmission impairment caused by combination of intrinsic effects (birefringence and mode coupling) and extrinsic effects on cable (bends, twists). Studies show, though, that transmission up to 250 miles is possible at OC-192.

PMD is caused by slight fiber asymmetry: during the preform fabrication or during the drawing process, a non-totally circular core and/or cladding may result. PMD is the result of the accumulation of weak birefringence along the various fiber spans (a link of any length exceeding 2 or 4 km is typically comprised of spliced fibers that originate from different manufacturing events.) An input light pulse of an initial polarization will decompose into two pulses with two different polarizations separated in time. The time separation leads to decreased system (signal) margin or even outages. PMD also depends on the temperature of the fiber, sometimes making transmission problematic on a time-of-year basis. This issue becomes more pronounced and problematic at higher speeds (i.e., OC-192 and OC-768).

Policy   (financial term) A contract of insurance, describing the term, coverage, premiums and deductibles. Also called insurance policy.

Policy Action (or) Action   A description of the middlebox treatment/service to be applied to a set of packets. Definition of what is to be done to enforce a policy rule, when the conditions of the rule are met. Policy actions may result in the execution of one or more operations to affect and/or configure network traffic and network resources. Network Address Translator (NAT) Address-BIND [or Port-BIND in the case of NAPT (Port NAT)] and firewall permit/deny action are examples of an Action [r037].

Policy Approving Authority (PAA)   The top-level signing authority of a Multilevel Information Systems Security Initiative (MISSI) certification hierarchy. The term refers both to that authoritative office or role and to the person who plays that role. A PAA registers MISSI a policy creation authorities (PCAs) and signs their X.509 public-key certificates. A PAA issues certificate revocation lists (CRL) but does not issue a CKL. A PAA may issue cross-certificates to other PAAs [r013].

Policy Certification Authority (Internet PCA) An X.509-compliant Certification Authority (CA) at the second level of the Internet certification hierarchy, under the Internet Policy Registration Authority (IPRA). Each policy creation authority (PCA) operates in accordance with its published security policy (see Certification Practice Statement) and within constraints established by the IPRA for all PCAs [r109, r013].

Policy Compliance   Tools and techniques that define, measure, and report on the compliance of information systems with security policies or government regulations.

Policy Creation Authority (PCA)   The second level of a Multilevel Information Systems Security Initiative (MISSI) certification hierarchy;

the administrative root of a security policy domain of MISSI users and other, subsidiary authorities. The term refers both to that authoritative office or role and to the person who fills that office. A MISSI PCA's certificate is issued by a policy approving authority. The PCA registers the Certification Authorities (CAs) in its domain, defines their configurations, and issues their X.509 public-key certificates. [The PCA may also issue certificates for subordinate certification authorities (SCAs), organizational registration authorities (ORAs), and other end entities, but a PCA does not usually do this.] The PCA periodically issues certificate revocation lists (CRLs) and Compromised Key Lists (CKLs) for its domain [r013].

Policy Decision Point (PDP)   See MIDCOM Policy Decision Point

Policy Enable Rule   (MIDCOM context) A policy rule containing an enable action. The policy condition consists of a descriptor of one or more unidirectional or bidirectional packet flows, and the policy action enables packets belonging to this flow to traverse the middlebox. The descriptor identifies the protocol, the flow direction, and the source and destination addresses, optionally with a range of port numbers [r030].

Policy Management   Enables users to set specific policies about how storage is implemented and used. Solutions containing policy management will automatically enforce those policies and take specific actions based on user-defined conditions [r029].

Policy Management Authority   (Canadian context) An organization responsible for public-key infrastructure (PKI) oversight and policy management in the Government of Canada.

Policy Mapping   Recognizing that, when a Certification Authority (CA) in one domain certifies a CA in another domain, a particular certificate policy in the second domain may be considered by the authority of the first domain to be equivalent (but not necessarily identical in all respects) to a particular certificate policy in the first domain [r061, r013].

Policy Qualifier   Policy-dependent information that may accompany a Certificate Policy (CP) identifier in an X.509 certificate. Such information can include a pointer to the URL of the applicable Certification Practice Statement (CPS) or relying party agreement. It may also include text (or number causing the appearance of text) that contains terms of the use of the certificate or other legal information [r011].

Policy Reserve Rule   (MIDCOM context) A policy rule containing a reserve action. The policy condition of this rule is always true. The action is the reservation of just an IP address or a combination of an IP address and a range of port numbers on neither side, one side, or both sides of the middlebox, depending on the middlebox configuration [r030].

Policy Rule(s)   The combination of one or more filters and one or more actions. Packets matching a filter are to be treated as specified by the associated action(s). The policy rules may also contain auxiliary attributes such as individual rule type, timeout values, creating agent, and so on [r037].

(MIDCOM context) In general, a policy rule is "a basic building block of a policy-based system. It is the binding of a set of actions to a set of conditions, where the conditions are evaluated to determine whether the actions are performed" (as described in RFC 3198). In the MIDCOM context the condition is a specification of a set of packets to which rules are applied. The set of actions always contains just a single element per rule, either action "reserve" or action "enable" [r030].

Policy, Security   See Security Policy

Poller   (Presence Services context) a fetcher that requests presence information on a regular basis [r015].

Polymorphic Virus   (aka evolutionary viruses) Virus that modifies itself each time it attaches to another program and cannot be detected by an anti-virus program [r057].

In laboratory experiments, F. Cohen produced viruses that had no common sequences of over three bytes between each subsequent generation by using encryption [r089, r388, r389]. Such viruses are called polymorphic viruses. Numerous polymorphic viruses have appeared in the wild. For example, the Tremor virus is a polymorphic virus that has almost 6,000,000,000 forms [r183].

A polymorphic virus can be a cryptovirus. If a polymorphic virus [r183, r182] contains and uses a public key then it is a cryptovirus. A polymorphic virus usually contains and uses a symmetric key for the purposes of obfuscating and de-obfuscating its own code. So, if this is the only cryptographic key it uses then it is not a cryptovirus.

Polymorphic viruses often decrypt and then send control to the main portion of their code, called the virus body, at run-time. They may generate new keys periodically and produce new ciphertexts of their bodies to make virus detection more difficult. The body also contains code that alters (morphs) the decryption code at the beginning of the virus. This makes it such that the virus changes its entire appearance. Although it would make sense to call this a "cryptovirus," this is not the way the computer term was originally defined [r172].

Polynomial Time   An algorithm operates in polynomial-time if the Turing machine halts after a number of steps polynomial in the length of its input [r032].

POP   See Point of Presence

POP3   See Post Office Protocol, version 3

Port   Either an endpoint to a logical connection, or a physical connection to a computer [r200].

Port (Physical)   Various I/O channels on the computer or server. For example, the ports to plug in the keyboard, the mouse, USB devices, monitor, parallel printer, and so on.

Port Restricted Cone Network Address Translator (NAT)   Similar to a restricted cone NAT, but the restriction includes port numbers. Specifically, an external host can send a packet, with source IP address X and source port P, to the internal host only if the internal host had previously sent a packet to IP address X and port P [r252].

Port Scan   (aka scan) An attack that sends client requests to a range of server port addresses on a host, with the goal of finding an active port and exploiting a known vulnerability of that service. A technique used by intruders and hackers to determine what Transmission Control Protocol/User Datagram Protocol (TCP/UDP) ports are open or in use on a system or network. By using various tools, a hacker can send data to TCP or UDP ports one at a time and based on the response received the port scan utility can determine if that port is in use. Using this information, the hacker or intruder can then focus their attack on the ports that are open and try to exploit any weaknesses to gain access [r035].

Portable Operating System Interface for Computer Environments (POSIX)   A standard (originally IEEE Standard P1003.1) that defines an operating system interface and environment to support application portability at the source code level. It is intended to be used by both application developers and system implementers. P1003.1 supports security functionality like those on most UNIX systems, including discretionary access control and privilege. IEEE Draft Standard P1003.6.1 specifies additional functionality not provided in the base standard, including (a) discretionary access control, (b) audit trail mechanisms, (c) privilege mechanisms, (d) mandatory access control, and (e) information label mechanisms [r013, r217].

Portal (or Internet Portal)/User Interface   A possible access mechanism to a computing grid; it provides the user with an interface to launch grid applications [r080]. A gateway or single point of entry through which the user can access related information from a variety of up-stream sources.

Port-Based Virtual Local Area Networks (VLANs)   For port-based VLANs, a switch port is manually configured to be a member of a specific VLAN. Any device connected to this port will belong to the same broadcast domain as all other ports configured with the same VLAN number. The challenge of port-based VLANs becomes documenting which port belongs to each VLAN. The VLAN membership information is not displayed on the front of the switch. As a result, the VLAN membership cannot be determined just by looking at the physical switch port. Only by looking at the configuration information can the membership be determined [r350].

Ports (Logical)   Virtual ports, referring to code points (within a defined range) in the Transmission Control Protocol/User Datagram Protocol (TCP/UDP) header. For example, HTTP traffic flows on port 80 at the TCP level, POP3 e-mail flows on port 110 at the TCP level, and many other ports are defined by the Internet Research Task Force (IRTF) set of TCP documentation. By blocking or opening these ports into and out of the network at the firewall level the firm can control what kinds of data can flow through the intranet.

POSIX   See Portable Operating System Interface for Computer Environments

Post Office Protocol, Version 3 (POP3)   An Internet Standard protocol by which a client workstation can dynamically access a mailbox on a server host to retrieve mail messages that the server has received and is holding for the client [r398, r013]. POP3 has mechanisms for optionally authenticating a client to a server and providing other security services.

Post Office Protocol, Version 3 (POP3) APOP   A POP3 "command" (better described as a transaction type, or a protocol within a protocol) by which a POP3 client optionally uses a keyed hash (based on MD5) to authenticate itself to a POP3 server and, depending on the server implementation, to protect against replay attacks [r013]. The server includes a unique timestamp in its greeting to the client. The subsequent APOP command sent by the client to the server contains the client's name and the hash result of applying Message Digest 5 (MD5) to a string formed from both the timestamp and a shared secret that is known only to the client and the server. APOP was designed to provide as an alternative to using POP3's USER and PASS (i.e., password) command pair, in which the client sends a cleartext password to the server [r013].

Post Office Protocol, Version 3 (POP3) AUTH
A "command" [r397] (better described as a transaction type, or a protocol within a protocol) in POP3, by which a POP3 client optionally proposes a mechanism to a POP3 server to authenticate the client to the server and provide other security services [r013]. If the server accepts the proposal, the command is followed by performing a challenge–response authentication protocol and, optionally, negotiating a protection mechanism for subsequent POP3 interactions. The security mechanisms used by POP3 AUTH are those used by Internet Message Access Protocol, Version 4 (IMAP4).

Power over Ethernet (PoE)   A technology for wired Ethernet Local Area Networks (LANs) that allows the electrical current necessary for the operation of each device to be carried by the data cables rather than by power cords [r101]. Motivations for use include [r247]: reduces installation costs greatly; reduces cable runs; power consumption is lower; it is quicker to install. This technology is useful for Voice over IP (VoIP) applications, monitoring cameras (security), and/or to support wireless Access Points (APs). Defined in IEEE 802.3af.

Power Over Ethernet (PoE) Elements   There are three elements to a PoE system [r247]:

Power Sourcing Equipment (PSE): The PSE is connected to a device and at once detects whether the device falls into two categories. Either it is a compliant device or it is noncompliant. If it is noncompliant no current is supplied to the device. This means that noncompliant equipment is not damaged and users will not find a 48-V electromotive force where they were not expecting it. This enables legacy equipment and cables to be used on an IEEE802.3af PSE without harm.

Powered Device (PD): This typically includes devices such as (but not limited to) VoIP Phone, camera, Wi-Fi access point, or other device. The device will provide the correct impedance to the PSE and ideally give a signature to the PSE to in-

dicate how much power it requires. The powered device has to decide which conductors in the Category 5 cable have the power connected and also the polarity of the power.

Cable: Category 5 cable or better is used to transmit the power; this means that legacy cables can be used for this application, which in turn keeps installation costs down. The maximum length of cable is 100 m and the delivered power is 12.95 W at the end of the cable.

PP   See Protection Profile

PPP   See Point-to-Point Protocol

PPTP   See Point-to-Point Tunneling Protocol

PPVPN   See Provider-Provisioned Virtual Private Network

PRACH   See Physical Random Access Channel

Pre-authorization   A capability of a Certification Authority Workstation (CAW) that enables certification requests to be automatically validated against data provided in advance to the Certification Authority (CA) by an authorizing entity [r013].

Prefix Discovery   The process by which a host discovers the network prefixes for local destinations [r024].

Prefix Filtering   A technique for eliminating routes from consideration as candidates for entry into a Routing Information Bases (RIBs) by matching the network prefix in a Border Gateway Protocol (BGP) Route against a list of network prefixes. A BGP Route is eliminated if, for any filter prefix from the list, the Route prefix length is equal to or longer than the filter prefix length and the most significant bits of the two prefixes match over the length of the filter prefix [r086].

Prefixes List   Linked prefixes list supported by each host. Each entry defines the directly reachable IP addresses range—that is, neighbors [r008].

Prefix-Length Notation   Notation used to represent network prefixes. The notation uses the address/prefix length form; this prefix length is the address' initial bits number that is employed to define the prefix [r008].

Presence   The willingness and ability of a user to

communicate with other users on the network [r237].

Presence Agent (PA)   A presence agent is a Session Initiation Protocol (SIP) user agent which is capable of receiving SUBSCRIBE requests, responding to them, and generating notifications of changes in presence state. A presence agent must have knowledge of the presence state of a presentity. This means that it must have access to presence data manipulated by Presence User Agents (PUA) for the presentity. One way to do this is by co-locating the PA with the proxy/registrar. Another way is to colocate it with the presence user agent of the presentity. However, these are not the only ways, and this specification makes no recommendations about where the PA function should be located. A PA is always addressable with a SIP Uniform Resource Identifier (URI) that uniquely identifies the presentity (i.e., sip:joe@example.com). There can be multiple PAs for a particular presentity, each of which handles some subset of the total subscriptions currently active for the presentity. A PA is also a notifier (defined in RFC 3265) that supports the presence event package [r227].

Presence Information   (Presence Services context) This consists of one or more presence tuples [r016].

Presence Protocol   (Presence Services context) The messages that can be exchanged between a presentity and a presence service, or a watcher and a presence service [r015].

Presence Server   A physical entity that can act as either a presence agent or as a proxy server for SUBSCRIBE requests. When acting as a Presence Agent (PA), it is aware of the presence information of the presentity through some protocol means. When acting as a proxy, the SUBSCRIBE requests are proxied to another entity that may act as a PA [r227].

Presence Service   (Presence Services context) This accepts, stores, and distributes presence information.

- It may require authentication of presentities and/or watchers.

- It may have different authentication requirements for different presentities.
- It may have different authentication requirements for different watchers, and may also have different authentication requirements for different presentities being watched by a single watcher.
- It may have an internal structure involving multiple servers and/or proxies. There may be complex patterns of redirection and/or proxying while retaining logical connectivity to a single presence service. Note that a presence service does not require having a distinct server—the service may be implemented as direct communication among presentity and watchers.
- It may have an internal structure involving other presence services, which may be independently accessible in their own right as well as being reachable through the initial presence service [r015].

Presence Tuple   (Presence Services context) This consists of a status, an optional communication address, and optional other presence markup [r015].

Presence User Agent (PUA)   (Presence Services context) This means for a principal to manipulate zero or more presentities. Motivation: This is essentially a "model/view" distinction: The presentity is the model of the presence being exposed, and it is independent of its manifestation in any user interface. The presence user agent, presentity, and presence service can be colocated or can be distributed across machines [r015].

A PUA manipulates presence information for a presentity. This manipulation can be the side effect of some other action (such as sending a Session Initiation Protocol (SIP) REGISTER request to add a new Contact) or can be done explicitly through the publication of presence documents. It allows multiple PUAs per presentity. This means that a user can have many devices [such as a cell phone and Personal Digital Assistant (PDA)], each of which is independently generating a component of the overall presence information for a presentity. PUAs push data into the presence system, but are outside of it, in that they do not receive SUBSCRIBE messages or send NOTIFY messages [r227].

Presentity (Presence Entity)   (Presence Services context) This provides presence information to a presence service. Note that the presentity is not (usually) located in the presence service: The presence service only has a recent version of the presentity's presence information. The presentity initiates changes in the presence information to be distributed by the presence service [r015].

Pretty Good Privacy (PGP)/Multipurpose Internet Mail Extensions (MIME) Digital Envelope   Security based on the Pretty Good Privacy (PGP) standard, integrated with MIME Security Multiparts.

Pretty Good Privacy (Trademark) (PGPTM)   Trademarks of Network Associates, Inc., referring to a computer program (and related protocols) that uses cryptography to provide data security for electronic mail and other applications on the Internet. PGP encrypts messages with International Data Encryption Algorithm (IDEA) in Cipher Feedback (CFB) mode, distributes the IDEA keys by encrypting them with Rivest–Shamir–Adleman (RSA), and creates digital signatures on messages with Message Digest 5 (MD5) and RSA. To establish ownership of public keys, PGP depends on the web of trust [r013].

PGP prevents a message from being altered in route from sender to receiver, although it does not protect the message from being altered once the receiver decodes it with a digital "key" [r062]. PGP-encrypted e-mail is an example of message-level security. The actual network transport need not be encrypted to ensure message security. The e-mail can be sent using a nonsecure transport over a hostile channel, because the body of the message is encrypted for confidentiality. A message hash ensures integrity and the digital signature provides identification and authentication (even nonrepudiation functions) [r276].

Preventive Control   Risk control established to prevent an event from occurring.

PRF   See Pseudo-Random Function

Primary Account Number (PAN)   (SET context) The assigned number that identifies the card issuer and cardholder. This account number is composed of an issuer identification number, an individual account number identification, and an accompanying check digit. PAN is defined by ISO 7812-1985" [r018, r013]. The PAN is embossed, encoded, or both on a magnetic-strip-based credit card. The PAN identifies the issuer to which a transaction is to be routed and the account to which it is to be applied unless specific instructions indicate otherwise. The authority that assigns the bank identification number part of the PAN is the American Bankers Association.

Primary Scrambling Code (PSC)   (3G Wireless context) A code transmitted via the Primary-SCH (Primary Synchronization Channel). With the help of the PSC, the User Equipment synchronizes itself to the timeslots of a cell [r007].

Primary Synchronization Channel (P-SCH)   (3G Wireless context) The Synchronization Channel (SCH) is used for cell search and for User Equipment synchronization. It is comprised of the Primary Synchronization Channel (P-SCH), and the Secondary Synchronization Channel (S-SCH). The Primary Synchronization Channel is used for the User Equipments' timeslot synchronization [r007].

Primary-Common Control Physical Channel (P-CCPCH)   (3G Wireless context) The Primary-Common Control Physical Channel carries the system information of a cell [r007].

Prime Number   A number that has no proper divisors. A number that has only the number "1" and itself as a divisors. The first few primes are 1, 2, 3, 5, 7, 11, 13, 17, 19, 23, 29, and so on. Number theory in general and prime numbers in particular play a role in encryption.

Prime Rate   (financial term) The interest rate that commercial banks charge their most creditworthy borrowers, such as large corporations. The prime rate is a lagging indicator. Also called prime.

Principal (Kerberos context) A string that names a specific entity to which a set of credentials may be assigned. A uniquely named client or server instance that participates in a network communication [r070]. It generally has three parts [r317]:

- *Primary:* The first part of a Kerberos principal. In the case of a user, it is the username. In the case of a service, it is the name of the service.
- *Instance:* The second part of a Kerberos principal. It gives information that qualifies the primary. The instance may be null. In the case of a user, the instance is often used to describe the intended use of the corresponding credentials. In the case of a host, the instance is the fully qualified hostname.
- *Realm:* The logical network served by a single Kerberos database and a set of Key Distribution Centers. By convention, realm names are generally all uppercase letters, to differentiate the realm from the Internet domain.

The typical format of a typical Kerberos principal is primary/instance@REALM.

(Human Presence Services context) Human, program, or collection of humans and/or programs that chooses to appear to the presence service as a single actor, distinct from all other principals.

Principle of Complete Mediation See Complete Mediation

Principle of Economy of Mechanism See Economy of Mechanism

Principle of Fail-Safe Defaults See Fail-Safe Defaults

Principle of Least Common Mechanism See Least Common Mechanism

Principle of Least Privilege See Least Privilege

Principle of Open Design See Open Design

Principle of Psychological Acceptability See Psychological Acceptability

Principle of Separation of Privilege See Separation of Privilege

Priority The degree of urgency with which a situation requires resolution of the problem.

Privacy The right of individuals to control or influence what information related to them may be collected and stored and by whom and to whom that information may be disclosed [r160].

Privacy Act as Applied to Internet Capture Under some circumstances are the programs/systems/logs that an entity may capture in monitoring Internet usage considered a System of Records and subject to all requirements of the Privacy Act of 1974. The Department of Justice determined that a network/Internet monitoring/logging/audit system is a System of Records for Privacy Act considerations if the system has the capability of attributing data to a person (whether or not it is used for this purpose) [r067].

Privacy Enhanced Mail (PEM) An Internet protocol to provide data confidentiality, data integrity, and data origin authentication for electronic mail [r399, r109]. PEM encrypts messages with Data Encryption Standard (DES) in cipher-block chaining (CBC) mode, provides key distribution of DES keys by encrypting them with Rivest–Shamir–Adleman (RSA), and signs messages with RSA over either MD2 or MD5. To establish ownership of public keys, PEM uses a certification hierarchy, with X.509 public-key certificates and X.509 certificate revocation lists (CRLs) that are signed with RSA and MD2. PEM is designed to be compatible with a wide range of key management methods, but is limited to specifying security services only for text messages and, like Multipurpose Internet Mail Extensions Object Security Services (MOSS), has not been widely implemented in the Internet [r013].

Private Branch Exchange (PBXs) Traditional on-premises (customer-owned) customer premises equipment to handle Time Division Multiplexing (TDM) voice in a building or campus. Many of these are now being replaced by Voice over IP (VoIP)-based systems known as IP-PBX systems.

Private Channel A channel that is a result of prior negotiation on a secure channel. In this context it may be used to handle media streams [r068a].

Private Component   A synonym for "private key."

Private Key   (aka private component) In a public-key cryptosystem, that key of a user's key pair which is known only by that user (i.e., is kept secret) [r061].

Private Key Cryptography   An encryption methodology in which the encryptor and decryptor use the same key, which must be kept secret.

Privilege   An authorization or set of authorizations to perform security-relevant functions, especially in the context of a computer operating system.

Privilege Asserter   A privilege holder using their attribute certificate or public-key certificate to assert privilege.

Privilege Management Infrastructure (PMI)   In X.509 the infrastructure able to support the management of privileges in support of a comprehensive authorization service and in relationship with a Public-Key Infrastructure [r068a].

Privilege Policy   The policy that outlines conditions for privilege verifiers to provide/perform sensitive services to/for qualified privilege asserters. Privilege policy relates attributes associated with the service as well as attributes associated with privilege asserters [r068a].

Privileged Process   A computer process that is authorized (and, therefore, trusted) to perform some security-relevant functions that ordinary processes are not [r013].

Probabilistic Cryptosystems   (aka Probabilistic Public-Key Cryptosystems) A probabilistic public-key cryptosystem consists of the following [r390]:

- A set K called the key space whose elements are called keys.
- A rule by which each $k \in K$ is associated with a partial-trap-door one-way function Ek with domain $Mk \times Rk$ and range Ck. (Here, Mk is called the plaintext space, Rk the randomization set, and Ck the ciphertext space.)
- A procedure for generating a random key $k \in K$ together with a partial-trap-door d for

Ek and the map $Dk : Ck \rightarrow Mk$ such that $Dk(Ek(m; r)) = m$; for all $m \in Mk$; $r \in Rk$.

The elements $k \in K$ are called the public keys and the partial trap-doors d the private keys. Obviously, the deterministic model is a special case of the probabilistic model in which Rk has only one element.

In order for the probabilistic model to be useful and secure, the following properties are needed:

- P1. Given a public key k, it is easy to compute $Ek(m; r)$ for $m \in Mk$ and $r \in Rk$.
- P2. Given a private key d, it is easy to compute $Dk(c)$ for $c \in Ck$.
- P3. Knowing k and $c \in Ck$ it is infeasible to decide for any $m \in Mk$ whether m can be encrypted to c under Ek. Thus, it is infeasible to determine Dk or d from the general information about the cryptosystem.
- P4. It is easy to generate a random key $k \in K$ and the corresponding private key d.

In the deterministic model it was required that it be infeasible to determine m from a knowledge of only Ek and c (as Ek is one-way). The corresponding requirement P3 for the probabilistic model is much stronger because if one cannot even decide whether a plaintext m can be encrypted to a given c, then certainly one cannot find a plaintext that can be encrypted to c. In this connection we note that in the deterministic model, it is trivial to decide if a plaintext $m \in Mk$ can be encrypted to a given ciphertext $c \in Ck$, as one can simply compute $Ek(m)$ and check whether or not it is c. Requirement P3 also implies that even when an adversary has a potentially matched pair $(m; c)$ of plaintext and ciphertext, he or she cannot even verify that there exists $r \in Rk$ such that $Ek(m; r) = c$. Therefore, a probabilistic cryptosystem can provide a higher level of security than a deterministic one.

The first such cryptosystem was developed by S. Goldwasser and S. Micali [r391, r392, r393], and is based on the difficulty of extracting quadratic residues modulo some composite n. This cryptosystem relies on the notion of Unapproximable Trapdoor Predicates. The idea is that one develops a function Q that is hard to compute without knowing some additional information, but given y, it is easy to find an element x such that $Q(x) = y$. A probabilistic public-key cryptosystem can be based, for example, on quadratic residues [r394].

Probabilistic Public-Key Cryptosystems   See Probabilistic Cryptosystems

Probability   A measure of how likely it is that some event will occur. Subjective probability view—Bayesian statistics—is where the probability is interpreted as the "degree of belief" in a stated proposition. Probability, in the frequentist view, which is the most common view (particularly in scientific environments), is the frequency of an experiment that is repeated infinitely-many times. Perform a certain well-defined experiment N times, and look at the times the outcome A fits a specified criterion; let this number be n. The observed frequency is freq $(A) = n/N$:

$$p(A) = \lim_{N \to \infty} (n/N) = \lim_{N \to \infty} f(A)$$

Probe   Mechanisms attempting to glean information about the target systems in an effort to support unauthorized access attempts. For example, an intruder could install sniffers to collect additional passwords and user Ids.

Production Honeypot   A honeypot used in a production environment.

Production, Input/Output Controls   Security procedures in place that support the operations of the information technology system. Some examples are: user support; procedures to ensure unauthorized individuals cannot read, copy, alter, or steal printed or electronic information; internal/external labeling of tapes, and procedures for restricting access to output products [r067].

Profile   Patterns of a user's activity that can detect changes in normal routines.

Profitability   (financial term) The ability to earn a profit.

Program Management   The management of the overall scope of the IT security program [r067].

Promiscuous Mode   Normally in a traditional shared Local Area Network (LAN) a Network Interface Card (NIC) reads all address information but it accepts only those frames destined for itself. When the interface is in promiscuous mode, it reads all information (sniffer), regardless of its destination. This situation is somewhat mitigated in switched LANs (because only frames destined for the specific user attached to that port are propagated: Virtual LANs (VLANs) may provide additional isolation.

Proposed Standard Protocol, Internet Engineering Task Force (IETF)   The entry-level maturity for the standards track is "Proposed Standard." A specific action by the Internet Engineering Steering Group (IESG) is required to move a specification onto the standards track at the "Proposed Standard" level [r280, r281].

Proprietary   Refers to information (or other property) that is owned by an individual or organization and for which the use is restricted by that entity [r013].

Protected Checksum   A checksum that is computed for a data object by means that protect against active attacks that would attempt to change the checksum to make it match changes made to the data object [r013].

Protected Distribution System   A wireline or fiber-optic system that includes sufficient safeguards (acoustic, electric, electromagnetic, and physical) to permit its use for unencrypted transmission of (cleartext) data [r013].

Protected Extensible Authentication Protocol (PEAP)   An improved version of the authentication protocol used in Wireless Local Area Networks (WLANs). It is based on Extensible Authentication Protocol (EAP) and is utilized in conjunction with Remote Authentication Dial-In User Service (RADIUS). Replaced the Cisco-specific Lightweight EAP (LEAP) protocol used in the early to mid-2000s. May eventually be replaced by Wi-Fi Protected Access Version 2 (WPA-2).

Protected Label Switched Path (LSP)   (MPLS

context) An LSP is said to be protected at a given hop if it has one or multiple associated backup tunnels originating at that hop [r083].

Protected Memory Space   Locations in a processor's memory that are protected by the Operating System (OS).

Protection Profile (PP)   An implementation-independent specification of information assurance security requirements. Protection profiles are a complete combination of security objectives, security related functional requirements, information assurance requirements, assumptions, and rationale [r401].

The purpose of a PP is to state a security problem rigorously for a given collection of system or products [known as the Target of Evaluation (TOE)] and to specify security requirements to address that problem without dictating how these requirements will be implemented.

Product vendors may respond to the security concerns defined by a PP by producing a Security Target (ST), which is similar to a PP except that it contains implementation-specific information that demonstrate how their product addresses those security concerns.

In accordance with their respective responsibilities under Public Law 100-235 (Computer Security Act of 1987), the National Institute of Standards and Technology (NIST) and the National Security Agency (NSA) have agreed to cooperate on the development of security requirements for key technology areas necessary for the protection of Federal information systems and networks, including those comprising the critical infrastructure within the United States. NIST and NSA are undertaking this effort [r401]:

- To ensure that the U.S. Government has a consistent comprehensive set of recommended protection profiles for key technology areas;
- To forge partnerships with public and private sector constituencies to develop and gain consensus on PPs important for critical infrastructure protection; and

- To facilitate national and international convergence of protection profiles in key technology areas.

Protection Ring   One of a hierarchy of privileged operation modes of a system that gives certain access rights to processes authorized to operate in that mode [r013].

Protocol   A format for transmitting data between devices [r200]. Agreed-upon methods of communications used by computers. A specification that describes the rules and procedures that products should follow to perform activities on a network, such as transmitting data. If they use the same protocols, products from different vendors should be able to communicate on the same network [r057].

A set of rules (i.e., formats and procedures) to implement and control some type of association (e.g., communication) between systems. (For example, see: Internet Protocol.) In particular, a series of ordered steps involving computing and communication that are performed by two or more system entities to achieve a joint objective [r339, r013].

Protocol Data Unit (PDU)   (aka datagram) A fragment of a data sequence that is transmitted through the network. A packet. Data objects corresponding to a concrete layer in a network architecture consisting of layers. During transmission the data unit of the n-layer turn into the payload of the $n - 1$ layer (the lower layer) [r008].

Protocol Key Format   This describes which octet string values represent valid keys. For encryption mechanisms that do not have perfectly dense key spaces, this describes the representation used for encoding keys. It need not describe invalid specific values; all key generation routines should avoid such values [r115].

Protocol Sublayer   The logical partitioning of a protocol layer [such as the layers defined by the Open Systems Interconnection Reference Model (OSIRM)] into distinct, nonoverlapping, hierarchical functional portions, which when considered in total, comprise the entire layer. The sublayers typically have formal interfaces between adjacent (neighboring) sublayers, similar, in concept, to the formal interfaces between adjacent layers.

Protocol Suite   A complementary (hierarchical) set of communication protocols used in a computer network.

Protocol-Based Virtual Local Area Networks (VLANs)   With Protocol-based VLANs, the Layer 3 protocol being carried by the frame is used to determine VLAN membership. While this may work in multi-protocol environments, in a predominately IP-based network, this method is not practical [r350].

Provably Secure   Algorithm that can be demonstrated by mathematical proof to be secure. For example, the cryptosystem introduced by Rivest, Shamir, and Adleman is based on the difficulty of factoring. Unfortunately, many of the public-key cryptosystems are not provably secure. Another example is the Diffie–Hellman Key exchange, where it is known that breaking the system is not harder then solving discrete logarithms, but one has no idea if a lower bound exists. Also, it is hard to prove security, as information could be retrieved from the ciphertext, by frequency analysis or any other method [r394].

Provider Edge (PE)   The name of the device or set of devices at the edge of the provider network with the functionality that is needed to interface with the customer. Without further qualifications, PE is very often used for naming the devices since it is made unambiguous by the context [r082]. Both routers and switches may be used to implement PEs; however, the scaling properties will be radically different depending on which type of equipment is chosen.

In naming PEs, there are three aspects that one needs to consider, the service they support, whether the functionality needed for service is distributed across more than one device and the type of device they are built on [r082].

Provider Edge (PE) Device   The equipment in the service provider's network that interfaces with the equipment in the customer's network.

Provider Edge (PE) Router   A router at the edge of a provider's network that speaks external Border Gateway Protocol (eBGP) to a BGP speaker in another Autonomous System (AS).

Provider Edge Router (PE-R)   A Layer 3 device that participates in the Packet Switched Network (PSN) routing and forwards packets based on the routing information.

Provider Edge Switch (PE-S)   A L2 device that participates in, for example, a switched Ethernet taking forwarding decision packets based on Layer 2 address information.

Provider Router   The Provider Router is a router in the service provider's core network that does not have interfaces directly toward the customer. A Provider Router is used to interconnect the Provider Edge (PE) routers. A provider router does not have to maintain Virtual Private Network (VPN) state and is thus VPN-unaware.

Provider-Provisioned Virtual Private Network (PPVPN)   A Virtual Private Network (VPN) that is configured and managed by the service provider (and thus not by the customer itself). Security is an integral aspect of PPVPN services [r058]. A PPVPN service is a private network service made available by a service provider to a PPVPN user. The service is implemented using virtual constructs built on a shared PPVPN core network. A PPVPN service interconnects sites of a PPVPN user. Extranets can be considered as VPNs in which multiple sites are controlled by different (legal) entities. Extranets are another example of PPVPN deployment scenarios wherein restricted and controlled communication is allowed between trusted zones, often via well-defined transit points [r058].

Provider-Provisioned Virtual Private Network (PPVPN) Security Threats   Threats that impact PPVPNs or that affect PPVPNs in unique ways. A successful attack on a particular PPVPN or on a service provider's PPVPN infrastructure may cause one or more of the following ill effects [r058]:

- observation, modification, or deletion of PPVPN user data,

- replay of PPVPN user data,
- injection of nonauthentic data into a PPVPN,
- traffic pattern analysis on PPVPN traffic,
- disruption of PPVPN connectivity, or
- degradation of PPVPN service quality.

Threats to a PPVPN, whether malicious or accidental, may come from different categories of sources. For example, they may come from [r058] (i) users of other PPVPNs provided by the same PPVPN service provider, (ii) the PPVPN service provider or persons working for it, (iii) other persons who obtain physical access to a service provider site, (iv) other persons who use social engineering methods to influence behavior of service provider personnel, (v) users of the PPVPN itself (i.e., intra-Virtual Private Network (VPN) threats), or (vi) others (i.e., attackers from the Internet at large).

Provisional Response (SIP context) A response used by the server to indicate progress, but that does not terminate a Session Initiation Protocol (SIP) transaction. 1xx responses are provisional, other responses are considered final [r025].

Provisioning Indicates the control of employee access rights to applications and intellectual property. This includes providing employees with user names and passwords, resetting passwords when users forget them, and removing user accounts [r062].

(telecommunications industry context) Indicates services and all associated transmission, wiring, and equipment.

Prowler A daemon that is run periodically to seek out and erase core files, truncate administrative logfiles, destroy directories, and otherwise delete information.

Proxy An intermediate relay agent between clients and servers of an application, relaying application messages between the two. Proxies use special protocol mechanisms to communicate with proxy clients and relay client data to servers and vice versa. A Proxy terminates sessions with both the client and the server, acting as server to

the end-host client and as client to the end-host server. Applications such as File Transfer Protocol (FTP), Service Initiation Protocol (SIP), and Real Time Streaming Protocol (RTSP) use a control session to establish data sessions. These control and data sessions can take divergent paths. While a proxy can intercept both the control and data sessions, it might intercept only the control session. This is often the case with real-time streaming applications such as SIP and RTSP [r037].

(Presence Services context) A server that communicates presence information, instant messages, subscriptions, and/or notifications to another server. Sometimes a proxy acts on behalf of a presentity, watcher, or instant inbox [r015].

Proxy Firewall A firewall that acts as a proxy server. It usually runs on a bastion host, which may support proxies for several protocols [e.g., File Transfer Protocol (FTP), HyperText Transfer Protocol (HTTP), and TELNET]. Instead of a client in the protected enclave connecting directly to an external server, the internal client connects to the proxy server which in turn connects to the external server. The proxy server waits for a request from inside the firewall, forwards the request to the remote server outside the firewall, gets the response, then sends the response back to the client. The proxy may be transparent to the clients, or they may need to connect first to the proxy server, and then use that association to also initiate a connection to the real server [r013].

Proxy Server A computer process, often used as, or as part of, a firewall, that relays a protocol between client and server computer systems, by appearing to the client to be the server and appearing to the server to be the client. (See Proxy firewall for more information on a firewall as a proxy server.)

Proxies are generally preferred over SOCKS for their ability to perform caching, high-level logging, and access control. A proxy can provide security service beyond that which is normally part of the relayed protocol, such as access control based on peer entity authentication of clients, or peer entity authentication of servers when clients do not have that capability. A proxy at Open Systems Interconnection Reference Model (OSIRM) layer 7 can also provide finer-grained security service than can a filtering router at OSIRM layer 3. For example, an FTP proxy could permit transfers out of, but not into, a protected network [r013].

Proxying   See Proxy

PS   See Packet-Switched Mode

PSC   See Primary Scrambling Code

P-SCH   See Primary Synchronization Channel

Pseudo-Wire (PW)   An emulated point-to-point connection over a packet switched network that allows the interconnection of two nodes with any Layer 2 technology. The PW shares some of the building blocks and architecture constructs with the point-to-multipoint solutions—for example, Provider Edge (PE) and Customer Edge (CE) [r082]. An early solution for PWs is described in references r402 and r403. Requirements for PWs are found in reference r404, and reference r405 presents an architectural framework for PWs.

Pseudo-Header   (IPv6 context) Provisional header that is built to calculate the needed checksum to associate the IPv6 header with the charge. IPv6 uses a new pseudo-header format to calculate User Datagram Protocol (UDP), Transmission Control Protocol (TCP) and of Internet Control Message Protocol v6 (ICMPv6) checksum [r008].

Pseudo-Integrity Protection   Mechanism where change in ciphertext produces random plaintext; used for example in IEEE P1619 [r279].

Pseudo-Periodic   (IPv6 context) Event that is repeated at intervals of various lengths. For example, the routes advertisement sent by an IPv6 router is made at intervals that are calculated between a minimum and a maximum [r008].

Pseudo-Random   A sequence of values that appears to be random (i.e., unpredictable) but is actually generated by a deterministic algorithm [r013].

Pseudo-Random Function (PRF)   A function with parameters (protocol-key, octet-string) →

(octet-string). This pseudo-random function should generate an octet string of some size that is independent of the octet string input. The PRF output string should be suitable for use in key generation, even if the octet string input is public. It should not reveal the input key, even if the output is made public [r115].

Pseudo-Random Number Generators (PRNGs)   A process used to deterministically generate a series of numbers (usually integers) that appear to be random according to certain statistical tests, but actually are pseudo-random. Mechanisms used to generate cryptographic keys. Pseudo-random number generators are usually implemented in software.

When a seed has sufficient entropy, from some appropriate source and possibly de-skewed and mixed, one can algorithmically extend that seed to produce a large number of cryptographically strong random quantities. Such algorithms are platform independent and can operate in the same fashion on any computer. For the algorithms to be secure, their input and internal workings must be protected from adversarial observation [r166].

Pseudo-Random Number Generators (PRNGs) Problems   PRNGs can result in little or no security. An attacker may find it much easier to reproduce the PRNG environment that produced the keys, searching the resulting small set of possibilities, rather than brute force searching the whole key space. The generation of quality random numbers is difficult. RFC 1750 offers important guidance in this area, and Appendix 3 of FIPS Pub 186 provides one quality PRNG technique [r138].

Pseudo-Random Processes Weaknesses   Security systems are built on strong cryptographic algorithms that foil pattern analysis attempts. However, the security of these systems is dependent on generating secret quantities for passwords, cryptographic keys, and similar quantities. The use of pseudo-random processes to generate secret quantities can result in pseudo-security. A sophisticated attacker may find it easier to reproduce the environment that produced the secret quantities and to search the resulting small set of possibilities than to locate the quantities in the whole of the potential number space. Choosing random quantities to foil a resourceful and motivated adversary is often difficult [r166].

Pseudo-Random Sequences A source of deterministic or "pseudo-random" numbers. Sequences typically start with a "seed" quantity and use simple numeric or logical operations to produce a sequence of values. A typical pseudo-random number generation technique is the linear congruence pseudo-random number generator. This technique uses modular arithmetic, where the value numbered $n + 1$ is calculated from the value numbered n by

$$Vn + 1 = (Vn * a + b)(\text{Mod } c)$$

These techniques are not suitable for cryptographic use; classical applications are simulations of natural phenomena, sampling, numerical analysis, testing computer programs, decision making, and games, none of which have the characteristics suitable for security uses [r166].

The quality of traditional pseudo-random number generator algorithms is measured by statistical tests on such sequences. Carefully chosen values a, b, c, and initial V or carefully chosen placement of the shift register tap in the above simple process can produce excellent statistics. These sequences may be adequate in simulations (Monte Carlo experiments) as long as the sequence is orthogonal to the structure of the space being explored. Even there, subtle patterns may cause problems. However, such sequences are clearly bad for use in security applications. They are fully predictable if the initial state is known. Depending on the form of the pseudo-random number generator, the sequence may be determinable from observation of a short portion of the sequence. For example, with the generators above, one can determine $Vn + 1$ given knowledge of Vn. In fact, it has been shown that with these techniques, even if only one bit of the pseudo-random values are released, the seed can be determined from short sequences [r166].

Pseudo-Security (aka weak security, superficial security, or infraction discouragement techniques) An environment where there is a false sense of security. For example, the claim that Virtual Local Area Networks (VLANs) are secure because of the labeling mechanism, or the claim that MultiProtocol Label Switching (MPLS) is secure because of the labeling mechanism [r406]. Related to security through obscurity.

PSN See Packet Switched Network

PSTN See Public Switched Telephone Network

Psychological Acceptability (aka Principle of Psychological Acceptability) One of Saltzer and Schroeder's Design Principles. Security mechanisms should not make the resource more difficult to access than if the security mechanisms were not present. Security mechanisms often entail additional burdens, but they should be as minimal as possible [r139a].

PTCCH See Packet Timing Advance Control Channel

PTM See Point-to-Multipoint

PTM-G See Point-To-Multipoint Group Call

PTO See Public Telecommunication Operator

PTP See Point-to-Point

PTP-CNLS See Point-to-Point Connectionless Network Service

PTP-CONS See Point-to-Point Connection Oriented Network Service

PU See Payload Units

PUA See Presence User Agent

Public Component A synonym for "public key."

Public Key (aka public component) The published and publicly available key in a Public-Key Cryptography system. This key is used to encrypt messages bound for its intended recipient and to decrypt signatures made by the sender.

Public-Key Certificate (PKC) A data structure containing the public key of an end entity and some other information, which is digitally signed with the private key of the Certification Authority (CA) which issued it [r105].

A digital certificate that binds a system entity's identity to a public key value, and possibly to additional data items. Also, a digitally signed data structure that attests to the ownership of a public key. The digital signature on a public-key certificate is unforgeable. Thus, the certificate can be published, such as by posting it in a directory, without the directory having to protect the certificate's data integrity [r013].

Public-Key Cryptography (aka asymmetric cryptography) A modern branch of cryptography in which the algorithms employ a pair of keys (a public key and a private key) and use a different component of the pair for different steps of the algorithm [r013].

Public-Key Cryptography Standards (PKCS) Specifications produced by RSA Laboratories in cooperation with secure systems developers worldwide for the purpose of accelerating the deployment of public-key cryptography. First published in 1991 as a result of meetings with a small group of early adopters of public-key technology, the PKCS documents have become widely referenced and implemented. Contributions from the PKCS series have become part of many formal and de facto standards, including ANSI X9 documents, Secure Electronic Transaction (SET), Secure Multipurpose Internet Mail Extensions (S/MIME), and Secure Sockets Layer (SSL).

- PKCS #1: RSA Cryptography Standard
- PKCS #3: Diffie–Hellman Key Agreement Standard
- PKCS #5: Password-Based Cryptography Standard
- PKCS #6: Extended-Certificate Syntax Standard
- PKCS #7: Cryptographic Message Syntax Standard
- PKCS #8: Private-Key Information Syntax Standard
- PKCS #9: Selected Attribute Types
- PKCS #10: Certification Request Syntax Standard
- PKCS #11: Cryptographic Token Interface Standard
- PKCS #12: Personal Information Exchange Syntax Standard

- PKCS #13: Elliptic Curve Cryptography Standard
- PKCS #15: Cryptographic Token Information Format Standard

Public-Key Cryptography Standards #10 (PKCS #10) A standard [r425] from the PKCS series; defines a syntax for requests for public-key certificates. A PKCS #10 request contains a Distinguished Name (DN) and a public key, may contain other attributes, and is signed by the entity making the request. The request is sent to a Certification Authority (CA), who converts it to an X.509 public-key certificate (or some other form) and returns it, possibly in PKCS #7 format.

Public-Key Cryptography Standards #11 (PKCS #11) A standard [r408] from the PKCS series; defines a software Cryptographic Application Programming Interface (CAPI) called Cryptoki (short for "cryptographic token interface") for devices that hold cryptographic information and perform cryptographic functions [r013].

Public-Key Cryptography Standards #7 (PKCS #7) A standard from the PKCS series; defines a syntax for data that may have cryptography applied to it, such as for digital signatures and digital envelopes.

Public-Key Cryptosystem Consists of three algorithms, K, E, and D. The key generation algorithm K is an efficient algorithm that takes a security parameter as input and outputs a public key pk and private key sk. The public key specifies among other things a finite set of possible messages and a finite set of possible ciphertexts, denoted by pkM and pkC. The encryption algorithm E is an efficient algorithm that takes a public key and a message as input and outputs a ciphertext. The decryption algorithm D is a deterministic polynomial-time algorithm that takes a private key and a ciphertext as input and outputs either a message or the special symbol. One requires that for any public–private key pair (pk, sk) and any message m in the set of messages specified by pk, $D(sk, E(pk, m)) = m$ [r032].

Public-Key Encryption, Original Articles Public-key encryption was first proposed by Diffie and Hellman, and widely popularized with the Rivest–Shamir–Adleman (RSA) cryptosystem. The following three papers are generally regarded as the seminal papers in the field of public-key cryptography: R. Rivest and A. Shamir, L. M. Adleman, "A Method for Obtaining Digital Signatures and Public-Key Cryptosystems," Communications of the ACM, 21(2):120–126, February 1978; W. Diffie and M. Hellman, "New Directions in Cryptography," *IEEE Transactions on Information Theory,* IT-22; and, R. Merkle, "Secure Communications Over Insecure Channels," *Communications of ACM,* vol. 17, no. 4, 294–299.

Public-Key Forward Secrecy (PFS)   (aka perfect forward secrecy) For a key agreement protocol based on asymmetric cryptography, the property that ensures that a session key derived from a set of long-term public and private keys will not be compromised if one of the private keys is compromised in the future [r013].

Public-Key Infrastructure (PKI)   A system of Certification Authorities (CAs) [and, optionally, registration authorities (RAs) and other supporting servers and agents] that perform some set of certificate management, archive management, key management, and token management functions for a community of users in an application of asymmetric cryptography [r013].

Public-Key Infrastructure X.509 (PKIX) usage: The set of hardware, software, people, policies, and procedures needed to create, manage, store, distribute, and revoke digital certificates based on asymmetric cryptography [r013].

The core PKI functions are (a) to register users and issue their public-key certificates, (b) to revoke certificates when required, and (c) to archive data needed to validate certificates at a much later time. Key pairs for data confidentiality may be generated (and perhaps escrowed) by CAs or RAs, but requiring a PKI client to generate its own digital signature key pair helps maintain system integrity of the cryptographic system, because then only the client ever possesses the private key it uses. Also, an authority may be es-

tablished to approve or coordinate Certificate Policy Statement (CPSs), which are security policies under which components of a PKI operate [r013].

A number of other servers and agents may support the core PKI, and PKI clients may obtain services from them. The full range of such services is not yet fully understood and is evolving, but supporting roles may include archive agent, certified delivery agent, confirmation agent, digital notary, directory, key escrow agent, key generation agent, naming agent who ensures that issuers and subjects have unique identifiers within the PKI, repository, ticket-granting agent, and time stamp agent [r013].

Public-Key Infrastructure X.509 (PKIX)   A contraction of "Public-Key Infrastructure (X.509)," the name of the IETF working group that addressed architecture and set of protocols needed to support an X.509-based Public-Key Infrastructure (PKI) for the Internet.

Also, a collective name for that architecture and set of protocols. The goal of PKIX is to facilitate the use of X.509 public-key certificates in multiple Internet applications and to promote interoperability between different implementations that use those certificates. The resulting PKI is intended to provide a framework that supports a range of trust and hierarchy environments and a range of usage environments. PKIX specifies (a) profiles of the v3 X.509 public-key certificate standards and the v2 X.509 certificate revocation list (CRL) standards for the Internet; (b) operational protocols used by relying parties to obtain information such as certificates or certificate status; (c) management protocols used by system entities to exchange information needed for proper management of the PKI; and (d) information about certificate policies and Certificate Policy Statements (CPSs), covering the areas of PKI security not directly addressed in the rest of PKIX [r013].

Public Land Mobile Network (PLMN)   (GSM context) The collective term for public mobile radio networks [r011].

Public Switched Telephone Network (PSTN)

The traditional voice network in the United States, managed, supported, and operated by telecom carriers. While business services have become nearly completely digital [Time Division Multiplexing (TDM)] [e.g., via Integrated Services Digital Network (ISDN) and/or T1 trunks], the consumers still utilize analog telephony for the "last mile."

Public Telecommunication Operator (PTO)
Term to describe telecommunication administrations, recognized operating agencies, private (customer and third party) administrations, and/or other organizations that operate or use a Telecommunications Management Network (TMN) [r068].

Pulse Code Modulation (PCM)   (GSM context) Pulse Code Modulation (PCM) describes the configuration of terrestrial interfaces in the Station Subsystem (BSS). There is the PCM 24 configuration with 24 traffic channels per frame (e.g., in the United States) and the PCM 30 configuration with 30 traffic channels per frame (e.g., in Europe) [r011].

Pulsed Laser   (optical transmission term) A laser that emits light in a series of pulses rather than continuously. Used in testing fiber systems.

Purpose-Built   (Storage context) Device designed for a specific purpose or application that includes specialized hardware/software to provide that function [r029].

PVC   See Permanent Virtual Circuit

PVCC   See Permanent Virtual Channel Connection

PVPC   See Permanent Virtual Path Connection

PW   See Pseudo-Wire

Q

Q Q Q Q Q Q Q Q Q Q Q Q Q Q Q Q Q Q Q Q Q Q Q

Q Adapter   A physical block that is characterized by a contained Q adapter function block and which connects network element (NE)-like or operations system (OS)-like physical entities with non-Telecommunications Management Network (TMN)-compatible interfaces (at m reference points) to Q interfaces [r068a].

Q Interface   An interface applied at *q* reference points.

Q Reference Points   A reference point located between network element function (NEF) and operations systems function (OSF), between Q adapter function (QAF) and OSF, and between OSF and OSF [r068a].

QoS   See Quality of Service

Qualified Learning   The learning decisions at the User facing Provider Edge (U-PE) are based on the customer Ethernet frame's Media Access Control (MAC) address and Virtual Local Area Network (VLAN) tag, if a VLAN tag exists. If no VLAN tag exists, the default VLAN is assumed [r082].

Quality of Service (QoS) Layer 2 Standard   Defined in IEEE 802.1p. Provides prioritized Ethernet frame handling as they travel from a client to the default gateway (router).

Quality of Service (QoS) Layer 3 Standards   See diffserv or intserv

Quantum   When used as a noun (plural quanta): a discrete quantity of energy, momentum or angular momentum; the smallest amount of energy that can be absorbed or radiated by matter at that frequency. When used as an adjective (as in quantum theory, quantum mechanics, quantum field theory): defines the theory as involving quantities that depend on Planck's constant h. In such theories radiation comes in discrete quanta [r144].

Quantum Computer (QuC) A computer that takes advantage of Quantum Theory properties (e.g., entanglement) present at the nanoscale. A significant expectation is that a QuC will be able to effectively factorize large integers into their primes, posing a threat to widely-used encryption methods [r427]. Quantum cryptography is considered to be the most advanced application of QuC; studies have suggested that quantum cryptography can provide absolutely secure (new) encryption methods [r144].

Quantum Computing Quantum computing is a massively parallel architecture at a level that is impossible in any classical architecture. In quantum computing, information is encoded in "quantum bits (qubits)." In contrast to classical logical bits, which can be in either state 1 or state 0, quantum bits exist as a combination (a linear superposition) of two quantum logic states, represented as $|1>$ and $|0>$. It is because of this capacity for parallel processing that a quantum computer is able to perform calculations much faster than classical computers. Quantum computing is presently at an (immature) experimental stage, but if many of the problems can be overcome, the potential power of the technique will allow many numerically intensive calculations to be completed that are presently impossible with classical computers. At this time only a few systems with up to 7 qubits have been demonstrated. For most applications such as factorization of large numbers for cryptography, 30,000 qubits or so are required, although even 50 qubits will quickly solve problems that are very slow on classical computers [r144].

Quantum Cryptography See Quantum Encryption

Quantum Encryption Encryption based on quantum algorithms. Based on current concepts for Quantum Computing and the development of concrete quantum algorithms, the possibility exists that several computational problems might be solved more efficiently by exploiting the principles of quantum mechanics in the computational process. The objectives of this research are to better understand this technological opportunity and to exploit it fully; topics include (i) quantum algorithms and complexity, (ii) cryptography, (iii) fault-tolerant computation, and (iv) information and communication theory. Anticipated results include new quantum polynomial time algorithms and few-qubit applications, complexity theory-based quantum cryptographic protocols, better QuC codes, self-testing/correcting quantum programs, advanced information theories, communication complexity, and the Kolmogorov complexity in the quantum domain [r427, r144].

Quantum Theory A theory that seeks to explain that the action of forces is a result of the exchange of subatomic particles. The theory used to describe physical systems that are very small, of atomic dimensions or less.

Qubits (Quantum bits) In quantum computing, information is be encoded in "quantum bits (qubits)." In contrast to classical logical bits, which can be in either state 1 or state 0, quantum bits exist as a combination (a linear superposition) of two quantum logic states, represented as $|1>$ and $|0>$ [r144].

R&D   See Research and Development

RA   See Registration Authority

RAB   See Radio Access Bearer

Rabin–Miller Test   An efficient probabilistic algorithm that can recognize a composite number of say 1000 digits without ever factoring that number, and the primality of a number can also be determined efficiently. Also, there have been developed over the years much improved factoring algorithms, but despite this progress, factoring a general composite number with as few as say 1000 digits is still a challenging problem using the best algorithms known today [r390].

RAC   See Routing Area Code

RACC   See Routing Area Color Code

Race Conditions   A time-of-change/time-of-use attack that exploits the time difference between when a security control was applied and the time the service was used.

RACH   See Random Access Channel

Radio Access Bearer (RAB)   (3G Wireless context) The connection between the User Equipment and the Core Network [r007].

Radio Frequency Identification (RFID)   Low-cost tags affixed to consumer items and inventories that are considered "smartlabels." For example, RFID are used in keyless entry systems, automated tollbooths, subway stations fare-paying cards, and in clothing. RFID systems are comprised of radio frequency (RF) tags (transponders), and RF tag readers (transceivers). Typically, tags consist of an antenna connected to an integrated circuit; the logic allows the tag to support capabilities such as writable storage, environmental sensors, access control, or encryption. Tag readers broadcast an RF signal that enables the reader to access data stored on tags (e.g., a unique identification number) [r078].

Privacy is an issue in a ubiquitous RFID system. Consumer products labeled with insecure tags could reveal sensitive information when queried by snoops in proximity. RFID technology has made headway in other sectors, such as the retail, defense, automotive, and information technology industries. Most notably, Wal-Mart stores and the U.S. Department of Defense have both recently set policy and guidelines requiring vendors to use RFID technology within their supply chains [r311].

Radio Link Control (RLC)   (3G Wireless context) Data link layer service; offers transport services to the overlying layer, such as acknowledged or unacknowledged data transfer [r007].

Radio Network Controller (RNC)   (3G Wireless context) Controls the Node Bs via the Iub interface [r007].

Radio Network Identifier (RNTI)   (3G Wireless context) Enables the Medium Access Control (MAC) layer to distinguish at which User Equipments the data on the common transport channels is directed [r007].

Radio Network Subsystem (RNS)   (3G Wireless context) Consists of the network elements Radio Network Controller (RNC) and Node B [r007].

Radio Resource Control (RRC)   (3G Wireless context) Used to control the procedures in the physical layer, as well as in the Medium Access Control (MAC) and the Radio Link Control (RLC) [r007].

RADIUS   See Remote Authentication Dial-In User Service

RAI   See Routing Area Identification

RAID   See Redundant Array of Independent Disks

Rainbow Series   A set of more than 30 technical and policy documents with colored covers, issued by the National Computer Security Center (NCSC), that discuss in detail the Trusted Computer System Evaluation Criteria (TCSEC) and provide guidance for meeting and applying the criteria [r013].

Rainbow Table   Hashing is a cryptographic technique where a mathematical function takes a text input and converts that to a fixed size output, say 128 bits. In a brute force attack, the attacker tries all password combinations as input and compares the output with the hash stored in the database to get a match. Password hashes are considered secure when it is not feasible to brute force the password in reasonable time. A rainbow table stores a fraction of the total number of hashes. The keys are organized in chains where only the first and the last element of the chain are stored in the table. A word is selected and hashed; the result is "reduced" so that it represents another possible password by converting each character into a printable American Standard Code for Information Interchange (ASCII) character. The reduced word is hashed again. The process is repeated over a few thousand times. The final value is stored in the second column of the table against the first word. None of the intermediate hashes are stored. The storage requirement is thus reduced considerably. A large number of such rows are pre-computed and stored in a database: these are called "rainbow chains." To obtain the password from the hash, the hash is looked up in the second column of the rainbow table. If no match is found, the hash is reduced and hashed. The resulting hash is again looked up in the second column of the table. This is repeated until a lookup succeeds. Once a match is obtained, it means the password is present somewhere in that chain. The chain is then recomputed forwards from the word in the first column to obtain the password.

RAM   See Random Access Memory

RAN   See Regional Area Network

Random   (General context) In mathematics, random means "unpredictable." A sequence of values is called random if each successive value is obtained merely by chance and does not depend on the preceding values of the sequence, and a selected individual value is called random if each of the values in the total population of possibilities has equal probability of being selected [r013].

(Security context) In cryptography and other security applications, random means not only unpredictable, but also "unguessable." When selecting data values to use for cryptographic keys, the requirement is for data that an adversary has a very low probability of guessing or determining. It is not sufficient to use data that only meets traditional statistical tests for randomness or which is based on limited range sources, such as clocks. Frequently such random quantities are determinable (i.e., guessable) by an adversary searching through a small space of possibilities [r410, r013].

Random Access Channel (RACH) (GSM context) A Common Control Channel in the uplink. It is used by the mobile station to initiate transactions and to transmit its identity and its request, like the request for registration [r011, r007].

Random Access Memory (RAM) Microprocessor (volatile) memory that holds all the real-time information for the execution of programs and tasks.

Random Access Memory (RAM) Slack The space from the end of the file to the end of the containing sector. Before a sector is written to disk, it is stored in a buffer somewhere in RAM. If the buffer is only partially filled with information before being committed to disk, remnants from the end of the buffer will be written to disk. In this way, information that was never "saved" can be found in RAM slack on disk [r057].

Random Early Detection (RED) One (of several) mechanisms for Active Queue Management that has been proposed to detect and address congestion in packet-switched networks. Mechanism is implemented in core and edge routers and is currently being deployed in the Internet.

Random Number (RAND) (GSM context) The random number, together with the key Kc and the Signed Response (SRES), forms the Authentication Triplet, which is generated in the Authentication Center (AuC) for the authentication of mobile subscribers [r011].

Random Number Generation in Microsoft Windows Microsoft's recommendation to users of the Windows operating system is to use the CryptGenRandom pseudo-random number generation call with the CryptAPI cryptographic service provider. This takes a handle to a cryptographic service provider library, a pointer to a buffer by which the caller can provide entropy and into which the generated pseudo-randomness is returned, and an indication of how many octets of randomness are desired. The Windows CryptAPI cryptographic service provider stores a seed state variable with every user. When CryptGenRandom is called, this is combined with any randomness provided in the call and with various system and user data such as the process ID, thread ID, system clock, system time, system counter, memory status, free disk clusters, and hashed user environment block. These data are fed to Secure Hash Algorithm 1 (SHA-1) (RFC 3174), and the output is used to seed a Rivest Cipher #4 (RC4) key stream. That key stream is used to produce the pseudo-random data requested and to update the user's seed state variable [r166].

Random Number Generator A process used to generate an unpredictable, uniformly distributed series of numbers (usually integers). True random number generators are hardware-based devices that depend on the output of a "noisy diode" or other physical phenomena [r410, r013].

Random Numbers Numbers spanning a (specified) interval $[a, b]$ such that the probability density function $f(x)$ describing the probability of finding such number at point $a \leq x \leq b$ is the uniform distribution. The practical generation of "quality" random numbers is difficult.

Randomized Algorithm An algorithm that can make random choices during its execution. A randomized algorithm will typically choose a different path of execution (based on the output of a random number generator, such as the flip of a coin) on each run and sometimes output a different result [r094].

Randomness in Update Trains An update train

used as a test stimulus has a considerable number of parameters that can be varied, to a greater or lesser extent, randomly and independently. A random update train will contain a route mixture randomized across [r086].

Random-to-Key Function (Kerberos) This function generates a key from a random bitstring of a specific size; namely, (bitstring[K]) → (protocol-key). All the bits of the input string are assumed to be equally random, even though the entropy present in the random source may be limited [r115].

Rapid Spanning Tree Protocol (RSTP) Refinements to the Spanning Tree Protocol (STP) defined in IEEE 802.1w. Enables faster convergence of topology reconfiguration at Layer 2. It is used in corporate Local Area Networks (LANs) and/or metro Ethernet services. Supports faster convergence to a new logical topology upon a link failure (subsecond convergence). In turn, this facilitates to transition from traditional carrier networks and (future) Ethernet-based Wide Area Networks (WANs).

Rate of Return (financial term) The annual rate of return on an investment, expressed as a percentage of the total amount invested. Also called return.

Rayleigh Scattering (optical transmission term) Impairment affecting optical transmission. This is caused by the microscopic nonuniformity of glass and its refractive index. These develop due to small variations in the density of glass as it cools. A ray of light is partially scattered into many directions, therefore, some of the light energy is lost. The attenuation due to scattering decreases with wavelength because the structure of glass is much finer than the wavelength. Rayleigh scattering lessens as wavelengths grow longer: scattering affects short wavelengths more than long wavelengths and limits the use of wavelengths below 800 nm.

RBAC See Role-Based Access Control

RC2 See Rivest Cipher #2

RC4 See Rivest Cipher #4

RD See Route Distinguisher

Read-Only Memory (ROM) Nonvolatile micro-processor memory that holds microcode to start/operate the system.

Real Evidence Tangible asset-based evidence (e.g., a computer, a printout) that may be used in a Court of Law to support legal proceedings.

Real-Time Variable Bit Rate (rtVBR) An Asynchronous Transfer Mode (ATM) service category that supports packet-oriented data traffic. rtVBR is useful for isochronous applications such as voice and video. The Service Level Agreement (SLA) is expressed (by the provider) in terms of end-to-end latency, jittter, and packet loss. The end-user will require the use of ATM Adaptation Layer 5 (AAL-5) in their clients/hosts/routers to utilize VBR-based services.

Realm (Kerberos context) The domain of authority of a Kerberos server (consisting of an authentication server and a ticket-granting server), including the Kerberized clients and the Kerberized application servers [r013].

Real-Time Streaming Protocol (RTSP) An application-level protocol for control over the delivery of data with real-time properties. Described in RFC 2326 [r257].

Real-Time Transport Protocol (RTP) A protocol used to carry streaming real-time multimedia data over IP Networks. Defined in RFC 1889 [r257].

Real Time Protocol (RTP) Sniffing The interception of RTP traffic [e.g., traffic containing Voice Over IP (VoIP) information].

Reassembly Procedure to rebuild the original charge of a datagram from several fragments [r008].

Receipt The functional message that is sent from a receiver to a sender to acknowledge receipt of an Electronic Data Interchange/e-Commerce (EDI/EC) interchange. This message may be either synchronous or asynchronous in nature [r164].

Reconnaissance Scans Scanning the victims looking for ways into their systems. The purpose is to map out the target network and systems.

Record-Keeping Server (RKS) The device that collects and correlates various Event Messages.

Recovery   The phase in Incident Handling that returns the system to a fully operational status.

Recovery Point Objective (RPO)   The point in time that the restarted infrastructure will reflect when recovered from a disaster or data loss scenario. Essentially, this is the roll-back that will be experienced as a result of a system recovery. Reducing RPO requires increasing synchronicity of data replication.

Recovery Time Objective (RTO)   The amount of time that will pass before a system is available following a disaster. Reducing RTO requires data to be online and available at a failover site.

Recursion   (SIP context) A client recurses on a 3xx response when it generates a new request to one or more of the Uniform Resource Identifier (URIs) in the Contact header field in the response [r025].

RED   Designation for information system equipment or facilities that handle (and for data that contains) only plaintext (or, depending on the context, classified information), and for such data itself. This term derives from U.S. Government COMSEC terminology [r013].

RED   (as acronym) See Random Early Detection

RED/BLACK Separation   An architectural concept for cryptographic systems that strictly separates the parts of a system that handle plaintext (i.e., RED information) from the parts that handle ciphertext (i.e., BLACK information). This term derives from U.S. Government COMSEC terminology [r013].

Redirect   (IPv6 context) Procedure included in the neighbors discovery mechanisms to inform a host about the IPv6 address of another neighbor that is more appropriate as next hop to a destination [r008].

Redirect Function   The process by which a router informs a host of a better first-hop IPv6 address to reach a destination. This is equivalent to the function of the IPv4 of Internet Control Message Protocol (ICMP) Redirect message [r024].

Redirect Server   (SIP context) A redirect server is a user agent server that generates 3xx responses to requests it receives, directing the client to contact an alternate set of Uniform Resource Identifiers (URIs) [r025].

Reduced Sign-on   A partial step to complete Single Sign-On (SSO) environment. Reduced sign-on reduces the number of passwords required across multiple applications, but not all the way to just one sign-on. Reduced sign-on to the network eliminates the need to authenticate multiple times; administrators provide enhanced security through streamlined management. For example, users can securely move between applications without having to authenticate multiple times. Without reduced sign-on (or SSO for that matter) users have too many credentials to remember, spend too much time logging on to various systems and applications; administrators have to provision multiple accounts and incur the overhead of maintaining multiple directories.

Redundant Array of Independent Disks (RAID)
A disk subsystem that is used to increase performance or provide fault tolerance. RAID can also be set up to provide both functions at the same time. RAID is a set of two or more ordinary hard disks and a specialized disk controller that contains the RAID functionality. Developed initially for servers and stand-alone disk storage systems, RAID is increasingly popular in desktop PCs. RAID can also be implemented via software only, but with less performance, especially when rebuilding data after a failure [r029].

RAID improves performance by disk striping, which interleaves bytes or groups of bytes across multiple drives, so more than one disk is reading and writing simultaneously. Fault tolerance is achieved by mirroring or parity. Mirroring is 100% duplication of the data on two drives (RAID 1), and parity is used (RAID 3 and 5) to calculate the data in two drives and store the results on a third: a bit from drive 1 is XOR'd with a bit from drive 2, and the result bit is stored on drive 3 (see OR for an explanation of XOR). A failed drive can be hot swapped with a new one, and the RAID controller automatically rebuilds the lost data. In addition, RAID systems may be built using a spare drive (hot spare) ready and waiting to be the replacement for a drive that fails [r029].

RAID systems come in all sizes from desktop units to floor-standing models. Any desktop PC can be turned into a RAID system by adding a RAID controller board and the appropriate number of IDE or SCSI disks. Stand-alone units may also include large amounts of cache as well as redundant power supplies [r029].

In the late 1980s, RAID used to mean an array of "inexpensive" disks, being compared to large computer disks or SLEDs (Single Large Expensive Disk). As hard disks became cheaper, the RAID Advisory Board changed the name to mean "independent" [r029].

Redundant Array of Independent Disks (RAID) LEVEL 0   Level 0 is disk striping only, which interleaves data across multiple disks for better performance. It does not provide safeguards against failure [r029].

Redundant Array of Independent Disks (RAID) LEVEL 1   Uses disk mirroring, which provides 100% duplication of data. Offers highest reliability, but doubles storage cost [r029].

Redundant Array of Independent Disks (RAID) LEVEL 2   Bits (rather than bytes or groups of bytes) are interleaved across multiple disks. The Connection Machine used this technique, but this is a rare method [r029].

Redundant Array of Independent Disks (RAID) LEVEL 3   Data are striped across three or more drives. Used to achieve the highest data transfer, because all drives operate in parallel. Parity bits are stored on separate, dedicated drives [r029].

Redundant Array of Independent Disks (RAID) LEVEL 4   Similar to RAID Level 3, but manages disks independently rather than in unison. Not often used [r029].

Redundant Array of Independent Disks (RAID) LEVEL 5   Most widely used RAID technology. Data are striped across three or more drives for performance, and parity bits are used for fault tolerance. The parity bits from two drives are stored on a third drive [r029].

Redundant Array of Independent Disks (RAID) LEVEL 6   Highest reliability, but not widely used. Similar to RAID 5, but does two different parity computations or the same computation on overlapping subsets of the data [r029].

Redundant Array of Independent Disks (RAID) LEVEL 10   A combination of RAID 1 and RAID 0 combined. Raid 0 is used for performance, and RAID 1 is used for fault tolerance [r029].

Reference Monitor   An access control concept that refers to an abstract machine that mediates all accesses to objects by subjects [r120]. A reference monitor should be complete (i.e., it mediates every access), isolated (i.e., it cannot be modified by other system entities), and verifiable (i.e., small enough to be subjected to analysis and tests to ensure that it is correct) [r013].

Reference Point   An architectural concept used to delineate management function blocks and which defines a service boundary between two management function blocks [r068a].

Reflection Attack   A type of replay attack in which transmitted data is sent back to its originator.

Regenerator   (optical transmission term) An active device that receives an incoming digital optical symbol and retransmits a new, cleaned-up digital optical symbol.

Regeneration with Retiming and Reshaping (3R)   (optical transmission term) The "cleaning-up" of a signal at discrete points along the transmission path, typically every 20–35 miles (with today's technology).

Regional Area Network (RAN)   Networks that exceed a Metropolitan Area Network (MAN) in geographic scope, but are not nationwide or global in nature.

Registrar   (SIP context) A registrar is a server that accepts REGISTER requests and places the information it receives in those requests into the location service for the domain it handles [r025].

Registration   An administrative act or process whereby an entity's name and other attributes are established for the first time at a Certification Authority (CA), prior to the CA issuing a digital certificate that has the entity's name as the subject. Registration may be accomplished either directly, by the CA, or indirectly, by a separate Registration Authority (RA). An entity is presented to the CA or RA, and the authority either records the name(s) claimed for the entity or assigns the entity's name(s). The authority also determines and records other attributes of the entity that are to be bound in a certificate (such as a public key or authorizations) or maintained in the authority's database (such as street address and telephone number). The authority is responsible, possibly assisted by an RA, for authenticating the entity's identity and verifying the correctness of the other attributes, in accordance with the CA's Certificate Policy Statement (CPS) [r013].

Registration Authority (RA) [aka Local Registration Authority (LRA)] An entity that is responsible for one or more of the following functions [r424]:

- The identification and authentication of certificate applicants
- The approval or rejection of certificate applications
- Initiating certificate revocations or suspensions under certain circumstances
- Processing subscriber requests to revoke or suspend their certificates
- Approving or rejecting requests by subscribers to renew or re-key their certificates

RAs, however, do not sign or issue certificates [i.e., an RA is delegated certain tasks on behalf of a Certification Authority (CA)] [r124, r105].

[Public-Key Infrastructure X.509 (PKIX) context] An optional PKI component, separate from the CA(s). The functions that the RA performs will vary from case to case but may include identity authentication and name assignment, key generation and archiving of key pairs, token distribution, and revocation reporting [r432].

(SET context) An independent third-party organization that processes payment card applica-

tions for multiple payment card brands and forwards applications to the appropriate financial institutions [r019].

Registration Authority (RA) Domains A capability of a Certification Authority Workstation (CAW) that allows a Certification Authority (CA) to divide the responsibility for certification requests among multiple RAs. This capability might be used to restrict access to private authorization data that is provided with a certification request, and to distribute the responsibility to review and approve certification requests in high volume environments. RA domains might segregate certification requests according to an attribute of the certificate subject, such as an organizational unit [r013].

Registration Key A key used in the Mobile Node-Foreign Agent (MN-FA) or Mobile Node-Home Agent (MN-HA) Mobility Security Association. A registration key is typically only used once or a very few times, and only for the purposes of verifying a small volume of authentication data [r012].

Registry A central hierarchical database used in Microsoft Windows Operating System to store information necessary to configure the system for one or more users, applications, and hardware devices. The registry contains information that Windows continually refreshes during operation, such as profiles for each user, the applications installed on the computer, and so on. The registry is the "local portion" of Active Directory (AD); AD has a more inclusive view of the entire network.

Registry Schema The definition for a registry type specifying the queries, results, and entity classes.

Registry Type A registry serving a specific function, such as a domain registry or an address registry. Each type of registry is assigned a Uniform Resource Name (URN).

Regrade Deliberately change the classification level of information in an authorized manner [r013].

Regression Analysis The rigorous and exhaustive testing of new features included in a new software, firmware, or hardware release to validate that it works (as advertised) and that is does not "regress" in the area of existing capabilities.

Regular Transaction (SIP context) A regular transaction is any transaction with a method other than INVITE, ACK, or CANCEL [r025].

Regulatory Compliance Measures, procedures, mechanisms, actions, and audit trails that enable an organization to meet the rules and regulations identified in applicable legislation.

Rekey Change the value of a cryptographic key that is being used in an application of a cryptographic system. For example, rekey is required at the end of a cryptoperiod or key lifetime [r013].

Relaying The act of passing an Internet message (such as e-mail or netnews) from machine to machine.

Relay Router 6to4 (IPv6 context) An IPv6/IPv4 router that redirects traffic directed to 6to4 addresses between 6to4 routers in the Internet and IPv6 Internet devices [r008].

Reliability The ability of a system to perform a required function under stated conditions for a specified period of time. The probability that a system operates through a given operation specification:

$R(t)$ = the reliability, the chance that the system will fail between $[t_0, t]$,

$z(t)$ = the failure rate,

$R(t) = e^{-\int z(t)\, dt}$

During the useful life of the product, one can approximate the failure rate as linear:

$\int z(t)\, dt \approx \lambda t$,

$R(t) = e^{-\lambda t}$ = The Exponential Failure Law.

Note that the failure rate is the expected number of failures per unit time, and is shown with the constant (lambda, λ), with the units of failures per hour.

Relying Party (RP) (Certification Authority context) (aka "certificate user") A recipient of a certificate who acts in reliance on that certificate

and/or any digital signatures verified using that certificate. The terms "certificate user" and "relying party" are often used interchangeably [r011, r105]. Used in a legal context to mean a recipient of a certificate who acts in reliance on that certificate [r013].

Relying Party Agreement (RPA) An agreement between a certification authority and relying party that typically establishes the rights and responsibilities between those parties regarding the verification of digital signatures or other uses of certificates [r011].

Remediation (aka add-on security) Mitigating a risk identified in a risk assessment after the system has been operationalized.

Remote Access Dial-In User Service (RADIUS) Protocol used for authentication and authorization, as well as billing information that details the service or services being delivered to the end user. Described in RFC 2138 and RFC 2139 [r157, r415]. RADIUS mediates users' authentication information and configuration information between a shared, centralized authentication server (the RADIUS server) and a network access server (the RADIUS client) that needs to authenticate the users of its network access ports. A user of the RADIUS client presents authentication information to the client, and the client passes that information to the RADIUS server. The server authenticates the client using a shared secret value, then checks the user's authentication information, and finally returns to the client all authorization and configuration information needed by the client to deliver service to the user [r013]. The RADIUS server can support a variety of methods to authenticate a user.

The RADIUS protocol is the basis for the Authentication, Authorization, and Accounting (AAA) server used in various networking applications.

Remote Control Mechanisms used to resolve workstation problems expeditiously and securely by logging into and taking command of the user's workstation. Typically, the user's workstation has the "server" software on it and the help desk personnel have the "client" software on their workstation with which to access the server software.

Remote Installation A general technique to transfer a program remotely [e.g., via File Transfer Protocol (FTP), e-mail, etc.] and install it into a target device (e.g., a PC).

Remote Installation Keylogger Mode Many keyloggers have a feature whereby it can attach to other programs and can be sent by e-mail to install on the remote PC in stealth mode. It will then send keystrokes, screenshots, and websites visited to the attacker by e-mail or via File Transfer Protocol (FTP) [r224].

Remote Network Monitoring (RMON) See Simple Network Management Protocol (SNMP), Remote Network Monitoring (RMON)

Renyi Entropy A continuous spectrum of entropies, called Renyi entropy, has been defined, specified by the parameter r. $r = 1$ is Shannon entropy and $r =$ infinity is min-entropy. When $r =$ zero, it is just log (n), where n is the number of nonzero probabilities. Renyi entropy is a nonincreasing function of r, so min-entropy is always the most conservative measure of entropy and usually the best to use for cryptographic evaluation [r166].

Replacement Value   (financial term) The value of an asset as determined by the estimated cost of replacing it.

Replay Attack   (aka session highjack) An attack in which a valid data transmission is maliciously or fraudulently repeated, either by the originator or by an adversary who intercepts the data and retransmits it, possibly as part of a masquerade attack [r013]. Such protection mechanisms as one-time password systems and nonces [r384, r416] are meant to counter replay attacks.

Replica Origin Server An origin server holding a replica of a resource that may act as an authoritative reference for client requests.

Replication Creating duplicate copies of media or systems configuration files for the purposes of backup and recovery.

Replicator Any program that acts to produce copies of itself; examples include a program, a worm, a fork bomb, or virus.

Repository A system for storing and distributing digital certificates and related information [including certificate revocation lists (CRLs), Certificate Policy Statements (CPSs), and certificate policies] to certificate users. "A trustworthy system for storing and retrieving certificates or other information relevant to certificates" [r111, r013]. A certificate is published to those who might need it by putting it in a repository. The repository usually is a publicly accessible, on-line server. In the Federal Public-Key Infrastructure, for example, the expected repository is a directory that uses Lightweight Directory Access Protocol (LDAP), but also may be the X.500 Directory that uses Directory Access Protocol (DAP), or a Hypertext Transfer Protocol (HTTP) server, or a File Transfer Protocol (FTP) server that permits anonymous login [r013].

Repudiability The ability for the sender to deny that he/she wrote any particular message. Digital signatures are often touted as great tools for achieving non-repudiability. Useful for electronic communiqués (e.g., contracts), but problematic for private communication. Note that the sender could just not sign the message, but then not even the intended receiver is assured of the message's authenticity [r381].

Repudiation Denial by one of the entities involved in a communication of having participated in all or part of the communication [r160].

Repudiation, False Denial of Origin   A repudiation action whereby the originator of data denies responsibility for its generation.

Repudiation, False Denial of Receipt   A repudiation action whereby the recipient of data denies receiving and possessing the data.

Request   (SIP context) A Session Initiation Protocol (SIP) message sent from a client to a server, for the purpose of invoking a particular operation [r025].

Request for Comment (RFC)   One of the documents in the archival series that is the official channel for Internet Standards Documentation

(ISDs) and other publications of the Internet Engineering Steering Group, the Internet Architecture Board, and the Internet community in general [r293, r417, r013].

Request Transaction   (MIDCOM context) Consists of a request message transfer from the agent to the middlebox, processing of the message at the middlebox, a reply message transfer from the middlebox to the agent, and the optional transfer of notification messages from the middlebox to agents other than the one requesting the transaction. A request transaction might cause a state transition at the middlebox [r030].

Required Checksum Mechanism   A checksum mechanism that must be available when a given encryption mechanism is used. For example, since Kerberos has no built in mechanism for negotiating checksum mechanisms, once an encryption mechanism is decided, the corresponding checksum mechanism can be used [r116].

Reroutable LSP   (MPLS context) Any Label-Switched Path (LSP) for which the head-end Label-Switching Router (LSR) requests local protection.

Research and Development (R&D)   Discovering new knowledge about products, processes, and services and then applying that knowledge to create new and improved products, processes, and services that fill market needs [r009].

Research Honeypot   An information-gathering honeypot.

Residual Data   Information that appears to be unavailable (erased), but is still recoverable from the computer system. This includes deleted files still extant on a disk surface. It also includes data existing in hardware such as buffer memories of printers and scanners/fax machines.

Residual Risk   The risk that remains after countermeasures have been applied.

Resilient Packet Ring (RPR)   Relatively new standard for packet-oriented Metropolitan Area Network (MAN) technology to compete with Synchronous Optical Network (SONET). Work undertaken by the Electrical and Electronics Engineers (IEEE) 802.17™ RPR Working Group.

Initial effort encompassed standardization of the RPR MAC. Some carriers are considering standardized RPR a cost-effective solution for the delivery of carrier-class voice, data, and video over existing SONET rings. The fully ratified IEEE 802.17 RPR Standard was expected to be published in mid-2004 [r419, r002, r003].

Resilient Packet Ring (RPR) Alliance   An industry advocacy group committed to the development of an RPR technology standard for the networking industry. The Alliance promotes the adoption of an RPR standard for Local Area Networks (LANs), Metropolitan Area Networks (MANs), and Wide Area Networks (WANs) by educating the networking industry about RPR technology and the benefits of a standard as well as by fostering multi-vendor interoperability.

Resolution Method   The technique used to locate an authority [r237].

Resource Records (RRs)   The DNS data records. Their format is defined in RFC 1035. The most important fields in a resource record are Name, Class, Type, and Data. Name is a domain name, Class and Type are two-byte integers, and Data is a variable-length field to be interpreted in the context of Class and Type. Almost all Internet applications use Class 1, the Internet Class. For the Internet Class, many standard Types have been defined [r418].

Resource Reservation Protocol (RSVP)   A protocol defined in RFC 2205 that has evolved to provide end-to-end quality of service (QoS) signaling services for application data streams (the alternative would be diffserv). Hosts use RSVP to request a specific QoS from the network for particular application flows. Routers use RSVP to deliver QoS requests to all routers along the data path. RSVP also can maintain and refresh states for a requested QoS application flow. RSVP carries QoS signaling messages through the network, visiting each node along the data path. To make a resource reservation at a node, the RSVP module communicates with two local decision modules, admission control and policy control. Admission control determines whether the node has sufficient available resources to supply the requested QoS. Policy control provides authorization for the QoS request. If either check fails, the RSVP module returns an error notification to the application process that originated the request. If both checks succeed, the RSVP module sets parameters in a packet classifier and packet scheduler to obtain the desired QoS [r420].

Resources   (IT context) Include, but are not limited to, processors, data storage, scientific equipment, and so on. Physical resources include servers, storage, and network. Above the physical resources are logical resources that provide additional function by virtualizing and aggregating the resources in the physical layer [r080].

Response   (SIP context) A Session Initiation Protocol (SIP) message sent from a server to a client, for indicating the status of a request sent from the client to the server [r025].

Restricted Cone Network Address Translation (NAT)   A NAT where all requests from the same internal IP address and port are mapped to the same external IP address and port. Unlike a full cone NAT, an external host (with IP address X) can send a packet to the internal host only if the internal host had previously sent a packet to IP address X [r252].

Retransmissions in Transmission Control Protocol (TCP)   TCP has two methods for triggering retransmissions. First, the TCP sender relies on incoming duplicate ACKs, which indicate that the receiver is missing some of the data. After a required number of successive duplicate ACKs have arrived at the sender, it retransmits the first unacknowledged segment and continues with a loss recovery algorithm such as NewReno or SACK-based loss recovery. Second, the TCP sender maintains a retransmission timer which triggers retransmission of segments, if they have not been acknowledged before the retransmission timeout (RTO) expires. When the retransmission timeout occurs, the TCP sender enters the RTO recovery where the congestion window is initialized to one segment and unacknowledged segments are retransmitted using the slow-start algo-

rithm. The retransmission timer is adjusted dynamically, based on the measured round-trip times [r421].

It has been pointed out that the retransmission timer can expire spuriously and cause unnecessary retransmissions when no segments have been lost. After a spurious retransmission timeout, the late acknowledgments of the original segments arrive at the sender, usually triggering unnecessary retransmissions of a whole window of segments during the RTO recovery. Furthermore, after a spurious retransmission timeout, a conventional TCP sender increases the congestion window on each late acknowledgment in slow start. This injects a large number of data segments into the network within one round-trip time, thus violating the packet conservation principle [r421].

Retrovirus   A virus that waits until all possible backup media are infected too, so that it is not possible to restore the system to an uninfected state [r057].

Return Loss   (optical transmission term) The relative power level (dB) reflected back to the input end in the backward direction referenced to the 0-dB reference level when a device is inserted.

Return on Security Investment (ROSI)   (financial term) As most computer security professionals are aware, making the case to invest in computer security is difficult at best. Defining clearly the internal rate of return for each computer security investment is critical for all organizations to be able to invest properly in specific computer security implementations. ROSI is a metric that takes into account what constitutes appropriate inputs for Information Technology (IT) security capital investment planning. National Institute of Standards and Security (NIST) has developed a guideline for Federal agencies to use to support successful integration of security into the capital investment planning process.

Return-to-libc Attack   An attack in which the return address on the stack is replaced by the address of another function. This kind of attack also can be the basis for assaults on a non-executable memory stack [r161].

Reverse Address Resolution Protocol (RARP) (aka Reverse ARP) Protocol used to host machines that do not know their IP address. RARP enables them to request their IP address from the gateway's ARP cache [r19].

Reverse Proxy   (aka surrogate) Accepts inbound requests on behalf of the actual target of the request, applies rules to determine where the request should be directed to (that is, it hides the actual physical address and location of the target of the request, making it less vulnerable to breaches of security), and can also check to see if the requestor is authorized to make such a request. In addition, a reverse proxy can be part of an overall scheme to develop a consistent enterprise-wide approach to security administration [r422].

Review of Security Controls   The routine evaluation, assessment, audit, or review of the security controls placed on an information technology system. Such reviews can be performed by the organization in question or by a third party. The type and rigor of reviews should be commensurate with the acceptable level of risk established for the system [r067].

Revocation Certificate   A security certificate issued by a security authority to indicate that a particular security certificate has been revoked.

Revocation Date   In an X.509 certificate revocation list (CRL) entry, a date-time field that states when the certificate revocation occurred—that is, when the Certification Authority (CA) declared the digital certificate to be invalid. The revocation date may not resolve some disputes because, in the worst case, all signatures made during the validity period of the certificate may have to be considered invalid. However, it may be desirable to treat a digital signature as valid even though the private key used to sign was compromised after the signing. If more is known about when the compromise actually occurred, a second date-time, an "invalidity date," can be included in an extension of the CRL entry [r013].

Revocation List Certificate   A security certificate that identifies a list of security certificates that have been revoked.

RFC   See Request for Comments

RFC 2547 Style Virtual Private Network (VPN) The term has been used for Layer 3 VPN (L3VPN) to describe the extensions of the VPNs defined in the informational RFC 2547 [r423]. This term has now been replaced by the term Border Gateway protocol/Multi-Protocol Label Switching (BGP/MPLS) IP VPNs [r082].

RFID   See Radio-Frequency Identification

RIB   See Routing Information Base

Rights Expression Languages   Policy languages for digital rights management, such as eXtensible rights Markup Language™ (XrML™) and Open Digital Rights Language (ODRL).

Ringback   (SIP context) The signaling tone produced by the calling party's application indicating that a called party is being alerted (ringing) [r025].

Ripple   (optical transmission term) The power difference (dB) between the minimum and maximum insertion loss within the entire passband or clear window for all polarizations.

Risk   The probability that a vulnerability may be exploited or that a threat may become harmful [r056]. Risk is the net negative impact of the exercise of a vulnerability, considering both the probability and the impact of occurrence [r315]. The potential for loss as a consequence of endogenous or exogenous events.

Also defined as an expectation of loss expressed as the probability that a particular threat will exploit a particular vulnerability with a particular harmful result [r013].

(SET context) The possibility of loss because of one or more threats to information (not to be confused with financial or business risk) [r018].

Risk Analysis   Process of analyzing a target environment and the relationships of its risk-related attributes. The analysis should identify threat vulnerabilities, associated these vulnerabilities of affected assets, identify the potential nature of an undesirable result, and identify and evaluate risk-reducing countermeasures [r425].

Risk Assessment   A process that systematically identifies valuable system resources and threats to those resources, quantifies loss exposures (i.e., loss potential) based on estimated frequencies and costs of occurrence, and (optionally) recommends how to allocate resources to countermeasures so as to minimize total exposure. The analysis lists risks in order of cost and criticality, thereby determining where countermeasures should be applied first. It is usually financially and technically infeasible to counteract all aspects of risk, and so some residual risk will remain, even after all available countermeasures have been deployed [r013, r426].

Management identifies the potential risks to business strategy and objectives based on internal and external historical risk events, input from subject matter experts, audit reports, and its own understanding of the internal and external business environment.

Risk Assessment and Management The total process of identifying, controlling, and mitigating information system-related risks. It includes risk assessment, cost–benefit analysis, and the selection, implementation, test, and security evaluation of safeguards. This overall system security review considers both effectiveness and efficiency, including impact on the mission and constraints due to policy, regulations, and laws [r315].

Risk Assessment Components Security services for information risk assessment. Examples include application testing tools, vendor site assessments, and enterprise risk assessments.

Risk Assessment Process Process for the identification and evaluation of risks and risk impacts, and for the recommendation of risk-reducing measures.

Risk Deficiencies Gaps in control structures that expose a firm to unacceptable risks.

Risk Evaluation Process Ongoing (repeatable) processes for environment evaluation leading to a high-assurance risk management program.

Risk Event The actual occurrence of something that generates a loss by materializing the risk.

Risk Governance Processes addressing accountability, ownership, roles, and responsibilities for risk management. Risk governance reflects the required structure and information flow and reporting, and it describes the rules and process for making risk-related decisions.

Risk Identification Identification of the potential risks to the business strategy based on previous internal and external risk events, input from subject matter experts, and audits.

Risk Impact The effect a risk would have on a firm's ability to achieve its mission if the risk occurred.

Risk Limits (aka risk threshold or risk tolerance) The boundaries for acceptable risk-taking.

Risk Management The process concerned with the identification, measurement, control, and minimization of security risks in information systems to a level commensurate with the value of the assets protected [r056]. Assessment of the probability (likelihood) of occurrence various risks and the potential impact such an event could have for the company.

Risk Management and Control The practices, processes, and activities that enable a firm to make informed risk-considering decisions.

Risk Management and Remediation Team Corporate/institutional team responsible for comprehensive risk management (identification, assessment, containment) and security assurance.

Risk Management Components Security services for information risk management. Maintains the residual risk at an acceptable and manageable level. Examples include associate awareness campaigns, Information Protection standards and procedures, and risk management models.

Risk Map The pictorial representation of risk (which has been identified through a risk assessment process). This pictogram often takes the form of a two-dimensional grid with likelihood of occurrence on one axis and with severity on the other axis. The Risk map is used as follows: The risks that fall in the high-frequency/high-severity quadrant are given priority risk management attention.

Risk Metrics Metrics that can be used to assess the occurrence of risk events or establish the probability of future risk events.

Risk Mitigation   Methods to increase security assurance. Involves risk identification, risk analysis, risk assessment, and risk management.

Risk Prioritization   The ranking of significant risk by frequency and/or severity. This ranking information drives to the understanding of the overall risk exposure and prioritization.

Risk Profile   A view of the overall set of risks, along with their degree of magnitude or significance.

Risk Response   A response strategy and action plan for mitigating risks that are determined to exceed desired risk limits. Additional mitigation activities may be appropriate for risks that are above desired risk limits if there is an appropriate cost benefit associated with those activities.

Risk Self-Assessment   The process by which an organization identifies, assesses, and determines the appropriate course of action for addressing risks that exceed acceptable limits.

Risk, Acceptable Limits   Risk limits acceptable to an organization.

Risk, Cause   A condition that allowed a risk to occur. Causes include internal problems or external matters.

Risk, Control   The process of comparing actual performance with planned performance, analyzing variances, evaluating possible alternatives, and taking appropriate corrective action as needed.

Risk, Effect   The consequence that a risk has to a firm. The effect can be measured qualitatively (low, moderate, high, extreme) or quantitatively (dollar amount) terms.

Risk, Exposure   The total financial value at risk because of a nefarious event. Exposure also deals with the degree to which a firm's reputation is at risk. Exposure relates to the possibility of loss without regard to the probability of actually experiencing the event.

Risk, Net Risk   The level of risk considering the effect of existing risk control.

Risk, Significant Risk   A risk or risks, to which a firm is exposed that may have an adverse effect. Such a risk has nontrivial probability of occurrence and then a nontrivial severity of impact.

Risk-Adjusted Measures   Metrics that incorporate the net impact of risks related to the objective that the metric supports.

Rivest Cipher #2 (RC2)   A block cipher developed by Ron Rivest at RSA Data Security, Inc. (now a wholly owned subsidiary of Security Dynamics, Inc) [r429, r430, r039].

Rivest Cipher #4 (RC4)   A stream cipher licensed by RSA Data Security (now a wholly owned subsidiary of Security Dynamics, Inc.) [r411, r413, r039].

Rivest–Shamir–Adleman (RSA)   An algorithm for asymmetric cryptography, invented in 1977 by Ron Rivest, Adi Shamir, and Leonard Adleman. RSA uses exponentiation modulo the product of two large prime numbers. The difficulty of breaking RSA is believed to be equivalent to the difficulty of factoring integers that are the product of two large prime numbers of approximately equal size.

To create an RSA key pair, randomly choose two large prime numbers, p and q, and compute the modulus, $n = pq$. Randomly choose a number e, the public exponent, that is less than n and relatively prime to $(p - 1)(q - 1)$. Choose another number d, the private exponent, such that ed-1 evenly divides $(p - 1)(q - 1)$. The public key is the set of numbers (n, e), and the private key is the set (n, d).

It is assumed to be difficult to compute the private key (n, d) from the public key (n, e). However, if n can be factored into p and q, then the private key d can be computed easily. Thus, RSA security depends on the assumption that it is computationally difficult to factor a number that is the product of two large prime numbers. (Of course, p and q are treated as part of the private key, or else destroyed after computing n.)

For encryption of a message, m, to be sent to Bob, Alice uses Bob's public key (n, e) to compute $m**e \pmod{n} = c$. She sends c to Bob. Bob computes $c**d \pmod{n} = m$. Only Bob knows d, so only Bob can compute $c**d \pmod{n} = m$ to recover m.

To provide data origin authentication of a message, m, to be sent to Bob, Alice computes $m{**}d$ (mod n) = s, where (d, n) is Alice's private key. She sends m and s to Bob. To recover the message that only Alice could have sent, Bob computes $s{**}e$ (mod n) = m, where (e, n) is Alice's public key.

To ensure data integrity in addition to data origin authentication requires extra computation steps in which Alice and Bob use a cryptographic hash function h (as explained for digital signature). Alice computes the hash value $h(m) = v$, and then encrypts v with her private key to get s. Alice sends m and s. Bob receives m' and s', either of which might have been changed from the m and s that Alice sent. To test this, Bob decrypts s' with Alice's public key to get v'. Bob then computes $h(m') = v''$. If v' equals v'', Bob is assured that m' is the same m that Alice sent [r013].

Rivest–Shamir–Adleman (RSA) Cryptography A very widely used public-key algorithm that can be used for either encryption or digital signing [r428, r039]. The algorithm is named for the initials of its inventors (Ronald L. Rivest, Adi Shamir, and Leonard M. Adleman).

Rivest–Shamir–Adleman (RSA) Operation To use the algorithm, keys are developed using two large prime numbers, p and q (256 bits and 258 bits, respectively), and d and e are large numbers with the property that $(de - 1)$ is divisible by $(p - 1)(q - 1)$. The encryption function E_K(P) is calculated by $P{\wedge}e$ mod pq, and the decryption function D_K(C) [where C is the encrypted plaintext that is the result of E_K(P)] is calculated by $C{\wedge}d$ mod pq. The mechanism works because E_K is easily calculated from (pq, e), but D_K is computationally difficult to be computed from the pair (pq, e). Hence it follows that the key (pq, e) can be relatively safely published [r202].

Rivest–Shamir–Adleman (RSA) Optimal Asymmetric Encryption Padding (OAEP) Encryption Scheme Encryption scheme proposed by Bellare and Rogaway in [r429]. The scheme is widely used in practice in the RSA-PKCS version. It is known to be plaintext aware under the RSA assumption in the random oracle model, and also chosen-ciphertext secure in the random oracle model [r430].

Rivest–Shamir–Adleman (RSA) Signature Algorithm The RSA signature algorithm is defined in RFC 2347. RFC 2347 specifies the use of the RSA signature algorithm with the Secure Hash Algorithm (SHA-1) and Message Digest 5 (MD5) message digest algorithms.

RKS See Record-Keeping Server

RLC See Radio Link Control

RMON See Remote Network Monitoring

RNC See Radio Network Controller

RNS See Radio Network Subsystem

RNTI See Radio Network Identifier

Rogue Access Point An unauthorized Access Points in a corporate Wireless Local Area Network (WLAN). For example, an employee of an organization might hook up an AP without the permission or knowledge of the firm.

Rogue Dynamic Host Configuration Protocol (DHCP) Server Attack method where attacker sets up a rogue DHCP server. The DHCP protocol can aid a hacker to redirect traffic through their machine (man in the middle attack) or send users to false web pages [via a rogue Domain Name System (DNS) server]. This could occur as a DHCP server can set various options such as what IP address to use for the default gateway and also what DNS servers to use [r199]. By starting a rogue DHCP server, the real DHCP server and the rogue server will fight to assign an interface an IP address. If a rogue server wins then the interface could be assigned a different default gateway. By assigning a different default gateway (i.e., a hacker's machine) all outgoing packets would be sent via the hackers machine thus sniffable. The machine acting as the default gateway would need to rewrite the Media Access Control (MAC) layer to enable the packets to be forwarded to the correct destination (i.e., the correct default gateway). The source code grabs an IP address from the DHCP server using the same method as the denial of service but instead of stealing all the IP addresses only one IP address is stolen. A rogue DHCP server is then started and listens for a client to send a discovery packet to the broadcast address. The rogue server and the valid server then both send an offer packet (the rogue server issues the IP address stolen at the start of the attack, this is to ensure that no IP address conflicts occur) and depending on which reaches the client first, determines which server the client uses. If the client uses the valid DHCP server then the man in the middle attack will fail; if the client uses the rogue DHCP server the man in the middle attack will succeed.

Role Assignment Certicate A certificate that contains the role attribute, assigning one or more roles to the certificate subject/holder [r068a].

Role-Based Access Control (RBAC) (aka role-based security) A form of identity-based access control where the system entities that are identified and controlled are functional positions in an organization or process [r013]. American National Standard 359-2004 is the Information Technology (IT) industry consensus standard for RBAC [r067].

Role-Based Security See Role-Based Access Control (RBAC)

Role Specification Certificate A certificate that contains the assignment of privileges to a role.

Rollback The ability to restore an environment after a service pack has been installed or some new configuration file has been uploaded, in case some unexpected problem arises.

ROM See Read-Only Memory

Root (UNIX context) A user account (also called "superuser") that has all privileges (including all security-related privileges) and thus can manage the system and its other user accounts [r013]. Generally, the system administrator will login with root privileges to administer the system.

(PKI context) The Certification Authority (CA) that is the highest level (most trusted) CA in a certification hierarchy—that is, the authority upon whose public key all certificate users base their trust. In a hierarchical PKI, a root issues public-key certificates to one or more additional CAs that form the second highest level. Each of these CAs may issue certificates to more CAs at the third highest level, and so on. To initialize operation of a hierarchical PKI, the root's initial public key is securely distributed to all certificate users in a way that does not depend on the PKI's certification relationships. The root's public key may be distributed simply as a numerical value, but typically is distributed in a self-signed certificate in which the root is the subject. The root's certificate is signed by the root itself because there is no higher authority in a certification hierarchy. The root's certificate is then the first certificate in every certification path [r013].

Root Certificate A certificate for which the subject is a root.

(PKI context) The self-signed public-key certificate at the top of a certification hierarchy.

Root Key A public key for which the matching private key is held by a root.

Root Private Key The private signing key of the highest-level Certification Authority (CA). It is normally used to sign public-key certificates for lower-level CAs or other entities [r068a].

Root Registry A name previously used for a Multilevel Information Systems Security Initiative policy approving authority.

Rootkit A collection of tools that allows a hacker to provide a backdoor into a system, collect information on other systems on the network, mask the fact that the system is compromised, and so on. Rootkit is a classic example of Trojan Horse software [r057]. Rootkits, once installed, are difficult to remove.

ROSI See Return on Security Investment

Route In general, a "route" is the *n*-tuple <prefix, nexthop, [other routing or nonrouting protocol attributes]>. A route is not end-to-end, but is defined with respect to a specific next hop that should take packets on the next step toward their destination as defined by the prefix. In this usage, a route is the basic unit of information about a target destination distilled from routing protocols. This term refers to the concept of a route common to all routing protocols. With reference to the definition above, typical nonrouting protocol attributes would be associated with diffserv or traffic engineering [r086].

Route Change Events A route can be changed implicitly by replacing it with another route or explicitly by withdrawal followed by the introduction of a new route. In either case, the change may be an actual change, no change, or a duplicate. The notation and definition of individual categorizable route change events is [r086]:

1. AADiff: Implicit withdrawal of a route and replacement by a route different in some path attribute.
2. AADup: Implicit withdrawal of a route and replacement by route that is identical in all path attributes.
3. WADiff: Explicit withdrawal of a route and replacement by a different route.
4. WADup: Explicit withdrawal of a route and replacement by a route that is identical in all path attributes.

Route Distinguisher (RD) An 8-byte value that, together with a 4-byte IPv4 address, identifies a VPN-IPv4 address family [r088]. If two Virtual Private Networks (VPNs) use the same IPv4 address prefix, the Provider Edges (PEs) translate these into unique VPN-IPv4 address prefixes. This ensures that if the same address is used in two different VPNs, it is possible to install two completely different routes to that address, one for each VPN [r082].

Route Flap A route flap is a change of state (withdrawal, announcement, attribute change) for a route. Route flapping can be considered a special and pathological case of update trains [r086].

Route Mixture The demographics of a set of routes.

Route Packing The number of route prefixes accommodated in a single Routing Protocol UPDATE Message, either as updates (additions or modifications) or as withdrawals.

Route Reflector A network element owned by a Service Provider (SP) that is used to distribute in Border Gateway Protocol (BGP) routes to the SP's BGP-enabled routers [r081, r082].

Route Set (SIP context) A collection of ordered Session Initiation Protocol (SIP) or Secure SIP (SIPS) Uniform Resource Identifiers (URIs) which represent a list of proxies that must be traversed when sending a particular request. A route set can be learned, through headers like Record Route, or it can be configured [r025].

Route Target (RT) An attribute that can be thought of as identifying a set of sites or, more precisely, a set of VPN Routing and Forwardings (VRFs) [r082, r088]. Associating a particular Route Target with a route allows that route to be placed in all VRFs used for routing traffic received from the corresponding sites. A Route Target attribute is also a BGP extended community used in [r423] and [r427]. A Route Target community is used to constrain VPN information distribution to the set of VRFs. A route target can be perceived as identifying a set of sites or, more precisely, a set of VRFs [r082].

Router (aka gateways in original parlance—this term now has limited use) A relaying device that operates at the network layer of the protocol model. Node that can forward datagrams not specifically addressed to it. An interconnection device that is similar to a bridge but serves packets or frames containing certain protocols. Routers interconnect logical subnets [e.g., implemented at a Local Area Network (LAN) level] at the network layer. A computer that is a gateway between two networks at Layer 3 of the Open Systems Interconnection Reference Model (OSIRM) and that relays and directs data packets through that internetwork. The most common form of router operates on IP packets [r013]. A router is a device or, in some cases, software in a computer, that determines the next network point to which a packet should be forwarded toward its destination [r029].

Internet usage: In the context of the Internet protocol suite, a networked computer that forwards Internet Protocol packets that are not addressed to the computer itself [r008].

Router Advertisement Neighbor discovery message sent by a router in a pseudo-periodic way or as a router solicitation message response. In IPv6 the advertisement includes, at least, information about a prefix that will be used later by the host to calculate its own unicast IPv6 address following the stateless mechanism [r008].

Router Discovery   The process by which a host discovers the local routers on an attached link and automatically configures a default router. In IPv4, this is equivalent to using of Internet Control Message Protocol v4 (ICMPv4) router discovery to configure a default gateway [r024].

Router's Cache   See Destination Cache

Routers Discovery   Neighbors' discovery process that allows for discovering of routers connected to a particular link [r008].

Routing   The process of moving information from its source to the destination [r200].

Routing Area Code (RAC)   (GSM context) An attribute of the Packet Control Unit (PCU) object [r014].

Routing Area Color Code (RACC)   (GSM context) An attribute of the Packet Control Unit (PCU) object [r014].

Routing Area Identification (RAI)   (GSM context) Area that can includes one or more cells or sectors [r014].

Routing Control   The application of rules during the process of routing so as to chose or avoid specific networks, links, or relays [r068a].

Routing Information Base (RIB)   The RIB collectively consists of a set of logically (not necessarily physically) distinct databases, each of which is enumerated below. The RIB contains all destination prefixes to which the router may forward, and one or more currently reachable next hop addresses for them. Routes included in this set potentially have been selected from several sources of information, including hardware status, interior routing protocols, and exterior routing protocols. RFC 1812 contains a basic set of route selection criteria relevant in an all-source context. Many implementations impose additional criteria. A common implementation-specific criterion is the preference given to different routing information sources [r086].

Routing Loop   Undesirable situation in a network that causes the traffic was relayed over a closed loop, so it never reaches its destination [r008].

Routing Policy   Routing Policy is "the ability to define conditions for accepting, rejecting, and modifying routes received in advertisements." RFC 1771 further constrains policy to be within the hop-by-hop routing paradigm. Policy is implemented using filters and associated policy actions such as Prefix Filtering. Many ASes formulate and document their policies using the Routing Policy Specification Language (RPSL) (RFC 2622) and then automatically generate configurations for the BGP processes in their routers from the RPSL specifications [r086].

Routing Policy Information Base   The set of incoming and outgoing policies.

RP   See Relying Party

RPA   See Relying Party Agreement

RP-Complexity Problem   RP (randomized polynomial time) is a class similar to BPP (bounded probabilistic polynomial time), except that the algorithms that solve the problems in this class may err only on inputs for which the answer is really supposed to be "yes." Co-RP is the analogous class of problems for which algorithms that solve the problems only err on inputs which are really suppose to be "no." In other words, a decisional problem is in Co-RP if its "complementary" problem is in RP. The problem complementary to that of deciding if an integer is prime is the problem of deciding if an integer is composite [r094].

RPO   See Recovery Point Objective

RPR   See Resilient Packet Ring

RR   See Resource Records

RRC   See Radio Resource Control

RSA   See Rivest–Shamir–Adleman

RSTP   See Rapid Spanning Tree Protocol

RSVP   See Resource Reservation Protocol

RT   See Route Target

RTO   See Recovery Time Objective

RTP   See Real-Time Transport Protocol

RTSP   See Real-Time Streaming Protocol

rtVBR   See Real-Time VBR

Rule of 72   (aka 72 Rule) (financial term) The estimation of doubling time on an investment, for which the compounded annual rate of return times the number of years must equal roughly 72 for the investment to double in value [r009].

Rule of 78   See 78 Rule

Rule-Based Security Policy   A security policy based on global rules imposed for all users. These rules usually rely on comparison of the sensitivity of the resource being accessed and the possession of corresponding attributes of users, a group of users, or entities acting on behalf of users [r160].

Rules-Based Detection   (aka misuse detection) The intrusion detection system detects intrusions by looking for activity that corresponds to known intrusion techniques (signatures) or system vulnerabilities [r057].

S

S/Key A security mechanism that uses a cryptographic hash function to generate a sequence of 64-bit, one-time passwords for remote user login [r431]. The client generates a one-time password by applying the Message Digest 4 (MD4) or Message Digest 5 (MD5) cryptographic hash function multiple times to the user's secret key. For each successive authentication of the user, the number of hash applications is reduced by one. (Thus, an intruder using wiretapping cannot compute a valid password from knowledge of one previously used.) The server verifies a password by hashing the currently presented password (or initialization value) one time and comparing the hash result with the previously presented password [r013].

S/KEY Algorithm A one-time password (OTP) algorithm described in RFC 1760 that is based on a one-way hash function [e.g., Message Digest 5 (MD5)]. S/Key has been a standard part of all FreeBSD distributions since version 1.1.5, and it is also implemented on many other systems.

S/MIME See Secure Multipurpose Internet Mail Extensions

SA See Security Association

SACCH See Slow Associated Control Channel

SAD See Security Association Database

Safeguard A risk-reducing measure that acts to detect, prevent, or minimize loss associated with the occurrence of specified threat or category of threats. Safeguards are also often described as controls or countermeasures [r425].

Safety The property of a system being free from risk of causing harm to system entities and outside entities.

Minoli–Cordovana's Authoritative Computer and Network Security Dictionary. By Daniel Minoli and James Cordovana
Copyright © 2006 John Wiley & Sons, Inc.

SAID   See Security Association Identifier

Salt   A random value that is concatenated with a password before applying the one-way encryption function used to protect passwords that are stored in the database of an access control system. Salt protects a password-based access control system against a dictionary attack [r013].

Saltzer and Schroeder Design Principles See Design Principles for Security (by Saltzer and Schroeder)

SAML   See Security Assertion Markup Language

SAN   See Storage Area Network

SAN-Based Vulnerabilities   The advent of Storage Area Networks (SANs) has made storage devices, which used to be directly connected to servers, vulnerable to more than one machine [r193].

Sandbox   Security mechanisms employed when executable code comes from unknown or untrusted sources (such as from the Internet) allowing the user to run untrusted code safely. An example is a Java Sandbox used in the Java development environment.

Sanitize   Delete sensitive data from a file, a device, or a system, such that data recovery is impossible. Sanitizing includes overwriting, degaussing, and destruction [r057].

SAR   See Suspicious Activity Report

Sarbanes–Oxley Act of 2002   (aka SarbOx) Legislation that requires certain companies to certify the accuracy of their internal financial controls. More specifically, legislation that authorizes the Security Exchange Commission to prescribe regulations requiring entities that produce annual financial reports pursuant to sections 13(a) or 15(d) of the Securities Exchange Act of 1934 to contain a report on the firm's internal financial controls. The report must state the responsibility of management for establishing and maintaining an adequate internal control structure and procedures for financial reporting and assess the effectiveness of those structures and controls. External audits must attest to and report on management's assessments. "Internal control" is defined as a process that provides assurance regarding the re-

liability of financial reporting. It pertains to the maintenance of records that accurately reflect the transactions and dispositions of assets and prevents or detects unauthorized acquisition, use, or disposition of assets. The security of information technology (systems, software, applications) is a critical element to assess [r208].

SarbOx   See Sarbanes–Oxley Act of 2002

SASL   See Simple Authentication and Security Layer

Sasser Worm   Exploiting a flaw in the Local Security Authority Subsystem Service (LSASS) component, the Sasser worm squirmed through unpatched Windows 2000 and Windows XP machines (May 2004). Sasser was particularly dangerous and spread rapidly through vulnerable network ports [r090].

SAT   See Security Access Token

SBGP   See Secure BGP

S-Boxes   Many modern block encryption functions, including Data Encryption Standards (DES) and Advanced Encryption Standard (AES), incorporate modules known as S-Boxes (substitution boxes). These produce a smaller number of outputs from a larger number of inputs through a complex non-linear mixing function that has the effect of concentrating limited entropy from the inputs into the output. S-Boxes sometimes incorporate bent Boolean functions (functions of an even number of bits producing one output bit with maximum nonlinearity). Looking at the output for all input pairs differing in any particular bit position, exactly half the outputs are different. An S-Box in which each output bit is produced by a bent function such that any linear combination of these functions is also a bent function is called a "perfect S-Box" [r166].

SBS   See Stimulated Brillouin Scattering

SCA   See Subordinate Certification Authority

Scalable   How well and easily a system can expand to meet future demands on the system. Demands on the system may include the need to service more users, better performance, more storage space, and so on.

Scan   (aka port scan) An attack that sends client requests to a range of server port addresses on a host, with the goal of finding an active port and exploiting a known vulnerability of that service. A technique used by intruders and hackers to determine what Transmission Control Protocol/User Datagram Protocol (TCP/UDP) ports are open or in use on a system or network. By using various tools, a hacker can send data to TCP or UDP ports one at a time and based on the response received the port scan utility can determine if that port is in use. Using this information, the hacker or intruder can then focus their attack on the ports that are open and try to exploit any weaknesses to gain access [r035].

Scavenging (Computational) Grid   A grid used to "locate processors cycles": Grid nodes are exploited for available CPU cycles and other resources. Nodes typically equate to desktop computers; a large number of processors are generally involved. Owners of the desktop processors are usually given control over when their resources are available to participate in the grid [r080].

SCCP   See Signaling Connection and Control Part

S-CCPCH   See Secondary Common Control Physical Channel

SCH   See Synchronization Channel

Scheduler Function   A grid-based system that is responsible for routing a job to a properly selected processor to be executed. The scheduling software identifies a processor on which to run a specific grid job that has been submitted by a user. Schedulers (along with) load balancers provide a function to route jobs to available resources based on Service Level Agreements (SLAs), capabilities, and availability [r080].

Schnorr Signatures Scheme   A digital signature scheme based on discrete logarithms (the discrete logarithms are defined in group theory in abstract algebra in analogy to ordinary logarithms). This signature is considered the simplest such scheme to be provably secure. It is efficient and generates short signatures. It is covered by a U.S. patent that expires in 2008. Signatures scheme described in [r432].

Scope   (IPv6 context) For IPv6 addresses, the scope is the portion of the network to which the traffic will be propagated to [r008].

Scope ID   (IPv6 context) Identifies a specific area within the reachability scope for nonglobal addresses. A node identifies each area of the same scope with a unique scope ID.

SCR   See Sustainable Cell Rate

Screening Router   See Filtering Router

Script Kiddie   A hacker or cracker who uses existing programs or compiles prewritten scripts in order to find weaknesses on target systems. These users do not always understand the complexities of the scripts they are executing and therefore do not always realize the damage they inflict [r062].

SCSI   See Small Computer System Interface

SDCCH   (GSM context) Together with the Slow Associated Control Channel (SACCH) and the Fast Associated Control Channel (FACCH), the Stand-alone Dedicated Control Channel SDCCH belongs to the group of the Dedicated Control Channels. The Dedicated Control Channels are bidirectional point-to-point channels. The SDCCH transmits Short Message Service (SMS) and the information necessary for call setup [r011].

SDE   See Software Development Environment or see Secure Data Exchange

SDE   See Secure Data Exchange

SDH   See Synchronous Digital Hierarchy

SDNS   See Secure Data Network System

SDOs   See Standards Developing Organizations

Seal   To encipher a record containing several fields in such a way that the fields cannot be individually replaced without either knowledge of the encryption key or leaving evidence of tampering [r070].

SEC   See Securities and Exchange Commission

SECAM (Séquential Couleur avec Memoire)   (video formats and coding) Analog French and Eastern Europe format. The video and broadcasting standard used in France, Eastern Europe, Russia, and most of Asia and Africa. SECAM has the same screen resolution of 625 lines and 50-Hz refresh rate as PAL [r203].

Second Generation Computing Grids Second generation grids that began with projects where underlying software services and communications protocols are used as a basis for developing distributed applications and services. 2G Grids offered basic building blocks, but deployment involved significant customization and filling-in lacunae. Example include Condor, I-WAY (the origin of Globus) and Legion (origin of Avaki) [r080].

Secondary Storage Any data storage medium other than a computer's random access memory (RAM)—typically tape or disk.

Secondary Synchronization Channel (S-SCH) (3G Wireless context) Channel used for cell search and for User Equipment synchronization. It is comprised of the Primary Synchronization Channel (P-SCH), and the Secondary Synchronization Channel (S-SCH). The Secondary Synchronization Channel is used for timeslot, as well as frame synchronization [r007].

Secondary-Common Control Physical Channel (S-CCPCH) (3G Wireless context) Control channel that is used for, among other things, pagings [r007].

Secrecy of Encryption Algorithm Less-commonly-used cryptographic methods. These rely on the secrecy of the encryption algorithms; such algorithms are only of historical interest and are not adequate for commercial needs [r036].

Secret The condition of information being protected from being known by any system entities except those who are intended to know it [r013].

Secret Access (aka back door) A hardware or software mechanism that provides access to a system and its resources by other than the usual procedure, was deliberately left in place by the system's designers or maintainers, and is usually not publicly known. For example, a way to access a computer other than through a normal login. Such access paths do not necessarily have malicious intent. For example, operating systems sometimes are shipped by the manufacturer with privileged accounts intended for use by field service technicians or the vendor's maintenance programmers [r013].

Secret Key A key that is used with a symmetric cryptographic algorithm. Possession of a secret key is restricted (usually to two entities).

Secret-Key Cryptography A synonym for symmetric cryptography.

Secret Splitting (aka secret sharing) A cryptographic technique that breaks a piece of data into two components; learning one of these components does not reveal half of the data, it actually reveals no information at all. In the most basic form of secret splitting, a secret is split into shares, that are stored on two servers. The secret can later be reassembled from the shares and used for some cryptographic purpose. The secret is thus protected from compromise in its "stored" state, while becoming available "in transit." In more advanced forms, the two servers can simulate the use of the secret without even reassembling it, thus not exposing the secret at all. Some examples of this split-key cryptography include digital signatures and verifying correct user entry of personal data [r078].

Sector A group of bytes within a track of a disk drive.

Secure BGP (SBGP) Internet routing is based on a distributed system composed of many routers, grouped into management domains called Autonomous Systems (ASes). Routing information is exchanged between ASes in Border Gateway Protocol (BGP) UPDATE messages. BGP is a critical component of the Internet's routing infrastructure. However, it is highly vulnerable to a variety of attacks due to the lack of a scalable means of verifying the authenticity and authorization of BGP control traffic. S-BGP addresses these vulnerabilities. The S-BGP architecture employs three security mechanisms. First, a Public-Key Infrastructure (PKI) is used to support the authentication of ownership of IP address blocks, ownership of Autonomous System (AS) numbers, an AS's identity, and a BGP router's identity and its authorization to represent an AS. This PKI parallels the IP address and AS number assignment system and takes advantage of the existing infrastructure (Internet registries, etc.) Second, a new, optional, BGP transitive path attribute is employed to carry digital signatures (in "attestations") covering the routing information in a BGP UPDATE. These signatures along with certificates from the S-BGP PKI enable the receiver of a BGP routing UPDATE to verify the address prefixes and path information that it contains. Third, IPsec is used to provide data and partial sequence integrity, and to enable BGP routers to authenticate each other for exchanges of BGP control traffic. However, a major obstacle to the deployment of S-BGP is that it requires the participation of several distinct organizations—the Internet registries, router vendors, and Internet service providers (ISPs). Because there will be no security benefits unless a few of each type of the organizations participate, each organization cannot justify the expense of investing in this new technology unless the others have also done so—a classic "chicken-and-egg" problem [r433, r434].

Secure Cookie A small file (known as a cookie) that is used to track user activity and maintain session state when accessing web content. The term secure cookie is often associated with persistent cookies (which are stored on the users' hard drive) that contain sensitive content that has been encrypted by the application that created the cookie. Some consider session cookies to be secure cookies because the cookie is removed from memory when the browser is closed, or in some cases, when the application that created the cookie is logged out of.

Secure Data Exchange (SDE) A Local Area Network (LAN) security protocol defined by the IEEE 802.10 standard.

Secure Data Network System (SDNS) A National Security Agency (NSA) program that developed security protocols for electronic mail (Message Security Protocol), Open System Interconnection Reference Model (OSIRM) layer 3 [Security Protocol for layer three (SP3)], OSIRM layer 4 [Protocol for layer four (SP4)], and Key Management Protocol (KMP).

Secure Electronic Transaction (SET) Private Extension One of the private extensions defined by SET for X.509 certificates. Carries information about hashed root key, certificate type, merchant data, cardholder certificate requirements, encryption support for tunneling, or message support for payment instructions [r013].

Secure Electronic Transaction (SET) Qualifier A certificate policy qualifier that provides information about the location and content of a SET certificate policy. In addition to the policies and qualifiers inherited from its own certificate, each Certification Authority (CA) in the SET certification hierarchy may add one qualifying statement to the root policy when the CA issues a certificate. The additional qualifier is a certificate policy for that CA.

Secure Electronic Transaction (SET)™ A protocol developed jointly by MasterCard International and Visa International and published as an open standard to provide confidentiality of transaction information, payment integrity, and authentication of transaction participants for payment card transactions over unsecured networks, such as the Internet [r013].

Secure File Transport Protocol (SFTP) [aka SSH (Secure Shell) File Transfer Protocol (sftp) or Secure FTP] Provides secure file transfer over a non-secure network [such as a Transmission Control Protocol/Internet Protocol (TCP/IP) network]. The SFTP component offers the features found in a standard File Transfer Protocol (FTP) program with the added ability to encrypt data using a secure SSH2 channel.

Secure FTP See Secure File Transfer Protocol (SFTP)

Secure Hash Algorithm (SHA) (aka SHA-1) A hash algorithm that is defined in FIPS PUB 180-1 [r436]. This cryptographic hash function produces a 160-bit output (hash result or message digest) for input data of any length $< 2^{64}$ bits.

Secure Hash Standard (SHS) See Secure Hash Algorithm (SHA)

Secure HyperText Transfer Protocol (Secure-HTTP, S-HTTP) An Internet protocol for providing client-server security services for HTTP communications. S-HTTP is designed to transmit individual messages securely. S-HTTP was originally specified by CommerceNet, a coalition of businesses interested in developing the Internet for commercial uses. S-HTTP has been approved by the Internet Engineering Task Force (IETF) as a standard. Secure Sockets Layer (SSL) and S-HTTP are considered complementary rather than competing technologies (SSL creates a secure connection between a client and a server, over which data can be sent securely).

Several message formats may be incorporated into S-HTTP clients and servers, particularly Cryptographic Message Syntax (CMS) and Multipurpose Internet Mail Extensions (MIME) Object Security Services (MOSS). S-HTTP supports choice of security policies, key management mechanisms, and cryptographic algorithms through option negotiation between parties for each transaction. S-HTTP supports both asymmetric and symmetric key operation modes. S-HTTP attempts to avoid presuming a particular trust model, but it attempts to facilitate multiply-rooted hierarchical trust and anticipates that principals may have many public-key certificates [r013].

Secure Interaction Rules   Security policy rules that regulate interactions between security domains.

Secure Multipurpose Internet Mail Extensions (S/MIME)   A format and protocol [r462] for adding cryptographic signature and/or encryption services to Internet MIME messages.

Secure Neighbor Discovery (SEND) Protocol   Protocol described in RFC 3971. SEND is designed to counter the threats to Neighbor Discovery Protocol (NDP). SEND is applicable in environments where physical security on the link is not assured (such as over wireless) and attacks on NDP are a concern. IPv6 defines the Neighbor Discovery Protocol (NDP) in RFC 2461 and RFC 2462. Nodes on the same link use NDP to discover each other's presence and link-layer addresses, to find routers, and to maintain reacha-

bility information about the paths to active neighbors. NDP is used by both hosts and routers. Its functions include Neighbor Discovery (ND), Router Discovery (RD), Address Autoconfiguration, Address Resolution, Neighbor Unreachability Detection (NUD), Duplicate Address Detection (DAD), and Redirection. The original NDP specifications called for the use of IPsec to protect NDP messages. However IPsec can only be used with a manual configuration of security associations, due to bootstrapping problems in using the Internet Key Exchange (IKE). Furthermore, the number of manually configured security associations needed for protecting NDP can be very large, making that approach impractical for most purposes. Hence, the use of SEND.

Secure Network Server   A device that acts as a gateway between a protected enclave and the outside world [r057].

Secure Opportunistic Hotspots (SOHs)   A novel architecture for secure shared use of a wireless local area network (WLAN) by members of the organization that owns the WLAN and visitors from the public at large. Visitors pay for access using an on-line payment method (e.g., PayPal) at the time of access. SOHs are "opportunistic" because (1) they allow an organization that needs to maintain a WLAN for its members (e.g., home or university) to use it to obtain extra revenues from eventual visitors, and (2) they allow a visitor to use any SOH that may happen to be within range, without requiring the visitor to have any previous or subsequent relationship with that SOH. SOHs allow any of the tens of millions of users with an on-line payment account to connect to any SOH, which in turn could be any of the millions of existing private, Wi-Fi (Wireless Fidelity) networks. SOHs may therefore be a significant contribution toward realizing the goal of ubiquitous connectivity [r437].

Secure POP3 (SPOP)   Secure e-mail protocol. When clients and servers use Secure POP3 to communicate, all messages and their contents are encrypted between server and client. The encryption uses the Secure Sockets Layer (SSL) standard [r438]. POP via SSL encrypted connection, used to remotely retrieve e-mail by clients. SPOP operates on Transmission Control Protocol (TCP) port 995.

Secure Profile Inspector (SPI)   A network monitoring tool for Unix, developed by the Department of Energy.

Secure Real-Time Transport Protocol (SRTP)   Secure real-time transport protocol that provides confidentiality, message authentication, and replay protection for Real-time Transport Protocol (RTP) [r257].

Secure Shell (SSH)   A protocol for encrypted, secure remote login (TELNET) and other secure network services over an insecure network. SSH consists of three major components [r013]:

- *Transport layer protocol:* Provides server authentication, confidentiality, and integrity. It may optionally also provide compression. The transport layer will typically be run over a Transmission Control Protocol/ Internet Protocol (TCP/IP) connection, but might also be used on top of any other reliable data stream.
- *User authentication protocol:* Authenticates the client-side user to the server. It runs over the transport layer protocol.
- *Connection protocol:* Multiplexes the encrypted tunnel into several logical channels. It runs over the user authentication protocol.

Secure Shell (SSH) Applicability   SSH can be used as a replacement for TELNET on most Unix-like systems. It uses Rivest–Shamir–Adleman (RSA) cryptography to encrypt connection information so that passwords and other sensitive material are not sent over the Internet in plain text. This counters the problem with many protocols being that they send passwords, etc. encapsulated in packets of information that can be easily "sniffed" and snooped upon, generally without the knowledge of the sender or the recipient. SSH provides secure alternatives to the plaintext-sending versions of these commonly used programs [r202].

Secure Sockets Layer (SSL)   An Internet protocol originally developed by Netscape Communications Corporation for transmitting confidential documents via the Internet and/or for general communication authentication and encryption over Transmission Control Protocol/Internet Protocol (TCP/IP) networks [r439]. It uses connection-oriented end-to-end encryption to provide data confidentiality service and data integrity service for traffic between a client (often a web browser) and a server, and that can optionally provide peer entity authentication between the client and the server. SSL is layered below HTTP and above a reliable transport protocol [Transmission Control Protocol (TCP)]. SSL is independent of the application it encapsulates, and any higher-level protocol can layer on top of SSL transparently [r013].

Nearly all browsers support SSL, and many websites use the protocol to obtain confidential user information, such as credit card numbers. By convention, Uniform Resource Locators (URLs) that require an SSL connection start with "*https:*" instead of "*http:*". SSL has been approved by the Internet Engineering Task Force (IETF) as a standard. The SSL protocol provides connection security that has three basic properties:

- The connection is private. Encryption is used after an initial handshake to define a secret key. Symmetric cryptography is used for data encryption [e.g., Data Encryption Standard (DES), Rivest Cipher #4 (RC4), etc.].
- The peer's identity can be authenticated using asymmetric, or public key, cryptography (e.g., RSA, etc.).
- The connection is reliable. Message transport includes a message integrity check using a keyed Message Authentication Code (MAC). Secure hash functions [e.g., Secure Hash Algorithm (SHA), Message Digest 5 (MD5), etc.] are used for MAC computations.

The SSL Protocol is composed of two layers.

- At the lowest level, layered on top of some reliable transport protocol [e.g., Transmission Control Protocol (TCP)], is the SSL Record Protocol. The SSL Record Protocol is used for encapsulation of various higher level protocols. One such encapsulated protocol, the SSL Handshake Protocol, allows the server and client to authenticate each other and to negotiate an encryption algorithm and cryptographic keys before the application protocol transmits or receives its first byte of data. One advantage of SSL is that it is application protocol independent.
- A higher-level protocol can layer on top of the SSL Protocol transparently. SSL's upper layer provides asymmetric cryptography for server authentication (verifying the server's identity to the client) and optional client authentication (verifying the client's identity to the server), and it also enables them to negotiate a symmetric encryption algorithm and secret session key (to use for data confidentiality) before the application protocol transmits or receives data. A keyed hash provides data integrity service for encapsulated data [r013].

Note that SSL and Secure Hypertext Transfer Protocol (Secure-HTTP, S-HTTP) are considered complementary rather than competing technologies.

Secure Sockets Layer (SSL) Authentication The server and client certificate verification process.

Secure Sockets Layer (SSL) Digital Certificates The de facto standard for secure websites/web servers (e.g., websites whose address starts with "https" are secured using SSL certificates). VeriSign is considered to be the leading provider of SSL certificates.

Secure Sockets Layer (SSL) Virtual Private Networks (VPNs) VPNs that run on HyperText Transport Protocol-Secure (HTTPS) protocol instead of IP security (IPsec). SSL VPNs allow for easy deployment (since standard web browsers can connect the SSL VPN service) and reduced infrastructure changes (because HTTPS ports are often already opened through corporate firewalls). SSL VPNs are particularly well-suited for remote users who need limited access to corporate services and who do not have access to company-owned workstations. The challenges for accessing corporate services through non-company-owned workstations (such as an airport kiosk) include:

- Appropriately authenticating the remote users
- Providing sufficient functionality while limiting access to sensitive services and data
- Ensuring that malicious logic (such as virus or keystroke loggers) is not being introduced to the corporate environment or is listening in on the communication
- Clearing the workstation cache of all activity

Secure Sockets Layer (SSL)/Transport Layer Security (TLS), Understructure Protocols SSL/TLS operates over Transmission Control Protocol (TCP), but does not operate on User Datagram Protocol (UDP). Note that IPsec supports both TCP and UDP Protocol Data Units (PDUs).

Secure Sockets Layer (SSL)-Encrypted Internet Message Access Protocol (IMAP) (SIMAP) IMAP via SSL encrypted connection, used to remotely retrieve e-mail by clients in a secure fashion. A version of IMAP that is tunneled through SSL for increased security. SIMAP operates on Transmission Control Protocol (TCP) port 993.

Secure State A system condition in which no subject can access any object in an unauthorized manner.

Secure Transaction Technology The use of the Secure Sockets Layer (SSL), Secure Hypertext Transfer Protocol (Secure-HTTP, S-HTTP), or both in on-line transactions, such as form transmission or credit card purchases [r435].

Secure Transmission Loop (EDI context) Process that involves one organization sending a signed and encrypted Electronic Data Interchange (EDI) interchange to another organization, requesting a signed receipt, followed later by the receiving organization sending this signed receipt back to the sending organization. In other words, the following transpires [r358]:

- The organization sending Electronic Data Interchange/e-commerce (EDI/EC) data signs and encrypts the data using either Pretty Good Privacy/Multipurpose Internet Mail Extensions (PGP/MIME) or Secure MIME (S/MIME). In addition, the message will request a signed receipt to be returned to the sender of the message.
- The receiving organization decrypts the message and verifies the signature, resulting in verified integrity of the data and authenticity of the sender.
- The receiving organization then returns a signed receipt to the sending organization in the form of a message disposition notification message. This signed receipt will contain the hash of the signature from the received message, indicating to the sender that the received message was verified and/or decrypted properly.

Secure Wide Area Network (SWAN)   A set of computers that communicate over a public network, such as the Internet, but use security measures, such as encryption, authentication, and authorization, to prevent their communications from being intercepted and understood by unauthorized users [r435].

Secure-HTTP   See Secure Hypertext Transfer Protocol

SecureID   RSA Security's access token.

Securing Storage Systems, Traditional Means of   Traditional means of securing storage systems involve physical defenses such as fences, locked doors, and guards. When storage devices are no longer used, mechanical destruction and disk sanitization render data unreadable. However, these approaches are expensive and often unreliable [r193].

Security   Measures taken to protect a system.

Also, the condition of a system that results from the establishment and maintenance of measures to protect the system.

Additionally, the condition of system resources being free from unauthorized access and from unauthorized or accidental change, destruction, or loss [r013].

Information Technologies (IT) security does not exist in a vacuum as a discipline. The field and mechanisms of IT security have evolved to meet the need to protect IT resources. These resources include, but are not limited to, hosts, systems, Operating Systems (OSs), databases, storage, information, communications links, communications network elements, clients, Personal Computers (PCs), Personal Digital Assistants (PDAs), wireless devices, e-mail, and so on [r435].

Security Access Token (SAT)   A mechanism in the Windows Operating System (OS) environment to identify a user to the computer that the user is utilizing, and is the user's identity on the network. The SAT is attached to all the processes that the user spins off. The SAT is comprised of the Security ID (SID) and the granted rights. When a user logs on to the desktop processor, the processor obtains the SID for the user account being employed and all the SIDs for all the groups that the user belongs to.

Security Administrator   A person who is responsible for the definition or enforcement of one or more parts of a security policy [r068a].

Security Algorithm   A set of rules for using input data and a secret key for producing data for use in security protocols.

Security Architecture   A plan and set of principles that describe (a) the security services that a system is required to provide to meet the needs of its users, (b) the system elements required to implement the services, and (c) the performance levels required in the elements to deal with the threat environment.

A complete system security architecture includes administrative security, communication security, computer security, emanations security, personnel security, and physical security (e.g., see reference r249). A complete security architecture needs to deal with both intentional, intelligent threats and accidental kinds of threats [r013].

Security Assertion Markup Language (SAML) An Extensible Markup Language (XML) standard that can be employed for business-to-business (B2B) and business-to-consumer (B2C) transactions, allowing a user to log on once for affiliated but separate websites in a Single Sign-On manner. The standard has been developed by Organization for the Advancement of Structured Information Standards (OASIS). SAML can make use of a number of protocols including HyperText Transfer Protocol (HTTP), Simple Mail Transfer Protocol (SMTP), and File Transfer Protocol (FTP).

SAML specifies three components: (1) assertions, (2) protocol, and (3) binding:

(1) There are three assertions: authentication, attribute, and authorization. Authentication assertion validates the user's identity. Attribute assertion contains specific information about the user. An authorization assertion identifies what the user is authorized to do.

(2) The protocol defines how SAML asks for and receives assertions.

(3) Binding defines how SAML message exchanges are mapped to Simple Object Access Protocol (SOAP) exchanges.

Security Assertion Markup Language (SAML) Assertion Framework As defined by the Organization for the Advancement of Structured Information Standards (OASIS) Security Services Technical Committee, it is a framework for exchanging security information between on-line business partners. It allows business entities to make assertions regarding the identity, attributes, and entitlements of a subject (an entity that is often a human user) to other entities, such as a partner company or another enterprise application. The SAML standard leverages core web services standards including eXtensible Markup Language (XML), Simple Object Access Protocol (SOAP), Transport Layer Security (TLS), XML Signature

(XMLsig), and XML Encryption (XMLenc). SAML Version 2.0 enables the secure exchange of authentication, attribute, and authorization information between disparate security domains, making vendor-independent web single sign-on and secure e-business transactions possible. Version 2.0 adds key functions to create and manage federated networks that combine and appropriately share preexisting repositories of identity information.

Security Assertion Markup Language (SAML) Assertions SAML provides a common language for three kinds of assertions [r205]:

- Authentication assertions: declarations about a user's identity
- Attribute assertions containing particular details about a user
- Authorization decision assertions, which specify what the user is allowed to do at a particular site

Assertions are issued by server-based applications known as SAML authorities. When a subject (person or computer) successfully requests access to a protected resource, a SAML authority issues a digitally signed token that the subject can use for further requests without re-authenticating within any domain that trusts the issuer of the token.

Security Association (SA) Security policies defined for communication between two or more entities; the relationship between the entities is represented by a key. The relationship is used to negotiate characteristics of protection mechanisms, but does not include the mechanisms themselves. A security association describes how entities will use security services. The relationship is represented by a set of information that is shared between the entities and is agreed upon and considered a contract between them [r013].

[IP security (IPsec) context] A simplex (uni-directional) logical connection created for security purposes and implemented with either Authentication Header (AH) or Encapsulating Security Payload (ESP) (but not both). The security services offered by a security association depend on the protocol selected, the IPsec mode (transport or tunnel), the endpoints, and the election of optional services within the protocol. A security association is identified by a triple consisting of (a) a destination IP address, (b) a protocol (AH or ESP) identifier, and (c) a Security Parameter Index [r013].

Security Association Database (SAD)   In transport mode, IP security (IPsec) inserts a security protocol header into outgoing IP packets between the original IP header and the packet payload. The contents of the IPsec header are based on the result of a "security association" (SA) lookup that uses the contents of the original packet header as well as its payload (especially transport layer headers) to locate an SA in the Security Association Database (SAD). When receiving packets secured with IPsec transport mode, a similar SA lookup occurs based on the IP and IPsec headers, followed by a verification step after IPsec processing that checks the contents of the packet and its payload against the respective SA. The verification step is similar to firewall processing [r282].

Security Association Identifier (SAID)   A data field in a security protocol [such as IEEE 802.10b Secure Data Exchange (SDE) Protocol], used to identify the security association to which a protocol data unit is bound. The SAID value is usually used to select a key for decryption or authentication at the destination [r013].

Security Audit   An independent review and examination of a system's records and activities to determine the adequacy of system controls, ensure compliance with established security policy and procedures, detect breaches in security services, and recommend any changes that are indicated for countermeasures [r160]. The basic audit objective is to establish accountability for system entities that initiate or participate in security-relevant events and actions. Thus, means are needed to generate and record a security audit trail and to review and analyze the audit trail to discover and investigate attacks and security compromises [r013].

Security Audit Trail   Data collected and potentially used to facilitate a security audit.

Security Authority   An entity that is responsible for the definition, implementation, or enforcement of security policy.

Security Certificate   A set of security-relevant data issued by a security authority or trusted third party, together with security information which is used to provide the integrity and data origin authentication services for the data. (*Note:* All certificates are deemed to be security certificates (see the relevant definitions in ISO 7498-2) [r068a].

Security Clearance   A determination that a person is eligible, under the standards of a specific security policy, for authorization to access sensitive information or other system resources [r013].

Security Compromise   A security violation in which a system resource is exposed, or is potentially exposed, to unauthorized access [r013].

Security Countermeasures   Countermeasures that are aimed at specific threats and vulnerabilities or involve more active techniques as well as activities traditionally perceived as security [r057].

Security Domain Authority   A security authority that is responsible for the implementation of a security policy for a security domain [r068a].

Security Domains   The sets of objects that an entity in question has the ability to access.

Security Environment   The set of external entities, procedures, and conditions that affect secure development, operation, and maintenance of a system [r013].

Security Event   An event that compromises the confidentiality, integrity, availability, or accountability of an information system [r200]. The term includes both events that are security incidents and those that are not. In a Certification Authority (CA) workstation, for example, a list of security events might include the following [r013]:

- Performing a cryptographic operation—for example, signing a digital certificate or certificate revocation list (CRL)

- Performing a cryptographic card operation: creation, insertion, removal, or backup
- Performing a digital certificate lifecycle operation: rekey, renewal, revocation, or update
- Posting information to an X.500 Directory
- Receiving a key compromise notification
- Receiving an improper certification request
- Detecting an alarm condition reported by a cryptographic module
- Logging the operator in or out
- Failing a built-in hardware self-test or a software system integrity check

Security Fault Analysis   A security analysis, usually performed on hardware at a logic gate level, gate-by-gate, to determine the security properties of a device when a hardware fault is encountered [r013].

Security Features   The security-relevant functions, mechanisms, and characteristics of hardware and software platforms.

Security for Storage Data-At-Rest   The mishandling of stored data (information at rest) is a significant threat to firms and their customers. Whether data are stolen, lost, or discarded, the results are the same: Information that should be confidential may no longer be. To address this deficiency, the Institute of Electrical and Electronics Engineers (IEEE) Computer Society's Security in Storage Working Group is developing Project 1619, *Standard Architecture for Encrypted Shared Storage Media*. P1619's goal is to enable the interoperable encryption of storage devices, provide methods for information owners to transfer key material, and facilitate product certification. The standard currently includes encryption at the physical level of disk and tape drives, and future efforts will extend it to objects and file systems [r193].

Security Forensics   Mechanisms for protecting the evidence related to an intrusion, infraction, or crime on a computer.

Security Framework   A construct to describe a security architecture. One of the first security frameworks is ISO 7498-2, the Open Systems Interconnection (OSI) Security Architecture. This standard covers the following: (i) security attacks relevant to Open System; (ii) general architectural elements that can be used to thwart such attacks, and (iii) circumstances under which the security elements can be used. A framework is broad in scope and covers general principles rather than detailed solutions.

Security Gateway   An intermediate system that acts as the communications interface between two networks. The set of hosts (and networks) on the external side of the security gateway is viewed as untrusted (or less trusted), while the networks and hosts on the internal side are viewed as trusted (or more trusted). The internal subnets and hosts served by a security gateway are presumed to be trusted by virtue of sharing a common, local, security administration. In the IPsec context, a security gateway is a point at which Authentication Header (AH) and/or Encapsulating Security Payload (ESP) is implemented in order to serve a set of internal hosts, providing security services for these hosts when they communicate with external hosts also employing IPsec (either directly or via another security gateway) [r186, r013].

Security Grid Tools   Tools that cover authentication, authorization, message integrity, and message confidentiality for grid-computing applications [r080].

Security IDs (SIDs)   Identification (ID) mechanism in the Windows Operating System (OS) environment where each user account, computer account, and group has a unique identifier that is used to specify "rights."

Security Implementation Layer   Security mechanisms can be located at any layer. In general, putting a mechanism at a lower layer protects a wider variety of higher-layer protocols, but may not be able to protect them as well. A link-layer encryptor can protect not just IP, but even Address Resolution Protocol (ARP) packets. However, its reach is just that one link. Conversely, a signed e-mail message is protected even if sent through many store-and-forward mail gateways; also, it can identify the actual sender, and the signature can be verified long after the message is delivered. However, only that one type of message is protected. Messages of similar formats, such as some Netnews postings, are not protected unless the mechanism is specifically adapted and then implemented in the news-handling programs [r170].

Security Incident   Any adverse event which compromises some aspect of computer or network security [r441].

Security information   Information needed to implement security services.

Security Intrusion   A security event, or a combination of multiple security events, that constitutes a security incident in which an intruder gains, or attempts to gain, access to a system (or system resource) without having authorization to do so [r013].

Security Kernel   The hardware, firmware, and software elements of a trusted computing base that implement the reference monitor concept. It must mediate all accesses, be protected from modification, and be verifiable as correct [r120]. That is, a security kernel is an implementation of a reference monitor for a given hardware base [r013].

Security Label   A marking that is bound to a system resource and that names or designates the security-relevant attributes of that resource [r160, r443]. The recommended definition is usefully broad, but usually the term is understood more narrowly as a marking that represents the security level of an information object—that is, a marking that indicates how sensitive an information object is [r120]. System security mechanisms interpret security labels according to applicable security policy to determine how to control access to the associated information, otherwise constrain its handling, and affix appropriate security markings to visible (printed and displayed) images thereof [r013].

Security Level   The combination of a hierarchical classification level and a set of nonhierarchical

category designations that represents how sensitive information is [r013].

Security Log   A log, generated by a firewall or other security device that lists events that could affect security, such as access attempts or commands, and the identifiers of the users involved [r437].

Security Management   Tools for a complete view into the security of the enterprise, enabling a firm to quickly take action in times of crisis.

Security Management Infrastructure (SMI) System elements and activities that support security policy by monitoring and controlling security services and mechanisms, distributing security information, and reporting security events. The associated functions are as follows [r160, r013]:

- Controlling (granting or restricting) access to system resources: This includes verifying authorizations and identities, controlling access to sensitive security data, and modifying access priorities and procedures in the event of attacks.
- Retrieving (gathering) and archiving (storing) security information: This includes logging security events and analyzing the log, monitoring and profiling usage, and reporting security violations.
- Managing and controlling the encryption process: This includes performing the functions of key management and reporting on key management problems.

Security Manager   (Java context) Mechanism used in a Java sandbox. The security manager is consulted whenever a dangerous operation is about to be carried out. The security manager can block the operation by generating a security exception.

Security Mechanism   A process (or a device incorporating such a process) that can be used in a system to implement a security service that is provided by or within the system. Some examples of security mechanisms are authentication exchange, checksum, digital signature, encryption, and traffic padding [r013].

Security Mechanisms in Internet Protocols   Security must be intrinsically incorporated into Internet Protocols for those protocols to offer their services securely. Many security problems can be traced to improper protocol implementations. However, even a proper implementation will have security problems if the fundamental protocol is itself exploitable. There are security compromises that are facilitated by the very protocols that are in use on the Internet. It is therefore vitally important that protocols developed for the Internet provide this fundamental security. Exactly how security should be implemented in a protocol will vary, because of the structure of the protocol itself. There are many protocols for which standard Internet security mechanisms, already developed, may be applicable. The precise one that is appropriate in any given situation can vary [r170]. Internet Security compromises can be divided into several classes, ranging from Denial of Service to Host Compromise. Host Compromise (most commonly caused by undetected Buffer Overflows) represent flaws in individual implementations rather than flaws in protocols. Nevertheless, carefully designed protocols can make such flaws less likely to occur and harder to exploit. However, it is not hard to envision an attack that targets a fundamental security flaw in a widely deployed protocol. It is therefore imperative that we strive to minimize such flaws in the protocols that are designed.

Security Model   A schematic description of a set of entities and relationships by which a specified set of security services are provided by or within a system. An example is the Bell-LaPadula Model [r013].

Security Parameters Index (SPI)   An arbitrary 32-bit value that assists in the identification of an Authentication, Authorization, and Accounting (AAA) or Mobility Security Association. The type of security association identifier used in IPsec protocols. A 32-bit value used to distinguish among different security associations terminating at the same destination (IP address) and using the same IPsec security protocol [Authentication Header (AH) or Encapsulating Security

Payload (ESP)]. Carried in AH and ESP to enable the receiving system to determine under which Security Association (SA) to process a received packet [r012].

The combination of a destination address, a security protocol, and an SPI uniquely identifies a security association. The SPI enables the receiving system to select the SA under which a received packet will be processed. An SPI has only local significance, as defined by the creator of the SA (usually the receiver of the packet carrying the SPI); thus an SPI is generally viewed as an opaque bit string. However, the creator of an SA may choose to interpret the bits in an SPI to facilitate local processing [r186].

Security Perimeter   The boundary of the domain in which a security policy or security architecture applies, that is, the boundary of the space in which security services protect system resources [r013].

Security Policy (or Policies)   A set of rules and practices that specify or regulate how a system or organization provides security services to protect sensitive and critical system resources [r013].

Security Policy Model   A formal presentation of the security policy enforced by the system. It identifies the set of rules and practices that regulate how a system manages, protects, and distributes sensitive information [r057].

Security Policy Rules   A representation of a security policy for a security domain within a real system.

Security Principles   "Common sense principles" to be used in design of network and/or computer systems. See Saltzer and Schroeder Design Principles.

Security Principles (other than Saltzer and Schroeder Design Principles)   "Common sense principles" such as follows [r449a]: (i) Secure the weakest link: Attackers will usually focus on the weakest part of the system (e.g., cryptography is usually not the weakest link and the attacker will try to access data before it gets encrypted or after it gets decrypted); (ii) Fail securely: Ensure that one handle errors in a safe manner (e.g., aim to keep the system stable and in a secure state all the time and on error, rollback changes already made by this operation, (iii) Compartmentalize (principle of least privilege): Manage access to different components with separate access controls; (iv) Promote privacy (principle of fail-safe defaults); (v) Be reluctant to trust: Do not trust anything which is not under sole control (do not put more trust in users than necessary), (vi) Use community resources: follow best practices which have shown to be a good choice

Security Products   Products (including software applications, appliances, servers/proxies) that support a security management function. Note that often it is not possible to categorize products simply by function, because many products combine multiple functions. Typical products include: Firewalls, IPsec Virtual Private Networks (VPNs), Secure Sockets Layer (SSL) VPNs, Intrusion detection, Intrusion prevention, Antivirus, and Uniform Resource Locator (URL) filtering.

Security Profile   A (sub)set of consistent, interoperable procedures and features.

Security Protocol 3 (SP3)   A protocol [r444] to provide connectionless data security at the top of Open Systems Interconnection Reference Model (OSIRM) layer 3.

Security Protocol 4 (SP4)   A protocol [r445] to provide either connectionless or end-to-end connection-oriented data security at the bottom of Open Systems Interconnection Reference Model (OSIRM) layer 4.

Security Recovery   Actions that are taken and procedures that are carried out when a violation of security is either detected or suspected to have taken place.

Security Requirements   Types and levels of protection necessary for equipment, data, information, applications, and Information Technology (IT) facilities.

Security Risk Scorecard   A scorecard that illustrates the organization's current risk profile [r190].

Security Risks, Outsourcing   Exposure to infraction, penetration, theft, compromise, or inappropriate disclosure. Typical security risks can include (but are not limited to) [r187]:

- Inappropriate access to, or disclosure of, information or loss of data integrity through inadequately secured physical facilities.
- Loss of accessibility and data integrity because of nonexistent or inadequate business continuity or disaster recovery policies and procedures.
- Inappropriate disclosure through inadequate screening of personnel, resulting (in extreme cases) in extortion, fraud attempts, or terrorist uses.
- Inappropriate access to, or disclosure of, information by reason of formal or informal government access (such as Law Enforcement or national security requests, or economic or political espionage).

Significant legal risks arising from security risks include violation of data protection and intellectual property laws (through the disclosure of third-party proprietary data), export and defense trade control laws and notice statutes (requiring notification of security breaches to the individuals) [r187].

Security Service   A processing or communication service that is provided by a system to give a specific kind of protection to system resources. Security services implement security policies, and are implemented by security mechanisms [r013].

Security Situation   (Internet Security Association and Key Management Protocol (ISAKMP) context) The set of all security-relevant information [for example, network addresses, security classifications, manner of operation (normal or emergency)] that is needed to decide the security services that are required to protect the association that is being negotiated [r013].

Security System Management   A set of security services that typically includes archiving, backup and restore, and security event mechanisms.

Security Templates   Files that contain security settings in a Windows Operating System (OS) environment, for example: password policy, account lockout policy, audit policy, etc.

Security Through Obscurity   A sense of security that is based on attackers not having insider knowledge of the system. This is not considered strong security because secrets degrade over time. An example would include web content that is on a website that has no hyperlinks to it. Related to pseudo-security.

Security Token   A set of data protected by one or more security services, together with security information used in the provision of those security services, that is transferred between communicating entities [r068a].

Security Violation   An act or event that violates security policy or controls.

Security/Vulnerability Testing   Testing performed (on behalf of the system owners) to discover and report on vulnerabilities on the systems tested.

Security-Aware Name Server   (DNSSEC context) An entity acting in the role of a name server (defined in RFC 1034) that understands the Domain Name System (DNS) security extensions. In particular, a security-aware name server is an entity that receives DNS queries, sends DNS responses, supports the Extension Mechanisms for DNS (EDNS0) (RFC 2671) message size extension and the "DNSSEC OK" (DO)bit (RFC 3225), and supports the Resource Record (RR) types and message header bits [r069].

Security-Aware Recursive Name Server   (DNSSEC context) An entity that acts in both the security-aware name server and security-aware resolver roles. A more cumbersome but equivalent phrase would be "a security-aware name server that offers recursive service" [r069].

Security-Aware Resolver   (DNSSEC context) An entity acting in the role of a resolver (defined in RFC 1034) that understands the DNS security extensions. In particular, a security-aware resolver is an entity that sends DNS queries, receives DNS responses, supports the Extension Mechanisms for DNS (EDNS0) (RFC 2671) message size extension and the "DNSSEC OK" (DO)bit (RFC 3225), and is capable of using the Resource Record (RR) types and message header bits defined in this document set to provide DNSSEC services [r069].

Security-Aware Stub Resolver   (DNSSEC context) An entity acting in the role of a stub resolver (defined in RFC 1034) that has enough of an understanding the DNS security extensions to provide additional services not available from a security-oblivious stub resolver. Security-aware stub resolvers may be either "validating" or "non-validating," depending on whether the stub resolver attempts to verify DNSSEC signatures on its own or trusts a friendly security-aware name server to do so [r069].

Security-Oblivious <anything>   (DNSSEC context) An <anything> that is not "security-aware" [r069].

SEED   A symmetric encryption algorithm developed by KISA (Korea Information Security Agency) and a group of experts since 1998. The input/output block size and key length of SEED is 128 bits. SEED has the 16-round Feistel structure. A 128-bit input is divided into two 64-bit blocks and the right 64-bit block is an input to the round function, with a 64-bit subkey generated from the key scheduling. SEED is easily implemented in various software and hardware because it takes less memory to implement than other algorithms and generates keys without degrading the security of the algorithm. In particular, it can be effectively adopted in a computing environment with restricted resources, such as mobile devices and smart cards. SEED is robust against known attacks including DC (Differential Cryptanalysis), LC (Linear Cryptanalysis), and related key attacks. SEED has gone through wide public scrutinizing procedures. SEED is widely used in South Korea for electronic commerce and financial services operated on wired and wireless communications [r446]. Highlights are [r447]:

- The Feistel structure with 16-round
- 128-bit input/output data block size
- 128-bit key length

- A round function strong against known attacks
- Two 8×8 S-boxes
- Mixed operations of XOR and modular addition

Selective Field Protection   The protection of specific fields within a message which is to be transmitted.

Self-Phase Modulation (SFM)   (optical transmission term) Optical impairment that introduces chirping, in turn interacts with fiber dispersion to cause pulse broadening or compression (depending on the dispersion profile of the fiber).

Self-Signed Certificate   A public-key certificate for which the public key bound by the certificate and the private key used to sign the certificate are components of the same key pair, which belongs to the signer. In a self-signed X.509 public-key certificate, the issuer's Distinguished Name (DN) is the same as the subject's DN [r013].

Semantic Data   See Metadata

Semantic Security   An attribute of an encryption algorithm that is a formalization of the notion that the algorithm not only hides the plaintext but also reveals no partial information about the plaintext. Whatever is efficiently computable about the plaintext when given the ciphertext is also efficiently computable without the ciphertext [r013].

Sender   (Presence Services context) Source of instant messages to be delivered by the instant message service [r015].

Sender User Agent   (Presence Services context) Means for a principal to manipulate zero or more senders [r015].

Senior Management   Management individuals that make decisions about the IT security budget.

Senior Officers   Chief Information Officers (CIOs) and Chief Security Officers (CSOs), along with Chief Financial Officers (CFOs), Chief Technology Officers (CTOs), and Chief Operating Officer (COO), all of whom make strategic decisions about the direction of the organization; the mission owners. The Chief Executive Officer (CEO) also bears (ultimate) responsibility in the area of security and information integrity.

Sensitive Information   Information is sensitive if disclosure, alteration, destruction, or loss of the information would adversely affect the interests or business of its owner or user [r013].

Sensitivity   Characteristic of a resource that implies its value or importance. The characteristic of a resource which implies its value or importance, and may include its vulnerability [r068a].

Sensor Network   (aka networked sensors or network of sensors) An infrastructure comprised of sensing (measuring), computing, and communication elements that grants the administrator the ability to instrument, observe, and react to events and phenomena in a specified environment. The administrator typically is some civil, government, commercial, or, industrial entity. The environment can be the physical world, a biological system, or a private or public Information Technology (IT) framework. Network(ed) sensor systems are seen by observers as an important technology that will experience major deployment in the next few years for a plethora of applications, not the least being Homeland Security. Typical applications include, but are not limited to, data collection, monitoring, surveillance, and medical telemetry. In addition to sensing, one is often also interested in control and activation [r021]. The network is often wireless, but this does not obligatorily have to be the case.

Sensor Networks Routing Protocols   Sensor networks often require special routing protocols (in place of/in addition to simple IP) [r021]:

Data-centric: The sink sends queries to certain Wireless Sensor Networks (WSN) regions and waits for data from the Wireless Nodes (WNs) located in the selected regions. Because data is being requested through queries, attribute-based naming is necessary to specify the properties of data. Due to the large number of nodes deployed, in many WSNs it is not practical to assign global identifiers to each node. This, along with potential random deployment of WNs makes it challenging to select a specific (or a specific set of) WN to be queried. Hence, data are typically transmitted from every WN within the deployment region; this, however, gives rise to significant redundancy along with inefficiencies in terms of energy consumption. It follows that it is desirable to have routing protocols that will be able to select a set of sensor nodes and utilize data aggregation during the relaying of data. This has led to the development of data-centric routing (in traditional address-based routing routes are created between addressable nodes managed in the network layer mechanism).

Examples: Sensor Protocols for Information via Negotiation (SPIN), Directed Diffusion, Rumor Routing, Gradient-based routing (GBR), Constrained anisotropic diffusion routing (CADR), COUGAR, and ACQUIRE.

Hierarchical: A single-tier (gateway or clusterpoint) network can cause the gateway node to become overloaded, particularly as the density of sensors increases. This, in turn, can cause latency in event status delivery. To permit WSNs to deal with a large population of WNs and to cover a large area of interest multipoint clustering has been proposed. The goal of hierarchical routing is to efficiently manage the energy consumption of WNs by establishing multihop communication within a particular cluster, and by performing data aggregation and fusion to decrease the number of transmitted packets to the sink.

Examples: Energy Adaptive Clustering Hierarchy (LEACH); Threshold sensitive Energy Efficient sensor Network protocol (TEEN) and Adaptive Threshold sensitive Energy Efficient sensor Network protocol (APTEEN); and Power-Efficient GAthering in Sensor Information Systems (PEGASIS).

Location-based: Location information about the WNs can be utilized in routing data in an energy-efficient manner. Location information is used to calculate the distance between two given nodes so that energy consumption can be determined (or at least, estimated). For example, if the region to be sensed is known, the query can be diffused only to that specific region, limiting and/or eliminating the number of transmission in the out-of-region space. Location-based routing is ideal for mobile ad hoc networks, but it can also be used for generic WSNs (note that non-energy-aware location-based protocols designed for wireless ad hoc networks, such as Cartesian and trajectory-based routing, are not desirable/ideal in WSNs).

Example: Minimum Energy Communication Network (MECN) and Small Minimum Energy Communication Network (SMECN), Geographic Adaptive Fidelity (GAF), and Geographic and Energy Aware Routing (GEAR).

QoS-oriented: Quality of Service (QoS)-aware protocols consider end-to-end delay requirements in setting up the paths in the sensor network.

Examples: Sequential Assignment Routing (SAR), and Stateless Protocol for end-to-end delay (SPEED).

Separation of Duties   The practice of dividing the steps in a system function among different individuals, so as to keep a single individual from subverting the process.

Separation of Privilege   (aka Principle of Separation of Privilege) One of Saltzer and Schroeder's Design Principles. A system should not grant permission based on a single condition [r139a] E.g., do not rely on a single security mechanism. An environment where a use has only the privileges that are needed for supporting a basic, well-defined function. With this approach, even if an intruder has compromised one part of the system the separation of privilege mechanism ensures that it is difficult for the intruder to subvert the rest of the system. From another perspective, the principle of separation of privilege asserts that a system should not grant permission based on a single condition.

Sequential Search   (SIP context) In a sequential search, a proxy server attempts each contact address in sequence, proceeding to the next one only after the previous has generated a final response. A 2xx or 6xx class final response always terminates a sequential search [r025].

Server   A computer or other device that manages a business (application) or network service.

(SIP context) A network element that receives requests in order to service them and sends back responses to those requests. Examples of servers are proxies, user agent servers, redirect servers, and registrars [r025].

(Presence Services context) an indivisible unit of a presence service or instant message service [r015].

Server Push–Pull   A combination of web client/server techniques individually called "server push" and "client pull." In server push, the server loads data to the client, but the data connection stays open. This allows the server to continue sending data to the browser as necessary. In client pull, the server loads data to the client, but the data connection does not stay open. The server sends a HyperText Markup Language (HTML) directive to the browser telling it to reopen the connection after a certain interval to get more data or possibly to open a new Uniform Resource Locator (URL) [r435].

Server Volume Management   Mechanisms to dynamically reconfigure volume sets or partitions, copy, resize, move, merge, or consolidate volumes/partitions on multiple storage devices.

Server Write Key   The key used to encrypt data written by the server [r039].

Server Write MAC Secret   The secret data used to authenticate data written by the server [r039].

Service   This term represents telecommunications capabilities that the customer buys or leases from a service provider. Includes but is not limited to telecommunication connectivity offering, such as a private line, a cell relay offering, a frame relay offering, and so on. Service is an abstraction of the network element-oriented or equipment-oriented view. Identical services can be provided by different network elements, and different services can be provided by the same network elements [r068a].

Also, any program or computer a user can accesses over a network [e.g., Web Service (WS)].

Service Management Layer   A management lay-er that is concerned with, and responsible for, the contractual aspects, including service order handling, complaint handling, and invoicing of services that are being provided to customers or available to potential new customers [r068a].

Service Optimal Routing (SOR)   (GSM context) A supplementary service that deals with forwarding calls directly to the subscriber's current location. It is up to the user whether a call is to be forwarded or not [r011].

Service Pack   A collection of updates and "hotfixes" rolled into one large installation package [e.g., in the Windows Operating System (OS) environment].

Service Provider   (Identity Management context) An entity that provides services within a federation. This entity acts as the recipient of a Single-Sign-On (SSO) event from an Identity Provider. Based on the trust relationship with the Identity Provider, a Service Provider is able to validate Identity Provider-provided SSO credentials for a user [r278].

Service-Oriented Architecture (SOA)   A (modeling approach) of building applications by integrating standardized subservice modules (components) over a well-defined (open) interface. The subservice modules could be local (all executing in one server) or could be distributed across a Storage Area Network (SAN), Local Area Network (LAN), Metropolitan Area Network (MAN), or Wide Area Network (WAN). The goal is to empower developers to treat applications as network services that can be chained together to create a complex business process in an expeditious manner. A strategy of SOA is code reuse: developers only need to figure out the interfaces for existing applications, rather than writing new applications from scratch each time new business rules are developed; there are significant economic advantages in using reusability across the enterprise.

Architecture that defines how two computing entities interact to enable one entity to perform a unit of work on behalf of another entity. The unit of work is referred to as a service, and the service interactions are defined using a description language. Each interaction is self-contained; each interaction is independent of any other interaction environment software components can be exposed as services on the network, and so can be re-used for different applications and purposes [r080].

CORBA (Common Object Request Broker Architecture)-based Object Request Brokers (ORBs) are one example of a service-oriented architecture. More recently, companies have been using Web Services (WS) to connect applications. CORBA is a standardized blueprint worked out by the Object Management Group (OMG) defining how application objects and ORBs can cooperate to deliver services or perform processes independent of platform, network or location. In CORBA, ORBs can communicate across a Transmission Control Protocol/Internet Protocol (TCP/IP) network via the Internet Inter-ORB Protocol (IIOP). This protocol that lets both applications (such as web browsers) and object request brokers communicate over a TCP/IP network.

An ORB establishes a client/server connection between two objects across a network with the goal of allowing applications, which may be running on completely different operating systems, to exchange and act on information. ORBs (i) abstractly define an application's interfaces so that other applications can use them; (ii) discover applications and the associated interfaces elsewhere in a network; and, (iii) allow applications to message and respond to one another.

Neither the programmers who create the objects, nor the object themselves, nor the end-users who use them need to know anything about the other objects in the network because the ORB is designed to handle the interactions. Interfaces are defined with an interface definition language. CORBA is one example of an attempt at ORB specifications.

ORBs were developed before the Extensible Markup Language (XML)-based protocol Simple Object Application Protocol (SOAP), which attempts to achieve similar goals (some vendors now offer tools to connect ORB and Web-services-based systems).

Serving GPRS Support Node (SGSN) (3G Wireless context) The Serving General Packet Radio Service (GPRS) Support Node comes after the Gateway GPRS Support Node. It is a new GPRS element. The SGSN takes over important functions such as security and Mobility Management [r007].

Serving Radio Network Controller (SRNC) (3G Wireless context) A controller that provides the main connection to the User Equipment in case of macrodiversity [r007].

Service Relationship References an established security association between two functional entities, assuming that at least a shared key is present [r068a].

Serving Radio Network Subsystem (SRNS) (3G Wireless context) The main connection of a User Equipment to the network is realized via the SRNS. The User Equipment, however, can also be connected to further Node Bs of another RNS. This is then called Drift Radio Network Subsystem [r007].

Session A user-to-host or host-to-host data-exchange instance where there are well-defined (long-duration) dialogue parameters.

(SIP context): A multimedia session is a set of multimedia senders and receivers and the data streams flowing from senders to receivers. A multimedia conference is an example of a multimedia session (as defined in RFC 2327) [r025].

Also, the context information of a Secure Sockets Layer (SSL) communication.

Session Border Controller A device used in Voice Over IP (VoIP) to deal with a number of interworking issues. The controller refreshes Network Address Translation (NAT) bindings for Session Initiation protocol (SIP) registrations. It compresses SIP packets to less than 1492 bytes [User Datagram Protocol (UDP) fragmentation]. It hides routing information to the outside world. It ensures that an end-to-end media path is established. It helps the teardown process after the call is completed.

Session Cookie   A small file (known as a cookie) that is used to track user activity and maintain session state when accessing web content. Unlike a persistent cookie, a session cookie is maintained in memory (instead of being on the hard drive). The session cookie is removed from memory when the browser is closed, or in some cases, when the application that created the cookie is logged out of.

Session Hijacking   (aka replay attack) An attack in which a valid data transmission is maliciously or fraudulently repeated, either by the originator or by an adversary who intercepts the data and retransmits it, possibly as part of a masquerade attack [r013]. Such protection mechanisms as one-time password systems [r384, r416] and nonces are meant to counter session highjacking.

An attack approach where a third party intercepts communications in a session and impersonates one of the parties involved in the session. More typically this involves Transmission Control Protocol (TCP) Session Hijacking. There is subtle difference between spoofing and hijacking. Spoofing is pretending to be someone else. This could be achieved by sniffing a logon/authentication process and replaying it to the server after the user has logged off. The server may then assume that the intruder is the user that the sniffed process actually belongs to. Hijacking is taking over an already established TCP session and injecting one's own packets into that stream so that your commands are processed as the authentic owner of the session [r483].

Session Identifier   A value generated by a server that identifies a particular session [r039].

Session Initiation Protocol (SIP)   An application-layer control protocol defined by Internet Engineering Task Force (IETF) that can establish, modify, and terminate multimedia sessions or calls. A stateless signaling protocol developed to support IP telephony and other "presence" services. Defined in RFC 3261 (Rosenberg, J., Schulzrinne, H., Camarillo, G., Johnston, A., Peterson, J., Sparks, R., Handley, M., and E. Schooler, "SIP: Session Initiation Protocol," RFC 3261, June 2002). Competes with ITU-T H.323 (which is a stateful signaling protocol). Multimedia sessions include invitations to both unicast and multicast conferences and Internet telephony applications. SIP can be used in conjunction with other call setup and signaling protocols, and it is described in RFC 2543 [r257].

Session Initiation Protocol (SIP) Proxy Server   (SIP context) An intermediary entity that acts as both a server and a client for the purpose of making requests on behalf of other clients. A proxy server primarily plays the role of routing, which means its job is to ensure that a request is sent to another entity "closer" to the targeted user. Proxies are also useful for enforcing policy (for example, making sure a user is allowed to make a call). A proxy interprets and, if necessary, rewrites specific parts of a request message before forwarding it [r025].

Session Initiation Protocol (SIP) Transaction   (SIP context) A SIP transaction occurs between a client and a server and comprises all messages from the first request sent from the client to the server up to a final (non-1xx) response sent from the server to the client. If the request is INVITE and the final response is a non-2xx, the transaction also includes an ACK to the response. The ACK for a 2xx response to an INVITE request is a separate transaction [r025].

Session Key   A temporary encryption key used between two principals, with a lifetime limited to the duration of a single login "session" [r070]. In the context of symmetric encryption, a key that is temporary or is used for a relatively short period of time. Usually, a session key is used for a defined period of communication between two computers, such as for the duration of a single connection or transaction set, or the key is used in an application that protects relatively large amounts of data and, therefore, needs to be rekeyed frequently [r013].

Session Management (SM)   (3G Wireless context) Mechanism that defines the setup, monitoring, and teardown of a packet-switched connection [r007].

SET See Secure Electronic Transaction

Set of Provisions A collection of practice and/or policy statements, spanning a range of standard topics, for use in expressing a Certificate Policy (CP) or Certification Practice Statement (CPS) [r011].

Severity Code Sev-0 Event (including security event) that has devastating impact. Extremely rare, catastrophic event that has a devastating impact (meaning actual or potential for long-term impact) on the operations of the majority or the entire enterprise.

Severity Code Sev-1 Event (including security event) that has immediate and high impact. A critical (continuity required) business function is unavailable or unable to be performed by an entire business unit, causing an immediate and high level of impact on the customers, economics, or operations. An incident where an outage of 5–15 minutes will in many instances make a difference to the firm's customers.

Severity Code Sev-2 Event (including security event) that has potentially high impact. An incident that impacts multiple customers or departments and has the potential to have a high level of impact on customers, economics, or operations. Alternatively, the incident causes a regulatory compliance breach.

Severity Code Sev-3 Event (including security event) that has immediate and moderate impact. An incident has an immediate and moderate level of impact on Operations. Typically, the incident is localized and a work-around can be implemented.

Severity Code Sev-4 Event (including security event) that has low or no impact. An incident has A low level of impact on Operations. Typically, this affects one individual and there is a work-around or the individual presents an issue that has little or no business impact.

SF See Spreading Factor

SFM See Self-Phase Modulation

sftp See SSH Secure File Transfer Protocol

SGSN See Serving GPRS Support Node

SHA See Secure Hash Algorithm

SHA-1 See Secure Hash Algorithm

Shallow Packet Inspection The examination of the header of a Protocol Data Unit (PDU), or packet [such as Transmission Control Protocol (TCP) PDU] to determine if there are potential security issues, for example, if the packet was a crafted packet.

Shared Risk Link Group (SRLG) (optical transmission term) Mechanism to provide an effective approach to plan for reliability in transport networks. An SRLG is associated with an entity at risk, typically a fiber span (however, more general risks might be modeled). SRLGs are basic inputs to resource management in the Generalized Multi-Protocol Label Switching (GMPLS) control plane for wavelength-routed optical networks. Planners typically look at three classes of SRLG-diverse path protection schemes: dedicated, shared, and unprotected. SRLGs can provide the technical foundation for Service Level Agreements (SLAs) with customers.

Shared Risk Link Group (SRLG) Disjoint (MPLS context) A path is considered to be SRLG disjoint from a given link or node if the path does not use any links or nodes which belong to the same SRLG as that given link or node [r083].

Shared Secret (aka keying material or cryptographic key) Data (such as keys, key pairs, and initialization values) needed to establish and maintain a cryptographic security association [r013]. The term shared secret implies a symmetric algorithm is used for encryption.

Shares (Security context) Files that can be shared in the Windows Operating System.

Shibboleth A project within the Internet2 higher education consortium to develop technical and policy frameworks and an open software system for the sharing of on-line resources among researchers, educators, and students.

Shielded Twisted-Pair (STP) Cable An electrically conducting cable, comprising one or more elements, each of which is individually shielded. There may be an overall shield, in which case the cable is referred to as shielded twisted-pair cable with an overall shield (from ISO/IEC 11801: 1995). Specifically for IEEE 802.3 100BASE-

TX, 150 ohms balanced inside cable with performance characteristics specified to 100 MHz (i.e., performance to Class D link standards as per ISO/IEC 11801: 1995). In addition to the requirements specified in ISO/IEC 11801: 1995, IEEE 802.3 Clauses 23 and 25 provide additional performance requirements for 100BASE-T operation over STP [r100].

Short-Message Service (SMS)   (GSM context) A data service for sending short messages [r011].

Short-Message Service Center (SMS-C)   (GSM context) Network operators, service-providers, and private customers can send short messages directly to any other subscriber's mobile phone via the SMS-C. There the short messages are stored temporarily, and forwarded to the recipient. The SMS-C has interfaces to several Mobile Services Switching Centers (MSCs), to the Operation & Maintenance Center (OMC), and to the Voice Mail System (VMS) [r011].

SHS   See Secure Hash Algorithm

S-HTTP   See Secure HTTP

SIDs   Security identifiers (IDs) used to uniquely identify a user, system, or session.

Signal   Under Unix and Linux, the signal is the most fundamental and common form of inter-process communications (IPC). It is also the basis for "event-driven" programming under these systems. Each Unix implementation defines a set of signals that are associated with various asynchronous events, such as a terminal sending an ''interrupt request" (SIGINT) or a change in window size (SIGWINCH) [r084].

Signal Type Values for Synchronous Optical Network/Synchronous Digital Hierarchy (SONET/SDH)   SONET and SDH each define a multiplexing structure. Both structures are trees whose roots are, respectively, a Synchronous Transport Signal level N (STS-N) or a Synchronous Transport Module level N (STM-N) and whose leaves are the signals that can be transported via the timeslots and switched between timeslots within an ingress port and timeslots within an egress port—that is, a Virtual Tributary x Synchronous Payload Envelope (VTx SPE), an STS-x SPE, or a

Virtual Channel x (VC-x). A SONET/SDH label will identify the exact position (i.e., first timeslot) of a particular VTx SPE, STS-x SPE, or VC-x signal in a multiplexing structure [r254]. Permitted Signal Type values for SONET/SDH are:

VT1.5: SPE / VC-11
VT2: SPE / VC-12
VT3: SPE
VT6: SPE / VC-2
STS-1: SPE / VC-3
STS-3c: SPE / VC-4
STS-1/STM-0
STS-3/STM-1
STS-12/STM-4
STS-48/STM-16
STS-192/STM-64
STS-768/STM-256

Signaling Compression   (aka "SigComp") A protocol for transportation of compressed messages between two network elements. One of the key features of SigComp is the ability of the sending node to request that the receiving node store state objects for later retrieval [r448].

Signaling Connection and Control Part (SCCP)   (GSM context) To guarantee virtual connections and connectionless signaling (i.e., signaling that is not related to a call), another protocol layer on top of Message Transfer Part (MTP) and parallel to Telephone User Part (TUP) is necessary in Signaling System No. 7 (SS7). This is the Signaling Connection and Control Part [r011].

Signaling System No. 7 (SS7)   The system (network and layered protocols) used to handle switch-to-switch message-based signaling in the Public Switched Telephone Network (PSTN). (GSM context) The protocol used in the Network Subsystem (NSS) [r011].

Signaling   (aka signalling) The messages and layered protocols used to handle switch-to-switch and user-to-switch call management (call establishment, call teardown) in the Public Switched Telephone Network (PSTN).

Signal-to-Interference Ratio (SIR)   (3G Wireless context) Ratio that describes the difference in power between the user and the interference signals [r007].

Signature Certificate   A public-key certificate that contains a public key that is intended to be used for verifying digital signatures, rather than for encrypting data or performing other cryptographic functions. A v3 X.509 public-key certificate may have a "keyUsage" extension which indicates the purpose for which the certified public key is intended [r013].

Signature Schemes with Appendix   Digital signature schemes that require the message as input to the verification algorithm. These schemes are more commonly used scheme as opposed to schemes with message recovery. The schemes rely on cryptographic hash functions rather than customized redundancy functions. Examples include Digital Signature Algorithm (DSA), ElGamal, Schnorr, and so on.

Signature Schemes with Message Recovery   A digital signature scheme that does not require a priori knowledge of the message for the verification; the message is recovered from the signature itself. Examples include Rivest–Shamir–Adleman (RSA), Rabin, Nyberg-Rueppel, and so on.

Signature Verification Procedure   To verify a (digital) signature, a recipient first determines whether it trusts that the key belongs to the person it is supposed to belong to (using a certificate or a priori knowledge) and then decrypts the signature using the public key of the person. If the signature decrypts properly and the information matches that of the message (proper message digest, etc.), the signature is accepted as valid. In addition to authentication, this technique also provides data integrity, which means that unauthorized alteration of the data during transmission is detected [r036].

Signature-Based Intrusion Detection System (IDS)   (aka Misuse Detection Model Intrusion Detection System) Approach where the intrusion detection system detects intrusions by looking for activity (i.e., signatures) that corresponds to known intrusion techniques or system vulnerabilities Intrusion Detection System [r076].

Signed Receipt   (EDI context) Electronic Data Interchange (EDI) receipt with a digital signature. The term used for both the functional activity and message for acknowledging receipt of an Electronic Data Interchange/E-commerce (EDI/EC) interchange is receipt, or signed receipt. The first term is used if the acknowledgment is for an interchange resulting in a receipt that is not signed. The second term is used if the acknowledgment is for an interchange resulting in a receipt that is signed. The method used to request a receipt or a signed receipt is defined in RFC 2298, "An Extensible Message Format for Message Disposition Notifications" [r358].

Signed Response (SRES)   (GSM context) Together with the Random Number (RAND) and the key Kc, the Signed Response belongs to the Authentication Triplet, which is generated in the Authentication Center (AuC) for the authentication of mobile subscribers [r011].

Signed Zone   Concept introduced in Domain Name System (DNS) Security Extensions (DNSSEC). A zone whose Resource Records sets (RRsets) are signed and that contains properly constructed DNSKEY, Resource Record Signature (RRSIG), Next Secure (NSEC), and (optionally) Delegation Signer (DS) records [r069]. To sign a zone, the zone's administrator generates one or more public/private key pairs and uses the private key(s) to sign authoritative RRsets in the zone [r215].

Signer   A human being or an organization entity that uses its private key to create a digital signature for a data object [r110].

Significant Risk   A risk, or a combination of risks, to which a firm is exposed. Such risk requires attention because of the probability of occurrence or the severity of impact or a combination of the two. That risk could have a material (quantitative or qualitative) adverse effect on a firm's earnings, reputation, and so on.

SIM   See Subscriber Identity Module

Simple Authentication   An authentication process that uses a password as the information needed to verify an identity claimed for an entity [r013].

Simple Authentication and Security Layer (SASL) An Internet specification for adding authentication service to connection-based protocols (RFC 2222) [r449]. It specifies a challenge–response protocol where data are exchanged between the client and the server for the purposes of authentication and (optional) establishment of a security layer on which to carry on subsequent communications. To use SASL, a protocol includes a command for authenticating a user to a server and for optionally negotiating protection of subsequent protocol interactions. The command names a registered security mechanism. SASL mechanisms include Kerberos, Generic Security Services Application Programming Interface (GSSAPI), S/KEY [S/KEY is a one-time password (OTP) scheme described in RFC 1760], and others. Some protocols that use SASL are Internet Message Access Protocol, version 4 (IMAP4) and Post Office Protocol, version 3 (POP3) [r013]. SASL is used with protocols such as Lightweight Directory Access Protocol Version 3 (LDAPv3) or Internet Message Access Protocol Version 4 (IMAPv4). There are various mechanisms defined for SASL. Each mechanism defines the data that must be exchanged between the client and server in order for the authentication to succeed. This data exchange required for a particular mechanism is referred to as its protocol profile [e.g., DIGEST-MD5 and RFC 2831 define how Hypertext Transfer Protocol (HTTP) Digest Authentication can be used as an SASL mechanism.]

Simple Key-Management for Internet Protocols (SKIP) A key distribution protocol that uses hybrid encryption to convey session keys that are used to encrypt data in IP packets [r450]. SKIP uses the Diffie–Hellman algorithm (or could use another key agreement algorithm) to generate a key-encrypting key for use between two entities. A session key is used with a symmetric algorithm to encrypt data in one or more IP packets that are to be sent from one of the entities to the other. The key-encrypting key (KEK) is used with a symmetric algorithm to encrypt the session key, and the encrypted session key is placed in a SKIP header that is added to each IP packet that is encrypted with that session key [r013].

Simple Mail Transfer Protocol (SMTP) Basic Internet protocol used to transfer e-mail messages between servers. A Transmission Control Protocol (TCP)-based, application-layer, Internet Standard protocol for moving electronic mail messages from one computer to another [r451]. SMTP e-mail server supports mail transfer from client to server [Mail User Agent (MUA) to Mail Transport Agent (MTA)] and server to server (MTA to MTA). Uses port 25.

Simple Network Management Protocol (SNMP) A set of protocols for managing networks. A User Datagram Protocol (UDP)-based, application-layer, Internet Standard protocol [r452, r453] for conveying management information between managers and agents. SNMP version 1 uses cleartext passwords for authentication and access control. Version 2 included cryptographic mechanisms based on Data Encryption Standards (DES) and Message Digest 5 (MD5). Version 3 provides enhanced, integrated support for security services, including data confidentiality, data integrity, data origin authentication, and message timeliness and limited replay protection.

SNMP operates by sending messages to different network elements (e.g., routers, switches, firewalls, etc.). SNMP-compliant devices store data about on specific parameters in Management Information Bases (MIBs) and return this data to the SNMP requesters. SNMP is the basis for most modern network management since it provides multi-vendor network management systems the ability to manage network devices from a central location. SNMP includes standard protocols, databases, and procedures that are used to monitor and manage devices connected to the network. Nearly all vendors of network-based components, computers, bridges, routers, switches, and so on, offer SNMP. Basic SNMP components are: Management Station or Console, MIB, Proxy Agent, and Remote Network Monitoring (RMON) [r245].

SNMP was developed to manage IP devices via in-band means, in which management access is primarily via the same interface(s) used to send and receive IP traffic. SNMP's wide adoption has resulted in its use for managing communication devices that do not support in-band IP access (e.g., Fibre Channel devices); a separate out-of-band IP interface is often used for management. Uniform Resource Identifiers (URIs) provide a convenient way to locate that interface and specify the protocol to be used for management. One possible scenario is for an in-band query to return a URI that indicates how the device is managed. A URI can permit SNMP to be designated as the management protocol. A URI can also refer to specific object instances within an SNMP MIB [r083].

Simple Network Management Protocol (SNMP), Management Agent   The program that resides on a given network device that responds to requests from the Management Console or generates events (traps) based on configured parameters [r245].

Simple Network Management Protocol (SNMP), Management Information Base (MIB)   The management database for a given network component. There is a standard definition of a MIB for every device that is supported by SNMP. The Management Station monitors and updates the values in the MIB, via the agent. SNMP provides three main functions—GET, SET, and TRAP—to retrieve, set device values, and receive notification of network events [r245].

Simple Network Management Protocol (SNMP), Management Station or Console   The user interface component of the network management system. It provides the applications to configure, monitor, analyze, and control the various components that comprise the network [r245].

Simple Network Management Protocol (SNMP), Proxy Agent   The program used to support devices that do not have an SNMP implementation available. The proxy is an SNMP management agent that services requests from the management console, on behalf of one or a number of non-SNMP devices [r245].

Simple Network Management Protocol (SNMP), Remote Network Monitoring (RMON)   A specification that was developed to provide a standard interface between a Management Station and remote monitoring agents or probes. Remote monitoring agents are used to gather network statistical information to diagnose network faults and performance issues. RMON defines additional MIBs that collect this performance information [r245].

Simple Network Management Protocol Agent   Software used to control network communications devices using Transmission Control Protocol/Internet Protocol (TCP/IP) [r057].

Simple Object Access Protocol (SOAP)   Transport mechanism that is independent of the underlying platform and protocol. For example, two disparate processes can communicate without the intimate knowledge of systems and platforms on which both of them are running. SOAP provides a mechanism of messaging between a service requestor and a service provider. It is a mechanism for formatting a Web Service (WS) invocation: a simple enveloping process for eXtensible Markup Language (XML) payloads that defines a Remote Procedure Call (RPC) convention and a messaging convention [r080].

Simple Traversal of UDP Through NAT (STUN) Client   A STUN client (also just referred to as a client) is an entity that generates STUN requests. A STUN client can execute on an end system, such as a user's PC, or can run in a network element, such as a conferencing server [r252].

Simple Traversal of UDP Through NAT (STUN) Server   An entity that receives STUN requests and sends STUN responses. STUN servers are generally attached to the public Internet [r252].

Simple Traversal of User Datagram Protocol (UDP) Through Network Address Translators (NATs) (STUN)   A lightweight protocol described in RFC 3489 that allows applications to discover the presence and types of NATs and firewalls between them and the public Internet. It also provides the ability for applications to determine the public IP addresses allocated to them by the NAT. STUN works with many existing NATs and does not require any special behavior from them; as a result, it allows a variety of applications to work through existing NAT infrastructure. STUN is a simple client–server protocol. A client sends a request to a server, and the server returns a response. There are two types of requests: Binding Requests, sent over UDP, and Shared Secret Requests, sent over TLS over Transmission Control Protocol (TCP). Shared Secret Requests ask the server to return a temporary username and password. This username and password are used in a subsequent Binding Request and Binding Response, for the purposes of authentication and message integrity [r252].

Single Loss Expectancy (SLE)   The loss from a single security infraction event.

Single Sign-On (SSO)   A system that enables a user to access multiple computer platforms (usually a set of hosts on the same network) or application systems after being authenticated just one time. Typically, a user logs in just once and then is transparently granted access to a variety of permitted resources with no further login being required until after the user logs out. Such a system has the advantages of being user-friendly and enabling authentication to be managed consistently across an entire enterprise, and it has the disadvantage of requiring all hosts and applications to trust the same authentication mechanism [r013].

Single Sign-On (SSO) Limitations   There are some possible limitations with an SSO-based approach, such as [r261]: (i) costs required to integrate with each application under the SSO banner; and (ii) providing a single entry point via a password to multiple systems makes an organization far less secure than a separate password for each system. Some organizations add a Public-Key Identification (PKI) infrastructure, but this increases complexity in implementation, IT management, and user operation.

Single-Factor Authentication   A scheme requiring authentication that satisfies only one of the following conditions:

- Authentication based on what you know—for example, a user identifier/password combination
- Authentication based on what you have—for example, hardware-based token (such as a smart card) or a software-based token (Public-Key Infrastructure (PKI) certificate)
- Authentication based on what you are—for example, fingerprint or retinal scan

Typical deployments of single-factor authentication include the use of a user identifier (ID) and the associated password.

SIP   See Session Initiation Protocol

SIR   See Signal-to-Interference Ratio

SirCam Worm   Malicious code that spread through e-mail and unprotected network shares. The damage from SirCam was somewhat limited, but what was to follow would set the tone for a spate of network worms that caused billions of dollars in business costs (2001) [r090].

Site Prefix   (IPv6 context) A 48-bit prefix used to refer to all site addresses. Site prefixes are stored in a prefixes table that is used to confine traffic associated to these site prefixes [r008].

Site Security Officer (SSO)   In the FORTEZZA environment the SSO is the Local Authority [r108].

Site-Level Aggregation Identifier (SLA ID)   (IPv6 context) A 16-bit field inside the global unicast address that uses an organization to identify subnetworks inside its own network [r008].

SKIP   See Simple Key Management for Internet Protocols

Skipjack   A National Security Agency (NSA)-developed encryption algorithm for the Clipper chip. A Type II block cipher with a block size of 64 bits and a key size of 80 bits. The algorithm was formerly classified at the U.S. Department of Defense "Secret" level; in 1998, NSA announced that Skipjack had been declassified.

SLA   See Service Level Agreement

SLA ID   See Site-Level Aggregation Identifier

Slammer Worm   Reminiscent of the Code Red

worm, Slammer exploited two buffer overflow vulnerabilities in Microsoft's SQL Server database, causing major congestion of Internet traffic throughout Asia, Europe, and North America. The worm infected about 75,000 hosts in the first 10 minutes and knocked several ISPs around the world offline for extended periods of time (2003) [r090].

SLE   See Single Loss Expectancy

Slot   A chassis port in hardware (e.g., router, switch, firewall) that can be used to add a plug-in board that supports additional user-level ports or some other hardware functionality.

(MISSI context) One of the FORTEZZA PC card storage areas that are each able to hold an X.509 certificate and additional data that is associated with the certificate, such as the matching private key [r013].

Slow Associated Control Channel (SACCH) (GSM context) Like the Stand-alone Dedicated Control Channel (SDCCH) and the Fast Associated Control Channel (FACCH), this channel belongs to the Dedicated Control Channels. These are bidirectional point-to-point-channels. The SACCH transmits network measurement reports [r011].

SM   See Session Management

Small Computer System Interface (SCSI)   A well-established, processor-independent standard, for system-level interfacing between a computer and intelligent devices including disk drives, CD-ROM reader/writers, printers, scanners, and many more. It uses a parallel bus that allows one to connect multiple devices to a single SCSI adaptor (or "host adaptor") on the computer's bus. SCSI can operate in either asynchronous or synchronous modes. The synchronous transfer rate is up to 5 MBps. The Universal Serial Bus (USB) has become a competitor technology to SCSI and is faster.

Smart Card   A device that is often the same size as a credit card but that is smart enough to hold its own data and applications and do its own processing. The device contains one or more integrated circuit chips, which perform the functions of a computer's central processor, memory, and input/output interface. Smart cards can be used to store personal information, hold digital cash, or prove identity. They are often contrasted with dumb cards that have magnetic strips or barcodes and rely more heavily on networks. Smart cards are popular in Europe but less so in the United States [r057].

Smart Rename Mode   This feature allows a user to rename all keylogger's executable files and registry entries [r224].

Smart Token   A device that conforms to the definition of smart card except that rather than having standard credit card dimensions, the token is packaged in some other form, such as a dog tag or door key shape [r013].

SMI   See Security Management Infrastructure

SMS   See Short-Message Service

SMS-C   See Short Message Service Center

SMTP   See Simple Mail Transfer Protocol

Smurf   See Smurfing

Smurfing   A denial of service attack in which an attacker spoofs the source address of an echo-request of Internet Control Message Protocol (ICMP) (ping) packet to the broadcast address for a network, causing the machines in the network to respond en masse to the victim, thereby clogging its network [r057].

(financial term) A money laundering technique. In the world of money laundering, a "smurf" is a person who deposits cash or monetary instruments into someone else's account. The smurf may be making deposits as a favor for a friend or for a total stranger. Often, the smurf has no idea that the money being deposited was obtained from illegal activities. Smurfing manifests as numerous deposits of small amounts of cash (or monetary instruments such as travelers checks or money orders) into a single account. The deposits may be made by one person or by several people, but none of them owns the account.

Snapshot   A fully usable copy of a defined collection of data that contains an image of the data as it appeared at the point in time at which the copy was initiated. A snapshot may be either a duplicate or a replicate of the data it represents [r029].

Snarf To appropriate a document or file for the purpose of using it with or without the author's permission.

Snarf Attack A Bluetooth-targeted hacking technique that allows hackers to access another Bluetooth device without the victim's knowledge. It is also possible for the attacker to use the phones commands through their own phone. Although it is obvious that the Snarf attack reveals sensitive information, what is not so obvious is what other malicious attacks can be initiated through a snarf attack. The Snarf attack allows the attacker to do the following. (i) Send SMS: Attackers are able to use the Bluetooth connection to send an SMS. This may be initiated to save on costs or to undertake criminal activities. (ii) Initiate a phone call: It is possible to make a phone call to virtually any other phone number. Once again, saving costs may be enough motivation for criminals to use this attack as some phone calls such as international calls can become quiet expensive. The attacker may also use the phone call for criminal activities. (iii) Write a Phone Book Entry: Attackers can delete, edit, or add to the victim's dialed number list, or phone book; criminals may find a malicious reason for such an attack.

SNDCP See Sub-Network-Dependent Convergence Protocol

Sneaker An individual hired to break into places in order to test their security. Related to tiger team [r057].

SNIA See Storage Networking Industry Association

Sniffer A program (or hardware) to capture data across a computer network. Used by hackers to capture user id names and passwords. Software tool that audits and identifies network traffic packets. Is also used legitimately by network operations and maintenance personnel to troubleshoot network problems [r057].

Sniffing (aka passive wiretapping) The passive interception of data transmissions.

SNM See Storage Network Management

SNMP See Simple Network Management Protocol

SOA See Source of Authority or Service Oriented Architecture

SOAP See Simple Object Access Protocol

Social Engineering Obtaining information from individuals by trickery. A euphemism for non-technical or low-technology means—such as lies, impersonation, tricks, bribes, blackmail, and threats—used to attack information systems [r013].

Social Engineering Attacks on Service Provider Infrastructure (PPVPN context) Attacks in which the service provider network is reconfigured or damaged, or in which confidential information is improperly disclosed, and may be mounted through manipulation of service provider personnel. These types of attacks are Provider Provisioned Virtual Private Network (PPVPN)-specific if they affect PPVPN-serving mechanisms. It may be observed that the organizational split (customer, service provider) that is inherent in PPVPNs may make it easier to mount such attacks against provider-provisioned Virtual Private Networks (VPNs) than against VPNs that are self-provisioned by the customer at the IP layer [r058].

Socket A socket on a certain host is defined as the combination of an IP address, a protocol, and a port number. Internet Assigned Numbers Authority (IANA) and now Internet Corporation for Assigned Names and Numbers (ICANN) are responsible for assigning Transmission Control Protocol (TCP) and User Datagram Format (UDP) port numbers to specific uses. Well-known ports are those in the range 0-1023. Registered port numbers are those in the range 1024-49151. Port numbers in the range 49152-65535 are private or dynamic ports, not used by any defined application. ICANN does not enforce this; it is simply a set of recommended uses.

Sometimes ports may be used for different applications or protocols than their official ICANN designation. This misuse may, for example, be by a Trojan horse or, alternatively, by a commonly used program that did not get an ICANN registered port or port range.

Examples include the following:

2181/tcp	EForward-document transport system	Official
2181/udp	EForward-document transport system	Official
2427/udp	Cisco MGCP	Official
3128/tcp	HTTP used by web caches and the default port for the Squid cache	Official
3306/tcp	MySQL Database system	Official
3389/tcp	Microsoft Terminal Server (RDP)	Official
3396/tcp	Novell NDPS Printer Agent	Official
3689/tcp	DAAP Digital Audio Access Protocol used by Apple's ITunes	Official
3690/tcp	Subversion version control system	Official

SOCKS An Internet protocol [r456] that provides a generalized proxy server that enables client–server applications—such as TELNET, File Transfer Protocol (FTP), and Hyper Text Transfer Protocol (HTTP) running over either Transmission Control Protocol (TCP) or User Datagram Protocol (UDP)—to use the services of a firewall. SOCKS is layered under the application layer and above the transport layer. When a client inside a firewall wishes to establish a connection to an object that is reachable only through the firewall, it uses TCP to connect to the SOCKS server, negotiates with the server for the authentication method to be used, authenticates with the chosen method, and then sends a relay request. The SOCKS server evaluates the request, typically based on source and destination addresses, and either establishes the appropriate connection or denies it [r013].

Soft Reset A reset performed on a per-neighbor basis. It does not clear the Border Gateway Protocol (BGP) session while re-establishing the peer-

ing relation and does not stop the flow of traffic [r086].

Soft TEMPEST The use of software techniques to reduce the radio-frequency information leakage from computer displays and keyboards [r013].

Software Computer programs (that are stored in and executed by computer hardware) and associated data (that also is stored in the hardware) that may be dynamically written or modified during execution [r013].

Software Architecture The organizational structure of an Information Technology (IT) system. Structure(s) of the IT system, which comprise software components, the externally visible properties of those components, and the relationships among them. An architecture can be recursively decomposed into parts that interact through interfaces, relationships that connect parts, and constraints for assembling parts. Parts that interact through interfaces include classes, components, and subsystems.

Software Cryptography Weaknesses Software cryptography is coming into wider use, although there is a long way to go until it becomes pervasive. Systems such as Secure Shell (SSH), IPSec, Transport Layer Security (TLS), Secure/Multipurpose Internet Mail Extensions (S/MIME), Pretty Good Privacy (PGP), Security Extensions for Domain Name System (DNS) Security (DNSSEC), and Kerberos are maturing and becoming a part of the network landscape. These systems provide substantial protection against snooping and spoofing. However, there is a potential flaw. At the heart of all cryptographic systems is the generation of secret, unguessable (i.e., random) numbers. The lack of generally available facilities for generating such random numbers (that is, the lack of general availability of truly unpredictable sources) forms an open wound in the design of cryptographic software. For the software developer who wants to build a key or password generation procedure that runs on a wide range of hardware, this is a very real problem [r166].

Software Development Environment (SDE)   Development environments (tools) for the creation of software. An effective software development environment includes both the SDE and an Integrated Development Environment (IDE).

An SDE typically includes: version control system, defect tracking system, loadbuild, update submission process (inspection and testing), loadbuild process, and sanity testing process.

An IDE typically includes: source-code editor, source-code debugger, low-level debugger, code browsers, compile and build tools, and simulation/emulation capabilities.

Software Distribution   Mechanisms to keep systems current and deploy or migrate software in a timely manner.

Software Keyloggers Using a Hooking Mechanism   Type logging is accomplished by using the Windows function SetWindowsHookEx() that monitors all keystrokes. The spyware is typically packaged as an executable file that initiates the hook function, plus a DLL file to handle the logging functions. An application that calls SetWindowsHookEx() is capable of capturing even autocomplete passwords [r224].

Software Vulnerabilities, Examples   Examples include, but are not limited to, out-of-date antivirus software, missing patches, poorly written applications (e.g., cross-site scripting), poorly written applications (e.g., SQL injection), poorly written applications (e.g., code weaknesses such as buffer overflows), deliberately placed weaknesses (e.g., vendor backdoors for management or system recovery; spyware such as keyloggers; Trojan horses), configuration errors (e.g., manual provisioning leading to inconsistent configurations; systems not hardened; systems not audited; systems not monitored) [r190].

SOH   See Secure Opportunistic Hotspots

Solicitation Class Keyword   Concept defined in RFC 3865; an arbitrary string or label which can be associated with an electronic mail message and transported by the ESMTP (SMTP with Service Extensions) mail service as defined in RFC 2821 and related documents. Solicitation class keywords are formatted like domain names, but reversed. For example, the zone administrator of "example.com" might specify a particular solicitation class keyword such as "com.example.adv" that could be inserted in a "No-Solicit:" header by the message sender or in a trace field by a message transfer agent (MTA). This solicitation class keyword is inserted by the sender of the message, who may also insert a variety of other solicitation class keywords as defined by the sender or by other parties. Note that a malicious sender could insert a large number of solicitation class keywords or improperly formatted solicitation keywords, thus performing a Denial of Service attack on the recipient's resources through the use of an excessive number of Domain Name System (DNS) lookups [r457].

Solicited-Node Address   (IPv6 context) Multicast address used by nodes during address resolution process. The solicited-node address facilitates efficient querying of network nodes during address resolution. IPv6 uses the Neighbor Solicitation message to perform address resolution. In IPv4, the Address Resolution Protocol (ARP) Request frame is sent to the Media Access Control (MAC)-level broadcast, disturbing all nodes on the network segment regardless of whether a node is running IPv4. For IPv6, instead of disturbing all IPv6 nodes on the local link by using the local-link scope all-nodes address, the solicited-node multicast address is used as the Neighbor Solicitation message destination. The solicited-node multicast address consists of the prefix FF02::1:FF00:0/104 and the last 24-bits of the IPv6 address that is being resolved [r008].

Solid-State Storage   Random Access Memory (RAM)-based disk devices.

Solution Integration   The planning and staging step of all technology elements prior to production deployment [r029].

Solution Integrity   Mechanisms that protect resources to ensure correct and reliable operation and detect deviation of the protection policies. Examples include system hardening, trusted time, patch management software, file encryption, elimination of single points of failure, code reviews and coding standards, and fault tolerance.

SONET   See Synchronous Optical Network

SONET, Next-gen   See Next-gen SONET

SOR   See System of Record or Service Optimal Routing

SORA   See SSO-PIN ORA

Source Integrity   The degree of confidence that can be placed in information based on the trustworthiness of its sources.

Source of Authority (SOA)   An Attribute Authority (AA) that a privilege verifier for a particular resource trusts as the ultimate authority to assign a set of privileges [r068a].

SP3   See Security Protocol 3

SP4   See Security Protocol 4

Spam   (aka junk mail) Noun: electronic "junk mail" [r458]. In sufficient volume, spam can cause denial of service.

Verb: To indiscriminately send unsolicited, unwanted, irrelevant, or inappropriate messages, especially commercial advertising in mass quantities.

(Presence Services context) Unwanted instant messages [r015].

Spamming   The act of sending out (in bulk) unsolicited electronic mail messages. Typically, spamming is performed in an effort to inexpensively perform mass advertising, but it can also be used for denial of service attacks.

Spanning Tree Standard (Traditional)   Defined in IEEE 802.1D Spanning Tree. Supports convergence of logical topology in a bridged network upon link failure. May take 30–60 seconds to achieve reconfiguration (convergence).

Spanning-Tree Protocol (STP) Manipulation Attack   An attack against switches that involves intercepting traffic by attacking the STP. This protocol is used in switched networks to prevent the creation of bridging loops in an Ethernet network topology. Upon bootup the switches begin a process of determining a loop-free topology. The switches identify one switch as a root bridge and block all other redundant data paths. By attacking STP, the network attacker hopes to spoof his or her system as the root bridge in the topology. To do this, the network attacker broadcasts out STP Configuration/Topology Change Bridge Protocol Data Units (BPDUs) in an attempt to force spanning-tree recalculations. The BPDUs sent out by the network attacker's system announce that the attacking system has a lower bridge priority. If successful, the network attacker can see a variety of frames [r156].

SPE   See Synchronous Payload Envelope

Specific Key Structure   A description of the keying material derived from the chosen key and used to encrypt or decrypt data or compute or verify a checksum. It may, for example, be a single key, a set of keys, or a combination of the original key with additional data [r115].

SPI   See Secure Profile Inspector or Security Parameters Index

Spiral   (SIP context) A Session Initiation Protocol (SIP) request that is routed to a proxy, forwarded onwards, and arrives once again at that proxy, but this time differs in a way that will result in a different processing decision than the original request. Typically, this means that the request's Request-Uniform Resource Identifier (URI) differs from its previous arrival. A spiral is not an error condition, unlike a loop. A typical cause for this is call forwarding. A user calls joe@att.com. The example.com proxy forwards it to Joe's PC, which, in turn, forwards it to bob@att.com. This request is proxied back to the example.com proxy. However, this is not a loop. Since the request is targeted at a different user, it is considered a spiral and is a valid condition [r025].

Split Key   A cryptographic key that is divided into two or more separate data items that individually convey no knowledge of the whole key that results from combining the items [r013].

Split Knowledge   A security technique under which two or more entities separately have key components which individually convey no knowledge of the plaintext key which will be produced when the key components are combined in the cryptographic module [r167].

Spoof   Attempt by an unauthorized entity to gain

access to a system by posing as an authorized user [r013].

Spoofed Sender The actual sender of the message (e.g., v-mail voice message) might not be the same as that specified in the Sender or From header fields of the message content header fields, or the MAIL FROM address from the Simple Mail Transfer Protocol (SMTP) envelope. It should be recognized that SMTP implementations do not provide inherent authentication of the senders of messages, nor are sites under obligation to provide such authentication [r459].

Spoofing (IP Address Spoofing) The creation of IP packets with counterfeit (spoofed) IP source addresses. A form of masquerading where a trusted IP address is used instead of the true IP address as a means of gaining access to a computer system [r200]. An attacker can use special programs to construct IP packets that originate from valid addresses inside the corporate intranet. Upon gaining access to the network with a valid IP address, the attacker can modify, reroute, or delete a user's data and can also conduct other types of attacks. Impersonating, masquerading, and mimicking are forms of spoofing [r057].

(Presence Services context) A principal improperly imitating another principal [r015].

Spoofing Attack (aka masquerade attack) A type of attack in which one system entity illegitimately poses as (assumes the identity of) another entity [r013].

SPOP See Secure POP3

Spreading Factor (SF) (3G Wireless context) The ratio between the code rate and the gross user data rate. It defines how far the data must be spread in order to make use of the entire bandwidth [r007].

Spy Programs See spyware

Spying Techniques Some spyware applications gather information about a user's web browsing habits, purely for marketing purposes, while others are far more malicious. In any case, the spyware attempts to uniquely identify the information sent across a network by using a unique identifier, such as a cookie on the user's hard disk

or a Globally Unique Identifier (GUID). The spyware then sends the logs directly to a remote user or a sever that is collecting this information. The collected information typically includes the infected user's hostname, IP address, and GUID, along with various login names, passwords, and other keystrokes [r224].

Spyware Stand-alone programs that can secretly monitor system activity and relay the information back to another computer. In some cases, spyware may be legitimate programs that are employed by corporations to monitor employee Internet usage. However, it may also represent less legitimate applications. Spyware programs can be surreptitiously placed on users' systems in order to gather confidential information such as passwords, login details, and credit card details. This can be done through keystroke logging and by capturing e-mail and instant messaging traffic. Because spyware can capture sensitive information before it is encrypted for transmission, it can bypass security measures such as firewalls, secure connections, and Virtual Private Networks (VPNs) [r460]. The effects of these programs range from unwanted pop-up ads and browser hijacking to more dangerous security breaches, which include (a) the theft of personal information changing dial-up ISP numbers to expensive toll numbers and (b) installing backdoors on a system that leave it open for hackers [r224]. Spyware is a particular concern because of its potential use in identity theft and fraud [r460]. The dividing line between adware and spyware is intent.

Spyware Vectors Mechanism of entry for spyware programs. Spyware usually gets into the computer through banner ad-based software where the user is enticed to install the software for free. Other sources of spyware include instant messaging, various peer-to-peer applications, popular download managers, on-line gaming, many porn/crack sites, and more. Most, but not all, spyware is targeted exclusively at Microsoft's Internet Explorer web browser. Users of modern web browser alternatives, such as Mozilla's Firefox and Apple's Safari, are generally not affected by spyware [r224].

SQL   See Structured Query Language

SRES   See Signed Response

SRM   See Storage Resource Management

SRNC   See Serving Radio Network Controller

SRNS   See Serving Radio Network Subsystem

SRTP   See Secure Real-time Transport Protocol

S-SCH   See Secondary Synchronization Channel

SSH   See Secure Shell

SSH (Secure Shell) File Transfer Protocol (SFTP)   [aka Secure FTP or Secure File Transfer Protocol (SFTP)] Provides secure file transfer over a nonsecure network (such as a Transmission Control Protocol/Internet Protocol (TCP/IP) network). The SFTP component offers the features found in a standard File Transfer Protocol (FTP) program with the added ability to encrypt data using a secure SSH2 channel.

SSL   See Secure Sockets Layer

SSMTP   Secure SMTP

SSO   See Single Sign-On, or System Security Officer, or Site Security Officer.

Stack   (MPLS context) Synonymous with label stack.

Stakeholders, IEEE 1471-2000   Individuals that have key roles in, or concerns about, the system—for example, as users, developers, or managers. Different stakeholders with different roles in the system will have different concerns. Stakeholders can be individuals, teams, or organizations.

Stalking   (Presence Services context) Using presence information to infer the whereabouts of a principal, especially for malicious or illegal purposes [r015].

Standard Protocol, Internet Engineering Task Force (IETF)   A specification for which significant implementation and successful operational experience has been obtained may be elevated to the Internet Standard level. An Internet Standard (which may simply be referred to as a standard) is characterized by a high degree of technical maturity and by a generally held belief that the specified protocol or service provides significant benefit to the Internet community [r280, r281].

Standard Security Mechanisms, Digital Signatures   One of the strongest forms of challenge/ response authentication is based on digital signatures. Using public-key cryptography is preferable to schemes based on secret key ciphers because no server needs a copy of the client's secret. Rather, the client has a private key; servers have the corresponding public key. Using digital signatures properly is tricky. A client should never sign the exact challenge sent to it, since there are several subtle number-theoretic attacks that can be launched in such situations. The Digital Signature Standard (DSS) and Rivest–Shamir–Adleman (RSA) are both good choices; each has its advantages. Signing with Digital Signature Algorithm (DSA) requires the use of good random numbers (RFC 1750). If the enemy can recover the random number used for any given signature or if one uses the same random number for two different documents, one's private key can be recovered. DSS has much better performance than RSA for generating new private keys, and somewhat better performance generating signatures, while RSA has much better performance for verifying signatures [r170].

Standard Security Mechanisms, Firewalls, and Topology   Firewalls are a topological defense mechanism. That is, they rely on a well-defined boundary between the good "inside" and the bad "outside" of some domain, with the firewall mediating the passage of information. While firewalls can be very valuable if employed properly, there are limits to their ability to protect a network. The first limitation is that firewalls cannot protect against inside attacks. While the actual incidence rate of such attacks is not known (and is probably unknowable), there is no doubt that it is substantial, and arguably constitutes a majority of security problems. More generally, given that firewalls require a well-delimited boundary, to the extent that such a boundary does not exist, firewalls do not help. Any external connections, whether they are protocols that are deliberately passed through the firewall, links that are tunneled through, unprotected wireless Local Area Networks (LANs), or direct external connections from nominally inside hosts, weaken the protection. Firewalls tend to become less effective over time because users tunnel protocols through them and may have inadequate security on the tunnel endpoints. If the tunnels are encrypted, there is no way for the firewall to censor them. An oft-cited advantage of firewalls is that they hide the existence of internal hosts from outside eyes. Given the amount of leakage, however, the likelihood of successfully hiding machines is rather low. In a more subtle vein, firewalls hurt the end-to-end model of the Internet and its protocols. Indeed, not all protocols can be passed safely or easily through firewalls. Sites that rely on firewalls for security may find themselves cut off from new and useful aspects of the Internet [r170].

Firewalls work best when they are used as one element of a total security structure. For example, a strict firewall may be used to separate an exposed web server from a back-end database, with the only opening the communication channel between the two. Similarly, a firewall that permitted only encrypted tunnel traffic could be used to secure a piece of a Virtual Private Network (VPN). On the other hand, in that case the other end of the VPN would need to be equally secured [r170].

Standard Security Mechanisms, Generic Security Service Application Programming Interface (GSS-API)   GSS-API (RFC 2744) provides a framework for applications to use when they require authentication, integrity, and/or confidentiality. Unlike Simple Authentication and Security Layer (SASL), GSS-API can be used easily with User Datagram Protocol (UDP)-based applications. It provides for the creation of opaque authentication tokens (aka chunks of memory) that may be embedded in a protocol's data units. Note that the security of GSS-API-protected protocols depends on the underlying security mechanism; this must be evaluated independently [r170].

Standard Security Mechanisms, Hash Message Authentication Code (HMAC)   HMAC (RFC 2104) is the preferred shared-secret authentication technique. If both sides know the same secret key, HMAC can be used to authenticate any arbitrary message. This includes random challenges, which means that HMAC can be adapted to prevent replays of old sessions. A disadvantage of using HMAC for connection authentication is that the secret must be known in the clear by both parties, making this undesirable when keys are long-lived. When suitable, HMAC should be used in preference to older techniques, notably keyed hash functions. Simple keyed hashes based on Message Digest 5 (MD5) (RFC 1321), such as that used in the Border Gateway Protocol (BGP) session security mechanism (RFC 2385), are especially to be avoided in new protocols, given the hints of weakness in MD5. HMAC can be implemented using any secure hash function, including MD5 and Secure Hash Algorithm (SHA-1) (RFC 3174). SHA-1 is preferable for new protocols because it is more frequently used for this purpose and may be more secure. It is important to understand that an HMAC-based mechanism needs to be employed on every protocol data unit (aka packet). It is a mistake to use an HMAC-based system to authenticate the beginning of a Transmission Control Protocol (TCP) session and then send all remaining data without any protection. Attack programs exist that permit a TCP session to be stolen. An attacker merely needs to use such a tool to steal a session after the HMAC step is performed [r170].

Standard Security Mechanisms, IPsec   The generic IP-layer encryption and authentication protocol defined in RFC 2401, RFC 2402, RFC 2406, RFC 2407, and RFC 2411. As such, it protects all upper layers, including both Transmission Control Protocol (TCP) and User Datagram Protocol (UDP). Its normal granularity of protection is host-to-host, host-to-gateway, and gateway-to-gateway. The specification does permit user-granularity protection, but this is comparatively rare. As such, IPsec is currently inappropriate when host-granularity is too coarse. Because IPsec is installed at the IP layer, it is rather intrusive to the networking code. Implementing it generally requires either new hardware or a new protocol stack. On the other hand, it is fairly transparent to applications. Applications running over IPsec can have improved security without changing their protocols at all. But at least until IPsec is more widely deployed, most applications should not assume they are running atop IPsec as an alternative to specifying their own security mechanisms. Most modern operating systems have IPsec available; most routers do not, at least for the control path. An application using Transport Layer Security (TLS) is more likely to be able to assert application-specific to take advantage of its authentication [r170].

Standard Security Mechanisms, Kerberos Kerberos, defined in RFC1510, provides a mechanism for two entities to authenticate each other and exchange keying material. On the client side, an application obtains a Kerberos "ticket" and "authenticator." These items, which should be considered opaque data, are then communicated from client to server. The server can then verify their authenticity. Both sides may then ask the Kerberos software to provide them with a session key that can be used to protect or encrypt data. Kerberos may be used by itself in a protocol. However, it is also available as a mechanism under Simple Authentication and Security Layer (SASL) and Generic Security Services Application Programming Interface (GSSAPI). It has some known vulnerabilities but it can be used securely [r170].

Standard Security Mechanisms, One-Time Passwords (OTP) One-time password schemes, such as that described in RFC 2289, are very much stronger than conventional passwords. The host need not store a copy of the user's password, nor is it ever transmitted over the network. However, there are some risks. Since the transmitted string is derived from a user-typed password, guessing attacks may still be feasible. (Indeed, a program to launch just this attack is readily available.) Furthermore, the user's ability to login necessarily expires after a predetermined number of uses. While in many cases this is a feature, an implementation most likely needs to provide a way

to reinitialize the authentication database, without requiring that the new password be sent in the clear across the network. There are commercial hardware authentication tokens. Apart from the session hijacking issue, support for such tokens (especially challenge/response tokens, where the server sends a different random number for each authentication attempt) may require extra protocol messages [r170].

Standard Security Mechanisms, Open Pretty Good Privacy (OpenPGP) and Secure/Multipurpose Internet Mail Extensions (S/MIME) Digital signatures can be used to build "object security" applications that can be used to protect data in store and forward protocols such as electronic mail. Two different secure e-mail protocols, OpenPGP and S/MIME, have been proposed to replace Privacy Enhanced Mail (PEM) (RFC 1421, RFC 1422, RFC 1423, RFC 1424). It is not clear which, if either, will succeed. While specified for use with secure e-mail, both can be adapted to protect data carried by other protocols. Both use certificates to identify users; both can provide secrecy and authentication of e-mail messages; however, the certificate formats are very different. Historically, the difference between PGP-based e-mail and S/MIME-based e-mail has been the style of certificate chaining. In S/MIME, users possess X.509 certificates; the certification graph is a tree with a very small number of roots. By contrast, PGP uses the so-called "web of trust," where any user can sign anyone else's certificate. This certification graph is really an arbitrary graph or set of graphs [r170].

S/MIME is designed to be "foolproof." That is, very little end-user configuration is required. Specifically, end-users do not need to be aware of trust relationships, etc. The idea is that if an S/MIME client says, "This signature is valid," the user should be able to "trust" that statement at face value without needing to understand the underlying implications. To achieve this, S/MIME is typically based on a limited number of "root" Certification Authorities (CAs). The goal is to build a global trusted certificate infrastructure. The downside to this approach is that it requires a deployed public key infrastructure before it will work. Two end-users may not be able to simply obtain S/MIME-capable software and begin communicating securely. This is not a limitation of the protocol, but a typical configuration restriction for commonly available software. One or both of them may need to obtain a certificate from a mutually trusted CA; furthermore, that CA must already be trusted by their e-mail handling software. This process may involve cost and legal obligations. This ultimately results in the technology being harder to deploy, particularly in an environment where end-users do not necessarily appreciate the value received for the hassle incurred [r170].

The PGP "web of trust" approach has the advantage that two end-users can just obtain PGP software and immediately begin to communicate securely. No infrastructure is required and no fees and legal agreements need to be signed to proceed. As such, PGP appeals to people who need to establish ad-hoc security associations. The downside to PGP is that it requires end-users to have an understanding of the underlying security technology in order to make effective use of it. Specifically, it is fairly easy to fool naive users to accept a "signed" message that is in fact a forgery. To date, PGP has found great acceptance between security-aware individuals who have a need for secure e-mail in an environment devoid of the necessary global infrastructure. By contrast, S/MIME works well in a corporate setting where a secure internal CA system can be deployed. It does not require a lot of end-user security knowledge. S/MIME can be used between institutions by carefully setting up cross certification [r170].

Standard Security Mechanisms, Secure Shell (SSH) SSH provides a secure connection between client and server. It operates very much like Transport Layer Security (TLS); however, it is optimized as a protocol for remote connections on terminal-like devices. One of its more innova-

tive features is its support for "tunneling" other protocols over the SSH-protected Transmission Control Protocol (TCP) connection. This feature has permitted knowledgeable security people to perform such actions as reading and sending e-mail or news via insecure servers over an insecure network. It is not a substitute for a true Virtual Private Network (VPN), but it can often be used in place of one [r170].

Standard Security Mechanisms, Security Extensions for Domain Name System (DNS) (DNSSEC) DNSSEC (RFC 2535) digitally signs DNS records. It is an essential tool for protecting against DNS cache contamination attacks; these in turn can be used to defeat name-based authentication and to redirect traffic to or past an attacker. The latter makes DNSSEC an essential component of some other security mechanisms, notably IPsec. Although not widely deployed on the Internet at the time of the writing of this document, it offers the potential to provide a secure mechanism for mapping domain names to IP protocol addresses. It may also be used to securely associate other information with a DNS name. This information may be as simple as a service that is supported on a given node, or a key to be used with IPsec for negotiating a secure session. Note that the concept of storing general purpose application keys in the DNS has been deprecated (RFC 3445), but standardization of storing keys for particular applications—in particular, IPsec— is proceeding [r170].

Standard Security Mechanisms, Security/Multipart Security/Multiparts (RFC 1847) are the preferred mechanism for protecting e-mail. More precisely, it is the Multipurpose Internet Mail Extensions (MIME) framework within which encryption and/or digital signatures are embedded. Both Open Pretty Good Privacy (OpenPGP) and Secure/Multipurpose Internet Mail Extensions (S/MIME) use Security/Multipart for their encoding. Conforming e-mail readers can easily recognize and process the cryptographic portions of the mail. Security/Multiparts represents one form of "object security," where the object of interest to the end-user is protected, independent of transport mechanism, intermediate storage, and so on. Currently, there is no general form of object protection available on the Internet [r170].

Standard Security Mechanisms, Simple Authentication and Security Layer (SASL) SASL (RFC 2222) is a framework for negotiating an authentication and encryption mechanism to be used over a Transmission Control Protocol (TCP) stream. As such, its security properties are those of the negotiated mechanism. Specifically, unless the negotiated mechanism authenticates all of the subsequent messages or underlying protection protocol such as Transport Layer Security (TLS) is used, TCP connections are vulnerable to session stealing. TLS makes extensive use of certificates for authentication. As commonly deployed, only servers have certificates, whereas clients go unauthenticated (at least by the TLS processing itself). SASL permits the use of more traditional client authentication technologies, such as passwords (one-time or otherwise). A powerful combination is (a) TLS for underlying protection and authentication of the server and (b) a SASL-based system for authenticating clients. Care must be taken to avoid man-in-the-middle vulnerabilities when different authentication techniques are used in different directions [r170].

Standard Security Mechanisms, Transport Layer Security (TLS) TLS (RFC 2246) provides an encrypted, authenticated channel that runs on top of Transmission Control Protocol (TCP). While TLS was originally designed for use by Web browsers, it is by no means restricted to such. In general, though, each application that wishes to use TLS will need to be converted individually. Generally, the server side is always authenticated by a certificate. Clients may possess certificates, too, providing mutual authentication, though this is rarely deployed. It's an unfortunate reality that even server side authentication is not as secure in practice as the cryptography would imply because most implementations allow users to ignore authentication failures (by clicking OK to a warning) and most users routinely do so. Designers should

thus be wary of demanding plaintext passwords, even over TLS-protected connections. (This requirement can be relaxed if it is likely that implementations will be able to verify the authenticity and authorization of the server's certificate.) Although application modification is generally required to make use of TLS, there exist toolkits, both free and commercial, that provide implementations. These are designed to be incorporated into the application's code. An application using TLS is more likely to be able to assert application specific certificate policies than one using IPsec [r170].

Standards Developing Organizations (SDOs) The U.S. has a voluntary standardization system. American National Standards Institute (ANSI) coordinates U.S. private sectors voluntary standardization system. It relies on SDOs. SDOs are technical organizations that work cooperatively to develop voluntary national consensus standards. There are hundreds of SDOs; the 20 largest SDOs produce 90% of standards. IEEE is an SDO. SDOs are typically comprised of Technical Committees, which are responsible for content of standards, and Special Interest Groups, which explore new ideas that may need coverage in published standards.

Standards for Interoperable LAN/MAN Security (SILS) A (defunct) set of Institute of Electrical and Electronics Engineers (IEEE) standards, which has eight parts: (a) Model, including security management, (b) Secure Data Exchange protocol, (c) Key Management, (d) [has been incorporated in (a)], (e) Secure Data Exchange (SDE) over Ethernet 2.0, (f) SDE Sublayer Management, (g) SDE Security Labels, and (h) SDE PICS Conformance. Parts b, e, f, g, and h are incorporated in IEEE Standard 802.10-1998 [r013].

Note: IEEE 802.10-1998, IEEE Standard for Local and Metropolitan Area Networks: Interoperable LAN/MAN Security (SILS) was administratively withdrawn by the IEEE on 16 January 04.

802.10-1992 Interoperable LAN/MAN Security (SILS) was superseded by 802.10-1998.

IEEE 802.10a-1999, Supplement to 802.10-1998, Standard for Interoperable LAN/MAN Security (SILS)—Security Architecture Framework was administratively withdrawn 16 January 04 IEEE 802.10c-1998, Supplement to 802.10-1998, Key management (Clause 3) was administratively withdrawn 16 January 04.

Stateful Compression   A compression method such as LZS (Lempel Ziv STAC), the data compression algorithm used in IP Security (IPsec) protocol, where the compressor maintains its state through all compressed records. Stateful compression requires both a reliable link and sequenced record delivery to ensure that all records can be decompressed in the same order they were compressed. Since Transport Layer Security (TLS) and lower-layer protocols provide reliable, sequenced record delivery, compression history information may be maintained and exploited when the LZS Compression Method is used.

Stateful Inspection   A packet filter firewall that undertakes protocol-deep analysis. While a packet filter only checks the packet header to determine the source and destination address and the source and destination ports to verify against its rules, stateful inspection checks the packet all the way to the application layer. Stateful inspection monitors incoming and outgoing packets to determine not only source and destination, but also context. By ensuring that only requested information is allowed back in stateful inspection helps protect against hacker techniques such as IP spoofing and port scanning [r035].

Stateful Proxy   (SIP context) A logical entity that maintains the client and server transaction state machines defined by this specification during the processing of a request, also known as a transaction stateful proxy. A (transaction) stateful proxy is not the same as a call stateful proxy [r025].

Stateless Compression   A compression method where the compressor compresses each record independently.

Stateless Proxy   (SIP context) A logical entity that does not maintain the client or server transaction state machines defined in this specification when it processes requests. A stateless proxy forwards

every request it receives downstream and every response it receives upstream [r025].

Static Routing   Utilization of routes, introduced by hand, into routers routing tables [r008].

Status   (Presence Services context) A distinguished part of the presence information of a presentity. Status has at least the mutually exclusive values open and closed, which have meaning for the acceptance of instant messages, and may have meaning for other communication means. There may be other values of status that do not imply anything about instant message acceptance. These other values of status may be combined with open and closed or they may be mutually exclusive with those values. Some implementations may combine status with other entities. For example, an implementation might make an instant inbox address visible only when the instant inbox can accept an instant message. Then, the existence of an instant inbox address implies open, while its absence implies closed [r015].

Status of a Trouble Report   The stage that has been reached by a trouble report since its instantiation/creation while the trouble is being resolved [r068a].

Stealth Mode   A keylogger mode where no icon is present in the taskbar and the keylogger is virtually hidden [r224].

Stealth Virus   Virus type that takes steps to avoid detection.

Steganography   Methods of hiding the existence of a message or other data. It is used to hide a file inside another. For example, an image can be hidden inside another graphic image file, audio file, or other file format [r057]. Steganography is different than cryptography, which hides the meaning of a message but does not hide the message itself [r013].

Stego   Abbreviation for steganography.

Stimulated Brillouin Scattering (SBS)   (optical transmission term) Optical transmission impairment that limits power that can be injected into a siglemode fiber. As more and more OC-48/OC-192 systems are placed over a fiber, the output power of the erbium-doped fiber amplifiers (EDFAs) can cause SBS problems. Techniques have recently been developed to boost the SBS threshold.

STM-N See Synchronous Transport Module (-N)

Storage Infrastructure (typically in the form of appliances) that is used for the permanent or semi-permanent on-line retention of structured (e.g., databases) and unstructured (e.g., business/e-mail files) corporate information. Typically includes (i) a controller that manages incoming and outgoing communications as well as the data steering onto the physical storage medium (e.g., RAIDs (redundant arrays of independent disks, semiconductor memory, etc.) and (ii) the physical storage medium itself. The communications mechanism could be a network interface (such as Gigabit Ethernet), a channel interface [such as Small Computer System Interface (SCSI)], or a SAN Interface [i.e., Fibre Channel (FC)].

Storage Appliances A storage platform designed to perform a specific task, such as Network Attached Storage (NAS), archival, etc. [r029].

Storage Area Network (SAN) A high-speed sub-network of shared storage devices. A set of standards defined by American National Standards Institute (ANSI). A storage device is a machine that contains disks or tapes for storing data. A network that transfers data between computer systems and storage devices via peripheral channels such as Small Computer System Interface (SCSI) or Fibre Channel (FC).

A SAN is used to attach storage devices to servers. Traditionally SANs have been implemented using the FC standards and networks; with the introduction of Internet SCSI (iSCSI), SAN usage has been expanded to include IP networks.

A network of storage disks. In large enterprises, a SAN connects multiple servers to a centralized pool of disk storage. Compared to managing hundreds of servers, each with their own disks, SANs improve system administration. By treating all the company's storage as a single resource, disk maintenance and routine backups are easier to schedule and control. In some SANs, the disks themselves can copy data to other disks for backup without any processing overhead at the host computers [r029].

The SAN network allows data transfers between computers and disks at the same high peripheral channel speeds as when they are directly attached. FC is a driving force with SANs and is typically used to encapsulate SCSI commands. ESCON channels are also supported [r029].

SANs can be centralized or distributed. A centralized SAN connects multiple servers to a collection of disks, whereas a distributed SAN typically uses one or more Fibre Channel or SCSI switches to connect nodes within buildings or campuses. For long distances, SAN traffic is transferred over Asynchronous Transfer Mode (ATM), Synchronous Optical Network (SONET) or dark fiber. To guarantee complete recovery in a disaster, dual, redundant SANs are deployed, one a mirror of the other and each in separate locations [r029].

Another SAN option is IP storage, which enables data transfer via IP over fast Gigabit Ethernet locally or via the Internet to anywhere in the world [r029].

Storage Area Network to Wide Area Network (SAN/WAN) Extension Gateways that connect geographically distributed SANs via existing WAN infrastructure. These solutions may use IP, Synchronous Optical Network (SONET), Dense Wavelength Division Multiplexing (DWDM), or Automatically Switched Optical network (ASON), transport technologies, and support protocols that carry Fibre Channel (FC) blocks via those WAN networks [Fibre Channel over Internet Protocol (FCIP), Internet FCP (iFCP), etc.] [r029].

Storage Attachment Modes Network-Attached Storage (NAS) is a disk subsystem that attaches to the Local Area Network (LAN) (e.g., a Gibabit Ethernet port). A NAS system is like any other file server on the network; however, rather than containing a full-blown operating system, it typically uses a slimmed-down microkernel specialized for handling only file reads and writes. Adding or removing a NAS device is similar to adding or removing any node in a network.

Channel attachment implies the use of a processor's Input/Output (I/O) channel rather than a communications port (e.g., a Gibabit Ethernet port). A channel-attached storage subsystem is typically (but not always) locally attached [e.g., via the Small Computer System Interface (SCSI) port].

A Directly Attached Storage (DAS) system is a system dedicated to a single server and is typically collocated with the server and attached via a SCSI port. (It is possible that DAS could be physically attached to a SAN port on the server, but this is less likely: when storage is local/dedicated/DAS-oriented is typically connected via SCSI.)

Storage subsystem can be shared and/or remotely attached (remote meaning at some distant point in the Data Center or at a geographically separate location) over a Storage Area Network (SAN). SANs use Fibre Channel (FC) standards/technology. A SAN can be utilized to "extend" and/or "virtualize" the channel; channel-attached SANs extend the peripheral channel to long distances [r213]. A server may have a built-in SAN port, in which case it can connect directly to a SAN network; currently, however, many servers (including whole classes of popular machines) are prevented from accessing FC SANs because they are only equipped with SCSI ports; in this case the storage can still be positioned over a SAN, but a bridging device (perhaps a switch/director port) is needed to convert from SCSI to FC.

Storage Implications for Encryption Fundamental differences between communications and storage have important implications for encryption, even though the basic encryption algorithms are the same [r193]:

Latency. Communication is ephemeral: Once the sender transmits data and it arrives at the receiver, the job is complete. Communication usually occurs at the speed of light; even in the case of multicast, where there may be more than one receiver, it still occurs within a short period of time. In any case, the receiver actually exists and can participate in a key agreement, authentication protocols, or other cryptographic methods that enable secure communications. One can think of storage as communications with a very long latency—possibly years. It is easy to imagine writing information to a storage device and then reading it with a machine that did not exist at the time the data were written. Such storage latencies make it impossible for the reader to participate in a key agreement protocol.

Interoperability. Standards for interoperability in communications ensure that it is not necessary for both ends of a link to be the same vendor. Replacing a vendor involves replacing both ends of a link and restarting the data traffic. However, interoperability is even more important for storage. Without a standard, it would be impossible to replace a vendor without re-encrypting all the data at rest. A user who has encrypted a petabyte of storage using one vendor should be able to replace that vendor without having to incur such an expense.

Key management. In communications, the well-known key management process involves creating, using, and then destroying a key. If the key is lost or some other problem with it occurs, the solution is to create or agree on a new unrelated key and continue operations. Because the old key is to previous (now complete) communications, this is not a significant hardship. With storage, however, if one loses access to the existing key, one loses access to all the stored data. Creating any new unrelated key to the previously encrypted data does not help.

Additional security. Communications generally occur in a variable-length stream that allows adding information before or after the encrypted data. The encryption protocol can use this additional information to implement extra security measures. Storage, particularly disk storage, organizes the data in a randomly accessible manner that makes adding integrity information a daunting task.

Storage Network Management (SNM) Storage software solutions that discover, monitor, manage, and display the physical elements that make up the storage network infrastructure [r029].

Storage Networking Industry Association (SNIA)

Not-for-profit trade organization for companies and individuals in various sectors of the storage industry.

Storage Networking Industry Association (SNIA) Shared Storage Model   This is the layered storage model advanced by the SNIA.

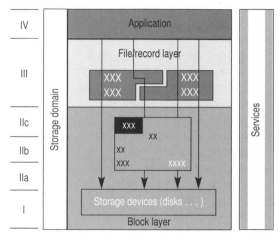

The SNIA Shared Storage Model is a layered model. The figure shows a picture of the stack with a numbering scheme for the layers. Roman numerals are used to avoid confusion with the ISO and IETF networking stack numbers. The layers are as follows:

- IV. Application
- III. File/record layer
  - ○ IIIb. Database
  - ○ IIIa. File system
- II. Block aggregation layer, with three function-placements:
  - ○ IIc. Host
  - ○ IIb. Network
  - ○ IIa. Device
- I. Storage devices

Storage Resource Management (SRM)   Storage software solutions that discover, assess, and report the usage patterns of storage systems [r029].

Storage Security   Hardware and/or software solutions that are designed specifically to protect storage assets and resident data from unauthorized access [r029].

Storage Systems, Traditional Security   Traditional means of securing storage systems involve physical defenses such as fences, locked doors, and guards. When storage devices are no longer used, mechanical destruction and disk sanitization render data unreadable; however, these ap-

proaches are expensive and often unreliable [r193].

Storage Temperature   (optical transmission term) The temperature range (°C) over which the device can be stored and cycled without damage, and can be operated properly according to its specifications over operating temperature.

Storage Virtualization   Software (sub)systems (typically middleware) that abstract the physical and logical storage assets from the host systems.

STP   See Shielded Twisted-Pair or Spanning Tree Protocol

Strategic Imperatives   High-level objectives that set the direction of a company.

Strategic Objectives   An organization's goals or activities to address competitiveness, business advantages, or change.

Strategic Planning   A process for long-term goal-setting, determining priorities and making decisions.

Stream Cipher   An encryption algorithm that breaks plaintext into a stream of successive bits (or characters) and encrypts the nth plaintext bit with the nth element of a parallel key stream, thus converting the plaintext bit stream into a ciphertext bit stream [r291, r013].

Strict Routing   (SIP context) A proxy is said to be strict routing if it follows the route processing rules of RFC 2543 and many prior work in progress versions of this RFC. That rule caused proxies to destroy the contents of the Request-Uniform Resource Identifier (URI) when a route header field was present. Strict routing behavior is not used in this specification, in favor of a loose routing behavior. Proxies that perform strict routing are also known as strict routers [r025].

Stringent Authentication Process   Password-based logins are weak from a security/authentication perspective. The use of digital certificates issued and verified by a Certification Authority (CA) as part of a public-key infrastructure is considered likely to become the norm, in the near future, for undertaking authentication on the Internet [r347].

String-to-Key Function (Kerberos)   This function generates a key from two UTF-8 (8-bit Unicode Transformation Format) strings and an opaque octet string; namely (UTF-8 string, UTF-8 string, opaque) → (protocol-key). One of the strings is usually the principal's pass phrase, but generally it is merely a secret string. The other string is a "salt" string intended to produce different keys from the same password for different users or realms. Although the strings provided will use UTF-8 encoding, no specific version of Unicode should be assumed; all valid UTF-8 strings should be allowed. Strings provided in other encodings must first be converted to UTF-8 before applying this function. The third argument, the octet string, may be used to pass mechanism-specific parameters into this function. Since doing so implies knowledge of the specific encryption system, generating nondefault parameter values should be an uncommon operation, and normal Kerberos applications should be able to treat this parameter block as an opaque object supplied by the Key Distribution Center or defaulted to some mechanism-specific constant value. The string-to-key function should be a one-way function so that compromising a user's key in one realm does not compromise it in another, even if the same password (but a different salt) is used [r115].

String-to-Key Parameter Format (Kerberos) This describes the format of the block of data that can be passed to the string-to-key function above to configure additional parameters for that function. Along with the mechanism of encoding parameter values, bounds on the allowed parameters should also be described to avoid allowing a spoofed Key Distribution Center (KDC) to compromise the user's password. If practical, it may be desirable to construct the encoding so that values unacceptably weakening the resulting key cannot be encoded [r115].

Strong Authentication An authentication process that uses cryptography (particularly public-key certificates) to verify the identity claimed for an entity. A strong authentication process uses something other than (or in addition to) user identifiers and passwords. Multi-factor authentication is an example of strong authentication.

Strong Random Sequence Generation One way to produce a strong random sequence is to take a seed value and hash the quantities produced by concatenating the seed with successive integers and then to mask the values obtained so as to limit the amount of generator state available to the adversary. It may also be possible to use an "encryption" algorithm with a random key and seed value to encrypt successive integers, as in counter (CTR) mode encryption. Alternatively, one can feedback all of the output value from encryption into the value to be encrypted for the next iteration. This is a particular example of output feedback mode (OFB) [r166].

Strong Unforgeability Attacks on Signature Schemes In strong unforgeability attacks on signature schemes the adversary is allowed to query a signature oracle and is considered to be successful if he/she later forges a signature for a new message, but also if he/she creates a new signature for a previously signed message. This security notion is, for example, important for blind signatures used as coins in e-cash systems: It should be infeasible to create another coin from a given coin, even for the same message [r016].

Structure of the "Subject:" Field Contained in RFC 2047, which species the mechanisms for character set encoding in mail headers. In addition to choosing a character set, RFC 2047 uses two algorithms, known as "Base64 Encoding" and "Quoted Printable," which are two different methods for encoding characters that fall outside the basic 7-bit American Standard Code for Information Interchange (ASCII) requirements that are specified in the core electronic mail standards. The basic definition of the "Subject:" of an electronic mail message is contained in RFC 2822. The normative requirements that apply to all headers are: (i) The maximum length of the header field is 998 characters. (ii) Each line must be no longer than 78 characters.

Structured Query Language (SQL) A defacto standard language that can be applied to query and update data sources in Relational Database Management Systems (RDBMS).

Structuring   (financial term) A money laundering technique. Laundered funds are typically placed into a financial institution via a series of structured transactions. This is a practice frequently used to hide proceeds from drug sales. Structuring is the process of regularly depositing cash in amounts just below the reporting thresholds amount. These deposits may occur several times a week or several times during a 30-day period. The deposits may even be at several different locations or offices of a financial institution on the same day, in an effort to better disperse the funds. Each of these deposits would be far below the reporting requirement so as not to arouse suspicion.

STS-N   See Synchronous Transport Signal-Level N

STUN   See Simple Traversal of User Datagram Protocol (UDP) Through Network Address Translators (NATs)

Subject   (Computer System context) A system entity that causes information to flow among objects or changes the system state; technically, a process-domain pair [r013].

(Digital Certificate context) The entity name that is bound to the data items in a digital certificate, and particularly a name that is bound to a key value in a public-key certificate [r013].

Subject Certification Authority (CA)   (aka subject CA) The CA whose public key is certified in the certificate [r011, r105].

Sublayer, Protocol   The logical partitioning of a protocol layer (such as the layers defined by the Open Systems Interconnection Reference Model) into distinct, nonoverlapping, hierarchical functional portions, which when considered in total, comprise the entire layer. The sublayers typically have formal interfaces between adjacent sublayers (neighboring), similar, in concept, to the formal interfaces between adjacent layers.

Subliminal Channel   An information transmission channel that can be used to send information out of (or potentially into) a cryptosystem. A subliminal channel is a type of covert channel; how-

ever, covert channels are broader in scope since they are not specific to cryptosystems [r162]. Many kleptographic attacks are based on the notion of a subliminal channel [r089].

A concrete example explains what a covert channel is. Suppose that Alice and Bob are connected to a computer that is running a multiuser operating system. In a secure operating system that can be used for sensitive (e.g., military) applications it should not be possible for a process that Alice is running to transmit information covertly to a process that Bob is running. But, suppose that a printer is connected to this machine. Each process can make an operating system call to print data. This call will return a result code indicating success or failure. The result code will also indicate if the printer is busy printing out a document. Alice's process can utilize a special communication protocol to speak with a process that Bob is running. For example, printing out two short documents with a brief pause in between could correspond to a binary "1" and printing out one document could be a binary "0." Bob's process calls the operating system routine in a busy waiting fashion to receive bits from Alice's process. This is not a subliminal channel, but it is a covert channel [r162, r089].

Subliminal channels are characterized by their inability to be detected when in use, their inability to be read even when it is assumed that they are in use, and their inherent channel capacity, or bandwidth. However, the code that transmits information over a subliminal channel is readily identifiable by cryptographers when they inspect the code. Therefore, that attacker must ensure that subliminal channels are only utilized in black-box cryptosystems. Gus Simmons investigated subliminal channels while assessing the security of a nuclear arms control verification protocol [r181, r454]. He then extended the notion to other scenarios. The classic use of a subliminal channel is in the prisoners' problem [r329].

In the prisoners' problem, two prisoners are allowed to communicate to each other but are not allowed to send encrypted messages to each other. They are only permitted to exchange public keys and digitally sign their messages. The problem is to devise a way, using the digital signature algorithm in question, for the two prisoners to communicate secretly with each other through digital signatures in such a way that the warden cannot detect or read the subliminal messages.

The applications of subliminal channels grew to encompass insider attacks against smartcards as well [r330]. A very general type of subliminal channel has been shown to exist that is based on the quadratic residuosity problem. The channel involves placing a small set of primes, which must remain secret, within a smartcard. It has been shown that this channel can be used by a malicious designer to covertly obtain the Digital Signature Algorithm (DSA) private signing key of the user of the smartcard [r455].

There have been efforts by the research community to try to eliminate subliminal channels in certain algorithms.

Subnet Anycast Router Address (IPv6 context) Anycast address (64 bits:: prefix) that is allocated to routers interfaces [r008].

Subnetwork An Open Systems Interconnection Reference Model (OSIRM) term for a system of packet relays and connecting links that implement the lower three protocol layers of the OSIRM to provide a communication service that interconnects attached end systems. Usually the relays operate at OSIRM layer 3 and are all of the same type [r013].

(IPv6 context) One or more links that use the same 64 bits prefix in IPv6 [r008].

Subnetwork Associated Path (IPv6 context) Path where the 64 bits prefix belongs to a concrete subnetwork [r008].

Sub-Network-Dependent Convergence Protocol (SNDCP) (GSM context) The Sub-Network Dependent Convergence Protocol compresses and segments data, like the Transmission Control Protocol/Internet Protocol (TCP/IP) header, in the Serving GPRS Support Node (SGSN) [r014].

Subordinate Certification Authority (SCA) A Certification Authority (CA) whose public-key certificate is issued by another (superior) CA.

[Multilevel Information System Security Initiative (MISSI) context] The fourth-highest (bottom) level of a MISSI certification hierarchy; a MISSI CA whose public-key certificate is signed by a MISSI CA rather than by a MISSI PCA. A MISSI SCA is the administrative authority for a subunit of an organization, established when it is desirable to organizationally distribute or decentralize the CA service. The term refers both to that authoritative office or role, and to the person who fills that office. A MISSI SCA registers end users and issues their certificates and may also register organizational registration authorities (ORAs), but may not register other CAs. An SCA periodically issues a certificate revocation list (CRL) [r013].

Subordinate Distinguished Name An X.500 Distinguished Name (DN) is subordinate to another X.500 DN if it begins with a set of attributes that is the same as the entire second DN except for the terminal attribute of the second DN [which is usually the name of a Certification Authority (CA)] [r013].

Subscriber (Certification Authority context) A subject of a certificate who is issued a certificate [r011].

(Presence Services context) A form of watcher that has asked the presence service to notify it immediately of changes in the presence information of one or more presentities [r015].

More generally, the registered user of a telecom voice or data service.

Subscriber Agreement An agreement between a Certification Authority (CA) and a subscriber that establishes the right and responsibilities of the parties regarding the issuance and management of certificates [r011].

Subscriber Edge Router A router at the edge of the subscriber's network that speaks external Border Gateway Protocol (eBGP) to its provider's Autonomous Systems (ASs).

Subscriber Identity Module (SIM) A smart card inside a Global System for Mobile Communications (GSM) phone that identifies the user account to the network, handles authentication, and provides data storage for user data such as phone numbers and network information. It may contain applications that run on the phone [r005, r011].

Subscriber Number (SN) (GSM context) Cellular number part of the Mobile Station Roaming Number (MSRN) and of the Handover Number (HON) [r011].

Subscription (Presence Services context) The information kept by the presence service about a subscriber's request to be notified of changes in the presence information of one or more presentities [r015].

Sub-session Key A temporary encryption key used between two principals, selected and exchanged by the principals using the session key, and with a lifetime limited to the duration of a single association [r070].

Substitution Altering or replacing valid data with false data that serves to deceive an authorized entity.

(Cryptography context) A cipher based on replacing a character in a message with another character (e.g., replace "a" with "u"). This is an extremely weak encryption mechanism.

Subversion Occurs when an intruder modifies the operation of the intrusion detector to force false negatives to occur.

Successful Delivery (Instant Messaging/Presence context) A situation in which an instant message was transmitted to an instant inbox for the intended recipient, and the instant inbox acknowledged its receipt. Successful delivery usually also implies that an inbox user agent has handled the message in a way chosen by the principal. However, successful delivery does not imply that the message was actually seen by that principal [r027].

Suitable Path Selection (IPv6 context) The algorithm used by the routes selection procedure to choose the routes from the routing table that are nearer to the destination address the packet should be sent [r008].

Summary of Control Solution Effectiveness A management report summarizing the degree to which the control solutions are mitigating risk [r190].

Sun Microsystems' N1 Data-center Architecture An approach based on clusters (Sun Grid Engine). N1 is Sun Microsystems' architecture, products, and services for supporting network computing. The marketing angle of the company is that N1 allows "managing n computers as 1" [r080].

Superencryption An encryption operation for which the plaintext input to be transformed is the ciphertext output of a previous encryption operation [r013].

Supplementary Service Call Forwarding on Mobile Subscriber Busy (CFB) (GSM context) A supplementary service that diverts calls if the line is busy [r011].

Supplicant The end of the link that responds to the authenticator in IEEE802.1X.

Suppressive Controls PHYSEC (Physical security) mechanisms to physically protect an environment, such as sprinklers and fire extinguishers.

Surrogate (aka reverse proxy) Accepts inbound requests on behalf of the actual target of the request, applies rules to determine where the request should be directed to (that is, it hides the actual physical address and location of the target of the request, making it less vulnerable to breaches of security), and can also check to see if the requestor is authorized to make such a request. In addition, a reverse proxy can be part of an overall scheme to develop a consistent enterprise-wide approach to security administration [r422].

Survivability The ability of a system to remain in operation or existence despite adverse conditions, including both natural occurrences, accidental actions, and attacks on the system [r013].

Suspicious Activity Report (SAR) (financial term) The Bank Secrecy Act (BSA) requires financial institutions to detect and report suspicious activity through Suspicious Activity Reports (SARs), to keep records of certain financial transactions, and to file Currency Transaction Reports (CTRs) to report large (over $10,000) cash transactions. SARs provide law enforcement with information about possible criminal activity, and CTRs and other transaction records provide a paper trail for law enforcement, which helps them build a better case against money launderers and other criminals.

Sustainable Cell Rate (SCR)   Traffic parameter used in Asynchronous Transfer Mode (ATM) services [e.g., real-time variable bit rate (rtVBR), non-real-time variable bitrate (nrtVBR)] that corresponds to the "average" arrival rate, measured in cells.

SVC   See Switched Virtual Circuit

SVCC   See Switched Virtual Channel Connection

SVPC   See Switched Virtual Path Connection

SWAN   See Secure Wide Area Network

Swap File   An area operating systems such as Windows uses to increase its Random Access Memory (RAM) memory by writing to the disk "temporarily." Like other deleted files, the SWAP remains until overwritten. There is a potential that these files can contain remnants of on-line e-mail messages, Internet browsing activity, database entries passwords, pre-encrypted files, and chat [r057].

Swiss Cheese   A colloquial term meaning that the security mechanisms are weak or not present. This is often associated with firewall rules that are not very restrictive.

Switched Connection   (Telecom context) A connection established via signaling [r289].

Switched Ethernet   (aka Switched LAN) An Ethernet network run through a high-speed switch instead of an Ethernet hub. A switched Ethernet involves dedicated bandwidth of 10 Mbps between stations rather than a shared medium [r435].

Switched LAN   (aka Switched Ethernet) An Ethernet network run through a high-speed switch instead of an Ethernet hub. A switched Ethernet involves dedicated bandwidth of 10 Mbps between stations rather than a shared medium [r435].

Switched Path   (MPLS context) Synonymous with label switched path [r042, r044–r052].

Switched Virtual Channel Connection (SVCC)

A connection that is established and taken down dynamically through control signaling. A Virtual Channel Connection (VCC) is an Asynchronous Transfer Mode (ATM) connection where switching is performed on the Virtual Path Identifier/Virtual Channel Identifier (VPI/VCI) fields of each cell [r042, r044–r052].

Switched Virtual Circuit (SVC)   In ATM services, a connection established via signaling. The user defines the endpoints when the call is initiated [r042, r044–r052].

Switched Virtual Path Connection (SVPC)   A connection that is established and taken down dynamically through control signaling. A Virtual Path Connection (VPC) is an Asynchronous Transfer Mode (ATM) connection where switching is performed on the VPI field only of each cell [r042, r044–r052].

Switches   Devices that reside in the network and direct traffic based on source and destination addresses. Most common examples are Fibre Channel (FC) or Ethernet switches [r029].

Symmetric Block Cipher   (aka block cipher) An encryption algorithm that processes plaintext in groups of bits. A common block size is 64 bits, and it is used in common encryption algorithms such as Data Encryption Standard (DES). Examples include Blowfish, Data Encryption Algorithm (DEA), International Data Encryption Algorithm (IDEA), RC2, and SKIPJACK.

Symmetric (Secret-Key Based) Cryptographic Algorithm   An algorithm for performing encipherment or the corresponding algorithm for performing decipherment in which the same key is required for both encipherment and decipherment [r068a].

Symmetric Cryptographic Algorithm   An algorithm for performing encipherment or the corresponding algorithm for performing decipherment in which the same key is required for both encipherment and decipherment [r068a].

Symmetric Cryptography   A branch of cryptography involving algorithms that use the same key for two different steps of the algorithm (such as encryption and decryption, or signature creation and signature verification). A modern example of a symmetric encryption algorithm is the U.S. Government's Data Encryption Algorithm. Symmetric cryptography is sometimes called "secret-key cryptography" (versus public-key cryptography) because the entities that share the key, such as the originator and the recipient of a message, need to keep the key secret. For example, when Alice wants to ensure confidentiality for data she sends to Bob, she encrypts the data with a secret key, and Bob uses the same key to decrypt. Keeping the shared key secret entails both cost and risk when the key is distributed to both Alice and Bob. Thus, symmetric cryptography has a key management disadvantage compared to asymmetric cryptography [r013].

Symmetric Encryption, Classes Symmetric algorithms can be classified as stream ciphers or block ciphers. Stream ciphers encrypt a single bit of plaintext at a time, whereas block ciphers take a number of bits (typically 64 bits in modern ciphers), and encrypt them as a single unit. Asymmetric ciphers (also called public-key algorithms) permit the encryption key to be public (it can even be published to a website), allowing anyone to encrypt with the key, whereas only the proper recipient (who knows the decryption key) can decrypt the message. The encryption key is also called the public key and the decryption key the private key. The security provided by these ciphers is based on keeping the private key secret [r036].

Symmetric Key A cryptographic key that is used in a symmetric cryptographic algorithm [r013].

Symmetric Key-Based Algorithm See Symmetric Cryptography

Symmetric Network Address Translation (NAT) A symmetric NAT is one where all requests from the same internal IP address and port, to a specific destination IP address and port, are mapped to the same external IP address and port. If the same host sends a packet with the same source address and port, but to a different destination, a different mapping is used. Furthermore, only the external host that receives a packet can send a User Data-

gram Protocol (UDP) packet back to the internal host [r252].

SYN Flood A denial of service attack that sends a host more Transmission Control Protocol (TCP) SYN packets (request to synchronize sequence numbers, used when opening a connection) than the protocol implementation can handle [r013].

Synchronization Channel (SCH) (GSM context) A channel that belongs to the group of the Broadcast Channels and only exists in the downlink. The Synchronization Channel contains information about the GSM system time. With its help, the mobile station can synchronize to one out of 8 timeslots sent out by the Base Transceiver Station (BTS). The SCH contains the Time Division Multiple Access (TDMA) frame number and the Base Station Identity Code (BSIC) and informs the mobile station of the relevant network operator [r011]. The Synchronization Channel is used for cell search and for User Equipment synchronization. It divides into the Primary Synchronization Channel (P-SCH), and the Secondary Synchronization Channel (S-SCH) [r007].

Synchronous Digital Hierarchy (SDH) European Time Division Multiplexing (TDM) digital transmission hierarchy similar (in ways) to Synchronous Optical Network (SONET).

Synchronous Optical Network (SONET) A physical-layer standard for supporting fiber-optic transmission systems. Covers optical parameters and management mechanisms. Intended principally for telecommunication carrier equipment. Basic SONET standards include, but are not limited to, ANSI T1.105 and ITU-T G.707.

Synchronous Optical Network (SONET) Higher-Order Virtual Container (optical transmission term) In the SONET multiplexing process, payloads are layered into lower-order and higher-order virtual containers, each including a range of overhead functions for management and error monitoring. Transmission is then supported by the attachment of further layers of overheads. It supports a layering of function for both traffic and management. High-order virtual concatenation containers (51 Mbps and 155 Mbps) are grouped when transporting high-speed data services such as Gigabit Ethernet and fiber channel. Low-order containers (1.5 Mbps or 2 Mbps) are used for low-speed data services such as 10-Mbps or 100-Mbps Ethernet. Supports next-gen SONET services. Supports operation up to 10 Gbps rates/OC-192. Also applicable internationally to Synchronous Digital Hierarchy (SDH).

Synchronous Optical Network (SONET) Virtual Concatenation (optical transmission term) Framing approach that enables SONET transport channels to be packed more efficiently (particularly in the context of data services) by grouping individual SONET containers into a virtual high-bandwidth "link," matched to the required service bandwidth. High-order virtual concatenation containers (51 Mbps and 155 Mbps) are grouped when transporting high-speed data services such as Gigabit Ethernet and Fibre Channel (FC). Low-order containers (1.5 Mbps or 2 Mbps) are used for low-speed data services such as 10-Mbps or 100-Mbps Ethernet. Supports next-gen SONET services. Also applicable internationally to Synchronous Digital Hierarchy (SDH).

Synchronous Receipt A receipt returned to the sender during the same HTTP session as the sender's original message.

Synchronous Transport Module (-N) (STM-N) A PHY-level data framing mechanism of Synchronous Digital Hierarchy (SDH).

Synchronous Transport Signal-Level N STS(-N) A PHY-level data framing standards for Synchronous Optical Network (SONET) transmission.

Synthetic Source A device or an embedded software program that generates a data packet (or packets) and injects it (or them) onto the path to a corresponding probe or existing server solely in support of a performance monitoring function. A synthetic source may talk intrusively to existing application servers [r357].

System A collection of components organized to accomplish a specific function or set of functions (IEEE Std. 610.12-1990). A system can be described by one or more models, possibly from different viewpoints. In the present context the

term is mainly used as an abbreviation for "automated information system."

System Binaries Binaries used in an Operating System to handle large quantities of untyped data.

System Entity An active element of a system (e.g., an automated process, a subsystem, a person or group of persons) that incorporates a specific set of capabilities [r013].

System High The highest security level supported by a system at a particular time or in a particular environment.

System High Security Mode A mode of operation of an information system, wherein all users having access to the system possess a security clearance or authorization, but not necessarily a need-to-know, for all data handled by the system [r013]. This mode is defined formally in U.S. Department of Defense (DoD) policy regarding system accreditation [r195], but the term is widely used outside the Defense Department and outside the Government.

System Integrity The quality that a system has when it can perform its intended function in a unimpaired manner, free from deliberate or inadvertent unauthorized manipulation [r120].

System Integrity Service A security service that protects system resources in a verifiable manner against unauthorized or accidental change, loss, or destruction [r013].

System Life Cycle There are, in general terms, five basic phases to the development of a computer system: initiation, development/acquisition, implementation, operation, and disposal phase. In the initiation phase the need for a system is expressed and the purpose of the system is documented. A sensitivity assessment should be performed which looks at the information to be processed and the security it will require. During the development/acquisition phase the security requirements should be developed at the same time system planners define the requirements of the system. In the implementation phase the system's security features should be configured and enabled, the system should be tested and installed, and the system should be authorized for processing. In the operation/maintenance phase the system is almost always being continuously modified by the addition of hardware and software and numerous other events. The security of the system should be documented and reviewed, also, risk-based choices should be made, and they should be re-authorized to process when major changes are made. In the disposal phase the disposition of information, hardware, and software is made [r067].

System Low   The lowest security level supported by a system at a particular time or in a particular environment.

System of Record (SOR)   (aka authoritative data source) The source of information from which all other system entities rely upon. Oftentimes, it is necessary to identify the system of record because numerous copies of data are sometimes performed in an enterprise.

System Resources   Capabilities that can be accessed by a user or program either on the user's machine or across the network. Capabilities can be services, such as file or print services, or devices, such as routers [r200].

System Security Officer (SSO)   A person responsible for enforcement or administration of the security policy that applies to the system.

System Security Officer (SSO) Personal Identifi-
cation Number (PIN)   One of two personal identification numbers that control access to the functions and stored data of a FORTEZZA PC card. Knowledge of the SSO PIN enables the card user to perform the FORTEZZA functions intended for use by an end user and also the functions intended for use by a Multilevel Information Systems Security Initiative (MISSI) certification authority [r013].

System Security Officer (SSO)–PIN Organizational Registration Authority (ORA) (SORA)
A Multilevel Information Systems Security Initiative (MISSI) organizational Registration Authority (RA) that operates in a mode in which the ORA performs all card management functions and, therefore, requires knowledge of the SSO Personal Identification Number (PIN) for an end user's FORTEZZA PC card [r013].

System Security Plan   A plan that documents the security requirements of the system and describes the controls that are in place or planned.

Systems (Applications) Solution Architecture
An architectural definition of the systems/application solution function.

Systems (Applications) Solution Function   The function that aims at delivering/supplying computerized IT system(s) required to support the plethora of specific functions needed by the Business function.

T

TACACS See Terminal Access Controller Access Control System

Tamper Willful alteration of a system's logic, data, or control information to interrupt or prevent correct operation of system functions.

Tangible Assets/Extranet Data These assets require protection considerations (among others): partner contract data; partner financial data; partner contact data; partner collaboration application; partner cryptographic keys; partner credit reports; partner purchase order data; supplier contract data; supplier financial data; supplier contact data; supplier collaboration application; supplier cryptographic keys; supplier credit reports; and supplier purchase order data [r190].

Tangible Assets/Internet Data These assets require protection considerations (among others):

website sales application; website marketing data; customer credit card data; customer contact data; public cryptographic keys; press releases; white papers; product documentation; and training materials [r190].

Tangible Assets/Intranet Data These assets require protection considerations (among others): source code; human resources data; financial data; marketing data; employee passwords; employee private cryptographic keys; computer system cryptographic keys; smart cards; intellectual property; data for regulatory requirements [Gramm–Leach–Bliley Act (GLBA), Health Insurance Portability and Accountability Act (HIPAA), CA SB1386, EU Data Protection Directive, etc.]; U.S. employee social security numbers; employee drivers' license numbers; strategic

Minoli–Cordovana's Authoritative Computer and Network Security Dictionary. By Daniel Minoli and James Cordovana
Copyright © 2006 John Wiley & Sons, Inc.

plans; customer consumer credit reports; customer medical records; employee biometric identifiers; employee business contact data; employee personal contact data; purchase order data; network infrastructure design; internal websites; and employee ethnographic data [r190].

Tangible Assets/Physical Infrastructure   These assets require protection considerations (among others): data centers; servers; desktop computers; mobile computers; Personal Digital Assistants (PDAs); cell phones; server application software; end-user application software; development tools; routers; network switches; fax machines; Private Branch Exchanges/Voice over IP (PBXs/VoIP) servers; removable media [e.g., tapes, floppy disks, Digital Vide Disks (DVDs), portable hard drives, PC card storage devices, Universal Serial Bus (USB) storage devices, etc.]; power supplies; uninterruptible power supplies; fire suppression systems; air conditioning systems; air filtration systems; and other environmental control systems [r190].

Target Refresh Request   (SIP context) A request that can modify the remote target of the dialog [r025].

TBS   See Transport Block Sets

TC   See Transcoder

TCAP   See Transaction Capabilities Application Part

TCB   See Trusted Computing Base

TCH   See Traffic Channels

TCO   See Total Cost of Ownership

TCP   See Transmission Control Protocol

TCP/IP   See Transmission Control Protocol/Internetwork Protocol

Tcpdump   One of the better-known freeware software sniffer that runs on Unix/Linux environments. Tcpdump prints out the headers of packets on a network interface that match the boolean expression. It can also be run with the -w flag, which causes it to save the packet data to a file for later analysis, and/or with the -b flag, which causes it to read from a saved packet file rather than to read packets from a network interface. In all cases, only packets that

match a specified expression are processed by tcpdump.

TCSEC   See Trusted Computer System Evaluation Criteria

TDD Mode   See Time Division Duplex Mode

TDM   See Time Division Multiplexing

TDMA   See Time Division Multiple Access

TE   See Traffic Engineering

Technical Security Support Personnel   The individuals responsible for security architecture, security policies, and security analysts.

Technical Support Personnel   The individuals who manage and administer security for the IT systems (e.g., network, system, application, and database administrators).

Technology Infrastructure Architecture   An architectural formulation (description) of the technology infrastructure function.

Technology Infrastructure Function   The complete technology environment required to support the information function and the (Systems/Application) solution function.

Telecommunications Fraud Prevention Committee (TFPC)   Alliance for Telecommunications Industry Solutions (ATIS)-based working group focusing on telecom fraud prevention. In recent years they have focused on how a person committing fraud would be identified in a Voice over Internet Protocol (VoIP) environment.

Telecommunications Industry Association (TIA)   A U.S. trade organization that specializes in the development of standards for telecommunications cabling and its support structures [r033].

Telecommunications Management Network (TMN)   An architecture for management, including planning, provisioning, installation, maintenance, operation, and administration of telecommunications equipment, networks and services [r068a].

Telephone User Part (TUP)   (GSM context) The protocol used for sending, receiving, and application from the user's point of view [r011].

Telephony Routing over IP (TRIP)   A policy-driven, dynamic routing protocol used for advertising a range of possible telephony destinations and their routing attributes. TRIP can serve as the telephony routing protocol for any signaling protocol. Described in RFC 2871 [r257].

Telnet Protocol (aka TELNET or telnet) A (nonsecure) Transmission Control Protocol (TCP)-based, application-layer, Internet Standard protocol [r461] for remote login from one host to another. User identifiers are passed in plaintext. Many enterprises have chosen to replace telnet services with Secure Shell (SSH) implementations, that provides enhanced features such as encryption and authentication options.

Telnet Based Intrusion A reconnaissance technique with the intent of discovering telnet applications in use.

TEMPEST A vernacular name for specifications and standards for limiting the strength of electromagnetic emanations from electrical and electronic equipment and thus reducing vulnerability to eavesdropping. This term originated in the U.S. Department of Defense (DoD).

Temporal Key Integrity Protocol (TKIP) Part of the IEEE 802.11i specification. Encryption standard for Wireless Local Areas Networks (WLANs). TKIP is the next generation of, the Wired Equivalency Protocol (WEP), which is used to secure 802.11 WLANs. TKIP provides per-packet key mixing, a message integrity check and a re-keying mechanism, thus fixing the flaws of WEP [r005].

Protocol addresses encryption for the wireless links in an IEEE 802.11 context (a different part of 802.11i addresses the per-message integrity problem). TKIP was designed with a number of constraints in place: Specifically, it had to operate on existing hardware and therefore it could not require computationally advanced encryption. TKIP is a "wrapper" that goes around the existing WEP encryption. TKIP comprises the same encryption engine and Rivest Cipher 4 (RC4) algorithm defined for WEP; however, the key used for encryption in TKIP is 128 bits long.

Temporary Mobile Subscriber Identity (TMSI) (GSM context) A temporary identity of the mo-

bile subscriber. It is changed at regular intervals and is transmitted over the air interface after the first Location Update, in lieu of the International Mobile Subscriber Identity (IMSI) [r011]. Temporary Mobile Subscriber Identity (a temporary subscriber identification). The TMSI is only of local importance within the Visitor Location Register (VLR) area and connects to the IMSI identification. It supports the anonymity of transactions—for example, in unciphered transmissions. It can be assigned by the VLR and used together with the LAI (Location Area Identity) after a successful authentication [r014].

Term Rule-Based Security Policy A security policy based on global rules imposed for all users. These rules usually rely on a comparison of the sensitivity of the resources being accessed and the possession of corresponding attributes of users, a group of users, or entities acting on behalf of users [r057].

Terminal Access Controller (TAC) Access Control System (TACACS) Mechanism used by Cisco Systems commonly used to provide Authentication, Authorization, and Accounting (AAA) solutions. A User Datagram Protocol (UDP)-based authentication and access control protocol [r462] in which a network access server receives an identifier and password from a remote terminal and passes them to a separate authentication server for verification. TACACS was developed for ARPANET and has evolved for use in commercial equipment. TACs were a type of network access server computer used to connect terminals to the early Internet, usually using dial-up modem connections. TACACS used centralized authentication servers and served not only network access servers like TACs but also routers and other networked computing devices. TACs are no longer in use, but TACACS+ is [r194, r013].

Terminal Access Controller (TAC) Access Control System plus (TACACS+) Mechanism used by Cisco Systems commonly used to provide Authentication, Authorization, and Accounting (AAA) solutions. "TACACS+" is a

Transmission Control Protocol (TCP)-based protocol that improves on TACACS by separating the functions of authentication, authorization, and accounting and by encrypting all traffic between the network access server and authentication server. It is extensible to allow any authentication mechanism to be used with TACACS+ clients [r013].

Terminal Hijacking   Allows an attacker, on a certain machine, to control any terminal session that is in progress. A hacker can send and receive terminal I/O while a user is on the terminal [r057].

Testing   Evaluating a system to find operation errors or security vulnerabilities.

Text Conversation   Text streams transmitted alone or in connection with other conversational facilities, such as video and voice, to form multimedia conversation services. Text in multimedia conversation sessions is sent character-by-character as soon as it is available, or with a small delay for buffering. The text is intended to be entered by human users from a keyboard, handwriting recognition, voice recognition or any other input method. The rate of character entry is usually at a level of a few characters per second or less. In general, only one or a few new characters are expected to be transmitted with each packet. Small blocks of text may be prepared by the user and pasted into the user interface for transmission during the conversation, occasionally causing packets to carry more payload. International Telecommunication Union (ITU) T.140 specifies that text and other T.140 elements must be transmitted in International Organization for Standardization (ISO) 10646-1 code with UTF-8 (8-bit Unicode Transformation Format) transformation [r463].

TF-ESP   See Transport-Friendly ESP Protocol

TGT   See Ticket-granting Ticket and/or Kerberos Operation

The Open Group   A vendor-neutral and technology-neutral consortium seeking to enable access to integrated information, within and among enterprises, based on open standards and global interoperability (http://www.opengroup.org/architecture/togaf/).

The Open Group Architecture Framework (TOGAF)   TOGAF is a framework—a detailed method and a set of supporting tools—for developing an enterprise architecture. It is described in a set of documentation published by The Open Group on its public web server, and it may be used freely by any organization wishing to develop an enterprise architecture for use within that organization. TOGAF was developed by The Open Group's own members, working within the Architecture Forum. Now in Version 8.1 (with Version 9 expected by 2007). The original development of TOGAF Version 1 in 1995 was based on the Technical Architecture Framework for Information Management (TAFIM), developed by the U.S. Department of Defense (DoD). The DoD gave The Open Group explicit permission and encouragement to create TOGAF by building on the TAFIM, which itself was the result of many years of development effort and many millions of dollars of U.S. government investment. Starting from this sound foundation, the members of The Open Group's Architecture Forum have developed successive versions of TOGAF each year and published each one on The Open Group's public website.

Theft of Data   Unauthorized acquisition and use of data.

Theft of Functionality   Unauthorized acquisition of actual hardware, software, or firmware of a system component.

Theft of Service   Unauthorized use of service by an entity.

Thin Client   A PC (or workstation) that only uses a browser for application access. Thin clients are used in a production mode (e.g., contact centers, reservation agents, etc.) where an application is configured to run only a fixed, predetermined, mostly repetitive function. This eases deployment issues typical of complex enterprises. Currently, Citrix's WinFrame and Microsoft's Terminal Server products are leading thin-client application server products.

Third Generation Grids Computational grids where standards define grids in a consistent way; this enables grid systems to become easily-built "off-the-shelf" systems. Grid architectures defined by the Global Grid Forum [r080].

Threat A potential for violation of security, which exists when there is a circumstance, capability, action, or event that could breach security and cause harm. A threat is a possible danger that might exploit a vulnerability. The means through which the ability or intent of a threat agent to adversely affect an automated system, facility, or operation can be manifest. A threat can be either "intentional" (i.e., intelligent; e.g., an individual cracker or a criminal organization) or "accidental" (e.g., the possibility of a computer malfunctioning, or the possibility of an "act of God" such as an earthquake, a fire, or a tornado). In some contexts the term is used narrowly to refer only to intelligent threats [r013]. A security architecture deals with both intentional acts (i.e., attacks) and accidental events.

(U.S. Government context) The technical and operational capability of a hostile entity to detect, exploit, or subvert friendly information systems and the demonstrated, presumed, or inferred intent of that entity to conduct such activity [r013].

Threat Action An assault on system security.

Threat Analysis An analysis of the probability of occurrences and consequences of damaging actions to a system [r013].

Threat Assessment Process of formally evaluating the degree of threat to an information system and describing the nature of the threat [r057].

Threat Consequence A security violation that results from a threat action. Includes disclosure, deception, disruption, and usurpation.

The following subentries describe four kinds of threat consequences, and also list and describe the kinds of threat actions that cause each consequence.

Note that each of the identified threat actions are separate terms in this dictionary, so their associated definitions are not replicated here. Also note that threat actions that are accidental events are marked by an asterisk* [r013]:

1. (Unauthorized) Disclosure (a threat consequence): A circumstance or event whereby an entity gains access to data for which the entity is not authorized. The following threat actions can cause unauthorized disclosure:

    A. Exposure: A threat action whereby sensitive data is directly released to an unauthorized entity. This includes Deliberate Exposure, Scavenging, * Human error, and * Hardware/software error.

    B. Interception: A threat action whereby an unauthorized entity directly accesses sensitive data traveling between authorized sources and destinations. This includes Theft, Wiretapping (passive), and Emanations analysis.

    C. Inference: A threat action whereby an unauthorized entity indirectly accesses sensitive data (but not necessarily the data contained in the communication) by reasoning from characteristics or byproducts of communications. This includes Traffic analysis and Signals analysis.

    D. Intrusion: A threat action whereby an unauthorized entity gains access to sensitive data by circumventing a system's security protections. This includes Trespass, Penetration, Reverse engineering, and Cryptanalysis.

2. Deception (a threat consequence): A circumstance or event that may result in an authorized entity receiving false data and believing it to be true. The following threat actions can cause deception:

    A. Masquerade: A threat action whereby an unauthorized entity gains access to a system or performs a malicious act by posing as an authorized entity. This includes Spoof and Malicious logic.

    B. Falsification: A threat action whereby false data deceives an authorized entity. This includes Substitution and Insertion.

C. Repudiation: A threat action whereby an entity deceives another by falsely denying responsibility for an act. This includes False denial of origin and False denial of receipt.

3. Disruption (a threat consequence): A circumstance or event that interrupts or prevents the correct operation of system services and functions. The following threat actions can cause disruption:

A. Incapacitation: A threat action that prevents or interrupts system operation by disabling a system component. This includes Malicious logic, Physical destruction, * Human error, * Hardware or software error, and * Natural disaster.

B. Corruption: A threat action that undesirably alters system operation by adversely modifying system functions or data. This includes Tamper, Malicious logic, * Human error, * Hardware or software error, and * Natural disaster.

C. Obstruction: A threat action that interrupts delivery of system services by hindering system operations. This includes Interference and Overload.

4. Usurpation (a threat consequence): A circumstance or event that results in control of system services or functions by an unauthorized entity. The following threat actions can cause usurpation:

A. Misappropriation: A threat action whereby an entity assumes unauthorized logical or physical control of a system resource. This includes Theft of service, Theft of functionality, and Theft of data.

B. Misuse: A threat action that causes a system component to perform a function or service that is detrimental to system security. This includes Tamper, Malicious logic, and Violation of permissions.

Threat Model   A model that identifies who may be expected to attack what resource, using what sorts of mechanisms. The most important factor in choosing a security mechanism is the threat model. A low-value target, such as a website that offers public information only, may not merit much protection. Conversely, a resource that if compromised could expose significant parts of the Internet infrastructure [e.g., a major backbone router or high-level Domain Name Server (DNS)], should be protected by very strong mechanisms. The value of a target to an attacker depends on the purpose of the attack. If the purpose is to access sensitive information, all systems that handle this information or mediate access to it are valuable. If the purpose is to wreak havoc, systems on which large parts of the Internet depend are exceedingly valuable. Even if only public information is posted on a website, changing its contents can cause embarrassment to its owner and could result in substantial damage. It is difficult when designing a protocol to predict what uses that protocol will someday have [r170].

Threats and Threat Identification   A threat is an event or activity that has the potential to cause harm to the information systems. Term defines an event (tornado, theft, or computer virus infection) the occurrence of which could have an undesirable impact [r056].

Threat Vector   A mechanism that is a vehicle for the launch of an attack. Examples include outsider attacks from the public data network (Internet); outsider attacks from the public voice network; insider attack from a local (internal) network.

Thumbprint   A pattern of curves formed by the ridges on the tip of a thumb.

TIA   See Telecommunications Industry Association

Ticket   A synonym for "capability." A ticket is usually granted by a centralized access control server (ticket-granting agent) to authorize access to a system resource for a limited time. Tickets have been implemented with symmetric cryptography, but can also be implemented as attribute certificates using asymmetric cryptography [r013].

(Kerberos context) A temporary set of electronic credentials that verify the identity of a client for a particular service. A record that helps a client authenticate itself to a server; it contains the client's identity, a session key, a timestamp, and other information, all sealed using the server's secret key. It only serves to authenticate a client when presented along with a fresh authenticator [r070].

Ticket-Granting Ticket (TGT)   See Kerberos Operations

Tiered Storage   A process for the assignment of different categories of data to different types of storage media. The purpose is to reduce total storage cost and optimize accessibility. Organizations are reportedly finding cost savings and improved data management with a tiered storage approach. In practice the assignment of data to particular media tends to be an evolutionary and complex activity. Storage categories may be based on a variety of design/architectural factors, including levels of protection required for the application or organization, performance requirements, and frequency of use. Software exists for automatically managing the process based on a company-defined policy. Tiered storage generally introduces more vendors into the environment and interoperability is important.

An example of tiered storage is as follows: Tier 1 data (e.g., mission-critical files) could be effectively stored high-quality Directly Attached Storage (DAS) (but relatively expensive) media such as double-parity redundant arrays of independent disks (RAIDs). Tier 2 data (e.g., quarterly financial records) could be stored on media affiliated with a storage area network (SAN); this media tends to be less expensive than DAS drives, but there may be network latencies associated with the access. Tier 3 data (e.g., e-mail backup files) could be stored on recordable compact discs (CD-Rs) or tapes. (Clearly, there could be more than three tiers, but the management of the multiple tiers than becomes fairly complex.)

Another example (in the medical field) is as follows: Real-time medical imaging information may be temporarily stored on DAS disks as a tier

1, say for a couple of weeks. Recent medical images and patient data may be kept on Fibre Channel (FC) drives (tier 2) for about a year. After that, less-frequently accessed images and patient records are stored on AT Attachment (ATA) drives (tier 3) for 18 months or more. Tier-4 consists of a tape library for archiving.

Tiger Team   Government- and industry-sponsored teams of computer experts who attempt to break down the defenses of computer systems in an effort to uncover, and eventually patch, security holes [r057].

Time Bomb   Like a logic bomb, the purpose of a time bomb is to wreak havoc with the system it is on. Unlike the logic bomb, the time bomb is set to activate based on the system date, not user input [r062].

Time Division Duplex (TDD) Mode   (3G Wireless context) In the Time Division Duplex Mode, multiple access is achieved by combining various spreading codes and by dividing the used frequency into timeslots for the uplink and the downlink [r007].

Time Division Multiple Access (TDMA)   Cellular service. The technology is used for digital transmissions such as moving a signal between a mobile phone and a base station. With TDMA, a frequency band is chopped into several channels or time slots that are then stacked into shorter time units, facilitating the sharing of a single channel by several calls. Each user is assigned definite time slots. Global System for Mobile communications (GSM) actually uses narrowband TDMA, enabling eight simultaneous calls on the same radio frequency. Standard: TDMA (IS-136) [r121].

Time Division Multiplexing (TDM)   Traditional voice and private line data transmission environments where the service is based on the classical digital hierarchy of dedicated timeslots based on DS0 (64 kbps slots), DS1 (24 DS0 slots), DS3 (28 DS1 slots), and SONET (OC-3, OC-12, OC-48, OC-192, OC-768) aggregates. In the voice world TDM is being replaced by Voice over IP (VoIP) constructs; in the transmission world (at least at the enterprise network level) TDM is being replaced by packet-oriented services such as Ethernet Private Lines, Resilient Packet Ring (RPR), and Multi-Protocol Label Switching (MPLS).

Time Memory Trade Off (TMTO) Attacks Password cracking techniques that use precomputed databases to reduce the time required to do the brute force attack. One such approach generate hashes of all possible passwords and store them sorted in a database. Once the database is created an attacker can just look up the database and find the password.

Timestamp The date and time signature associated with when a message or file was created or altered.

Timestamping The action of applying a timestamp. One example is with the RTP (Real Time Protocol) used in VoIP, Video over IP, and in IP-based TV (IPTV).

Tinkerbell Program A monitoring program used to scan incoming network connections and generate alerts when calls are received from particular sites, or when logins are attempted using certain IDs [r057].

TKIP See Temporal Key Integrity Protocol

TLA ID See Maximum-Level Aggregation Identifier

TLS See Transport Layer Security or Transparent LAN Service

TLSP See Transport Layer Security Protocol

TLVs See Type Length Value

TMN See Telecommunications Management Network

TMSI See Temporary Mobile Subscriber Identity

TMTO See Time Memory Trade Off (TMTO) Attacks.

TOE See TCP/IP Offload Engine

TOGAF See The Open Group Architecture Framework

Token (General context) An object that is used to control access and is passed between cooperating entities in a protocol that synchronizes use of a shared resource. Usually, the entity that currently holds the token has exclusive access to the resource [r013]. An example would be a driver's license.

(Authentication context) [aka access token (in this context)] A type of credential that satisfies the "what you have" element of an authentication transaction. The token is in the form of a hardware device [such as a one-time password fob, smart card, or portable Universal Serial Bus (USB) device] or a software asset (such as an X.509 certificate or a secured cookie). A token is often used along with a password, which "unlocks" the token, thereby creating a multifactor authentication mechanism.

(SET context) Portable device (e.g., smart card) specifically designed to store cryptographic information and possibly perform cryptographic functions in a secure manner [r018].

Token Backup A token management operation that stores sufficient information in a database [e.g., in a Certification Authority Workstation (CAW)] to recreate or restore a security token (e.g., a smart card) if it is lost or damaged [r013].

Token Copy A token management operation that copies all the personality information from one security token to another. However, unlike in a token restore operation, the second token is initialized with its own, different local security values such as Personal Identification Numbers (PINs) and storage keys [r013].

Token Management The process of initializing security tokens, loading data into the tokens, and controlling the tokens during their life cycle. May include performing key management and certificate management functions, generating and installing Personal Identification Numbers (PINs), loading user personality data, performing card backup, card copy, card restore operations, and updating firmware [r013].

Token Restore A token management operation that loads a security token with data for the purpose of recreating (duplicating) the contents previously held by that or another token [r013].

Token Storage Key A cryptography key used to protect data that is stored on a security token.

Top Certification Authority A Certification Authority (CA) that is the highest level (i.e., is the most trusted CA) in a certification hierarchy.

Top-Level Aggregation Identifier (TLA ID)   See Maximum-Level Aggregation Identifier

Top-Level Specification   A non-procedural description of system behavior at the most abstract level; typically a functional specification that omits all implementation details [r120]. A top-level specification may be descriptive or formal [r013]:

- Descriptive top-level specification: One that is written in a natural language like English or an informal design notation.
- Formal top-level specification: One that is written in a formal mathematical language to enable theorems to be proven that show that the specification correctly implements a set of formal requirements or a formal security model.

Topology   The map or plan of the network. The physical topology describes how the wires or cables are laid out, and the logical or electrical topology describes how the information flows [r057].

Total Cost of Ownership (TCO)   TCO is a financial metric designed to establish a final cost figure that reflects the true cost of purchase when all related expenses are considered. As noted in [r465], when one considers (for example) deploying a network (or network element), all of the following costs need to be taken into account (although many are often ignored): "Equipment costs, cables, software, software licenses, documentation, initial communication costs, recurring communication costs, Rental costs for housing equipment (e.g., towers, remote concentrators, switches), real estate, floor space, air conditioning, lighting, sensors, security, planning and administration, electrical power (principal, backup, planning and administration), project feasibility study (staff time), project pilots, project evaluation, management review, project implementation costs (construction, delivery costs, testing and validating, integration,

delays and overruns, cost of service overlap, specialized installation staff), fees (rights-of-way, licenses), taxes, system/network operations and management (staff, benefits, management of staff, facilities, test equipment, training, turnover, ad hoc maintenance, routine maintenance, insurance, cost of documentation, capacity planning, planning and administration, costs of network/system security—including appropriate tools), cost to backup system (including disaster recovery), financial management (i.e., bookkeeping and accounting), cost of capital, cost of eventual replacement, decommissioning costs." It follows that TCO needs to account for all of the costs associated with procuring, deploying and owning IT systems. Some industry studies show that cost of the hardware and software is only 15% of the total cost of owning the asset. Management, support and indirect expenses account for 85% of the total cost. TCO is an annual cost figure that is an average cost of ownership over a five-year period, without regard to the benefits of owning or using the asset [for comparison, Return on Investment (ROI) looks at the implementation costs as they occur to account for the total positive and negative impacts of a planned project and its financial viability].

Total Quality Management (TQM)   A management philosophy that became popular in the 1980s and 1990s. TQM is focused on continuously improving the performance of all individuals and processes in achieving customer satisfaction [r057].

TQM   See Total Quality Management

Trace Packet   In a packet-switching network, a unique packet that causes a report of each stage of its progress to be sent to the network control center from each visited system element [r057].

Traceroute   An operation of sending trace packets for determining information; traces the route of User Datagram Protocol (UDP) packets for the local host to a remote host. Normally traceroute displays the time and location of the route taken to reach its destination computer [r057].

Traffic Analysis The inference of information from observation of traffic flows (presence, absence, amount, direction and frequency) [r068a].

Traffic Analysis Activities Network administrators and engineers often need the ability to monitor and analyze traffic from a network to perform variety of tasks like load/traffic control, capacity planning, diagnosis, intrusion detections, and firewalls. These tasks often require the ability to access upper-layer protocol headers within packets (some security mechanisms such as IPsec encryption can make such analysis more difficult) [r022]. Nonetheless, appropriate controls need to be put in place so that these capabilities are not exploited for nefarious reasons.

Traffic Channels (TCH) (GSM context) Bidirectional channels that transmit speech data. TCHs are service channels and are used for transmitting encoded user information. No signaling is transmitted via the TCHs. These channels are not used for signaling information [r014]. The Traffic Channel Halfrate (TCH/H) offers a bit rate of 5.6 kbps, and the Traffic Channel Fullrate (TCH/F) offers a bit rate of 13 kbps. Assuming that the bitrate of both channels is the same, the Traffic Channel Enhanced Fullrate (TCH/EFR) can achieve a higher speech quality than the normal TCH/F [r011].

Traffic Engineering (TE) (MPLS context) Multiprotocol Label Switching (MPLS) supports traffic engineering (a process of selecting the paths chosen by data traffic in order to balance the traffic load on the various links, routers, and switches in the network). MPLS offers capabilities to control the paths taken by different flows. Using these capabilities, traffic could be rerouted to avoid congestion points in a network. Key performance objectives of TE are (a) traffic-oriented (includes aspects that enhance the QoS of traffic streams); and (b) resource-oriented (includes aspects that pertain to the optimization of resource utilization).

Mechanism that discriminates between flows inside the network (generally called flow classification). The flow information in IPv4 is encoded in both the IP header and the upper-layer protocol headers, such as Transmission Control Protocol (TCP) or User Datagram Protocol (UDP) port numbers. Flow classification is essential in providing rich classes of services and quality-of-service (QoS) support. These include flow-based and class-based queueing, Random Early Detection (RED), router-based congestion control and policing, integrated services [intserv, implemented with resource reservation protocol (RSVP)] and differentiated services (diffserv, used for example in MPLS) and so on. TE mechanisms need to access the upper-layer protocol headers; if this is done inside the network (as opposite to classification at endpoints), it may conceivably conflict with IPsec [r022].

Traffic Flow Confidentiality A confidentiality service to protect against traffic analysis [r160].

Traffic Interception The process of using a network element to examine network traffic to determine whether it should be redirected.

Traffic Padding The generation of spurious instances of communication, spurious data units, and/or spurious data within data unit [r160].

Traffic Redirection Redirection of client requests from a network element performing traffic interception to a proxy. Used to deploy (caching) proxies without the need to manually reconfigure individual user agents, or to force the use of a proxy where such use would not otherwise occur.

Training The staff education and competency development step that typically follows deployment and includes knowledge transfer [r029].

Transaction Capabilities Application Part (TCAP) (GSM context) A Signaling System No. 7 (SS7) protocol layer that resides directly on top of Signaling Connection and Control Part (SCCP). It coordinates the sequence and allocation of many different requests and replies within the Network Subsystem (NSS) [r011].

Transaction User (TU) (SIP context) The layer of protocol processing that resides above the transaction layer. Transaction users include the user agent client (UAC) core, user agent server (UAS) core, and proxy core [r025].

Transceiver (TRX)   (GSM context) The transceiver is the central working unit of the Base Transceiver Station (BTS), which holds connections to up to 8 mobile stations via one high-frequency pair [r011].

Transcoder (TC)   (GSM context) The transcoder is the third element in the Base Station Subsystem (BSS) after the Base Transceiver Station (BTS) and the Base Station Controller (BSC). It is necessary for processing speech data. Speech data coming from the Network Subsystem (NSS) over the A interface at a bit rate of 64 Kbps are reduced to 16 kbps by the transcoder [r011].

Transcoding and Rate Adaptation Unit (TRAU) (GSM context) A special transmitting component of the Global System for Mobile communications (GSM) system, which belongs to the Base Transceiver Station (BTS), according to specifications. It is responsible for transcoding and converting the data exchanged between the Mobile Station (MS) and the Network Subsystem (NSS) [r014].

Transformation Function   A function block that translates between a Telecommunications Management Network (TMN) reference point and a non-TMN) (either proprietary or otherwise standardized) reference point. The non-TMN part of this function block is outside the TMN boundary [r068a].

Transition   (IPv6 context) Conversion of IPv4-only nodes into dual stack nodes or IPv6-only nodes [r008].

Transmission Control Protocol (TCP)   Basic networking protocols used in most modern computer networks (including the Internet). TCP is an end-to-end Layer 4 protocol providing message sequentiality and completeness. The original reference for the IP protocol is Postel, J., "Transmission Control Protocol," RFC 761,USC/Information Sciences Institute, January 1980, and later RFC 793 [r464]. An Internet Standard protocol that reliably delivers a sequence of datagrams (discrete sets of bits) from one computer to another in a computer network. TCP is designed to fit into a layered hierarchy of protocols that support internetwork applications. TCP assumes it can obtain a simple, potentially unreliable datagram service (such as the Internet Protocol) from the lower-layer protocols [r013].

TCP is responsible for segmenting large data messages into smaller frames called packets and handling the reassembly at the remote end (packets are generally in the 1500-byte range). To achieve this, TCP assigns each packet a sequence number and then passes them on to be transmitted to their destination. In an IP network constituent packets may not take the same path to get to its destination. TCP has the responsibility of reassembling the packets at the destination in the correct sequence and performing error-checking to ensure that the complete data message arrived reliably [r035].

Transmission Control Protocol (TCP) Flow Identification   Flow identification used to segregate TCP sessions for each TCP packet. It consists of source and destination IP addresses (both stored in IP header), as well as source and destination port numbers (both stored in TCP header) [r022].

Transmission Control Protocol (TCP) Performance Enhancing Proxy (PEP)   Refers to the category of techniques where intermediate nodes in the network interact with the TCP layer and influence its end-to-end behavior [r033]. TCP does not provide optimal performance when operated as wireless networks. This is because many such networks possess certain characteristics that are "unfriendly" to TCP, such as noncongestion losses, long delays, variable bandwidth, and dynamic changing topology. Transport-aware link layer mechanisms are often necessary to correct these problems. For example, TCP snooping can improve TCP performance over a lossy wireless link if the base station can inspect every TCP packet and deliberately delay or drop certain ones. Other similar techniques like indirect connections and explicit notifications also provide improvements in wireless networks. Furthermore, many satellite networks have deployed TCP spoofing and booster mechanisms to reduce the impact of latency.

Also, TCP performance over a wireless ad-hoc network can be enhanced if intermediate nodes can send explicit link failure notifications to the TCP sender [r033].

TCP PEP operates on the TCP flow identification and sequence numbers within the flow. However, when a TCP session is transported by an IPsec Encapsulating Security Payload (ESP) protocol, the TCP header is encrypted inside the ESP header. It is, thus, impossible for an intermediate gateway outside sender or receiver's security enclaves to analyze an IPsec header to extract TCP flow identification and sequence number. Proposals have been made to use multilayer IP-security (ML-IPsec) to resolve issue [r022].

Transmission Control Protocol (TCP) Sequence Numbers   The sequence numbers are used to match acknowledgments with the data segments. This number is stored in TCP header [r022].

Transmission Control Protocol (TCP) Session Hijacking   The taking over an already established TCP session and injecting one's own packets into that stream so that your commands are processed as the authentic owner of the session. One problem with TCP is that it was not built with security in mind. Any TCP session is identified by the (client IP address + client port number) and (server IP address + server port number). Any packets that reach either machine that have those identifiers are assumed to be part of the existing session. So if an attacker can spoof those items, they can pass TCP packets to the client or server and have those processed as someone else [r483].

To establish a session with a TCP peer, a client must follow the 3-Way Handshake. For two TCP-enabled devices to talk to each other, they must synchronize, specifically they must inform the other machine of their communication settings such as Sequence Number (SEQ) and Window size (WIN). All packets transmitted in a TCP connection must have a sequence number since TCP is a connection-oriented protocol; every single packet has to be assigned a session unique number that will enable the receiving machine to re-

assemble the stream of packets back into their original and intended order. If the packets arrive out of order, as can happen regularly over the Internet, then the SEQ is used to stream them correctly. To complete a hijack, an intruder must perform three actions.

1. Monitor or track a session.
2. Desynchronize the session.
3. Inject the intruder's own commands.

To monitor a session, one can simply sniff the traffic, if that is possible. An intruder can desynchronize a session by "Sequence Packet Prediction." If one can predict the next sequence number to be used by a client (or server), one can use that sequence number before the client (or server) gets a chance to. Predicting the number may seem a difficult task to do since there are possible 4 billion combinations, but the ACK packet actually tells the next expected sequence number. If one has access to the network and can sniff the TCP session, one does not have to guess, we are told what sequence number to use. This is known as "Local Session Hijacking." If one does not have the ability to sniff the TCP session between client and server, one will have to attempt "Blind Session Hijacking." This attack vector is much less reliable since the intruder is transmitting data packets with guessed sequence numbers [r483].

Transmission Control Protocol (TCP) Snooping   A mechanism implemented via a Performance Enhancing Proxy to improve operation of certain wireless networks. The wireless base station inspects each TCP packet in transit and matches the TCP data packet in one direction with the TCP acknowledgments in the other direction. If packet losses are detected, the base station will retransmit the lost segments and suppress the "loss signals" (such as three duplicated packets) from reaching back to the TCP sender. Studies have shown that this improves the performance significantly [r022].

Transmission Control Protocol (TCP) Vulnerabilities   See Transmission Control Protocol/Internet Protocol (TCP/IP) fields used for passive fingerprinting

Transmission Control Protocol/Internet Protocol (TCP/IP)   A synonym for "Internet Protocol Suite" in which the Transmission Control Protocol (TCP) and the Internet Protocol (IP) are the networking and transport layer protocols. Basic Layer 4 and Layer 3 computer networking protocol suite (hierarchical pair) used in most modern computer networks (including the Internet). TCP is an end-to-end Layer 4 protocol providing message sequentiality and completeness; IP is a node-to-node Layer 3 networking protocol supporting dynamic routing (packet forwarding).

Transmission Control Protocol/Internet Protocol (TCP/IP) Fields Used For Passive Fingerprinting   Passive fingerprinting tools tend to focus on the following TCP/IP fields [r387]:

- IP Time to Live (TTL): Different operating systems have different default TTL values they set on outbound packets.
- IP Don't Fragment (DF): A number of IP devices set the DF field on by default. So the use of this field for passive finger printing is of limited value.
- IP Type of Service (TOS): Because it has been found that what TOS is set tends to be governed a lot more by the protocol than by the operating system, it is also of limited value.
- TCP Window Size: It has been found that TCP Window Size can be a useful way to determine the sending operating system. This involves not only the default size that is set to an outbound packet, but also how the window size changes throughout a session.
- Other fields that can also be used to passively determine the IP device of a packet are: IP ID numbers, TCP-selective acknowledgment (SackOK), and TCP maximum segment size (MSS).

Transmission Control Protocol/Internet Protocol (TCP/IP) Offload Engine (TOE)   Network In-

terface cards with hardware or firmware onboard which is designed to offload the majority of all TCP/IP processing from the host Central Processing Unit (CPU). The intent is to speed up I/O by increasing the speed of TCP/IP processes [r029].

Transmission Protocols   Provide the mechanism for the transfer of information. The most common protocol pair of this type is Transmission Control Protocol/Internet Protocol (TCP/IP).

Transparent LAN Service (TLS)   An early name used to describe the Virtual Private LAN Services (VPLS) service. TLS has been replaced by VPLS, which is the current term [r082].

Transport Block Sets (TBS)   (3G Wireless context) Every 10 ms, the transport channels transmit one or more TBSs. A TBS is composed of one or more transport blocks [r007].

Transport-Friendly Encapsulating Security Payload (TF-ESP) Protocol   A proposed protocol/format that modifies the original Encapsulating Security Payload (ESP) protocol to include limited Transmission Control Protocol (TCP) state information, such as flow identifications and sequence numbers, in a disclosure header outside the encryption scope (but authenticated) [r022]. There are no known implementations.

Transport Layer Security (TLS)   A general communication authentication and encryption protocol whose primary goal is to provide privacy and data integrity between two communicating applications [r492]. Developed by the Internet Engineering Task Force (IETF), TLS is the successor protocol to Secure Sockets Layer (SSL) Version 3.0 [r039]. The TLS protocol is misnamed, because it operates well above the transport layer (Open System Interconnection Reference Model (OSIRM) Layer 4).

The protocol is composed of two layers: the TLS Record Protocol and the TLS Handshake Protocol. At the lowest level, layered on top of some reliable transport protocol (e.g., Transmission Control Protocol (TCP) [r464]), is the TLS Record Protocol. The TLS Record Protocol provides connection security that has two basic properties [r039]:

- The connection is private. Symmetric cryptography is used for data encryption [e.g., Data Encryption Standard (DES) [r191], Rivest Cipher 4 (RC4) [r413], etc.]. The keys for this symmetric encryption are generated uniquely for each connection and are based on a secret negotiated by another protocol (such as the TLS Handshake Protocol). The Record Protocol can also be used without encryption.
- The connection is reliable. Message transport includes a message integrity check using a keyed Message Authentication Code (MAC). Secure hash functions [e.g., Secure Hash Algorithm (SHA), Message Digest 5 (MD5), etc.] are used for MAC computations. The Record Protocol can operate without a MAC, but is generally only used in this mode while another protocol is using the Record Protocol as a transport for negotiating security parameters.

Note that the TLS Record Protocol is used for encapsulation of various higher-level protocols.

Transport Layer Security (TLS) Applications TLS is used extensively to secure client-server connections on the World Wide Web (TLS is a stateful protocol). Although these connections can often be characterized as short-lived and exchanging relatively small amounts of data, TLS is also being used in environments where connections can be long-lived and the amount of data exchanged can extend into thousands or millions of octets. For example, TLS is now increasingly being used as an alternative Virtual Private Network (VPN) connection. Compression services have long been associated with IPsec and PPTP VPN connections, so extending compression services to TLS VPN connections preserves the user experience for any VPN connection. Compression within TLS is one way to help reduce the bandwidth and latency requirements associated with exchanging large amounts of data while preserving the security services provided by TLS [r344].

Transport Layer Security (TLS) Compression

The Transport Layer Security (TLS) protocol (RFC 2246) includes features to negotiate selection of a lossless data compression method as part of the TLS Handshake Protocol and then to apply the algorithm associated with the selected method as part of the TLS Record Protocol. TLS defines one standard compression method, which specifies that data exchanged via the record protocol will not be compressed. An additional compression method associated with the Lempel–Ziv–Stac (LZS) lossless data compression algorithm can be used with TLS [r344].

Compression methods used with TLS can be either stateful (the compressor maintains its state through all compressed records) or stateless (the compressor compresses each record independently), but there seems to be little known benefit in using a stateless compression method within TLS.

Transport Layer Security (TLS) Protocol Components The TLS Record Protocol is used for encapsulation of various higher level protocols. One such encapsulated protocol, the TLS Handshake Protocol, allows the server and client to authenticate each other and to negotiate an encryption algorithm and cryptographic keys before the application protocol transmits or receives its first byte of data. The TLS Handshake Protocol provides connection security that has three basic properties [r039]:

- The peer's identity can be authenticated using asymmetric, or public key, cryptography [e.g., Rivest–Shamir–Adleman (RSA) [r428], Digital Signature Standard (DSS) [r205], etc.]. This authentication can be made optional, but is generally required for at least one of the peers.
- The negotiation of a shared secret is secure: the negotiated secret is unavailable to eavesdroppers, and for any authenticated connection the secret cannot be obtained, even by an attacker who can place himself in the middle of the connection.
- The negotiation is reliable: no attacker can

modify the negotiation communication without being detected by the parties to the communication.

One advantage of TLS is that it is application protocol independent. Higher level protocols can layer on top of the TLS Protocol transparently. The TLS standard, however, does not specify how protocols add security with TLS; the decisions on how to initiate TLS handshaking and how to interpret the authentication certificates exchanged are left up to the judgment of the designers and implementors of protocols which run on top of TLS [r039].

Transport Layer Security (TLS) Protocol Goals The goals of TLS Protocol, in order of their priority, are [r039]:

- Cryptographic security: TLS should be used to establish a secure connection between two parties.
- Interoperability: Independent programmers should be able to develop applications utilizing TLS that will then be able to successfully exchange cryptographic parameters without knowledge of one another's code.
- Extensibility: TLS seeks to provide a framework into which new public key and bulk encryption methods can be incorporated as necessary. This will also accomplish two sub-goals: to prevent the need to create a new protocol (and risking the introduction of possible new weaknesses) and to avoid the need to implement an entire new security library.
- Relative efficiency: Cryptographic operations tend to be highly processor-intensive, particularly public-key operations. For this reason, the TLS protocol has incorporated an optional session caching scheme to reduce the number of connections that need to be established from scratch. Additionally, care has been taken to reduce network activity.

Transport Layer Security (TLS) Session An as-

sociation between a client and a server. Sessions are created by the handshake protocol. Sessions define a set of cryptographic security parameters, that can be shared among multiple connections. Sessions are used to avoid the expensive negotiation of new security parameters for each connection [r039].

Transport Layer Security Protocol (TLSP) An end-to-end encryption protocol [International Organization for Standardization (ISO) Standard 10736] that provides security services at the bottom of Open System Interconnection Reference Model (OSIRM) Layer 4—that is, directly above Layer 3 [r013].

Transport Mode, IPsec IP security (IPsec) mode as defined in RFC 2401, "Security Architecture for the Internet Protocol." Transport mode is allowed between two end hosts only; tunnel mode is required when at least one of the endpoints is a security gateway (intermediate system that implements IPsec functionality, e.g., a router) [r282]. Transport mode secures portions of the existing IP header and the payload data of the packet, and inserts an IPsec header between the IP header and the payload. The contents of the IPsec header are based on the result of a security association (SA) lookup that uses the contents of the original packet header as well as its payload (especially transport layer headers) to locate an SA in the Security Association Database (SAD). When receiving packets secured with IPsec transport mode, a similar SA lookup occurs based on the IP and IPsec headers, followed by a verification step after IPsec processing that checks the contents of the packet and its payload against the respective SA. The verification step is similar to firewall processing [r282].

Transposition A type of cipher based on orientation, ordering, or permutation of characters.

Trap Door A hidden computer flaw known to an intruder, or a hidden computer mechanism (usually software) installed by an intruder, who can activate the trap door to gain access to the computer without being blocked by security services or mechanisms [r013].

TRAU   See Transcoding and Rate Adaptation Unit

TRIP   See Telephony Routing over IP

Triple DES   (aka 3DES) Encryption with the Data Encryption Standard (DES) algorithm with the application of three keys in succession. The Triple DES algorithm is described in ANSI X9.52. This block cipher transforms each 64-bit plaintext block by applying the Data Encryption Algorithm three successive times. Triple DES uses either two or three different keys, for an effective key length of 112 or 168 bits. [r467, r013].

The Triple DES is composed from three sequential DES operations: encrypt, decrypt, and encrypt. Three-Key Triple DES uses a different key for each DES operation. Two-Key Triple DES uses one key for the two encrypt operations and different key for the decrypt operation. The same algorithm identifiers are used for Three-Key Triple DES and Two-Key Triple DES [r138].

Triple DES, IPsec Usage   The algorithm variation proposed for Encapsulating Security Payload (ESP) uses a 168-bit key, consisting of three independent 56-bit quantities used by the Data Encryption Algorithm, and a 64-bit initialization value. Each datagram contains an Initialization Vector (IV) to ensure that each received datagram can be decrypted even when other datagrams are dropped or a sequence of datagrams is reordered in transit [r310, r013].

Triple-wrapped   (S/MIME context) Data that has been signed with a digital signature, and then encrypted, and then signed again [r468].

Tripwire   A software tool for security. Typically works with a database that maintains information about the byte count of files. If the byte count has changed, it will identify it to the system security manager [r057].

Trojan Horse   A computer program that appears to have a useful function, but also has a hidden and potentially malicious function that evades security mechanisms, sometimes by exploiting legitimate authorizations of a system entity that invokes the program [r013].

Also, the term is sometimes defined as an unknown computer program that has a hidden and potentially malicious function.

Trojan, Denial Of Service Trojans Type   With Denial of Service trojans, a hacker infects a large number of victims with a DDoS trojan, then using the client part of the trojan he can connect either to all of them at once or he sends his commands to a drone (a master server) that then sends the commands out to all the victims to attack a single website or persons pc. These types of trojans have been used to bring down big sites such as yahoo.com [r469].

Trojan, File Server Trojan Type   File server trojans create a file server, usually an ftp server on the remote victims computer allowing a hacker to upload or download files, this is commonly used to upload a powerful remote administration trojan. Because some of these file server trojans are small, (some are just 8 kB) they are easily bound to other files making no significant size change [r469].

Trojan, Key Logger Trojans Type   Key logger trojans log everything the victim types and either send the info to the hacker by way of e-mail or store the typed info in a secret file located on the victims computer that the hacker then downloads using the client part of the trojan [r469].

Trojan, Password Sending Trojans Type   Password sending trojans have one purpose—to steal passwords from the victim's computer and send them back to the hacker. The most common way these trojans communicate with the hacker is by e-mail [r469].

Trojan, Remote Administration Type   Remote administration-type trojans (being the most common type) (e.g., Subseven, netbus) give the hacker more power over the victim's computer then the victim may have originally had. They include such functions as the ability to (a) steal all passwords cached or not (this is done using key logging technology), (b) modify the victims registry, (c) upload, (d) download, (e) execute (run) files, and various other things like turning on a web cam and spying on a victim [r469].

Trojan, Types   Remote access trojan types typically fall into the following five categories [r469]:

- Remote administration type: Give the attacker more power over the victim's computer than the victim may have originally had.
- File server trojan: Create a file server, usually an ftp server on the remote victims computer allowing a hacker to upload or download files.
- Password sending trojans: Steal passwords.
- Key logger trojans: Log everything the victim types.
- Distributed denial of service trojans or DDoS: Play a rile in DOS attacks.

Trouble   Any cause that may lead to or contribute to a user (or more formally to a manager-entity) perceiving a degradation in the quality of service of one or more network services or one or more network resources being managed [r068a].

Trouble Administration   In a telecom network, a set of functions that enable troubles to be reported and their status tracked (also applicable to an enterprise network). Trouble administration services include request trouble report format, enter trouble report, add trouble information, cancel trouble report, request trouble report status, review trouble history, attribute value change notification (e.g., trouble report status/commitment time), object creation/deletion (trouble report), verify trouble repair completion, and modify trouble administration information [r068a].

Trouble History Record   In a telecom network, a record of selected information from a trouble report that is retained for historical purposes after the trouble report is closed [r068a].

Trouble Management   In a telecom network, the trouble reporting and tracking between Conformant Management Entities (CMEs) interoperating cooperatively toward resolution of a trouble [r068a].

Trouble Reporting   The act of communicating that a trouble has been detected so that trouble management may be used in its resolution [r068a].

Trouble Resolution   The process of diagnosis and repair action required to clear a problem. It includes the process of assigning specific work items or overall responsibility for clearing and closing the trouble report [r068a].

Trouble Tracking   The ability to follow the progress of a trouble report from its creation through to its closure.

Trouble Type   The description or category of the trouble that was detected.

True Negative   (Security context) The correct identification of an normal activity as being normal benign behavior. Typically done by an Intrusion Detection System (IDS). This condition does not generate alerts for the security administrator to process.

True Positive   (Security context) The correct flagging of an anomalous activity as anomalous behavior that may be malicious. Typically done by an Intrusion Detection System (IDS). This generates alerts for the security administrator to process.

Trust   With any certificate scheme, trust depends on two primary characteristics. First, it must start from a known reliable source, either an X.509 root or someone highly trusted by the verifier, often him or herself. Second, the chain of signatures must be reliable. That is, each node in the certification graph is crucial; if it is dishonest or has been compromised, any certificates it has vouched for cannot be trusted. All other factors being equal (and they rarely are), shorter chains are preferable. Some of the differences reflect a tension between two philosophical positions represented by these technologies. Others resulted from having separate design teams [r170].

(Information System context) The extent to which someone who relies on a system can have confidence that the system meets its specifications—that is, that the system does what it claims to do and does not perform unwanted functions. The term "trusted" describes a system that operates as expected, according to design and policy.

When the trust can also be guaranteed in some convincing way, such as through formal analysis or code review, the system is termed "trustworthy"; this differs from the ABA Guidelines definition [r013].

(Public- Key Infrastructure context) A relationship between a certificate user and a Certification Authority (CA) in which the user acts according to the assumption that the CA creates only valid digital certificates. "Generally, an entity can be said to 'trust' a second entity when it (the first entity) makes the assumption that the second entity will behave exactly as the first entity expects. This trust may apply only for some specific function. The key role of trust in [X.509] is to describe the relationship between an entity and a [certification] authority; an entity shall be certain that it can trust the certification authority to create only valid and reliable certificates" [r061, r013].

Trust Anchor   (DNSSEC context) A configured DNSKEY Resource Record (RR) or Delegation Signer (DS) RR hash of a DNSKEY RR. A validating security-aware resolver uses this public key or hash as a starting point for building the authentication chain to a signed Domain Name System (DNS) response. In general, a validating resolver will have to obtain the initial values of its trust anchors via some secure or trusted means outside the DNS protocol. Presence of a trust anchor also implies that the resolver should expect the zone to which the trust anchor points to be signed [r069].

Trust Level   A characterization of a standard of security protection to be met by a computer system. The Trusted Computer System Evaluation Criteria (TCSEC) defines eight trust levels. From the lowest to the highest, they are D, C1, C2, B1, B2, B3, and A1. A trust level is based not only on the presence of security mechanisms but also on the use of systems engineering discipline to properly structure the system and implementation analysis to ensure that the system provides an appropriate degree of trust [r013].

Trust Management   As described in RFC 2704, it is a unified approach to specifying and interpreting security policies, credentials, and relationships; it allows direct authorization of security-critical actions.

Trust Management Systems   As described in RFC 2704, it is a system that provides standard, general-purpose mechanisms for specifying application security policies and credentials. Trust-management credentials describe a specific delegation of trust and subsume the role of public key certificates; unlike traditional certificates, which bind keys to names, credentials can bind keys directly to the authorization to perform specific tasks. Examples include SPKI/SDSI, Binder, and Cassandra.

Trust Negotiation   In open systems like the Internet, strangers can establish trust in each other by learning about each other's attributes, described in digital credentials that are disclosed during trust negotiation to gradually build up enough trust to complete a sensitive interaction.

Trusted Certificate   A certificate upon which a certificate user relies as being valid without the need for validation testing, especially a public-key certificate that is used to provide the first public key in a certification path. A trusted public-key certificate might be (a) the root certificate in a hierarchical Public-Key Infrastructure (PKI), (b) the certificate of the Certification Authority (CA) that issued the user's own certificate in a mesh PKI, or (c) any certificate accepted by the user in a trust-file PKI.

Trusted Computer System   (MISSI context) A system that employs sufficient hardware and software assurance measures to allow its use for simultaneous processing of a range of sensitive or classified information [r120].

Trusted Computer System Evaluation Criteria (TCSEC)   A standard for evaluating the security provided by operating systems [r496]. Called the "Orange Book" because of the color of its cover (it is the first document in the Rainbow Series).

Trusted Computing Base (TCB)   The sum of protection mechanisms within a computer system, including hardware, firmware, and software, the combination of which is responsible for enforcing a security policy [r120]. By installing and using the TCB, the administrator can define user access to the trusted communication path, which allows for secure communication between users and the TCB. TCB is the ensemble of protection mechanisms within a computer system including hardware, firmware, and software—the combination of which are responsible for enforcing a security policy. TCB everything in a computing system that provides a secure environment. TCB includes the operating system and intrinsic security mechanisms, hardware, network hardware and software, physical protection, and supportive procedures. Generally, there are provisions for controlling access, providing authorization, supporting user authentication, guarding against viruses and other forms of system penetration, and backup of data.

Trusted Distribution A trusted method for distributing the Trusted Computing Base (TCB) hardware, software, and firmware components, both originals and updates. This mechanism provides methods for protecting the TCB from modification during distribution and for detection of any changes to the TCB that may occur [r120].

Trusted Entity An entity that can violate a security policy, either by (a) performing actions that it is not supposed to do or (B) by failing to perform actions which it is supposed to do [r068a].

Trusted Functionality Functionality perceived to be correct with respect to some criteria—for example, as established by a security policy [r068a].

Trusted Host A network computer or system that can be trusted.

Trusted Key A public key upon which a user relies; especially a public key that can be used as the first public key in a certification path. A trusted public key might be (a) the root key in a hierarchical Public-Key Infrastructure (PKI), (b) the key of the Certification Authority (CA) that issued the user's own certificate in a mesh PKI, or (c) any key accepted by the user in a trust-file PKI [r013].

Trusted Network Interpretation The specific security features, the assurance requirements and the rating structure of the Orange Book as extended to networks of computers ranging from Local Area Networks (LANs) to Wireless LANS (WLANs), to Metropolitan Area Networks (MANs), to Wide Area Networks (WANs).

Trusted Path (COMPUSEC context) A mechanism by which a person or process can communicate directly with a cryptographic module and that can only be activated by the person, process, or module, and cannot be imitated by untrusted software within the module [r168, r013].

Trusted Process A system process that has privileges that enable it to affect the state of system security and that can, therefore, through incorrect or malicious execution, violate the system's security policy [r013].

Trusted Subnetwork A subnetwork containing hosts and routers that trust each other not to engage in active or passive attacks. There also is an assumption that the underlying communications channel [e.g., a Local Area network (LAN)] is not being attacked by other means [r186].

Trust-File Public-Key Infrastructure A non-hierarchical Public-Key Infrastructure (PKI) in which each certificate user has a local file (which is used by application software) of public-key certificates that the user trusts as starting points (i.e., roots) for certification paths. For example, popular browsers are distributed with an initial file of trusted certificates, which often are self-signed certificates. Users can add certificates to the file or delete from it. The file may be directly managed by the user, or the user's organization may manage it from a centralized server [r013].

Trustworthy System [American Bar Association (ABA) Digital Signature Guidelines] Computer hardware, software, and procedures that: (a) are reasonably secure from intrusion and misuse, (b) provide a reasonably reliable level of availability, reliability, and correct operation, (c) are reasonably suited to performing their intended functions, and (d) adhere to generally accepted security principles [r110].

TRX   See Transceiver

TTY Watcher   A hacker tool that allows hackers with even a small amount of skill to hijack terminals.

TU   See Transaction User

Tunable Lasers Systems   (optical transmission term) The lasers have a fixed frequency, may be tunable over a limited range, or may be tunable over the entire range of wavelengths supported by the Dense Wavelength Division Multiplexing (DWDM).

Tunnel   A communication channel created in a computer network by encapsulating (carrying, layering) a communication protocol's data packets in (on top of) a second protocol that normally would be carried above, or at the same layer as, the first one. Tunneling can involve almost any Open Systems Interconnection Reference Model (OSIRM) or Transmission Control Protocol/Internet Protocol (TCP/IP) protocol layer; for example, a TCP connection between two hosts could conceivably be tunneled through e-mail messages across the Internet. Most often, a tunnel is a logical point-to-point link (i.e., an OSIRM Layer 2 connection) created by encapsulating the Layer 2 protocol in a transport protocol (such as TCP in a network or internetwork layer protocol (such as IP), or in another link layer protocol. Often, encapsulation is accomplished with an extra, intermediate protocol—that is, a tunneling protocol [such as Layer 2 Tunneling Protocol (L2TP)] that is layered between the tunneled Layer 2 protocol and the encapsulating protocol. Tunneling can move data between computers that use a protocol not supported by the network connecting them. Tunneling also can enable a computer network to use the services of a second network as though the second network were a set of point-to-point links between the first network's nodes [e.g., virtual private network (PVN)].

A tunnel is connectivity through a Packet Switched Network (PSN) that is used to send traffic across the network from one Provider Edge (PE) equipment to another. The tunnel provides a means to transport packets from one PE

to another. Separation of one customer's traffic from another customer's traffic is done based on tunnel multiplexers. How the tunnel is established depends on the tunneling mechanisms provided by the PSN; for example, the tunnel could be based on the IP-header, a Multi-Protocol Label Switching (MPLS) label, the L2TP Session ID, or the Generic Routing Encapsulation (GRE) Key field [r082].

(IPv6 context) An IPv6 over IPv4 tunnel, in which endpoints are specified by manual configuration [r008].

(SET context) The name of a SET private extension that indicates whether the Certification Authority (CA) or the payment gateway supports passing encrypted messages to the cardholder through the merchant. If so, the extension lists Object Identifiers (OIDs) of symmetric encryption algorithms that are supported.

Tunnel Mode, IPsec   IPsec mode as defined in RFC 2401, "Security Architecture (SA) for the Internet Protocol." Tunnel mode is required when at least one of the endpoints is a "security gateway" (intermediate system that implements IPsec functionality, e.g., a router.) By contrast, transport mode is allowed between two end-hosts only [r282]. Transport mode secures portions of the existing IP header and the payload data of the packet, and inserts an IPsec header between the IP header and the payload; tunnel mode adds an additional IP header before performing similar operations. When using tunnel mode, IPsec prepends an IPsec header and an additional IP header to the outgoing IP packet. In essence, the original packet becomes the payload of another IP packet, which IPsec then secures. This has been described as "a tunnel mode SA is essentially a [transport mode] SA applied to an IP tunnel." In IPsec tunnel mode, the IP header of the original outbound packet together with its payload (especially transport headers) determines the IPsec SA, as for transport mode. However, a tunnel mode SA also contains encapsulation information, including the source and destination IP addresses for the outer tunnel IP header, which is also based on the original outbound packet header and its payload [r282].

Tunnel Multiplexor   An entity that is sent with the packets traversing the tunnel to make it possible to decide which instance of a service a packet belongs to and from which sender it was received [r082]. The tunnel multiplexor is formatted as a Multi-Protocol Label Switching (MPLS) label [r471].

Tunneling   The encapsulation of protocol Alpha within protocol Beta, such that Alpha treats Beta as though it were a datalink layer. Tunneling is employed to transfer data between administrative domains that use a protocol that is not supported by the intervening network (e.g., Internet) connecting those domains.

Tunneling Attack   An attack that attempts to exploit a weakness in a system at a low level of abstraction.

Tunneling of a Security Protocol Within Another   It is possible to tunnel Secure Socket Later/Transport Layer Security (SSL/TLS) inside an IPsec Encapsulating Security Payload (ESP), thereby allowing SSL/TLS to protect the Transmission Control Protocol (TCP) data and allowing IPsec protect the TCP header. However because IPsec encrypts both TCP header and TCP payload (SSL/TLS-protected data) as a whole, the encryption/authentication/decryption has to be done twice on the TCP data part, which is undesirable [r022].

Tunneling Protocols   Over the past several years, there has been a number of "tunneling" protocols specified by the Internet Engineering Task Force (IETF). Tunnels inIPv4 and IPv6 networks include Generic Routing Encapsulation (GRE) (RFC 1701, RFC 1702), IP-in-IP (RC 2003), Minimal Encapsulation (RFC 2004), Layer 2 Tunneling Protocol (L2TP) (RFC 2661), Point-to-Point Tunneling Protocol (PPTP) (RFC 2637), Layer 2 Forwarding (L2F) (RFC 2341), User Datagram Protocol (UDP) [e.g., (RFC 1234)], Ascend Tunnel Management Protocol (ATMP) (RFC 2107), and IPv6-in-IPv4 (RFC 2893) tunnels, among others [r472].

Tunneling Service   Any network service enabled by tunneling protocols such as Point to Point Tunneling Protocol (PPTP), Cisco Layer Two Forwarding (Protocol) (L2F), Level 2 Tunneling Protocol (L2TP), and IPsec tunnel mode. One example of a tunneling service is secure access to corporate intranets via a Virtual Private Network (VPN).

TUP   See Telephone User Part

Turing Machine   A mathematical model of a device that changes its internal state and reads from, writes on, and moves a potentially infinite tape, all in accordance with its present state. It is utilized as a model for computer-oriented behavior.

Two-Factor Authentication   A multifactor authentication scheme requiring authentication that satisfies two of the following conditions:

- Authentication based on what you know—for example, a user identifier/password combination
- Authentication based on what you have—for example, hardware-based token (such as a smart card) or a software-based token [Public-Key Infrastructure (PKI) certificate]
- Authentication based on what you are—for example, fingerprint or retinal scan

Typical deployments employ the use of a hardware or software-based device used along with a password which "unlocks" the token.

Two-Factor Authentication, Deployment Status   Currently the deployment of two-factor authentication remains limited. Notwithstanding increasingly higher levels of threats and attacks, most Internet applications still rely on weak authentication schemes for policing user access. The lack of interoperability among hardware and software technology vendors has been a limiting factor in the adoption of two-factor authentication technology. In particular, the absence of open specifications has led to solutions where hardware and software components are tightly coupled through proprietary technology, resulting in high cost solutions, poor adoption and limited innovation.

The rapid rise of network threats has exposed the inadequacies of static passwords as the primary mean of authentication on the Internet. At the same time, the current approach that requires an end-user to carry an expensive, single-function device that is only used to authenticate to the network is clearly not the right answer. For two-factor authentication to propagate on the Internet, it will have to be embedded in more flexible devices that can work across a wide range of applications [r263].

Two-Person Control   The tight surveillance and control of a system, process, or materials (especially with regard to cryptography) at all times by a minimum of two appropriately authorized persons. Each individual is capable of detecting incorrect and unauthorized procedures with respect to the tasks to be performed, and each is familiar with established security requirements [r013].

Type I Cryptography   A cryptographic algorithm or device approved by the National Security Agency (NSA) for protecting classified information.

Type II Cryptography   A cryptographic algorithm or device approved by the National Security Agency (NSA) for protecting sensitive unclassified information [as specified in section 2315 of Title 10 United States Code, or section 3502(2) of Title 44, United States Code].

Type III Cryptography   A cryptographic algorithm or device approved as a Federal Information Processing Standard.

Type Length Value (TLVs)   Protocol descriptors that provide information on the Protocol Data Unit (PDU) format, along with field lengths and permitted ranges of values.

U

U U U U U U U U U U U U U U U U U U U U U U

UA See User Agent

UAC See User Agent Client

UAC Core (SIP context) The set of processing functions required of a User Agent Client (UAC) that reside above the transaction and transport layers [r025].

UAS See User Agent Server

UAS Core (SIP context) The set of processing functions required at a User Agent Server (UAS) that resides above the transaction and transport layers [r025].

UBR See Unspecified Bit Rate

UCE See Unsolicited Commercial E-mail

UDC See Hewlett-Packard's Utility Data Center

UDDI See Universal Description, Discovery and Integration

UDP See User Datagram Protocol

UE See User Equipment

UL See Underwriters Laboratories

Um (GSM context) The air interface between the Base Transceiver Station (BTS) and the Mobile Station (MS) [r011].

UMA See Unlicensed Mobile Access

Umask A setting in a Unix process that modifies the permissions on newly created files. It is generally represented as a three-digit octal number that will be logically ANDed against the mode 666 (rw-rw-rw). Execute bits are not on newly created files in any case [r084].

UML Unified Modeling Language

UMTS See Universal Mobile Telecommunications System

Unallocated File Space The content that remains when files are erased or deleted in DOS/Win-

  Minoli–Cordovana's Authoritative Computer and Network Security Dictionary. By Daniel Minoli and James Cordovana
Copyright © 2006 John Wiley & Sons, Inc.

dows, and as a result, the data remains behind for discovery through the use of data recovery and/or computer forensics software utilities [r057].

Unauthorized Access   The use of an Information Technology (IT) resource, such as a Personal Computer (PC), host computer, database, network, and so on, without permission.

Unauthorized Deletion of Data Traffic on a Provider Provisioned Virtual Private Networks (PPVPN)   Refers to causing packets to be discarded as they traverse the Virtual Private Network (VPN). This is a specific type of Denial-of-Service attack [r058].

Unauthorized Disclosure   A circumstance or event whereby an entity gains access to data for which the entity is not authorized.

Unauthorized Observation of Data Traffic on a Provider Provisioned Virtual Private Networks (PPVPN)   This refers to "sniffing" Virtual Private Network (VPN) packets and examining their contents. This can result in exposure of confidential information. It can also be a first step in other attacks in which the recorded data is modified and re-inserted, or re-inserted unchanged [r058].

Unauthorized Traffic Pattern Analysis on a Provider Provisioned Virtual Private Networks (PPVPN)   Refers to "sniffing" Virtual Private Network (VPN) packets and examining aspects or meta-aspects of them that may be visible even when the packets themselves are encrypted. An attacker might gain useful information based on the amount and timing of traffic, packet sizes, source and destination addresses, and so on. For most PPVPN users, this type of attack is generally considered significantly less of a concern than are the other types of infractions.

Unclassified   Not classified.

Underwriters Laboratories (UL)   A nonprofit corporation established to maintain and operate laboratories for the examination and testing of devices, systems, and materials to determine their relation to hazards to life and property. Underwriters "Listing" mark on a product is generally accepted by the public and government agencies

as evidence of a "safe" product, not necessarily a "quality" product [r033].

Undocumented Access   A backdoor to a host computer system or a network element (such as a router or switch). Programs may have backdoors placed by the programmer to allow them to gain access to troubleshoot or change the program. Some backdoors are placed by hackers once they gain access to allow themselves an easier way in next time or in case their original entrance is discovered [r035].

Unencrypted   Not encrypted.

Unforgeable   The property of a cryptographic data structure (i.e., a data structure that is defined using one or more cryptographic functions) that makes it computationally infeasible to construct (i.e., compute) an unauthorized but correct value of the structure without having knowledge of one or more keys. This definition is narrower than general English usage, where "unforgeable" means unable to be fraudulently created or duplicated. In that broader sense, anyone can forge a digital certificate containing any set of data items whatsoever by generating the to-be-signed certificate and signing it with any private key whatsoever. For Public-Key Infrastructure (PKI) purposes, the forged data structure is invalid if it is not signed with the true private key of the claimed issuer; thus, the forgery will be detected when a certificate user uses the true public key of the claimed issuer to verify the signature [r013].

Unicast Address   An address that identifies an interface and allows network layer point-to-point communication. It identifies a single interface within the scope of the unicast address type [r008]. The following list shows the types of IPv6 addresses:

- Aggregatable global unicast addresses
- Link-local addresses
- Site-local addresses
- Special addresses, including unspecified and loopback addresses
- Compatibility addresses, including 6to4 addresses

With the appropriate unicast routing topology, packets addressed to a unicast address are delivered to a single interface.

Unicast Reverse Path Forwarding (uRPF) Mechanism that helps mitigate problems caused by the introduction of malformed or forged (spoofed) IP source addresses into a network by discarding IP packets that lack a verifiable IP source address.

Unified Modeling Language™ (UML) A specification of the OMG (Object Management Group) that permits one to model not only application structure, behavior, and architecture, but also business process and data structure. UML, along with the Meta Object Facility (MOF™), also provides a key foundation for OMG's Model-Driven Architecture®, that unifies steps of development and integration from business modeling, through architectural and application modeling, to development, deployment, maintenance, and evolution.

UML standardizes representation of object oriented analysis and design. A graphical language, its dozen diagram types include Use Case and Activity diagrams for requirements gathering, Class and Object diagrams for design, and Package and Subsystem diagrams for deployment. UML lets architects and analysts visualize, specify, construct, and document applications in a standard way. UML is a language with a broad scope that covers a large and diverse set of application domains; not all of its modeling capabilities are necessarily useful in all domains or applications; for this reason the language is structured modularly, with the ability to select only those parts of the language that are of direct interest.

Uniform Resource Identifier (URI) A type of formatted identifier that encapsulates the name of an Internet object, and labels it with an identification of the name space, thus producing a member of the universal set of names in registered name spaces and of addresses referring to registered protocols or name spaces [r473]. URIs are used in HyperText Markup Language (HTML) to identify the target of hyperlinks. In common practice, URIs include uniform resource locators and relative Uniform Resource Locators (URLs), and may be Uniform Resource Names (URNs) [r474, r013].

Uniform Resource Identifiers (URIs) for Extensible Markup Language (XML) Security A number of URIs intended for use with XML Digital Signatures, Encryption, and Canonicalization have been defined in RFC 4051. These URIs identify algorithms and types of keying information. Extensible Markup Language (XML), Digital Signatures, Canonicalization, and Encryption have been standardized by the W3C and the joint IETF/W3C XMLDSIG working group. All of these are now W3C Recommendations and IETF Informational or Standards Track documents. They are available as follows [r476]:

IETF Level	W3C Recommendations	Topic
RFC3275 Draft Std	XMLDSIG	XML Digital Signatures
Draft Std RFC3076 Info	CANON XMLENC	Canonical XML XML Encryption
RFC3741 Info	EXCANON	Exclusive XML Canonicalization

All of these standards and recommendations use URIs to identify algorithms and keying information types. Additional algorithms are given URIs that start with http://www.w3.org/2001/04/xmldsig-more#. For example, one hashttp://www.w3.org/2001/04/xmldsig-more#md5 (the MD5 algorithm described in RFC1321 takes no explicit parameters).

As another example, one has http://www.w3.org/2001/04/xmldsig-more#sha224 (the SHA-224 algorithm described in FIPS-180-2 and RFC3874 takes no explicit parameters).

Uniform Resource Locator (URL) The logical identifier to locate various resources on the World Wide Web. A type of formatted identifier that describes the access method and location of an information resource object on the Internet [r475].

A URL is a Uniform Resource Identifier (URI) that provides explicit instructions on how to access the named object. For example, "ftp://bbnarchive.bbn.com/foo/bar/picture/cambridge.zip" is a URL. The part before the colon specifies the access scheme or protocol, and the part after the colon is interpreted according to that access method. Usually, two slashes after the colon indicate the host name of a server (written as a domain name). In a File Transfer Protocol (FTP) or Hyper-Text Transfer Protocol (HTTP) URL, the host name is followed by the path name of a file on the server. The last (optional) part of a URL may be either a fragment identifier that indicates a position in the file, or a query string [r013].

Uniform Resource Locator (URL) Filtering (aka content filtering) Limiting users' access to certain Internet sites (or stripping out the content that is obtained) in order to restrict objectionable content (such as pornography), productivity-reducing content (such as humor or news sites), or performance reducing content (such as video streams or music files).

Uniform Resource Locator (URL)-Based Switching Methods and techniques for switching packets based on Open Systems Interconnection reference Model (OSIRM) Layer 7 information content, such as Uniform Resource Locator (URL) data. URL-based packet switching allows better management of server based applications and improves the performance and reliability of Internet services.

Uniform Resource Locator (URL)-Encoded (SIP context) A character string encoded according to RFC 2396 [r025].

Uniform Resource Name (URN) The term used to identify an Internet resource, without the use of a scheme, and can be specified in a single line of text. A Uniform Resource Identifier (URI) that has an institutional commitment to persistence and availability.

The difference between the Uniform Resource Locator (URL), URN, and URI is subtle. A URL refers to a Web page, including the scheme, but without a name location. A URN may also include the location of a code fragment. A URI refers to a Web page including the location of the code fragment, if one exists, and the scheme.

Union Relay Time passed between the sending of a Multicast Listener Report message by a new member of a multicast group in a subnetwork that has no members group, and the sending of multicast packets of this group over the subnetwork.

Universal Description, Discovery and Integration (UDDI) A repository that stores the descriptions of Web Services. UDDI is used to create a searchable directory of Web Services. It is an Extensible Markup Language (XML)-based registry [r080].

Universal Mobile Telecommunications System (UMTS) (GSM context) Describes a standard that enables the fast and flexible transmission of any kind of data over the air interface [r011]. It is defined as the next generation of global cellular that should be in place by mid decade; it is also referred to as third generation mobile radio (3G). Proposed data rates can approach around 2 Mbps, using combination Time Division Multiple Access (TDMA) and Sideband Code Division Multiple Access (W-CDMA). Operates at around 2 GHz [r121].

Universal Product Code (UPC) Linear, or one-dimensional bar code designed in the early 1970s; a familiar optical Auto-ID system found on many consumer items.

Universal Serial Bus (USB) A physical port (bus) (of plug-in connection) for PCs and peripherals (e.g., keyboards, scanners, mice, and digital cameras). Version 1.x supported 12-Mbps transfer rates; the speed has been increased to 480 Mbps for USB 2.0. USB 2.0 competes with FireWire for transmission speed.

Universal Serial Bus (USB) Token An access token with a USB interface. USB tokens are often used in multifactor authentication mechanisms.

Universal Terrestrial Radio Access (UTRA) (3G Wireless context) Universal Terrestrial Radio Access is a term for the air interface Uu between the User Equipment and the Universal Terrestrial Radio Access Network (UTRAN) [r007].

Universal Terrestrial Radio Access Network (UTRAN)   (3G Wireless context) The Universal Terrestrial Radio Access Network resembles the Base Station Subsystem (BSS) of the GSM network. It consists of two network elements: the Radio Network Controller and the Node B [r007].

UNIX   The operating system after which Linux is modeled. Although often used to refer to any operating system that provides features and programming interfaces that emulate UNIX, the term is a trademark legally held by The Open Group [r084].

UNIX Operating System Random Numbers   Several versions of the UNIX operating system provide a kernel-resident random number generator. Some of these generators use events captured by the Kernel during normal system operation. For example, on some versions of Linux, the generator consists of a random pool of 512 bytes represented as 128 words of 4 bytes each. When an event occurs, such as a disk drive interrupt, the time of the event is XORed into the pool, and the pool is stirred via a primitive polynomial of degree 128. The pool itself is treated as a ring buffer, with new data being XORed (after stirring with the polynomial) across the entire pool [r166]. Example event-based actions are keyboard interrupts, disk access-based interrupts, and mouse motion.

Unknown Key-Share Attacks   Attacks that show weaknesses in the station-to-station key agreement protocol. Discussed by Simon Blake-Wilson and Alfred Menezes [in paper "Unknown Key-Share Attacks on the Station-to-Station (STS) Protocol," Public-Key Cryptography (PKC)'99, Volume 1560 of Lecture Notes in Computer Science, pp. 154–170. Springer-Verlag, 1999]. Here the adversary is given a signature s for message m under some public verification key vk and her task is to find a different key pair (sk*, vk*) such that s is also a valid signature for m under vk* (called key-substitution attack). Signature schemes like Schnorr signatures are secure against this kind of attack [r016].

Unlicensed Mobile Access (UMA)   Any Radio Frequency (RF) spectrum that does not require a government license—for example, the Industrial Scientific and Medical (ISM) band.

Unqualified Learning   Learning that is based on a customer Ethernet frame's Media Access Control (MAC) address only.

Unshielded Twisted-Pair (UTP) Cable   An electrically conducting cable, comprising one or more pairs, none of which is shielded. There may be an overall shield, in which case the cable is referred to as unshielded twisted pair with overall shield [r100].

Unshielded Twisted-Pair Cable (UTP)   Wiring used to support standards Local Area Networks (LANs). For example, Category 5 Balanced Cable, or Category 5e Cable. Speeds up to 100 Mbps can be supported at 100 m; speeds of up to 1 Gbps can be supported over shorter distances (e.g., 25 m)

Unsigned Zone   (DNSSEC context) A zone that is not signed [r069].

Unsolicited Commercial E-mail (UCE)   (aka spam) "Junk" e-mail (i.e., unwanted e-mail) that is oftentimes sent in bulk to numerous e-mail addresses.

Unsolicited Voice Mail   Assigning an Internet mail address to a voice mailbox opens the possibility of receiving unsolicited messages (either text or voice mail). Traditionally voice mail systems operated in closed environments and were not susceptible to unknown senders. Voice mail users have a higher expectation of mailbox privacy and may consider such messages as a security breach. Many Internet mail systems are choosing to block all messages from unknown sources in an attempt to curb this problem [r459].

Unspecified Bit Rate (UBR)   An Asynchronous Transfer Mode (ATM) service category that does not specify traffic related service guarantees. Specifically, UBR does not include the notion of a per-connection negotiated bandwidth. No numerical commitments are made with respect to the cell loss ratio experienced by a UBR connection, or as to the cell transfer delay experienced by cells on the connection.

Untrusted Process   A system process that is not able to guarantee system security and prevent incorrect or malicious operation.

UORA   See User Personal Identification Number (PIN) Organizational Registration Authority (ORA)

UPC   See Universal Product Code

Update Train   A set of Routing Protocol UPDATE messages sent by a router to a Border Gateway Protocol (BGP) peer [r086].

U-PE   See User Facing PE

Uplink State Flag (USF)   (GSM context) Flag that indicates the destination of the data packets [r014].

Upstream   (SIP context) A direction of message forwarding within a transaction that refers to the direction that responses flow from the user agent server back to the user agent client [r025].

Uptime   (aka availability) A measure of the system's readiness for use by a system entity. Availability is diminished when the system entity does not have reliable access to data or a system. An example cause of this is a Denial of Service (DoS) attack. Related to downtime.

URI   See Uniform Resource Identifier

URL   See Uniform Resource Locator

URN   See Uniform Resource Name

US DoD Recommendations for Password Generation   The United States Department of Defense has specific recommendations for password generation. It suggests using the U.S. Data Encryption Standard (DES) in Output Feedback Mode as follows [r166]:

> Use an initialization vector determined from
> the system clock,
> system ID,
> user ID, and
> date and time;
> use a key determined from
> system interrupt registers,
> system status registers, and
> system counters; and
> as plain text, use an external randomly generated 64-bit quantity such as the American

Standard Code for Information Interchange (ASCII) bytes for 8 characters typed in by a system administrator.

The password can then be calculated from the 64-bit "cipher text" generated by DES in 64-bit Output Feedback Mode. As many bits as are needed can be taken from these 64 bits and expanded into a pronounceable word, phrase, or other format if a human being needs to remember the password.

USA PATRIOT Act   An act that was passed in the wake of the September 11, 2001 terrorist attacks on the United States. The law provides for stronger surveillance powers for law enforcement, stronger criminal laws against terrorism, improved intelligence-gathering capabilities, and improved anti-money laundering capabilities. Section 326 of the USA PATRIOT Act amended the BSA and required financial institutions to create and implement a Customer Identification Program (CIP) by October 1, 2003. The goal of CIP is to support Anti-Money Laundering (AML) compliance efforts by ensuring that financial institutions obtain and verify certain customer information when opening accounts so that they can be more certain about the true identity of their customers.

USB   See Universal Serial Bus

Use Cases   Use cases are a means for specifying required usages of a system. Typically, they are used to capture the requirements of a system, that is, what a system is supposed to do.

User   (aka end user) A person, organization entity, or automated process that accesses a system, whether authorized to do so or not [r013].

(Identity Management context) The end user or delegate agent acting on the user's behalf, who participates in the federation, using services from both the Identity Provider and the Service Providers, while directly authenticating only to the Identity Provider [r278].

User Agent (UA)   (SIP context) A logical entity that can act as both a user agent client and user agent server.

User Agent Client (UAC) (SIP context) A logical entity that creates a new request, and then uses the client transaction state machinery to send it. The role of UAC lasts only for the duration of that transaction. In other words, if a piece of software initiates a request, it acts as a UAC for the duration of that transaction. If it receives a request later, it assumes the role of a user agent server for the processing of that transaction [r025].

User Agent Server (UAS) (SIP context) A logical entity that generates a response to a Session Initiation Protocol (SIP) request. The response accepts, rejects, or redirects the request. This role lasts only for the duration of that transaction. In other words, if a piece of software responds to a request, it acts as a UAS for the duration of that transaction. If it generates a request later, it assumes the role of a user agent client for the processing of that transaction [r025].

User and Account Creation The process by which a user obtains their system credentials (user identifier, password, PKI credentials, etc.).

User Datagram Protocol (UDP) Member of Transmission Control Protocol/Internet Protocol (TCP/IP) suite of protocols used for datagram ("connectionless") communications over an intranet or Internet. Specified in RFC 768, published in 1980 [r478]. Utilized in a number of environments such as Simple Network Management protocol (SNMP), Real-time Transport Protocol (RTP), broadcast applications, and so on. It is simpler than TCP in that it offers limited error-checking and does not establish a connection (in terms of aggregated multipacket communication based on packet counters/reassembly).

UDP is a transport layer protocol, and it assumes that IP is the underlying protocol. UDP enables application programs to send transaction-oriented data to other programs with minimal protocol mechanism. UDP does not provide reliable delivery, flow control, sequencing, or other end-to-end services that TCP provides [r013].

UDP is defined to make available a datagram mode of packet-switched computer communication in the environment of an interconnected set of computer networks. This protocol assumes that the Internet Protocol (IP) is used as the underlying protocol. This protocol provides a procedure for application programs to send messages to other programs with a minimum of protocol mechanism. The protocol is transaction oriented, and delivery and duplicate protection are not guaranteed. Applications requiring ordered reliable delivery of streams of data should use the Transmission Control Protocol (TCP).

```
0     7 8    15 16    23 24    31
-|- - - -|- - - -|- - - - - -|- - - -|
|   Source          Destination   |
|   Port              Port        |
-|- - - -|- - - -|- - - - - -|- - - -|
|   Length          Checksum      |
-|- - - -|- - - -|- - - - - -|- - - -|
|           data octets . . .     |
-|- - - -|- - - -|- - - - - -|- - - -|
```

Source Port is an optional field, when meaningful, it indicates the port of the sending process, and may be assumed to be the port to which a reply should be addressed in the absence of any other information. If not used, a value of zero is inserted.

Destination Port has a meaning within the context of a particular Internet destination address.

Length is the length in octets of this user datagram including this header and the data. (This means the minimum value of the length is eight.)

Checksum is the 16-bit one's complement of the one's complement sum of a pseudo header of information from the IP header, the UDP header, and the data, padded with zero octets at the end (if necessary) to make a multiple of two octets.

The pseudo header conceptually prefixed to the UDP header contains the source address, the destination address, the protocol, and the UDP length. This information gives protection against misrouted datagrams. This checksum procedure is the same as is used in TCP.

User Equipment (UE) (3G Wireless context) In a Universal Mobile Telecommunications System

(UMTS) network, the mobile terminal is called User Equipment [r007].

User Facing PE (U-PE) The U-PE is the device to which the functions needed to take forwarding or switching decisions at the ingress of the provider network.

User Identifier A character string or symbol that is used in a system to uniquely name a specific user or group of users. Often verified by a password in an authentication process [r013].

User Personal Identification Number (PIN) One of two personal identification numbers in a Multilevel Information System Security Initiative (MISSI) system that controls access to the functions and stored data of a FORTEZZA PC card. Knowledge of the user PIN enables the card user to perform the FORTEZZA functions that are intended for use by an end user [r013].

User Personal Identification Number (PIN) Organizational Registration Authority (ORA) (UORA) A Multilevel Information System Security Initiative (MISSI) organizational registration authority that operates in a mode in which the ORA performs only the subset of card management functions that are possible with knowledge of the user PIN for a FORTEZZA PC card [r013].

User Rights In the Windows Operating System (OS) environment a user right references a general capability that is not tied to any particular object. In contrast, a permission is attached to some particular object (e.g., read access to a file).

User Security Function A mechanism to support security. Specifically, it provides authentication, authorization, data confidentiality, data integrity, and availability, particularly from a user's point of view [r080].

User Self-registration Mechanisms where users (typical external entities such as in an e-commerce context) provide some information in order to activate an account with limited capabilities (e.g., to download a White Paper). An e-mail confirmation is typically sent to the user to confirm that (limited) access has been granted. In general users may be added to the user databas-

es by the administrative manager; or through external software in the case when user data is stored externally; or through user self-registration.

User-Created Files Files created by users that may be used as evidence against the user's activity that is considered suspicious. File types may include digital images, e-mail, and other electronic documents.

User-ID and Password The most prevalent user authentication methodology, which consists of an identifier (ID) to identify the system/user and a password which is used to verify the identify of the system/user. This single factor authentication, based in "something you know," is considered less secure as most two-factor authentication mechanisms.

User-Protected Files Files that are compressed, encrypted, password-protected, or hidden.

USF See Uplink State Flag

Usurpation A circumstance or event that results in control of system services or functions by an unauthorized entity. The following threat actions can cause usurpation [r013]:

- Misappropriation: A threat action whereby an entity assumes unauthorized logical or physical control of a system resource.
- Theft of service: Unauthorized use of service by an entity.
- Theft of functionality: Unauthorized acquisition of actual hardware, software, or firmware of a system component.
- Theft of data: Unauthorized acquisition and use of data.
- Misuse: A threat action that causes a system component to perform a function or service that is detrimental to system security.
- Tamper: In context of misuse, deliberate alteration of a system's logic, data, or control information to cause the system to perform unauthorized functions or services.
- Malicious logic: In context of misuse, any hardware, software, or firmware intentionally introduced into a system to perform or

control execution of an unauthorized function or service.

- Violation of permissions: Action by an entity that exceeds the entity's system privileges by executing an unauthorized function.

UTCTime   The ASN.1 data-type "UTCTime" contains a calendar date (YYMMDD) and a time to a precision of either one minute (HHMM) or one second (HHMMSS), where the time is either (a) Coordinated Universal Time or (b) the local time followed by an offset that enables Coordinated Universal Time to be calculated.

Utility   A program used to configure or maintain systems, or to make changes to stored or transmitted data [r200].

(Storage context) Storage capable of providing quality of service, carrier class availability and serviceability, on-line expansion, or reallocation of resources [r029].

Utility Competing   A synonym for Grid Computing.

UTP   See Unshielded Twisted-Pair Cable

UTRA   See Universal Terrestrial Radio Access

UTRAN   See Universal Terrestrial Radio Access Network

Uu   (3G Wireless context) The air interface between the User Equipment and the Universal Terrestrial Radio Access Network (UTRAN) [r007].

UUencode   Method for converting files from Binary code to American Standard Code for Information Interchange (ASCII) code (text) so that these files can be sent across an intranet or the Internet via e-mail [r057].

v1 Certificate Ambiguously refers to either an X.509 public-key certificate in its version 1 format, or an X.509 attribute certificate in its version 1 format. However, many people who use this term are not aware that X.509 specifies attribute certificates that do not contain a public key [r013].

v1 CRL An abbreviation for "X.509 Certificate Revocation List (CRL) in version 1 format."

v2 Certificate An abbreviation for "X.509 public-key certificate in version 2 format."

v2 CRL An abbreviation for "X.509 Certificate Revocation List (CRL) in version 2 format."

v3 Certificate An abbreviation for "X.509 public-key certificate in version 3 format."

Vaccine A program that attempts to detect and disable viruses.

Valid Certificate A digital certificate for which the binding of the data items can be trusted; one that can be validated successfully.

Validate vs. Verify The community uses words inconsistently when describing what a certificate user does to make certain that a digital certificate can be trusted. Usually, one says "verify the signature," but means to say "validate the certificate"—that is, one "verifies" atomic truths but "validates" data structures, relationships, and systems that are composed of or depend on verified items [r013].

Validating Security-Aware Stub Resolver (DNSSEC context) A security-aware resolver that sends queries in recursive mode but that performs signature validation on its own rather than just blindly trusting an upstream security-aware recursive name server [r069].

Validating Stub Resolver (DNSSEC context) A term that refers to validating a security-aware stub resolver [r069].

Validation (Certification Authority context) The process of identification of certificate applicants. "Validation" is a subset of "identification" and refers to identification in the context of establishing the identity of certificate applicants [r011].

Validity Period A data item in a digital certificate that specifies the time period for which the binding between data items (especially between the subject name and the public key value in a public-key certificate) is valid, except if the certificate appears on a Certificate Revocation List (CRL) or the key appears on a Compromised Key List (CKL).

Value-Added Network (VAN) (older term) A computer network or subnetwork (which is usually a commercial enterprise) that transmits, receives, and stores Electronic Data Interchange (EDI) transactions on behalf of its customers. A VAN may also provide additional services, ranging from EDI format translation, to EDI-to-FAX conversion, to integrated business systems [r013].

VAN See Value-Added Network

Variable Bitrate (VBR) An Asynchronous Transfer Mode (ATM) service category that supports packet-oriented data traffic. The variability of the traffic is described with the average (Sustainable Cell Rate) and peak (Peak Cell Rate) traffic parameters. There is Real-Time VBR (rtVBR) version of the service and a non-Real-Time VBR (nrtVBR) version. rtVBR is useful for isochronous applications such as voice and video, while nrtVBR is more suited to data (IP)/bulk transfer applications. The difference in these services (the SLA) is expressed (by the provider) in terms of end-to-end latency, jitter, and packet loss (different values of these parameters are applicable to the two classes). The end-user will require the use of ATM Adaptation Layer 5 (AAL-5) in their clients/hosts/routers to utilize VBR-based services.

VBR See Variable Bitrate

VBScript A scripting language that supports active scripting. VBScript can be used within HyperText Markup Language (HTML) to execute small programs to generate a dynamic web page. This language (based on Visual Basic) was developed by Microsoft to compete with Netscape's JavaScript.

VC See Virtual Circuit

VCC See Virtual Channel Connection

VCI See Virtual Channel Identifier

VCL See Virtual Channel Link

VC-n Virtual Container-n ad defined in Synchronous Digital Hierarchy (SDH).

VE See VPLS Edge

Verification The process of ensuring that information has not been changed in transit or in storage, either intentionally or accidentally.

System verification: The process of comparing two levels of system specification for proper correspondence, such as comparing a security policy with a top-level specification, a top-level specification with source code, or source code with object code [r120, r013].

Identification verification: Presenting information to establish the truth of a claimed identity.

Vernam Cipher (aka one-time pad) Of all the methods of encryption ever devised, only one has been mathematically proved to be completely secure: the Vernam cipher. The worth of all other ciphers is based on computational security. If a cipher is computationally secure this means the probability of cracking the encryption key using current computational technology and algorithms within a reasonable time is supposedly extremely small, yet not impossible. In theory, every cryptographic algorithm except for the Vernam cipher can be broken given enough ciphertext and time [r477].

In 1917 during the First World War the American scientist Gilbert Vernam was given the task of inventing an encryption method the Germans could not break. What was devised was the only provably unbreakable encryption scheme known to this day. Compared with most cryptosystems it is very simple. To use a one-time pad, one needs two copies of the "pad" (also known as the key) which is a block of truly random data at least as long as the message one wishes to encode. If the data on the pad are not truly random, the security of the pad is compromised [r477].

Very Small Aperture Terminal (VSAT)   Satellite-based two-way systems that employ small satellite dishes (e.g., as used by PrimeStar and DirecTV). In addition to tuning in satellite TV, they can be used to receive data such as IP multicasting. Some companies (particularly in remote areas, Third-World environments, or oceanic territories) use this technology to construct a Wide Area Network (WAN) infrastructure [r203].

VFI   See VPN Forwarding Instance

View, IEEE 1471-2000   A representation of entire system from the perspective of a related set of concerns.

Violation of Permissions   Action by an entity that exceeds the entity's system privileges by executing an unauthorized function.

Virtual Channel Connection (VCC)   An Asynchronous Transfer Mode (ATM) connection where switching is performed on the Virtual Path Identifier (VPI)/Virtual Channel Identifier (VCI) fields of each cell. A concatenation of Virtual Channel Links (VCLs) that extends between the points where the ATM service users access the ATM layer. The points at which the ATM cell payload is passed to, or received from, the users of the ATM Layer (i.e., a higher layer or ATM entity) for processing signify the endpoints of a VCC. VCCs are unidirectional.

Virtual Channel Identifier (VCI)   A unique numerical tag as defined by a 16-bit field in the Asynchronous Transfer Mode (ATM) cell header that identifies a virtual channel, over which the cell is to travel [r042, r044–r052].

Virtual Channel Link (VCL)   A means of unidirectional transport of Asynchronous Transfer Mode (ATM) cells between the point where a Virtual Channel Identifier (VCI) value is assigned and the point where that value is translated or removed.

Virtual Circuit (VC)   A circuit used by a connection-oriented Layer 2 technology such as Asynchronous Transfer Mode (ATM) or Frame Relay, requiring the maintenance of state information in Layer 2 switches [r042, r044–r052]. Specifically, a communications channel that provides for the sequential unidirectional transport of ATM cells.

Virtual Circuit (VC) Merge   Label merging where the Multi-Protocol Label Switching (MPLS) label is carried in the Asynchronous Transfer Mode (ATM) Virtual Channel Identifier (VCI) field (or combined Virtual Path Identifier/Virtual Channel Identifier VPI/VCI field), so as to allow multiple VCs to merge into one single VC [r042, r044–r052].

Virtual Interface   A nonexistent interface that binds itself to a real interface. This virtual interface can be assigned its own IP address and will access the network through the real interface its bound to. For example, interface eth0 can have eth0:X bound to it, with 'X' being replaced by the virtual interface number [r084].

Virtual Keyboard   A graphical keypad where a user clicks on the characters rather than types them on the keyboard. An example is a mechanism for entering the username and password on a web server to (attempt to) avoid keystroke capture.

Virtual LAN (VLAN) Tagging   VLAN tags are used to indicate VLAN membership within a frame going across the network. These tags are attached to the frame as it enters a switch port belonging to a VLAN and the tags are removed when the frame leaves a port belonging to the VLAN. The type of port within the VLAN will determine whether the VLAN tag is stripped from the frame or whether it remains attached to the frame. The two port types within a VLAN environment are known as access ports and trunk ports [r350].

Access ports: Access ports are used where a frame enters or exits the VLAN. When an access port receives a frame, the frame does not contain a VLAN tag. As the frame enters the access port, the VLAN tag is attached to the frame. While the frame is within the switch, it carries the VLAN tag that was attached when it entered through the access port. As the frame leaves the switch through the destination access port, the VLAN tag is removed. The transmitting device and the receiving device are not aware that the VLAN tag was ever attached.

Trunk ports: In networks containing more than one switch, it becomes necessary to be able to send VLAN tagged frames from one switch to another. The difference between trunk ports and access ports is that trunk ports do not strip off the VLAN tag before sending the frame. With the VLAN tag preserved, the receiving switch will know the membership of the transmitted frame. This frame can then be sent out the appropriate ports on the receiving switch.

Virtual LAN (VLAN) Tagging Approaches Each VLAN tagged frame contains fields that denote its VLAN membership. There are two predominant formats for the VLAN tags, Cisco's Inter-Switch Link (ISL) format and the standardized IEEE 802.1Q format [r350].

Virtual LAN (VLAN) Tagging Standard Defined in IEEE 802.1Q tagging VLAN.

Virtual LAN (VLAN) Trunk Protocol Protocol for the maintenance of the VLAN configuration across multiple switches (without a centralized means of configuring and maintaining the VLAN information, the network administrator must configure the VLANs on each switch individually). Example: Cisco's VLAN Trunk Protocol [r350].

Virtual LAN (VLAN) Trunk Protocol (VTP) Vendor-proprietary protocol (Cisco) that allows one to configure VLANs on a single device, the VTP server, and have this configuration information propagated out through the switched network. This reduces the amount of time required to administer the VLANs. Within a VTP environment, a switch can be in one of three different roles. The switch can operate as a VTP server, a VTP client, or it can be in transparent mode [r350].

Virtual LAN (VLAN) Types VLAN methods to assign a device to a VLAN include the following methods: (1) Port-based VLANs. (2) Protocol-based VLANs. (3) Media Access Control (MAC)-based VLANs (refer to each entry for additional details.)

Virtual Local Area Network (VLAN) A method for administratively segregating logical LAN segments within an actual LAN segment. A customer VLAN identification using some scheme such as IEEE 802.1Q tags, port configuration, or any other means [r042, r044–r052].

A logical grouping of two or more devices. This logical grouping may extend across many switches. The devices are grouped based on a number of factors depending on the configuration of the network. Network administrators typically create one or more logical groupings of devices. In most cases, these reasons are broadcast control, (pseudo-) security, Layer-3 address management, and consolidation of networking resources [r350].

The term VLAN was specified by IEEE 802.1Q; it defines a method of differentiating traffic on a LAN by tagging the Ethernet frames. By extension, VLAN is used to mean the traffic separated by Ethernet frame tagging or similar mechanisms [r082].

Virtual Local Area Network (VLAN) Hopping Attack VLAN hopping is a network attack whereby an end system sends out packets destined for a system on a different VLAN that cannot normally be reached by the end system. This traffic is tagged with a different VLAN ID to which the end system belongs. Alternatively, the attacking system may be trying to behave like a switch and negotiate trunking so that the attacker can send and receive traffic between other VLANs [r156].

Switch Spoofing: In a VLAN hopping attack, the network attacker configures a system to spoof itself as a switch. This requires that the network attacker be capable of emulating 802.1Q signaling along with Dynamic Trunk Protocol (DTP) signaling. Using this method a network attacker can make a system appear to be a switch with a trunk port. If successful, the attacking system then becomes a member of all VLANs.

Double Tagging: Another version of this network attack involves tagging the transmitted frames with two 802.1Q headers in order to forward the frames to the wrong VLAN. The first switch to encounter the double-tagged frame (1) strips the first tag off the frame and forwards the frame. The result is that the frame is forwarded with the inner 802.1Q tag out all the switch ports (2) including trunk ports configured with the native VLAN of the network attacker. The second switch then forwards the packet to the destination based on the VLAN identifier in the second 802.1Q header.

Virtual Network (VN)   VNs connect subsets of resources of an underlying base network, and present the result as a virtual network layer to upper-layer protocols. Similar to a real network, virtual networks consist of virtual hosts (packet sources and sinks) and virtual routers (packet transits), both of which can have a number of network interfaces, and links, which connect multiple network interfaces together. Virtual links (also called tunnels, especially when point-to-point) are one-hop links in the VN topology, but are either direct links or paths (sequences of connected links) in the underlying base network. Base network hosts and routers can be part of multiple virtual networks at the same time, and their role in the base network does not need to coincide with their role in a virtual network (i.e., base network hosts may act as VN routers or hosts, as may base network routers) [r282].

IPsec can be used to secure the links of a VN, creating a secure VN. In a secure VN, trusted routers inside the network dynamically forward packets in the clear (internally), and exchange the packets on secure tunnels, where paths may traverse multiple tunnels. Contrast this to the conventional Virtual Private Network (VPN), which often assumes that paths tend to traverse one secure tunnel to resources in a secure core. A general secure VN allows this secure core to be distributed, composed of trusted or privately managed resources anywhere in the network [r282].

Virtual Path (VP)   In Asynchronous Transfer Mode (ATM) services, a unidirectional logical association or bundle of Virtual Circuits (VCs).

Virtual Path (VP) Merge   Label merging where the Multi-Protocol Label Switching (MPLS) label is carried in the Asynchronous Transfer Mode (ATM) Virtual Path Identifier (VPI) field, so as to allow multiple VPs to be merged into one single VP. In this case, two cells would have the same Virtual Channel Identifier (VCI) value only if they originated from the same node. This allows cells from different sources to be distinguished via the VCI.

Virtual Path Connection (VPC)   In Asynchronous Transfer Mode (ATM) services, a concatenation of Virtual Path Links (VPLs) between Virtual Path Terminators (VPTs). VPCs are unidirectional [r042, r044–r052].

Virtual Path Identifier (VPI)   An eight-bit field in the Asynchronous Transfer Mode (ATM) cell header that indicates the virtual path over which the cell should be routed. VPI value is assigned and the point where that value is translated or removed [r042, r044–r052].

Virtual Path Identifier/Virtual Channel Identifier (VPI/VCI)   A label used in Asynchronous Transfer Mode (ATM) networks to identify circuits.

Virtual Path Link (VPL)   A means of unidirectional transport of Asynchronous Transfer Mode (ATM) cells between the point where a Virtual Path Identifier (VPI) value is assigned and the point where that value is translated or removed.

Virtual Path Terminator (VPT)   In Asynchronous Transfer Mode (ATM) services, a system that unbundles the Virtual Circuits (VCs) of a Virtual Path (VP) for independent processing of each VC.

Virtual Private Local Area Network (LAN) Service (VPLS)   Transparent LAN service based on Multi-Protocol Label Switching (MPLS). End-to-end Wide Area Network (WAN)-scope service whose point-of-demarcation is an Ethernet handoff.

Virtual Private Local Area Network (LAN) Service (VPLS)   A VPLS is a provider service that emulates the full functionality of a traditional

LAN. A VPLS makes it possible to interconnect several LAN segments over a packet switched network (PSN) and makes the remote LAN segments behave as one single LAN [r082, r479, r480, [r366]. In a VPLS, the provider network emulates a learning bridge, and forwarding decisions are taken based on Media Access Control (MAC) addresses or MAC addresses and Virtual LAN (VLAN) tag.

Virtual Private Local Area Network (LAN) Service (VPLS) Edge (VE)   Originates from a dated Internet Draft on a distributed transparent LAN service and was used to describe the device used by a provider network to hand off a VPLS to a customer. In this document, the VE is called a VPLS-PE. This name is dated [r082].

Virtual Private Local Area Network (LAN) Service (VPLS) System   A collection of communication equipment, related protocols, and configuration elements that implements VPLS Services. A VPLS service can be extended to recognize customer's VLANs.

Virtual Private Local Area Network (LAN) Service (VPLS) Virtual Port   The logical port of a virtual switch. It is connected to virtual circuit.

Virtual Private Local Area Network (LAN) Service (VPLS) Virtual Switch   A logical switch that has logical ports (e.g., virtual circuits) as its interfaces. Therefore, it has the ability to do regular bridge/switch functionality such as Media Access Control (MAC) address learning/aging, flooding, forwarding (unicasting, ulticasting/broadcasting), and running Spanning Tree Protocol (STP) (if needed) per broadcast domain but based on its logical ports.

Virtual Private Local Area Network (LAN) Service (VPLS)/Virtual Private Wire Service (VPWS) Scaling   For scaling reasons, in the VPLS/VPWS cases sometimes it is desired to distribute the functions in the VPLS/VPWS-Provider Edge (PE) across more than one device. For example, is it feasible to allocate Access Control (MAC) address learning on a comparatively small and inexpensive device close to the customer site, while participation in the PSN signal-

ing and setup of PE to PE tunnels are done by routers closer to the network core [r082]. When distributing functionality across devices, a protocol is needed to exchange information between the Network facing PE (N-PE) and the User facing PE (U-PE).

Virtual Private Local Area Network (LAN) Service (VPLS)-Customer Edge (CE)   The device or set of devices on the customer premises that attaches to a provider provisioned VPLS.

Virtual Private Local Area Network (LAN) Service (VPLS)-Provider Edge (PE)   A device or set of devices at the edge of the provider network interfacing the customer network, with the functionality needed for a VPLS.

Virtual Private Network (VPN)   A restricted-use, logical (i.e., artificial or simulated) computer network that is constructed from the system resources of a relatively public, physical (i.e., real) network (such as the Internet), often by using encryption (located at hosts or gateways), and often by tunneling links of the virtual network across the real network [r013]. VPN is a generic term that covers the use of public or private networks to create groups of users that are separated from other network users and that may communicate among them as if they were on a private network. A network tunnel that restricts communication between a set of sites using an IP backbone shared by traffic that is not going to or coming from those sites [r082, r481]. In reference r081, the term VPN is used to refer to a specific set of sites as either an intranet or an extranet that have been configured to allow communication. Note that a site is a member of at least one VPN and may be a member of many.

For example, if a corporation has Local Area Networks (LANs) at many different sites, each connected to the Internet by a firewall, the corporation could create a VPN by (a) using encrypted tunnels to connect from firewall to firewall across the Internet and (b) not allowing any other traffic through the firewalls. A VPN is generally less expensive to build and operate than a dedicated real network, because the virtual network shares the cost of system resources with other users of the real network [r013]. VPNs are now remote access connectivity approaches that are quickly replacing traditional dial-up modem pools. With a VPN, remote users typically connect to an ISP or a private IP-based network and from there establish a secure connection with network servers via an encrypted tunnel. VPNs can also be used for secure communication across a LAN or Wide Area Networks (WAN) [r057].

Virtual Private Network (VPN) Building Blocks A way of describing the building blocks and allocation of functions in VPN solutions has been developed, starting with specifications of Layer 3 VPNs (L3VPNs) (e.g., the RFC 2547 specification [r423, r088] and Virtual Routers [r482]). Examples of the building blocks include Customer Edge Device (CE), Customer Edge Router (CE-R), Provider Edge (PE), Provider Edge Switch (PE-S), and Provider Edge Router (PE-R), among others. The building blocks are often used in day-to-day speech as if they were physical boxes, common for all services; however, for different reasons, this is an oversimplification since any of the building blocks could be implemented across more than one physical box [r082].

Virtual Private Network (VPN) Forwarding Instance (VFI) A logical entity that resides in a Provider Edge (PE) that includes the router information base and forwarding information base for a VPN instance [r081, r082].

Virtual Private Network (VPN) Routing and Forwarding (VRF) A per-site forwarding table. In networks running RFC 2547 VPNs [r442], Provider Edge (PE) routers maintain VRFs. Every site to which the PE router is attached is associated with one of these tables. A particular packet's IP destination address is looked up in a particular VRF only if that packet has arrived directly from a site that is associated with that table [r082].

Virtual Private Networking (VPN) Components A security services for flow control. Provides a tunnel over both untrusted and trusted networks, and grants access to services based on rules. Ex-

amples: Router-to-router (site-to-site) encryption, VPN client connections.

Virtual Private Wire Service (VPWS) A point-to-point circuit (link) connecting two Customer Edge (CE) devices. The link is established as a logical through a packet switched network. The CE in the customer network is connected to a Provider Edge (PE) in the provider network via an Attachment Circuit; the Attachment Circuit is either a physical or a logical circuit [r082]. The PEs in the core network are connected via a PW. The CE devices can be routers, bridges, switches, or hosts. In some implementations, a set of VPWSs is used to create a multi-site Layer 2 Virtual Private Network (L2VPN). An example of a VPWS solution is described in reference r471. A VPWS differs from a Virtual Private LAN Service (VPLS) in that the VPLS is point to multipoint, while the VPWS is point to point [r082, r308].

Virtual Private Wire Service Customer Edge (VPWS-CE) The device or set of devices on the customer premises that attaches to a provider provisioned VPWS.

Virtual Router (VR) Software and hardware based emulation of a physical router. Virtual routers have independent IP routing and forwarding tables, and they are isolated from each other [r082, r482].

Virtual Router (VR) Style A Provider Edge (PE)-based Virtual Private Network (VPN) approach in which the PE router maintains a complete logical router for each VPN that it supports. Each logical router maintains a unique forwarding table and executes a unique instance of the routing protocols [r082, r482].

Virtual Switch Instance (VSI) In a Layer 2 context, a VSI is a virtual switching instance that serves one single Virtual Private Local Area Network (LAN) Service (VPLS) [r308]. A VSI performs standard LAN (i.e., Ethernet) bridging functions. Forwarding done by a VSI is based on Media Access Control (MAC) addresses and Virtual LAN (VLAN) tags, and possibly on other relevant information on a per VPLS basis. The

VSI is allocated to VPLS-PE or, in the distributed case, to the U-PE [r082].

Virtual Tape A system that presents itself as a tape device (drive, autoloader, or library) that actually contains disk drives and memory (and also tape devices possibly), in order to provide performance improvement, and possibly increased connectivity to multiple backup software environments concurrently [r029].

Virtualization An approach that allows several operating systems to run simultaneously on one (large) computer. More generally, it is the practice of making resources from diverse devices accessible to a user as if they were a single, larger, homogenous, appear-to-be-locally-available resource. Dynamically shifting resources across platforms to match computing demands with available resources: the computing environment can become dynamic, enabling autonomic shifting applications between servers to match demand. The abstraction of server, storage, and network resources in order to make them available dynamically for sharing by Information Technology (IT) services, both internal to and external to an organization. In combination with other server, storage, and networking capabilities, virtualization offers customers the opportunity to build more efficient IT infrastructures. Virtualization is seen by some as a step on the road to utility computing [r080].

Storage software solutions that abstract the physical and logical storage assets from the host systems [r029].

Virus A hidden, self-replicating section of computer software, usually malicious logic, that propagates by infecting (i.e., inserting a copy of itself into and becoming part of) another program. A virus cannot run by itself; it requires that its host program be run to make the virus active [r013].

Visa USA Cardholder Information Security Program (CISP) Defines a standard of due care and enforcement for protecting sensitive information associated with credit cards. Currently, it applies to e-commerce merchants allowing online Visa transactions, including some colleges and universities. Among other things, CISP specifies the "Digital Dozen," a list of 12 basic security requirements with which all Visa payment system constituents need comply (e.g., requiring a firewall to protect data, encryption of data sent across public networks, and use of regularly updated anti-virus software).

Visibility Rules (Presence Services context) Constraints on how a presence service makes watcher information available to watchers. For each watcher's watcher information, the applicable visibility rules are manipulated by the watcher user agent of a principal that controls the watcher [r015].

Visitor Location Register (VLR) (GSM context) A dynamic database in the Network Subsystem (NSS). It supplies the serving Mobile Services Switching Center (MSC) with the necessary information on the current location of the mobile station [r011].

VLAN See Virtual Local Area Network

VLR See Visitor Location Register

VMS See Voice Mail System

VN See Virtual Network

Voice Mail System (GSM context) A memory system for speech, data and fax messages, spread over the entire Global System for Mobile Communications (GSM) network like a sort of large-scale answering machine [r011].

Voice over IP (VoIP) A packet-oriented technique to handle voice transmission. Fundamental work originally done in the mid to late 1970s [r484–r493]. Typically requires vocoding methods for low data rate encoding (e.g., 8 kbps), along with a suitable protocol stack for handling the stream either over a public IP network (e.g., Internet, carriers' MultiProtocol Label Switching [MPLS] networks) or over a private intranet. The stack is generally defined by ITU-T H.323, and includes Real-Time Protocol (RTP), User Datagram Protocol (UDP), IP, and appropriate lower layer protocols. H.323 is a stateful protocol suite developed on the Integrated Services Digital Network (ISDN) model. Of late there also has been a lot of interest in a stateless protocol based on Session Initiation (SIP). Quality of Service (QoS) is key to handling the isochroous nature of voice [r494–r496, r053].

Voice over IP (VoIP) Address Spoofing With VoIP, the source of the call can usually be determined by the IP address of the device that originates the call. However in some cases, the address is not permanent and can be manipulated by changing networks or by losing the "lease" for the address that is being used. As the IP address is not a stable source of identification, it cannot be used to identify location or as a point to deny service [r311].

Voice over IP (VoIP) Directories Large-scale deployments of IP video and voice services have demonstrated the need for complementary directory services middleware. Service administrators need call servers that are aware of enterprise directories to avoid duplication of account management processes. Users need "white pages" to locate other users with whom they wish to communicate. All of these processes should pull their information from canonical data sources in order to reduce redundant administrative processes and ensure information accuracy. The following are desiderata [r074]:

(1) Enable endpoint information to be associated with people. Alternately it enables endpoint information to be associated with resources such as conference rooms or classrooms.

(2) Enable on-line searchable "white pages" where dialing information (e.g., endpoint addresses) can be found, along with other "traditional" directory information about a user, such as name, address, telephone, e-mail, etc.

(3) Enable all endpoint information to be stored in a canonical data source (the Directory), rather than local to the call server, so that endpoints can be managed through manipulations of an enterprise directory, rather than by direct entry into the call server.

(4) Support the creation of very large-scale distributed directories. These include white pages "portals" that allow searching for users across multiple institutional directories. In this application, each enterprise directory registers itself with (or is unknowingly discovered by) a directory of directories that is capable of searching across multiple Lightweight Directory Access Protocol (LDAP) directories.

(5) Be able to support multiple instances of endpoints per user or resource.

(6) Represent endpoints that support more than one protocol, for example, endpoints that are both H.320 and H.323.

(7) Store enough information about endpoint configuration so that correct configuration settings can be documented to end users on a per-endpoint basis, as a support tool, or loaded automatically into the endpoint.

(8) Be extendible as necessary to allow implementation-specific attributes to be included.

(9) Be noninvasive to the enterprise directory, so that support for multimedia conferencing can be added in a modular fashion without significant changes to the enterprise directory.

Voice over IP (VoIP) Domain Name System (DNS) Protocol Vulnerability A flaw some IP phones running the DNS protocol. DNS handles the translation of domain names into IP addresses. DNS servers are located throughout the Internet to perform this translation and to ensure that IP packets arrive at their proper destinations. To expedite lookups on DNS servers, log files are often compressed. The VoIP vulnerability is caused by an error that occurs during the decompression of compressed DNS messages. The flaw can be exploited using specially crafted DNS packets containing invalid information in the compressed section of the message. This results in an error in processing on the IP phones, which could cause the phones to malfunction or crash [r497].

Voice over IP (VoIP) Media Gateway A device that converts a (digital or analog) linear data stream to a digital packetized data stream or vice versa. Usually a VoIP Media Gateway does some processing on the data it converts besides packetization or depacketization—that is, echo cancellation or dual tone multifrequency (DTMF) detection, and especially a coding/decoding. But there is a class of data streams that does not rely on or allow any data processing within the VoIP Media Gateway except for packetization or depacketization. Integrated Services Digital Network (ISDN) data terminals will produce data streams that are not compatible with a nonlinear encoding as used for voice [r313b].

Voice over IP (VoIP) Security   As VoIP becomes more widespread, so will the instances of fraud. Using VoIP, it is possible for a caller to control components of a call that are used to identify information about the originator, including the physical location. By doing so, a perpetrator can manipulate caller information to make it appear as if the calls are originating from a trusted source—possibly gaining them access to valuable personal information and leaving a virtually untraceable trail [r311]. The fraud-related challenges of IP-based services are substantially different from those of the traditional Public Switched Telephone Network (PSTN). Carriers that want to be successful in the VoIP world need to understand how their customers are using and misusing their networks [r311].

Voice over IP (VoIP) Security Alliance (VOIPSA) Industry group that aims to fill the void of VoIP security. VOIPSA's mission is to drive adoption of VoIP by promoting the current state of VoIP security research, VoIP security education and awareness, and free VoIP testing methodologies and tools.

Voice over IP (VoIP) Threats   Potential threats to VoIP networks include, but are not limited to, theft of service, spamming, intentional disruption of services, and number harvesting. Also, there are many other threats inherited from traditional data networks [worms, Distributed Denial of Service (DDoS), etc.].

Voice Profile for Internet Mail (VPIM)   Mechanism for interworking between multi-vendor

voice messaging systems (RFC 2421). Voice mail server-to-server communication protocol using Internet Mail Support of voice and fax attachments. Interworking between voice messaging systems and Internet mail also supports interworking between voice messaging systems and desktops. The voice message interchange format is a profile of the Internet Mail Protocol Suite.

Voice Response Unit (VRU)   [aka Interactive Voice Response (IVR) system] Automated systems that are used to manage the interaction of a customer population either as a simple filter/routing mechanism to a contact center or as a source of more sophisticated "self-serve" account information (when used in conjunction with a database system).

VoIP   See Voice over IP

VOIPSA   See Voice over IP (VoIP) Security Alliance

Volatile Memory   Computer memory that does not retain its content when power is turned off or lost.

VP   See Virtual Path

VPC   See Virtual Path Connection

VPI   See Virtual Path Identifier

VPL   See Virtual Path Link

VPLS   See Virtual Private LAN Service

VPN   See Virtual Private Network

VPN Consortium   Industry advocacy group (www@vpnc.org).

VPT   See Virtual Path Terminator

VPWS   See Virtual Private Wire Service

VR   See Virtual Router

VRF   See VPN Routing and Forwarding

VRU   See Voice Response Unit

VSAT   See Very Small Aperture Terminal

VSI   See Virtual Switch Instance (VSI)

VTn   Virtual Tributary-n (SONET).

Vulnerability   A flaw or weakness in a system's design, implementation, or operation and management that could be exploited to violate the system's security policy.

Most systems have vulnerabilities of some sort, but this does not mean that the systems are too flawed to use. Not every threat results in an attack, and not every attack succeeds. Success depends on the degree of vulnerability, the strength of attacks, and the effectiveness of any counter-measures in use. If the attacks needed to exploit a vulnerability are very difficult to carry out, then the vulnerability may be tolerable. If the perceived benefit to an attacker is small, then even an easily exploited vulnerability may be tolerable. However, if the attacks are well understood and easily made, and if the vulnerable system is employed by a wide range of users, then it is likely that there will be enough benefit for someone to make an attack [r013].

Vulnerability Analysis   Systematic examination of a network or product to determine the adequacy of security measures, identify security deficiencies, provide data from which to predict the effectiveness of proposed security measures, and confirm the adequacy of such measures after implementation [r057].

Vulnerability, Communications   Includes (among others) unencrypted network protocols, unnecessary protocols allowed, connections to multiple networks, and no filtering between network segments [r190].

Vulnerability, Exploited   A majority of compromises are a result of machines running well-known operating systems and applications. Intruders often use tools, often left behind on the system in "hidden" directories, to exploit known vulnerabilities and gain unauthorized access [r057].

Vulnerability, Hardware   Includes (among others) missing patches, outdated firmware, misconfigured systems, systems not physically secured, and management protocols allowed over public interfaces [r190].

Vulnerability, Human   Includes (among others) poorly defined procedures (insufficient incident response preparedness, manual provisioning, insufficient disaster recovery plans, testing on production systems, violations not reported, poor change control), and stolen credentials [r190].

Vulnerability Management   Mechanisms to proactively prevent the exploitation of potential breaches that threaten the security and availability of business systems.

Vulnerability, Media   Infraction risks to transmission mechanisms or storage mechanisms. Potential electrical interference either as jamming (channels) or physical damage (e.g., storage) [r190].

Vulnerability, Natural   Includes a facility located on a fault line, a facility located in a flood zone, and a facility located in an avalanche area [r190].

Vulnerability, Physical   Includes unlocked doors, unguarded access to computing facilities, insufficient fire suppression systems, poorly designed buildings, poorly constructed buildings, flammable materials used in construction, flammable materials used in finishing, unlocked windows, walls susceptible to physical assault, and interior walls that do not completely seal the room at both the ceiling and floor [r190].

Vulnerability Scanner   A tool to scan one's own environment [network, demilitarized zone (DMZ), or hosts] to determine what vulnerabilties may exist.

Vulnerability, Software   Includes out-of-date antivirus software, missing patches, poorly written applications (e.g., cross-site scripting), poorly written applications (e.g., SQL injection), poorly written applications (e.g., code weaknesses such as buffer overflows), deliberately placed weaknesses (e.g., vendor backdoors for management or system recovery, spyware such as keyloggers, Trojan horses), configuration errors (e.g., manual provisioning leading to inconsistent configurations, systems not hardened, systems not audited, and systems not monitored) [r190].

Vulnerability, Traditional Encryption Schemes   While traditional encryption schemes [e.g., Cramer–Shoup encryption scheme, Rivest–Shamir–Adleman Optimal Asymmetric Encryption Padding (RSA-OAEP) encryption scheme, Schnorr signature scheme] are secure against ordinary attacks, all suffer from weaknesses with respect to complete nonmalleability. These schemes still satisfy their designated security goals like chosen-ciphertext security or unforgeability, but they do not withstand the stronger kind of attack [r016].

W W W W W W W W W W W W W W W W W W W W W

WAIS   See Wide Area Information Service

Walled-garden   A service island that typically entails the use of proprietary protocols. Somewhat similar to closed user groups.

WAN   See Wide Area Network

War Dialer   (aka wardialer) A program that dials a given list or range of telephone numbers and records those which answer with handshake tones (these lines supporting modems), so that an intruder can attempt to break into the systems.

Warchalking   The practice of marking temporary symbols using chalk on physical landmarks indicating the presence of an open node, or connection point, on a Wireless Local Area Network (WLAN) network. Laptop computer users can connect to the Internet wirelessly (and for free) [r062].

Wardialing   An approach to circumvent perimeter security on a network by identifying systems with modems residing inside the network.

Wardriving   The act of driving (or walking, taking the bus, or sitting in a public space) with equipment used to detect wireless networks. Often, people that wardrive eventually publish the results in an open forum (such as the Internet).

Warehouse Attack   The compromise of systems that store authenticators [r200].

Wassenaar Arrangement   The Wassenaar Arrangement on Export Controls for Conventional Arms and Dual-Use Goods and Technologies is a global, multilateral agreement approved by 33 countries in July 1996 to contribute to regional and international security and stability, by promoting information exchange concerning, and greater responsibility in, transfers of arms and

Minoli–Cordovana's Authoritative Computer and Network Security Dictionary. By Daniel Minoli and James Cordovana
Copyright © 2006 John Wiley & Sons, Inc.

dual-use items, thus preventing destabilizing accumulations.

Watcher (Presence Services context) Requests presence information about a presentity, or watcher information about a watcher, from the presence service. Special types of watcher are fetcher, poller, and subscriber [r015].

Watcher Information (Presence Services context) Information about watchers that have received presence information about a particular presentity within a particular recent span of time. Watcher information is maintained by the presence service, which may choose to present it in the same form as presence information; that is, the service may choose to make watchers look like a special form of presentity. Motivation: if a presentity wants to know who knows about it, it is not enough to examine only information about subscriptions. A watcher might repeatedly fetch information without ever subscribing. Alternately, a watcher might repeatedly subscribe, then cancel the subscription. Such watchers should be visible to the presentity if the presence service offers watcher information, but will not be appropriately visible if the watcher information includes only subscriptions [r015].

Watcher User Agent (Presence Services context) Means for a principal to manipulate zero or more watchers controlled by that principal. Motivation: as with presence user agent and presentity, the distinction here is intended to isolate the core functionality of a watcher from how it might appear to be manipulated by a product. Watcher user agent, watcher, and presence service can be colocated or can be distributed across machines.

Waveguide (optical transmission term) A structure that guides electromagnetic waves along its length. An optical fiber is an optical waveguide.

Waveguide Dispersion (optical transmission term) The portion of chromatic dispersion that arises from the different speeds light travels in the core and cladding of a single-mode fiber.

Wavelength (optical transmission term) The distance between successive crests, troughs, or identical parts of a periodic wave. Also, in quantum terms, the electron wavelength, λ, is related to electron energy via the de Broglie relationship.

Wavelength Division Multiplexing (WDM) (optical transmission term) Multiplexing of optical signals by transmitting them at different wavelengths through the same fiber.

Wavelength Range (optical transmission term) The spectral region (nm) over which the device is operated. All signal channels are confined within this wavelength range—for example, C-band or L-band.

WCCP   See Web Cache Control Protocol

WDM   See Wavelength Division Multiplexing

Web Cache Control Protocol (WCCP) Cisco proprietary protocol used to communicate between a cache appliance and a properly configured Cisco router, for example, to support content switching. Cisco's Cisco Cache Engine product provides transparent caching for World Wide Web pages retrieved via HyperText Transfer Protocol (HTTP). The Cache Engine uses WCCP to communicate the router and register as a cache service provider; the router then diverts HTTP traffic to the Cache Engine.

Web Connectivity Provides connectivity to the Web—that is, to services supported through a "web browser" (such as Firefox, Internet Explorer, Mozilla, Netscape, Lynx, or Opera), particularly those services using the HyperText Transfer Protocol (HTTP) or Secure HTTP (HTTPS) protocols. Other services are generally not supported. In particular, there may be no access to Post Office Protocol Version 3 (POP3) or Internet Message Access Protocol Version 4 (IMAP4) e-mail, encrypted tunnels or other Virtual Private Network (VPN) mechanisms. The addresses used may be private and/or not globally reachable. They are generally dynamic (see the discussion of dynamic addresses in Section 3 for further discussion of this terminology and its implications) and relatively short-lived (hours or days rather than months or years). These addresses are often announced as "dynamic" to those who keep lists of dial-up or dynamic addresses. The provider may impose a filtering web proxy on the connections; that proxy may change and redirect Uniform Resource Locators (URLs) to other sites than the one originally specified by the user or embedded link [r034].

Web of Trust [Pretty Good Privacy® (PGP) context] A trust-file public-key infrastructure (PKI) technique used in PGP for building a file of validated public keys by making personal judgments about being able to trust certain people to be holding properly certified keys of other people [r013]. Environment where a PKI does not obligatorily require a universally accepted hierarchy or roots, and each party may have different trust points [r036].

Web Server A software process that runs on a host computer typically connected to the Internet to respond to HyperText Transfer Protocol (HTTP) requests for documents from client web browsers [r013].

Web Service (WS) Security Currently the dominant/de facto approach in Extensible Markup Language (XML) and Web Service security is to reuse the traditional HyperText Transfer Protocol/Secure Sockets Layer (HTTP/SSL) apparatus. However, WS and XML messages are assumed to require more that the traditional web security model. The major lacuna is that the HTTP/SSL model does not decouple security and transport, nor does it secure the XML messages themselves. XML firewalls are aimed at addressing this issue [r276].

Web Service Definition Language (WSDL) <binding> The communication protocols used by the Web Service. Describes how the operation is invoked by specifying concrete protocol and data format specifications for the operations and messages [r080].

Web Service Definition Language (WSDL) <message> The messages used by the Web Service. An abstract definition of the data being communicated [r080].

Web Service Definition Language (WSDL) <port> Specifies a single endpoint as an address for the binding, thus defining a single communication endpoint [r080].

Web Service Definition Language (WSDL) <port-Type> The operations performed by the Web Service. An abstract set of operations supported by one or more endpoints [r080].

Web Service Definition Language (WSDL) <service> Specifies the port address(es) of the binding. The service is a collection of network endpoints or ports [r080].

Web Service Definition Language (WSDL) <types> The data types used by the Web Service. Provides information about any complex data types used in the WSDL document. When simple types are used, the WSDL document does not need this section [r080].

Web Services (WS) A series of specifications that describe software components to be accessed, methods for accessing these components, and discovery methods that enable the identification of relevant service providers. WS use the Internet for application-to-application invocation and data transfer [r080, r286]. Simple Object Access Protocol (SOAP), Universal Description, Discovery and Integration (UDDI), and Web Service Definition Language (WSDL) are typical protocols used in this environment. Whereas HyperText Transfer Protocol (HTTP) is suited for client-to-server communication, SOAP is designed for server-to-server communication.

Web Services are programming language-, programming model-, and system software-neutral. In other words, they are Internet-based services that provide standard infrastructure for data exchange between two different distributed applications. Web Services are small units of code and are independent of operating systems and programming languages. They are designed to handle a limited set of tasks. Web Services are expected to play a key constituent role in the standardized definition of Grid Computing, since Web Services have emerged as a standards-based approach for accessing network applications (keeping in mind that grids provide an infrastructure for aggregation of high-end resources for solving large-scale problems). Web Services standards are being defined within the W3C and other standards bodies and form the basis for major new industry initiatives such as IBM (Dynamic e-Business), Microsoft (.NET), and Sun (Sun ONE) [r080].

Web Services Definition Language (WSDL) A language that provides a way of describing the specific interfaces of Web Services and APIs and is used by Universal Description, Discovery, and Integration (UDDI). An Extensible Markup Language (XML) mechanism for describing Web Services as a set of endpoints operating on messages. These messages contain either document-oriented (messaging) or Remote Procedure Call (RPC) payloads. Service interfaces are defined abstractly in terms of message structures and sequences of message exchanges [r080].

Web Services Inspection Language (WSIL) An Extensible Markup Language (XML)-based format utilized to facilitate the discovery and aggregation of Web Service descriptions in a simple and extensible fashion. A simple, lightweight mechanism for Web Service discovery that complements Universal Description, Discovery, and Integration (UDDI). WSIL is an XML document format designed to facilitate the discovery and aggregation of Web Service descriptions in a simple and extensible fashion. Created by IBM and Microsoft [r080].

Website Defacement The intentional and/or malicious defacement of a website.

Well-Known Ports Well-known ports are those in the range 0–1023. On Unix/Linux operating systems, opening a port in this range to receive incoming connections requires root privileges. Sometimes ports may be used for applications or protocols that are different from their official designation and this misuse may, for example, be by a Trojan horse or, alternatively, be by a commonly used program that did not get an Internet Assigned Numbers Authority registered port or port range.

WEP See Wired Equivalent Privacy

White Hat/Black Hat Hackers Hackers purportedly fall into two camps: Black Hat and White Hat. While Black Hat hackers illegally crack into systems for malicious reasons, their White Hat counterparts probe and test for security flaws and Information Technology (IT) research [r062].

White Pages An application that allows end-users to look up the address of another user. This may be web-based or may use some other user interface [r074].

WICIS See Wireless Intercarrier Communications Interface Specifications

Wide Area Information Service (WAIS) A pre-Web Internet service that allows one to search a large number of specially indexed databases [r057].

Wide Area Network (WAN) A physical or logical network spanning a topology in geographic areas larger than those served by local area networks (LANs). These networks are usually built utilizing carrier-provided telecommunication services.

Wide Area Network/Storage Area Network (WAN/SAN) Extension Gateways that connect geographically distributed SANs via existing WAN infrastructure. These solutions may use IP, Dense Wavelength Division Multiplexing (DWDM), or Synchronous Optical network (SONET) transport technologies and support protocols that carry Fibre Channel (FC) blocks via those WAN networks [Fibre Channel over IP (FCIP), Internet Fibre Channel Protocol (iFCP), etc.] [r029].

Wide Area Networks (WANs) Ethernet-Based In the late 1990s, competitive carriers started to offer new transport services which were cheaper, faster, and more flexible than the traditional leased lines or Frame Relay access services. These new services were based on Ethernet, serving as both a service User-to-Network Interface (UNI) for end-users but also as a switching/transport technology [r362].

Initially, regular Ethernet switches were used for this transport. Requirements were to support the full range of 802.1Q Virtual Local Area Network (VLANs) (4096) and the ability to support a large number of Media Access Control (MAC) addresses. New requirements quickly emerged in order to scale and cost-effectively operate service Provider (SP) Ethernet backbones [r362]:

- The ability to support VLAN translation to handle customers with overlapping VLANs
- The ability to transparently carry customer Spanning Tree Bridge Protocol Data Units (BPDUs)
- The ability to handle a full range of VLANs per customer, independently of the SP VLANs, known as Q-in-Q

These extensions have recently been standardized by the IEEE 802.1ad working group.

It quickly became necessary to provide a more scalable approach to operate such networks. This implied that switches used for transport had to become carrier-class. In other words, they had to provide the same reliability, scalability, and security capabilities that traditional Time Division Multiplexing (TDM) or Asynchronous Transfer Mode (ATM) switches offered. Multi-Protocol Label Switching (MPLS) has most of the attributes required to meet such challenges by supporting strong tunneling, traffic engineering, Quality of Service (QoS), and fast protection capabilities. Complementary hardware and software capabilities deliver the additional reliability necessary. This is the reason for using MPLS-based technology to support evolving Virtual Private LAN Service (VPLS) [r362].

Wideband Code Division Multiple Access (W-CDMA)   One of the latest components of Universal Mobile Telecommunications System (UMTS), along with Time Division Multiple Access (TDMA) and cdma2000. It has a 5-MHz air interface and is the basis of higher-bandwidth data rates [r121].

Wi-Fi   See Wireless Fidelity

Wi-Fi Protected Access 2 (WPA-2)   Security protocol for Wireless Fidelity (Wi-Fi) described in IEEE 802.11i.

Wind-up   A Microsoft Windows version of the TCPdump sniffer.

Wipe   (aka nuked) Deliberately overwriting a

piece of media and removing any trace of files or file fragments [r057].

Wired Equivalent Privacy (WEP)   The security mechanism originally included in the IEEE Wireless Local Area Network (WLAN) standard (IEEE 802.11, 802.11a, and 802.11b).

Now widely recognized as flawed, WEP was a data encryption method used to protect the transmission between 802.11 wireless clients and Access Points (APs.) However, it used the same key among all communicating devices. WEP's weaknesses are well known, including an insufficient key length and no automated method for distributing the keys. WEP can be easily cracked in a couple of hours with off-the-shelf tools [r005].

Wireless Community Networks   There are efforts by volunteer groups in the U.S. and/or municipal communities to establish wireless community networks to provide free wireless connectivity to the public.

Wireless Fidelity (Wi-Fi)   The marketing name for the IEEE 802.11 set of Wireless LAN standards (the term IEEE 802.11 is also used specifically for the original version; to avoid confusion this original WLAN is sometimes called "802.11-legacy").

The 802.11 family currently includes three separate protocols that focus on encoding (a, b, g); security was originally included, but is now part of other family standards (e.g., 802.11i). Other standards in the family (c–f, h–j, n) are service enhancement and extensions.

IEEE 802.11b was the first widely accepted wireless networking standard, followed, paradoxically, by IEEE 802.11a and IEEE 802.11g. IEEE 802.11b and IEEE 802.11g standards make use of the unlicensed (and, so, unprotected) 2.4 GHz band. The IEEE 802.11a standard uses the 5 GHz band. Operating in an unregulated frequency band, IEEE 802.11b and IEEE 802.11g gears can incur interference from microwave ovens, cordless phones, and other appliances using the same 2.4-GHz range.

Wireless Frequencies, Wi-Fi   The following are supported:

Standard	Transfer Method (FHSS= Frequency Hopping Spread Spectrum; DSSS = Direct Sequence Spread Spectrum)	Frequencies	Data Rates Supported (Mbps)
802.11 legacy	FHSS, DSSS, infrared	2.4 GHz, IR (infrared)	1, 2
802.11b	DSSS, HR-DSSS	2.4 GHz	1, 2, 5.5, 11
"802.11b+" nonstandard	DSSS, HR-DSSS (PBCC)	2.4 GHz	1, 2, 5.5, 11, 22, 33, 44
802.11a	OFDM	5.2, 5.8 GHz	6, 9, 12, 18, 24, 36, 48, 54
802.11g	DSSS, HR-DSSS, OFDM	2.4 GHz	1, 2, 5.5, 11; 6, 9, 12, 18, 24, 36, 48, 54

Wireless Intercarrier Communications Interface Specifications (WICIS) Specification for Wireless Local Number Portability published by the Alliance for Telecommunications Industry Solutions (ATIS). The WICIS defines the operational requirements and technical specifications for the intercarrier exchange of information when a consumer changes wireless service providers and ports their existing number to a new carrier. The WICIS 3.0.0 document replaces version 2.1.0. Carriers were expected to begin using version 3.0.0 on the "sunrise" date of May 22, 2005. The transition will take place over several months, and the sunset for WICIS 2.1.0 is set for February 12, 2006. Benefits of WICIS 3.0.0 [r311]:

- Carriers determined that the ability to support two versions in production allows them to better manage software releases in support of industry changes.
- Backwards compatibility, including test and broadcast messages, provides connectivity status and operations support.
- The document outlines a specific character set for each value to avoid interoperability issues between trading partners.

- Updates to the Interface Definition Language (IDL) removes outdated code, particularly that referring to a single TN structure. The IDL also has been changed to define test and broadcast messages.

Wireless Local Area Network (WLAN) A LAN technology that utilizes short-range radio waves in the ISM (Industrial, Scientific, and Medical) 2.4 GHz band to transmit information. WLAN technologies are formalized in IEEE standards IEEE 802.11, 802.11a, 802.11b, 802.11g, 802.11n, 802.11e, 802.11i, and 802.11r.

Wireless Local Loop (WLL) Wireless local loop technology for limited-number systems, usually found in remote areas where fixed-line usage is impossible. Many WLL systems use Code Division Multiple Access (CDMA) technology [r121]. WiMax may be used in the future for these kinds of applications.

Wireless Markup Language (WML) An Extensible Markup Language (XML) language that is used to specify content and the user interface for Wireless Application Protocol (WAP) devices. WML is supported by almost every mobile phone browser in the world. It allows the text portions of web pages to be presented on mobile phones and Personal Digital Assistants (PDAs) via a wireless connection. WML pages are requested and served in the same way as HyperText Markup Language (HTML) pages. For web servers to serve WML pages, they must contain the text/vnd.wap.wml mime type [r005].

Wireless Networks, Higher Layer Protocols The Transmission Control Protocol (TCP) is the standard transport protocol for all-IP wireless networks, including third-generation/fourth-generation (3G/4G) cellular networks, satellite networks, wireless Personal Area Network (PAN), and mobile ad-hoc networks [r022].

Wireless Node (WN) The wireless sensor node in a Wireless Sensor Network (WSN).

Wireless Personal Area Networks (WPANs) Personal-area networks (PANs) defined by IEEE 802.15.

Wireless Quality of Service (QoS)   IEEE 802.11e provides QoS support for Local Area Network (LAN) applications. QoS is critical for delay-sensitive applications such as Voice over Wireless IP (VoWIP). The standard will provide classes of service with managed levels of QoS for data, voice, and video applications.

Wireless Security   Principally (but not only) related to full security for Wireless LANs (e.g., data encryption mechanisms). Confidentiality and integrity of data are two critical issues for wireless, mobile networks. A number of standards exists to address issue. For example, IEEE 802.11i is intended to improve WLAN security. It describes the encrypted transmission of data between systems of 802.11a and 802.11b WLANs. IEEE 802.11i defines new encryption key protocols including the Temporal Key Integrity Protocol (TKIP) and the Advanced Encryption Standard (AES).

The most widely accepted method for ensuring data confidentiality and integrity is to pass encrypted data end-to-end using a mechanism such as IPsec. This approach, however, limits the types of performance enhancing services that can be provided within a network. In particular, this model is not ideal for the wireless, mobile environment because it makes data transmission less efficient, and it precludes the network from performing many operations that are designed to mitigate the effects of wireless links [r502]. The use of Multilayer IPsec has been suggested.

Wireless Sensor Network (WSN) Types   WSNs can be coarsely taxonomized (commercial) sensor networks/systems into two categories:

- Category 1 WSNs (C1WSNs): Almost-invariably mesh-based systems with multihop radio connectivity among/between Wireless Nodes (WNs), utilizing dynamic routing in both the wireless portion and the wireline portion of the network. Military-theater systems typically belong to this category.
- Category 2 WSNs (C2WSNs): Point-to-point or multipoint-to-point (star-based)

systems generally with single-hop radio connectivity to WNs, utilizing static routing over the wireless network; typically, there will be only one route from the WNs to the companion terrestrial/wireline forwarding node—WNs are pendent nodes. Residential control systems typically belong to this category.

Wireless Sensor Networks (WSN)   A sensor networks that is wireless; most sensor networks are, in fact, WSNs. This is a network of dispersed sensors that collect and transmit data to a central processing location [r021].

Wireless Sensor Networks (WSN) Applications   WSNs support a broad spectrum of applications ranging from environmental sensing to vehicle tracking; from perimeter security to inventory management; and from habitat monitoring to battlefield management [r021]. For example, WSNs may be deployed outdoors in large sensor fields to detect and control the spread of wild fires, to detect and track enemy vehicles, or to support environmental monitoring including precision agriculture. With WSNs one can monitor and control factories, offices, homes, vehicles, cities, the ambiance, and the environment. For example, one can detect structural faults (e.g., fatigue-induced cracks) in ships, aircrafts, and buildings; public-assembly locations can be equipped to detect toxins and to trace the source of the contamination. Volcanic eruption, earthquake detection, and tsunami alerting can be useful environmental-monitoring systems; these kinds of applications generally require Wireless Nodes (WNs) that are deployed in remote, even hard-to-reach locations.

Wireless Sensor Networks (WSN) Protocol Stack   The following is a typical protocol stack for WSNs:

- Upper Levels: In-network applications including application processing, data aggregation, external querying query processing, external database
- Layer 4: Transport, including data dissemi-

nation/accumulation, caching, storage
- Layer 3: Networking, including adaptive topology management, topological routing
- Layer 2: Link Layer: (Contention) Channel Sharing [Media Access Control (MAC)], timing, locality
- Layer 1:Physical Medium: Communication channel, sensing, actuation, signal processing

Wiretapping   An attack that intercepts and accesses data and other information contained in a flow in a communication system. Although the term originally referred to making a mechanical connection to an electrical conductor that links two nodes, it is now used to refer to reading information from any sort of medium used for a link or even directly from a node, such as gateway or subnetwork switch. Active wiretapping attempts to alter the data or otherwise affect the flow, while passive wiretapping only attempts to observe the flow and gain knowledge of information it contains [r013].

WLAN   See Wireless Local Area Network

WML   See Wireless Markup Language

WN   See Wireless Node

Work Factor   (General Security context) The estimated amount of effort or time that can be expected to be expended by a potential intruder to penetrate a system, or defeat a particular countermeasure, when using specified amounts of ex-

pertise and resources [r013].

(Cryptography context) The estimated amount of computing time and power needed to break a cryptographic system [r013].

World Wide Web ("the Web", WWW, W3)   The global, hypermedia-based collection of information and services that is available on Internet servers and is accessed by browsers using Hypertext Transfer Protocol (HTTP) and other information retrieval mechanisms [r499, r013, r504].

Worm   A computer program that can run independently, can propagate a complete working version of itself onto other hosts on a network, and may consume computer resources destructively [r013]. The worm may do damage and compromise the security of the computer. Oftentimes, worms are introduced to networks via e-mail (as an attachment), via download from websites, or via portable digital medial brought into an enterprise. Some well-known worms include My-Doom, CodeRed, SQL Slammer.

WPA-2   See Wi-Fi Protected Access 2

WPANs   See Wireless Personal Area Networks

Wrap   To use cryptography to provide data confidentiality service for a data object.

WS   See Web Services

WSIL   See Web Services Inspection Language

WSN   See Wireless Sensor Networks

WWW   See World Wide Web

X

X.25 A packet technology used in public networks of the 1970s and 1980s. It is still used in Europe. For example, an X.25 packet data network can provide the connection between two General Packet Radio Service (GPRS) networks (backbone) used in Global System for Mobile communications (GSM).

X.400 An International Telecommunications Union–Telecommunications (ITU-T) Recommendation [r500] that is one part of a joint ITU-T/International Organization for Standardization (ISO) multipart standard (X.400-X.421) that defines the Message Handling Systems. [The ISO equivalent is International Standard (IS) 10021, parts 1–7.]

X.500 Directory An International Telecommunications Union–Telecommunications (ITU-T) Rec-ommendation [r498] that is one part of a joint ITU-T/International Organization for Standardization (ISO) multipart standard (X.500-X.525) that defines the X.500 Directory, a conceptual collection of systems that provide distributed directory capabilities for OSI entities, processes, applications, and services. [The ISO equivalent is International Standard (IS) 9594-1 and related standards, IS 9594-x.] The X.500 Directory is structured as a tree (the Directory Information Tree), and information is stored in directory entries. Each entry is a collection of information about one object, and each object has a Distinguished Name (DN). A directory entry is composed of attributes, each with a type and one or more values. For example, if a Public-Key Infrastructure (PKI) uses the Directory to distribute

Minoli–Cordovana's Authoritative Computer and Network Security Dictionary. By Daniel Minoli and James Cordovana
Copyright © 2006 John Wiley & Sons, Inc.

certificates, then the X.509 public-key certificate of an end user is normally stored as a value of an attribute of type "userCertificate" in the Directory entry that has the DN that is the subject of the certificate [r013].

X.509 An authentication certificate scheme recommended by the International Telecommunications Union–Telecommunications (ITU-T) [r061, r424]. Among other applications, this mechanism is used for Secure Sockets Layer/Transport Layer Security (SSL/TLS) authentication. The recommendation defines a framework to provide and support data origin authentication and peer entity authentication services, including formats for X.509 public-key certificates, X.509 attribute certificates, and X.509 Certificate Revocation Lists (CRLs). [The International Organization for Standardization (ISO) equivalent is International Standard (IS) 9498-4.] X.509 describes two levels of authentication: (a) simple authentication based on a password and (b) strong authentication based on a public-key certificate [r013].

X.509 Attribute Certificate An attribute certificate in the version 1 (v1) format defined by X.509. [The v1 designation for an X.509 attribute certificate is disjoint from the v1 designation for an X.509 public-key certificate, as well as from the v1 designation for an X.509 Certificate Revocation List (CRL).] An X.509 attribute certificate has a subject field, but the attribute certificate is a separate data structure from that subject's public-key certificate. A subject may have multiple attribute certificates associated with each of its public-key certificates, and an attribute certificate may be issued by a different Certification Authority (CA) than the one that issued the associated public-key certificate [r013].

X.509 Authority Revocation List (ARL) One of the formats defined by X.509—version 1 (v1) or version 2 (v2). A specialized kind of certificate revocation list.

X.509 Certificate Revocation List (CRL) One of the formats defined by X.509—version 1 (v1) or version 2 (v2). (The v1 and v2 designations for an X.509 CRL are disjoint from the v1 and v2 designations for an X.509 public-key certificate, as well as from the v1 designation for an X.509 attribute certificate.) [r013].

X.509 Certificates Either an X.509 public-key certificate or an X.509 attribute certificate. International Telecommunications Union–Telecommunications (ITU-T) X.509 (formerly CCITT X.509) or ISO/IEC/ITU 9594-8 defines a standard certificate format.

X.509 Certificates, History and Usage The standard was first published in 1988 as part of the X.500 Directory set of recommendations. The X.509 certificate format in the 1988 standard is called the Version 1 (v1) format. When X.500 was revised in 1993, two more fields were added, resulting in the Version 2 (v2) format (these two fields may be used to support directory access control). The Internet Privacy Enhanced Mail (PEM) RFCs, published in 1993, include specifications for a public-key infrastructure based on X.509 v1 certificates. The experience gained in attempts to deploy RFC 1422 made it clear that the v1 and v2 certificate formats are deficient in several respects. Most importantly, more fields were needed to carry information that PEM design and implementation experience has proven necessary. In response to these new requirements, ISO/IEC/ITU and ANSI X9 developed the X.509 Version 3 (v3) certificate format. The v3 format extends the v2 format by adding provision for additional extension fields. Particular extension field types may be specified in standards or may be defined and registered by any organization or community. In 1996, standardization of the basic v3 format was completed. ISO/IEC/ITU and ANSI X9 have also developed standard extensions for use in the v3 extensions field. These extensions can convey such data as additional subject identification information, key attribute information, policy information, and certification path constraints. However, the ISO/IEC/ITU and ANSI X9 standard extensions are broad in their applicability and in order to develop interoperable implementations of X.509 v3 systems for Internet use it is necessary to specify a profile tailored for the Internet [r103].

X.509 Public-Key Certificate A public-key certificate in one of the formats defined by X.509—version 1 (v1), version 2 (v2), or version 3 (v3). [The v1 and v2 designations for an X.509 public-key certificate are disjoint from the v1 and v2 designations for an X.509 Certificate Revocation List (CRL), as well as from the v1 designation for an X.509 attribute certificate.] An X.509 public-key certificate contains a sequence of data items and has a digital signature computed on that sequence. In addition to the signature, all three versions contain items 1 through 7 listed below. Only v2 and v3 certificates may also contain items 8 and 9, and only v3 may contain item 10 [r013]:

1. Version: Identifies v1, v2, or v3.
2. SerialNumber: Certificate serial number; an integer assigned by the issuer.
3. Signature: Object Identifier (OID) of algorithm that was used to sign the certificate.
4. Issuer: Distinguished Name (DN) of the issuer (the Certification Authority who signed).
5. Validity: Validity period; a pair of UTC-Time values: "not before" and "not after."
6. Subject: DN of entity who owns the public key.
7. SubjectPublicKeyInfo: Public key value and algorithm OID.
8. IssuerUniqueIdentifier: Defined for v2, v3; optional.
9. SubjectUniqueIdentifier: Defined for v2, v3; optional.
10. Extensions: Defined only for v3; optional.

X.509 Warranty Certificate Extension Identifies the warranty policy associated with a X.509 public-key certificate. Often the Certification Authority (CA) will obtain an insurance policy to ensure coverage of the warranty. The certificate warranty provides an extended monetary coverage for the end entities. The certificate warranty primarily concerns the use, storage, and reliance on a certificate by a subscriber, a relying party, and the CA. It is common for a CA to establish reliance limits on the use of a certificate. It is not uncommon for a CA to attempt through contractual means to exclude its liability entirely. However, this undermines the confidence that commerce requires to gainfully use certificates. Alternatively, a CA may provide extended coverage for the use of the certificate. Usually, the subscriber pays for the extended warranty coverage. In turn, subscribers are covered by an appropriately drafted insurance policy. The certificate warranty is backed by an insurance policy issued by a licensed insurance company, which results in a financial backing that is far greater than that of the CA. This extra financial backing provides a further element of confidence necessary to encourage the use of certificates in commerce [r501].

X9.82 Pseudo-Random Number Generation The American National Standards Institute (ANSI) X9F1 committee is in the final stages of creating a standard for random number generation covering both true randomness generators and pseudo-random number generators. It includes a number of pseudo-random number generators based on hash functions, one of which will probably be based on Hash Message Authentication Code (HMAC) Secure Hash Algorithm (SHA) hash constructs (RFC 2104) [r166].

XACML See eXtensible Access Control Markup Language

XML (eXtensible Markup Language) A meta-language used to describe grammatical descriptions of objects and describing data structures in an open manner. It is similar in appearance to HyperText Markup Language (HTML), is platform-neutral, and can be used to represent both documents and data [r080, r503, r505].

XML Firewall See Extensible Markup Language (XML) Firewall

XOR Digital operation where "0" is generated if the compared bits are the same, and "1" is generated if they are different. This operation is often used in ciphers.

XrML See eXtensible rights Markup Language

XSS See Cross-Site Scripting

Zachman Framework An Enterprise Architecture framework developed by John Zachman providing a view of the subjects and models needed to develop a complete enterprise architecture. The framework is described pictorially by a two-dimensional table. A picture of this framework is available at the Zachman Institute for Framework Advancement (ZIFA) website (www.zifa.com). The Zachman Framework is a widely used approach for developing and/or documenting an enterprise-wide information systems architecture. Zachman based his framework on practices in traditional architecture and engineering. This resulted in an approach which on the vertical axis provides multiple perspectives of the overall architecture, and on the horizontal axis a classification of the various artifacts of the architecture.

Zero Dispersion Wavelength (optical transmission term) A wavelength at which the net chromatic dispersion of an optical fiber is nominally zero. This arises when waveguide dispersion cancels out material dispersion.

Zero-Error Probabilistic Polynomial-Time (ZPP)–Complexity Problem The class of problems that can be solved with zero error, but for which the algorithm may, with low probability, run for a long time (it should be that the expected time is polynomial in the input length) [r094].

Zeroize Use erasure or other means to render stored data unusable and unrecoverable, particularly a key stored in a cryptographic module or other device [r013].

ZigBee A standardized middleware that operates on top of the recently-approved IEEE protocols

(IEEE 802.15.4) used for sensor networks and telemetry applications [r021]. (IEEE 802.15.4 is the physical radio and ZigBee as the logical network and application software.)

Zombie   (aka zombie army or botnet) A computer that has been hijacked by a hacker and used (without its owner's knowledge) to send spam or participate in other malicious activity. Often, a collection of these zombies, called a zombie army, is used to perform distributed denial of service attacks (DDoS).

Zombie Army   A collection of highjacked computers (zombies) that are collectively used for malicious activities. Often, zombie armies are used to perform distributed denial of service attacks (DDoS).

Zone   Term used in various contexts. A logical group of network devices.

Zone Apex   (in DNSSEC context) Term used to describe the name at the child's side of a zone cut [r069].

Zone Signing Key (ZSK)   (DNSSEC context) An authentication key that corresponds to a private key used to sign a zone. Typically, a zone-signing key will be part of the same DNS public-key (DNSKEY) RRset as the key-signing key whose corresponding private key signs this DNSKEY RRset, but the zone-signing key is used for a slightly different purpose and may differ from the key-signing key in other ways, such as validity lifetime. Designating an authentication key as a zone-signing key is purely an operational issue; DNSSEC validation does not distinguish between zone signing keys and other DNSSEC authentication keys, and it is possible to use a single key as both a key signing key and a zone signing key [r069].

Zone Transfer   Transfer when a secondary name server for a zone, also sometimes referred to as a slave server, gets the zone data from another name server that is authoritative for the zone, called its master server. When a secondary name server starts up, it contacts its master server and requests a copy of the zone data for which it is responsible, storing it in the event a request is made for information in that zone [r084].

References and Sources

[r001] IEEE P802.3ae 10Gb/s Ethernet Task Force, http://grouper.ieee.org/groups/802/3/ae/

[r002] D. Minoli, *Ethernet-Based Metro Area Networks—Planning and Designing the Provider Network* (co-authored), McGraw-Hill, New York, 2002.

[r003] D. Minoli, *Next-Generation SONET-Based Metro Area Networks—Planning and Designing the Provider Network,* McGraw-Hill, New York, 2002.

[r004] Ethernet Hardware, http://wiki.ethereal.com/EthernetHardware

[r005] http://www.devx.com/wireless/Door/11314

[r006] M. Garcia-Martin, Input 3rd-Generation Partnership Project (3GPP) Release 5 Requirements on the Session Initiation Protocol (SIP), RFC 4083, May 2005.

[r007] *Essentials in Telecommunications,* UMTS Essentials, Wiley, 2003, Chichester, West Sussex, U.K.

[r008] IPv6 Portal, http://www.ipv6tf.org/meet/faqs.php

[r009] http://www.investorwords.com/ Copyright © 1997–2005 by InvestorGuide.com, Inc.

[r010] http://www.moneyextra.com/glossary/gl00009.htm

[r011] *Essentials in Telecommunications,* GSM Essentials, Wiley, 2003, Chichester, West Sussex, U.K.

[r012] C. Perkins and P. Calhoun, "Authentication, Authorization, and Accounting (AAA) Registration Keys for Mobile IPv4," RFC 3957, March 2005.

[r013] R. Shirey, Internet Security Glossary, RFC 2828, May 2000, Copyright © The Internet Society, 2000. All Rights Reserved. This document and translations of it may be copied and furnished to others, and derivative works that comment on or otherwise explain it or assist in its implementation may be prepared, copied, published, and distributed, in whole or in part, without restriction of any kind, provided that the above copyright notice and this paragraph are included on all such copies and derivative works.

Minoli–Cordovana's Authoritative Computer and Network Security Dictionary. By Daniel Minoli and James Cordovana
Copyright © 2006 John Wiley & Sons, Inc.

[r014] *Essentials in Telecommunications,* GPRS Essentials, Wiley, 2003, Chichester, West Sussex, U.K.

[r015] M. Day, J. Rosenberg, and H. Sugano, "A Model for Presence and Instant Messaging," RFC 2778, February 2000.

[r016] M. Fischlin, "Completely Non-Malleable Schemes," Institute for Theoretical Computer Science, ETH Zurich, Switzerland, marc.fischlin@inf.ethz.ch, http://www.fischlin.de/

[r017] MasterCard and Visa, "SET Secure Electronic Transaction Specification, Book 1: Business Description," version 1.0, May 31, 1997.

[r018] MasterCard and Visa, "SET Secure Electronic Transaction Specification, Book 2: Programmer's Guide," version 1.0, May 31, 1997.

[r019] http://searchcio.techtarget.com/sDefinition/0, sid19_gci809833,00.html

[r020] International Telecommunications Union—Telecommunication Standardization Sector (formerly "CCITT"), Recommendation X.680, "Information Technology—Abstract Syntax Notation One (ASN.1) —Specification of Basic Notation," 15 November 1994 (equivalent to ISO/IEC 8824-1).

[r021] D. Minoli, *Wireless Sensor Networks* (co-authored with K. Sohraby and T. Znati), Wiley, New York 2006.

[r022] Y. Zhang, "A Multilayer IP Security Protocol for TCP Performance Enhancement in Wireless Networks," *IEEE Journal on Selected Areas in Communications,* Vol. 22, No. 4, pp. 767–776, May 2004.

[r023] Microsoft Windows CE .NET 4.2, "IPv6 addresses," MSDN, May 18, 2004, http://msdn.microsoft.com/library/default.asp?url=/library/en-us/wcetcpip/html/cmconmulticastipv6addresses.asp

[r024] T. Narten, E. Nordmark, and W. Simpson, RFC 2461, Neighbor Discovery for IP Version 6 (IPv6), December 1998.

[r025] J. Rosenberg, H. Schulzrinne, G. Camarillo, A. Peterson, R. Sparks, M. Handley, and E. Schooler, "SIP: Session Initiation Protocol," RFC 3261, June 2002. This document and translations of it may be copied and furnished to others, and derivative works that comment on or otherwise explain it or assist in its implementation may be prepared, copied, published, and distributed, in whole or in part, without restriction of any kind, provided that the above copyright notice and this paragraph are included on all such copies and derivative works.

[r026] V. Manral, R. White, and A. Shaikh, OSPF Benchmarking Terminology and Concepts," RFC 4062, April 2005.

[r027] M. Day, S. Aggarwal, G. Mohr, and J. Vincent, Instant Messaging/Presence Protocol Requirements, RFC 2779, February 2000.

[r028] D. McGrew and J. Viega, The Use of Galois Message Authentication Code (GMAC) in IPsec ESP, March 2005, IETF draft-mcgrew-aes-gmac-esp-00.txt

[r029] http://www.zzyzx.com/Services/Technical_Support/Glossary/

[r030] M. Stiemerling, J. Quittek, and T. Taylor, "Middlebox Communications (MIDCOM) Protocol Semantics," RFC 3989, February 2005.

[r031] Air Force Fact Sheets, Air Intelligence Agency, http://usmilitary.about.com/library/milinfo/affacts/blairintelligenceagency.htm

[r032] K. Gjøsteen, "Subgroup Membership Problems and Public Key Cryptosystems," Dr. ing. Thesis, Department of Mathematical Sciences, Norwegian University of Science and Technology, 2004.

[r033] http://www.hubbell-premise.com/Technical/Standards.htm

[r034] J. Klensin, "Terminology for Describing Internet Connectivity," RFC 4084, May 2005 (BCP: 104).

[r035] T. Bradley, Glossary, http://netsecurity.about.com/library/glossary/bldef-appg.htm

[r036] SSH Communications Security, Cryptography White Papers, Valimotie 17, FI-00380 Helsinki, Finland, Phone: +358 20 500 7000, http://www.ssh.com

[r037] P. Srisuresh, J. Kuthan, J. Rosenberg, A. Molitor, and A. Rayhan, "Middlebox Communication Architecture and Framework," RFC 3303, August 2002.

[r038] R. P. Swale, P. A. Mart, P. Sijben, S. Brim, and M. Shore, "Middlebox Communications (midcom) Protocol Requirements," RFC 3304, August 2002.

[r039] T. Dierks and C. Allen, The TLS Protocol, Version 1.0, IETF RFC 2246, January 1999. Copyright © The Internet Society (1999). All Rights Reserved. This document and translations of it may be copied and furnished to others, and derivative works that comment on or otherwise explain it or assist in its implementation may be prepared, copied, published, and distributed, in whole or in part, without restriction of any kind, provided that the above copyright notice and this paragraph are included on all such copies and derivative works.

[r040] D. Newman, "Benchmarking Terminology for Firewall Performance," IETF RFC 2647, 1999.

[r041] M. V. Hayden, National Information Assurance

(IA) Glossary, CNSS Instruction No. 4009, Revised May 2003, Committee on National Security Systems, CNSS Secretariat (I42). National Security Agency. 9800 Savage Road, STE 6716, Ft Meade, MD, 20755-6716. Phone: (410) 854-6805. Fax: (410) 854-6814, nstissc@radium.ncsc

[r042] D. Minoli, *Enterprise Networking: Fractional T1 to SONET, Frame Relay to BISDN,* Artech House, Norwood, MA, 1992.

[r43]ATA-ATAPI.COM Information, Test Software and Consulting Services for Developers of Products using ATA (PATA, IDE/EIDE), Serial ATA (SATA), ATAPI, and CE-ATA and Other ATA Related Interfaces, http://www.ata-atapi.com/

[r044] D. Minoli, *MPOA: Building State-of-the Art ATM Intranets* (co-authored), Prentice-Hall/Manning, Englewood Cliffs, NJ, 1998.

[r045] D. Minoli, *Client/Server Applications on ATM Networks* (co-authored), Prentice-Hall/Manning, Englewood Cliffs, NJ, 1997.

[r046] D. Minoli, *Planning and Managing Corporate ATM-Based Network* (co-authored), Prentice-Hall/Manning, Englewood Cliffs, NJ, 1997.

[r047] D. Minoli, *LAN, LAN Emulation, and ATM* (co-authored), Artech House, Norwood, MA, 1997.

[r048] D. Minoli, *Cell Relay Service and ATM for Corporate Environments* (co-authored), McGraw-Hill, New York, 1994.

[r049] D. Minoli, *IP Applications with ATM* (co-authored), McGraw-Hill, New York, 1998.

[r050] D. Minoli, *Video Dialtone Technology: Digital Video over ADSL, HFC, FTTC, and ATM* McGraw-Hill, New York, 1995.

[r051] D. Minoli, *IP Applications with ATM* (co-authored) (Chinese translation), McGraw-Hill, 2002.

[r052] D. Minoli, *Planning and Managing ATM Networks* (coauthored) (Chinese translation), McGraw-Hill, 1998.

[r053] D. Minoli, *Voice over MPLS,* McGraw-Hill, New York, 2002.

[r054] D. Minoli, *Network Layer Switched Services* (co-authored), Wiley, New York, 1998.

[r055] D. Minoli, *Telecommunication Technologies Handbook,* 2nd edition, Artech House, Norwood, MA, 2003.

[r056] R. K., Nichols, *Defending Your Digital Assets,* McGraw-Hill, New York, 2000.

[r057] http://www.infosec.uga.edu/glossary.html

[r058] L. Fang (Ed.), "Security Framework for Provider-Provisioned Virtual Private Networks (PPVPNs)," RFC 4111, July 2005.

[r059] B. Kaliski, "On Hash Function Firewalls in Signature Schemes," Topics in Cryptology—Cryptographer's Track, RSA Conference (CT-RSA) 2002, Vol. 2271 of Lecture Notes in Computer Science, Springer-Verlag, New York, 2002, pp. 1–16.

[r060] Collaborative ITU and ISO/IEC meeting on the Directory, "Final Proposed Draft Amendment on Certificate Extensions," April 1999.

[r061] International Telecommunications Union—Telecommunication Standardization Sector (formerly "CCITT"), Recommendation X.509, "Information Technology—Open Systems Interconnection—The Directory: Authentication Framework" (equivalent to ISO 9594-8).

[r062] http://www.csoonline.com/glossary/category.cfm?ID=13

[r063] National Institute of Standards and Technology, "SKIPJACK and KEA Algorithm Specifications," version 2, May 29, 1998 (http://csrc.nist.gov/encryption/skipjack-kea.htm)

[r064] http://www.anti-keyloggers.com/glossary.html

[r065] Critical Infrastructure Glossary of Terms and Acronyms, http://www.ciao.gov/CIAO_Document_Library/glossary/A.htm

[r066] New Technologies, Inc. (NTI) Promotional Material, http://www.forensics-intl.com/def2.html

[r067] NIST, http://csrc.nist.gov/fasp/index.html

[r068] R. Pearce-Moses, "A Glossary of Archival and Records Terminology," http://www.archivists.org/glossary/term_details.asp?DefinitionKey=915

[r068a] ITU-T, "Security In Telecommunications And Information Technology, An Overview of Issues and the Deployment of Existing ITU-T Recommendations for Secure Telecommunications," 2003. Geneva, CH.

[r069] R. Arends, R. Austein, M. Larson, D. Massey, and S. Rose, "DNS Security Introduction and Requirements," RFC 4033, March 2005.

[r070] J. Kohl and C. Neuman, "The Kerberos Network Authentication Service (V5)," RFC 1510, September 1993.

[r071] S. Kent and R. Atkinson, "IP Authentication Header," RFC 2402, November 1998.

[r072] J. Schiller, "Strong Security Requirements for Internet Engineering Task Force Standard Protocols," RFC 3365, BCP: 61, August 2002.

[r073] D. Stanley, J. Walker, and B. Aboba, "Extensible

Authentication Protocol (EAP) Method Requirements for Wireless LANs," RFC 4017, March 2005.

[r074] T. Johnson, S. Okubo, and S. Campos, "H.350 Directory Services," RFC 3944, December 2004.

[r075] GAO Executive Report—B-266140, *Information Security—Computer Attacks at Department of Defense Pose Increasing Risks,* May 1996.

[r076] http://www.cerias.purdue.edu/about/history/coast_resources/idcontent/ids.html

[r077] NSA Glossary of Terms Used in Security and Intrusion Detection, http://www.sans.org/newlook/resources/glossary.htm

[r078] RSA Laboratories, Industry Liaison information.

[r079] D. Papadimitriou, J. Drake, J. Ash, and L. Ong, "Requirements for Generalized MPLS (GMPLS) Signaling Usage and Extensions for Automatically Switched Optical Network (ASON), RFC 4139, July 2005.

[r080] D. Minoli, *A Networking Approach to Grid Computing,* Wiley, Hoboken, NJ, 2005.

[r081] A. Nagarajan, "Generic Requirements for Provider Provisioned Virtual Private Networks (PPVPN)," RFC 3809, June 2004.

[r082] L. Andersson and T. Madsen, Provider Provisioned Virtual Private Network (VPN) Terminology, IETF RFC 4026, March 2005.

[r083] P. Pan, G. Swallow, and A. Atlas (Eds.), "Fast Reroute Extensions to RSVP-TE for LSP Tunnels," RFC 4090, May 2005.

[r084] Glossary, http://infocenter.guardiandigital.com/manuals/SecureProfessional/node277.html

[r085] http://www.ppiaf.org/Reports/LaborToolkit/Toolkit/module7/assessing_financial_returns.html

[r086] H. Berkowitz, E. Davies (Eds.), S. Hares, P. Krishnaswamy, and M. Lepp, "Terminology for Benchmarking BGP Device Convergence in the Control Plane," RFC 4098, June 2005.

[r087] Staff, "AGMA and KPMG Spotlight Counterfeiting as Significant Threat to Information Technology Sector; Whitepaper Highlights Dangers and Early Warning Signs of IT Counterfeiting; Offers Detection and Prevention Strategies," BUSINESS WIRE, August 16, 2005, http://www.nasdaq.com//aspxcontent/newsstory.aspx?selected=NT&symbol=CSCO%60&symbol=T%60&symbol=LU%60&symbol=NT%60&symbol=COF%60&textpath=20050816%5CAC-QBIZ200508161100BIZWIRE%5FUSPR%5F%5F%5F%5F%5FBW5253%2Ehtm&cdtime=08%2F16%2F2005+11%3A00AM. Also www.agmaglobal.org

[r088] E. Rosen, "BGP/MPLS IP VPNs," Work in Progress, IETF, October 2004.

[r089] A. L. Young, Cryptovirology FAQ, Version 1.24, Last updated: June 5, 2005, http://www.cryptovirology.com/cryptovfiles/cryptovirologyfaqver1.html. This document is copyright © 2004–2005 Adam L. Young. Permission to copy, and distribute the contents of this document, in any medium for any purpose and without fee or royalty is hereby granted, provided that you include a link or URL to the original FAQ on www.cryptovirology.com and provided that ALL copies retain the copyright and any other proprietary notices contained therein. Furthermore, a copy of this FAQ must include this copyright notice.

[r090] R. Naraine, "From Melissa to Zotob: 10 Years of Windows Worms," August 24, 2005, eweek.com, http://www.eweek.com/article2/0,1895,1851792,00.asp

[r091] L. Blum, M. Blum, and M. Shub, "A Simple Unpredictable Pseudo-Random Number Generator," *SIAM Journal on Computing,* Vol. 15, No. 2, pp. 364–383, 1986.

[r092] http://searchsmb.techtarget.com/sDefinition/0,sid44_gci213813,00.html

[r093] WhatIs@lists.techtarget.com, April 28, 2005.

[r094] A. Stiglic, "The PRIMES is in P little FAQ, Last Updated," October 25, 2004, http://crypto.cs.mcgill.ca/~stiglic/PRIMES_P_FAQ.html

[r095] http://www.protocols.com

[r096] S. Ostrowski, Computing Technology Industry Association Inc. (CompTIA), a nonprofit trade organization in Chicago.

[r097] W. Sawyer, "Management Information Base for Data over Cable Service Interface Specification (DOCSIS) Cable Modem Termination Systems for Subscriber Management," RFC 4036, April 2005.

[r098] S. Moriai, A. Kato, and M. Kanda, "Addition of Camellia Cipher Suites to Transport Layer Security (TLS)," RFC 4132, August 2005.

[r099] American National Standards Institute, "Financial Institution Message Authentication (Wholesale)," ANSI X9.9-1986, August 15, 1986.

[r100] D. Minoli, *First, Second, and Next Generation LANs,* McGraw-Hill, New York, 1994.

[r101] http://searchnetworking.techtarget.com/sDefinition/0,,sid7_gci954712,00.html

[r102] http://www.dqcs.com/networking/cabling.htm

[r103] R. Housley, W. Ford, W. Polk, and D. Solo, *Internet X.509 Public Key Infrastructure Certificate and CRL Profile,* RFC 2459, January 1999. Copyright © The In-

ternet Society (1999). This document and translations of it may be copied and furnished to others, and derivative works that comment on or otherwise explain it or assist in its implementation may be prepared, copied, published, and distributed, in whole or in part, without restriction of any kind, provided that the above copyright notice and this paragraph are included on all such copies and derivative works.

[r104] S. Chokhani and W. Ford, "Internet X.509 Public Key Infrastructure, Certificate Policy and Certification Practices Framework," RFC 2527, March 1999.

[r105] EuroPKI Certificate Policy, *VERSION 1.1,* January 2004, OID: 1.3.6.1.4.1.5255.1.1.1, http://www.europki.org/ca/root/cps/en_cp.pdf

[r106] U.S. Department of Commerce, "Public Key Infrastructure (PKI) Technical Specifications: Part A—Technical Concept of Operations," National Institute of Standards, September 4, 1998.

[r107] U.S. Department of Commerce, "Guideline for Computer Security Certification and Accreditation," FIPS PUB 102, September 27, 1983.

[r108] Security Policy for FORTEZZA Crypto Card, July 27, 1999, DOC. NO. D1014, CIIN: CE100 REV. D, http://csrc.nist.gov/cryptval/140-1/140sp/140sp069.pdf

[r109] S. Kent, "Privacy Enhancement for Internet Electronic Mail, Part II: Certificate-Based Key Management," RFC 1422, February 1993.

[r110] American Bar Association, "Digital Signature Guidelines: Legal Infrastructure for Certification Authorities and Secure Electronic Commerce," Chicago, IL, August 1, 1996.

[r111] D. Atkins, "Threat Analysis of the Domain Name System (DNS)," IETF RFC 3833, August 2004.

[r112] W. Simpson, "PPP Challenge Handshake Authentication Protocol (CHAP)," RFC 1994, August 1996.

[r113] J. Klensin, R. Catoe, and P. Krumviede, "IMAP/POP AUTHorize Extension for Simple Challenge/Response," RFC 2195, September 1997.

[r114] H. Krawczyk, M. Bellare, and R. Canetti, "HMAC: Keyed- Hashing for Message Authentication," RFC 2104, February 1997.

[r115] K. Raeburn, "Encryption and Checksum Specifications for Kerberos 5," RFC 3961," February 2005.

[r116] U.S. Department of Commerce, "DES Modes of Operation," FIPS PUB 81, December 2, 1980.

[r117] P. Karn, P. Metzger, and W. Simpson, "The ESP DES-CBC Transform," RFC 1829, August 1995.

[r118] R. Pereira and R. Adams, "The ESP CBC-Mode Cipher Algorithms," RFC 2451, November 1998.

[r119] D. Teare, C. Paquet, "CCNP Self-Study: Advanced IP Addressing," Cisco Press, Jun 11, 2004, http://www.ciscopress.com/articles/article.asp?p=174107&seqNum=4&rl=1

[r120] National Computer Security Center, "Glossary of Computer Security Terms," NCSC-TG-004, version 1, October 21, 1988 (part of the Rainbow Series).

[r121] The Wireless Developer Network (http://www.wirelessdevnet.com/newswire-less/feb012002.html) is an on-line community for information technology professionals interested in mobile computing and communications.

[r122] http://en.wikipedia.org/wiki/Coding_theory

[r123] Thomas M. Cover and Joy A. Thomas, *Elements of Information Theory,* Wiley, New York, 1991. ISBN 0471062596.

[r124] S. Roman, J. H. Ewing (Ed.), F. W. Gehring (Ed.), and P. R. Halmos (Ed.), *Coding and Information Theory,* Springer-Verlag, New York, January 1992.

[r125] C. Xing, S. Lingayah, and San Ling, *Coding Theory: A First Course,* Cambridge University Press, Boston, January 2004.

[r126] T. M. Cover and J. A. Thomas, *Elements of Information Theory,* Wiley, New York, March 1991.

[r127] P. B. Garrett, *Making, Breaking Codes: Introduction to Cryptology,* Pearson Education, Englewood Cliffs, NJ, August 2000.

[r128] H. Niederreiter (Ed.), *Coding Theory and Cryptology, Lecture Notes Series,* Vol. 1, Contribution by University Press Singapore, August 2002.

[r129] J. Justesen and T. Hoholdt, *A Course in Error-Correcting Codes,* American Mathematical Society, Washington, DC, May 2004.

[r130] D. Stinson, *Cryptography: Theory and Practice,* 2nd edition, CRC Press, Boca Raton, FL, February 2002.

[r131] D. J. C. MacKay, *Information Theory, Inference and Learning Algorithms,* Cambridge University Press, Boston, October 2003.

[r132] W. Stallings, *Cryptography and Network Security: Principles and Practice,* 3rd edition, August 2002, Pearson Education, Englewood Cliffs, NJ.

[r133] S. Lin and D. J. Costello, *Error Control Coding,* 2nd edition, Prentice Hall, Englewood Cliffs, NJ, February 2002.

[r134] G. Di Crescenzo, J. Katz, R. Ostrovsky, and A. Smith, "Efficient and Non-Interactive Non-Mal-

leable Commitment," Telcordia Technologies, Inc., Department of Computer Science, Columbia University, Laboratory for Computer Science, MIT, http://www.cs.ucla.edu/~rafail/PUBLIC/52.pdf#search='nonmalleable%20Commit%20Decommit%20public%20key'

[r135] Common Criteria Implementation Board, "Common Criteria for Information Technology Security Evaluation, Part 1: Introduction and General Model," version 2.1, CCIB-99-01, August 1999.

[r136] http://www.networkdictionary.com/protocols/cmip.php

[r137] International Telecommunications Union—Telecommunication Standardization Sector (formerly "CCITT"), Recommendation X.520, "Information Technology—Open Systems Interconnection—The Directory: Selected Attribute Types."

[r138] R. Housley, "Cryptographic Message Syntax," RFC 2630, June 1999.

[r139] http://www.askcalea.net/

[r139a] J. H. Saltzer and M. D. Schroeder, "The Protection of Information in Computer Systems," *Communications of the ACM*, 17, 7 (July 1974). Also in *Proceedings of the IEEE*, Vol. 63, No. 9, September, 1975, pp. 1278–1308.

[r140] U.S. Department of Commerce, "General Procedures for Registering Computer Security Objects," National Institute of Standards Interagency Report 5308, December 1993.

[r141] IBM Corp, Promotional Material, Autonomic Computing Glossary, IBM Corporation, 1133 Westchester Avenue, White Plains, NY 10604, United States, http://www.ibm.com

[r142] Steering Committee for Cyberinfrastructure Research and Development in the Atmospheric Sciences (CyRDAS) (http://www.cyrdas.org), Division of Atmospheric Sciences of the National Science Foundation, http://www.geo.nsf.gov/atm/, 4201 Wilson Boulevard, Room 775, Arlington, VA, 22230, Phone: (703) 292-8500, Fax: (703) 292-9042.

[r143] R. Bajcsy, Assistant Director for Computer and Information Science and Engineering at the National Science Foundation, House Science Committee Hearing on *Beyond Silicon Computing: Quantum and Molecular Computing*, September 12, 2000.

[r144] D. Minoli, *Nanotechnology Applications to Telecommunications and Networking*, Wiley, Hoboken, NJ, 2005.

[r145] National Institute of Standards and Technology, "Pervasive Computing 2001," May 1–2, 2001, Gaithersburg MD, http://www.nist.gov/pc2001/

[r146] J. West, *The Quantum Computer, An Introduction*, 2000, Computer Science Department, California Institute of Technology, 1200 E. California Boulevard, MC 256-80, Pasadena, CA 91125. Phone: (626) 395-6251.

[r147] D. Deutsch, "Quantum Theory, The Church–Turing Principle and The Universal Quantum Computer," *Proceedings of the Royal Society of London, Series A,* Vol. 400, pp. 96–117, 1985.

[r148] D. Deutsch and A. Ekert, "Quantum Computation," *Physics World,* Vol. 11, No. 3, pp. 47–52, March 1998.

[r149] R. P. Feynman, "Simulating Physics with Computers," *International Journal of Theoretical Physics,* Vol. 21, 467, p. 1982.

[r150] B. J. Rhodes et al., "Wearable Computing Meets Ubiquitous Computing: Reaping The Best of Both Worlds," In: *The Proceedings of the Third International Symposium on Wearable Computers (ISWC '99)*, San Francisco, CA, October 18–19, 1999, pp. 141–149.

[r151] Mahi Networks, "Implementing A Constraint-Based Shortest Path First Algorithm in Intelligent Optical Networks," White Paper.

[r152] S. Suri, M. Waldvogel, D. Bauer, and P. R. Warkhede, "Profile-Based Routing and Traffic Engineering," Computer Communications, 2002.

[r153] T. Korkmaz and M. Krunz, "Multi-Constrained Optimal Path Selection," INFOCOM 2001.

[r154] K. Kar, M. Kodialam, and T. V. Lakshman, "Minimum Interference Routing of Bandwidth Guaranteed Tunnels with MPLS Traffic Engineering Applications," *IEEE Journal on Selected Areas in Communications,* Vol. 18, No. 12, pp. 2566–2579, December 2000.

[r155] G. Li, D. Wang, C. Kalmanek, and R. Doverspike, "Efficient Distributed Path Selection for Shared Restoration Connections," INFOCOM 2002.

[r156] Cisco, SAFE Layer 2 Security In-depth Version 2, http://www.cisco.com/en/US/netsol/ns340/ns394/ns171/ns128/networking_solutions_white_paper09186a008014870f.shtml#wp1002384

[r157] IT Governance Institute, 3701 Algonquin Road, Suite 1010, Rolling Meadows, IL, 60008. Phone: +1.847.590.7491, http://www.itgi.org/

[r158] http://guide.darwinmag.com/technology/web/intranet/

[r159] http://cipp.gmu.edu/cip/

[r160] International Standards Organization, "Information Processing Systems—Open Systems Interconnec-

tion Reference Model—[Part 1:] Basic Reference Model," ISO/IEC 7498-1. (Equivalent to ITU-T Recommendation X.200). "Part 2: Security Architecture," ISO/IEC 7499-2. "Part 4: Management Framework," ISO/IEC 7498-4.

[r161] G. Keizer, "Researcher: CPU No-Execute Bit Is No Big Security Deal," TechWeb.com, July 28, 2005, http://www.techweb.com/wire/security/166403451

[r162] R. J. Anderson, *Security Engineering: A Guide to Building Dependable Distributed Systems,* Chapter 7, Subsection 7.5.3—Covert Channels, Wiley, Hoboken, NJ, 2001.

[r163] V. Smyslov, "Simple Cryptographic Program Interface," RFC 2628, June 1999.

[r164] D. Moberg and R. Drummond, "MIME-Based Secure Peer-to-Peer Business Data Interchange Using HTTP," Applicability Statement 2, AS2, RFC 4130, July 2005.

[r165] R. Housley, Protecting Multiple Contents with the Cryptographic Message Syntax (CMS), IETF RFC 4073, May 2005.

[r166] D. Eastlake, 3rd, J. Schiller, and S. Crocker, "Randomness Requirements for Security," RFC 4086, June 2005.

[r167] U.S. Department of Commerce, "Security Requirements for Cryptographic Modules," FIPS PUB 140-1, January 11, 1994.

[r168] T. Aura, "Cryptographically Generated Addresses (CGA)," RRFC 3972, March 2005.

[r169] T. Aura, "Cryptographically Generated Addresses (CGA)," 6th Information Security Conference (ISC'03), Bristol, UK, October 2003.

[r170] S. Bellovin, J. Schiller, and C. Kaufman (Eds.), "Security Mechanisms for the Internet," RFC 3631, December 2003. Copyright © The Internet Society, 2003. All Rights Reserved. This document and translations of it may be copied and furnished to others, and derivative works that comment on or otherwise explain it or assist in its implementation may be prepared, copied, published and distributed, in whole or in part, without restriction of any kind, provided that the above copyright notice and this paragraph are included on all such copies and derivative works.

[r171] I. Damgard, "Definitions and results for Cryptosystems," October 12, 2004, http://www.daimi.au.dk/~ivan/cryptosystems.pdf

[r172] A. Young and M. Yung, "Cryptovirology: Extortion-Based Security Threats and Countermeasures,"

IEEE Symposium on Security & Privacy, pp. 129–141, May 6–8, 1996.

[r173] A. Young and M. Yung, *Malicious Cryptography: Exposing Cryptovirology,* Wiley, Hoboken, NJ, 2004.

[r174] S. Schechter and M. Smith, "How Much Security Is Enough to Stop a Thief?" In: *Proceedings of Financial Crypto,* Springer-Verlag, Berlin, 2003.

[r175] A. Young, "Cryptovirology and the Dark Side of Black-Box Cryptography," Master's Thesis, Moti Yung (Advisor), Computer Science S6902, Columbia University Department of Comp. Science, Summer, 1995.

[r176] A. Young and M. Yung, "Deniable Password Snatching: On the Possibility of Evasive Electronic Espionage," *IEEE Symposium on Security & Privacy,* pp. 224–235, May 4–7, 1997.

[r177] S. Schechter and M. Smith, "Access for Sale—A New Class of Worm," In: *Proceedings of WORM '03,* ACM, 2003.

[r178] National Institute for Standards and Technology (NIST), "Security Requirements for Cryptographic Modules," FIPS PUB 140-2, May 25, 2001.

[r179] National Institute for Standards and Technology (NIST), "Digital Signature Standard (DSS)," FIPS PUB 186-2, January 27, 2000.

[r180] A. Young, "Non-Zero Sum Games and Survivable Malware," 4th Annual IEEE Information Assurance Workshop, United States Military Academy, West Point, NY, 2003.

[r181] G. J. Simmons, "Subliminal Channels: Past and Present," *IEEE European Transactions on Telecommunication,* Vol. 5, No. 4, pp. 459–473, 1994.

[r182] M. Bishop, *Computer Security: Art and Science,* Addison-Wesley-Longman, Reading, MA, 2003.

[r183] R. Slade, *Robert Slade's Guide to Computer Viruses,* Springer-Verlag, New York, 1994.

[r184] U.S. Department of Commerce, "Computer Data Authentication," FIPS PUB 113, 30 May 1985.

[r185] U.S. Department of Commerce, "Data Encryption Standard (DES)," FIPS PUB 46-2, December 30, 1993.

[r186] S. Kent and R. Atkinson, "Security Architecture for the Internet Protocol," RFC 2401 November 1998 (Obsoletes RFC 1825 and Updated by RFC 3168).

[r187] M. Lesk, M. R. Stytz, and R. L. Trope, "Averting Security Missteps in Outsourcing," IEEE Computer Society, 1540-7993/05/$20.00, IEEE Security & Privacy.

[r188] H. Chaskar and R. Koodli, "MPLS and DiffServ for UMTS QoS in GPRS Core Network Architecture,"

Nokia Research Center White Paper, http://www.isoc.org/isoc/conferences/inet/01/CD_proceedings/T56/MPLSDiff.htm, 2000.

[r189] J. Pagonis, "GPRS Facts for the Internet Application Developer—Part I," Symbian White Paper, July 2003, www.symbian.com

[r190] http://www.microsoft.com/technet/security/topics/policiesandprocedures/secrisk/srsgch06.mspx

[r191] ANSI X3.106, "American National Standard for Information Systems—Data Link Encryption," American National Standards Institute, 1983.

[r192] W. Tuchman, "Hellman Presents No Shortcut Solutions to DES," *IEEE Spectrum,* Vol. 16, No. 7, pp. 40–41, July 1979.

[r193] J. Hughes, IEEE Standard for Encrypted Storage, IEEE Security in Storage Working Group, http://www.computer.org/computer/homepage/1104/standards/

[r194] G. Malkin (Ed.), "Internet Users' Glossary," FYI 18, RFC 1983, August 1996.

[r195] U.S. Department of Defense, Directive 5200.28, "Security Requirements for Automated Information Systems (AISs)," March 21, 1988.

[r196] D. Hamlet, "Foundations of Software Testing: Dependability Theory," *ACM SIGSOFT Software Engineering Notes,* Vol. 19, No. 5, pp. 128–139, December 1994.

[r197] M. Thomas, "Software in Practice: A Series of Four Lectures on Why Software Projects Fail, and What You Can Do About It," Praxis High Integrity Systems Ltd., Oxford University Computing Laboratory, web.comlab.ox.ac.uk/oucl/courses/topics04-05/poc/2005Lecture4.ppt

[r198] S. Park, P. Kim, and B. Volz, "Rapid Commit Option for the Dynamic Host Configuration Protocol version 4 (DHCPv4)," RFC 4039, March 2005.

[r199] http://www.networkpenetration.com/dhcp_flaws.html

[r200] U.S. National Information Systems Security Glossary. Also http://www.ffiec.gov/ffiecinfobase/booklets/information_secruity/08_glossary.html

[r201] Infosec@UGA, The University of Georgia, Office of Information Security, Athens, GA, 30602-1911.

[r202] University of Sydney, http://luddite.cst.usyd.edu.au/cgi-bin/twiki/view/Catie/MiniEssayThree

[r203] http://www.scala.com/definition/activex.html

[r204] A. Durand, B. Field-Elliot, E. Norlin, D. Waite, and G. Caruolo, SourceID, "Digital Identity Basics," Open Source Federated Identity Management http://www.sourceid.org/content/primer

[r205] NIST FIPS PUB 186, "Digital Signature Standard," National Institute of Standards and Technology, U.S. Department of Commerce, May 18, 1994.

[r206] U.S. Department of Commerce, "Digital Signature Standard (DSS)," FIPS PUB 186, 19 May 1994.

[r207] D. Minoli, *The Telecommunications Handbook,* K. Terplan and P. Morreale (Eds.), IEEE Press, 2000, Major Video Section.

[r208] J. Moteff, "Computer Security: A Summary of Selected Federal Laws, Executive Orders, and Presidential Directives," April 16, 2004, Congressional Research Service, The Library of Congress, Science and Technology Policy Resources, Science, and Industry Division.

[r209] International Telecommunications Union—Telecommunication Standardization Sector (formerly "CCITT"), Recommendation X.519, "Information Technology—Open Systems Interconnection—The Directory: Protocol Specifications."

[r210] International Telecommunications Union—Telecommunication Standardization Sector (formerly "CCITT"), Recommendation X.690, "Information Technology—ASN.1 Encoding Rules—Specification of Basic Encoding Rules (BER), Canonical Encoding Rules (CER) and Distinguished Encoding Rules (DER)," November 15, 1994 (equivalent to ISO/IEC 8825-1.)

[r211] International Telecommunications Union—Telecommunication Standardization Sector (formerly "CCITT"), Recommendation X.501, "Information Technology—Open Systems Interconnection—The Directory: Models."

[r212] C. Kaufman, "DASS: Distributed Authentication Security Service," RFC 1507, September 1993.

[r213] http://www.iqss.com/d2d.html

[r214] U.S. Department of Defense, "Department of Defense Trusted Computer System Evaluation Criteria," DoD 5200.28-STD, December 26, 1985.

[r215] R. Arends, R. Austein, M. Larson, D. Massey, and S. Rose, "Protocol Modifications for the DNS Security Extensions," RFC 4035, March 2005.

[r216] http://www.spampal.us/usermanual/glossary.htm

[r217] International Standards Organization, "Portable Operating System Interface for Computer Environments," ISO/IEC 9945-1:1990.

[r218] P. Mockapetris, "Domain Names—Concepts and Facilities," STD 13, RFC 1034, November 1987.

[r219] J. Kohl and C. Neuman, "Domain Name System Structure and Delegation," March 1994.

[r220] D. Eastlake, 3rd, "Domain Name System Security Extensions," RFC 2065, January 1997.

[r221] D. Eastlake, "Secure Domain Name System Dynamic Update," RFC 2137, April 1997.

[r222] D. EastLake, "DSA KEYs and SIGs in the Domain Name System (DNS)," RFC 2536, March 1999.

[r223] D. Piper, "The Internet IP Security Domain of Interpretation for ISAKMP," RFC 2407, November 1998.

[r224] *Sachin Shetty,* Introduction to Spyware Keyloggers, April 14, 2005, http://www.securityfocus.com/infocus/1829

[r225] S. Hollenbeck, "E.164 Number Mapping for the Extensible Provisioning Protocol (EPP)," FRC 4114, June 2005.

[r226] D. Minoli and E. Minoli, *Web Commerce Technology Handbook,* McGraw-Hill, New York, 1997.

[r227] J. Rosenberg, A Presence Event Package for the Session Initiation Protocol (SIP), RFC 3856, August 2004.

[r228] D. Minoli, *Telecommunication Technologies Handbook,* 1st edition, Artech House, Norwood, MA, 1991.

[r229] D. Minoli, *Technologias de Telecomunicaciones, Asociacion Hispanoamericana de Centros de Investigacion y Empresas de Telecomunicaciones,* 1994 (Spanish translation of *Telecommunication Technologies Handbook*).

[r230] D. Eastlake 3rd, "Electronic Commerce Modeling Language (ECML) Version 2 Specification," RFC 4112, June 2005.

[r231] S. Blake-Wilson, G. Karlinger, Y. Wang, "Using the Elliptic Curve Signature Algorithm (ECDSA) for XML Digital Signatures," IETF RFC 4050, April 2005.

[r232] American National Standards Institute, "Public Key Cryptography for the Financial Services Industry: The Elliptic Curve Digital Signature Algorithm (ECDSA)," X9.62-1998, ANSI approval 7 January 1999.

[r233] Network Appliance, Inc. (NetApp), NearStore® Online Archival Solutions, http://www.netapp.com/solutions/nearstore_archival.html

[r234] C. Malamud, "Policy-Mandated Labels Such as 'Adv:' in Email Subject Headers Considered Ineffective at Best," RFC 4096, May 2005.

[r235] S. Kent and R. Atkinson, "IP Encapsulating Security Payload (ESP)," RFC 2406, November 1998.

[r236] M. Carugi and D. McDysan, "Service require-ments for Layer 3 Virtual Private Networks," Work in Progress, IETF, July 2004.

[r237] A. Newton and M. Sanz, "IRIS: The Internet Registry Information Service (IRIS) Core Protocol," RFC 3981, January 2005.

[r238] U.S. Department of Commerce, "Glossary for Computer Systems Security," FIPS PUB 39, February 15, 1976.

[r239] U.S. Department of Commerce, "Escrowed Encryption Standard," FIPS PUB 185, February 9, 1994.

[r240] D. Minoli, *Expert Systems Applications in Integrated Network Management* (co-authored), Artech House, Norwood, MA, 1989.

[r241] H. Danisch, "The Exponential Security System TESS: An Identity-Based Cryptographic Protocol for Authenticated Key-Exchange (E.I.S.S. Report 1995/4)," RFC 1824, August 1995.

[r242] Cisco Systems Documentation.

[r243] L. Blunk and J. Vollbrecht, "PPP Extensible Authentication Protocol (EAP)," RFC 2284, March 1998.

[r244] D. Minoli, "Next-generation e-commerce/extranets," Session Chair, Supercomm, ENTNET, Chicago, IL, June 2005.

[r245] http://www.symbol.com/products/whitepapers/whitepapers_network_mgmt_in_wi.html

[r246] Federal Financial Institutions Examination Council's (FFIEC), http://www.ffiec.gov/

[r247] PowerOverEthernet.com Staff, "Quick Guide to Power Over Ethernet Technology," 27th April 2005, http://www.poweroverethernet.com/articles.php?article_id=271

[r248] J. Postel and J. Reynolds, "File Transfer Protocol (FTP)," STD 9, RFC 959, October 1985.

[r249] A. Gwinn, "Network Security for Trade Shows," RFC 2179, July 1997.

[r250] U.S. Department of Commerce, "Security Requirements for Cryptographic Modules," FIPS PUB 140-1, January 11, 1994.

[r251] http://www.computerhope.com/jargon/f/forwarde.htm

[r252] J. Rosenberg, J. Weinberger, C. Huitema, and R. Mahy, "STUN—Simple Traversal of User Datagram Protocol (UDP) Through Network Address Translators (NATs)," RFC 3489, March 2003. This document and translations of it may be copied and furnished to others, and derivative works that comment on or otherwise explain it or assist in its implementation may be prepared, copied, published, and distributed, in whole or in part, without restriction of any kind, provided

that the above copyright notice and this paragraph are included on all such copies and derivative works.

[r253] http://en.wikipedia.org/wiki/Fuzzy_logic

[r254] E. Mannie and D. Papadimitriou, "Generalized Multi-Protocol Label Switching (GMPLS) Extensions for Synchronous Optical Network (SONET) and Synchronous Digital Hierarchy (SDH) Control," RFC 3946, October 2004.

[r255] J. Linn, "Generic Security Service Application Program Interface, Version 2," RFC 2078, January 1997.

[r256] M. Baugher, R. Canetti, L. Dondeti, and F. Lindholm, Multicast Security (MSEC) Group Key Management Architecture, RFC 4046, April 2005.

[r257] Staff, "Protocols," http://www.Vovida.org/

[r258] P. Cheng and R. Glenn, "Test Cases for HMAC-MD5 and HMAC- SHA-1," RFC 2202, Sepember 1997.

[r259] C. Madson and R. Glenn, "The Use of HMAC-MD5-96 within ESP and AH," RFC 2403, November 1998.

[r260] C. Madson and R. Glenn, "The Use of HMAC-SHA-1-96 within ESP and AH," RFC 2404, November 1998.

[r261] H. Bondar, "Biometric Password Automation in the Enterprise—Issues and Solutions," Whitepaper, August 2004, DigitalPersona, Inc., 805 Veterans Boulevard Redwood City, CA 94063. Phone: (650) 261-6070, www.digitalpersona.com

[r262] Protegrity USA, Inc., 15 Bank Street, Stamford CT 06901. Phone: (203) 326-7200, http://www.protegrity.com/whitepapers/whitepapers/The_Protegrity_Compliance_Series_HIPAA.pdf

[r263] D. M'Raihi, M. Bellare, F. Hoornaert, D. Naccache, and O. Ranen, "HOTP: An HMAC-Based One Time Password Algorithm," IETF Internet Draft draft-mraihi-oath-hmac-otp-03.txt, October 2004.

[r264] Symantec Internet Security Threat Report, Attack Trends for Q3 and Q4 2002, Vol. III, February 2003.

[r265] D. Minoli and R. Bear, "Hyperperfect Numbers," *PME (Pi Mu Epsilon) Journal,* University of Oklahoma, Fall 1975, pp. 153–157.

[r266] D. Minoli, "Sufficient Forms for Generalized Perfect Numbers," *Annals, Faculty of Sciences, University Nation. Zaire,* Section Mathem, Vol. 4, No. 2, pp. 277–302, December 1978.

[r267] D. Minoli, Structural Issues for Hyperperfect Numbers, *Fibonacci Quarterly,* Vol. 19, No. 1, pp. 6–14, February 1981.

[r268] D. Minoli, "Issues In Non-Linear Hyperperfect

Numbers," *Mathematics of Computation,* Vol. 34, No. 150, pp. 639–645, April 1980.

[r269] D. Minoli, "New Results for Hyperperfect Numbers," *Abstracts American Mathematical Society,* Vol. 1, Issue 6, pp. 561, October 1980.

[r270] D. Minoli and W. Nakamine, "Mersenne Numbers Rooted On 3 for Number Theoretic Transforms," *1980 IEEE International Conference on Acoustics, Speech and Signal Processing.*

[r271] J. S. McCranie, "A Study of Hyperperfect Numbers," *Journal of Integer Sequences,* Vol. 3, 2000, http://www.math.uwaterloo.ca/JIS/VOL3/mccranie.html

[r272] http://en.wikipedia.org/wiki/Hyperperfect_number

[r273] D. Minoli, *Internet and Intranet Engineering,* McGraw-Hill, New York, 1997.

[r274] T. Berners-Lee, "Hypertext Markup Language—2.0," RFC 1866, November 1995.

[r275] R. Fielding, J. Gettys, J. Mogul, H. Frystyk, L. Masinter, P. Leach, and T. Berners-Lee, "Hypertext Transfer Protocol—HTTP/1.1," RFC 2616, June 1999.

[r276] G. Wrenn, "Securing Web services: A Job for The XML Firewall," March 8, 2004, http://searchsecurity.techtarget.com/tip/1,289483,sid14_gci954170,00.html?Offer=SEcpwslg25

[r277] M. St. Johns, "Identification Protocol," RFC 1413, February 1993.

[r278] Verisign Corporation, Identity Federation White Paper, http://www.verisign.com/static/016556.pdf

[r279] F. Maino, "IEEE P1619- Security for Storage Data at Rest," Cisco Systems, http://www.t10.org/ftp/t10/document.04/04-146r0.pdf

[r280] S. Bradner, IETF BCP-9 (RFC 2026), "The Internet Standards Process," Revision October 29, 1996.

[r281] IETF RFC Index—Anne & Lynn Wheeler—2005/05/15, http://www.garlic.com/~lynn/rfcietf.htm

[r282] J. Touch, L. Eggert, and Y. Wang, "Use of IPsec Transport Mode for Dynamic Routing," RFC 3884, September 2004.

[r283] J. Myers, "IMAP4 Authentication Mechanisms," RFC 1731, December 1994.

[r284] Steve Duplessie, "A Blueprint for Tiered Storage," An *IT Briefing* produced by SearchStorage.com, 2004, http://images.apple.com/xserve/raid/pdf/Tiered_Storage_Whitepaper.pdf#search='Tiered%20Storage'

[r285] Information Assurance Technical Framework Forum, http://www.iatf.net/protection_profiles/overview.cfm

[r286] http://en.wikipedia.org/wiki/Information_theory

[r287] C. E. Shannon and Warren Weaver, *The Mathematical Theory of Communication,* University of Illinois Press, Champaign, IL, 1963.

[r288] C. Madson and N. Doraswamy, "The ESP DES-CBC Cipher Algorithm with Explicit IV," RFC 2405, November 1998.

[r289] D. Minoli, *Signaling Principles for Frame Relay and Cell Relay Services* (co-authored), Artech House, Norwood, MA, 1994.

[r290] X. Lai, "On the Design and Security of Block Ciphers," *ETH Series in Information Processing,* Vol. 1, Hartung-Gorre Verlag, Konstanz, 1992.

[r291] B. Schneier, *Applied Cryptography,* Wiley, New York, 1994.

[r292] J. Postel, "Internet Control Message Protocol," STD 5, RFC 792, September 1981.

[r293] S. Bradner, "The Internet Standards Process—Revision 3," BCP 9, RFC 2026, March 1994.

[r294] A. Ramos, "IETF Identification and Security Guidelines," RFC 2323, 1 April 1998.

[r295] P. Hoffman and S. Bradner, "Defining the IETF," RFC 3233, February 2002.

[r296] P. Hoffman, "Algorithms for Internet Key Exchange Version 1 (IKEv1)," RFC 4109, May 2005.

[r297] S. Andersen, A. Duric, H. Astrom, R. Hagen, W. Kleijn, and J. Linden, "Internet Low Bit Rate Codec (iLBC)," RFC 3951, December 2004.

[r298] M. Crispin, "Internet Message Access Protocol—Version 4 Revision 1," RFC 2060, December 1996.

[r299] J. Postel, "Internet Protocol," STD 5, RFC 791, September 1981.

[r300] S. Deering and R. Hinden, "Internet Protocol, Version 6 (IPv6) Specification," RFC 2460, December 1998.

[r301] D. Maughan, M. Schertler, M. Schneider, and J. Turner, "Internet Security Association and Key Management Protocol (ISAKMP)," RFC 2408, November 1998.

[r302] B. Carpenter (Ed.), "Architectural Principles of the Internet," RFC 1958, June 1996.

[r303] I. Kantzavelou and A. Patel, "An Attack Detection System for Secure Computer Systems—Design of ADS." In: *Proceedings of the 12th International Information Security Conference,* May 1996, pp. 1–16.

[r304] I. Kantzavelou and S. K. Katsikas, "An Attack Detection System For Secure Computer Systems—Outline of the Solution." In: *Proceedings of the 13th International Information Security Conference,* May 1997, pp. 123–135.

[r305] P. Innella, "A Brief History of Intrusion Detection, Navy Information Assurance," https://infosec.navy .mil/ps/?t=infosecprodsservices/infosecprodsser-vices.tag&bc=infosecprodsservices/bc_ids.html, Tetrad Digital Integrity, LLC.

[r306] D. Lehmann, Siemens CERT, http://www.sans .org/resources/idfaq

[r307] R. Hinden and S. Deering, "IP Version 6 Addressing Architecture," RFC 2373, July 2998.

[r308] L. Andersson and E. Rosen, "Framework for Layer 2 Virtual Private Networks (L2VPNs)," Work in Progress, IETF, June 2004.

[r309] D. Harkins and D. Carrel, "The Internet Key Exchange (IKE)," RFC 2409, November 1998.

[r310] P. Karn, P. Metzger, and W. Simpson, "The ESP Triple DES Transform," RFC 1851, September 1995.

[r311] Alliance for Telecommunications Industry Solutions (ATIS), www.atis.org

[r312] Cisco Systems, VPN Services, Managed VPN—Comparison of MPLS, IPSec, and SSL Architectures, http://www.cisco.com/en/US/netsol/ns341/ns121/ns19 3/networking_solutions_white_paper0900aecd801b1b 0f.shtml

[r313] R. Kreuter, RTP Payload Format for a 64 kbit/s Transparent Call, RFC 4040, April 2005.

[r314] M-K. Shin, Ed., Y-G. Hong, J. Hagino, P. Savola, E. M. Castro, "Application Aspects of IPv6 Transition," RFC 4038, March 2005.

[r315] G. Stoneburner, A. Goguen, and A. Feringa, "Risk Management Guide for Information Technology Systems—Recommendations of the National Institute of Standards and Technology," Special Publication 800-30, July 2002, Computer Security Division Information Technology Laboratory, National Institute of Standards and Technology Gaithersburg, MD 20899-8930. [This document may be used by non-governmental organizations on a voluntary basis. It is not subject to copyright.]

[r316] D. Minoli, *Imaging in Corporate Environments—Technology and Communication,* McGraw-Hill, New York, 1994.

[r317] Kerberos Glossary, http://www.lns.cornell.edu/ public/COMP/krb5/user-guide/user-guide_4.html

[r318] A. Young, and M. Yung, "The Dark Side of Black-Box Cryptography, or: Should We Trust Capstone?" In: *Proceedings of Crypto '96,* Neal Koblitz (Ed.), LNCS 1109, Springer-Verlag, New York, 1996, pp. 89–103.

[r319] A. Young and M. Yung, "Kleptography: Using Cryptography Against Cryptography." In: *Proceedings of Eurocrypt '97,* W. Fumy (Ed.), LNCS 1233, Springer-Verlag, New York, 1997, pp. 62–74.

[r320] A. Young and M. Yung, "The Prevalence of Kleptographic Attacks on Discrete-Log Based Cryptosystems." In: *Proceedings of Crypto '97,* B. S. Kaliski (Ed.), LNCS 1294, Springer-Verlag, New York, 1997, pp. 264–276.

[r321] A. Young, "Kleptography: Using Cryptography Against Cryptography," PhD Thesis, Moti Yung (Advisor), Columbia University, 2002.

[r322] V. Rijmen and B. Preneel, "A Family of Trapdoor Ciphers." In: *Proceedings of Fast Software Encryption,* E. Biham (Ed.), Springer-Verlag, New York, 1997, pp. 139–148.

[r323] J. Patarin and L. Goubin, "Asymmetric Cryptography with S-Boxes." In: *Proceedings of ICICS,* LNCS 1334, Springer-Verlag, New York, 1997, pp. 369–380.

[r324] A. Young, M. Yung, "Monkey: Black-Box Symmetric Ciphers Designed for Monopolizing Keys." In: *Proceedings of Fast Software Encryption,* Springer-Verlag, 1998, pp. 122–133.

[r325] A. Young and M. Yung, "Backdoor Attacks on Black-Box Ciphers Exploiting Low-Entropy Plaintexts." In: *Eighth Australasian Conference on Information Security and Privacy (ACISP),* LNCS 2727, Springer-Verlag, New York, 2003, pp. 297–311.

[r326] H. Wu, F. Bao, R. Deng, and Q. Ye, "Cryptanalysis of Rijmen–Preneel Trapdoor Ciphers." In: *Proceedings of Asiacrypt '98,* 1998, pp. 126–132.

[r327] Y. Ding-Feng, L. Kwok-Yan, and D. Zong-Duo. "Cryptanalysis of the "2R" schemes." In: *Proceedings of Crypto '99,* 1999, pp. 315–325.

[r328] E. Biham, "Cryptanalysis of Patarin's 2-Round Public Key System S Boxes (2R)." In: *Proceedings of Eurocrypt '00,* 1999, pp. 408–416.

[r329] G. J. Simmons, "The Prisoners' Problem and the Subliminal Channel." In: *Proceedings of Crypto '83,* D. Chaum (Ed.), Plenum Press, New York, 1984, pp. 51–67.

[r330] G. J. Simmons, "The Subliminal Channel and Digital Signatures." In: *Proceedings of Eurocrypt '84,* T. Beth, N. Cot, and I. Ingemarsson (Eds.), LNCS 209, Springer-Verlag, 1985, pp. 364–378.

[r331] Y. Desmedt, C. Goutier, and S. Bengio, "Special Uses and Abuses of the Fiat–Shamir Passport Protocol." In: *Proceedings of Crypto '87,* C. Pomerance (Ed.), LNCS 293, Springer-Verlag, New York, 1988, pp. 21–39.

[r332] Y. Desmedt, "Abuses in Cryptography and How to Fight Them." In: *Proceedings of Crypto '88,* S. Goldwasser (Ed.), LNCS 403, Springer-Verlag, New York, 1988, pp. 375–389.

[r333] Y. Desmedt, "Subliminal-Free Authentication and Signature." In: *Proceedings of Eurocrypt '88,* LNCS 330, Springer-Verlag, New York, 1988.

[r334] A. Juels and J. Guajardo, "RSA Key Generation with Verifiable Randomness." In: *Proceedings of Public Key Cryptography,* D. Naccache and P. Paillier (Eds.), Springer-Verlag, New York, 2002, pp. 357–374.

[r335] M. E. Smid and D. K. Branstad, "Response to Comments on the NIST Proposed Digital Signature Standard." In: *Proceedings of Crypto '92,* E. F. Brickell (Ed.), LNCS 740, Springer-Verlag, New York, 1992, pp. 76–87.

[r336] A. Young, "Mitigating insider threats to RSA Key Generation," *CryptoBytes, RSA Laboratories,* Vol. 7, No. 1, Spring, 2004.

[r337] R. Weis and S. Lucks, "All Your Key Bit Are Belong to Us—The True Story of Black Box Cryptography." In: *Proceedings of SANE,* May 27–31, 2002.

[r338] C. Crepeau and A. Slakmon, "Simple Backdoors for RSA Key Generation." In: *Proceedings of CT-RSA,* Marc Joye (Ed.), LNCS 2612, Springer-Verlag, New York, 2003, pp. 403–416.

[r339] American National Standards Institute, "Public Key Cryptography for the Financial Service Industry: Agreement of Symmetric Keys Using Diffie–Hellman and MQV Algorithms," X9.42, 29 January 1999.

[r340] American National Standards Institute, "Financial Institution Key Management (Wholesale)," X9.17, April 4, 1985. [Defines procedures for the manual and automated management of keying material and uses DES to provide key management for a variety of operational environments.]

[r341] P. Metzger and W. Simpson, "IP Authentication Using Keyed MD5," RFC 1828, August 1995.

[r342]   http://www.anti-keyloggers.com/spy_v_antispy.html

[r343] D. E. Denning, "A Lattice Model of Secure Information Flow," *Communications of the ACM,* Vol. 19, No. 5, pp. 236–243, May 1976.

[r344] R. Friend, "Transport Layer Security (TLS) Protocol Compression Using Lempel–Ziv–Stac (LZS)," RFC 3943, November 2004.

[r345] W. Yeong, T. Howes, and S. Kille, "Lightweight Directory Access Protocol," RFC 1777, March 1995.

[r346] D. Eastlake, "Physical Link Security Type of Service," RFC 1455, May 1993.

[r347] http://searchsecurity.techtarget.com/gDefinition/0,,sid14_gci211621,00.html?Offer=SEcpswlg25

[r348] D. Minoli, *Hotspot Networks: Wi-Fi for Public Access Locations,* McGraw-Hill, New York, 2002.

[r349] J. Strand (Ed.) and A. Chiu (Ed.), "Optical Layer Routing," IETF RFC 4054, May 2005.

[r350] Fluke Networks, VLAN Best Practices, Whitepaper, Fluke Corporation, P.O. Box 777, Everett, WA 98206-0777, www.flukenetworks.com/contact, 2004.

[r351] B. Kaliski, "The MD2 Message-Digest Algorithm," RFC 1319, April 1992.

[r352] R. Rivest, "The MD4 Message-Digest Algorithm," RFC 1320, April 1992.

[r353] R. Rivest, "The MD5 Message-Digest Algorithm," RFC 1321, April 1992.

[r354] These definitions were prepared by ATIS Committee T1A1. For more information on the work related to these definitions, visit the ATIS website.

[r355] U.S. Department of Defense, National Security Agency, "Secure Data Network System, Message Security Protocol (MSP)," document SDN.701, Revision 4.0, 7 June 1996, with Corrections to Message Security Protocol, SDN.701, Rev 4.0," 96-06-07, August 30, 1996.

[r356] http://www.lightreading.com

[r357] C. Kalbfleisch, R. Cole, and D. Romascanu, "Definition of Managed Objects for Synthetic Sources for Performance Monitoring Algorithms," RFC 4149, August 2005.

[r358] T. Harding, R. Drummond, C. Shih, "MIME-Based Secure Peer-to-Peer Business Data Interchange over the Internet," RFC 3335, September 2002. This document and translations of it may be copied and furnished to others, and derivative works that comment on or otherwise explain it or assist in its implementation may be prepared, copied, published and distributed, in whole or in part, without restriction of any kind, provided that the above copyright notice and this paragraph are included on all such copies and derivative works.

[r359] H. Ohta, "A Description of the MISTY1 Encryption Algorithm," RFC 2994, November 2000.

[r360] J. Conner, Foresight Institute, Judy@foresight.org. Phone: (650) 917-1122.

[r361] Intel, Promotional Materials. Intel, 2200 Mission College Blvd., Santa Clara, CA 95052.

[r362] MPLS/VPLS Evolution—A Riverstone Perspective, Riverstone Networks Whitepaper, 2004, 5200 Great America Parkway, Santa Clara, CA 95054. Phone: (408) 878-6500.

[r363] N. Freed and N. Borenstein, "Multipurpose Internet Mail Extensions (MIME) Part One: Format of Internet Message Bodies," RFC 2045, November 1996.

[r364] D. Crocker, "Standard for the Format of ARPA Internet Text Messages," STD 11, RFC 822, August 1982.

[r365] S. Crocker, N. Freed, J. Galvin, and S. Murphy, "MIME Object Security Services," RFC 1848, October 1995.

[r366] K. Kompella, "Virtual Private LAN Service," Work in Progress, IETF, January 2005.

[r367] The Globus Alliance (a partnership of Argonne National Laboratory's Mathematics and Computer Science Division, the University of Southern California's Information Sciences Institute, the University of Chicago's Distributed Systems Laboratory, the University of Edinburgh in Scotland, and the Swedish Center for Parallel Computers). This material is licensed for use under the terms of the Globus Toolkit Public License.

[r368] Nanotechnology Research Directions: IWGN Workshop Report, September 1999.

[r369] http://www.ind.alcatel.com/library/e-briefing/eBrief_NetworkManagement.pdf

[r370] M. Bellare and A. Sahai, "Non-Malleable Encryption: Equivalence Between Two Notions, and an Indistinguishability-Based Characterization." In *Advances in Cryptology—Crypto 99 Proceedings, Lecture Notes in Computer Science,* Vol. 1666, M. Wiener (Ed.), Springer-Verlag, New York, 1999.

[r371] D. Dolev, C. Dwork, and M. Naor, "Non-malleable Cryptography," *SIAM Journal on Computing,* Vol. 30, No. 2, pp. 391–437, 2000.

[r372] IBM, "Cryptographic Protocols and Theoretical Foundations," http://www.almaden.ibm.com/cs/k53/crypt.html

[r373] D. Dolev, C. Dwork, and M. Naor, "Non-malleable Cryptography." In: *Proceedings of the 22nd Annual Symposium on Foundations of Computer Science,* IEEE, New York, 1981, pp. 542–552.

[r374] M. Bellare and P. Rogaway, "Optimal Asymmetric Encryption," In: *Proceedings of Eurocrypt '94,* Springer-Verlag, New York, 1995, pp. 92–111.

[r375] V. Shoup and R. Cramer, "A Practical Public Key Cryptosystem Provably Secure Against Adaptive Chosen Ciphertext Attack, In: *Proceedings of Crypto '98,* Springer-Verlag, New York, 1999.

[r376] R. Glenn and S. Kent, "The NULL Encryption Algorithm and Its Use with IPsec," RFC 2410, November 1998.

[r377]   http://en.wikipedia.org/wiki/Category:Number_ theory

[r378] H. Orman, "The OAKLEY Key Determination Protocol," RFC 2412, November 1998.

[r379] Object Management Group Documentation, http://www.omg.org

[r380] http://www.smartcomputing.com/editorial/dictionary/detail.asp?guid=&searchtype=1&DicID=9895&RefType=Dictionary

[r381] I. Goldberg, "Off-the-Record Messaging, or When Not to Use PGP," Black Hat Briefings, July 31, 2002, Zero-Knowledge Systems (ian@zeroknowledge.com), http://blackhat.com/presentations/bh-usa-02/bh-us-02-goldberg-messaging.pdf

[r382] L. Lamport, "Password Authentication with Insecure Communication," *Communications of the ACM,* 24.11, pp. 770–772, November 1981.

[r383] Computer Emergency Response Team (CERT), "IP Spoofing and Hijacked Terminal Connections," CA-95:01, January 1995. Available via anonymous ftp from info.cert.org in /pub/cert_advisories

[r384] N. Haller, C. Metz, P. Nesser, M. Straw, A One-Time Password System, RFC 2289, February 1998. Copyright © The Internet Society (1998). All Rights Reserved. This document and translations of it may be copied and furnished to others, and derivative works that comment on or otherwise explain it or assist in its implementation may be prepared, copied, published, and distributed, in whole or in part, without restriction of any kind, provided that the above copyright notice and this paragraph are included on all such copies and derivative works.

[r385] N. Haller and C. Metzion, "A One-Time Password System," RFC 1938, May 1996.

[r386] A. Rousskov, "Open Pluggable Edge Services (OPES) Callout Protocol (OCP) Core," RFC 4037, March 2005.

[r387] B. Doyle, Intrusion Detection FAQ, Passive Fingerprinting Utilizing the Telnet Protocol Negotiation data, http://www.sans.org/resources/idfaq/fingerp_ telnet.php

[r388] F. Cohen, "Computer Viruses—Theory and Experiments," *IFIP-TC11 Computers and Security,* Vol. 6, pp. 22–35, 1987.

[r389] F. Cohen, Computer Viruses, PhD Thesis, University of Southern California, ASP Press, 1988.

[r390] J. Brawley and S. Gao, Mathematical Models in Public-Key Cryptology," May 26, 1999, http://www .mat.clemson.edu/faculty/Gao/papers/crypto_mod.pdf

[r391] S. Goldwasser and S. Micali, "Probabilistic Encryption," *JCSS,* Vol. 28, No. 2, pp. 270–299, April 1984.

[r392] S. Micali, C. Rackoff, and R. Sloan, "The Notion of Security for Probabilistic Cryptosystems." In: *Proceedings of Crypto '86,* Springer-Verlag, New York, LNCS 263, 1987, pp. 381–392.

[r393] S. Micali, C. Rackoff, and R. Sloan, "The Notion of Security for Probabilistic Cryptosystems," *SIAM Journal on Computing,* Vol. 17, No. 2, pp. 412–426, 1988.

[r394] I. Hekimi, "A Survey of Cryptographic Schemes," September 4, 2005, http://www.math.mcgill.ca/darmon/courses/usra/hekimi.pdf

[r395] B. Lloyd and W. Simpson, "PPP Authentication Protocols," RFC 1334, October 1992.

[r396] W. Simpson (Ed.), "The Point-to-Point Protocol (PPP)," STD 51, RFC 1661, July 1994.

[r397] J. Myers, "POP3 AUTHentication Command," RFC 1734, December 1994.

[r398] J. Myers and M. Rose, "Post Office Protocol—Version 3," STD 53, RFC 1939, May 1996.

[r399] J. Linn, "Privacy Enhancement for Internet Electronic Mail, Part I: Message Encryption and Authentication Procedures," RFC 1421, February 1993.

[r400] Collaborative ITU and ISO/IEC Meeting on the Directory, "Final Proposed Draft Amendment on Certificate Extensions," April 1999.

[r401] National Institute of Standards and Technology, http://niap.nist.gov/pp/index.html

[r402] L. Martin and N. El-Aawar, "Transport of Layer 2 Frames Over MPLS," Work in Progress, IETF, June 2004.

[r403] L. Martini, "Encapsulation Methods for Transport of Layer 2 Frames Over IP and MPLS Networks," Work in Progress, IETF, September 2004.

[r404] X. Xiao, D. McPherson, and P. Pate, "Requirements for Pseudo-Wire Emulation Edge-to-Edge (PWE3)," RFC 3916, September 2004.

[r405] S. Bryant and P. Pate, "PWE3 Architecture," Work in Progress, IETF, March 2004.

[r406] D. Minoli, work experience with marquee Fortune

200 firms, carriers, technology establishments, universities, Venture capitalist, and publishers at AIG; ARPA think tanks; Bell Telephone Laboratories; ITT; Prudential Securities; Bell Communications Research; DVI Communications; Teleport Communications Group; AT&T; InfoPort Communications Group; Global Wireless Services; Capital One Financial; New York University; Rutgers University; Carnegie-Mellon University; Stevens Institute of Technology; Monmouth University; AT&T Wireless/Shiff Harding & Waite; Computer-World; NetworkWorld; Network Computing; Datapro/Gartner; Probe Research Corporation; Societe' General de Financiament de Quebec; Caisse de Depot et Placement Quebec; Les Funds De Solidarite' Des Travailleurs; MRC; NHC; Cifra; Uniforce; Memotec; Miranda; Lumenon; Medisys; Tri-Link; Maxima; ACE*COMM; Artech House; McGraw-Hill; Wiley; Prentice-Hall; SUPERCOMM ENTNET 2005; SUPERCOMM ENTNET 2004; Web Week 2001; Institute for International Research 2001; Next Generation Switching and Routing 2000; VoiceNet 2000; HP Industry Advisory Council Meeting 1999; UNISYS User Group 1999; ICM Broadband Networking Conference 1999; Institute For International Research Conference 1999; Advanced Internet Protocols Conference 1999; Institute for International Research 1998; Fall Condex 1998; ICM Broadband Networking Conference 1998; Interop 1998; 2nd Texas A&M Symposium on Communications 1998; 1997 Broadband Networking Symposium; International Engineering Symposium 1997; Annual ECI Telecom Technical & Planning Symposium 1997; Nordex Wall Street Seminar 1997; 1997 Comdex; ITEC Expo 1997; 1997 Interop; 1997 Conference on Emerging Technologies; 1996 Integrated OSS For ATM Broadband Technologies; Supercomputing 1996; IEEE Convergence of Networks and Services 1996; 1996 First Annual Telecommunications Conference; TCG Industry Seminar 1996; 1996 Global Telemedicine and Federal Technologies; CMA Spring Session 1996; CMA Winter Session 1996; 1995 Broadband And Multimedia Comforum; Systems Support Expo 1995; Interop 1995; CMA Show 1995; Conference on Outsourcing Support Services in Hospitals 1995; TechCon/NeoCon June 1995; Nortel's Forum 1995; Developing an Outsourcing Strategy Conference 1995; ICA 1995; Futures Industry Association Meeting 1995; The Information Technology Outsourcing Institute 1995; Mt. Jade Science & Technology 1994; ICA Summer Program 1994; United Technologies Engineering Coordination Activities Engineering Operations Subcommittee For Computer Maintenance 1994; Central New York Communications Association 1994; Comnet 1993; Texpro (Pacific Bell Technology Fair) 1993; Unix Expo 1992; The 10th North American ISDN User Forum 1990; ORSA/TIMS Conference 1990; 1st ORSA Telecom SIG Conference 1990; 1988 Enterprise Networking Event; Bellcore Artificial Intelligence Symposium 1988; International Communications Conference 1988; University of Utah Fourth Annual Management Information Systems Seminar 1988; Computer Networking Symposium 1988; Interface 1986; Computer Networking Symposium 1986; 1981 International Electrical/Electronics Conference; International Communication Conference 1980; Networks 80 Conference 1980; INTELCOM 80 Conference 1980; IEEE International Conference on Acoustics; Speech and Signal Processing 1980; International Electrical/Electronics Conference 1979; International Communication Conference 1979; NCC Conference 1979; IEEE Canadian Conference on Communication and Power 1978; 28th IEEE Vehicular Technology 1978; International Communication Conference 1978; Polytechnic Engineer 1975; PME Journal 1975; The Matrix and Tensor Quarterly 1975; Att. Accad. Naz. Linc, Rendiconti 1975; IEEE Transactions on Communication 1977; Rev. Col. Matem. 1977; Alta Frequenza, 1978; IEEE Transactions on Communication 1978; IEEE Transactions on Communication, 1979; Frequenz 1979; Alta Frequenza 1979; IEEE Transactions on Aerospace and Electrical Systems 1979; Annals, Faculty of Sciences, University Nation. Zaire, Section Mathem; 1978; Australian Electronics Engineer 1979; Fibonacci Quarterly 1981; Proceedings of IEE 1979; IEEE Transactions on Communication, Special Issue on Digital Radio 1979; IEEE Transactions on Communication 1980; Telecommunications Journal 1979; Mathematics of Computation 1980; IEEE Transactions on Communication, Special Issue on Military Communications 1980; Notices of American Mathematical Society 1979; Data Communications 1979; Audio 1980; Electrical Communication 1980; Comunicaciones Electricas, Elektriches Nachrichtenwesen 1980; Revue des Telecommunicationes 1980; Abstracts of the American Math. Society 1980; SIGCOMM Computer Communications Review 1979; Data Communication and Computer Networks, edited by S. Ramani; IEEE Transactions on Communication 1980; Data Communications 1980; Computer Communication 1980; Abstracts

American Soc. 1980; Computer Networks 1980; Computer Communications 1980; Telephony 1980; Telephony 1981; Computer Communications 1981; Computer Networks 1983; Infosystems 1986; IEEE Spectrum; Teleconnect 1986; LAN Magazine 1986; Business Week 1987; Communications News 1987; WAN Connections/Communications Week 1993; Network World Collaboration 1994.

[r407] RSA Laboratories, "PKCS #10: Certification Request Syntax Standard," version 1.0, RSA Laboratories Technical Note, November 1, 1993.

[r408] RSA Laboratories, "PKCS #11: Cryptographic Token Interface Standard," version 1.0, April 28, 1995.

[r409] Asian Technology Information Program (ATIP), "Quantum Computation in Europe," Report ATIP01.019r. Publisher: Asian Technology Information Program, Harks Roppongi Building 1F, 6-15-21 Roppongi, Minato-ku, Tokyo 106, JAPAN. Phone: +81 3 5411-6670, Fax: +81 3 5411-6671.

[r410] D. Eastlake, S. Crocker, and J. Schiller, "Randomness Recommendations for Security," RFC 1750, December 1994.

[r411] Contact RSA Data Security, Inc. Phone: 415-595-8782.

[r412] R. Rivest, "A Description of the RC2(r) Encryption Algorithm," IETF RFC 2268, January 1998.

[r413] R. Thayer and K. Kaukonen, "A Stream Cipher Encryption Algorithm," IETF, Work in Progress.

[r414] C. Adams and S. Farrell, "Internet X.509 Public Key Infrastructure Certificate Management Protocols," RFC 2510, March 1999.

[r415] C. Rigney, A. Rubens, W. Simpson, and S. Willens, "Remote Authentication Dial In User Service (RADIUS)," RFC 2138, April 1997.

[r416] N. Haller and R. Atkinson, "On Internet Authentication," IETF RFC 1704, October 1994.

[r417] J. Postel, "Instructions to RFC Authors," RFC 2223, October 1997.

[r418] http://www.freesoft.org/CIE/Topics/78.htm

[r419] J. Guinan, "IEEE 802.17 RPR Draft Standard Moves to Sponsor Approval," Press Release, San Francisco, CA, November 19, 2003, Sage Strategic Marketing, Jennifer@sagestrat.com, (610) 415-9659.

[r420] J. Manner and X. Fu, "Analysis of Existing Quality-of-Service Signaling Protocols," RFC 4094, May 2005.

[r421] P. Sarolahti and M. Kojo, "Forward RTO-Recovery (F-RTO): An Algorithm for Detecting Spurious Retransmission Timeouts with TCP and the Stream Control Transmission Protocol (SCTP)," RFC 4138, August 2005.

[r422]   http://www-106.ibm.com/developerworks/patterns/glossary/reverse-proxy-node.html

[r423] E. Rosen and Y. Rekhter, "BGP/MPLS VPNs," RFC 2547, March 1999.

[r424] S. Chokhani, W. Ford, R. Sabett, C. Merrill, and S. Wu, "Internet X.509 Public Key Infrastructure Certificate Policy and Certification Practices Framework," RFC 3647, November 2003. This document and translations of it may be copied and furnished to others, and derivative works that comment on or otherwise explain it or assist in its implementation may be prepared, copied, published, and distributed, in whole or in part, without restriction of any kind, provided that the above copyright notice and this paragraph are included on all such copies and derivative works.

[r425] H. F. Tipton, and M. Krause, *Information Security Management Handbook,* 4th edition. Boca Raton, FL, Auerbach, 2000.

[r426] B. Fraser, "Site Security Handbook," FYI 8, RFC 2196, September 1997.

[r427] H. Ould-Brahim, E. Rosen, and Y. Rekhter, "Using BGP as an Auto-Discovery Mechanism for Layer-3 and Layer-2 VPNs," Work in Progress, IETF, May 2004.

[r428] R. Rivest, A. Shamir, and L. M. Adleman, "A Method for Obtaining Digital Signatures and Public-Key Cryptosystems," *Communications of the ACM,* Vol. 21, No. 2, February 1978, pp. 120–126.

[r429] M. Bellare and P. Rogaway "Optimal Asymmetric Encryption—How to Encrypt with RSA," *Advances in Cryptology—Eurocrypt '94,* Lecture Notes in Computer Science, Vol. 950, Springer-Verlag, New York, 1995, pp. 92–111.

[r430] E. Fujisaki, T. Okamoto, David Pointcheval, and Jacques Stern, "RSA-OAEP is Secure Under the RSA Assumption." *Advances in Cryptology—Crypto 2001,* Lecture Notes in Computer Science, Vol. 2139, Springer-Verlag, New York, 2001.

[r431] N. Haller, "The S/KEY One-Time Password System," RFC 1760, February 1995.

[r432] C. P. Schnorr, "Efficient Signature Generation by Smart Cards," *Journal of Cryptology,* Vol. 4, pp. 161–174, 1991.

[r433] Secure BGP Project (S-BGP), http://www.ir.bbn.com/projects/sbgp/

[r434] C. Lynn, J. Mikkelson, K. Seo, Secure BGP (S-BGP), *S-BGP Protocol Specification, http://www.ir .bbn.com/projects/sbgp/draft-clynn-s-bgp-protocol-01.txt.,* Internet Draft, June 2003.

[r435] http://support.microsoft.com/default.aspx?scid=% 2Fsupport%2Fglossary%2Fs.asp

[r436] U.S. Department of Commerce, "Secure Hash Standard," FIPS PUB 180-1, April 17, 1995.

[r437] "Multi-use Wireless Gateways," University of Pittsburgh, http://www.digitalgreenhouse.com/default. aspx?id=round_8

[r438] http://www.gordano.com/kb.htm?q=308

[r439] A. Frier, P. Karlton, and P. Kocher, "The SSL 3.0 Protocol," Netscape Communications Corp., November 18, 1996.

[r440] B. Ramsdell (Ed.), "S/MIME Version 3 Message Specification," RFC 2633, June 1999.

[r441] N. Brownlee and E. Guttman, "Expectations for Computer Security Incident Response," RFC 2350, June 1998.

[r442] S. Kent and R. Atkinson, "Security Architecture for the Internet Protocol," RFC 2401, November 1998.

[r443] R. Housley, "Security Label Framework for the Internet," RFC 1457, May 1993.

[r444] U.S. Department of Defense, National Security Agency, "Secure Data Network Systems, Security Protocol 3 (SP3)," document SDN.301, Revision 1.5, May 15, 1989.

[r445] U.S. Department of Defense, National Security Agency, "Security Protocol 4 (SP4)," document SDN.401, Revision 1.2, July 12, 1988.

[r446] J. Park, S. Lee, J. Kim, and J. Lee, "Use of the SEED Encryption Algorithm in Cryptographic Message Syntax (CMS)," RFC 4010, February 2005.

[r447] J. Park, S. Lee, J. Kim, and J. Lee, "The SEED Encryption Algorithm," RFC 4009, February 2005.

[r448] A. B. Roach, A Negative Acknowledgement Mechanism for Signaling Compression," RFC 4077, May 2005.

[r449] J. Myers, "Simple Authentication and Security Layer (SASL)," RFC 2222, October 1997.

[r449a] J. Viega and G. McGraw, *Building Secure Software,* Addison-Wesley, ISBN 0-201-72152-X.

[r450] C. Montenegro and V. Gupta, "Sun's SKIP Firewall Traversal for Mobile IP," RFC 2356, June 1998.

[r451] J. Postel, "Simple Mail Transfer Protocol," STD 10, RFC 821, August 1982.

[r452] J. Case, R. Mundy, D. Partain, and B. Stewart, "Intro-duction to Version 3 of the Internet-Standard Network Management Framework," RFC 2570, April 1999.

[r453] U. Blumenthal, and B. Wijnen, "User-based Security Model (USM) for Version 3 of the Simple Network Management Protocol (SNMPv3)," RFC 2574, April 1999.

[r454] G. J. Simmons, "The History of Subliminal Channels," *IEEE Journal on Selected Areas in Communication,* Vol. 16, No. 4, pp. 452–462, 1998.

[r455] G. J. Simmons, "Subliminal Communication is Easy Using the DSA," In: *Proceedings of Eurocrypt '93,* T. Helleseth (Ed.), LNCS 765, Springer-Verlag, New York, 1993, pp. 218–232.

[r456] M. Leech, M. Ganis, Y. Lee, R. Kuris, D. Koblas, and L. Jones, "SOCKS Protocol Version 5," RFC 1928, March 1996.

[r457] C. Malamud, "Attaching Meaning to Solicitation Class Keywords," RFC 4095, May 2005.

[r458] S. Hambridge and A. Lunde, "Don't Spew: A Set of Guidelines for Mass Unsolicited Mailings and Postings," RFC 2635, June 1999.

[r459] P. Amsden, J. Amweg, P. Calato, S. Bensley, and G. Lyons, "Cabletron's Light-weight Flow Admission Protocol Specification Version 1.0," IETF RFC 2124, March 1997.

[r460] http://enterprisesecurity.symantec.com/article.cfm ?articleid=5589

[r461] J. Postel and J. Reynolds, "TELNET Protocol Specification," STD 8, RFC 854, May 1983.

[r462] C. Finseth, "An Access Control Protocol, Sometimes Called TACACS," RFC 1492, July 1993.

[r463] G. Hellstrom, and P. Jones, "Text Conversation Session Contents Are Specified in ITU-T Recommendation T.140," RFC 4103, June 2005.

[r464] J. Postel (Ed.), "Transmission Control Protocol," STD 7, RFC 793, September 1981.

[r465] D. Minoli, *Broadband Network Analysis and Design,* Artech House, Norwood, MA, 1993.

[r466] RFC 2246 The TLS Protocol Version 1.0 January 1999, Copyright © The Internet Society, 1999. All Rights Reserved. This document and translations of it may be copied and furnished to others, and derivative works that comment on or otherwise explain it or assist in its implementation may be prepared, copied, published, and distributed, in whole or in part, without restriction of any kind, provided that the above copyright notice and this paragraph are included on all such copies and derivative works.

[r467] American National Standards Institute, "Triple

Data Encryption Algorithm Modes of Operation," X9.52-1998, ANSI approval, November 9, 1998.

[r468] P. Hoffman (Ed.), "Enhanced Security Services for S/MIME," RFC 2634, June 1999.

[r469] http://www.anti-trojan.com/

[r470] U.S. Department of Defense, "Department of Defense Trusted Computer System Evaluation Criteria," DoD 5200.28-STD, December 26, 1985.

[r471] K. Kompella, "Layer 2 VPNs over Tunnels," IETF, June 2002.

[r472] D. Thaler, "IP Tunnel MIB," RFC 4087, June 2005.

[r473] T. Berners-Lee, "Universal Resource Identifiers in WWW," RFC 1630, June 1994.

[r474] R. Fielding, "Relative Uniform Resource Locators," RFC 1808, June 1995.

[r475] J. Myers, L. Masinter, and M. McCahill (Eds.), "Uniform Resource Locators (URL)," RFC 1738, December 1994.

[r476] D. Eastlake 3rd, "Additional XML Security Uniform Resource Identifiers (URIs)," IETF RFC 4051, April 2005.

[r477] Cryptology and Data Secrecy: The Vernam Cipher, http://www.pro-technix.com/information/crypto/pages/vernam_base.html

[r478] J. Postel, "User Datagram Protocol," STD 6, RFC 768, August 1980.

[r479] W. Augustyn and Y. Serbest, "Service Requirements for Layer 2 Provider Provisioned Virtual Private Networks," Work in Progress, IETF, October 2004.

[r480] M. Lasserre and V. Kompella, "Virtual Private LAN Services over MPLS," Work in Progress, IETF, September 2004.

[r481] B. Gleeson, A. Lin, J. Heinanen, G. Armitage, and A. Malis, "A Framework for IP Based Virtual Private Networks," RFC 2764, February 2000.

[r482] P. Knight, H. Ould-Brahim, and B. Gleeson, "Network Based IP VPN Architecture Using Virtual Routers," Work in Progress, IETF, April 2004.

[r483] Lee Lawson, "Session Hijacking Packet Analysis," SecurityDoc.com, Security Whitepapers and Articles, 07/25/2005, http://www.securitydocs.com/library/3479

[r484] D. Minoli, "General Geometric Arrival, Constant Server Queueing Problem With Applications to Packetized Voice," ICC 1978 Conference Record, Vol. 3, pp. 36.6.1–36.6.5.

[r485] D. Minoli, "Optimal Packet Length for Packet Voice Communication," *IEEE Transactions on Communication,* Concise paper, Vol. COMM-27, pp. 607–611, March 1979.

[r486] D. Minoli, "Packetized Speech Network, Part 3: Delay Behavior And Performance Characteristics," *Australian Electronics Engineer,* pp. 59–68, August 1979.

[r487] D. Minoli, "Packetized Speech Networks, Part 2: Queueing Model," *Australian Electronics Engineer,* July 1979, pp. 68–76.

[r488] D. Minoli, "Packetized Speech Networks, Part 1: Overview," *Australian Electronics Engineer,* April 1979, pp. 38–52.

[r489] D. Minoli, "Satellite On-Board Processing of Packetized Voice," ICC 1979 Conference Record, pp. 58.4.1–58.4.5.

[r490] D. Minoli, "Issues In Packet Voice Communication," *Proceedings of IEE,* Vol. 126, No. 8, pp. 729–740, August 1979.

[r491] D. Minoli, "Some Design Parameters for PCM Based Packet Voice Communication," 1979 International Electrical/Electronics Conference Record.

[r492] D. Minoli, "Packet Length Considerations In Carrier Sense Multiple Access Packet Radio Systems," INTELCOM 80 Conference Record (with E. Paterno and W. Nakamine).

[r493] D. Minoli, "Digital Voice Communication over Digital Radio Links," *SIGCOMM Computer Communications Review,* Vol. 9, No. 4, pp. 6–22, October 1979.

[r494] D. Minoli, *Delivering Voice over IP Networks,* 1st edition (co-authored), Wiley, Hoboken, NJ, 1998.

[r495] D. Minoli, *Delivering Voice over IP and the Internet,* 2nd edition (co-authored), Wiley, Hoboken, NJ, 2002.

[r496] D. Minoli, *Delivering Voice over Frame Relay and ATM,* (co-authored), Wiley, New York, 1998.

[r497] M. Reardon, "Cisco Targets Net Phone Software Flaw," CNET News.com, May 24, 2005, 4:42 PM PDT.

[r498] International Telecommunications Union—Telecommunication Standardization Sector (formerly "CCITT"), Recommendation X.500, "Information Technology—Open Systems Interconnection—The Directory: Overview of Concepts, Models, and Services" (equivalent to ISO 9594-1).

[r499] G. Bossert, S. Cooper, and W. Drummond, "Considerations for Web Transaction Security," RFC 2084, January 1997.

[r500] International Telecommunications Union—Telecommunication Standardization Sector (formerly "CCITT"), Recommendation X.400, "Message Handling Services: Message Handling System and Service Overview."

[r501] D. Linsenbardt, S. Pontius, and A. Sturgeon, Warranty Certificate Extension, IETF RFC 4059, May 2005.

[r502] "Mobile Multi-Layered IP Security," Pennsylvania State University, http://www.digitalgreenhouse.com/default.aspx?id=round_8

[r503] T. Bray, E. Maler, J. Paoli, and C. M. Sperberg-McQueen, Extensible Markup Language (XML) 1.0 (2nd edition), W3C Recommendation, October 2000. http://www.w3.org/TR/2000/REC-xml-20001006

[r504] D. Minoli, *Internet Architectures* (co-authored), Wiley, New York, 1999.

[r505] D. Minoli, *Internet Architectures* (co-authored), Publishing House of Electronics Industry (Chinese translation), 1999.